A
Consumer's
Dictionary
of
Food
Additives

A Consumer's Dictionary of Food Additives

UPDATED FOURTH EDITION

Ruth Winter, M.S.

Crown Trade Paperbacks   New York

Published by Crown Trade Paperbacks, 201 East 50th Street, New York, New York 10022. Member of the Crown Publishing Group.

Random House, Inc. New York, Toronto, London, Sydney, Auckland

CROWN TRADE PAPERBACKS and colophon are trademarks of Crown Publishers, Inc.

Manufactured in U.S.A.

Library of Congress Cataloging-in-Publication Data

Winter, Ruth, 1950–
    A consumer's dictionary of food additives / Ruth Winter. — Updated
4th ed.
          p.   cm.
    Includes bibliographical references.
    1. Food additives—Dictionaries.   I. Title.
TX553.A3W55   1994
664'.06'03—dc20   94-27332
                                                                  CIP

ISBN 0-517-88195-0

10   9   8   7   6   5   4   3   2   1

Fourth Revised Edition

A
Consumer's
Dictionary
of
Food
Additives

INTRODUCTION

With this book, you will be better able to:

- Evaluate foods and choose the best sources of nutrients.
- Plan your diet to avoid certain additives.
- Find foods abundant in desirable ingredients.

You will, in this edition of *A Consumer's Dictionary of Food Additives,* learn not only about the more than two thousand additives deliberately added to your food but also about the myriad of indirect additives from packaging, processing, pesticides, and animal drugs. Whenever possible, the U.S. government residue tolerances are given. You may be surprised at some of the information. Did you know, for example:

- Tranquilizing drugs are injected into many pigs immediately before transport to slaughter, making a withdrawal period impossible and giving diners unexpected sedation with their pork dish?[1]

- Apple growers lost a fortune over the scare about the pesticide Alar (diaminozide) in 1988–89, but at the time residues permitted on peaches, cherries, and nectarines were much higher?[2]

- From 70 to 80 percent of food is packaged in various polymers, some of which contain potential cancer-causing agents that migrate into our food every day?[3]

- Sixty percent of all herbicides, 90 percent of all fungicides, and 30 percent of all insecticides are carcinogens?[4]

The World Health Organization and U.S. government agencies are concerned about certain direct and indirect food additives, but the efforts at identification and protection move slowly. The U.S. Environmental Protection Agency (EPA) reviews the scientific data on pesticide products before they can be registered (or licensed) for use. If a product is intended for use on food crops, the EPA also establishes a tolerance. The U.S. Food and Drug Administration (FDA) is responsible for enforcing these tolerances on all foods except meat, poultry, and certain egg products, which are monitored by the U.S. Department of Agriculture (USDA). In this "alphabet soup" of regulators, the FDA works with the EPA to set "action levels"— enforcement guidelines for residues of pesticides that may remain in the environment after their use is dis-

---

1. *WHO Technical Report Series* 799 (1991):40. (Evaluation of certain veterinary drug residues in food: thirty-seventh report of the Joint FAO/WHO Expert Committee on Food Additives.)
2. *U.S. Food and Drug Investigations Operations Manual: Food Additives Status List.* Corrected to January 30, 1992, page 293.
3. Robert J. Scheuplein, "Perspectives on Toxicological Risk—An Example: Foodborne Carcinogenic Risk," *Critical Reviews in Food Science and Nutrition* 32(2) (1992):105–21.
4. National Research Council, *Toxicity Testing: Strategies to Determine Needs and Priorities* (Washington, D.C.: National Academy Press, 1984).

continued. In the past fifty years, 8,500 separate residue-tolerance licenses have been awarded for pesticides.[5] The residue amounts are based on the effects on a 160-pound man. Nearly 1 billion pounds of pesticides are applied to crops each year.[6] The EPA in June 1993 acknowledged that federal safety guidelines for the use of pesticides on food crops should be made ten times more stringent. This move by the EPA to reduce the use of pesticides was in response to a $1.1-million, five-year study of children's health risks from pesticides commissioned by the National Academy of Sciences (NAS).[7] The report stated that infants and young children might be uniquely sensitive to pesticides on food. Early in life, youngsters consume more than sixty times the amount of fruits as adults for their body weight and so tend to get higher doses of the pesticides used on fruits. The report also stated that infants and children—as well as adults—routinely encounter residues from more than one pesticide on individual food items. Government risk-assessment procedures assume that we are exposed to only one pesticide at a time.

Prof. John Wargo of Yale, who spent five years with the NAS panel sifting through data on pesticide risks to infants and children and trying to make sense of the patchwork system of federal regulations, says, "Children are particularly vulnerable to having a neurological response called cholinesterase inhibition when exposed to toxic chemicals, which causes the pattern of electronic-signal transfer between nerves to be disrupted, and my research indicates that between one point two and five percent of two-year-old children consume pesticides at a level above that which the EPA has identified as safe."[8]

In other regulatory developments since the last edition of this book, a new plan has evolved to require companies to demonstrate their products meet a safety standard of "reasonable certainty of no harm to consumers of food." This proposed regulation—which will require passage of legislation—is in response to a federal appeals court decision in 1992. In that case, the court in San Francisco struck down a Bush administration effort to begin applying a *negligible-risk* standard to processed food without first getting the Delaney clause repealed. The new standard, which would apply to raw and processed foods, is aimed at replacing the much stricter Delaney Amendment.

The Delaney Amendment

Written by Congressman James Delaney, the amendment was part of the 1958 law requested by the Food and Drug Administration. The law stated that food and chemical manufacturers had to test additives before they were put on the market, and the results had to be submitted to the FDA. Delaney's

---

5. John Wargo, associate professor of natural resource policy at Yale School of Forestry and Environmental Studies and chief policy analyst for the National Academy of Sciences, quoted in *Yale University Science News* 57 (September 30, 1993).

6. Keith Schneider, "Pesticide Plan Could Uproot U.S. Farming," *New York Times,* October 10, 1993, p. 6.

7. "Pesticides in the Diets of Infants and Children," National Academy of Sciences report, released June 29, 1993, Washington, D.C.

8. Wargo, op. cit.

amendment states that "no additive may be permitted in any amount if the tests show that it produces cancer when fed to man or animals or by other appropriate tests." Ever since it was enacted, it has been severely attacked by food and chemical manufacturers, the Nutrition Council of the American Medical Association, and several FDA commissioners. The FDA commissioners claim it is unenforceable and point to the problem with saccharin, a proven carcinogen. The artificial sweetener has been in use since 1879. When it was shown to cause cancer in laboratory animals in 1977, the FDA announced the use of saccharin in foods and beverages would be banned. There was a public outcry from dieters led by The Calorie Control Council, a trade organization that spent over a million dollars in just six months to stop the ban. Saccharin is still on the market, the FDA having postponed the ban several times in response to "public" pressure. The Delaney standard has never been enforced to the letter, as you can determine by scanning many of the direct and indirect additives in this book. Incidentally, sales of sugar substitutes—including saccharin—totaled more than $235,200,000[9] in 1993.

Food processors and scientists frequently say that with new detection apparatus such minute amounts of a cancer-causing agent can be detected that for all practical purposes the chemicals would have a "no-observed-effect level" (see page 15). Indeed, some residues are measured in nanograms—one billionth of a gram. A small quantity, it is true, yet consider that a human female produces a mere one-half teaspoonful of estrogen in her entire lifetime and think of the emotional and physiological effects of that tiny amount. How much exposure to a carcinogen does it take to damage a gene or to cause cancer in a child or an adult? No one knows for certain.

The new government proposals would allow the FDA and the EPA to determine the level at which a substance posed a "negligible" risk to human health. For cancer-causing substances, that would be the level of residues that would lead to one additional cancer case for every million people. (If you or a loved one are that one in a million, then that is one too many.) For substances that cause other health problems, regulators would determine the level below which there are no detectable adverse effects in laboratory animals. Then they would increase the safety factor by a hundredfold.

Initiators and Promoters of Cancer

Since the 1960s, scientists have believed that cancer develops in two steps:[10]

Step One: Initiation. Some substances, such as tobacco smoke, serve as initiators that start but cannot finish the cancer-causing process without the help of promoters.

Step Two: Promotion. Most promoters cannot work in cells that have not been initiated. Interfering with promoters offers the best approach in our lifetime of reducing cancer incidence. This was demonstrated, for example, when the

---

9. "NutraSweet still king of aspartame hill," *Advertising Age,* September 20, 1993, p. 12.
10. "Highlights of National Cancer Institute's Carcinogenesis Studies," National Institutes of Health, June 23, 1993.

"promoter" estrogen supplementation given to postmenopausal women was found to cause cancer of the uterine lining. When the estrogen medication was curtailed, the cases of endometrial cancer in postmenopausal women dropped dramatically. Saccharin is another cancer promoter (although a weak one), hence the warning on the artificial sweetener's packaging.

It is feasible, scientists believe, that we all may be victims of Step One, but that if Step Two does not occur, we don't get cancer. Identifying cancer initiators and promoters is difficult because:

• In most instances exposure to cancer-causing agents (carcinogens) takes place twenty to thirty years before a statistically significant increase in cancer can be detected. Only then can it be adduced that the increase in cancer may have been caused by exposure to specific cancer-causing agents.

• Animal studies may give clues, but laboratory conditions and the bodies of other creatures may not result in valid conclusions for us.

• Each of us is unique in the way our bodies process chemicals based on our age, sex, heredity, medical history, diet, and behavior. Epidemiologists estimate that approximately one-third of all cancer deaths can be attributed to diet.[11]

Robert J. Scheuplein, of the Office of Toxicological Sciences, Center for Food Safety and Applied Nutrition, U.S. Food and Drug Administration, believes there is greater danger from natural carcinogens in food than from additives or pesticides. He says:

"An individual's entire exposure history probably affects his or her susceptibility to any single carcinogenic chemical, and therefore most cancers are unlikely to be solely the result of any single chemical insult. Just as a person's carcinogenic risk from asbestos, alcohol, or inhaled radon is not independent of his or her smoking history—nor can the risks be simply added—it is also probably true that the risks from the low-dose exposure of any single carcinogenic chemical is influenced nonadditively by hundreds, if not thousands, of concomitant exposures. It is also probably true that the total, cumulative exposure to various carcinogenic initiators bears no simple relationship to the probability of developing a cancer in any given individual."

Since it is unethical to deliberately feed humans cancer-causing agents, researchers must rely on epidemiological studies, which can be confounded by many factors, including the environment. If there is a history of cancer in your family, for example, your risk from cancer-causing agents in food would be greater than for somebody who doesn't have those vulnerable genes.

Once an additive—direct or indirect—has been identified as a cancer-causing agent, it is not easy to get that substance out of our food supply. Carcinogenic pesticides are a prime example. Even if everyone cooperated with the EPA and proposed legislation were passed today, it would still be more than five years before the pesticide companies had to begin their long leeway—up to seven years—to show their products are not dangerous to the public food supply.

---

11. Scheuplein, op. cit.

Drug Residues from Animals

Pesticides are one type of indirect food additive of concern, but another involves residues from animal drugs. The Food and Drug Administration has been trying to rein in the use of antibiotics in animal feed since 1972, but the cattle and poultry are still being fed antibiotic-laced feed to increase their growth. More and more antibiotic-resistant infections in humans are occurring and scientists world-wide are blaming "animal husbandry practices" as an "important" cause.[12]

Consumers and scientists have been fighting for more than two decades to have hormones used to increase the growth of cattle, swine, and poultry stopped, but these powerful drugs are still widely employed. It is not just estrogen added directly to the food supply that may have adverse effects. The EPA announced in October 1993 that emerging evidence indicates that the insecticide endosulfan, and other chemicals that imitate estrogen, may be associated with instances of breast cancer.[13] Perhaps things will move more swiftly now that there are increasing reports estrogen residues "in the environment" may also be responsible for the great drop in male sperm count.[14]

The Food and Agriculture Organization of the United Nations and the World Health Organization (FAO/WHO) Expert Committee on Food Additives agrees there is a problem. It notes:

Of particular relevance to the FAO/WHO Committee are residues of drugs used in animal medications or as aids to animal production, and the frequency with which the consumer might be exposed to them. A drug whose toxicity profile was unsatisfactory and that was used widely and for lengthy periods during food-animal production would cause the highest level of concern. Human exposure to such a drug in food could be expected to occur widely and repeatedly.

Also of concern to the Committee would be a drug whose presence in food could result in a pharmacological effect in the consumer in the absence of conventional toxicological effects. This would constitute an intrusion into the body's homeostasis, against which consumers could reasonably expect to be protected. Drugs still present in the animal at the time of slaughter and at a concentration compatible with a pharmacological effect pose the greatest risk in this respect.[15]

The Committee says the sedative Azaperone, the phenothiazine tranquilizers chlorpromazine and propiomazine, and the beta-blocker carazolol (*see all*) fall into this category.

"In particular," the Committee said, "chlorpromazine is known to persist for very long periods in the human body (up to eighteen months), and it is therefore possible that repeated intake could result in accumulation of the drug, thereby increasing the pharmacological response."

12. Emilio Perez-Trallero, Mercedes Urbieta, Carmen Lopategul, Carmen Zigorraga, and Isabel Ayestaran, "Antibiotics in Veterinary Medicine and Public Health," *Lancet,* vol. 342, November 27, 1993, p. 1371.
13. "EPA to Study an Insecticide for Links to Cancer," *New York Times,* October 24, 1993, p. 21.
14. Cristophe Lambton, "Mamas Maketh Man," *Guardian* [S12 (2) February 11, 1993.
15. "Evaluation of Certain Veterinary Drug Residues," World Health Organization Technical Report Series, 1991, 815:1–64.

The Committee said examples of types of use that may cause high levels of residues include:

• Administration of a drug before slaughter, as when pigs are given tranquilizer drugs by injection immediately before transport to slaughter (the full pharmacological effect of the drug is exerted right up to the moment of slaughter, rendering a withdrawal period impossible). The potential of drug effect in the consumer is then of concern in addition to conventional toxicity.

• Veterinary drug treatment of animals slaughtered for human consumption before appropriate withdrawal times are observed.

• Implantation or injection of long-acting drugs with slow rates of absorption, such as anabolics (hormones), in edible tissue.

Such problems could be avoided the FAO/WHO Committee says "by ensuring that the injection site is excised and discarded at slaughter. In practice, this is difficult to achieve because the site is not readily recognizable unless the drug is colored or implanted in an inedible tissue. The site, its dimensions, and the efficiency of its removal would be liable to considerable variation. To accommodate these variables, a relatively large amount of tissue would have to be discarded, and it is probable that this practice would be seen as uneconomic."

The Committee recommends that measures be taken to limit the need for drugs used immediately prior to slaughter and thus likely to leave significant levels of residues in food. With regard to pigs, such measures may include improved preslaughter handling, transport, and shelter, and the elimination of stress-susceptible pigs from production.

With respect to residues at sites of injected drugs, the Committee recommended that implants or injections of long-acting and slowly absorbed substances should preferably be located in tissues that are discarded at slaughter, such as in the ears of cattle.

Chemicals in animal feed are also a big problem. For example, consider the following entry:

CARBADOX • An antibacterial used in animal feed for swine. The Expert Committee on Food Additives of the World Health Organization would not set an ADI or NOEL (*see both*) for this drug since it is a cancer-causing agent. FDA tolerance for carbadox residues in swine is zero.

You can't see carbadox in pork with the naked eye. Detection requires expensive chemical tests and trained personnel. We must then rely on the swine producer's honor to stop the antibacterial so that the residue is zero, as the FDA tolerance is set.

What About Additives Added Directly to Human Food?

What do you want from your food? You are part of the market force. By using this book to understand the labels and by selecting wisely, you can affect the sales of more wholesome foods and protect the health of your family.

There are more than three thousand indirect and direct common food additives in our diet, nearly two-thirds of them flavorings used to replace the natural flavors lost during processing. Contrary to public belief, food additives are not a modern innovation. Adding chemicals to food began in the dawn of civilization when man first discovered that by adding salt to meat, the meat would last longer.

The father of modern food-additives laws was Dr. Harvey W. Wiley, who in the early 1900s led the fight against chemical preservatives such as boric acid, formaldehyde, and salicylic acid. He dramatized the problem by his famous "Poison Squad," composed of young men willing to be guinea pigs, which meant eating measured amounts of these chemicals to determine toxicity.

As a result of Dr. Wiley's pioneering work, the first Federal Food and Drug Act was passed in 1906.

Food processors have in their armamentaria an estimated ten thousand chemicals they can add to what we eat. Some are deleterious, some are harmless, and some are beneficial.

Every one of these chemicals used in food processing must serve one or more of the following purposes:[16]

- Improve nutritional value.
- Enhance quality or consumer acceptability.
- Improve the keeping quality.
- Make the food more readily available.
- Facilitate its preparation.

The majority of food additives have nothing to do with nutritional value, as anyone can see from the contents of this dictionary.

Most of the chemicals added to enhance consumer acceptability are to feed our illusions. All our lives we have been subjected to the beautiful pictures of foods in our magazines and on television. We have come to expect an advertiser's concept of perfection in color and texture, even though Mother Nature may not turn out all her products that way. As a result, the skins of the oranges we eat are dyed bright orange to match our mental image of an ideal orange. Our poultry is fed a chemical to turn the meat yellower and more appetizing, and our fruits and vegetables are kept unblemished by fungicides, pesticides, herbicides, and other antispoilants.

To improve the keeping quality of some products, processors embalm them. Bread has sixteen chemicals to keep it feeling "fresh." One type of bread, balloon bread, undergoes rigor mortis thanks to its additive plaster of paris. Ironically, when nothing is added to the foods, they cost us considerably more. Unbleached flour is four times as much as bleached; untreated tomatoes, five times as much as regular canned tomatoes; and unsulfured raisins are six times the cost of treated ones.

---

16. According to the Food Protection Committee of the National Academy of Sciences, which evaluates the safety of additives.

Food companies ostensibly test additives for acute toxicity. Additives are fed to animals in large amounts at one time. Although most companies do not use control groups—for comparison, animals not fed any additive—or perform autopsies to determine any effects on tissues, they observe the animals for symptoms of ill effects. They also usually determine the lethal dose (if in fact the additive can be determined to be lethal) based on what kills 50 percent of the animals (LD 50). In subacute (*see*) studies, which have also been done for a number of food additives, the food chemical is fed to groups of animals in varying amounts nearly to the point of death. These tests usually last a minimum of three months and are made on at least two species of animals, most often rats and dogs. The data collected during the study includes appetite, thirst, growth rates, weight, blood and urine analyses, and behavior patterns. At the end of the study, all surviving animals are autopsied. These tests are expensive and time-consuming, often costing more than $250,000 for a single chemical.

In the mid-1970s, the FDA discovered that some of the 130 laboratories doing food-additive testing had serious deficiencies, and in the 1980s, several laboratory executives were indicted for fraud. The federal agency had relied on the basic accuracy and integrity of the data submitted to make decisions about approving food and color additives for the market. The FDA officials noted: "The submission of faulty, erroneous, or distorted data increases the potential for reaching invalid judgments about the safety of these additives."

In September 1980, the National Toxicology Program (NTP) contracted with the National Research Council (NRC) and the National Academy of Sciences for a study[17] with two principal charges:

1. To determine toxicity-testing needs for substances to which humans are exposed so that the federal agencies responsible for the protection of public health would have the information needed to assess the toxicity of such substances.

2. To develop and validate uniformly applicable and wide-ranging criteria by which to set priorities for research on substances with potentially adverse public-health impact.

The NRC considered 65,725 substances of possible concern, among them 8,627 food additives and 3,410 cosmetic ingredients approved for use. Through a random-sample program, one hundred of these substances were selected because they had at least some toxicity information. An in-depth examination of this subsample led to the conclusion that enough toxicity and exposure information is available for a complete health-hazard assessment to be conducted on only a small fraction of the subsample. On the great majority of the substances, data considered essential for conducting a health-hazard assessment are lacking. The NRC drew the following conclusions:

• When judged against current standards for toxicity testing, 92 percent of the tests in the subsample were inadequate.

17. National Research Council, op. cit.

- Of eighteen standard tests, only one—the oral administration in rodents—was judged adequate. The other seventeen tests necessary to meet the standards needed repetition or were not done at all in from 67 to 100 percent of the food additives.

- For food additives, a large variety of test types were found to be needed, such as chronic studies, inhalation studies, and more complex studies such as neurotoxicity, genetic toxicity, and effects on the fetus.

- There is no toxicity information available on 46 percent of the additives, and for only 5 percent is complete health-hazard assessment possible.

The National Research Council reports that although the number and uses of chemicals are voluminous, little is known about their hazards. A committee of the NRC found that no toxicity data is available for about 80 percent of 49,000 commercially used chemicals. Toxicity data were either inadequate or nonexistent for 64 percent of 1,800 drugs, and 80 percent of 8,600 food additives.

The fact is that a large percentage of the food additives have not been tested long-term—a great problem in determining chemical safety. Cancer, for instance, may take twenty years to develop in humans, and often more than two years in animals. Long-term safety is determined from rats, which live from eighteen to twenty-four months. However, researchers point out that laboratory animals are in a nonnatural, sterile environment and that in two years, 70 to 90 percent of them would be dead anyway and only two or three would be left for evaluation. Therefore, long-term tests may have invalid assurances of safety.

One partial solution, although not accepted by all scientists, is the Ames Test. In the early 1970s, Dr. Bruce Ames, a biochemist at the University of California at Berkeley, developed a simple test using common bacteria that reveals whether a chemical is a mutagen. The test can be done quickly and is relatively inexpensive. Mutagens act by changing the genetic material that is transferred to daughter cells when cell division occurs. Carcinogens also act by fouling up the genetic material within a cell. Almost all of the chemicals known to be carcinogenic have also been shown to be mutagenic by the Ames Test.

How valid are animal studies? All but two of the known human carcinogens—benzene and arsenic—are also carcinogenic in rodents. None of the approximately 143 "rodent" carcinogens have been proven to be noncarcinogenic in humans. Animal assays have predicted several human carcinogens, including three that may be contaminants in food: the mold found on nuts, aflatoxin; the plastic used in packaging, vinyl chloride; and the hormone once used to increase the weight of meat, diethylstilbestrol.

Incidentally, the FDA has set a limit for aflatoxins in nuts of fifteen parts per billion. If a batch exceeds that, the producers can add noncontaminated nuts to the batch to reduce levels, a system a number of food processors advocate for other undesirable additives such as low-potency carcinogens.[18]

18. "Public Issues, Private Medicine," symposium by Smith Kline Corp. and the College of Physicians of Philadelphia, December 6, 1978, in Philadelphia.

Another great problem with testing additives is how they interact with each other and with the 63,000 other chemicals in common use today. In 1976, *The Journal of Food Science* carried a report on a small-scale attempt to determine the extent of the problem. When three additives were tested one at a time on rats, the animals stayed well. Two at a time, the rats became ill, and with a three-additive combination, all the animals died within fourteen days.

As can be determined from the contents of this dictionary, not all questions concerning food-additive safety have been answered.

In the mid-1950s, when Food and Drug Administration scientists pushed for further laws, the FDA could not stop the use of a chemical simply because it was questionable or had not been adequately tested. It had to be provable in court that the chemical was poisonous or deleterious. But on September 6, 1958, the Food Additives Amendment was passed. Food and chemical manufacturers, as of that date, were required to run extensive tests on additives before they were marketed. Results of these tests had to be submitted to the FDA.

When the FDA finds data about an additive are sufficient to meet current criteria, the agency issues a Food Additive regulation approving the petitioned use of that specific substance. Previously regulated additives, though safe, might not entirely satisfy current criteria.

The FDA's Bureau of Foods has set up a computerized data bank, Priority Based Assessment of Food Additives (PAFA). Its primary function is to serve as a data repository on the toxicological effects of direct food additives as reported in the literature. PAFA is composed of an umbrella file, EAFUS (Everything Added to Food in the United States), containing all compounds identified by a National Academy of Sciences survey taken every six years. There are 2,945 additives now in the bank. PAFA does not include indirect food additives, food contaminants, or natural food constituents, although the FDA believes the inclusion of such chemicals in the future would be desirable.[19]

How is the information obtained? The FDA has a contract with five individuals to search the literature for toxicology information from internal of the agency and from external records in the community, including those in Russian or any other language. The researchers are assigned four chemicals per month. Some additives may take a short time to research because there is so little information about them, and some may take more than four years, such as caffeine, because there is so much data. The searchers also update up to sixty chemicals a month.[20]

Once the contractor has researched the literature on an additive, the result is checked by a second contractor. The information is then submitted to the FDA, where it is checked again and, finally, put into a "computer folder."

Daniel Benz, Ph.D., supervisor toxicologist, says the data bank can be accessed by the FDA should a question be raised about a particular additive. Once the additive is on the market, however, the FDA does not have the

---

19. "What is PAFA?" document supplied by the FDA to author, November 15, 1993.
20. Daniel Benz, Ph.D., personal contact with author, November 15, 1993.

authority to order a manufacturer to do additional testing. If a red flag is raised, the FDA can contract experts to study the toxicology.[21]

Alan Rules, Ph.D., who heads the project, is optimistic about the results of the computerization of information about food additives. In 1978, he said, they had little information about individual food additives. He said his department hopes to set up a system where food processors and scientists can tap into the database and obtain the latest information on the chemicals used. Additionally the database has been useful for international exchange of toxicological information and for prioritizing additives for review.

To date, the problem has not only been setting up a government fee and retrieval system, but also that some of the information on the database includes trade secrets.[22] The software is not yet available to enable outsiders to tap into the PAFA data bank. Under the Freedom of Information Act, however, any citizen can request printed information about a specific chemical.

The *Redbook*

While the testing of additives in our food for carcinogenicity may be imperfect, little if any testing is being done to determine if food additives may be toxic to the brain and nerves, although a number of scientists believe that neurotoxins are even more of a problem in food than carcinogens.[23, 24]

In 1982, the FDA started publishing *Redbook: Toxicological Principles for the Safety Assessment of Direct Food Additives and Color Additives Used in Food.* It set guidelines and priorities for testing additives. In 1992, the FDA started revising the book in light of developments in toxicological testing methods and comments from the scientific community and the public. The suggested revisions in the *Redbook* will emphasize neurotoxic hazards as a specific and important element in the routine safety assessment of proposed food chemicals, according to the FDA's Thomas J. Sobotka, Ph.D. He said the public has become alarmed and has demanded some assurances that appropriate and effective measures are being taken to minimize the environmental presence of neurotoxic substances, particularly in the daily food supply. The fact that some chemicals can adversely affect the nervous system is not a new concept in regulatory toxicology. In evaluating the safety of proposed food chemicals, he noted, the traditional concept of neurotoxicity focused on obvious pathological changes in the structure of the brain and nerves. Dr. Sobotka says:

> This view, however, does not reflect the full spectrum of adverse effects that a neurotoxicant may exert on the nervous system. Neurotoxicity is now understood to be a complex multidimensional process involving a sequence of interactive events. Invariably, this process is initiated at the molecular level through some neurochemical change that may subsequently result in an array of structural and functional

21. Ibid.
22. Personal communication with Alan Rules, Ph.D., August 11, 1988.
23. Bernard Weiss, Ph.D., *Nutrition Update* 1 (1983):21–38.
24. Charles Vorhees and R. E. Butcher, *Developmental Toxicology,* ed. K. Snell (London: Croom Helm, 1982), 247–98.

alterations. In humans, neurotoxicants can adversely affect a broad spectrum of behavioral functions, including the ability to learn, to interact appropriately with others, and to perceive and respond to environmental stimuli; basically these represent everyday functions that enable people to live productive lives. The focus placed on neurotoxicity will encourage the development of more relevant information about the potential adverse effects of chemicals on the structural and functional integrity of the nervous system and should help obtain the information needed for a reasonable assessment of potential neurotoxic hazard.[25]

Suspect Neurotoxic Additives

One of the major questions that will hopefully be answered in the new *Redbook* is the effect on the brain and nerves of such "excitotoxin" food additives as monosodium glutamate (MSG) or aspartame (NutraSweet). Excitotoxins are either extracted from natural sources or manufactured in the laboratory and have biologic properties that make them useful as food additives.[26] Glutamic acid (glutamate is its salt) derives its flavor-enhancing effects from its excitatory (depolarizing) action on sensory taste receptors. Aspartame, when combined with phenylalanine, also interacts with the taste receptors, resulting in the perceived sweet taste. The FDA does not place regulatory restriction on the use of glutamic acid (*see*) nor does it have a program for monitoring how or in what amount glutamate is used. Although glutamate is no longer being added to baby foods as it once was, young children are exposed to large loads of it through commercially available soups (1,300 mg) and in everything from bubble gum to soda.

Glutamate and aspartate cause lesions in the hypothalamic center of the brain in young mice. Hydrolyzed vegetable protein (HVP) is added to many of the same foods that are seasoned with glutamic acid. Since both glutamic acid and aspartame are released from protein during hydrolysis, HVP includes high concentrations of both of these excitotoxins. The brain-damaging properties of systemically administered protein hydrolysate have been demonstrated.

Cysteine-S-sulfonic acid (CSS) is another excitotoxin and is five to ten times more potent than glutamic acid. It is generated in foods because of the sulfite (*see*) that is added during processing. The excitotoxic amino acids are unique agents that interact with the central nervous system in ways that are different from other known neurotoxins.

John Olney, M.D., professor of psychiatry, University of Washington, St. Louis, Missouri, has long been a critic of glutamate, especially where it may affect the brains of children.[27] He says it is sometimes argued that glutamic acid and aspartame are safe food additives because humans have been exposed to

25. Thomas J. Sobotka, Ph.D., "Revisions to the FDA's *Redbook* Guidelines for Toxicity Testing: Neurotoxicity," *Critical Reviews in Food Science and Nutrition* 32(2) (1992):165–71.

26. J. W. Olney, "The Toxic Effects of Glutamate and Related Compounds," the Ophthalmic Communications Society, presented at the Symposium on Nutrition, Pharmacology, and Vision, sponsored by the Committee on Vision, National Research Council, National Academy of Sciences, Washington, D.C., November 16–17, 1981.

27. Ibid.

these compounds in one form or another for many years without sustaining harm. This argument overlooks the fact that brain and retinal damage from glutamic acid or aspartame is a silent phenomenon. When infant animals are given neurotoxic doses of glutamate or aspartame, they fail to manifest overt signs of distress while nerves in the brain and eye are actually degenerating. Indeed, there are no obvious changes in the animal's appearance or behavior until it is approaching adulthood. Thus, if glutamate or aspartame damage the hypothalamus of a human infant or child, delayed sequelae such as obesity and subtle disturbances in neuroendocrine status are the types of effects to be expected, and it would not be until adolescence or perhaps early adulthood that such effects would become clearly evident.

The hypothalamus is the brain area involved in emotions, movement, and eating. Less than the size of a peanut and weighing a quarter of an ounce, this small area deep within the brain also oversees appetite, blood pressure, sexual behavior, and sleep, and sends orders to the pituitary gland.

Researchers at Albert Einstein College of Medicine in New York, for example, have been working with a substance isolated from chickpeas that causes nerve damage similar to amyotrophic lateral sclerosis (ALS), Lou Gehrig's disease. They have been collaborating with Indian and Israeli scientists. The toxic component BOAA is chemically related to the two approved food additives glutamate and aspartate (the ingredients in the sweetener aspartame.)

The FDA has been evaluating MSG's safety since 1970. While some people admittedly have adverse reactions to MSG, the FDA maintains that the additive is safe. Indeed, the European Communities' Scientific Committee for Food and the Joint Expert Committee on Food Additives of the United Nations Food and Agricultural Organization and the World Health Organization have also placed MSG in the safest category of food additives.[28] It is up to you to decide for yourself about MSG's safety based on the above. Ask yourself if MSG is a necessary additive.

Setting Food Additive Amounts Worldwide

When we sit down to eat, our fruits may be from South America, our vegetables from the Middle East, our wine and cheese from Europe, and our crackers from Sweden. Our market baskets are, whether we are aware of it or not, filled with foods grown and processed in other lands.

The Food and Agriculture Organization of the United Nations/World Health Organization (FAO/WHO) Expert Committee on Food Additives evaluates the safety and residue information concerning direct and indirect additives. It makes recommendations that countries may or may not follow. The FAO/WHO experts, based on information given to them, calculate the following:

Acceptable Daily Intake (ADI)

This is an estimate of the amount of a substance in food or drinking water, expressed on a body-weight basis, that can be ingested daily over a lifetime with-

---

28. *FDA Backgrounder,* October 1991, Washington, D.C.

out appreciable health risk. The standard weight used for humans is sixty kilograms (132 pounds). The Committee has to take into consideration the ingestion for people who are regular eaters of those foodstuffs that contain the additive. For example, if they calculate the mean intake of the whole population for soft drinks, they obtain a daily per capita intake of about 150 ml per day. This figure is halfway between two groups of population: those who almost never use soft drinks and those who are regular drinkers. FAO/WHO calculates consumers who regularly use soft drinks actually ingest 600 ml per day (not quite a quart per day).

The level of intake of additives is closely related to the type of authorization given by a country's regulatory agencies. The FAO/WHO experts must consider the following when making their recommendations:

• Is the additive authorized in a large number of foodstuffs or in a restricted number? (It is difficult to calculate the intake of an additive when many additives are authorized in the same foodstuff and for the same reason [preservation]). For example, in some countries, due to its higher acceptable daily intake (ADI) designation, the preservative sorbic acid is authorized in more foodstuffs than the preservative benzoic acid (*see both*). Also, different production techniques, various climates, and other basic approaches for authorization must be taken into account.[29]

• Are those foodstuffs ingested in rather large amounts: grams a day, such as mustard, or a few hundred grams a day, such as bread, or even great amounts as with soft drinks?

• Is the level of authorized use a few parts per million (ppm) or a few thousand ppm, and, closely related to this point, is the additive really used in all the foodstuffs where it is authorized and is it used at the maximum level? Very often an industry tries to get higher levels than those really needed.

The FAO/WHO Expert Committee has priorities about certain food additives that need further investigation. In the top priority group is sulfur dioxide (*see*), which has a rather low acceptable daily intake but is widely used. It is followed in priority by benzoic acid and nitrates (*see both*). Nitrates are present in large amounts in some types of vegetables (salads, carrots, spinach, cabbage). The FAO/WHO experts want to know the risk of reduction of nitrates to potentially cancer-causing and blood-damaging nitrites and where that reduction can occur.

Maximum Residue Limits

In addition to setting the acceptable daily intakes (ADIs), the joint FAO/WHO Expert Committee on Food Additives also sets maximum residue limits (MRLs) based on the ADIs and covering the whole range of biological activity of a compound including its toxic, drug, and pest-killing potential. The

---

29.   M. Fondu, "Food Additives Intake," *Food Additives and Contaminants* 9, no. 5 (1992):535–39. Taylor & Francis Ltd.

ADI is expressed as a range extending from zero to the upper limit. The Committee tries to set the MRL below the upper limit of the ADI to reduce the potential exposure of the consumer to residues of veterinary drugs. The Committee establishes a Maximum Residue Limit for a drug based on the results of studies submitted to it. The Committee says it attempts to set a MRL that can be achieved through realistic withdrawal times and established good practices.

Noel Is Not a Celebration

The FAO/WHO Committee and other regulators are increasingly citing NOEL—the *No-Observed-Effect Level*—derived from the most appropriate study. The safety factor usually has a value of one hundred in the case of a NOEL derived from a long-term animal study, on the assumption that humans are ten times as sensitive as the test animal used and that there is a tenfold range of sensitivity within the human population. They keep talking about "no-effect levels" and pointing out that one part per billion is equal to one inch in sixteen thousand miles. The FDA estimates that exposure to DES—diethylstilbestrol—as low as one part per trillion may be associated with the risk of one cancer per million consumer lifetimes.

The FAO/WHO Committee and regulatory agencies worldwide obtain information from another United Nations organization, the International Agency for Research on Cancer (IARC). This entity gathers information on suspected environmental carcinogens and summarizes available data with appropriate references. Included in these reviews are synonyms, physical and chemical properties, uses and occurrence, and biological data relevant to the evaluation of the risk of cancer to humans. The more than forty monographs in the series contain an evaluation of about nine hundred materials.

United States Food Supply Guardians

Three federal agencies protect our food supply from harmful direct and indirect additives—the U.S. Department of Agriculture (USDA), the U.S. Environmental Protection Agency (EPA), and the U.S. Food and Drug Administration (FDA). The Food and Drug Administration oversees the majority of direct and indirect additives to food. The National Toxicology Program (NTP) is a U.S. government agency that has a Carcinogenesis Testing Program and makes recommendations to the FDA and EPA.

The food industry has been pushing for changes in the food laws. Among the new legislation they want:

• Define the term *safe* since a zero-risk standard is neither realistic nor desirable, they claim.

• Allow the comparison of risk and benefits when issuing or revoking approval for an additive since there is no need to ban a product where risk has been shown to be small or unproven, according to the industry. (This is now being touted as the *de minimis* approach with respect to carcinogens in the food supply. This common law is generally interpreted as meaning that the law does not care for or take notice of small or trifling matters.) By not banning all the carcinogens or carcinogen-containing foods or food ingredients being used, the FDA has been applying a *de minimis* concept.[30, 31]

• Permit a *gradual* phaseout of a product, they ask, since immediate bans on food additives disrupt the food supply and can cause severe economic hardship.

The advocates of such changes point out nitrites as an example of risk and benefit. Nitrites combine with natural stomach chemicals to cause nitrosamines, powerful cancer-causing agents, but nitrites also prevent botulism, a potentially fatal illness caused by contaminated food. Since, advocates claim, there is no good substitute for nitrites, their benefits outweigh their risks.

Unfortunately, when it comes to potentially harmful food additives, we take the risk while the food processor takes the benefits.

It is more important than ever that you read and understand the labels on food and have enough knowledge about what is claimed to make an informed choice. This book tells you about the additives in your food, where they come from, how they are used, and what is known about how they may affect your health.

Pick up a can, box, or any package of food. Do you understand the label? Do you know what is not on the label but may be added to the food?

What the food processor is offering has changed greatly since this book was first published in 1972. There were thirty-five widely used additives that had been approved as safe for food use then but have since been removed as unsafe, most of them because they were found to be capable of causing cancer. In 1978, food additives were a $1.3-billion-a-year business. Today, it is a more than $4.5-billion enterprise. In 1978, there were 164.1 million pounds of food additives in processed meat alone. Today, there are more than 363 million pounds.[32]

In order to get you to buy, the package has to be attractive, placed properly, priced right, and usually have "new" on it. Approximately eight thousand new food products are introduced in a year, some with new additives and many with new combinations of additives.[33]

A food additive is a substance, or mixture of substances other than basic foodstuffs, present in food as a result of any aspect of production, processing, storage, or packaging. The term does not include chance contaminants.

The FDA's requested 1994 budget was $209,000,000 for food and cosmetics. Of the 1,854 field officers, 1,149 are assigned to consumer safety for food, drugs, cosmetics, and medical devices; 29 are toxicologists; and 20 are food technolo-

---

30. "Congress Eyes Major Rewrite of Nation's Food Safety Laws," *American Medical News,* June 24, 1983.

31. Roger D. Middlekauf, "Delaney Meets De Minimis," *Food Technology,* November 1985, pp. 62–69.

32. *Food Product Development* (December 1980):36–40.

33. Ed Fitch, "Life in the food chain becomes predatory," Special Report, *Advertising Age,* May 9, 1988.

gists.[34, 35] They must cover the multibillion-dollar food, drug, medical-devices, and cosmetics industries with their hundreds of thousands of products. The FDA personnel, while well intentioned, do not have the resources to prevent all potentially harmful food additives from reaching the market. Your knowledge is your best protection.

Generally Recognized as Safe (GRAS) List

The GRAS list was established in 1958 by Congress. Those substances that had been added to food over a long time, which under the conditions of their intended use were generally recognized as safe by qualified scientists, would be exempt from premarket clearance. Congress had acted on a very marginal response—on the basis of returns from those scientists sent questionnaires. Only 355 out of 900 responded, and only about 100 of those responses had substantive comments. Three items were removed from the originally published list.

In recent years, developments in science and in consumer awareness have brought to light the inadequacies of the testing of food additives and, ironically, the complete lack of testing of the generally-recognized-as-safe category.

Cyclamates, the artificial sweeteners, were shown to be cancer-causing agents in laboratory animals and were removed from the market. They had been on the GRAS list. As a result, in 1969, Pres. Richard Nixon directed the FDA to reevaluate all of the items on the GRAS list. The study of the GRAS-list substances has been conducted by an expert advisory group—the Select Committee on GRAS Substances of the Federation of American Societies for Experimental Biology.

By 1980, 415 substances that had been in use prior to the 1958 Food Additives Amendment to the Food, Drug and Cosmetic Act were reviewed. The committee's evaluations were based on review of medical and scientific literature and unpublished reports. In some cases the research extended back sixty years. The number of references obtained for a given GRAS substance ranged from twenty-three reports for carnauba wax to two thousand for vitamin A. Of the 415 substances reviewed, 305 were given Class 1 status, which means they are considered safe for use at current levels and future anticipated levels under the conditions of good manufacturing practices.

Sixty-eight were placed in Class 2. They are considered safe for use at current levels, but the committee advised that more research is needed to determine whether a significant increase in consumption would constitute a dietary hazard. This category includes certain zinc salts, alginates, iron, tannic acid, sucrose, and vitamins A and D.

Class 3 status was given to nineteen substances for which the committee recommended additional studies because of unresolved questions in research data. The FDA issued interim regulations for this class of ingredients requiring that certain safety tests be undertaken within a specific time, but meanwhile permitting current use of the substances. Caffeine, BHA, and BHT were listed in this class.

34. FDA budget, provided author, October 20, 1993.
35. *FDA Field Officers Series for Scientific Employees,* provided by the FDA, October 25, 1993.

Five substances—salt and four modified starches—were placed in Class 4, which means the committee recommended that FDA establish safer conditions of use or prohibit addition of the ingredients to food.

The committee said there is no evidence that salt hurts most people but suggested that a reduction of salt in processed foods would benefit the 10 to 30 percent of the U.S. population genetically predisposed to high blood pressure and might thus reduce the frequency of hypertension.

Restrictions were also recommended on some starches—distarch glycerol and hydroxypropyl, acetylated and succinyl distarch glycerol—used primarily as thickening agents.

In addition, the use of lactic acid and calcium lactate was placed in this category for exclusion from infant formulas, because of reports of adverse effects. They are no longer used in infant formulas, except when needed in special medical compounds.

Class 5 had eighteen substances about which, the committee said, there were insufficient data to make any evaluation. These substances include some glycerides and certain iron salts. The FDA proposes removing these substances from the GRAS list unless sufficient data becomes available for evaluation.

Approximately one hundred new flavoring substances were designated as GRAS between 1980 and 1985, bringing the total of GRAS flavoring substances to 1,750.[36] Flavorings are added to our foods to replace the flavoring taken out of the food during processing.

The expert-committee evaluations and the questions raised about food additives continue. In the meantime, over 31 million Americans who are allergic even to the tiniest amount of some chemicals in foods (with allergic reactions ranging from a mild skin rash to death) can't wait.

The disturbing questions of long-term toxicity and carcinogenicity remain.

The purpose of this dictionary is to enable you to look up any additive under its alphabetical listing to determine whether to continue with a product because it is beneficial or reject it in favor of its betters.

Categories of Additives

The dictionary includes most of the food additives in common use. For the sake of clarity and ease of use, their nearly fifty functions are grouped under the following broad categories:

Preservatives

"Antispoilants" are used to help prevent microbiological spoilage and chemical deterioration. They are of many different types, of which about one hundred are in common use.

Preservatives for fatty products are called antioxidants, which prevent the production of off-flavors and off-odors. These include benzoic acid, used in margarine, and butylated hydroxyanisole (BHA), used in lard, shortenings, crackers, soup bases, and potato chips. In bread, preservatives are "mold" and

---

36. B. L. Oser et al., "GRAS Substances," *Food Technology* 39 (11) (November 1985):107–8, 110, 112.

"rope" inhibitors. They include sodium and calcium propionate, sodium diacetate, and such acidic substances as acetic acid and lactic acid. Sorbic acid and sodium and potassium salts are preservatives used in cheeses, syrups, and pie fillings. Preservatives used to prevent mold and fungus growth on citrus fruits are called fungicides.

Sequestering agents, still another type of preservative, prevent physical or chemical changes that affect color, flavor, texture, or appearance. Ethylenediaminetetraacetic acid (EDTA) and its salts, for instance, are used to prevent the adverse effects of the presence of metals in such products as soft drinks, where metal ions can cause clouding. Sequestrants used in dairy products to keep them "fresh and sweet" include sodium, calcium, and potassium salts of citric, tartaric, and pyrophosphoric acids. Other common multipurpose preservatives are the gas sulfur dioxide, propyl gallate, and, of course, sugar, salt, and vinegar.

Irradiated Food

When food is irradiated, it is loaded onto a conveyor belt and passed through a radiation cell where it is showered with beams of ionizing radiation produced by highly radioactive isotopes. The radiation can inhibit ripening and kill certain bacteria and molds that induce spoilage, so that food looks and tastes fresh for up to several weeks. The process does not make food radioactive or change the food's color or texture in most cases. Does it destroy nutrients? Does it create radiolytic products in food after exposure that may cause genetic damage? Is irradiation less dangerous than some of the other chemicals added to foods as preservatives? These questions are being hotly debated. Since bacteria in hamburgers caused several deaths in 1993, increased efforts to kill such contaminants in meat by irradiation are under way at this writing.

The FDA requires foods that have been irradiated to say so on the label and to display an international logo, a flower in a circle.

Fresh Refrigerated Products

Fresh refrigerated products now account for $500 million of the $450 billion U.S. food industry and are expected to grow at 14 percent per year. These processed foods are designed to offer the convenience of frozen and canned foods while providing homemade taste and appearance. Typically, they are cooked just enough to ward off spoilage for a short period of time. As a further aid to freshness, they are often sealed in packaging that contains little or no oxygen, which can extend shelf life for several weeks. Scientists, however, are concerned that some dangerous bacteria may not be killed during the minimal precooking and that microorganisms that cause botulism can flourish in an oxygen-free environment. One publicized outbreak of botulism associated with this category could devastate it.

Acids, Alkalies, Buffers, Neutralizers

The degree of acidity or alkalinity is important in many processed foods. An acid such as potassium acid tartrate, sodium aluminum phosphate, or tartaric acid acts on the leavening agent in baked goods and releases the gas that causes the desired "rising." The flavor of many soft drinks, other than cola types, is modified by the use of an acid such as citric acid from citrus fruits, malic acid from apples, or tartaric acid, a component of grapes. Phosphoric acid is used to give colas the "tangy" taste. The same acids that are used in soft drinks are also used in churning cream to help preserve the flavor and keeping quality of butter. Alkalies such as ammonium hydroxide in cocoa products and ammonium carbonate in candy, cookies, and crackers are employed to make the products more alkaline. Buffers and neutralizing agents are chemicals added to foods to control acidity or alkalinity, just as acids and alkalies are added directly. Some common chemicals in this class are ammonium bicarbonate, calcium carbonate, potassium acid tartrate, sodium aluminum phosphate, and tartaric acid.

Moisture Content Controls

Humectants are necessary in the production of some types of confections and candy to prevent drying out. Without a humectant, shredded coconut, for example, would not remain soft and pliable. Substances used for this purpose include glycerine, which retains the soft, moist texture in marshmallows, propylene glycol, and sorbitol. On the other hand, calcium silicate is used to prevent table salt from caking due to moisture absorption from the air.

Coloring Agents

Food colors of both natural and synthetic origin are extensively used in processed foods, and they play a major role in increasing the acceptability and attractiveness of these products. However, the indiscriminate use of color can conceal damage or inferiority or make the product appear better than it actually is. The World Health Organization, in delineating some 140 different kinds of colorants, found many to be unsafe. Coal-tar colors were subject to a special provision in a 1938 law that required every coal-tar color used in food to be listed with the government as "harmless and suitable for use," and every batch of the color intended for use in food had to be certified by a government agency as safe. Some of the colors originally listed as "harmless" were found to produce injury when fed to animals and were removed from the list. In 1960, the federal government required manufacturers to retest all artificial colors to determine safety. At present, nine are permanently listed as safe. Among them, FD and C Blue No. 1 and FD and C Citrus Red No. 2 have been shown to cause tumors at the site of injection in animals, but the FDA does not consider this significant because the experiment concerned injection by needle and not by ingestion in food or application on the skin. FD and C Red No. 40, one of the most widely used colorings, is also being questioned because it is made from a base known to be carcinogenic and because many scientists feel that it should not have been given permanent listing based solely on the manufacturer's tests.

Among the natural colors used in foods are alkanet, annatto, carotene, chlorophyll, cochineal, saffron, and turmeric. Foods that are frequently colored include candies, baked goods, soft drinks, and such dairy products as butter, cheese, and cream.

Flavorings

Of the three thousand food additives known to be added to our food supply, two thousand are flavorings to replace the flavors lost during processing. Of these, some five hundred are natural and the balance synthetic. A wide variety of spices, natural extractives, oleoresins, and essential oils are used in processed foods in addition to what the modern flavor chemist has synthetically produced. Both types of products are used extensively in soft drinks, baked goods, ice cream, and confectionery. They are usually employed in amounts ranging from a few to three hundred parts per million. Amyl acetate, benzaldehyde, carvone, ethyl acetate, ethyl butyrate, and methyl salicylate are typical compounds employed in the preparation of flavoring materials. However, many of the compounds used in synthetic flavorings are also found in natural products or derive from natural acids. Essential oils, such as oil of lemon and oil of orange, are natural flavors made by extraction from the fruit rind. There are also flavor enhancers, the commonest being monosodium glutamate (MSG) and maltol.

Physiologic Activity Controls

The chemicals in this group are added to fresh foods to serve as ripeners or antimetabolic agents. For instance, ethylene gas is used to hasten the ripening of bananas, and maleic hydrazide is used to prevent potatoes from sprouting. Coming into increasing use are enzymes that are of natural origin and generally believed to be nontoxic. Of all food enzyme additives, amylases, which act on starch, have the most numerous applications. Various amylases from plant, animal, fungal, and bacterial sources have been used to break down the components of starch to make it more digestible. Enzymes are also used in the fermentation of sugar to make candy, in the brewing industry, and in the manufacture of artificial honey, bread, and frozen milk concentrates.

Bleaching and Maturing Agents/Bread Improvers

Fresh-ground flour is pale yellow. Upon storage, it slowly becomes white and undergoes an aging process that improves its baking qualities. For more than fifty years, processors have added oxidizing agents to the flour to accelerate this process, thus reducing storage costs, spoilage, and the opportunity for insect infestation. Compounds such as benzoyl peroxide bleach the flour without effect on baking qualities. Other compounds, such as oxides of nitrogen, chlorine dioxide, nitrosyl chloride, and chlorine, have both a bleaching and maturing or "improving" ability. Bread improvers used by the baking industry contain oxidizing substances such as potassium bromate, potassium iodate, and calcium peroxide. They also contain inorganic salts such as ammonium or calcium sulfate and ammonium phosphates, which serve as yeast foods and dough conditioners. Quantities used are relatively small since these can easily result in an inferior product. Bleaching agents may also be used in other foods, such as cheese, to improve the appearance of the finished product.

Processing Aids

Many chemicals fall into this category. Sanitizing agents, for instance, to clean bacteria and debris from products, are considered such aids. So are clarifying agents, which remove extraneous materials. Tannin, for instance, is used for clarifying liquids in the wine and brewing industries. Gelatin and albumen remove small particles and minute traces of copper and iron in the production of vinegar and some beverages. Emulsifiers and emulsion stabilizers help to maintain a mixture and assure a consistency. They affect such characteristics as volume, uniformity, and fineness of grain (bakery products have a softer "crumb" and slower "firming" rate). They influence ease of mixing and smoothness, such as the whipping property of frozen desserts and the smoothness of cake mixes. They help maintain homogeneity and keeping quality in such products as mayonnaise, candy, and salad dressing. Some common emulsifiers are lecithin, the monoglycerides and diglycerides, and propylene glycol alginate. Sorbitan derivatives are used to retard "bloom," the whitish deposits of high-melting components of cocoa butter that occasionally appear on the surface of chocolate candy. Food chemists sometimes call emulsifiers "surfactants" or "surface-active agents."

Texturizers or stabilizers are added to products to give them "body" and maintain a desired texture. For instance, calcium chloride or some other calcium salt is added to canned tomatoes and canned potatoes to keep them from falling apart. Sodium nitrate and sodium nitrite are used in curing meats to develop and stabilize the pink color. Nitrogen, carbon dioxide, and nitrous oxide are employed in pressure-packed containers of certain foods to act as whipping agents or as propellants. The texture of ice cream and other frozen desserts is dependent on the size of the ice crystals in the product. By addition of agar-agar, gelatin, cellulose gum, or some other gum, the size of the ice crystals is stabilized. Texturizer gums are also used in chocolate milk to increase the viscosity of the product and to prevent the settling of cocoa particles to the bottom of the container. Gelatin, pectin, and starch are used in confectionery products to give a desired texture. Artificially sweetened beverages also need products to give a desired texture, plus bodying agents because they do not contain the "thickness" normally contributed by sugar. The thickeners employed include such natural gums as sodium alginate and pectins. The foaming properties of brewed beer can also be improved by the addition of texturizers.

Nutrition Supplements

Enrichment of food means that the natural nutrients have been removed during processing and then replaced. Enrichment of cereal foods, much touted by the big producers, according to them provides 12 to 23 percent of the daily supply of thiamine, niacin, and iron, and 10 percent of the riboflavin recommended for human consumption.

Fortification of food means that additional nutrients are added to the product to make it more nutritious than it was before. For instance, vitamin C is added to orange drinks and vitamin A to margarine. Vitamin D is used to fortify milk to prevent rickets, and potassium iodide is added to iodized salt to prevent goiter, a thyroid tumor caused by iodine deficiency.

Amino acids, the building blocks of protein, may become commonly used as additives. The amino acid used most often in the food industry today is monosodium glutamate, which enhances flavor. Actually, the human body needs certain amino acids not manufactured in the body in sufficient amounts, and some processors add these to increase the protein component of their product.

A number of additional substances are employed for various purposes. Certain sugar substitutes are used in food for people who must restrict their intake of ordinary sweets. Saccharin and sorbitol are commonly used for this purpose. Glazes and polishes such as waxes and gum benzoin are used on coated confections to give luster to an otherwise dull surface. Magnesium carbonate and tricalcium phosphate are employed as anticaking agents in table salt, and calcium stearate is used for a similar purpose in garlic salt.

More Information Is Needed on Food Additives

Although officially the FDA claims to know what additives are being used in food, FDA researchers report that it is impossible to check small manufacturers. Efforts have been made through the years to have food manufacturers register and provide the information, but as yet, there is no law requiring them to do so.

There is still much to learn about additives. As you will conclude when you read the entries in this book, many additives are beneficial and necessary, and others should be removed from our food supply as soon as possible.

Labeling

A food label is a contract between us and the manufacturer. Like most contracts, it may be difficult to understand, and what is not included may be as important as what is.

The provisions of the Nutrition Labeling and Education Act (NLEA) and the Dietary Supplement Act of 1992 are the first major changes in food-labeling regulations since 1974. As of May 8, 1994, food producers had to comply with most of FDA's new labeling requirements. (Advertising is not covered by NLEA; the Federal Trade Commission, however, has indicated it may apply the same criteria to advertising that FDA does to labels.)

Experts believe that the new labels will lead to fewer diet-related diseases and a lower incidence of cancer because shoppers will have the information they need to make informed food choices. The government estimates that over the next twenty years, the new labels will reduce national health-care costs substantially by making it easier for the public to choose more healthful diets.

The new regulations have more realistic serving sizes. Instead of a food manufacturer presenting a low calorie or fat count for half a teaspoonful, they will have to give the count for half a cup—the realistic serving size.

Many more products will have labels because the regulations, for the first time, make nutrition labeling mandatory for almost all processed foods. Also, uniform point-of-purchase nutrition information will accompany many fresh foods, such as fruits and vegetables and raw fish, meat, and poultry.

The FDA and USDA previously established a standard of identity for about three hundred foods such as peanut butter, mayonnaise, and fruit cocktails, fixing the ingredients by law. Many of these foods were exempted from the need to list ingredients. The new labeling requires full ingredient listing for *all* foods. It also allows manufacturers for the first time to produce healthier versions of some products and still use the recognized name. For instance, a reduced-fat ice cream does not have to be called "imitation" or "ice milk" but can be called "low-fat ice cream."

The FDA says under the new Nutrition Labeling and Education Act any term used to describe the nutrient content of a food will mean the same on every product on which it appears. Also, the list of acceptable claims now includes such descriptors as *free, low, light* (or *lite*), *reduced, less,* and *high. Lean* and *extra lean* also have been defined and will apply specifically to the fat content of meat, including game meat, poultry, and fish (see page 28).

The following are explanations set forth by the FDA of the new labeling changes. *Daily values (DVs)* comprise two sets of references for nutrients, *daily reference values (DRVs)* and *reference daily intakes (RDIs)*.

Daily Reference Values (DRVs)

These are for nutrients for which no set of standards previously existed, such as fat, cholesterol, carbohydrates, proteins, and fibers. DRVs for these energy-producing nutrients are based on the number of calories consumed per day. For labeling purposes, two thousand calories has been established as the reference for calculating the percent of daily values. This level was chosen, in part, because many health experts say it approximates the maintenance calorie requirements of the group most often targeted for weight reduction: postmenopausal women.

DRVs for the energy-producing nutrients are calculated as follows:

- Fat based on 30 percent of calories.
- Saturated fat based on 10 percent of calories.
- Carbohydrates based on 60 percent of calories.
- Protein based on 10 percent of calories.
- Fiber based on 11.5 grams of fiber per 1,000 calories.

The DRVs for cholesterol, sodium, and potassium, which do not contribute calories, remain the same no matter what the calorie level.

Because of the links between certain nutrients and specific diseases, DRVs for some nutrients represent the uppermost limit considered desirable. Eating too much fat or cholesterol, for example, has been linked to heart disease, and too much sodium to the risk of high blood pressure. Therefore, the label shows DVs for fats and sodium as follows:

- Total fat: less than 65 g.
- Saturated fat: less than 20 g.
- Cholesterol: less than 300 mg.
- Sodium: less than 2,400 mg.

Reference Daily Intakes (RDIs)

A set of dietary references based on and replacing the *recommended dietary allowances* (*RDAs*) for essential vitamins and minerals and, in selected groups, protein. You will continue to see vitamins and minerals expressed as percentages on the label, but these figures now refer to the daily values.

Here are the RDIs—once familiar to us as RDAs:

Nutrient	Amount
vitamin A	5,000 international units (IU)
vitamin C	60 milligrams (mg)
thiamine	1.5 mg
riboflavin	1.7 mg
niacin	20 mg
calcium	1 gram (g)
iron	18 mg
vitamin D	400 IU
vitamin E	30 IU
vitamin B_6	2.0 mg
folic acid	0.4 mg
vitamin B_{12}	6 micrograms (mcg)
phosphorus	1 g
iodine	150 mcg
magnesium	400 mg
zinc	15 mg
copper	2 mg
biotin	0.3 mg
pantothenic acid	10 mg

Based on National Academy of Sciences 1968 recommended dietary allowances.

The dietary components on the new label and the order in which they must appear are:

- total calories
- calories from fat
- calories from saturated fat
- total saturated fat
- stearic acid (on meat and poultry products only)
- polyunsaturated fat
- monounsaturated fats
- cholesterol
- sodium
- potassium
- total carbohydrate

- dietary fiber
- soluble fiber
- insoluble fiber
- sugars
- sugar alcohol (for example, the sugar substitutes xylitol, mannitol, and sorbitol)
- other carbohydrate (the difference between total carbohydrate and the sum of dietary fiber, sugars, and sugar alcohol, if declared)
- protein
- vitamin A
- percent of vitamin A present as beta-carotene
- vitamin C
- calcium
- iron
- other essential vitamins and minerals

If a food is fortified or enriched with any of the optional components, or a claim is made about any of them, pertinent additional nutrition information becomes mandatory. These mandatory and voluntary components are the only ones allowed on the nutrition panel.

No Nutrition Information

Some foods are exempt from nutrition labeling. Due to space limitations, small packages such as a candy bar do *not* have to provide nutrition information on the label. However, the address or telephone number must be provided for shoppers who wish to obtain this material. Other foods that do not have to provide nutrition labeling include:

- Food produced by small businesses. (As mandated by NLEA, FDA defines a small business as one with food sales of less than $50,000 a year or total sales of less than $500,000. The U.S. Department of Agriculture's Food and Safety Inspection Service (FSIS) defines a small business as one employing five hundred or fewer employees and producing no more than a certain amount of product per year.)

- Food served for immediate consumption, such as that served in restaurants and hospital cafeterias, on airplanes, and by food-service vendors (such as mall cookie counters, sidewalk vendors, and vending machines).

- Ready-to-eat foods that are not for immediate consumption, as long as the food is primarily prepared on-site—for example, many bakery, deli, and candy-store items.

- Food shipped in bulk, as long as it is not for sale in that form to consumers.

- Medical foods.

- Plain coffee and tea, flavor extracts, food colors, some spices, and other foods that contain no significant amounts of any nutrients.

- Donated foods.

- Products intended for export.

- Individually wrapped FSIS-regulated products weighing less than half an ounce and making no nutrient content claims.

Although these foods are exempt, they are free to carry nutrition information when appropriate as long as it complies with the new regulations.

A great controversy was occurring at this writing concerning the labeling of bioengineered foods such as the new "flavr Savr" tomato and milk produced with bovine somatotropin (BST) (see). The FDA is saying that there is no need to identify genetically engineered foods on the label and in fact warned dairy food producers not to say that no BST was used in their products.[37]

The following are other label terms:

- *Standards of quality* . . . ensure that only those fruits and vegetables of high quality, free of defects, are used. Products of lesser quality have to signify that on the label (for example mandarin orange pieces instead of segments).

- *Standards of composition* . . . regulate the amounts of cooked meat and poultry that processed products must contain. These standards dictate how much chicken goes into a chicken pot pie along with the peas and gravy. When shopping, you can compare foods for overall content. In "beef with noodles," beef is the main ingredient. In "noodles with beef," noodles are the main ingredient.

- *Standards of fill* . . . guarantee that a minimum amount of food is placed in a container and prohibits excessive amounts of air or water.

- *As packaged* . . . refers to the state of the product as it is marked for purchase, while *as prepared* refers to the product after it has been made ready for consumption (e.g., ingredients added per instructions and cooked, such as a cake mix that has been prepared and baked or a condensed or dry soup that has been reconstituted).

- *Food grading* and *inspection* . . . assure purity, wholesomeness, and appearance. The USDA has established grades for more than three hundred food products. Grading for most products is done voluntarily at the manufacturer's request (and expense) by a USDA inspector, and a USDA grade symbol may then appear on the package; lack of a symbol does not mean substandard product. Unfortunately, these grades lack continuity across product categories (Grade AA is the highest grade for eggs; Grade A is the highest for milk). Meat and poultry, however, whether fresh or processed and packaged must be inspected and carry an inspection stamp.

- *Low calorie* . . . fewer than forty calories per serving.

- *Low sodium* . . . 140 mg or less per serving.

- *Very low sodium* . . . less than 35 mg per serving.

37. Keith Schneider, "FDA Warns the Dairy Industry Not to Label Milk Hormone-Free," *New York Times,* February 8, 1994, p. 1.

- *Sodium free* . . . less than 5 mg per serving.

- *Low fat* . . . 3 g or less per serving.

- *Low saturated fat* . . . means 1 g or less per serving.

- *Low cholesterol* . . . signifies 20 mg or less per serving.

- *High* or *source of* . . . denotes the beneficial presence of a nutrient, such as fiber or vitamins.

- *High* or *excellent source of* . . . contains 20 percent or more of the daily value (*see*) for a particular nutrient in a serving.

- *Good source of* . . . supplies 10 to 19 percent of the daily value for a particular nutrient.

- *Reduced, less, light,* and *more* . . . are terms that compare to a regular product or comparable food.

- *Reduced* . . . means a product has been nutritionally altered and contains at least 25 percent less of a nutrient (such as fat) or 25 percent fewer calories than the regular product.

- *Less* . . . means a product contains 25 percent less of a nutrient or 25 percent fewer calories than the reference food. For example, pretzels that have 25 percent less fat than potato chips could carry a "less" claim.

- *Light* or *lite* . . . signifies a product contains one-third fewer calories or one-half the fat of the comparison food. "Light in sodium" may be used on food in which the sodium content has been reduced by at least 50 percent.

- *More* . . . means a product contains at least 10 percent more of the daily value for a desirable nutrient, such as fiber, than the regular food.

- *Fresh* . . . signifies a food that has not been heat-processed or frozen and contains no preservatives.

- *Lean* and *extra lean* . . . describe the fat content of meats, poultry, seafood, and game meats. *Lean* = fewer than 10 g fat per serving. *Extra lean* = fewer than 5 g fat per serving.

- *Percent fat free* . . . is used only to describe foods that qualify as low fat.

- *Natural* or *organic* . . . appears on many products, but they have no legal meaning, and food labels may claim that a product is "natural" and contains "no preservatives or MSG." The very same product may be next to it on the shelf, make no health claims, also contain no preservatives or MSG, and be a fraction of the price. "Natural Food" sales, never-the-less totaled $5.28 billion in 1992, up 13.8% from the year before.[38]

Interpreting Label Language

Requiring nutrients to be declared as a percent of the daily value, daily reference values, reference daily intakes, and all the other new labeling changes

---

38.   Laura Loro, "Sales Bloom for Natural Foods," *Advertising Age,* November 8, 1993, p. 39.

are intended to help us understand the role of individual foods in our total daily diet. Confusing? The FDA believes that understanding it will soon become second nature for us label readers.

Whether or not the new terms inform or confuse, there will still be terms on packages that may be misleading. For example, *unsalted, processed without salt,* or *no salt added* can signify the producer didn't put any additional salt in during processing, but the food may still be naturally high in sodium. The basic sources of cereals, on the other hand, are salt free—wheat, corn, rice, and oats. Yet instant oatmeal contains about 360 mg per serving, instant corn grits 590 mg, and instant cream of wheat 180 mg. If you're willing to cook the cereals a little bit, you can avoid the high salt. It's providing the "instant" that dishes out the sodium. Some seventy sodium compounds are used in foods, as you will see in this book. The National Academy of Sciences, whose experts establish dietary guidelines, recommends that we ingest no more than 1,100 to 3,000 milligrams of sodium for the entire day. The average American ingests 5,000 to 7,000 milligrams. If the numbers for sodium look very low on a label, look again and be aware of the difference between milligrams (mg) and grams (g). Some companies make you think there is less by saying 2 grams of sodium, for example, which is really 2,000 milligrams.

Sugar also masquerades under a variety of names, as you will also read in this book, and sometimes it is difficult to avoid. Common table sugar (sucrose), fructose, and corn syrup are among the types of calorie-containing sweeteners found in foods. A food can be labeled *sugar free* or *sugarless* and still contain calories from sugar alcohols (xylitol, sorbitol, and mannitol), provided the basis for the claim is explained (but not necessarily understood). Saccharin is a nonnutritive sweetener—that is, it has no calories. Aspartame has the same calories as sugar, but is so much sweeter that only small amounts are needed to provide the desired sweetness in a product.

We may even be getting more than we bargained for when we get our sweets from fruit juice. A popular brand of diet fruit juice has a beautiful picture of an open pineapple and a cut orange on its label proclaiming it to be "sugar free" and "low sodium." It is, however, colored with FD and C Yellow No. 5 and No. 6, both recognized allergens, flavored with benzoate of soda, also a common allergen, and artificially sweetened with saccharin and aspartame. Now, from what tree was that concoction harvested?

Who Checks the Nutritional Analysis of a Product?

The author, being on a low-salt diet, has often wondered who checks the analysis of a product for the amount of sodium or any other ingredient. The FDA does not approve and is not in a position to endorse or recommend specific laboratories. The FDA tells food processors: "Assistance may be available through the following sources: trade and professional associations, trade publications, colleges and universities, and by looking in local phone books under testing or analytical laboratories. For compliance purposes, FDA uses appropriate methods published by the Association of Analytical Chemists in *Official Methods of Analysis of the AOAC International,* 15th edition (1990), or other methods needed. You [the food processor] may wish to ascertain if the laboratory is familiar with these methodologies when selecting a laboratory."

When researchers at Columbia University, New York, checked the calorie content of packaged foods, they found the actual calories as much as three-and-one-half times higher than the labels indicated. The blatant underestimations occurred with regionally sold foods rather than with national brands.[39]

Raw Information

Safety labels on raw meat and poultry under federal safety rules in effect since August 1993 require all uncooked products to carry labels with cooking and handling instructions. This regulation is aimed at cutting down on the incidence of food poisoning due to improper food handling.

What Do You Want to Eat?

Food processors and vendors attempt to sell us what we demand. In our fast-paced and complicated world today, we are in the market for:

- Instant food
- Instant health

Instant Food

We want convenience, which by definition means ease and speed of preparation or use, and higher costs. If we spend the day on the job outside the home, we no longer have the time or energy to shop frequently or to spend hours preparing a meal. Households have shrunk in size, and the traditional sit-down family dinner has gone the way of handheld can opener.

The growing use of the microwave oven has also encouraged the use of convenience foods. In 1978, only 11 percent of American homes had the quick-cooking devices. Now, an estimated 80 percent of homes have them, and processed food products for microwaving are burgeoning.[40]

Those foods that are easier to prepare pass through many hands to be mashed, mushed, mangled, and loaded with chemicals so that we can have cake mixes and peeled and sliced potatoes and instant everything.

Technology has so advanced, or retreated, depending upon one's view, that some foods are almost pure ersatz. One well-known orange-flavored drink aimed at athletic-minded adults and children claims it "works 30 percent faster than water" as a thirst quencher. Its main ingredient is water, followed by glucose syrup solids (sugar), sucrose (sugar), citric acid, natural orange flavor with other natural flavors, salt, sodium citrate (another salt), monopotassium phosphate, ester gum, yellow 6 (to which many people are allergic), and brominated vegetable oil. It claims to "speed refreshment where you need it—deep down." If you think this product will make you perform better and longer, sit down. It

39. Roger Field, "Calorie Counts on Food Labels Can Be Misleading," *Medical Tribune,* October 21, 1993, p. 3.
40. "Scouts Agree: It's Hot If It's Microwavable," *Advertising Age,* May 9, 1988, p. S-16.

is orange-colored water laced with sugar and salt and a lot of hype. It also contains fifty calories, while water has none.

Plain water is good for you and so is plain rice. But one popular product on supermarket shelves contains, in addition to rice, 700 mg of sodium, 1 gram of fat, 130 calories, plus monosodium glutamate, corn syrup, brown sugar, molasses, caramel color, artificial flavors, disodium inosinate, disodium guanylate, and sodium sulfite for color retention. Look up all those additives in this dictionary and then opt for a nice package of plain brown rice.

By law, the label must identify the product in a language the consumer can understand. It must indicate the manufacturer, the packer or distributor, and declare the quantity of contents either in net weight or volume, with the ingredients listed in order of predominance. The label must be accurate in any statement about the product. Also, if a vignette or picture of the product is placed on the label, it is supposed to be truly representative of the container's contents. Can a packaged or processed food contain "instant health"?

Instant Health

The idea that food could prevent diseases such as cancer and heart attacks had been assigned by health and government agencies to the health "nut" category when the first edition of this book was published in 1972. In 1980, the Surgeon General's Office issued a report setting nutritional objectives for the nation by 1990 for improving the health of Americans. Some of the specific objectives were weight control, reduction in the population's serum cholesterol levels; reduced daily sodium intake; reduced consumption of potentially carcinogenic foods; and increased promotion and awareness of U.S. Department of Agriculture dietary guidelines.

The National Food Processors Association reaction to the Surgeon General's report was cited in an editorial in the March 1981 issue of *Food Product Development,* a trade journal:

> It should not be government's role in a free society to intervene or interfere in the production of manufactured foodstuffs to ensure their nutritional quality and content, a "technologic measure" suggested in the report. Such a policy could lead to government control over the food processing industry, lessening of competition, and stagnation in the development of new products with attributes desired by consumer.
>
> Nor is the positioning of products in the supermarkets to make nutrition information readily apparent, also suggested in the report, a province of government. So many factors are involved in shelf positioning of products that it is absurd to suggest that the presentation of nutrition information might become the overriding consideration.
>
> The food processing industry is opposed to promulgation of guidelines to maintain or improve the nutritional quality of the food supply. Again, development of food products should be unfettered by government regulation, even in the guise of guidelines, and left to the play of market forces.[41]

41. Fran LaBell, Editorial, *Food Product Development* (March 1981):70.

Now, many of the largest food processors have changed their collective minds. Health claims sell! As of this writing, labels are now carrying health claims citing recommendations for preventive diets from such staid organizations as the National Cancer Institute, the American Heart Association, and the American Cancer Society.

The FDA began to tolerate health messages on food packages when in October 1984 the Kellogg Company began displaying "Preventive health tips from the National Cancer Institute" including high-fiber, low-fat foods. Of course, their bran flakes were high fiber, low fat. The campaign not only helped boost sales of high-fiber cereals in general but also cut into the consumer purchase of low-fiber cereals.

In 1987, the FDA said that it "believes it is important to consider ways to improve the public's understanding about health benefits that can result from adhering to a sound and nutritious diet . . . the rapid growth of scientific and public interest in nutrition argues for recognition and dissemination of such new knowledge, and food labels offer one appropriate vehicle for this dissemination."[42]

The FDA cited three principal factors for proposing the change in its former policy:

• The growing scientific evidence that suggests a link between diet and various illnesses, such as cancer and coronary heart disease, and that people can reduce their risk of those diseases by eating more or less of various types of foods.

• Consumer interest in learning more about how to improve their diets, avoid diet-related illness, and generally stay healthier.

• Food industry interest in marketing and promoting products for their potential health benefits.

Health Claims

The FDA lists the following criteria to determine the "propriety of the health-related claims and information": the health message or claims made on food labels must be truthful and not misleading to consumers, and they "should not imply that a particular food [can] be used as part of a druglike treatment or therapy-oriented approach to health care." Further, the information "must not overemphasize or distort the role of a food" in promoting good health.

Claims linking a nutrient or a food to the risk of a disease or health-related condition are allowed only under certain circumstances on FDA-regulated products. At this writing, the FDA only permits statements about the relationships between:

• calcium and osteoporosis

• fat and cancer

• saturated fat and cholesterol and coronary heart disease (CHD)

---

42. "Selling Nutrition: Should Food Packages Carry Health Messages?" *FDA Consumer* (November 1987):22–25.

- fiber-containing grain products, fruits, and vegetables and cancer
- fruits, vegetables, and grain products that contain fiber, particularly soluble fiber and coronary heart disease
- sodium and hypertension

The claims must be supported by "valid, reliable, publicly available scientific evidence . . . and should conform to generally recognized medical and nutritional principles" for a sound, total diet. The "weight of scientific evidence" must support a health claim to ensure that the "substance of the message has achieved sufficient scientific recognition to be appropriate and nonmisleading."

The claims must clearly indicate that good nutrition is the result of the total diet and not a result of eating a specific food or foods. That requirement conforms to the traditional advice of most nutrition experts that people should eat a varied but balanced diet of nutritious foods.

Nutrition labeling is mandatory on any product making a health claim. In general, the purpose of the nutrition label is to inform consumers of the calories, protein, carbohydrate, fat, sodium, and certain essential vitamins and minerals present in each serving of a product.

But should you "swallow" everything a food processor puts on the label about the health benefits of a product? A soup company, for example, created a conflict when it claimed: "You can get as much fiber from a serving of home style bean soup as you can from a serving of many bran cereals . . . and fiber is important because the National Cancer Institute says that a diet high in fiber and low in fat may help reduce the risk of some kinds of cancer."

The Cancer Institute found the advertisement misleading because the company's bean and pea soups contained six hundred to seven hundred milligrams of sodium, much higher than the Department of Health and Human Services maintains is prudent. The Cancer Institute's name was removed from advertising in 1987–88.

Likewise, the Dairy Board highlighted the benefits of calcium, which is high in dairy products, but left out that they are also high in fat and sodium.

Even that old home remedy chicken soup is not immune. How about a product that is promoted as very low sodium? *Chicken* and *bouillon* are in big letters on the package, and in between in smaller letters is the word *flavor*. The ingredients in descending order of amount are dextrose, potassium chloride, hydrolyzed cereal solids, autolyzed yeast, chicken fat, onion powder, monoammonium glutamate, gelatin, natural chicken flavor, spices, garlic powder, turmeric, disodium inosinate, disodium guanylate, and carrot powder. Chances are neither your mother nor a chicken would recognize it. Very low sodium is desirable for people with cardiovascular problems, but chicken fat and the largest ingredient, dextrose (a sugar), are not.

Another "instant" chicken soup aimed at the general public proclaims "no preservatives," but it not only has sugar, cottonseed oil, sodium pyrophosphate and potassium pyrophosphate (both questionable antioxidants considered preservatives), sodium carbonate, potassium carbonate, monosodium glutamate, but a whopping 1,435 milligrams of sodium.

How to Use This Book

While unique in content, this dictionary follows the format of most standard dictionaries. The following are sample entries with any explanatory notes that may be necessary.

MARJORAM, POT • Sweet Marjoram. *Marjorana onites.* The natural extract of the flowers and leaves of two varieties of the fragrant marjoram plant. The *oleoresin* (*see*) is used in sausage and spice flavorings for condiments and meats. The *seed* is used in sausage and spice flavorings for meats (3,500 ppm) and condiments. Sweet marjoram is used in sausage and spice flavorings for beverages, baked goods (2,000 ppm), condiments, meats, and soups. The *sweet oil* is used in vermouth, wine, and spice flavorings for beverages, ice creams, ices, candy, baked goods, and condiments. Also used in hair preparations, perfumes, and soaps. Can irritate the skin. The redness, itching, and warmth experienced when marjoram is applied to the skin are caused by the local dilation of the blood vessels or by local reflex. May produce allergic reactions. Essential oils such as marjoram are believed to penetrate the skin easily and produce systemic effects. GRAS.

We have learned that pot marjoram is a natural flavoring extract, that there are pot and sweet marjoram, that they are utilized as an oleoresin, a seed, and sweet oil. By looking up *oleoresin* we learn that it means a natural plant product consisting of essential oil and resin extracted from a substance, such as ginger, by means of alcohol, ether, or acetone and that oleoresins are usually more uniform and more potent than the original product. The *ppm* stands for "parts per million," that is, 3,500 parts of marjoram is added to a million parts of meat. However, because ppm amounts (they do not appear on labels) represent maximum rather than actual usage, they are not reliable estimates of consumption and are included here only to show how amounts can be relatively large or small. *GRAS* means, of course, that the item is on the government's generally recognized as safe list, without having undergone thorough laboratory testing. ("GRAS in packaging" means that even though substances from the containers may migrate into the food, they are assumed not harmful.)

WORMWOOD • Absinthium. A European woody herb with a bitter taste, used in bitters and liquor flavorings for beverages and liquors. The *extract* is used in bitters, liquor, and vermouth flavorings for beverages, ice cream, candy, and liquors, and in making absinthe. The *oil* is a dark green to brown and a narcotic substance. Used in bitters, apple, vermouth, and wine flavorings for beverages, ice cream, ices, candy, baked goods, and liquors. In large doses or frequently repeated doses, it is a narcotic poison, causing headache, trembling, and convulsions. Ingestion of the volatile oil or of the liquor, absinthe, may cause gastrointestinal symptoms, nervousness, stupor, coma, and death.

Absinthium, of course, is another name for wormwood and is cross-referenced in the dictionary. Source materials for the comments on toxicity are indicated in the notes at the end of the dictionary. A similar example is the entry for lye.

SODIUM SESQUICARBONATE • Lye. White crystals, flakes, or powder produced from sodium carbonate. Soluble in water. Used as a neutralizer for butter, cream, fluid milk, ice cream, in the processing of olives before canning, cacao products, and canned peas. Used as an alkalizer in bath salts, shampoos, tooth powders, and soaps. Irritating to the skin and mucous membranes. May cause allergic reaction in the hypersensitive. The final report to the FDA of the Select Committee on GRAS Substances stated in 1980 that it should continue its GRAS status with no limitations other than good manufacturing practices.

Under the entry *ACACIA. Gum Arabic. Catechu,* the first two terms are used interchangeably. *Catechu* (from the Latin *Acacia catechu*) is less commonly used. Under the entry *ACETALDEHYDE. Ethanal,* the term *ethanal* is used interchangeably with *acetaldehyde.*

Some chemicals that are derived from a natural source are considered synthetic because they represent only a portion of the original compound or because other chemicals have been added. For instance:

NONANAL • Pelargonic Aldehyde. Colorless liquid with an orange-rose odor. A synthetic flavoring that occurs naturally in lemon oil, rose, sweet orange oil, mandarin, lime, orris, and ginger. Used in lemon and fruit flavorings for beverages, ice cream, ices, candy, baked goods, chewing gum, and gelatin desserts. Used also in perfumery. No known toxicity. *See* Aldehyde.

Terminology has generally been kept to a middle road between technician and the citizen of average interest, while at the same time oversimplification of data has been avoided. If in doubt, look up any term, listed alphabetically, such as *isolate* (used in its chemical context) or *extract* or *anhydride* or *oleoresin* or *mutagenic, teratogenic, subacute,* and so on.

With *A Consumer's Dictionary of Food Additives* you will be able to work with the current labels to determine the purpose and the desirability or toxicity of the additives listed. You will be able to assert your right to wholesome food along with a wholesome environment. By having options in the marketplace, by rejecting those products that are needlessly costly or unsafe or unpalatable in favor of "clean" food, you strike back at greed and ignorance as practiced by too many in the food industry. And you reward those manufacturers who deserve your purchases.

There is little doubt that what we eat affects our health. Our bodies are wonderful machines that can detoxify and render harmless many poisons we ingest; however, we don't want to overburden our bodies by taking unnecessary chances. Certainly, not all food additives are harmful. Some, in fact, are greatly beneficial. It is all a matter of judgment. Hopefully, this book will allow you to make wiser choices.

This book takes some of the guesswork out of the chemicals you eat.

Consumer Complaints

The widespread distribution of food additives and consequent public safety concerns necessitate timely and reliable evaluation of suspected adverse reactions. However, few criteria exist to evaluate consumer-initiated reports of adverse medical reactions after products have been marketed.

Currently, consumer complaints related to food additives as well as other food products are monitored by passive surveillance, carried out primarily by the Food and Drug Administration. Therefore, it is important that if you have had an adverse reaction to a food, you report it. To report an incident or to ask a question about a processed-food ingredient, write to:

The Office of Consumer Affairs, Food and Drug Administration, HFE-88, 5600 Fishers Lane, Rockville, MD 20857.

For a question about meat or storage, call the USDA's Meat and Poultry Hotline, 1-800-535-4555. Operates toll free weekdays, ten to four EST.

A

ABIES ALBA MILLS • *See* Pine Needle Oil.

ABIETIC ACID • Sylvic Acid. Chiefly a texturizer in the making of soaps. A widely available natural acid, water insoluble, prepared from pine rosin, usually yellow, and composed of either glassy or crystalline particles. Used also in the manufacture of vinyls, lacquers, and plastics. Employed to carry nutrients that are added to enriched rice in amounts up to .0026 percent of the weight of the nutrient mixture. Little is known about abietic acid toxicity; it is harmless when injected into mice but causes paralysis in frogs and is slightly irritating to human skin and mucous membranes. May cause allergic reactions.

ABSINTHIUM • Extract or Oil. *See* Wormwood.

ABSOLUTE • The term refers to a plant-extracted material that has been concentrated but remains essentially unchanged in its original taste and odor. For example, *see* Jasmine Absolute. Often called "natural perfume materials" because they are not subjected to heat and water as are distilled products. *See* Distilled.

ACACIA • Acacia vera. Gum Arabic. Catechu. Egyptian Thorn. Acacia is the odorless, colorless, tasteless dried exudate from the stem of the acacia tree grown in Africa, the Near East, India, and the southern United States. Its most distinguishing quality among the natural gums is its ability to dissolve rapidly in water. The use of acacia dates back four thousand years to when the Egyptians employed it in paints. Its principal use in the confectionery industry is to retard sugar crystallization and as a thickener for candies, jellies, glazes, and chewing gum. As a stabilizer, it prevents chemical breakdown in food mixtures. Gum acacia is a foam stabilizer in the soft-drink and brewing industries. Also used for mucilage, the gum gives form and shape to tablets. In 1976 the FDA placed acacia in the GRAS category as an emulsifier, flavoring agent, processing aid, and stabilizer in beverages at 2.0 percent, chewing gum at 5.6 percent; as a formulation aid, stabilizer, and humectant in confections and frostings at 12.4 percent; as a humectant stabilizer and formulation aid in hard candy at 46.5 percent; in soft candy at 85 percent; in nut formulations at 1.0 percent; and in all other food categories at 8.3 percent of the product. It is permitted as an optional ingredient in standardized foods (which are not required to list ingredients on the label). Medically, it is used as a demulcent to soothe irritations, particularly of the mucous membranes. It slightly reduces cholesterol in the blood. It can cause allergic reactions such as skin rash and asthmatic attacks. Oral toxicity is low. The FDA data bank, PAFA (see page 10) has fully up-to-date toxicology information on this additive. *See also* Vegetable Gums and Catechu Extract. GRAS.

ACCEPTABLE DAILY INTAKE (ADI) • It is defined as an estimate of the amount of a food additive, expressed on a body-weight basis, that can be ingested daily over a lifetime without appreciable health risk, according to the World Health Organization (1987).

ACENAPHTHENE • White needles derived from coal tar, insoluble in water. Used as a dye intermediate in pharmaceuticals, insecticides, fungicides, and plastics. *See* Coal Tar.

ACEPHATE (0-S-DIMETHYL ACETYLPHOSPHERAMIDO THIOATE and O-S-DIMETHYL PHOSPHORAMIDO THIOATE) • A contact and systemic pesticide in cottonseed meal resulting from application to growing crops. FDA permits 8 ppm in cottonseed and 4 ppm in soybean meal resulting from application to growing crop.

ACER SPICATUM LAM • *See* Mountain Maple Extract.

ACEROLA • Used as an antioxidant. Derived from the ripe fruit of the West Indian or Barbados cherry grown in Central America and the West Indies. A rich source of ascorbic acid. Used in vitamin C. No known toxicity.

ACESULFAME K • Acesulfame Potassium. Sunette. In a petition filed in September 1982, the American Hoechst Corporation asked for approval to make this nonnutritive sweetener, two hundred times sweeter than table sugar, for use in chewing gum, dry beverage mixes, confections, canned fruit, gelatins, puddings, custards, and as a tabletop sweetener. The petition, including fifteen volumes of research studies, said the sweetener is not metabolized and would not add calories to the diet. The FDA approved Acesulfame K on July 27, 1988, for use in dry food products and for sale in powder form or tablets that can be applied directly by the consumer. It has about the same sweetening power as aspartame (*see*), but unlike aspartame, has no calories. As of this writing, Hoechst was seeking approval to use acesulfame K as an ingredient in liquids and baked goods and candies. The sweetener has previously been approved for use in twenty countries including France and Britain.

The Food and Drug Administration said that four long-term animal studies in dogs, mice, and rats had not shown any toxic effects from the sweetener. However, the Center for Science in the Public Interest, a Washington, D.C.–based consumer group, sent a warning to the FDA more than six months before the sweetener's approval saying that animals fed acesulfame K in two different studies suffered more tumors than others that did not receive the compound. In another study cited by CSPI, diabetic rats had a higher blood level of cholesterol when fed the sweetener.

The FDA said in a press release that it had considered the Center's concerns and concluded that "any tumors found were typical of what could routinely be expected and were not due to feeding with acesulfame K."

Hoechst said that Sunette is not metabolized by the body and is excreted unchanged by humans and animals. When heated to decomposition, it emits toxic fumes. The FDA data bank, PAFA (see page 10), has fully up-to-date toxicology information on this additive.

ACETAL • A volatile liquid derived from acetaldehyde (*see*) and alcohol and used as a solvent in synthetic perfumes such as jasmine. Also used in fruit flavorings (it has a nutlike aftertaste) and as a hypnotic in medicine. It is a central nervous system depressant, similar in action to paraldehyde but more toxic. Paraldehyde is a hypnotic and sedative whose side effects are respiratory depression, cardiovascular collapse, and possible high blood pressure reactions. No known skin toxicity.

ACETALDEHYDE • Ethanal. An intermediate (*see*) and solvent in the manufacture of perfumes. A flammable, colorless liquid, with a characteristic odor, occurring naturally in apples, broccoli, cheese, coffee, grapefruit, and other vegetables and fruit. Also used in the manufacture of synthetic rubber and in the silvering of mirrors. It is irritating to the mucous membranes, and ingestion of large doses may cause death by respiratory paralysis. Its ability to depress the central nervous system is greater than that of formaldehyde (*see*), and ingestion produces symptoms of drunkenness. Acetaldehyde is thought to be a factor in the toxic effect caused by drinking alcohol after taking the anti-alcohol drug Antabuse. Inhalation, usually limited by intense irritation of the lungs, can also be toxic. Skin toxicity not identified. GRAS. The FDA data bank, PAFA (see page 10), has fully up-to-date toxicology information on this additive.

ACETALDEHYDE, BUTYL PHENETHYL ACETAL • *See* Aldehyde and Butanol.

ACETALDEHYDE ETHYL CIS-3-HEXENYL ACETAL • One of the newer synthetic flavorings. The FDA's data bank has not yet done a thorough toxicology search, as of this writing. *See* Acetaldehyde.

ACETALDEHYDE PHENETHYL PROPYL ACETAL PETITAL • A synthetic fruit flavoring agent for beverages, ice cream, ices, candy, and baked goods. The FDA data bank, PAFA (see page 10), has fully up-to-date toxicology information on this additive. *See* Acetaldehyde for toxicity.

p-ACETAMIDO BENZOIC ACID • *See* Benzoic Acid.

ACETANISOLE • A synthetic flavoring agent, colorless to pale yellow solid, with an odor of hawthorn or hay, moderately soluble in alcohol and most fixed oils. Acetanisole is used in butter, caramel, chocolate, fruit, nut, and vanilla flavorings, which go into beverages, ice cream, ices, candy, baked goods, and chewing gum. The FDA data bank, PAFA (see page 10), has fully up-to-date toxicology information on this additive.

ACETATE • Salt of acetic acid (*see*) used in liquor, nut, coffee, vanilla, honey, pineapple, and cheese flavorings for beverages, ice cream, sherbets, cakes, cookies, pastries, and candy. Also used in perfumery. May be irritating to the stomach if consumed in large quantities.

ACETIC ACID • It occurs naturally in apples, cheese, cocoa, coffee, grapes, skimmed milk, oranges, peaches, pineapples, strawberries, and a variety of other fruits and plants. Vinegar is about 4 to 6 percent acetic acid, and essence of vinegar is about 14 percent. It is used in cheese, baked goods, and animal feeds. Can be used in standardized foods and thus need not be listed on the label. Solvent for gums, resins, and volatile oils. Styptic, it stops bleeding when applied to a cut on the skin. It is also used in freckle-bleaching lotions, hand lotions, and hair dyes. Potential adverse skin reactions include irritation or itching, hives, and overgrowth of organisms that do not respond to germ-killers. In its glacial form (without much water) it is highly corrosive, and its vapors are capable of producing lung obstruction. Less than 5 percent acetic acid in solution is mildly irritating to the skin. It caused cancer in rats and mice when given orally or by injection. The FDA data bank, PAFA (see page 10), has fully up-to-date toxicology information on this additive. GRAS.

ACETIC ACID, CITRONELLYL ESTER • A flavoring agent found in oils of citronella geranium and about twenty other oils. Colorless liquid; fruity odor.

Used as a flavoring agent in mayonnaise, salad dressings, and sauces. Mildly toxic by ingestion. A human skin irritant.

ACETIC ANHYDRIDE • Acetyl Oxide; Acetic Oxide. Colorless liquid with a strong odor, derived from oxidation of acetaldehyde (*see*). It is used as a dehydrating and acetylating agent (*see* Dehydrated and Acetylated) and in the production of dyes, perfumes, plastics, food starch, and aspirin. It is a strong irritant and may cause burns and eye damage. The FDA says there is no reported use of the chemical and no toxicology information is available.

ACETIC ETHER • A synthetic agent, transparent, colorless liquid with a fragrant, refreshing odor, used in butter, butterscotch, fruit, nut, and spice flavorings for beverages, ice cream, ices, candy, baked goods (1,000 ppm), and chewing gum (4,000 ppm). Also used to coat vegetables.

ACETISOEUGENOL • White crystals with a clove odor, used as a flavoring agent. It is moderately toxic by ingestion. When heated to decomposition, it emits acrid smoke and irritating fumes. The FDA permits its use at a level not to exceed an amount reasonably required to accomplish the intended effect.

ACETOACETIC ESTER • *See* Ethyl Acetoacetate.

ACETOIN • Acetyl Methyl Carbinol. A flavoring agent and aroma carrier used in perfumery, it occurs naturally in broccoli, grapes, pears, cultured dairy products, cooked beef, and cooked chicken. As a product of fermentation and of cream ripened for churning, it is a colorless or pale yellow liquid or a white powder, has a buttery odor, and must be stored in a light-resistant container. It is used in raspberry, strawberry, butter, butterscotch, caramel, coconut, coffee, fruit, liquor, rum, nut, walnut, vanilla, cream soda, and cheese flavorings for beverages, ice cream, ices, candy, baked goods, margarine, gelatin desserts, cottage cheese, and shortenings. Mildly toxic by injection under the skin. A moderate skin irritant. When heated to decomposition, it emits acrid smoke and fumes. GRAS. The FDA data bank, PAFA (see page 10), has fully up-to-date toxicology information on this additive.

2-ACETONAPHTHONE • Orange Crystals. 2-Naphthyl Ketone. White crystalline solid with an orange-blossom odor. Used as a flavoring agent. Moderately toxic by ingestion. A human skin irritant. When heated to decomposition, it emits acrid smoke and fumes.

ACETONE • A colorless ethereal liquid derived by oxidation or fermentation and used as a solvent for spices. Not more than 30 ppm may be a residual in the product. It is also frequently used in nail polish removers and nail finishes and as a solvent for airplane dope, fats, oils, and waxes. It can cause peeling and splitting of the nails, skin rashes on the fingers and elsewhere, and nail brittleness. Inhalation may irritate the lungs, and in large amounts it is narcotic, causing symptoms of drunkenness similar to ethanol (*see*). In 1992, the FDA proposed a ban on acetone in astringent (*see*) products, because it had not been shown to be safe and effective as claimed. It is used in food processing. The FDA says that it has fully up-to-date toxicology information available on acetone.

ACETONE PEROXIDE • Acetone (*see*) to which an oxygen-containing compound has been added. A maturing agent for bleaching flour and dough. It has a sharp, acrid odor similar to hydrogen peroxide. A strong oxidizing agent, it can be damaging to the skin and eyes. The FDA says that although it is allowed as a food additive, there is no current reported use of the chemical, and therefore, although toxiocology information may be available, it is not updated.

ACETOPHENONE • Acetyl Benzene. Benzoyl Methide. A synthetic agent derived from coal tar, with an odor of bitter almonds, used in strawberry, floral, fruit, cherry, almond, walnut, tobacco, vanilla, and tonka-bean flavorings for beverages, ice creams, ices, candy, baked goods, gelatin desserts, and chewing gum. It occurs naturally in strawberries and tea and may cause allergic reactions. Poisonous by injection. Moderately toxic by ingestion. A skin and severe eye irritant. Narcotic in high concentrations. When heated to decomposition, it emits acrid smoke and fumes. The FDA has fully up-to-date toxicology information available on this additive.

ACETOSTEARIN • Obtained from fats and oils, it is a glyceride (*see*) that the Select Committee on GRAS Substances in 1980 stated should be GRAS with no limitations. It is used as a protective coating for food and as a plasticizer. *See also* Stearic Acid.

ACETYL ACETONE • Acetoacetone. Diacetyl methane. Colorless to slightly yellow liquid with a pleasant odor. Used as a flavoring agent in food. The FDA requires it not be used in excess of the amount reasonably required to accomplish the intended effect. Moderately toxic if ingested, injected, or inhaled.

ACETYL BENZENE • *See* Acetophenone.

ACETYL BENZOYL PEROXIDE • White crystals decomposed by water and organic matter. Used in medicine as a germicide and disinfectant. It is used to bleach flour. Toxic when ingested.

ACETYL BUTYRYL • *See* 2,3-Hexandione.

ACETYL-*o*-CREOSOL • *See o*-Tolyl Acetate.

3-ACETYL-2,5-DIMETHYL FURAN • Yellow liquid with a strong roasted-nut-like odor used as a flavoring agent. When heated to decomposition, it emits acrid smoke and irritating fumes. The FDA's data bank, PAFA (see page 10), claims to have fully up-to-date toxicology information on this food additive. GRAS.

2-ACETYL-3,(5 or 6)-DIMETHYLPYRAZINE, MIXTURE OF ISOMERS • Flavoring agent. The FDA's data bank, PAFA, claims to have fully up-to-date toxicology information on this food additive.

3-ACETYL-2,5-DIMETHYLTHIOPHENE • A flavoring agent. The FDA's data bank, PAFA, claims to have fully up-to-date toxicology information on this food additive.

2-ACETYL-3-ETHYLPYRAZINE • A flavoring agent. The FDA's data bank, PAFA (see page 10), claims to have fully up-to-date toxicology information on this food additive.

ACETYL EUGENOL • *See* Eugenyl Acetate.

ACETYL FORMALDEHYDE • *See* Pyruvaldehyde.

ACETYL FORMIC ACID • *See* Pyruvaldehyde.

ACETYL HEXAMETHYL TETRALIN • Used in perfumes. It is closely related to acetyl ethyl tetramethyl tetralin, which was voluntarily removed from perfumes when it was reported to have caused nerve damage in animals. The "hexa" component was inserted to make the fragrances less volatile and less allergenic.

N-ACETYL-L-METHIONINE • (Free, Hydrated, Anhydrous, or Sodium or Potassium Salts). Nutrient in foods except infant foods and products containing added nitrites/nitrates (*see both*). Limited to 3.1 percent by weight of the total protein in the food. When heated to decomposition, emits toxic fumes. The FDA's data bank, PAFA (see page 10), claims to have fully up-to-date toxicology information on this food additive.

ACETYL METHYL CARBINYL ACETATE • The FDA's data bank, PAFA, claims to have fully up-to-date toxicology information on this food additive. *See* Acetoin.

2-ACETYL-5-METHYLFURAN • A synthetic flavoring. The FDA's data bank, PAFA, claims to have fully up-to-date toxicology information on this food additive.

4-ACETYL-2-METHYLPYRIMIDINE • There is no reported use of this synthetic flavoring, and no toxicology information is available.

ACETYL NONYRYL • *See* 2,3-Undecadione.

ACETYL PELARGONYL • *See* 2,3-Undecadione.

ACETYL PENTANOYL • *See* 2,3-Heptanedione.

ACETYL PROPIONYL • Yellow liquid. Soluble in water. Used as a butterscotch or chocolate-type flavoring. *See* 2,3-Pentanedione.

2-ACETYL PYRAZINE • Colorless to pale yellow crystals or liquid with a sweet popcornlike odor. Used as a flavoring agent. Skin and eye irritant. When heated to decomposition, emits toxic fumes. GRAS. The FDA's data bank, PAFA (see page 10), claims to have fully up-to-date toxicology information on this food additive.

2-ACETYL PYRROLE • Light beige to yellow crystals with a breadlike odor used as a flavoring agent. When heated to decomposition, emits toxic fumes. GRAS when used at a level not in excess of the amount reasonably required.

4-ACETYL-6-TERT-BUTYL-1,1-DIMETHYL-INDANE • A synthetic flavoring. The FDA's data bank, PAFA, claims to have fully up-to-date toxicology information on this additive.

p-ACETYL TOLUENE • *See* 4-Methylacetophenone.

ACETYL-p-TOLYL ACETATE • *See* p-Tolyl Acetate.

ACETYL TRIBUTYL CITRATE • *See* Citric Acid.

ACETYL TRIETHYL CITRATE • A clear, oily, essentially odorless liquid used as a solvent and plasticizer. Moderately toxic by ingestion. When heated to decomposition, it emits acrid smoke and fumes. *See* Citric Acid.

ACETYL TRIOCETYL CITRATE PECTIN • Citrus Pectin. A jelly-forming powder obtained from citrus peel and used as a texturizer and thickening agent to form gels with sugars and acids. Light in color. It has no known toxicity.

ACETYL VALERYL • Yellow liquid used as cheese, butter, and miscellaneous flavors. *See* 2,3-Heptanedione.

ACETYL VANILLIN • *See* Vanillin Acetate.

ACETYLAMINO-5-NITROTHIAZOLE • Acinitrazole. Trichloral. Tritheom. An animal drug used in turkeys and limited to 0.1 ppm in the birds' flesh by the FDA. When heated to decomposition, emits toxic fumes.

ACETYLATED • Any organic compound that has been heated with acetic anhydride or acetyl chloride to remove its water. Acetylation is used to coat candy and other foods to hold in moisture. Acetic anhydride produces irritation and necrosis of tissues in the vapor state and carries a warning against contact with skin and eyes.

ACETYLATED DISTARCH ADIPATE and PHOSPHATE • Starches (*see*) that have been modified to change their solubility and digestibility. The Select Committee on GRAS Substances stated in 1980 that there is no available evidence of a hazard to the public when they are used at levels now current and in the manner now practiced. However, it is not possible to determine, without additional data, whether a significant increase in consumption would constitute a dietary hazard. They can continue GRAS with limitations on amounts that can be added to food.

ACETYLATED DISTARCH PROPANOL • A starch (*see*) that has been modified to change its solubility and digestibility. The final report to the FDA of the Select Committee on GRAS Substances stated in 1980 that although no available information demonstrates a hazard to the public at current use levels, uncertainties exist that require additional studies. GRAS status is continued while tests are being completed, the FDA said in 1980. Since then, no action has been reported.

ACETYLATED HYDROGENATED COTTONSEED GLYCERIDE • *See* Cottonseed Oil.

ACETYLATED HYDROGENATED LARD GLYCERIDE • *See* Lard.

ACETYLATED HYDROGENATED VEGETABLE GLYCERIDE • *See* Vegetable Oils.

ACETYLATED MONOGLYCERIDES • Acetylated Mono- and Diglycerides. Esters (*see*) of glycerin with acetic acid and edible fat-forming fatty acids. May be white to pale yellow liquids or solids. Bland tasting. Used as coating agents, emulsifiers, lubricants, solvents, and texture-modifying agents in baked goods, cake shortening, desserts, fruits, ice cream, margarine, meat products, nuts, oleomargarine, peanut butter, puddings, shortening, and whipped toppings. Use permitted by the FDA at a level not in excess of the amount reasonably required to accomplish the intended effect. When heated to decomposition, it emits acrid smoke and irritating fumes.

ACETYLATED SUCROSE DISTEARATE • The acetyl ester of sucrose distearate (*see* Ester and Sucrose Distearate).

ACETYLISOEUGENOL • Isoeugenol Acetate. White crystals with a spicy, clovelike odor; used as an aroma and flavor carrier in foods. In perfumery, it is used especially for carnation-type odors.

ACETYLMETHYL CARBINOL • Slightly yellow liquid or crystals used as an aroma and flavor carrier. *See* Acetoin.

2- or 3-ACETYLPYRIDINE • Additives used in making synthetic food additives. The FDA's data bank, PAFA, claims to have fully up-to-date toxicology information on these food additives.

2-ACETYLTHIAZOLE • Used in the manufacture of fungicides and dyes. The FDA's data bank, PAFA, claims to have fully up-to-date toxicology information on this food additive.

ACHILLEIC ACID • *See* Aconitic Acid.

ACID • An acid is a substance capable of turning blue litmus paper red and of forming hydrogen ions when dissolved in water. An acid aqueous solution is one that has a pH (*see*) of less than 7. Citric acid (*see*) is an example of a widely used acid in foods.

ACID-HYDROLYZED PROTEINS • Hydrolyzed Milk Protein. Hydrolyzed Plant Protein. Hydrolyzed Vegetable Protein. Used as a flavoring agent in bologna, salami, sauces, and stuffing. Use at level not in excess of the amount reasonably required to accomplish the intended effect. When heated to decomposition, it emits acrid smoke and irritating fumes.

ACID-MODIFIED STARCHES • Usually made by mixing an acid—such as hydrochloric or sulfuric—water, and starch at temperatures too low for gelatinization. When the starch has been reduced in viscosity to the degree desired, the acid is neutralized and the starch is filtered, washed, and dried. It is done so that starches can be cooked and used at higher concentrations than unmodified starches. Acid-modified starches are often used for salad dressings and puddings and as inexpensive thickening agents. The final report to the FDA of the Select Committee on GRAS Substances stated in 1980 that acid-modified starches are GRAS with no limitations.

ACID POTASSIUM SULFITE • *See* Sulfites.

ACIDOPHILUS • A type of bacteria that ferments milk and has been used medically to treat intestinal disorders.

ACIDS • *See* Acidulants.

ACIDULANTS • Acids. An acid is a substance capable of turning blue litmus paper red and of forming hydrogen ions when dissolved in water. An acid aqueous solution is one with a pH less than 7 (*see* pH). Acidulants are acids that make a substance more acid and function as flavoring agent to acidify taste, to blend unrelated flavoring characteristics, and to mask any undesirable aftertaste. Acidulants are also used as preservatives to prevent germ and spore growths that spoil foods. Acidulants control the acid-alkali (pH) balance and are used in meat curings to enhance color and flavor and as a preservative. Among the most common acids added to foods are acetic, propionic, and sorbic (*see* all).

ACIFLUOREN, SODIUM • Herbicide. FDA tolerances are 0.02 ppm residues in cattle and sheep, kidney and liver.

ACIMETON • Banthionine. Cynaron. Methilanin. Neston. White crystalline platelets with a characteristic odor. Used as a dietary supplement and nutrient. Moderately toxic by ingestion and other routes. When heated to decomposition, it emits toxic fumes. *See* Methionine.

ACONITIC ACID • Citridic Acid. Equisetic Acid. Achilleic Acid. A flavoring agent found in beetroot and cane sugar. Most of the commercial aconitic acids, however, are manufactured by sulfuric-acid dehydration of citric acid. It is used in fruit, brandy, and rum flavorings for beverages, ice cream, ices, candy, baked goods, liquors, and chewing gum. Also used in the manufacture of plastics and Buna rubber. As of this writing, the FDA's data bank has not yet done a toxicology search of the literature concerning this additive. GRAS.

ACROLEIN • A yellow, transparent liquid byproduct of petroleum produced by the oxidation of propylene. Sources include combustion of wood, paper, cotton, petroleum products, and polyolefins. Used in modifying food starch. Used in making plastics and metal products. Toxic, causes tearing and intense irritation of the upper respiratory tract. It is also a skin irritant and a fire hazard from heat and flame. The FDA's data bank reports no use of the chemical and no toxicology information is available.

ACRYLAMIDE • Colorless, odorless crystals soluble in water and derived from acrylonitrile and sulfuric acid. It is used in the manufacture of dyes, adhesives, and in permanent-press fabrics, nail enamels, and face masks. It is toxic by skin absorption. The FDA's PAFA data bank (see page 10) says it has fully up-to-date toxicology information available concerning this additive.

ACRYLIC RESINS • Polymers (see) of acrylics. Used in waxy oils, base coats, protective coatings, and waterproofing. Acrylates (see Acrylic acid), if inhaled, can cause allergic reactions in humans.

ACRYLATE-ACRYLAMIDE RESIN • Acrylic Acid. Colorless, odorless crystals soluble in water and derived from acrylonitrile and sulfuric acid. It is used as a clarifying agent in beet-sugar and cane-sugar juice and liquor or cornstarch hydrolysate (5 ppm by weight of juice, 10 ppm by weight of liquor or hydrolysate). The acid is the synthesis of this acrylic resin. It is also used in the manufacture of dyes, adhesives, and in permanent-press fabrics, nail enamels, and face masks. It is toxic by skin absorption. The FDA's PAFA data bank (see page 10) says it has fully up-to-date toxicology information available concerning this additive.

ACRYLAMIDE-SODIUM ACRYLATE RESIN • Although allowed as a food additive, there is no current reported use of the chemical, and therefore, although toxicology information may be available, it is not being updated by the FDA data bank.

ACRYLIC ACID • Colorless liquid with an acrid odor, it is derived by condensing ethylene oxide with hydrocyanic acid followed by reaction with sulfuric acid. It is used for making plastics and resins. Although allowed as a food additive, there is no current reported use of the chemical, and therefore, although toxicology information may be available, it is not being updated by the FDA data bank.

ACRYLONITRILE COPOLYMERS • Used in packaging materials. When heated to decomposition, it emits acrid smoke and irritating fumes.

ACRYLONITRILE POLYMER WITH STYRENE • Used in coatings and films in packaging materials. No restrictions, but cyanide and its compounds are on the Community Right-To-Know List. (See also Styrene.)

ACTADECYLSILOXYDIMETHYLSIOLOXYPOLYSILOXANE • A component of defoaming agents (see) used in processing beets and yeast. No known toxicity.

ACTIVATED CHARCOAL (CARBON) • Charcoal is obtained by destructive distillation of organic material such as vegetables or animal bones and is activated by heating with steam or carbon dioxide, which results in a porous material. It is used to relieve intestinal discomfort and diarrhea and to counteract poisons. It is the main ingredient in the "universal antidote." Activated charcoal is recognized by the FDA for the treatment of swallowed poisons. It adheres to many drugs and chemicals, inhibiting their absorption from the GI tract. Potential adverse reactions include black stools and nausea. Used to remove impurities that cause undesirable color, taste, or odor in liquid. The major sources are lignite, coal, and coke. The Select Committee of the Federation of American Societies for Experimental Biology (FASEB), under contract to the FDA, concluded that it is not a hazard to human health at current or possible future use levels. However, the Committee said because the substance is extensively used in the food industry, it would be prudent to have purity specifications for food-grade activated carbon to assure the absence of any cancer-causing hydrocarbons in food. It can cause a dust irritation, particularly to the eyes and mucous membranes. The FDA's data bank, PAFA (see page 10), says it has fully up-to-date toxicology information available concerning this chemical.

ACTIVATED 7-DEHYDROCHOLESTEROL • *See* Vitamin D₃.

ADENOSINE • White, crystalline powder with mild saline or bitter taste. It is isolated by the hydrolysis of yeast nucleic acid.

ADENOSINE PHOSPHATE • *See* Adenosine Triphosphate.

ADENOSINE TRIPHOSPHATE • Adenylic Acid. An organic compound that is derived from adenosine (*see*). A fundamental unit of nucleic acid, it serves as source of energy for biochemical transformation in plants, photosynthesis, and also for many chemical reactions in the body, especially those associated with muscular activity.

ADI • Abbreviation for Acceptable Daily Intake (*see*).

ADIPATES • The salt of adipic acid (*see*) used in food packaging. Some are suspected cancer-causing agents.

ADIPIC ACID • Hexanedioic Acid. Colorless needlelike formations, fairly insoluble in water; found in beets. A buffering and neutralizing agent impervious to humidity. Used in flavorings for baked goods, baking powder, condiments, dairy products, meat products, oils, oleomargarine, relishes, snack foods, canned vegetables, beverages, and gelatin desserts (5,000 ppm) to impart a smooth-tart taste. Also used as a buffer and neutralizing agent in confections, but limited to 3 percent of contents, and in the manufacture of plastics and nylons, and as a substitute for tartaric acid (*see*) in baking powders because it is impervious to humidity. No known toxicity. The final report to the FDA of the Select Committee on GRAS Substances stated in 1980 that it should continue its GRAS status with no limitations other than good manufacturing practices. Poison by injection and moderately toxic by other routes. A severe eye irritant. Combustible when exposed to flame; can react with oxidizing materials. The FDA's data bank, PAFA (see page 10), says it has fully up-to-date toxicology information available concerning this chemical.

ADIPIC ANHYDRIDE • A starch-modifying agent, not to exceed 0.12 percent of the starch compound. There is no reported use of the chemical, and no toxicology information is available, according to the FDA's data bank. *See* Modified Starch.

ADSORBATE • A powdered flavor made by coating liquid flavoring on the surface of a powder such as cornstarch, salt, or maltodextrin (*see all*).

AEROSOL • Small particles of material suspended in gas.

AFLATOXIN • A mold that contaminates corn and peanuts. Poisonous by ingestion and moderately toxic by other routes. Carcinogenic and mutagenic.

AGAR-AGAR • Japanese Isinglass. A stabilizer and thickener, it is transparent, odorless, and tasteless and obtained from various seaweeds found in the Pacific and Indian oceans and the Sea of Japan. Agar was the first seaweed to be extracted, purified, and dried. Discovered by a Japanese innkeeper around 1658 and introduced in Europe and the United States by visitors from China in the 1800s as a substitute for gelatin, it goes into beverages, ice cream, ices, frozen custard, sherbet, meringue, baked goods, jelly, frozen candied sweet potatoes, icings, confections, and artificially sweetened jellies and preserves. It can be 1.2 percent of candy and 0.25 percent of frozen desserts, jelly, and preserves. Agar is used for thickening milk and cream. It is also a bulk laxative and, aside from causing an occasional allergic reaction, is nontoxic. The final report to the FDA of the Select Committee on GRAS Substances stated in 1980 that there is no available evidence that it is a hazard to the public when used as it is now and that it should continue its GRAS status with limitations on amounts that can be added to food. Mildly toxic by ingestion. The FDA says its data bank, PAFA (see page 10), has fully up-to-date toxicology information available concerning this chemical.

AGAVE LECHUGUILLA • American Aloe. Native to the warm part of the United States and known by its heavy, stiff leaf and tall panicle or spike of candelabralike flowers. The leaves are used for a juice employed in cosmetics as an adhesive and in medicines as a diuretic. The fermented juice is popular in Mexico for its distilled spirit (mescal). Some species are cultivated for their fibers, which are used in thread and rope. No known toxicity.

AGRIMONY EXTRACT • An extract of *Agrimonia eupatoria,* an herb found in northern temperate regions. It has yellow flowers and bristly fruit.

AKLOMIDE • Gray scales from alcohol used as an animal drug to combat fungus infections in chickens. The FDA residue tolerances are 4.5 ppm in liver and muscle of uncooked edible tissue of chickens and 3 ppm in skin and fat.

ALACHLOR • Lasso. Alanex. A preemergent herbicide. The FDA permits its use. The EPA has determined it is a cancer-causing agent in rats and mice.

ALANEX • *See* Alachlor.

ALANINE (B-, L-, and DL-) • Colorless crystals derived from protein. Believed to be a nonessential amino acid. It is used in microbiological research and as a dietary supplement in the L and DL forms. The FDA has asked for supplementary information. It is now GRAS for addition to food. It caused cancer of the skin in mice, and tumors when injected into their abdomens. The FDA says its data bank, PAFA (see page 10), has fully up-to-date toxicology information available concerning this chemical.

ALAR • *See* Diaminozide.

ALBENDAZOLE • Zental. Valbazen. A worm medicine given to cattle. The FDA tolerances for residues are 0.2 ppm in uncooked edible cattle tissue, 0.6 in muscle, 1.2 ppm in liver, 1.8 ppm in kidney, 2.4 ppm in fat.

ALBUMIN (ALBUMEN) • A group of simple proteins composed of nitrogen, carbon, hydrogen, oxygen, and sulfur that are soluble in water. Albumin is usually derived from egg white and employed as an emulsifier in foods and cosmetics. May cause a reaction to those allergic to eggs. In large amounts can produce symptoms of lack of biotin, a growth factor in the lining of the cells. The FDA says its data bank, PAFA (see page 10), has fully up-to-date toxicology information available concerning this chemical.

ALBUMIN MACRO AGGREGATES • Used as a binder and firming agent in sausage, soups, stews, and wine. Poisonous by injection.

ALCOHOL • Ethyl Alcohol. Ethanol. Alcohol is widely used as a solvent in the cosmetic and food fields. Alcohol is manufactured by the fermentation of starch, sugar, and other carbohydrates. It is clear, colorless, and flammable, with a somewhat pleasant odor and a burning taste. Medicinally used externally as an antiseptic and internally as a stimulant and hypnotic. *Absolute alcohol* is ethyl alcohol to which a substance has been added to make it unfit for drinking. *Rubbing alcohol* contains not less than 68.5 percent and not more than 71.5 percent by volume of absolute alcohol and a remainder of denaturants, such as perfume oils. Toxic in large doses. *See also* Anisyl Alcohol.

ALCOHOL, DENATURED • There is no reported use of the chemical, and no toxicology information is available according to the FDA's data bank.

ALDEHYDE, ALIPHATIC • A class of organic chemical compounds intermediate between acids and alcohols. Aldehyde contains less oxygen than acids and less hydrogen than alcohols. Formaldehyde (*see*), a preservative, is an example of an aldehyde widely used in cosmetics. Benzaldehyde and cinnamic aldehydes are used to scent perfumes. Most are irritating to the skin and gastrointestinal tract.

ALDICARB • Temik. Crystals from isopropyl ether used as an insecticide, spider killer, and worm killer on citrus pulp in growing crops. FDA tolerance is 0.6 ppm, 0.3 ppm in cottonseed hulls, and 0.5 ppm in sorghum.

ALDRIN • Aldrex. Altox. Drinox. A pesticide. Poison by ingestion, skin contact, intravenous, intraperitoneal, and other routes. Causes tumors, cancer, and birth defects. Human systemic effects by ingestion: excitement, tremors, and nausea or vomiting. Continued acute exposure causes liver damage.

ALFALFA • Herb and Seed. Lucerne. Extract of *Medicago sativa.* A natural cola, liquor, and maple flavoring agent for beverages and cordials. Alfalfa is widely cultivated for forage and is a commercial source of chlorophyll. The FDA's data bank, PAFA (see page 10), has not yet done a toxicology search of the literature on this additive.

ALGAE, BROWN • Kelp. Ground, dried seaweed used to carry natural spices, seasonings, and flavorings. A source of alginic acid (*see*). Also used in chewing-gum base. All derivatives of alginic acid are designated "algin." The food industry is one of the major users of alginates (*see*) along with the pharmaceutical, cosmetic, rubber, and paper industries. The United States is the largest producer of alginates. Algae is claimed to prevent wrinkles and to moisturize the skin, but the American Medical Association denies any validity for algae's therapeutic benefits. However, seaweed products are widely used in cosmetics for many purposes. The final report to the FDA of the Select Committee on GRAS Substances stated in 1980 that it should continue its GRAS status with no limitations other than good manufacturing practices. Nontoxic. There is no reported use of algaes in food, according to the FDA, and there is no toxicology information available, according to the FDA's data bank, PAFA.

ALGAE MEAL, DRIED • Permanently listed to be used in chicken feed to enhance the color of chicken skin and egg yolks. No known toxicity.

ALGAE, RED • A natural extract of seaweed used to carry natural spices, seasonings, and flavorings. Nontoxic. GRAS. *See* Alginates.

ALGANET • Coloring agent used in casings and rendered fats.

ALGIN • The sodium salt of alginic acid (*see*), it is used in cheeses, frozen desserts, soda water, jellies, and preserves as a stabilizer. GRAS.

ALGINATES • Ammonium, Calcium, Potassium, and Sodium. All derivatives of alginic acid are designated "algin." Gelatinous substances obtained from certain seaweeds and used as stabilizers and water retainers in beverages, ice cream, ices, frozen custard, emulsions, desserts, baked goods, and confectionery ingredients. A clarifying agent for wine, chocolate milk, meat, toppings, cheeses, cheese spreads, cheese snacks, salad dressings, and artificially sweetened jelly and jam ingredients. Alginates are also used as stabilizers in gassed cream (pressure-dispensed whipped cream). The alginates assure a creamy texture and prevent formation of ice crystals in ice creams. Alginates have been used in the making of ice pops to impart smoothness of texture by ensuring that the fruit flavors are uniformly distributed throughout the ice crystals during freezing, helping the pops to retain flavor and color, and to stop dripping. The final report to the FDA of the Select Committee on GRAS Substances stated in 1980 that there is no available evidence that it is a hazard to the public when used as it is now and it should continue its GRAS status with limitations on the amounts that can be added to food. Alginates are also used as emulsifiers in hand lotions and creams, and as thickening agents in shampoos, wave sets, and lotions. They are also used as barrier agents (*see*) in hand creams and lotions, in the manufacture of celluloid, as an emulsifier in mineral oil, and in mucilage. Sodium alginate from brown seaweed is used as a thickener in dentifrices, but the FDA is testing the sodium form (largest use in ice cream) for short-term mutagenic birth-deforming, reproduction, and subacute effects. The FDA data bank, at this writing, was researching the literature concerning the toxicology of this food additive.

ALGINIC ACID • It is obtained as a highly gelatinous precipitate from seaweed. It is odorless and tasteless and is used as a stabilizer in ice cream, frozen custard, ice milk, fruit, sherbet, water ices, beverages, icings, cheeses, cheese spreads, cheese snacks, French dressing, and salad dressing. It is also used as a defoaming agent in processed foods. Capable of absorbing two hundred to three hundred times its weight of water and salts. Also used in sizing paper and textiles and as a stabilizer in cosmetics. The sodium carbonate (*see*) extracts of dried brown seaweed are treated with acid to achieve the result. Resembles albumin or gelatin (*see both*). Alginic acid is slowly soluble in water, forming a thick liquid. The World Health Organization on Food Additives observed that a ninety-day study in rats, 15 percent alginate in the diet, resulted in an enlarged, distended, heavy lower intestine, bumpy urinary bladder, and calcium deposits in the renal pelvis. A slight decrease in growth was also seen. The Committee noted that alginic acid and its salts have a laxative effect at a high level of intake. The Committee did not offer a ADI (*see*) for alginic acid. The FDA's data bank, PAFA (see page 10), has not yet done a search of the toxicology literature concerning this additive.

ALKALI • The term originally covered the caustic and mild forms of potash and soda. Now a substance is regarded as an alkali if it gives hydroxyl ions in solution. An alkaline aqueous solution is one with a pH (*see*) greater than 7. Sodium bicarbonate is an example of an alkali that is used to neutralize excess acidity in cosmetics.

ALKANET ROOT • A red coloring obtained by extraction from the herblike tree root grown in Asia Minor and the Mediterranean. Used as a copper or blue coloring (when combined with metals) for hair oils and other cosmetics. It is also used as a coloring for wines, inks, and sausage casings. May be mixed with synthetic dyes for color tints. Formerly used as an astringent. Once commonly used, the authorization for use was withdrawn by the FDA in 1988.

ALKANNIN • A red powder and the principal ingredient of alkanet root (*see*). Used as an astringent in cosmetics and to color cosmetics and food.

ALKANOMIDE • Produced by condensation of coconut-oil fatty acids and diethanolamine (*see*); used in delinting cottonseeds. FDA tolerance is less than 0.2 percent of weight by application. The FDA's data bank, PAFA (see page 10), has fully up-to-date toxicology information available on this food additive.

ALKYL • Meaning "from alcohol," usually derived from alkane. Any one of a series of saturated hydrocarbons such as methane. One or more alkyls are added to a compound to make the product more soluble. The mixture is usually employed with surfactants (*see*), which have a tendency to float when not alkylated.

ALKYL BETAINES • *See* Alkyl Sulfates.

ALKYL ETHER SULFATES • *See* Alkyl Sulfates.

ALKYL SULFATES • Surfactants (*see*) used in foods, drugs, and cosmetics. These compounds were developed by the Germans during World War II when vegetable fats and oils were scarce. A large number of alkyl sulfates have been prepared from primary alcohols by treatment with sulfuric acid; the alcohols are usually prepared from fatty acids (*see*). Alkyl sulfates are low in acute and chronic toxicity but may cause skin irritation.

ALKYLENE OXIDE ADDUCTS OF ALKYL ALCOHOLS • Used to assist in lye peeling of fruits and vegetables. FDA permits less than 0.2 percent in lye.

ALLANTOIN • Used in cold creams, hand lotions, hair lotions, after-shave lotions, and other skin-soothing cosmetics because of its ability to help heal wounds and skin ulcers and to stimulate the growth of healthy tissue. Colorless crystals, soluble in hot water, it is prepared synthetically by the oxidation of uric acid (*see*) or by heating uric acid with dichloroacetic acid. It is nontoxic.

ALLERGEN • A substance that provokes an allergic reaction in the susceptible but does not normally affect other people. Plant pollens, fungi spores, and animal danders are some of the common allergens.

ALLERGIC CONTACT DERMATITIS • ACD. Skin rash caused by direct contact with a substance to which the skin is sensitive. Symptoms include a red rash, swelling, and intense itching. Blisters may develop and break open, forming a crust. ACD may develop at any age and may be acute or chronic. Symptoms may appear seven to ten days after the first exposure to an allergen. More often, the allergic reaction doesn't develop for many years and may require many repeated low-level exposures. Once the sensitivity does develop, however, contact with the triggering allergen will produce symptoms within 24–48 hours. An attack builds in severity from one to seven days. Even without treatment, healing often occurs in one or two weeks, though it may take a month or longer.

ALLERGIC REACTION • An adverse immune response following repeated contact with otherwise harmless substances such as pollens, molds, foods, cosmetics, and drugs.

ALLERGY • An altered immune response to a specific substance, such as ragweed or pollen, on reexposure to it.

ALLOMALEIC ACID • *See* Fumaric Acid.

ALLSPICE • A natural flavoring from the dried berries of the allspice tree. Allspice is used in liquor, meat, and spice flavorings for beverages, ice cream, ices, candy, baked goods (1,400 ppm), chewing gum, condiments (1,000 ppm), and meats. *Allspice oleoresin* (a natural mixture of oil and resin) is used in sausage flavoring for baked goods, meat, and condiments. *Allspice oil* is used in sausage, berry cola, peach, rum, nut, allspice, cinnamon, ginger, nutmeg, and eggnog flavorings for beverages, ice cream, ices, candy, baked goods, chewing gum (1,700 ppm), condiments, pickles, meats, liquors, and soups. A weak sensitizer that may cause skin rash on contact. GRAS. The FDA's data bank, PAFA (see page 10), has not yet done a toxicology literature search on this food additive.

ALLYL • Prefix meaning "derived from allyl alcohol" (*see*).

ALLYL ALCOHOL • A colorless, pungent liquid made chiefly from allyl chloride heated to a thick substance in the presence of oxygen. It is used to make resins and plasticizers and as the basis for many synthetic flavorings.

p-**ALLYL ANISOLE** • Esdragol. Isoanethole. Tarragon. Isolated from the rind of *Persea gratissima garth,* and from oil of estragon, found in oils of Russian anise, basil, fennel, turpentine, and others. A flavoring agent used in bakery products, both alcoholic and nonalcoholic beverages, chewing gum, confections, fish, ice cream, salads, sauces, and vinegar.

ALLYL ANTHRANILATE • A synthetic citrus fruit and grape flavoring agent for beverages, ice cream, ices, candy, baked goods, and gelatin desserts. No known toxicity. The FDA's data bank, PAFA (see page 10), has fully up-to-date toxicology information available on this additive.

ALLYL BUTYRATE • A synthetic butter, fruit, and pineapple flavoring agent for beverages, ice cream, ices, candy, baked goods, and gelatin desserts. No known toxicity. The FDA's data bank, PAFA, has fully up-to-date toxicology information available on this additive.

ALLYL CAPROATE • 2-Propenyl-N-Hexanoate. Flavoring agent used in candy, dessert gels, puddings. Poison by ingestion and skin contact. An irritant to human skin.

ALLYL CINNAMATE • A light to yellow liquid with a cherry odor, used as a synthetic fruit and grape flavoring agent for beverages, ice cream, ices, candy, baked goods. Moderately toxic by ingestion. Human skin irritant. When heated to decomposition, emits acrid smoke and irritating fumes. The FDA's data bank, PAFA, has fully up-to-date toxicology information available on this additive.

ALLYL CROTONATE • Used in the manufacture of vitamins and flavorings. The FDA's data bank, PAFA, has fully up-to-date toxicology information available on this additive.

ALLYL CYCLOHEXANE ACETATE • A synthetic pineapple flavoring agent for beverages, ice cream, ices, candy, baked goods. The FDA's data bank, PAFA, has fully up-to-date toxicology information available on this additive.

ALLYL CYCLOHEXANE BUTYRATE • A synthetic pineapple flavoring agent for beverages, ice cream, ices, candy, baked goods. The FDA's data bank, PAFA, has fully up-to-date toxicology information available on this additive.

ALLYL CYCLOHEXANE HEXANOATE • A synthetic fruit flavoring agent for beverages, ice cream, ices, candy, baked goods. The FDA's data bank, PAFA, has fully up-to-date toxicology information available on this additive.

ALLYL CYCLOHEXANE PROPIONATE • A synthetic, colorless liquid with a pineapplelike odor, used in pineapple flavorings for beverages, ice cream, ices, candy, baked goods, gelatin desserts, puddings, chewing gum, and icings. No known toxicity. Poisonous by ingestion. When heated to decomposition, it emits acrid smoke and irritating fumes. The FDA's data bank, PAFA, has fully up-to-date toxicology information available on this additive.

4-ALLYL-1,2-DIMETHOXY PHENOL • White, crystalline solid derived from coal tar. Used in disinfectants, solvents, fungicides, and in the manufacture of wetting agents and dyestuffs. Toxic by ingestion and a skin irritant. May be mutagenic. The FDA's data bank, PAFA (see page 10), says there is no reported use of the chemical and no toxicology information is available.

ALLYL DISULFIDE • Found naturally in garlic and leeks, but considered a synthetic flavoring. It is used in garlic, onion, and spice flavorings for meats and condiments. No known toxicity.

ALLYL ENANTHATE • *See* Allyl Heptanoate.

ALLYL 2-ETHYLBUTYRATE • A synthetic berry, fruit, and brandy flavoring agent for beverages, ice cream, ices, candy, baked goods, gelatin desserts, and puddings. The FDA's data bank, PAFA, has fully up-to-date toxicology information available on this additive. GRAS.

ALLYL 2-FUROATE • A synthetic coffee and pineapple flavoring agent for beverages, ice cream, ices, candy, baked goods, and gelatin desserts. The FDA's data bank, PAFA, has fully up-to-date toxicology information available on this additive. GRAS.

ALLYL HEPTANOATE • A synthetic berry, fruit, and brandy flavoring agent for beverages, ice cream, ices, candy, baked goods, gelatin desserts, and chewing gum. Moderately toxic by ingestion and skin contact. A human skin irritant. Combustible liquid. When heated to decomposition, it emits acrid smoke and irritating fumes. The FDA's data bank, PAFA, has fully up-to-date toxicology information available on this additive. GRAS.

ALLYL HEXANOATE • A synthetic orange, strawberry, apple, apricot, peach, pineapple, and tutti-frutti flavoring agent for beverages, ice cream, ices, candy, baked goods, gelatin desserts, and toppings. The FDA's data bank, PAFA (see page 10), has fully up-to-date toxicology information available on this additive. GRAS.

ALLYL a-IONONE • Cetone V. A synthetic agent, yellow, with a strong fruity, pineapplelike odor, used in fruit flavorings for beverages, ice cream, ices, candy, baked goods, gelatin desserts, and toppings. A skin irritant. GRAS.

ALLYL ISOTHIOCYANATE • Mustard Oil. A naturally occurring agent in mustard, horseradish, and onion used in meat and spice flavorings for beverages, ice cream, ices, candy, condiments, meat, and pickles. Colorless or pale yellow with a pungent, irritating odor and acrid taste. It is also used in the manufacture of war gas. Can cause blisters and other skin problems. Toxic. The FDA's data bank, PAFA, has fully up-to-date toxicology information available concerning this additive.

ALLYL ISOVALERATE • Derived from valeric acid (*see*), it is used as a flavoring. The FDA's data bank, PAFA, has fully up-to-date toxicology information available concerning this additive.

ALLYL MERCAPTAN • A synthetic spice flavoring agent for beverages, ice cream, ices, candy, baked goods, and meats. Poison by inhalation and ingestion. Strong irritant to the skin and mucous membranes. Dangerous fire hazard. The FDA's data bank, PAFA, has fully up-to-date toxicology information available concerning this additive.

4-ALLYL-2-METHOXYPHENOL • *See* Eugenol.

ALLYL METHYL DISULFIDE • A synthetic flavoring. *See* Allyl Alcohol and Sulfides. The FDA's data bank, PAFA, has fully up-to-date toxicology information available concerning this additive.

ALLYL METHYL TRISULFIDE • *See* Allyl Alcohol and Sulfides. The FDA's data bank, PAFA, has fully up-to-date toxicology information available concerning this additive.

ALLYL NONANOATE • A synthetic fruit and wine flavoring agent for beverages, ice cream, ices, candy, baked goods, and meats. The FDA's data bank, PAFA, has fully up-to-date toxicology information available concerning this additive.

ALLYL OCTANOATE • A synthetic pineapple flavoring agent for beverages, ice cream, ices, candy, baked goods, and gelatin desserts. Moderately toxic by ingestion. A skin irritant. The FDA's data bank, PAFA, has fully up-to-date toxicology information available concerning this additive.

ALLYL PELARGONATE • Liquid with a fruity odor, used in flavors and perfumes.

ALLYL PHENOXYACETATE • Acetate PA. A synthetic fruit and grape flavoring agent for beverages, ice cream, ices, candy, baked goods, and gelatin desserts. Moderately toxic by ingestion and skin contact. The FDA's data bank, PAFA (see page 10), has fully up-to-date toxicology information available concerning this additive.

ALLYL PHENYLACETATE • A synthetic pineapple and honey flavoring agent for beverages, ice cream, ices, candy, baked goods. The FDA's data bank, PAFA, has fully up-to-date toxicology information available concerning this additive.

ALLYL PROPIONATE • A synthetic pineapple flavoring agent for beverages, ice cream, ices, candy, baked goods. The FDA's data bank, PAFA, has fully up-to-date toxicology information available concerning this additive.

ALLYL SORBATE • A synthetic fruit and grape flavoring agent for beverages, ice cream, ices, candy, baked goods, and gelatin desserts. The FDA's data bank, PAFA, has fully up-to-date toxicology information available concerning this additive.

ALLYL SULFHYDRATE • *See* Allyl Mercaptan.

ALLYL SULFIDE • A synthetic fruit and grape flavoring agent for beverages, ice cream, ices, candy, baked goods, condiments, and meats. Occurs naturally in garlic and horseradish. Produces irritation of the eyes and respiratory tract. Readily absorbed through the skin. Acute exposure can cause unconsciousness. Long-term exposure can cause liver and kidney damage. The FDA's data bank, PAFA (see page 10), has fully up-to-date toxicology information available concerning this additive.

ALLYL THIOPROPIONATE • A flavoring derived from the onion. The FDA's data bank, PAFA, has fully up-to-date toxicology information available concerning this additive.

ALLYL TIGLATE • A synthetic fruit and grape flavoring agent for beverages, ice cream, ices, candy, baked goods. The FDA's data bank, PAFA, has fully up-to-date toxicology information available concerning this additive.

ALLYL 10-UNDECENOATE • A synthetic fruit flavoring agent for beverages, ice cream, ices, candy, baked goods. The FDA's data bank, PAFA, has fully up-to-date toxicology information available concerning this additive.

ALLYL UNDECYLENATE • *See* Allyl 10-Undecenoate.

***p*-ALLYLANISOLE** • *See* Estragole.

ALLYLTHIOL • *See* Allyl Mercaptan.

4-ALLYLVERATROLE • *See* Eugenyl Methyl Ether.

ALMOND OIL • Bitter Almond Oil. A flavoring agent from the ripe seed of a small tree grown in Italy, Spain, and France. Colorless or slightly yellow, strong almond odor, and mild taste. Used in cherry and almond flavorings for beverages, ice cream, ices, candy, baked goods, chewing gums, maraschino cherries, and gelatin desserts. Used also in the manufacture of liqueurs and perfumes. It is distilled to remove hydrocyanic acid (prussic acid), which is very toxic. Nontoxic without the hydrocyanic acid. GRAS. The FDA's data bank, PAFA, has not yet done a search of the toxicology literature on this additive.

ALOE VERA • An anthraquinone compound expressed from the aloe plant leaf from a South African lilylike plant. Used for supposed softening benefits in skin creams. It contains 99.5 percent water, with the remaining 0.5 percent composed of some twenty amino acids (*see*) and carbohydrates. There is no scientific evidence that aloe vera has any benefits in cosmetics according to the American Medical Association. Used in bitters, vermouth, and spice flavorings for beverages (2,000 ppm) and alcoholic drinks. It has been used as a cathartic but was found to cause severe intestinal cramps and sometimes kidney damage. Cross-reacts with benzoin and balsam of Peru in those who are allergic to these ingredients.

ALPHA-GALACTOSIDASE from MORTIERELLA VINACEAE • An enzyme used in the production of sugar beets to increase sugar yield. No residue is permitted in the finished product.

(ALPHA RS, 2R)-FLUVALINATE (RS)-ALPHA-CYANO-3-PHENOXYBENZYL(R)-2[2-CHLORO-4-TRIFLUOROMETHYL)ANILINO]-3-METHYL BUTONATE • An insecticide. FDA residue tolerances are 1.0 ppm as a residue on cottonseed; 1.0 ppm as a residue in cottonseed oil; 0.3 ppm in cottonseed hulls; 0.05 ppm as a residue in the meat byproducts and fat of cattle, goats, hogs, poultry, and sheep; 0.01 ppm as residues in milk, eggs, and the meat of cattle, goats, hogs, poultry, and sheep. Contains cyanide (see).

ALPHA TOCOPHEROL • See Tocopherols and Vitamin E.

ALTHEA ROOT • Marshmallow Root. A natural flavoring substance from a plant grown in Europe, Asia, and the United States. The dried root is used in strawberry, cherry, and root-beer flavorings for beverages. The boiled root is used as a demulcent in ointments to soothe mucous membranes. The roots, flowers, and leaves are used externally as a poultice. Nontoxic.

ALUM • Potash Alum. Aluminum Ammonium. Potassium Sulfate. A colorless, odorless, crystalline, water-soluble solid used in astringent lotions, aftershave lotions, and as a styptic (stops bleeding). A double sulfate of aluminum and ammonium potassium, it is also employed to harden gelatin, size paper, or waterproof fabrics. In concentrated solutions alum has produced gum damage and fatal intestinal hemorrhages. It has a low toxicity in experimental animals, but ingestion of thirty grams (an ounce) has killed an adult human. It is also known to cause kidney damage. Liquid alum has been found by Penn State researchers to be capable of removing over 99 percent of phosphates from waste water. GRAS when used in packaging only.

ALUMINUM • Silvery white, crystalline solid. It is frequently used in food additives and cosmetics. Ingestion or inhalation of aluminum can aggravate kidney and lung disorders. Aluminum deposits have been found in the brains of Alzheimer's victims, but its part, if any, in this degenerative brain disorder is not clear.

ALUMINUM AMMONIUM SULFATE • Odorless, colorless crystals with a strong astringent taste. Used in purifying drinking water, in baking powders, as a buffer and neutralizing agent in milling, and in the cereal industries. Used also for fireproofing and in the manufacture of vegetable glue and artificial gems. In medicine, it is an astringent and styptic (stops bleeding). Ingestion of large amounts may cause burning in mouth and pharynx, vomiting, and diarrhea. The final report to the FDA of the Select Committee on GRAS Substances stated in 1980 that it should continue its GRAS status with no limitations other than good manufacturing practices.

ALUMINUM CALCIUM SILICATE • Anticaking agent used so that it is 2 percent of table salt. Used also in vanilla powder to prevent caking. Essentially harmless when given orally. GRAS.

ALUMINUM DISTEARATE • A binder that holds loose powders together when compressed into a solid-cake form. *See* Aluminum Stearates.

ALUMINUM HYDROXIDE • An alkali used as a leavening agent in the production of baked goods. Mild astringent and alkali used in antiperspirants, dentifrices, and dusting powders. A white gelatinous mass used as a drying agent, catalyst, adsorbent, and coloring agent in many cosmetic processes. Also used as a gastric antacid in medicine. Practically insoluble in water but not in alkaline solutions. Aluminum hydroxide has a low toxicity but may cause constipation if ingested. The final report to the FDA of the Select Committee on GRAS Substances stated in 1980 that it should continue its GRAS status for packaging only with no limitations other than good manufacturing practices.

ALUMINUM ISOSTEARATES/LAURATES/STEARATES • The aluminum salt of a mixture of isostearic acid, lauric acid, and stearic acid (*see all*). Used as a gelling agent. No known toxicity.

ALUMINUM ISOSTEARATES/MYRISTATES • Myristates is the aluminum salt of a mixture of isostearic acid and myristic acid (*see both*). Used as a gelling agent. No known toxicity.

ALUMINUM ISOSTEARATES/PALMITATES • Palmitates is the aluminum salt of palmitic acid (*see*) and isostearic acid (*see*). Used as a gelling agent. No known toxicity.

ALUMINUM LACTATE • The aluminum salts of lactic acid (*see both*).

ALUMINUM MONOSTEARATE • Anticaking agent, binder, emulsifier, and stabilizer used in packaging materials and various foods. Must conform to FDA specifications for salts or fats or fatty acids derived from edible oils.

ALUMINUM MYRISTATES/PALMITATES • Myristates is the aluminum salt of a mixture of palmitic acid and isostearic acid (*see both*). Used as a gelling agent. No known toxicity.

ALUMINUM NICOTINATE • Used as a source of niacin in special diet foods, also as a medication to dilate blood vessels and to combat fat. Tablets of 625 milligrams are a complex of aluminum nicotinate, nicotinic acid, and aluminum hydroxide. Side effects are flushing, rash, and gastrointestinal distress when taken in large doses.

ALUMINUM OLEATE • A yellow, thick, acidic mass practically insoluble in water. Used in packaging, as lacquer for metals, in waterproofing, and for thickening lubricating oils. Low toxicity. The final report to the FDA of the Select Committee on GRAS Substances stated in 1980 that it should continue its GRAS status for packaging only with no limitations other than good manufacturing practices.

ALUMINUM PALMITATE • White granules, insoluble in water, used as a lubricant and waterproofing and packaging material. Also used to thicken petroleum and as an antiperspirant. The final report to the FDA of the Select Committee on GRAS Substances stated in 1980 that it should continue its GRAS status for packaging only with no limitations other than good manufacturing practices.

ALUMINUM PHOSPHIDE • Used to fumigate processed foods including corn grits, brewers' malt, and brewers' rice. The FDA requires that processors aerate the finished food for forty-eight hours before it is offered to the consumer. It further warns that under no conditions should the formulation containing aluminum phosphide be used so that it or its unreacted residues will come into contact with any processed food. Reacts with moist air to produce the highly toxic phosphine. Residues of phosphine in or on processed food may not exceed .01 parts per million, according to the FDA. Phosphine may cause pain in the region of the diaphragm, a feeling of coldness, weakness, vertigo, shortness of breath, bronchitis, edema, lung damage, convulsions, coma, and death.

ALUMINUM POTASSIUM SULFATE • Colorless, odorless, hard, transparent crystals or powder with a sweet antiseptic taste used for clarifying sugar and as a firming agent and carrier for leaching agents. It is used in the production of sweet and dill pickles, cereal, flours, bleached flours, and cheese. Ingestion of large quantities may cause burning in the mouth and throat and stomach distress. The final report to the FDA of the Select Committee on GRAS Substances stated in 1980 that it should continue its GRAS status with no limitations other than good manufacturing practices.

ALUMINUM SALTS OF FATTY ACIDS • Used as binders, emulsifiers, and anticaking agents. Regulated and used according to good manufacturing practices. *See* Aluminum Sodium Sulfate.

ALUMINUM SODIUM SULFATE • Colorless crystals used as a buffer, firming agent, neutralizing agent, and carrier for bleaching agents. For other uses, *see* Aluminum Potassium Sulfate. The final report to the FDA of the Select Committee on GRAS Substances stated in 1980 that it should continue its GRAS status with no limitations other than good manufacturing practices. A weak sensitizer. Local contact may cause skin rash.

ALUMINUM STEARATES • Hard, plasticlike materials used in waterproofing fabrics, thickening lubricating oils, and as a chewing-gum base component and a defoamer component used in processing beet sugar and yeast. *Aluminum tristearate* is a hard plastic material used as a thickener and coloring in cosmetics. No known toxicity.

ALUMINUM SULFATE • Cake Alum. Patent Alum. Colorless crystals, soluble in water. Odorless, with a sweet, mildly astringent taste. Used in producing sweet and dill pickles and as a modifier for starch. It is used in packaging materials, pickle relish, potatoes, and shrimp packs. Also used as an antiseptic, astringent, and detergent in antiperspirants, deodorants, and skin fresheners; also purifies water. It may cause pimples under the arm when in antiperspirants and/or allergic reactions in some people. Moderately toxic by ingestion and injection. May affect reproduction. The final report to the FDA of the Select Committee on GRAS Substances stated in 1980 that it should continue its GRAS status with no limitations other than good manufacturing practices.

AMARANTH • Red No. 2, banned by the FDA in 1976. The ban was reaffirmed in 1980. *See* FD and C Colors.

AMARANTH FLOUR • A grain grown in Central and South America for thousands of years, it is high in protein and fiber. Because it costs more than other grains, it is usually found only in health-food stores.

AMBERGRIS • Concretion from the intestinal tract of the sperm whale found in tropical seas. About 80 percent cholesterol, it is a gray to black, waxy mass and is used for fixing delicate odors in perfumery. It is also used in a flavoring for food and beverages. No known toxicity. GRAS.

AMBRETTE • A natural flavoring agent from the seed of the hibiscus plant, clear yellow to amber as a liquid, with a musky odor. Seed used in berry and floral flavorings for beverages, ice cream, ices, candy, baked goods. The tincture is used in black-walnut and vanilla flavorings for the same products and in cordials. The seed oil is used in fruit flavoring for beverages, ice cream, candy, and baked goods. No known toxicity. GRAS.

AMBRETTOLID • Formed in ambrette-seed oil. Used as a flavoring, perfume fixative. No known toxicity.

AMBUSH • Ectiban. Exmin. Permethrin. A pesticide. Poisonous by inhalation and injection. Moderately toxic by ingestion. May be mutagenic. A skin irritant.

AMERICAN DILLSEED OIL • *See* Dill.

AMES TEST • Dr. Bruce Ames, a biochemist at the University of California, developed a simple, inexpensive test in the early 1970s using bacteria that reveals whether a chemical is a mutagen. Almost all chemicals that are known carcinogens have also been shown to be mutagenic on the Ames Test. Whether the test can identify carcinogens is still controversial.

AMINE OXIDES • Surfactants derived from ammonia (*see both*).

AMINO ACIDS • The body's building blocks, from which proteins are constructed. Of the twenty-two known amino acids, eight cannot be manufactured in the body in sufficient quantities to sustain growth health. These eight are called "essential" because they are necessary to maintain good health. A ninth, histidine, is thought to be necessary for growth only in childhood. Widely used in moisturizers and emollients because they are thought to help penetrate the skin. Certain amino acid deficiencies appear to have tumor-suppressing action. The amino acids of protein foods are separated by digestion and go into a general pool from which the body takes the ones it needs to synthesize its own proteins.

4-AMINO-6-tert-BUTYL-3-(METHYL THIO)-1,2,4-TRIAZIN-5-ON • Metribuzin. Sencoral. Secorex. An herbicide used on barley, potato chips, processed potatoes, sugar cane, molasses, and wheat, except flour. Under the EPA Genetic Toxicology Program. Poison by ingestion.

4-AMINO-6-(1,1-DIMETHYL-ETHYL)-3-(METHYL THIO)-1,2,4-TRIAZINE-5(4H)-ONE • Metribuzin. Herbicide used on processed potatoes, including potato chips, resulting from application of the herbicide on the raw agricultural commodity. The FDA tolerances are 3 ppm in processed potatoes and potato chips; 3 ppm in animal feed using wheat; 2 ppm in animal feed using tomato pomace; 0.3 ppm in animal feed using sugarcane molasses; and 0.5 ppm in animal feed using sugarcane bagasse. Toxic.

4-AMINO-3,5,6-TRICHLOROPICOLINIC ACID • Amdon Grazon. Borolin. Chloramp. An herbicide and defoliant used on barley, oats, and wheat. An experimental cancer-causing agent and teratogen. Moderately toxic by ingestion.

***p*-AMINOBENZOIC ACID** • *See* para-Aminobenzoic Acid.

para-AMINOBENZOIC ACID • The colorless or yellowish acid found in vitamin B complex. In an alcohol and water solution plus a little light perfume, it is sold under a wide variety of names as a sunscreen lotion. It is also used as a local anesthetic in sunburn products. It is used medicinally to treat arthritis. However, it can cause allergic eczema, a skin disorder, and a sensitivity to light in susceptible people, whose skin may react to sunlight by erupting with a rash, sloughing, and/or swelling.

AMINOBENZYLPENICILLIN • Acillin. Ado Bacillin. Alpen. Penbritin. Vicilin. Animal drug used in beef, milk, and pork. Under the EPA Genetic Toxicology Program. Moderately toxic by injection. Human systemic effects by ingestion: fever, agranulocytosis, and other blood effects. May be mutagenic.

6-AMINOCAPROIC ACID • See Amino Acids and Caproic Acid.

AMMONIA • Liquid used in permanent wave (cold) and hair bleaches. Obtained by blowing steam through incandescent coke. Ammonia is also used in the manufacture of explosives and synthetic fabrics. It is extremely toxic when inhaled in concentrated vapors and is irritating to the eyes and mucous membranes. It may cause hair breakage when used in permanent waves and hair bleaches.

AMMONIATED GLYCYRRHIZIN • GRAS. See Licorice.

AMMONIUM ALGINATE • A stabilizer and water retainer. The report to the FDA of the Select Committee on GRAS Substances stated in 1980 that there is no available evidence that it is a hazard to the public when used as it is now and it should continue its GRAS status with limitation on amounts that can be added to food. See Alginates.

AMMONIUM BICARBONATE • An alkali used as a leavening agent in the production of baked goods, confections, and cacao products. Usually prepared by passing carbon dioxide gas through concentrated ammonia water. Shiny, hard, colorless or white crystals; faint odor of ammonia. Used also in powder formulas in cooling baths. Used medicinally as an expectorant and to break up intestinal gas. Also used in compost heaps to accelerate decomposition. The final report to the FDA of the Select Committee on GRAS substances stated in 1980 that it should continue its GRAS status with no limitations other than good manufacturing practices.

AMMONIUM BITARTRATE • White crystals, soluble in water, derived from tartaric acid. Used in baking powder. No known toxicity.

AMMONIUM CARBONATE • A white, solid alkali derived partly from ammonium bicarbonate (see) and used as a neutralizer and buffer in permanent-wave solutions and creams. It decomposes when exposed to air. Also used in baking powders, for defatting woolens, in fire extinguishers, and as an expectorant. Ammonium carbonate can cause skin rashes on the scalp, forehead, or hands. The final report to the FDA of the Select Committee on GRAS Substances stated in 1980 that it should continue its GRAS status with no limitations other than good manufacturing practices.

AMMONIUM CASEINATE • The ammonium salt of casein, a protein occurring in milk and cheese. It is used in standard foods, particularly bakery products. Therefore, it does not have to be listed on the label. See Casein.

AMMONIUM CHLORIDE • Ammonium salt that occurs naturally. Colorless, odorless crystals or white powder, saline in taste, and incompatible with alkalies. Used as a dough conditioner and a yeast food in bread, rolls, buns, and so on. Also used as an acidifier in permanent-wave solutions, eye lotions, and as a cooling and stimulating skin wash. Industrially employed in freezing mixtures, batteries, dyes, safety explosives, and in medicine as a urinary acidifier and diuretic. Keeps snow from melting on ski slopes. If ingested, can cause nausea, vomiting, and acidosis in doses of 0.5 to 1 gram. Lethal as an intramuscular dose in rats and guinea pigs. As with any ammonia compound, concentrated solutions can be irritating to the skin. The final report to the FDA of the Select Committee on GRAS Substances stated in 1980 that it should continue GRAS status for packaging only with no limitations other than good manufacturing practices.

AMMONIUM CITRATE • The salt of citric acid (*see*), it is a natural constituent of plants and animals and dissolves easily in water, releasing free acid. Used as a sequestrant, flavor enhancer, and firming agent. The final report to the FDA of the Select Committee on GRAS Substances stated in 1980 that it should continue its GRAS status with no limitations other than good manufacturing practices.

AMMONIUM GLUCONATE • Prepared from gluconic acid with ammonia. It is used as an emulsifying agent for cheese and salad dressings. No known toxicity.

AMMONIUM HYDROXIDE • Ammonium Bicarbonate. Ammonia Water. A weak alkali formed when ammonia dissolves in water; exists only in solution. A clear, colorless liquid with an extremely pungent odor. Used as a buffer and neutralizer in cocoa products and in animal feeds. Also used as an alkali (*see*) in metallic hair dyes, hair straighteners, and in protective skin creams. Also used in detergents and for removing stains. It is irritating to the eyes and mucous membranes. It may cause hair breakage. A human poison by ingestion. The final report to the FDA of the Select Committee on GRAS Substances stated in 1980 that it should continue its GRAS status for packaging only with no limitations other than good manufacturing practices. GRAS.

AMMONIUM ISOVALERATE • *See* Isovaleric Acid.

AMMONIUM OLEATE • The ammonium salt of oleic acid (*see*) used as an emulsifying agent.

AMMONIUM PERSULFATE • Ammonium Peroxydisulfate. Odorless crystals or white powder. Used as an oxidizer and bleacher and as a modifier for food starch. *See* Modified Starch. The FDA's data bank, PAFA (see page 10), has not yet done a toxicology literature search on this additive.

AMMONIUM PHOSPHATE • Monobasic and Dibasic. Ammonium Salt. An odorless, white or colorless crystalline powder with a cooling taste used in mouthwashes. It is used as an acidic constituent of baking powder. Used as a buffer, leavening agent, and bread, roll, and bun improver up to 10 percent of product. Used in the brewing industry, in fireproofing textiles, paper, and wood, for purifying sugar, and in yeast cultures and fertilizers. Monobasic is used as baking powder with sodium bicarbonate. Medically used for its saline action. It has a diuretic effect (reducing body water) and makes urine more acid. No known toxicity. The final report to the FDA of the Select Committee on GRAS Substances stated in 1980 that it should continue its GRAS status with no limitations other than good manufacturing practices. An FDA toxicology literature search was in progress at this writing.

AMMONIUM POTASSIUM HYDROGEN • A stabilizer used in packaging.

AMMONIUM SACCHARIN • *See* Saccharin.

AMMONIUM SULFATE • Ammonium Salt. A yeast food, dough conditioner, and buffer in bakery products. Colorless, odorless, white crystals or powder. A neutralizer in permanent-wave lotions. Industrially used in freezing mixtures, fireproofing fabrics, and tanning. Used medicinally to prolong analgesia. No known toxicity when used cosmetically. Rats were killed when fed large doses. No known toxicity. The final report to the FDA of the Select Committee on GRAS Substances stated in 1980 that it should continue its GRAS status with no limitations other than good manufacturing practices. An FDA database toxicology literature search was in progress at this writing. *See* Ammonium Phosphate for other uses.

AMMONIUM SULFIDE • A salt derived from sulfur and ammonium used as a synthetic spice flavoring agent for baked foods and condiments. Also used as a neutralizer in permanent-wave lotions, as a depilatory, to apply patina to bronze, and in film developers. May evolve into toxic hydrogen sulfide, and a fatality has been reported from ingestion of ammonium sulfide permanent-wave solution. Irritating to the skin when used in depilatories. The FDA's data bank, PAFA (see page 10), has fully up-to-date toxicology information available concerning this additive.

AMOXICILLIN TRIHYDRATE • An animal drug used in meat and milk. Tolerance is 0.01 ppm in milk and uncooked edible tissues of meat. Moderately toxic.

AMP • The abbreviation for adenosine monophosphate (*see* Adenosine).

AMPHO • Means "double" or "both."

AMPHOTERIC • A material that can display both acid and basic properties. Used primarily in surfactants (*see*) and containing betaines and imidazoles (*see both*).

AMPICILLIN TRIHYDRATE • Amcill. Princillin. Vidopen. Animal drug used in meat. FDA tolerance is 0.01 ppm residue in uncooked tissue of cattle and swine and in milk.

AMPROLIUM • Crystals from methanol and ethanol (*see both*) used as an animal drug in beef, chicken, eggs, pheasant, and turkey. Limitation in chickens and turkeys of 1 ppm in liver and kidney, 0.5 ppm in muscle. Limitation of 8 ppm in egg yolks, 4 ppm in whole eggs.

AMYL • Prefix meaning "derived from amyl alcohol" (*see*).

AMYL ACETATE • Banana Oil. Pear Oil. Obtained from amyl alcohol, with a strong fruity odor. Used in nail finishes and nail-polish remover as a solvent, and as an artificial fruit essence in perfume. Also used in food and beverage flavoring and for perfuming shoe polish. Amyl acetate is a skin irritant and causes central nervous system depression when ingested. Exposure of 950 ppm for one hour has caused headache, fatigue, chest pain, and irritation of the mucous membranes.

AMYL ALCOHOL • A synthetic berry, chocolate, apple, banana, pineapple, liquor, and rum flavoring agent for beverages, ice cream, ices, candy, baked goods, gelatin desserts, and chewing gum. Used as a solvent in nail polish. It occurs naturally in cocoa and oranges and smells like camphor. Highly toxic and narcotic; ingestion of as little as thirty milligrams has killed humans. Inhalation causes violent coughing. The FDA's data bank, PAFA (see page 10), has fully up-to-date toxicology information available concerning this additive.

AMYL ALDEHYDE • *See* Valeraldehyde.

AMYL BUTYRATE • A synthetic flavoring agent, colorless, with a strong apricot odor. Occurs naturally in cocoa. Used in raspberry, strawberry, butter, butterscotch, fruit, apple, apricot, banana, cherry, grape, peach, pineapple, and vanilla flavorings for beverages, ice cream, ices, candy, baked goods, cherry syrup, and chewing gums. Used in some perfume formulas for its apricotlike odor. The FDA's data bank, PAFA, has fully up-to-date toxicology information available concerning this additive.

AMYL CAPRATE • *See* Cognac Oil.

AMYL CINNAMIC ALDEHYDE • Liquid with a strong floral odor suggesting jasmine. Used in perfumes and flavorings. The FDA's data bank, PAFA, has fully up-to-date toxicology information available concerning this additive. *See* Cinnamic Acid.

AMYL DECANOATE • Approved as a synthetic flavoring, but there is no current reported use of the chemical, and therefore, although toxicology information may be available, it is not being updated by the FDA.

AMYL FORMATE • A synthetic flavoring. The FDA's data bank, PAFA (see page 10), has fully up-to-date toxicology information available concerning this additive.

AMYL 2-FUROATE • A synthetic rum and maple flavoring agent for beverages, candy, baked goods, and condiments. The FDA's data bank, PAFA, has fully up-to-date toxicology information available concerning this additive.

AMYL GALLATE • An antioxidant obtained from nutgalls and from molds. No known toxicity.

AMYL HEPTANOATE • A synthetic lemon, coconut, fruit, and nut flavoring agent for beverages, ice cream, ices, candy, baked goods, gelatin desserts, puddings, and chewing gum. The FDA's data bank, PAFA, has fully up-to-date toxicology information available concerning this additive.

AMYL HEXANOATE • A synthetic citrus, chocolate, fruit, and liquor flavoring agent for beverages, ice cream, ices, candy, baked goods, and gelatin desserts. The FDA's data bank, PAFA (see page 10), has fully up-to-date toxicology information available concerning this additive.

2-AMYL-59 OR 60-KETO-1,4-DIOXANE • A synthetic fruit flavoring agent for beverages, ice cream, ices, candy, baked goods, and shortening. The FDA's data bank, PAFA, has fully up-to-date toxicology information available concerning this additive.

AMYL OCTANOATE • Occurs naturally in apples. A synthetic chocolate, fruit, and liquor flavoring agent for beverages, ice cream, ices, candy, baked goods, and gelatin desserts. The FDA's data bank, PAFA, has fully up-to-date toxicology information available concerning this additive.

a-**AMYL-B-PHENYLACROLEIN BUXINE** • *See a*-Amylcinnamaldehyde.

AMYL PROPIONATE • Colorless liquid with a fruity, applelike odor used in perfumes, flavors, and in lacquers. When heated to decomposition, it emits acrid smoke and irritating fumes.

AMYL SALICYLATE • There is no reported use of the additive, and no toxicology information is available about it. *See* Salicylates.

AMYLASE (swine) • An enzyme prepared from the hog pancreas used in flour to break down starch into smaller sugar molecules. Then, in turn, the enzymes produced by yeast in the dough again split these sugar molecules to form carbon dioxide gas, which causes the dough to rise. It improves crumb softness and shelf life. Used as a texturizer in cosmetics and medically to combat inflammation. Nontoxic.

AMYLASE (batenal) • Derived from *Aspergillus flavus, niger,* or *oryzae* or *Bacillus subtilis,* these enzymes are used as antibacterial agents. The FDA's data bank, PAFA (see page 10), has not done a toxicology search concerning these additives as yet.

a-**AMYLCINNAMALDEHYDE** • A synthetic agent, yellow, with a strong floral odor of jasmine, used in strawberry, apple, apricot, peach, and walnut flavorings for beverages, ice cream, ices, candy, baked goods, gelatin desserts, and chewing gum. Moderately toxic by ingestion. A mild skin irritant. Susceptible to oxidation by air.

a-**AMYLCINNAMALDEHYDE DIMETHYL ACETAL** • A synthetic fruit flavoring agent for beverages, ice cream, candy, and baked goods. No known toxicity.

AMYLCINNAMATE • Colorless to pale yellow liquid with a cocoa odor. Used as a flavoring agent.

a-**AMYLCINNAMYL ACETATE** • A synthetic chocolate, fruit, and honey flavoring agent for beverages, ice cream, ices, candy, baked goods, and chewing gum. No known toxicity.

a-**AMYLCINNAMYL ALCOHOL** • A synthetic chocolate, fruit, and honey flavoring agent for beverages, ice cream, ices, candy, baked goods, and chewing gum. No known toxicity.

a-**AMYLCINNAMYL FORMATE** • A synthetic chocolate, fruit, nut, and maple flavoring agent for beverages, ice cream, ices, candy, baked goods, and chewing gum. No known toxicity.

a-**AMYLCINNAMYL ISOVALERATE** • A synthetic chocolate, fruit, grape, and nut flavoring agent for beverages, ice cream, ices, candy, baked goods, and chewing gum. No known toxicity.

AMYLOGLUCOSIDASE • A sweet enzyme derived from *Rhizopus niveus* with a growth-encouraging potential. Used in the production of gelatinized starch into sugars and in the production of distilled spirits and vinegar. The FDA has not yet searched the toxicology literature concerning this additive.

AMYLOPECTIN • Amioca. Derived from starch, it is the almost insoluble outer portion of the starch granule. The gel constituent of starch. It forms a paste with water. Used as a texturizer in foods and cosmetics. Obtained from corn. Gives a red color when mixed with iodine and does not gel when mixed with water. No known toxicity.

AMYLOSE • Starches commonly processed from plants contain 18 to 27 percent amylose. It is the inner, relatively soluble portion of starch granules. Cornstarch solutions often form opaque gels after cooking and cooling; this is because of the presence of amylose. It is used as a dispersing and mixing agent for oleoresins. Nontoxic.

AMYRIS OIL • Sandalwood Oil. The volatile oil obtained from a gummy wood and used as a flavoring agent in chewing gum and candy. It is a clear, pale yellow, viscous liquid with a distinct odor of sandalwood. The FDA's data bank, PAFA (see page 10), has not yet done a toxicology search on this additive.

ANCHUSIN EXTRACT • *See* Alkanet Root.

ANETHOLE • A flavoring agent used in fruit, honey, licorice, anise, liquor, nut, root beer, sarsaparilla, spice, vanilla, wintergreen, and birch beer flavorings for beverages, ice cream, ices, candy, baked goods, chewing gum (1,500 ppm), and liquors (1,400 ppm). Obtained from anise (*see*) oil, fennel, and other sources. Colorless or faintly yellow liquid with a sweet taste and a characteristic aniselike odor. Chief constituent of anise. Anethole is affected by light and caused irritation of the gums and throat when used in a denture cream. When applied to the skin, anethole may produce hives, scaling, and blisters. GRAS. The FDA's data bank, PAFA, has fully up-to-date toxicology information available concerning this additive.

ANETHUM GRAVEOLENS L • *See* Dill.

ANGELIC ACID • *See* Angelica.

ANGELICA • Used in inexpensive fragrances, toothpastes, and mouthwashes. Grown in Europe and Asia, the aromatic seeds, leaves, stems, and roots have been used in medicine for flatus (gas), to increase sweating, and to reduce body water. When perfume is applied, skin may break out with a rash and swell when exposed to sunlight. The *bark* is used medicinally as a purgative and emetic. The *root oil* is used in fruit, gin, and rum flavorings for beverages, ice cream, ices, candy, baked goods, gelatin desserts, chewing gum, and liquors. The *root extract* is used in berry, liquor, wine, maple, nut, walnut, and root beer flavorings for the same foods, up to baked goods, plus syrups. The *seed extract* is used in berry, fruit, walnut, maple, and spice flavorings for beverages, candy, baked goods, syrups, and condiments. The *seed oil* is used for fruit and gin flavoring for beverages, ice cream, ices, candy, baked goods, gelatin, desserts, and liquors. The *stem oil* is used for fruit flavoring for the same foods as is seed oil, excepting liquors. Angelica can induce sensitivity to light. GRAS. The FDA's data bank, PAFA (see page 10), has not yet done a search on this additive.

ANGOLA WEED • A weed from West Africa used as a flavoring agent in alcoholic beverages only. The FDA says there is no reported use of the additive, and no toxicology information is available.

ANGOSTURA • Flavoring agent from the bark of trees, grown in Venezuela and Brazil. Unpleasant musty odor and bitter aromatic taste. The light yellow liquid extract is used in bitters, liquor, root beer, and spice flavorings for beverages and liquors (1,700 ppm). Formerly used to lessen fever. The FDA has not done a toxicology literature search on this additive as yet. GRAS.

ANHYDRIDE • A residue resulting from water being removed from a compound. An oxide—combination of oxygen and an element—that can combine with water to form an acid, or that is derived from an acid by the abstraction of water. Acetic acid (*see*) is an example.

ANHYDROUS • Describes a substance that contains no water.

ANIMAL COLLAGEN AMINO ACIDS • The major protein of the white fibers of connective tissue, cartilage, and bone, which is insoluble in water but easily altered to gelatins by boiling in water, dilute acids, or alkalies. *See* Hydrolyzed Protein.

ANIMAL KERATIN AMINO ACIDS • A mixture of amino acids from the hydrolysis of keratin (*see*). *See also* Hydrolyzed Keratin.

p-**ANISALDEHYDE** • A colorless oil with a hawthorn odor used as a flavoring agent in various foods. Moderately toxic by ingestion. A skin irritant.

ANISE • Anise Seed. Dried ripe fruit of Asia, Europe, and the U.S. Used in licorice, anise, pepperoni sausage, spice, and vanilla flavorings for beverages, ice cream, ices, candy, baked goods, condiments (5,000 ppm), and meats (1,200 ppm). The *oil* is used for butter, caramel, licorice, anise, rum, sausage, nut, root beer, sarsaparilla, spice, vanilla, wintergreen, and birch beer flavorings for the same foods as above excepting condiments but including chewing gum (3,200 ppm) and liquors. Sometimes used to break up intestinal gas. Used in masculine-type perfumes, cleaners, and shampoos. Can cause contact dermatitis. GRAS. The FDA's data bank, PAFA (see page 10), has not yet done a toxicology search on this additive. *See* Star Anise.

ANISOLE • A synthetic agent with a pleasant odor used in licorice, root beer, sarsaparilla, wintergreen, and birch beer flavorings for beverages, ice cream, ices, candy, and baked goods. The FDA's data bank, PAFA, has fully up-to-date toxicology information available concerning this additive. Also used in perfumery.

ANISYL ACETATE • Colorless liquid with a lilac odor used in perfumery and flavorings. The FDA's data bank, PAFA, has fully up-to-date toxicology information available concerning this additive. *See* Anise and Anisyl Alcohol.

ANISYL ALCOHOL • A synthetic berry, chocolate, cocoa, fruit, and vanilla flavoring agent for beverages, ice cream, ices, candy, baked goods, gelatin desserts, and chewing gum. The FDA's data bank, PAFA (see page 10), has fully up-to-date toxicology information available concerning this additive.

ANISYL BUTYRATE • A synthetic fruit and licorice flavoring agent for beverages, ice cream, ices, candy, and baked goods. The FDA's data bank, PAFA, has fully up-to-date toxicology information available concerning this additive.

ANISYL FORMATE • Formic Acid. A synthetic raspberry, fruit, licorice, and vanilla flavoring agent for beverages, ice cream, ices, baked goods, and gelatin desserts. Also used in perfumery. Found naturally in currant and vanilla. The

FDA's data bank, PAFA, has fully up-to-date toxicology information available concerning this additive. *See* Formic Acid for toxicity.

ANISYL PHENYLACETATE • A synthetic honey flavoring agent for beverages, ice cream, ices, candy, and baked goods. The FDA's data bank, PAFA, has fully up-to-date toxicology information available concerning this additive.

ANISYL PROPIONATE • Occurs naturally in quince, apple, banana, cherry, peach, and pineapple. A raspberry, cherry, and licorice flavoring agent for beverages, ice cream, ices, candy, baked goods, and gelatin desserts. No known toxicity.

ANNATTO • Extract and Seed. A vegetable dye from a tropical tree, yellow to pink, used in dairy products, baked goods, margarine, and breakfast cereals. It is also used to color such meat-product casings as bologna and frankfurters. A spice flavoring for beverages, ice cream, baked goods (2,000 ppm), margarine, breakfast cereals (2,000 ppm), and baked goods. The FDA's data bank, PAFA (see page 10), has fully up-to-date toxicology information available concerning this additive. Permanently listed in 1963 but certification not necessary for use (*see* Certified).

ANOXOMER • An antioxidant used up to 5,000 ppm.

ANTHOCYANINS • Intensely colored, water-soluble pigments responsible for nearly all the reds and blues of flowers and other plant parts. Such color, which is dissolved in plant sap, is markedly affected by the acidity and alkalinity of substances: red at low pH (*see*) and blue at higher pH values. There are about two hundred known anthocyanins, including those obtained from grapes, cranberries, cherries, and plums. They can be used to color acid compounds such as wines and cranberry juice cocktail. The twenty anthocyanins in grapes are the major source of anthocyanin pigment for food color. No known toxicity.

ANTHRANILIC ACID • o-aminobenzoic acid. Yellowish crystals with a sweet taste used in flavorings, dyes and perfumes. *See* Benzoic Acid.

ANTHRANILIC ACID, CINNAMYL ESTER • Reddish yellow powder with the odor of balsam used in baked goods, beverages, and candy as a flavoring agent. May be a cancer-causing agent.

ANTHRANILIC ACID, METHYL ESTER • A flavoring agent used in various foods. May cause tumors. Moderately toxic by ingestion. A skin irritant.

ANTIBIOTICS • For growth promotion and feed efficiency. *See* Bacitracin, Bambermycin, Chlortetracycline, Erythromycin, Lincomycin, Monesin, Oleandomycin, Oxytetracycline, Thiocyanate, Tylosin, and Virginiamycin.

ANTIBODY • Protein in blood formed in response to invasion by a germ, virus, or other foreign body. In sensitive individuals, a special antibody, IgE (*see*), is responsible for the allergic reaction.

ANTICAKING AGENTS • These keep powders and salt free-flowing, such as with calcium phosphate (*see*) in instant breakfast drinks and soft-drink mixes.

ANTIFOAMING AGENT • Defoaming Agent. A substance used to reduce foaming due to proteins, gases, or nitrogenous materials that may interfere with processing.

ANTIGEN • Any substance that provokes an immune response when introduced into the body.

ANTIOXIDANTS • Substances added to food to keep oxygen from changing the food's color or flavor. Apples, for instance, will turn brown when exposed to air, and fats will become rancid after exposure. Among the most widely used antioxidants are butylated hydroxyanisole (BHA) and butylated hydroxytoluene (BHT) (*see both*). Vitamin E and vitamin C are natural antioxidants.

ANTIPROTOZOAL • A medication that combats single-celled parasites that are slightly bigger than bacteria. Many live in human and animal intestines and are harmless, but some cause a variety of ills including dysentery.

***b*-APO-8'-CAROTENAL** • A fine crystalline powder used as a color additive in orange beverages, cheese, desserts, and ice cream. The FDA's data bank, PAFA (see page 10), has fully up-to-date toxicology information available concerning this additive.

APPLE ACID • *See* Malic Acid.

APPLE ESSENCE, NATURAL • A flavoring. The FDA's data bank has not done a toxicological search on this additive as yet.

APRAMYCIN • Ambylan. An animal drug used in pork. FDA tolerance: 0.1–0.4 ppm in swine.

APRICOT • Fruit and Oil. Persic Oil. The tart, orange-colored fruit is used as a natural cherry flavoring agent for beverages, ice cream, ices, candy, baked goods, and soups. The oil is used in brilliantine and the crushed fruit as a facial mask to soften the skin. No known toxicity. GRAS.

APRICOT KERNEL OIL • The oil from the kernel of *Prunus armeniaca*. The FDA has not yet done a toxicology data search on this additive.

ARABIC GUM • *See* Acacia.

ARABINOGALACTAN • A polysaccharide extracted with water from larch wood used in the minimum quantity required to be effective as an emulsifier, stabilizer, binder, or bodying agent in essential oils. Used in nonnutritive sweeteners, flavor bases, nonstandardized dressings, and pudding mixes. The FDA's data base, PAFA (see page 10), has fully up-to-date toxicology information available on this additive.

L-ARABINOSE • A common vegetable gum, especially from gum arabic. Used as a culture medium. The FDA data bank, PAFA, has fully up-to-date toxicology information available on this additive.

ARACHIDIC ACID • A fatty acid, also called eicosanoic acid, that is widely distributed in peanut oil fats and related compounds. It is used in lubricants, greases, waxes, and plastics. No known toxicity.

ARACHIDONIC ACID • A liquid, unsaturated fatty acid that occurs in the liver, brain, glands, and fat of animals and humans. The acid is generally isolated from animal liver. Used essentially for nutrition and in skin creams and lotions to soothe eczema and rashes. No known toxicity.

ARACHIDYL PROPIONATE • The ester of arachidyl alcohol and N-propionic acid, used as a wax. *See* Arachidic Acid.

L-ARGININE • An essential amino acid (*see*), strongly alkaline. It plays an important part in urea excretion. It has been used for the treatment of liver disease. Banned as not safe by the FDA, February 10, 1992, for use in over-the-counter diet pills. The FDA data bank, PAFA, has fully up-to-date toxicology information available on this additive.

ARHEOL • *See* Sandalwood Oil, Yellow.

ARNICA • Wolf's Bane. The dried flowerhead has long been used as an astringent to treat skin disorders. It is used as a flavoring in alcohol beverages only. Ingestion can lead to severe intestinal upset, nervous disturbances, irregular heartbeat, and collapse. Ingestion of one ounce has caused severe illness but not death. Active irritant on the skin. Not recommended for use in toilet preparation and should never be used on broken skin. The FDA's data bank, PAFA (see page 10), has fully up-to-date toxicology information available on this additive.

ARNOTTA EXTRACT AND SEED • *See* Annatto.

AROMATIC • In the context of cosmetics, a chemical that has an aroma.

AROMATIC BITTERS • Usually made from the maceration of bitter herbs and used to intensify the aroma of perfume. The herbs selected for aromatic bitters must have a persistent fragrance. Ginger and cinnamon are examples.

ARROWROOT STARCH • From the rhizome of *Maranta arundinacea,* a plant of tropical America. It is used in the diet of babies and invalids because it is easy to digest. An ingredient in dusting powders and hair dyes made from the root starch of plants. Arrowroot was used by the American Indians to heal wounds from poisoned arrows. It is used as a culture medium and as a medicine. In cosmetics, it is used to help moisturizers penetrate the skin. The final report to the FDA of the Select Committee on GRAS Substances stated in 1980 that it should continue its GRAS status with no limitations other than good manufacturing practices. No known toxicity.

ARSANILIC ACID • Aminobenzene Arsonic Acid. Used in animal feed. Poison by ingestion and injection. A human cancer-causing agent. Arsenic and its compounds are on the Community Right-To-Know List. Can cause blindness.

ARSENIC • Silvery, black crystals used as an animal drug to promote growth in livestock and poultry. Tolerance set by the FDA of 0.5 ppm in muscle, 2 ppm in uncooked edible byproducts, 0.5 ppm in eggs from chickens and turkeys. Limitation of 2 ppm in liver. A human carcinogen. Poison by subcutaneous, intramuscular, and intraperitoneal routes. Human systemic skin and gastrointestinal effects by ingestion. May cause birth defects.

ARTEMISIA • Mugwort. A shrub and herb native to north and south temperate climate having strongly scented foliage and small, rayless flower heads. Used as a flavoring in alcoholic beverages. The FDA says there is no reported use of the extract and no toxicology information is available. As for the oil, the FDA has not yet done a toxicology search. *See* Wormwood.

ARTICHOKE LEAVES • A tall herb that resembles a thistle. Used as a flavoring in beverages only. The FDA's data bank, PAFA (see page 10), has not yet done a toxicology search on this additive.

ARTIFICIAL • In foods, the term follows the standard meaning: a substance not duplicated in nature. A flavoring, for instance, may have only natural ingredients, but it must be called artificial if it has no counterpart in nature.

AS PACKAGED • Refers to the state of the product as it is marked for purchased, while *as prepared* refers to the product after it has been made ready for consumption (e.g., ingredients added per instructions and cooked, such as a cake mix that has been prepared and baked or a condensed or dry soup that has been reconstituted).

ASAFOETIDA EXTRACT • Asafetida. Devil's Dung. A gum or resin obtained from the roots or rhizome of *Ferula assafoetida,* any of several plants grown in Iran, Turkestan, and Afghanistan. The soft lumps, or "tears," have a garlicky odor and are used as a natural flavoring. The *fluid extract* is used in sausage, onion, and spice flavorings for beverages, ice cream, ices, candy, baked goods, meat, condiments, and soups. The *gum* is used in onion and spice flavorings for beverages, ice cream, ices, candy, baked goods, and seasonings. The gums have also been used medicinally as an expectorant and to break up intestinal gas. The *oil* is used for spice flavoring in candy, baked goods, and condiments. Asafoetida has a bitter taste, an offensive charcoal odor, and is used in India and Iran particularly as a condiment. The FDA's data bank, PAFA (see page 10), has not yet done a toxicology search on this additive. GRAS.

ASCORBATE • Calcium and Sodium. Vitamin C Salts. Antioxidants used in concentrated milk products, cooked, cured, or pulverized meat products, and in the pickle in which pork and beef products are cured or packed. The FDA's data bank, PAFA (see page 10), has not yet done a toxicology search on this additive.

ASCORBIC ACID • Vitamin C. A preservative and antioxidant used in frozen fruit, particularly sliced peaches, frozen fish dip, dry milk, beer and ale, flavoring oils, apple juices, soft drinks, fluid milk, candy, artificially sweetened jellies and preserves, canned mushrooms, cooked, cured, and pulverized meat products, and the pickle in which beef or pork is cured or packed (seventy-five ounces of vitamin C per one hundred gallons). Vitamin C is necessary for normal teeth, bones, and blood vessels. The white or slightly yellow powder darkens upon exposure to air. Reasonably stable when it remains dry in air, but deteriorates rapidly when exposed to air while in solution. Nobel laureate Linus Pauling caused a run on vitamin C in 1970 by endorsing it as a cold medicine. Although his theories were not widely accepted by the medical community, a great deal of study is now in progress on vitamin C and immunity. Vitamin C is known to affect the excretion of medications, such as barbiturates, and to make them more toxic. Pharmaceutically incompatible with sodium salicylate, sodium nitrate, theobromine, and methenamine. The final report to the FDA of the Select Committee on GRAS Substances stated in 1980 that it should continue its GRAS status with no limitations other than good manufacturing practices. The FDA's data bank, PAFA, has not yet done a toxicology search on this additive.

ASCORBYL PALMITATE • A salt of ascorbic acid (*see*), it is used as a preservative and antioxidant for candy. Like ascorbic acid, it prevents rancidity, browning of cut apples and other fruits, and is used in meat curing. Nontoxic. The final report to the FDA of the Select Committee on GRAS Substances stated in 1980 that it should continue its GRAS status with no limitations other than good manufacturing practices. The FDA's data bank, PAFA, has not yet done a toxicology search on this additive.

ASCORBYL STEARATE • Although allowed as a food additive, the FDA says there is no current reported use of the chemical, and therefore, although toxicology information may be available, it is not being updated. *See* Ascorbyl Palmitate.

ASPARAGINE • L Form. A nonessential amino acid (*see*). It is widely found in plants and animals both free and combined with proteins. It is used as a dietary supplement, a culture medium, and as a medicine. In cosmetics, it is used to help moisturizers penetrate the skin. The FDA's data bank, PAFA (see page 10), has fully up-to-date toxicology information available on this additive.

ASPARAGUS SEED and ROOT EXTRACT • *Asparagus officinalis.* Sparrow Grass. The root is used in Chinese medicine as a tonic. In India, it is used as a hormonal tonic for the female reproductive system. It is prescribed for women, to promote fertility, relieve menstrual pains, increase breast milk, and generally nourish and strengthen the female reproductive system. It is also used as a tonic for the lungs in consumptive diseases and for AIDS wasting. Asparagus contains glycosides, asparagine, sucrose, starch, and mucilage. In 1992, the FDA proposed a ban on asparagus in oral menstrual drug products because it has not been shown to be safe and effective for its stated claims. The FDA's data bank, PAFA (see page 10), has not yet done a toxicology search on these additives.

ASPARTAME • NutraSweet. A compound prepared from aspartic acid and phenylalanine (*see both*), with about two hundred times the sweetness of sugar, discovered during routine screening of drugs for the treatment of ulcers. The G. D. Searle Company sought FDA approval in 1973. The FDA approved it in 1974, but objections that aspartame might cause brain damage led to a stay, or legal postponement, of that approval. Another problem arose. An FDA investigation of records of animal studies conducted for Searle drug approvals and for aspartame raised questions. The FDA arranged for an independent audit, which took more than two years, and concluded that the aspartame studies and results were authentic. The agency then organized an expert board of inquiry, and the members concluded that the evidence did not support the charge that aspartame might kill clusters of brain cells or cause other damage. However, persons with phenylketonuria, or PKU, must avoid protein foods such as meat that contain phenylalanine—one of two components of aspartame. The board did, however, recommend that aspartame not be approved until further long-term animal testing could be conducted to rule out a possibility that aspartame might cause brain tumors. The FDA's Bureau of Foods reviewed the study data already available and concluded that the board's concern was unfounded. Aspartame was approved for use as a tabletop sweetener in certain dry foods on October 22, 1981.

In 1984, news reports fueled by the announcement that the Arizona Department of Health Services was testing soft drinks containing aspartame to see if it deteriorated into toxic levels of methyl alcohol under storage conditions created alarm. The Arizona Health Department acted after the director of the Food Sciences and Research Laboratory at Arizona State submitted a study alleging that higher than normal temperatures could lead to a dangerous breakdown in the chemical composition. The author checked with representatives of the Food and Drug Administration. They said that there are higher levels of methyl alcohol in regular fruit juices, and as far as the agency was concerned, the fears about decomposition products were unfounded.

Aspartame lowers the acidity of urine and therefore reportedly makes the urinary tract more susceptible to infection.

In 1988, the Mexican government stopped soda and food processors from using *nutra* in the brand name because it was "misleading." The Mexicans also required labeling with the following warning: "This product should not be used by individuals who are allergic to phenylalanine. Consumption by pregnant women and children under 7 years is not recommended. Users should follow a balanced diet. Consumption by diabetics must be authorized by a physician." The FDA's data bank, PAFA (see page 10), has fully up-to-date toxicology information available on this additive.

ASPARTIC ACID • DL and L Forms. Aminosuccinate Acid. A nonessential amino acid (*see*) occurring in animals and plants, sugarcane, sugar beets, and molasses. It is usually synthesized for commercial purposes. No known toxicity.

ASPERGILLUS • A genus of fungi. It contains many species of molds and spores that produce the antibiotic aspergillic acid. An *Aspergillus flavus-oryzae* group of mold has been cleared by the U.S. Department of Agriculture's Meat Inspection Division to soften tissues of beef cuts, to wit: "Solutions containing water, salt, monosodium glutamate, and approved proteolytic enzymes applied or injected into cuts of beef shall not result in a gain of more than 3 percent above the weight of the untreated product." It is also used in bakery products such as bread, rolls, and buns. Toxicity is unknown, but because of the use of the fungi antibiotics and monosodium glutamate, allergic reactions would certainly be possible. The FDA says that there is no current reported use of *Aspergillus niger* for fermentation production of citric acid, and therefore no toxicology information is available.

ASTRINGENT • A substance that causes skin or mucous membranes to pucker and shrink by reducing their ability to absorb water. Often used in skin cleansers and to help stop bleeding.

ATOPIC DERMATITIS • A chronic, itching inflammation of the skin, also called eczema (*see*).

ATTAR OF ROSES • *See* Rose Bulgarian.

AUBERPINE LIQUID • *See p*-Methoxybenzaldehyde.

AVERMECTIN B and DELTA • Broad-spectrum antiparasitic and antibiotics used on dried citrus pulp and cottonseeds. FDA tolerance 0.1 ppm on citrus pulp and 0.005 ppm on cottonseed.

AVOIDANCE • Measures taken to avoid contact with allergy-producing substances. Since there are no cures for allergies, as of yet, avoiding allergens is the best way to combat them.

AZAPERONE • A tranquilizer and sedative used to treat swine.

AZINPHOS METHYL • Crystals or a brown, waxy solid used as an insecticide for citrus pulp, soybean oil, and sugarcane. Poison by inhalation, ingestion, skin contact, intravenous, intraperitoneal, and possibly other routes. May cause tumors and birth defects.

AZO DYES • A large category of colorings used in both the food and cosmetics industries, the dyes are characterized by the way they combine with nitrogen. Made from diazonium compounds and phenol, the dyes usually contain a mild acid, such as citric or tartaric. Among the foods in which they are used are "penny" candies, caramels and chews, Life Savers, fruit drops, filled chocolates (but not pure chocolate); soft drinks, fruit drinks, and ades; jellies, jams, marmalades, stewed fruit sauces, fruit gelatins, fruit yogurts; ice cream, pie fillings, vanilla, butterscotch, and chocolate puddings, caramel custard, whips, dessert sauces such as vanilla, and cream in powdered form; bakery goods (except plain rolls), crackers, cheese puffs, chips, cake and cookie mixes, waffle/pancake mixes, macaroni and spaghetti (certain brands); mayonnaise, salad dressings, catsup (certain brands), mustard, ready-made salads with dressings, remoulade, béarnaise, and hollandaise sauces, as well as sauces such as curry, fish, onion, tomato, and white cream; mashed rutabagas, purees, packaged soups and some canned soups; canned anchovies, herring, sardines, fish balls, caviar, and cleaned shellfish. Azo dyes can cause allergic reactions, particularly hives. People who become sensitized to permanent hair dyes containing p-phenylene diamine also develop a cross-sensitivity to azo dyes. That is, a person who is allergic to permanent p-phenylene diamine dyes will also be allergic to azo dyes. Also used in nonpermanent hair rinses and tints. There are reports that azo dyes are absorbed through the skin.

AZODICARBONAMIDE • A bleaching and maturing agent for flour. Yellow to orange red, a crystalline powder, practically insoluble in water. Used in amounts up to 45 ppm. The FDA wants further study of this chemical for both short-term and long-term effects. Although allowed as a food additive, there is no current reported use of the chemical, and therefore, although toxicology information may be available, it is not being updated.

B

BABASSU OIL • A nondrying edible oil expressed from the kernels of the babassu palm, which grows in Brazil. Used in foods and soaps but is expensive. No known toxicity.

BACITRACIN • An antibiotic. White to pale with a slight odor. Used as an animal drug. In beef, chicken, eggs, milk, pheasant, pork, and turkey. Tolerance set by the FDA is 0.5 ppm in uncooked tissue of cattle, swine, chickens, turkeys, pheasants, quail, and in milk and eggs. Moderately toxic by ingestion and injection. Possibly mutagenic.

BACITRACIN METHYLENE DISALICYLATE and BACITRACIN ZINC • White to brownish gray powder used as an animal feed drug that the FDA permits at a level not in excess of the amount reasonably required to accomplish the intended effect.

BACTERIA • Microscopic single-cell organisms. Bacteria are among the most common microorganisms responsible for diseases in humans.

BACTERIAL CATALASE • A catalase is an enzyme in plant and animal tissues. It exerts a chemical reaction that converts hydrogen peroxide into water and oxygen. Derived from bacteria by a pure-culture fermentation process, bacterial catalase may be used safely, according to the FDA, in destroying and removing the hydrogen peroxide that has been used in the manufacture of cheese—providing "the organism *Micrococcus lysodeikticus* from which the bacterial catalase is to be derived is demonstrated to be nontoxic and nonpathogenic." The organism is removed from the bacterial catalase prior to the use of the catalase, the catalase to be used in an amount not in excess of the minimum required to produce its intended effect. There is no reported current use of the chemical and no toxicology information is available, according to the FDA.

BAKERS' YEAST EXTRACT • The FDA has not yet done a search of the toxicology literature on this additive. *See* Bakers' Yeast Protein.

BAKERS' YEAST GLYCAN • Used as an emulsifier, thickener, and stabilizer in frozen desserts, sour cream, cheese spread, and flavored snack dips. The FDA's data bank, PAFA, has fully up-to-date toxicology information available on this additive. *See* Bakers' Yeast Protein.

BAKERS' YEAST PROTEIN • *Saccharomyces cerevisiae.* A yeast strain yielding high growth and used in leavening bakery products and as a dietary supplement. The FDA's data bank, PAFA (see page 10), has fully up-to-date toxicology information available on this additive.

BAKING POWDER • In baking, any powders used as a substitute for yeast, usually a mixture of sodium bicarbonate, starch as a filler, and harmless acid, such as tartaric. Cream of tartar is often used as the necessary acid. Nontoxic.

BAKING SODA • A common name for sodium bicarbonate (*see*).

BALM, LEMON • *See* Lemon Balm.

BALM OIL • *Melissa officinalis.* A natural fruit and liquor flavoring agent for beverages, ice cream, ices, candy, and baked goods. The balm-leaves extract is also used in fruit flavors for beverages. The FDA has not yet done a search of the toxicology literature concerning this additive. GRAS.

BALSAM PERU • Obtained from Peruvian balsam in Central America near the Pacific Coast. A dark brown, viscous liquid with a pleasant, lingering odor and a warm, bitter taste extracted from a variety of evergreens. Used in strawberry, chocolate, cherry, grape, brandy, rum, maple, walnut, coconut, spice, and vanilla flavoring for beverages, ice cream, ices, candy, baked goods, gelatin desserts, chewing gum, and syrups. The *oil* is used in berry, coconut, fruit, rum, maple, and vanilla flavoring for beverages, ice cream, ices, candy, and baked goods. *Balsam fir oil* is a natural pineapple, lime, and spice flavoring for beverages, ice cream, ices, candy, baked goods, and gelatin desserts. *Balsam fir oleoresin* is a natural fruit and spice flavoring for beverages, ice cream, ices, candy, and baked goods. Fir balsam is a yellowish green, thick, transparent liquid with a pinelike smell and a bitter aftertaste. It is also used in the manufacture of chocolate. Used also in face masks, perfumes, cream hair rinses, and astringents. Mildly antiseptic and irritating to the skin and may cause contact dermatitis and a stuffy nose. It is one of the most common sensitizers and may cross-react with benzoin, rosin, benzoic acid, benzyl alcohol, cinnamic acid, essential oils, orange peel, eugenol, cinnamon, clove, tolu balsam, storax, benzyl benzoate, and wood tars. GRAS. The FDA has not yet done a search of the toxicology literature concerning this additive.

BAMBERMYCINS • Antibiotics used as an antibacterial in feed for poultry, cattle, and swine. *See* Antibiotics.

BANTHIONINE • *See* Acimeton.

BARLEY FLOUR • A cereal grass cultivated since prehistoric times. Used in the manufacture of malt beverages, as a breakfast food, and as a demulcent (*see*) in cosmetics. No known toxicity.

BARRIER AGENT • A protective for hand creams and lotions, which acts as a barrier against irritating chemicals, including water and detergents. The water-repellent types deposit a film that acts as a barrier to water and water-soluble agents that irritate the skin; oil-repellent types act as barriers against oil and oil-soluble irritants. Silicones (*see*) are widely used as barrier agents. Other skin protective ingredients in barrier agents include petrolatum, paraffin, ozokerite, vegetables, beeswax, casein, various celluloses, alginic acid, zein, gum tragacanth, pectin, quince seed, bentonite, zinc oxide, zinc stearate, sodium silicate, talc, stearic acid, and titanium dioxide (*see all*). Covering one's hands with Vaseline or zinc oxide ointment will protect them well and inexpensively.

BASES • Alkalies, such as ammonium hydroxide (*see*), used to control the acidity-alkalinity balance of food products. *See* pH.

BASIL EXTRACT • Sweet Basil. The extract of the leaves and flowers of *Ocimum basilicum,* an herb having spikes of small white flowers and aromatic leaves used as a seasoning. Has a slightly yellowish color and a spicy odor. Used in sausage and spice flavorings for beverages, candy, ice cream, baked goods, condiments, and meats. The *oleoresin* is used in spice flavorings for baked goods and condiments. The *oil* is used in loganberry, strawberry, orange, rose, violet, cherry, honey, licorice, basil, muscatel, meat, and root beer flavorings for beverages, ice cream, ices, candy, baked goods. Moderately toxic by ingestion. A skin irritant. The FDA has not yet done a search of the toxicology literature concerning this additive. GRAS.

BAY, SWEET • *Laurus nobilis.* A natural flavoring from a Mediterranean plant with stiff, glossy, fragrant leaves. Used in vermouth, sausage, and spice flavorings for beverages, ice cream, ices, candy, baked goods, condiments, and meats. The *oil,* from the laurel, is used in fruit and spice flavorings for beverages, ice cream, ices, candy, baked goods, chewing gum, meats, and condiments. Moderately toxic by ingestion. The FDA has not yet done a search of the toxicology literature concerning this additive.

BAY LEAVES • *Pimenta racemosa.* The West Indian extract is a natural flavoring used in vermouth and spice flavorings for beverages, ice cream, ices, candy, baked goods, meat, and soups. The *oil* is used in fruit, liquor, and bay flavorings for beverages, ice cream, ices, candy, baked goods, condiments, and meats. The *oleoresin* (*see*) is used in sausage flavoring for meats and soups. No known toxicity. The FDA has not yet done a search of the toxicology literature concerning this additive.

BEECHWOOD, CREOSOTE • *See* Creosote.

BEEF TALLOW • *See* Tallow Flakes. GRAS for packaging.

BEESWAX • From virgin bees and primarily used as an emulsifier. Practically insoluble in water. Yellow beeswax from the honeycomb is yellowish, soft to brittle, and has a honeylike odor. White beeswax is yellowish white and slightly different in taste but otherwise has the same properties as yellow beeswax. Used as a candy glaze and polish. Also used in many cosmetics including baby creams, brilliantine hair dressings, cold cream, emollient creams, wax depilatories, eye creams, eye shadow, foundation creams and makeup, lipstick, mascara, nail whiteners, protective creams, and paste rouge. Can cause contact dermatitis (*see*). The FDA has not yet done a search of the toxicology literature concerning this additive. The final report to the FDA of the Select Committee on GRAS Substances stated in 1980 that it should continue its GRAS status with no limitations other than good manufacturing practices. *See* Beeswax, Bleached.

BEESWAX, BLEACHED • White Wax. Yellow wax bleached and purified from the honeycomb of the bee. Remains yellowish white, is solid, somewhat translucent, and fairly insoluble in water. Differs slightly in taste from yellow beeswax. Used in fruit and honey flavorings for beverages, ice cream, ices, baked goods, and honey. *See* Yellow Beeswax for medicinal uses. Mild allergen. The final report to the FDA of the Select Committee on GRAS Substances stated in 1980 that it should continue its GRAS status with no limitations other than good manufacturing practices. The FDA has not yet done a search of the toxicology literature concerning this additive.

BEET • Juice and Powder. Vegetable dye used to color dairy products. Listed for food use in 1967. No known toxicity.

BEETROOT JUICE POWDER • The powdered stem of the beet used for its reddish color in powders and rouges. No known toxicity.

BEHENIC ACID • Docosanoic acid. Colorless water, soluble, constituent of seed fats, animal fats, and marine animal oils. It is a fatty acid (*see*) used to opacify shampoos. No known toxicity.

BENOMYL • (Methyl-l-[butyl carbamoyl]-2-benzimidazole-carbamate). Tersan 1991. Bonide. White crystalline solid, a carbamate (*see*). It is the generic name for a fungicide used on peaches, apples, and other fruits after they are picked. The FDA tolerances for residues in animal feed are 70 ppm in dried apple pomace resulting from application to apples; 125 ppm in dried grape pomace and raisin waste resulting from application to growing grapes; 50 ppm in raisins resulting from application to growing grapes; 50 ppm in dried citrus pulp when present therein as a result of application to the raw agricultural citrus fruits; 50 ppm in concentrated tomato products resulting from application to growing crop; and 50 ppm in rice hulls resulting from application to raw agricultural rice. It is also used as an oxidizer in sewage treatment. It is extremely toxic by ingestion. It may cause birth defects. It is a mild irritant to human skin.

BENTAZON • Herbicide. FDA residue tolerance is 4 ppm in or on mint hay used for feed resulting from application to growing mint.

BENTONITE • A colloidal clay (aluminum silicate) that has a high swelling capacity in water. Used as a food additive, as a thickener, and as a colorant in wine. Poison if given by vein, causing blood clots, and may cause tumors. The FDA's data bank, PAFA (see page 10), has fully up-to-date toxicology information available on this additive.

BENZALDEHYDE • Artificial Almond Oil. A colorless liquid that occurs in the kernels of bitter almonds. Lime is used in its synthetic manufacture. As the artificial essential oil of almonds, it is used in berry, butter, coconut, apricot, cherry, peach, liquor, brandy, rum, almond, pecan, pistachio, spice, and vanilla flavoring. Occurs naturally in cherries, raspberries, tea, almonds, bitter oil, cajeput oil, cassia bark. Used in beverages, ice cream, ices, candy, baked goods, chewing gum, and cordials. Also used in cosmetic creams and lotions, perfumes, soaps, and dyes. May cause allergic reactions. A skin irritant; contact may cause a rash. Highly toxic. Produces central nervous system depression and convulsions. Fatal dose is estimated to be two ounces. The FDA's data bank, PAFA, has fully up-to-date toxicology information available on this additive. GRAS.

BENZALDEHYDE DIMETHYL ACETAL • A synthetic agent used in fruit, cherry, nut, and almond flavorings for beverages, ice cream, ices, candy, baked goods, gelatin, and puddings. The FDA's data bank, PAFA, has fully up-to-date toxicology information available on this additive. *See* Benzaldehyde for toxicity.

BENZALDEHYDE GLYCERYL ACETAL • A synthetic agent used in fruit, cherry, nut, and almond flavorings for beverages, ice cream, ices, candy, baked goods, and chewing gum. The FDA's data bank, PAFA, has fully up-to-date toxicology information available on this additive. *See* Benzaldehyde for toxicity.

BENZALDEHYDE PROPYLENE GLYCOL ACETAL • A synthetic agent used in fruit, cherry, nut, and almond flavorings for beverages, ice cream, ices, candy, baked goods, and chewing gum. The FDA's data bank, PAFA (see page 10), has fully up-to-date toxicology information available on this additive. *See* Benzaldehyde for toxicity.

BENZALKONIUM CHLORIDE (BAK) • A widely used ammonium detergent. It is a germicide with an aromatic odor and a very bitter taste. Soluble in water and alcohol but incompatible with most detergents and soaps. Used medicinally as a topical antiseptic and detergent. Allergic conjunctivitis has been reported when used in eye lotions. Lethal to frogs in concentrated oral doses. Highly toxic. The FDA proposed a ban in 1992 for the use of benzalkonium chloride to treat insect bites and stings and in astringent (*see*) drugs because it has not been shown to be safe and effective for stated claims in OTC products.

BENZENE • A solvent obtained from coal and used in nail-polish remover. Also used in varnishes, airplane dopes, lacquers, and as a solvent for waxes, resins, and oils. Highly flammable. Poisonous when ingested and irritating to the mucous membranes. Harmful amounts may be absorbed through the skin. Also can cause sensitivity to light in which the skin may break out in a rash or swell. Inhalation of the fumes may be toxic. The Consumer Product Safety Commission voted unanimously in February 1978 to ban the use of benzene in the manufacture of many household products. The Commission took the action in response to a petition filed by the Consumer Health Research Group, an organization affiliated with consumer advocate Ralph Nader. Earlier in the year, OSHA and the EPA both cited benzene as a threat to public health. For more than a century, scientists have known that benzene is a powerful bone-marrow poison, causing such conditions as aplastic anemia. In the past several decades evidence has been mounting that it also causes leukemia. Derived from toluene or gasoline, it is used in the manufacture of detergents, nylon, artificial leather, as an antiknock in gasoline, and in airplane fuel. It has a chronic effect on bone marrow, destroying the marrow's ability to produce blood cells. Safety standards for cosmetic-manufacturing workers and other workers have been set at 10 ppm during an eight-hour day, but OSHA wants it reduced to 1 ppm. Although allowed as a food additive, there is no current reported use of the chemical, and therefore, although toxicology information may be available, it is not being updated, according to the FDA.

BENZENE ACETALDEHYDE • Oily, colorless liquid that grows thicker on standing. Has a hyacinth odor. Used as a flavoring agent in bakery products, beverages, chewing gum, confections, gelatin desserts, ice cream, maraschino cherries, and puddings. Moderately toxic by ingestion. Human skin irritant.

BENZENE HEXACHLORIDE (BHC) • Hexachlorane. Hexylan. A pesticide widely used. Poison by ingestion and by subcutaneous injection. Moderately toxic by skin contact. An experimental cancer-causing and tumor-causing agent by ingestion and skin contact. Human systemic effects by inhalation: headache, nausea or vomiting, and fever. Implicated in aplastic anemia. Possible reproductive effects. It is persistent in the environment and accumulates in mammalian tissue.

BENZENE METHYLAL • *See* Benzaldehyde.

BENZENECARBONAL • *See* Benzaldehyde.

BENZENECARBOXYLIC ACID • *See* Benzoic Acid.

BENZIN • Dark straw-colored to colorless liquid made from coal and oil. Used to dilute color, as a solvent, and as a protective coating for eggshells, fresh fruits, and vegetables. A human poison if injected into the vein. Chronic exposure may cause headache, lack of appetite, dizziness, and other symptoms of intoxication. The FDA permits its use at a level not in excess of the amount reasonably required to accomplish intended use.

1,2-BENZISOTHIAZOL-3 (2H)-ONE-1,1-DIOXIDE • Benzosulfimide. Zaharina. Saccharina. Saccharin Acid. Sucrette. Saccarinose. White crystals or powder, odorless with a sweet taste. Used as a masticatory substance in chewing-gum base. A nonnutritive sweetener used in artificial sweetener, bacon, beverage mixes, beverages, chewing gum, desserts, fruit-juice drinks, and jams. The FDA limits it to 12 mg per fluid ounce in beverages, fruit-juice drinks, and beverage mixes. Limitation of 20 mg per teaspoon of sugar-sweetening equivalent and 230 mg per designated size in processed foods. Sufficient evidence of carcinogenicity in animals but not in humans, although it is a possible human cancer-causing agent. Mild acute toxicity by ingestion.

BENZOATE OF SODA • *See* Sodium Benzoate.

1,2-BENZODIHYDROPYRONE • *See* Dihydrocoumarin.

BENZOE • *See* Benzoin.

BENZOEPIN • Brown crystals used as an insecticide in dried tea. Residue tolerance of 25 ppm in dried tea. Poison by ingestion, inhalation, skin contact, and other routes. Causes tumors in laboratory animals and birth defects. A central nervous system stimulant producing convulsions in humans. A highly toxic organochlorine pesticide that does not accumulate in human tissue. Absorption is normally slow, but is increased by alcohol, oil, and emulsifiers.

BENZOFUROLINE • 5-Benzyl-3-Furyl Methyl(+)-cis, trans-Chrysanthemate. A pesticide used in various food products. Poison by inhalation, ingestion, and intravenous routes. Moderately toxic by skin contact. When heated to decomposition, it emits acrid and irritating fumes.

BENZOIC ACID • A preservative that occurs in nature in cherry bark, raspberries, tea, anise, and cassia bark. First described in 1608 when it was found in gum benzoin. Used in chocolate, lemon, orange, cherry, fruit, nut, and tobacco flavorings for beverages, ice cream, ices, candy, baked goods, icings, and chewing gum. Also used in margarine and pickles. Also an antifungal agent. Used as a chemical preservative and a dietary supplement up to 0.1 percent. A mild irritant to the skin. It can cause allergic reactions such as asthma, red eyes, and skin rashes, especially in people sensitive to aspirin. Listed by the FDA as GRAS in a reevaluation of safety in 1976. The final report to the FDA of the Select Committee on GRAS Substances stated in 1980 that it should continue its GRAS status with no limitations other than good manufacturing practices.

BENZOIC ALDEHYDE • *See* Benzaldehyde.

BENZOIN • Gum Benjamin. Gum Benzoin. Any of several resins containing benzoic acid (*see*), obtained as a gum from various trees. Used as a preserving ointment for fumigating, in perfumes and cosmetics as a compound tincture of benzoin, as a skin protectant and respiratory inhalant. The resin is used as a flavoring agent in chocolate, cherry, rum, spice, and vanilla for beverages, ice cream, ices, candy, baked goods, and chewing gum. Benzoin is also a natural flavoring agent for butterscotch, butter, fruit liquor, and rum. Nontoxic. It was tested by the National Cancer Institute and found not to be a cancer-causing agent in rats and mice but may be mutagenic. The FDA's data bank, PAFA (see page 10), has fully up-to-date toxicology information available on this additive.

BENZOPHENONES (1–12) • At least a dozen different benzophenones exist. Synthetic agents used in berry, butter, fruit, apricot, peach, nut, and vanilla for beverages, ice cream, ices, candy, and baked goods. They are used as fixatives (*see*) for heavy perfumes (geranium, for example) and soaps (the smell of "new-mown hay"). Obtained as a white, flaky solid with a delicate, persistent roselike odor, and soluble in most fixed oils and in mineral oil. Also used in the manufacture of hairsprays and in sunscreens. They help prevent deterioration of ingredients that might be affected by the ultraviolet rays found in ordinary daylight. May produce hives and contact sensitivity. In sunscreens they may cause immediate hives as well as other photoallergic reactions. Toxic when injected. The FDA's data bank, PAFA (see page 10), has fully up-to-date toxicology information available on these additives.

2,3-BENZOPYRROLE • *See* Indole.

BENZOYL BENZENE • A fixative for heavy perfumes such as geranium, used especially in soaps. *See* Benzophenones.

BENZOYL EUGENOL • *See* Eugenyl Benzoate.

BENZOYL PEROXIDE • A bleaching agent for flours, blue cheese, Gorgonzola, and milk. A catalyst for hardening certain fiberglass resins. A drying agent in cosmetics. Toxic by inhalation. A skin allergen and irritant. The FDA's data bank, PAFA, has fully up-to-date toxicology information available on these additives.

BENZYL ACETATE • A colorless liquid with a pear or flowerlike odor obtained from a number of plants, especially jasmine, for use in perfumery and soap. A synthetic raspberry, strawberry, butter, violet, apple, cherry, banana, and plum flavoring agent for beverages, ice cream, ices, candy, baked goods, chewing gum, and gelatin desserts. Can be irritating to the skin, eyes, and respiratory tract. Ingestion causes intestinal upset, including vomiting and diarrhea. The FDA's data bank, PAFA (see page 10), has fully up-to-date toxicology information available on these additives.

BENZYL ACETOACETATE • A synthetic berry and fruit flavoring agent for beverages, ice cream, ices, candy, baked goods, gelatin desserts, and chewing gum. The FDA's data bank, PAFA, has fully up-to-date toxicology information available on these additives. *See* Benzyl Acetate for toxicity.

BENZYL ACETYL ACETATE • *See* Benzyl Acetoacetate.

BENZYL ALCOHOL • A flavoring that is derived as a pure alcohol and is a constituent of jasmine, hyacinth, and other plants. It has a faint sweet odor. Used in synthetic blueberry, loganberry, raspberry, orange, floral, rose, violet, fruit, cherry, grape, honey, liquor, muscatel, nut, walnut, root beer, and vanilla flavorings for beverages, ice cream, ices, candy, baked goods, gelatin desserts, and chewing gum. A solvent in perfumes, a preservative in hair dyes, and a topical antiseptic. Irritating and corrosive to the skin and mucous membranes. Ingestion of large doses causes intestinal upsets. It may cross-react in the sensitive with balsam Peru (*see*). The FDA's data bank, PAFA, has fully up-to-date toxicology information available on these additives.

BENZYL BENZOATE • Plasticizer in nail polishes, solvent and fixative for perfumes. Occurs naturally in balsams Tolu and Peru and in various flower oils. Colorless, oily liquid or white crystals with a light floral scent and sharp burning taste. The FDA's data bank, PAFA (see page 10), has fully up-to-date toxicology information available on these additives.

BENZYL BUTYL ETHER • Synthetic fruit flavoring agent for beverages, ice cream, ices, candy, baked goods, gelatin desserts, and puddings. The FDA's data bank, PAFA, has fully up-to-date toxicology information available on these additives.

BENZYL BUTYRATE • Butyric Acid. A synthetic flavoring agent, a colorless liquid with a plumlike odor. Used in loganberry, raspberry, strawberry, butter, apricot, peach, pear, liquor, muscatel, cheese, and nut flavorings for beverages, ice cream, ices, candy, baked goods, chewing gum, and gelatin desserts. The FDA's data bank, PAFA, has fully up-to-date toxicology information available on these additives.

BENZYL CARBINOL • *See* Phenethyl Alcohol.

BENZYL CINNAMATE • Sweet Odor of Balsam. Colorless prisms, used to give artificial fruit scents to perfumes. A synthetic flavoring agent found in balsams of Peru, Tolu, styrax, copaiba, and others. Used in raspberry, chocolate, apricot, cherry, peach, pineapple, plum, prune, honey, liquor, and rum for beverages, ice cream, ices, candy, baked goods, chewing gum, and gelatin desserts. Moderately toxic by ingestion. A mild allergen and skin irritant. The FDA's data bank, PAFA (see page 10), has fully up-to-date toxicology information available on these additives. *See* Balsam Peru for toxicity.

BENZYL DIMETHYL CARBINYL ACETATE • *See* *a,a,*-Dimethylphenethyl Acetate.

BENZYL DIMETHYL CARBINYL BUTYRATE • The FDA's data bank, PAFA, has fully up-to-date toxicology information available on these additives. *See* *a,a,*-Dimethylphenethyl Butyrate.

BENZYL DIMETHYL CARBINYL FORMATE • *See* *a,a,*-Dimethylphenethyl Formate.

BENZYL 2,3-DIMETHYLCROTONATE • A synthetic fruit and spice flavoring agent for beverages, ice cream, ices, candy, and baked goods.

BENZYL DIMETHYLDODECYLAMMONIUM CHLORIDE • Benzyl Ammonium Chloride. An antimicrobial agent used in beets and sugarcane. A skin and eye irritant.

BENZYL DIPROPYL KETONE • *See* 3-Benzyl-4-Heptanone.

BENZYL DISULFIDE • A synthetic fruit flavoring agent for beverages, ice cream, ices, and candy. The FDA's data bank, PAFA (see page 10), has fully up-to-date toxicology information available on these additives.

BENZYL ETHYL ETHER • Colorless, oily liquid, aromatic odor, insoluble in water, miscible in alcohol. Used in flavoring for beverages, ice cream, ices, candy, and baked goods. Narcotic in high concentrations. May be a skin irritant. The FDA's data bank, PAFA, has fully up-to-date toxicology information available on these additives.

BENZYL FORMATE • Formic Acid. A synthetic chocolate, apricot, cherry, peach, pineapple, plum, prune, honey, and liquor flavoring agent for beverages, ice cream, ices, candy, baked goods, and chewing gum. Pleasant fruity odor. Practically insoluble in water. There is no specific data for toxicity, but it is believed to be narcotic in high concentrations. The FDA's data bank, PAFA, has fully up-to-date toxicology information available on these additives.

3-BENZYL-4-HEPTANONE • Synthetic fruit flavoring for beverages, ice cream, ices, candy, and baked goods. The FDA's data bank, PAFA, has fully up-to-date toxicology information available on these additives.

BENZYL o-HYDROXYBENZOATE • *See* Benzyl Salicylate.

BENZYL ISOAMYL ALCOHOL • *See* *a*-Isobutylphenethyl Alcohol.

BENZYL ISOBUTYL CARBINOL • *See* *a*-Isobutylphenethyl Alcohol.

BENZYL ISOBUTYRATE • A synthetic strawberry and fruit flavoring for beverages, ice cream, ices, candy, and baked goods. The FDA's data bank, PAFA (see page 10), has fully up-to-date toxicology information available on these additives.

BENZYL ISOEUGENOL • A synthetic spice flavoring for beverages, ice cream, ices, candy, and baked goods. No known toxicity.

BENZYL ISOVALERATE • A synthetic raspberry, apple, apricot, banana, cherry, pineapple, walnut, and cheese flavoring agent for beverages, ice cream, ices, candy, baked goods, gelatin desserts, and chewing gum. The FDA's data bank, PAFA, has fully up-to-date toxicology information available on these additives.

BENZYL MERCAPTAN • A synthetic coffee flavoring agent used for beverages, ice cream, ices, candy, and baked goods. The FDA's data bank, PAFA, has fully up-to-date toxicology information available on these additives.

BENZYL METHOXYETHYL ACETAL • Synthetic fruit and cherry flavoring agent for beverages, ice cream, ices, candy, and baked goods. The FDA's data bank, PAFA (see page 10), has fully up-to-date toxicology information available on these additives.

BENZYL PHENYLACETATE • A synthetic butter, caramel, fruit, and honey flavoring agent for beverages, ice cream, ices, candy, baked goods, and toppings. A colorless liquid with a sweet floral odor, it occurs naturally in honey. The FDA's data bank, PAFA, has fully up-to-date toxicology information available on these additives.

BENZYL B-PHENYLACRYLATE • *See* Benzyl Cinnamate.

BENZYL PROPIONATE • A synthetic flavoring substance, colorless liquid, with a sweet fruity odor. Used in berry, apple, banana, grape, pear, and pineapple flavorings for beverages, ice cream, ices, candy, baked goods, chewing gum, and icings. The FDA's data bank, PAFA, has fully up-to-date toxicology information available on these additives.

BENZYL SALICYLATE • Salicylic Acid. Used in floral and peach flavorings for beverages, ice cream, ices, candy, and baked goods. A fixative in perfumes and a solvent in sunscreen lotions. A thick liquid with a light, pleasant odor, it is mixed with alcohol or ether. As with other salicylates it may interact adversely with such medications as antidepressants and anticoagulants and may cause the skin to break out with a rash and swell when exposed to sunlight. The FDA's data bank, PAFA (see page 10), has fully up-to-date toxicology information available on these additives. *See* Salicylates.

BENZYLACETIC ACID • *See* Cinnamic Acid.

BENZYLACETONE • *See* 4-Phenyl-3-Buten-2-One.

BENZYLETHYL ALCOHOL • *See* 3-Phenyl-1-Propanol.

1-BENZYLOXY (B-METHOXY) ETHOXY ETHANE • *See* Benzyl Methoxyethyl Acetal.

BENZYLPROPYL ACETATE • *See* a,a-Dimethylphenethyl Acetate.

BENZYLPROPYL ALCOHOL • *See* a,a-Dimethylphenethyl Acetate.

BENZYLPROPYL CARBINOL • *See* a-Propylphenethyl Alcohol.

BENZYLTHIOL • *See* Benzyl Mercaptan.

BERGAMOL • *See* Linalyl Acetate.

BERGAMOT • Bergamot Orange or Red. Oswego Tea. An orange flavoring extracted from a pear-shaped fruit whose rind yields a greenish brown oil much used in perfumery and brilliantine hairdressings. Used in strawberry, lemon, orange, tangerine, cola, floral, banana, grape, peach, pear, pineapple, liquor, spice, and vanilla flavorings for beverages, ice cream, ices, candy, baked goods, gelatin desserts, chewing gum, and icings. The oil can cause brown skin stains (berloque) when exposed to sunlight and is considered a prime photosensitizer (sensitivity to light). The FDA's data bank, PAFA (see page 10), has not yet searched the toxicology literature concerning this additive. *See* Berloque Dermatitis. GRAS.

BERLOQUE DERMATITIS • Some perfumes, which contain oil of bergamot (*see*) and other photosensitizers, may produce increased pigmentation (brown spots) in the area where the perfume has been applied, especially when it is immediately exposed to sunlight. There is no effective treatment and the pigmentation generally persists for some time.

BETA-APO-8'-CAROTENAL • Orange coloring agent for solid or semisolid foods. Nontoxic.

BETA-CAROTENE • Provitamin A. Beta Carotene. Found in all plants and in many animal tissues. It is the chief yellow coloring matter of carrots, butter, and egg yolk. Extracted as red crystals or crystalline powder, it is used as a coloring in food and cosmetics. Also used in the manufacture of vitamin A. Too much carotene in the blood can lead to carotenemia, a pale yellow-red pigmentation of the skin that may be mistaken for jaundice. It is a benign condition, and withdrawal of carotene from the diet cures it. Beta-carotene has less serious side effects than vitamin A and was given to 22,000 physicians as part of a five-year study to determine whether aspirin could protect against heart disease and beta-carotene against tumors. It is nontoxic. GRAS.

BETA-CITRAURIN • Excellent raw material for the extraction of carotenoids (*see* Carotene), or orange coloring. Found in tangerine and orange peels. Soluble in alcohol.

BETAINE • Used as a coloring and as a dietary supplement. Occurs in common beets and in many vegetables as well as animal substances. Used in resins. Has been employed medically to treat muscle weakness. No known toxicity.

BETAINE, ANHYDROUS • Betaine (*see*) with the water removed.

BETULA • Obtained from the European white birch and a source of asphalt and tar. Used in hair tonics; it reddens the scalp and creates a warm feeling due to an increased flow of blood to the area. Also used in moisturizing creams and astringents. Betula leaves were formerly used to treat rheumatism. *See* Salicylates.

BHA • *See* Butylated Hydroxyanisole.

BHT • *See* Butylated Hydroxytoluene.

BIACETYL • *See* Diacetyl.

BICARBONATE OF SODA • A buffer and neutralizing agent used in self-rising cornmeal. *See* Sodium Bicarbonate.

BIFENTHRIN • A synthetic pyrethroid pesticide. Used to combat insects and mites. FDA tolerances are 0.02 ppm in milk, 0.10 ppm in fat, meat, and meat byproducts of cattle, goats, hogs, and sheep, and 0.50 as a residue in cottonseed. Lower toxicity than most pesticides.

BILBERRY EXTRACT • The extract of *Vaccinium myrtillus,* a plant found in North America and the Alps that differs from typical blueberries in having single flowers or very small buds.

BILE SALTS and OX BILE EXTRACT • *See* Ox Bile.

BINDER • A substance, such as gum arabic, gum tragacanth, glycerin, or sorbitol (*see all*) that dispenses, swells, or absorbs water, increases consistency, and holds ingredients together. For example, binders are used to make powders in compacts retain their shape and to help dispense the paste in toothpaste smoothly.

BIOFLAVONOIDS • Vitamin P Complex. Citrus-flavored compounds needed to maintain healthy blood-vessel walls. Widely distributed among plants, especially citrus fruits and rose hips. Usually taken from orange and lemon rinds and used as a reducing agent (*see*). No known toxicity. Any claim for special dietary use, according to FDA regulations, renders the food misbranded.

BIOTIN • Vitamin H. Vitamin B Factor. A whitish crystalline powder used as a texturizer in cosmetic creams. Present in minute amounts in every living cell and in larger amounts in yeast and milk. Vital to growth. It acts as a coenzyme in the formation of certain essential fatlike substances and plays a part in reactions involving carbon dioxide. It is needed by humans for healthy circulation and red blood cells. The FDA's data bank, PAFA (see page 10), has not yet searched the toxicology literature concerning this additive. *See* Berloque Dermatitis.

BIPHENYL • Derived from benzene. Used as a fungistat in packaging of citrus fruits and in manufacturing processes. The FDA's data bank, PAFA, has fully up-to-date toxicology information available concerning this additive.

BIRCH • Betulaceae. Sweet Oil and Tar Oil. A flavoring agent from the bark and wood of deciduous trees common in the Northern Hemisphere. The oils are obtained by distillation. It is a clear, dark brown liquid with a strong leatherlike odor. *Birch sweet oil* is used in synthetic strawberry, pineapple, maple, nut, root beer, sarsaparilla, spice, wintergreen, and birch beer flavorings for beverages, ice cream, ices, candy, baked goods, gelatins, puddings (4,300 ppm), and syrups. *Birch tar oil,* which is refined, is used in chewing gum and has also been used for preserving leather. Used as an astringent in creams and shampoos, it is an ancient remedy. The medicinal properties of the plant tend to vary, depending upon which part of the tree is used. It has been used as a laxative, as an aid for gout, to treat rheumatism and dropsy, and to dissolve kidney stones. It is supposedly good for bathing skin eruptions. The FDA's data bank, PAFA, has not yet done a search of the toxicology literature on this food additive. *See* Betula.

BIS- • A prefix meaning twice.

BISABOLENE • A colorless, oily sesquiterpene found in many essential oils such as oil of bisabol and lime oil. Used as a flavoring. The FDA's data bank, PAFA (see page 10), has fully up-to-date toxicology information available concerning this additive.

BIS(2-CARBOXYETHYL)SULFIDE • Thiodipropionic Acid. TDPA. An antioxidant used in packaging material. Poisonous by injection. Moderately toxic by ingestion. A skin and eye irritant.

1,1-BIS(*p*-CHLOROPHENYL)-2,2,2-TRICHLOROETHANOL • Acarin. Decofol. An insecticide used on dried tea. Poison by ingestion and skin contact. May cause cancer and mutations in humans.

2,4-BIS(ETHYLAMINO)-6-CHLORO-s-TRIAZINE • Aktinit S. Aquazine. Zeapur. An herbicide used in animal feed, molasses, potable water, sugarcane byproducts, sugarcane syrups. The FDA's residue tolerances are 1 ppm in sugarcane byproducts, molasses, and syrup, and 0.01 ppm in potable water. Limitation of 1 ppm sugarcane byproduct molasses when used for animal feed. It is in the EPA Genetic Toxicology Program (*see*). Poison by intravenous route. Causes tumors in experimental animals. A skin and eye irritant in humans.

BIS(2-ETHYLHEXYL)PHTHALATE • BEHP. Witcizer 312. A plasticizer used in packaging materials for foods of high water content. Suspected human cancer-causing agent and teratogen. Affects the human gastrointestinal tract. A mild skin and eye irritant.

N,N-BIS(2-HYDROXYETHYL)DODECAN AMIDE • Lauryl Diethanolamide. Lauric Acid Diethanolamide. Antistatic agent used in packaging materials and limited to 0.5 percent in polyethylene containers.

BIS(8-OXYQUINOLINE)COPPER • Bioquin. Quinondo. Furitdo. A preservative for wood. Copper and its compounds are on the Community Right-To-Know List.

BIS(TRIS[BETA,BETA-DIMETHYLPHENETHYL]TIN)OXIDE • Bendex. An insecticide used in animal feed, dried apples, dried citrus pulp, dried grapes, dried prunes, and raisins. The FDA's tolerances are 20 ppm in prunes and in raisins. Limitations of 75 ppm in dried apple pomace, 35 ppm in dried citrus pulp, 100 ppm in dried grape pomace, and 20 ppm in raisin waste when used for animal feed. Moderately toxic by ingestion and skin contact.

BITTER ALMOND OIL • Almond Oil. Sweet Almond Oil. Expressed Almond Oil. A colorless to pale yellow, bland, nearly odorless essential and expressed oil from the ripe seed of the small sweet almond grown in Italy, Spain, and France. It has a strong almond odor and a mild taste. Used as a flavoring and in the manufacture of perfumes and as an oil in hair creams, nail whiteners, nail-polish remover, eye creams, emollients, soaps, and perfumes. Many users are allergic to cosmetics with almond oil. It causes stuffy nose and skin rashes.

BITTER ASH EXTRACT • *See* Quassia Extract.

BITTER ORANGE OIL • The pale yellow volatile oil expressed from the fresh peel of a species of citrus and used in perfumes and flavorings. May cause skin irritation and allergic reactions.

BITTERWOOD EXTRACT • *See* Quassia Extract.

BIURET • A nutrient in animal feed for ruminants except for those producing milk for human consumption. *See* Urea.

BIX ORELLANA • A solvent extraction of *Bixa orellana L.* seeds. A yellow carotenoid (*see*) solution or powder, it is a color additive in ink used for marking foods and in oleomargarine, poultry, sausage casings, and shortening. May cause contact dermatitis.

BIXIN • Norbixin. The active ingredients of annatto, both carotenoidlike compounds, but with five times the coloring power of carotene, and with better stability. They impart a yellow coloring to food. *See* Annatto.

BLACK COHOSH • Cimicifuga. Snakeroot. Bugbane. Used in astringents, perennial herb with a flower that is supposedly distasteful to insects. Grown from Canada to North Carolina and Kansas. It has a reputation for curing snake bites. It is used in ginger ale flavoring. A tonic and antispasmodic. No known toxicity.

BLACK CURRANT EXTRACT • The extract of the fruit of *Ribes nigrum,* a European plant that produces hanging yellow flowers and black aromatic fruit.

BLACK CUTCH EXTRACT • *See* Catechu Extract.

BLACK PEPPER OIL • From steam distillation of the dried fruit of *Piper nigrum L.* A colorless or greenish liquid with the odor and taste of pepper. A flavoring agent used in meat, salads, soups, and vegetables. A moderate skin irritant.

BLACK WALNUT EXTRACT • Extract of the leaves or bark of the black walnut tree, *Juglans nigra,* found in eastern North America. It produces nuts with a thick oil and is used as a black coloring.

BLACKBERRY BARK EXTRACT • *Rubus fruiticosus.* A natural flavoring agent extracted from the woody plant. Used in berry, pineapple, grenadine, root beer, sarsaparilla, wintergreen, and birch beer flavorings for beverages, ice cream, ices, candy, baked goods, and liquor. The berries, leaves, and root bark are also used to treat fevers, colds, sore throats, vaginal discharge, diarrhea, and dysentery. The berries contain isocitric and malic acids, sugars, pectin, monoglycoside of cyanidin, and vitamins C and A. The leaves and bark are said to lower fever, are astringent, and stop bleeding. The leaves are used for a soothing bath. The FDA's data bank, PAFA (see page 10), has not yet done a search of the toxicology literature on this food additive.

BLACKTHORN BERRIES • *See* Sloe Berries.

BLEACHING AGENTS • Used by many industries, particularly flour milling, to make dough rise faster. Certain chemical qualities, which pastry chefs call "gluten characteristics," are needed to make an elastic, stable dough. Such qualities are acquired during aging, but in the process, flour oxidizes, that is, combines with oxygen, and loses its natural gold color. Although mature flour is white, it possesses the qualities bakers want. But proper aging costs money and makes the flour more susceptible to insects and rodents, according to food manufacturers. Hence, the widespread use of bleaching and maturing agents.

BLOOM INHIBITOR • Bloom is an "undesirable effect" caused by the migration of cocoa fat from the cocoa fibers to the chocolate's surface. Chocolate that has bloomed has a gray-white appearance. Nonbloomed chocolate has a bright, shiny surface with a rich appearance. A bloom inhibitor—a surfactant (*see*) such as sorbitan or lecithin (*see both*)—controls the size of the chocolate crystals and reduces the tendency of the fat to mobilize.

BLUE • *See* FD and C Blue No. 1.

BLUE NO. 1 • *See* FD and C Blue No. 1.

BOILER WATER ADDITIVES • Most are used in food processing as cleaning agents. Those regulated by the FDA include ammonium alginate, cobalt sulfate, lignosulfonic acid, monbutyl ether of polyoxyethylene glycol or potassium tripolyphosphate, sodium carboxymethyl cellulose, sodium glucoheptonate, sodium humate, sodium meta silicate, sodium metabisulfite, polyoxypropylene glycol, polyoxyethylene glycol, potassium carbonate, sodium acetate, sodium alginate, sodium aluminate, sodium carbonate, sodium hexametaphosphate, sodium hydroxide, sodium lignosulfonate, sodium nitrate, sodium phosphate (mono-, di-, and tri-), sodium poly acrylate, sodium poly methacrylate, sodium silicate, sodium sulfate, sodium sulfite, sodium tripolyphosphate, tannin, tetrasodium EDTA, tetrasodium pyrophosphate, 1-hydroxy-ethylidene-1, 1-diphosphonic acid and its sodium and potassium salt. Hydrazine (*see*) must be zero in steam contacting food; acrylamide-sodium acrylate resin is restricted to 0.05 percent of acrylamide monomer in steam contacting food. Cyclohexylamine or morpholine must be less than 10 ppm in steam contacting food except milk and milk products. Octadecylamine must be less than 3 ppm; diethylaminoethanol must be less than 15 ppm; trisodium nitrilotriacetate must be less than 5 ppm in feed water; polymaleic acid and/or its sodium salt must be less than 1 ppm in feed water and in steam contacting food.

BOIS DE ROSE OIL • A fragrance from the chipped wood of the tropical rosewood tree obtained through steam distillation. The volatile oil is colorless to pale yellow, with a light camphor odor. Used in citrus, floral, fruit, meat, and spice flavorings for beverages, ice cream, ices, candy, baked goods, and chewing gum. The FDA's data bank, PAFA (see page 10), has not yet done a search of the toxicology literature on this food additive. GRAS.

BOLDUS LEAVES • Flavoring used in alcoholic beverages only, from a Chilean fir tree with a sweet, edible fruit. There is no reported use of the chemical and no toxicology information is available.

BOLETIC ACID • *See* Fumaric Acid.

BORAGE EXTRACT • The extract of the herb *Borago officinalis*. Contains potassium and calcium and has emollient properties and is used in a "tea" for sore eyes.

BORIC ACID • An antiseptic with bactericidal and fungicidal properties used as a fungus control on citrus fruit (FDA tolerance: 8 ppm boron residues). Also used in baby powders, bath powders, eye creams, liquid powders, mouthwashes, protective creams, after-shave lotions, soaps, and skin fresheners. It is still widely used despite repeated warnings from the American Medical Association of possible toxicity. Severe poisonings have followed both ingestion and topical application to abraded skin. There is no reported use of the chemical and no toxicology information is available.

BORNEO CAMPHOR • *See* Borneol.

BORNEOL • A flavoring agent with a peppery odor and a burning taste. Occurs naturally in coriander, ginger oil, oil of lime, rosemary, strawberries, thyme, citronella, and nutmeg. Toxicity is similar to camphor oil (*see*). Used as a synthetic nut or spice flavoring for beverages, syrups, ice cream, ices, candy, baked goods, chewing gum. Used in perfumery. Can cause nausea, vomiting, convulsions, confusion, and dizziness. The FDA's data bank, PAFA (see page 10), has fully up-to-date toxicology information available concerning this additive.

BORNYL ACETATE • It may be obtained from various pine-needle oils. Strong piney odor. As a yarrow herb and iva herb extract, it is used as a synthetic fruit and spice flavoring for beverages, ice cream, ices, candy, baked goods, chewing gum, and syrups. A colorless liquid derived from borneol (*see*), it is also used in perfumery and as a solvent. The FDA's data bank, PAFA, has fully up-to-date toxicology information available concerning this additive.

BORNYL FORMATE • Formic Acid. A synthetic fruit flavoring agent for beverages, ice cream, ices, candy, baked goods, and syrups. Used in perfumes, soaps, and as a disinfectant. The FDA's data bank, PAFA, has fully up-to-date toxicology information available concerning this additive. *See* Borneol.

BORNYL ISOVALERATE • A synthetic fruit flavoring agent with a camphor-like smell used for beverages, ice cream, ices, candy, baked goods, and syrups. Used in perfumes, soaps, and as a disinfectant. Also used medicinally as a sedative. The FDA's data bank, PAFA (see page 10), has fully up-to-date toxicology information available concerning this additive. *See* Borneol.

BORNYL VALERATE • A synthetic fruit flavoring agent for beverages, ice cream, ices, candy, and baked goods. The FDA's data bank, PAFA, has fully up-to-date toxicology information available concerning this additive. *See* Borneol.

BORNYVAL • *See* Bornyl Isovalerate.

BORON SOURCES • Boric Acid. Sodium Borate. Boron occurs in the earth's crust (in the form of its compounds, not the metal), and borates are widely used as antiseptics even though toxicologists warn about possible adverse reactions. Used in modified hops extract. Boric acid and sodium borate are astringents and antiseptics. Borates are absorbed by the mucous membranes and can cause such symptoms as gastrointestinal bleeding, skin rash, and central nervous system stimulation. The adult lethal dose is thirty grams (one ounce). Infants and young children are more susceptible. Boron is used as a dietary supplement up to one milligram per day. Cleared for use by the FDA in modified hops extract up to 310 ppm.

BORONIA, ABSOLUTE • A synthetic violet and fruit flavoring agent extracted from a plant. Used as a flavoring for beverages, ice cream, ices, and baked goods. The FDA has not done a search of the toxicology literature concerning this additive.

BOSWELLIA SPECIES • *See* Olibanum Extract.

BOURBONENE • *See* Ethyl Vanillin.

BOVINE SOMATOTROPIN • BST. A genetically engineered recombinant growth hormone introduced on the market in 1994 to increase the milk production of cows. The producers of the hormone, the FDA and some other experts claim that there is no difference in the milk of cows given the hormone since cow's milk naturally contains the hormone. Consumer groups, some scientists, small farmers, and a number of dairy product producers are against the use of the hormone. Among the reasons: it increases inflammation of the udder in cows, has unknown potential effects on humans, and is unnecessary because the U.S. government already supports milk prices because there is an overabundance of milk on the market.

BRAN • The outer indigestible shell of cereal grain that is usually removed before the grain is ground into flour. It provides bulk and fiber.

BRASSICA ALBA • *See* Mustard.

BREWER'S YEAST • Originally used by beer brewers, it is a good source of B vitamins and protein. It can cause allergic reactions.

BRILLIANT BLUE • *See* FD and C Blue No. 1.

BROMATED • Combined or saturated with bromine, a nonmetallic, reddish, volatile, liquid element. *See* Bromates.

BROMATES • *Calcium bromate* is a maturing agent and dough conditioner in bromated flours and bromated whole-wheat flour. *Potassium bromate* is a bread improver. Sugar contaminated with potassium bromate caused a food-poisoning outbreak in New Zealand. The lethal dose is not certain, but two to four ounces of a 2 percent solution causes serious poisoning in children. Death in animals and man apparently is due to kidney failure, but central nervous system problems have been reported. Also used in permanent-wave neutralizers. Topical application to abraded skin has also caused poisoning. Bromates may also cause skin eruptions.

BROMELIN • Bromelain. A protein-digesting and milk-clotting enzyme found in pineapple. Used for tenderizing meat, chill-proofing beer, and as an antiinflammatory medication. Federal government rules say: "Solutions consisting of water, salt, monosodium glutamate, and approved proteolytic enzymes applied or injected into cuts of beef shall not result in a gain of more than 3 percent of the weight of the untreated product." A search of the toxicology literature concerning this additive has not yet been performed by the FDA's data bank.

BROMIC ACID, POTASSIUM SALT • White crystals used as a dough conditioner and maturing agent used in baked goods, beverages, and confectionery products. A poison by ingestion. An experimental carcinogen. A powerful oxidizer. An irritant to skin, eyes, and mucous membranes.

BROMIDES, INORGANIC • Used as fumigants.

BROMINATED VEGETABLE OIL • Bromine, a heavy, volatile, corrosive, nonmetallic, liquid element, added to vegetable oil or other oils. Dark brown or pale yellow, with a bland or fruity odor. These high-density oils are blended with low-density essential oils to make them easier to emulsify. Used largely in soft drinks, citrus-flavored beverages, ice cream, ices, and baked goods. The FDA has them on the "suspect list." The FDA data bank, PAFA (see page 10), is conducting a search of the toxicology literature concerning this additive at this writing. *See* Bromates for toxicity.

0-(4-BROMO-2-CHLOROPHENYL)-O-ETHYL-S-PROPYL PHOSPHOROTHIO-ATE • Curacron. Profenofos. Selecron. An insecticide used in animal feed and cottonseed hulls. Poison by ingestion and skin contact.

BROMO METHANE • A colorless, volatile liquid that is used as a fumigant in animal feed, apples, barley, cereal grains, corn, cracked rice, fava beans, fermented malt beverages, flour, grain sorghum, kiwi fruit, lentils, macadamia nuts, oats, pistachio nuts, rice, rye, sweet potatoes, and wheat. FDA residue tolerances include 125 ppm in cereal grain, 25 ppm in fermented malt beverages,

400 ppm in dog food, and 125 ppm in barley, corn, grain sorghum, oats, rice, rye, and wheat when used for animal feed. Extremely hazardous, especially by inhalation. Death following acute poisoning is usually caused by lung irritation. In chronic poisoning, death is due to injury to the central nervous system.

BROOM EXTRACT • *See* Genet, Absolute.

BRYONIA • A small herb used for flavoring in alcoholic beverages. There is no reported use of the chemical and no toxicology information is available.

BST • Abbreviation for Bovine Somatotropin (*see*) Hormone.

BUCHU LEAF OIL • A natural flavoring agent from a South African plant used in berry, fruit, chocolate, mint, and spice flavorings for beverages, ice cream, ices, candy, baked goods, liquors, and condiments. Has been used as a urinary antiseptic and mild diuretic. A search of the toxicology literature concerning this additive has not yet been performed by the FDA's data bank.

BUCKBEAN LEAVES • Flavoring in alcoholic beverages only. There is no reported use of the chemical and no toxicology information is available, according to the FDA.

BUCKTHORN • Frangula. A shrub or tree grown on the Mediterranean coast of Africa, it has thorny branches and often contains a purgative in the bark or sap. Its fruits are used as a source of yellow and green dyes. No known toxicity.

BUFFER • Usually a solution with a relatively constant acidity-alkalinity ratio, which is unaffected by the addition of comparatively large amounts of acid or alkali. A typical buffer solution would be a mixture of hydrochloric acid (*see*) and sodium hydroxide (*see*).

BUQUINOLATE • An animal drug used in chicken feed to combat parasites. FDA limitations are 0.4 ppm in uncooked liver, kidney, and skin of chickens and 0.1 ppm in uncooked chicken muscle. Limitation of 0.5 ppm in egg yoke and 0.2 ppm in whole eggs.

BUTADIENE-STYRENE COPOLYMER • A component for a chewing-gum base. Butadiene is produced largely from petroleum gases and is used in the manufacture of synthetic rubber. It may be irritating to the skin and mucous membranes and narcotic in high concentrations. Styrene, obtained from ethyl benzene, is an oily liquid with a penetrating odor. It has the same uses and toxicity. The FDA's data bank, PAFA (see page 10), has fully up-to-date toxicology information available on this additive.

BUTADIENE-STYRENE RUBBER • Latex. A chewing-gum base. No known toxicity.

BUTAN-3-ONE-2YL BUTYRATE • White to yellow liquid used as a flavoring agent in various foods. The FDA's data bank, PAFA (see page 10), has fully up-to-date toxicology information available on this food additive. GRAS.

BUTANAL • *See* Butyraldehyde.

BUTANDIONE • *See* Diacetyl.

BUTANE • N-Butane. Methylsulfonal. Bioxiran. Dibutadiene Dioxide. A flammable, easily liquefiable gas derived from petroleum. A solvent, refrigerant, and food additive. Also used as a propellant or aerosol in cosmetics. The principal hazard is that of fire and explosion, but it may be narcotic in high doses and cause asphyxiation. It has been determined by the National Institute of Occupational Safety and Health to be an animal carcinogen. There is no reported use of the chemical and no toxicology information is available, according to the FDA. GRAS.

1,4-BUTANE DICARBOXYLIC ACID • *See* Adipic Acid.

1,3-BUTANEDIOL • A thick liquid used as a flavoring agent and solvent for flavorings. Mildly toxic by ingestion. An eye irritant. The FDA's data bank, PAFA (see page 10), has fully up-to-date toxicology information available on this food additive.

2,3-BUTANEDIONE • A greenish yellow liquid with a strong odor used as a flavoring agent with margarine. Moderately toxic by ingestion. A skin irritant. GRAS.

BUTANOIC ACID • *See* Butyric Acid.

1-BUTANOL • *See* Butyl Alcohol.

4-BUTANOLIDE • A colorless liquid with a caramel odor, it is used as a flavoring agent in candy and soy milk. Moderately toxic by ingestion. May cause skin tumors. GRAS.

2,3-BUTANOLONE • The FDA's data bank, PAFA, has fully up-to-date toxicology information available on this food additive. *See* Acetoin.

2-BUTANONE • Colorless liquid with an acetonelike odor used as a flavoring agent in various foods. On the Community Right-To-Know List and in the EPA Genetic Toxicology Program. Moderately toxic by ingestion, skin contact, and injection. The FDA's data bank, PAFA, has fully up-to-date toxicology information available on this food additive.

(trans)-BUTENEDIOIC ACID • *See* Fumaric Acid.

BUTOXYPOLYETHYLENE • A synthetic antifoaming agent used in beet sugar manufacture. No known toxicity.

BUTTER FAT • The oily portions of the milk of mammals. Cow's milk contains about 4 percent butter fat.

BUTTERMILK • The fluid remaining after butter has been formed from churned cream. It can also be made from sweet milk by the addition of certain organic cultures. Used as an astringent right from the bottle. Apply liberally and let dry about ten minutes. Rinse off with cool water.

BUTTERS • Acids, Esters, and Distillate. *Butter acids* are synthetic butter and cheese flavoring agents for beverages, ice cream, ices, candy (2,800 ppm), baked goods. *Butter esters* are synthetic butter, caramel, and chocolate flavoring agents for beverages, ice cream, ices, baked goods, toppings, and popcorn (1,200 ppm). *Butter starter distillate* is a synthetic butter flavoring agent for ice cream, ices, baked goods, and shortening (12,000 ppm). In cosmetology, substances that are solid at room temperature but that melt at body temperature are called butters. Cocoa butter is one of the most frequently used in both foods and cosmetics. Newer butters are made from natural fats by hydrogenation (*see*), which increases the butter's melting point or alters its plasticity. Butters may be used in stick or molded cosmetics such as lipsticks or to give the proper texture to a variety of finished products. Nontoxic.

BUTYL ACETATE • Acetic Acid. Butyl Ester. A synthetic flavoring agent, a clear liquid with a strong fruit odor, prepared from acetic acid and butyl alcohol. Used in raspberry, strawberry, butter, banana, and pineapple flavorings for beverages, ice cream, ices, candy, baked goods, chewing gum, and gelatin desserts. Used in perfumery, nail polish, and nail-polish remover. Also used in the manufacture of lacquer, artificial leather, plastics, and safety glass. It is an irritant and may cause eye irritation (conjunctivitis). It is a narcotic in high concentrations, and toxic to man when inhaled at 200 ppm. The FDA's data bank, PAFA (see page 10), has fully up-to-date toxicology information available on this food additive.

BUTYL ACETOACETATE • A synthetic berry and fruit flavoring agent for beverages, ice cream, candy, and baked goods. The FDA's data bank, PAFA, has fully up-to-date toxicology information available on this food additive.

BUTYL ACETYL RICINOLEATE • *See* Ricinoleate.

BUTYL ALCOHOL • A synthetic butter, cream, fruit, liquor, rum, and whiskey flavoring agent for beverages, ice cream, ices, candy, baked goods, cordials, and cream. A colorless liquid with an unpleasant odor, it occurs naturally in apples and raspberries. Used as a clarifying agent (*see*) in shampoos; also a solvent for waxes, fats, resins, and shellac. It may cause irritation of the mucous membranes, headache, dizziness, and drowsiness when ingested. Inhalation of as little as 25 ppm causes pulmonary problems in man. It can also cause contact dermatitis when applied to the skin. The FDA's data bank, PAFA, has fully up-to-date toxicology information available on this food additive.

t-**BUTYL ALCOHOL** • *See* Butyl Alcohol.

BUTYL ALDEHYDE • *See* Butyraldehyde.

BUTYL ANTHRANILATE • A synthetic grape, mandarin, and pineapple flavoring agent for beverages, ice cream, ices, candy, and baked goods. The FDA's data bank, PAFA (see page 10), has fully up-to-date toxicology information available on this food additive.

n-**BUTYL** *n*-**BUTANOATE** • Colorless liquid with pineapple odor used as a flavoring agent in various foods. Mildly toxic by ingestion. Moderately irritating to eyes, skin, and mucous membranes by inhalation. Narcotic in high concentrations.

BUTYL BUTYRATE • A colorless liquid used as a flavoring. It is an irritant and narcotic. The FDA's data bank, PAFA, has fully up-to-date toxicology information available on this food additive.

BUTYL BUTYROLLACTATE • Colorless liquid with a buttery, creamlike odor used as a flavoring agent in baked goods and candy. A skin irritant. The FDA's data bank, PAFA (see page 10), has fully up-to-date toxicology information available on this food additive.

BUTYL BUTYRYLLACTATE • A colorless, synthetic flavoring agent from butyl alcohol, with a fruity odor. Used in berry, butter, apple, banana, peach, pineapple, liquor, scotch, and nut flavoring for beverages, ice cream, ices, candy, baked goods, chewing gum, and gelatin desserts. The FDA's data bank, PAFA, has fully up-to-date toxicology information available on this food additive.

BUTYL CARBOBUTOXYMETHYL PHTHALATE • A plasticizer used in packaging material. Mildly toxic via injection. Causes birth defects in laboratory animals. An eye irritant in humans.

_a_-BUTYL CINNAMALDEHYDE • A synthetic fruit, nut, spice, and cinnamon flavoring agent for beverages, ice cream, ices, candy, and baked goods. The FDA's data bank, PAFA, has fully up-to-date toxicology information available on this food additive.

BUTYL CINNAMATE • A synthetic chocolate, cocoa, and fruit flavoring for beverages, ice cream, ices, candy, baked goods, and liquor. The FDA's data bank, PAFA, has fully up-to-date toxicology information available on this food additive.

BUTYL 2-DECENOATE • A synthetic apricot and peach flavoring agent for beverages, ice cream, ices, candy, baked goods, chewing gum (2,000 ppm). The FDA's data bank, PAFA, has fully up-to-date toxicology information available on this food additive.

BUTYL DECYLENATE • _See_ Butyl 2-Decanoate.

BUTYL DODECANOATE • _See_ Butyl Laurate.

BUTYL ETHYL MALONATE • A synthetic fruit and apple flavoring for beverages, ice cream, ices, candy, and baked goods. The FDA's data bank, PAFA (see page 10), has fully up-to-date toxicology information available on this food additive.

BUTYL FORMATE • Formic Acid. A synthetic fruit, plum, liquor, and rum flavoring for beverages, ice cream, ices, candy, and baked goods. _See_ Formic Acid for toxicity. The FDA's data bank, PAFA, has fully up-to-date toxicology information available on this food additive.

BUTYL HEPTANOATE • A synthetic fruit and liquor flavoring for beverages, ice cream, ices, candy, and baked goods. The FDA's data bank, PAFA, has fully up-to-date toxicology information available on this food additive.

BUTYL HEXANOATE • A synthetic butter, butterscotch, pineapple, and rum flavoring agent for beverages, ice cream, ices, candy, and baked goods. The FDA's data bank, PAFA, has fully up-to-date toxicology information available on this food additive.

BUTYL _p_-HYDROXYBENZOATE • Butyl Paraben. Butyl _p_-Oxybenzoate. Almost odorless, small, colorless crystals or a white powder used as an antimicrobial preservative. The FDA's data bank, PAFA, has fully up-to-date toxicology information available on this food additive.

tert-BUTYL HYDROQUINONE • White, crystalline solid used as an antioxidant in beef products, dry cereals, edible fats, margarine, meat, pizza toppings, pork, potato chips, poultry, sausage, and vegetable oils. Moderately toxic by ingestion. May be mutagenic. FDA limitations in food of 0.02 to 0.01 ppm. The FDA's data bank, PAFA (see page 10), has fully up-to-date toxicology information available on this food additive.

BUTYL ISOBUTYRATE • A synthetic raspberry, strawberry, butter, banana, and cherry flavoring agent for beverages, ice cream, ices, candy, baked goods, and chewing gum (2,000 ppm). The FDA's data bank, PAFA, has fully up-to-date toxicology information available on this food additive.

BUTYL ISOVALERATE • A synthetic chocolate and fruit flavoring for beverages, ice cream, ices, candy, puddings, and gelatin desserts. No known toxicity.

2-BUTYL-5 (or 6)-KETO-1,4-DIOXANE • A synthetic fruit and spice flavoring for beverages, ice cream, ices, candy, baked goods, and shortenings. No known toxicity.

BUTYL LACTATE • A synthetic butter, butterscotch, caramel, and fruit flavoring agent for beverages, ice cream, ices, candy, baked goods. No known toxicity.

BUTYL LAURATE • A synthetic fruit flavoring for beverages, ice cream, ices, candy, and baked goods. No known toxicity.

BUTYL LEVULINATE • A synthetic butter, fruit, and rum flavoring agent for beverages, ice cream, ices, candy, baked goods. No known toxicity.

BUTYL PARASEPT • See Butyl p-Hydroxybenzoate.

BUTYL PHENYLACETATE • Synthetic butter, honey, caramel, chocolate, rose, fruit, and nut flavoring agent for beverages, ice cream, ices, candy, baked goods, gelatin desserts, and puddings. No known toxicity.

BUTYL PHOSPHOROTRITHIOATE • Butifos. A defoliant found in animal feed and cottonseed hulls. A poison by ingestion, skin contact, and possibly other routes. Caused mutations in animals and affects nerve transmission. FDA limitations of 6 ppm in cottonseed hulls when used for animal feed.

BUTYL PROPIONATE • A synthetic butter, rum butter, fruit, and rum flavoring agent for beverages, ice cream, ices, candy, and baked goods. May be an irritant.

BUTYL RUBBER • A synthetic rubber used as a chewing gum base component. No known toxicity.

BUTYL SEBACATE • See Dibutyl Sebacate.

BUTYL STEARATE • A synthetic antifoaming agent used in the production of beet sugar. Also a synthetic banana, butter, and liquor flavoring for beverages, ice cream, ices, candy, baked goods, chewing gum, and liqueurs. The FDA's data bank, PAFA (see page 10), has fully up-to-date toxicology information available on this food additive.

BUTYL SULFIDE • A synthetic floral, violet, and fruit flavoring for beverages, ice cream, ices, candy, baked goods. The FDA's data bank, PAFA, has fully up-to-date toxicology information available on this food additive.

BUTYL 10-UNDECENOATE • A synthetic butter, apricot, cognac, and nut flavoring agent for beverages, ice cream, ices, candy, baked goods, chewing gum, icing, and liquor. The FDA's data bank, PAFA, has fully up-to-date toxicology information available on this food additive.

BUTYL VALERATE • A synthetic butter, fruit, and chocolate flavoring agent for beverages, ice cream, ices, candy, baked goods, puddings, and gelatin desserts. The FDA's data bank, PAFA (see page 10), has fully up-to-date toxicology information available on this food additive.

BUTYLAMINE • Colorless, volatile liquid with an ammonia odor derived from butanol or butyl chloride with ammonia. Used as an intermediate for emulsifying agents, insecticides, and dyes. The FDA's data bank, PAFA (see page 10), has fully up-to-date toxicology information available on this food additive.

sec-BUTYLAMINE • Tutane. A fungicide used in animal feed, limited to 90 ppm in citrus molasses and dried citrus pulp when used for cattle feed. Poisonous by ingestion. A powerful irritant. Moderately toxic by skin contact. The FDA's data bank, PAFA, has fully up-to-date toxicology information available on this food additive.

BUTYLATED HYDROXYANISOLE (BHA) • A preservative and antioxidant in many products, including beverages, ice cream, ices, candy, baked goods, chewing gum, gelatin desserts, soup bases, potatoes, glacéed fruits, potato flakes, sweet potato flakes, dry breakfast cereals, dry yeast, dry mixes for desserts, lard, shortening, unsmoked dry sausage, and in emulsions for stabilizers for shortenings. It is a white or slightly yellow, waxy solid with a faint characteristic odor. Insoluble in water. Total content of antioxidants is not to exceed .02 percent of fat or oil content of food; allowed up to 1,000 ppm in dry yeast, 200 ppm in shortenings, 50 ppm in potato flakes, and 50 ppm with BHT (*see* Butylated Hydroxytoluene) in dry cereals. Can cause allergic reactions. BHA affects the liver and kidney functions (the liver detoxifies it). BHA may be more rapidly metabolized than BHT, and in experiments at Michigan State University it appeared to be less toxic to the kidneys of living animals than BHT. Can cause allergic reactions. The final report to the FDA of the Select Committee on GRAS substances stated in 1980 that while no available evidence on it demonstrates a hazard to the public at current use levels, uncertainties exist, requiring that additional studies be conducted. The FDA said in 1980 that GRAS status should continue while tests on BHA are being completed and evaluated. In the *1990 Annual Review of Pharmacology and Toxicology,* scientists from the United Kingdom and the United States reviewed Japanese reports of a high incidence of cancerous and benign tumors in the forestomach of rats fed BHA. The reviewers concluded that because we humans don't have forestomachs, as rats do, and because the doses of BHA administered to the animals were so high, there was no cause for alarm. In November 1990, Glenn Scott, MD, a Cincinnati physician, filed a petition with the FDA asking the agency to prohibit the use of BHA in food. Before acting on Scott's petition, however, the FDA asked the Federation of American Societies for Experimental Biology (FASEB) to reexamine the scientific data on BHA and make a report by March 1992. The FDA's data bank, PAFA (see page 10), has fully up-to-date toxicology information available on this food additive.

BUTYLATED HYDROXYMETHYLPHENOL • A new antioxidant, a nearly white, crystalline solid with a faint characteristic odor. Insoluble in water and propylene glycol; soluble in alcohol. No known toxicity, but the formula, 4-hydroxymethyl-2,6-di-tert-butylphenol, contains phenol, which is very toxic.

BUTYLATED HYDROXYTOLUENE (BHT) • A preservative and antioxidant employed in many foods. Used as a chewing gum base, added to potato and sweet potato flakes and dry breakfast cereals, an emulsion stabilizer for shortenings, used in enriched rice, animal fats, and shortenings containing animal fats. White, crystalline solid with a faint characteristic odor. Insoluble in water. Total content of antioxidants in fat or oils not to exceed .02 percent. Allowed up to 200 ppm in emulsion stabilizers for shortenings, 50 ppm in dry breakfast cereals and potato flakes. Used also as an antioxidant to retard rancidity in frozen pork sausage and freeze-dried meats up to .01 percent based on fat content.

Can cause allergic reactions. Loyola University scientists reported on April 14, 1972, that pregnant mice fed a diet consisting of one-half of one percent of BHT (or BHA, butylated hydroxyanisole) gave birth to offspring that frequently had chemical changes in the brain and subsequently abnormal behavior patterns. BHT and BHA are chemically similar, but BHT may be more toxic to the kidney than BHA (*see* Butylated Hydroxyanisole), according to researchers at Michigan State University. The Select Committee of the American Societies for Experimental Biology, which advises the FDA on food additives, recommended further studies to determine "the effects of BHT at levels now present in foods under conditions where steroid hormones or oral contraceptives are being ingested." They said the possibility that BHT may convert other ingested substances into toxic or cancer-causing agents should be investigated. BHT is prohibited as a food additive in England. The FDA is pursuing further study of BHT. GRAS. The FDA's data bank, PAFA (see page 10), has fully up-to-date toxicology information available on this food additive.

1,3-BUTYLENE GLYCOL • A clear, colorless, viscous liquid with a slight taste. A solvent and humectant most resistant to high humidity and thus valuable in foods and cosmetics. It retains scents and preserves against spoilage. It has a similar toxicity to ethylene glycol (*see*), which when ingested may cause transient stimulation of the central nervous system, then depression, vomiting, drowsiness, coma, respiratory failure and convulsions; renal damage may proceed to uremia and death. One of the few humectants not on the GRAS list, although efforts to place it there have been made through the years. The FDA's data bank, PAFA, has fully up-to-date toxicology information available on this food additive.

BUTYLPARABEN • Widely used in food and cosmetics as an antifungal preservative, it is the ester of butyl alcohol and *p*-hydroxybenzoic acid (*see both*). No known toxicity.

BUTYRALDEHYDE • A synthetic flavoring agent found naturally in coffee and strawberries. Used in butter, caramel, fruit, liquor, brandy, and nut flavorings for beverages, ice cream, ices, candy, baked goods, alcoholic beverages, and icings. Used also in the manufacture of rubber, gas accelerators, synthetic resins, and plasticizers. May be an irritant and a narcotic. The FDA's data bank, PAFA (see page 10), has fully up-to-date toxicology information available on this food additive.

BUTYRIC ACID • N-Butyric Acid. Butanoic Acid. A clear, colorless liquid present in butter at 4 to 5 percent with a strong, penetrating rancid-butter odor. Butter, butterscotch, caramel, fruit, and nut flavoring agent for beverages, ice cream, ices, candy, baked goods, gelatin desserts, puddings, chewing gum, and margarine. Found naturally in apples, butter acids, geranium, rose oil, grapes, strawberries, and wormseed oil. It has a low toxicity but can be a mild irritant. It caused tumors when applied to the skin of mice in 108-mg doses per kilogram of body weight and cancer when injected into the abdomen of mice in 18-mg doses per kilogram of body weight. A NIOSH review has determined it is a positive animal carcinogen. The FDA's data bank, PAFA, has fully up-to-date toxicology information available on this food additive. GRAS.

BUTYRIC ALDEHYDE • *See* Butyraldehyde.

BUTYRIN • *See* (tri-) Butyrin.

(tri-) BUTYRIN • A synthetic flavoring agent found naturally in butter. Butter flavoring for beverages, ice cream, ices, candy (1,000 ppm), baked goods, margarine, and puddings. No known toxicity.

BUTYROIN • *See* 5-Hydroxy-4-Octanone.

BUTYROLACTONE • Butanolide. Liquid lactone used chiefly as a solvent for resins. It is also an intermediate (*see*) in the manufacture of polyvinylpyrrolidone (*see*) and a solvent for nail polish. Human toxicity is unknown.

BUTYRONE • *See* 4-Heptanone.

BUXINE • *See* a-Amylcinnamaldehyde.

BUXINOL • *See* a-Amylcinnamyl Alcohol.

C

CACAO SHELL • Cocoa shells of the seeds of trees grown in Brazil, Central America, and most tropical countries. Weak chocolatelike odor and taste, thin and peppery with a reddish brown color. Used in the manufacture of caffeine (*see*); also theobromine, which occurs in chocolate products and is used as a diuretic and nerve stimulant. Occasionally causes allergic reactions from handling. GRAS.

CACHOU EXTRACT • *See* Catechu Extract.

CACTUS ROOT EXTRACT • *See* Yucca Extract.

CADINENE • A general fixative that occurs naturally in juniper oil and pepper oil. It has a faint, pleasant smell. Used in candy, baked goods (1,200 ppm), and chewing gum (1,000 ppm). The FDA's data bank, PAFA (see page 10), has fully up-to-date toxicology information available on this food additive.

CAFFEINE • Guaranine. Methyltheobromine. Theine. Trimethylxanthine. An odorless, white powder with a bitter taste that occurs naturally in coffee, cola, guarana paste, tea, and kola nuts. Caffeine is the number one psychoactive drug. Obtained as a byproduct of caffeine-free coffee. Used as a flavor in root beer beverages and other foods. It is a central nervous system, heart, and respiratory system stimulant. Caffeine can alter blood sugar release and cross the placental barrier. It can cause nervousness, insomnia, irregular heartbeat, noises in the ear, and in high doses, convulsions. It has been linked to spontaneous panic attacks in persons sensitive to caffeine. Because of its capability of causing birth defects in rats, the FDA proposed regulations to request new safety studies and to encourage the manufacture and sale of caffeine-free colas. One regulation would make the food industry's continued use of caffeine as an added ingredient in soft drinks and other foods conditional upon its funding of studies of caffeine's effects on children and the unborn. A University of Montreal study published in *The Journal of the American Medical Association,* December 22, 1993, said that women who consume the amount of caffeine in one and a half to three cups of coffee a day may nearly double their risk of miscarriage. Under present regulations, a soft drink, except one artificially sweetened, must contain caffeine if it is to be labeled as *cola* or *pepper* and the FDA wants soda producers to be able to use this name when caffeine is not used. The FDA has asked for studies on the long-term effects of the additive to determine whether it may cause cancer or birth defects. The final report to the FDA of the Select Committee on GRAS Substances stated in 1980 that while no evidence or information is available on it that demonstrates a hazard to the public at current use levels, uncertainties exist, requiring that additional studies be conducted. GRAS status continues while tests are being conducted. The FDA's data bank, PAFA (see page 10), has fully up-to-date toxicology information available on this food additive.

CAJEPUT OIL • A spice flavoring from the cajeput tree native to Australia. The leaves yield an aromatic oil. Used for beverages, ice cream, ices, candy, and baked goods. The FDA data bank has not yet done a search of the toxicology literature concerning this additive.

CAJEPUTENE • *See d*-Limonene.

CAJEPUTOL • *See* Eucalyptol.

CALAMUS • Sweet Flag. Sweet Sedge. *Acorus calamus*. The rhizome contains essential oil, mucilage, glycosides, amino acid, and tannins. The oil is obtained by steam distillation of the stem or root and is used as a flavoring agent and in perfumery. Calamus root is an ancient Indian and Chinese herbal medicine used to treat acid stomach, irregular heart rhythm, low blood pressure, coughs, and lack of mental focus. Native Americans would chew the root to enable them to run long distances with increased stamina. Externally, it was used to induce a state of tranquillity.

CALCIUM ACETATE • Brown Acetate of Lime. A white, amorphous powder that has been used medicinally as a source of calcium. It is used in the manufacture of acetic acid and acetone and in dyeing, tanning, and curing skins and as a corrosion inhibitor in metal containers. Used cosmetically for solidifying fragrances and as an emulsifier and firming agent. Low oral toxicity. The final report to the FDA of the Select Committee on GRAS Substances stated in 1980 that it should continue its GRAS status with no limitations other than good manufacturing practices. The FDA's data bank, PAFA (see page 10), has fully up-to-date toxicology information available on this food additive.

CALCIUM ACID PHOSPHATE • *See* Calcium Phosphate.

CALCIUM ALGINATE • A stabilizer, thickener, gelling agent, and texturizer. Also used as a solvent and vehicle for flavorings. Found in ice cream and popsicles, soft and cottage cheeses, cheese snacks, dressings and spreads, fruit drinks, beverages, and instant desserts. *See* Alginates. GRAS.

CALCIUM ASCORBATE • A preservative and antioxidant prepared from ascorbic acid (vitamin C) and calcium carbonate (*see*). Used in concentrated milk products; in cooked, cured, or pulverized meat products; in pickles in which pork and beef products are cured and packed (up to seventy-five ounces per hundred gallons). *See* Ascorbic Acid for toxicity. The final report to the FDA of the Select Committee on GRAS Substances stated in 1980 that it should continue its GRAS status with no limitations other than good manufacturing practices. The FDA's data bank, PAFA, has fully up-to-date toxicology information available on this food additive.

CALCIUM BENZOATE • *See* Benzoic Acid.

CALCIUM BROMATE • A maturing agent and dough conditioner used in bromated flours. The FDA's data bank, PAFA (see page 10), has fully up-to-date toxicology information available on this food additive. *See* Bromates.

CALCIUM CARBONATE • Chalk. Absorbent that removes shine from talc. A tasteless, odorless powder that occurs naturally in limestone, marble, and coral. Used as a white food dye and as an alkali to reduce acidity in wine up to 2.5 percent, a neutralizer for ice cream and in cream syrups up to 0.25 percent, in confections up to 0.25 percent, and in baking powder up to 50 percent. Employed as carrier for bleaches. Though once widely used as a white coloring in foods and cosmetics, the authorization by the FDA was withdrawn in 1988. Calcium carbonate is also used as a firming agent and in dentifrices as a tooth polisher, in deodorants as a filler, in depilatories as a filler, and in face powder as a buffer. A gastric antacid and antidiarrhea medicine, it may cause constipation. Female mice were bred after a week on diets supplemented with calcium carbonate at 220 and 880 times the human intake of this additive. At all dosage levels, the first and second litters of newly weaned mice were lower in weight and number, and mortality was increased. The highest level caused heart enlargement. Supplementing the maternal diet with iron prevented this, so the side effects were attributed to mineral imbalance due to excessive calcium intake. In humans, five hundred milligrams per kilogram of body weight was fed to ulcer victims for three weeks. The amount ingested was 145 times the normal amount ingested as an additive. Some patients developed an excess of calcium in the blood and suffered nausea, weakness, and dizziness. The FDA's data bank, PAFA, has fully up-to-date toxicology information available on this food additive.

CALCIUM CARRAGEENAN • *See* Carrageenan.

CALCIUM CASEINATE • Used as a nutrient supplement for frozen desserts, creamed cottage cheese. The FDA's data bank, PAFA (see page 10), has fully up-to-date toxicology information available on this food additive. *See* Casein.

CALCIUM CHLORIDE • The chloride salt of calcium. Used in its anhydrous (*see*) form as a drying agent for organic liquids and gases. Used as a firming agent for sliced apples and other fruits, in apple pie mix; as a jelly ingredient; in certain cheeses to aid coagulation; in artificially sweetened fruit jelly; and in canned tomatoes. An emulsifier and texturizer in cosmetics and an antiseptic in eye lotions. Also used in fire extinguishers, to preserve wood, and to melt ice and snow. Employed medicinally as a diuretic and a urinary acidifier. Ingestion can cause stomach and heart disturbances. The final report to the FDA of the Select Committee on GRAS Substances stated in 1980 that it should continue its GRAS status with no limitations other than good manufacturing practices. The FDA's data bank, PAFA (see page 10), has fully up-to-date toxicology information available on this food additive.

CALCIUM CITRATE • A fine, white, odorless powder prepared from citrus fruit. Used as a buffer to neutralize acids in confections, jellies, jams, and in saccharine at the rate of three ounces per hundred pounds of the artificial sweetener. It is also used to improve the baking properties of flour. *See* Citrate Salts for toxicity. The final report to the FDA of the Select Committee on GRAS Substances stated in 1980 that it should continue its GRAS status with no limitations other than good manufacturing practices. The FDA is currently searching the toxicology literature concerning this additive.

CALCIUM DIACETATE • A sequestrant used in cereal. *See* Calcium Acetate. GRAS.

CALCIUM DI-L-GLUTAMATE • The salt of glutamic acid (*see*). A flavor enhancer and salt substitute. Almost odorless, white powder. The FDA says that it needs further study. As of this writing, nothing has been reported.

CALCIUM DIOXIDE • Used in cereal flours. *See* Calcium Peroxide.

CALCIUM DISODIUM EDTA • Edetate Calcium Disodium. Calcium Disodium Ethylenediamine Tetraacetic Acid. A preservative and sequestrant, a white, odorless powder with a faint salty taste. Used as a food additive to prevent crystal formation and to retard color loss. Used in canned and carbonated soft drinks for flavor retention; in canned white potatoes and cooked canned clams for color retention; in crab meat to retard struvite (crystal formation); in dressings as a preservative; in cooked and canned dried lima beans for color retention; in fermented malt beverages to prevent gushing; in mayonnaise and oleomargarine as a preservative; in processed dried pinto beans for color retention; and in sandwich spreads as a preservative. Residue tolerances set by the FDA for this additive are cereal flours, 25 ppm; fermented malt beverages, 25 ppm; spice extractives, 60 ppm; pecan pie filling, 100 ppm; clams (cooked-canned) to promote color retention, 340 ppm; lima beans to promote color, 310 ppm; crabmeat (cooked-canned) to retard struvite formation, 275 ppm; shrimp (cooked-canned) to retard struvite and to promote color retention, 250 ppm; carbonated soft drinks to promote flavor, 33 ppm; canned white potatoes to promote color retention, 110 ppm; canned mushrooms, 200 ppm; pickled cucumbers or pickled cabbage to promote color, flavor, and texture retention, 220 ppm; artificially colored lemon- and orange-flavored spreads, 100 ppm; potato salad preservative, 100 ppm; French dressing, mayonnaise, and salad dressing, nonstandardized dressings and sauces, preservative, 75 ppm; sandwich spread as a preservative, 100 ppm; 200 ppm by weight of egg yolk portion; distilled alcoholic beverages to promote stability of color, flavor, and/or product clarity; oleomargarine as a preservative, 75 ppm. Used medically as a chelating agent to detoxify poisoning by lead and other heavy metals. May cause intestinal upsets, muscle cramps, kidney damage, and blood in urine. On the FDA priority list of food additives to be studied for mutagenic, teratogenic, subacute, and reproductive effects.

CALCIUM GLUCONATE • Odorless, tasteless, white, crystalline granules, stale in air. Used as a buffer, firming agent, sequestrant. It is soluble in water. May cause gastrointestinal and cardiac disturbances. The final report to the FDA of the Select Committee on GRAS Substances stated in 1980 that it should continue its GRAS status with no limitations other than good manufacturing practices. The FDA's data bank, PAFA (see page 10), has fully up-to-date toxicology information available on this food additive.

CALCIUM GLYCEROPHOSPHATE • A fine, white, odorless, nearly tasteless powder used in dentifrices, baking powder, and as a food stabilizer and dietary supplement. A component of many over-the-counter nerve-tonic foods. Administered medicinally for numbness and debility. *See* Calcium Sources. The final report to the FDA of the Select Committee on GRAS Substances stated in 1980 that it should continue its GRAS status with no limitations other than good manufacturing practices. The FDA's data bank has not yet done a search of toxicology literature concerning this additive.

CALCIUM 5'-GUANYLATE • Flavor potentiator. Odorless, white crystals or powder having a characteristic taste. *See* Flavor Potentiators.

CALCIUM HEXAMETAPHOSPHATE • An emulsifier, sequestering agent, and texturizer used in breakfast cereals, angel food cake, flaked fish (prevents struvite), ice cream, ices, milk, bottled beer, reconstituted lemon juice, puddings, processed cheeses, artificially sweetened jellies and preserves, potable water supplies to prevent scale formation and corrosion, and in pickle for curing hams. No known toxicity. The final report to the FDA of the Select Committee on GRAS Substances stated in 1980 that it should continue its GRAS status with no limitations other than good manufacturing practices. There is no reported use of the chemical and no toxicology information is available, according to the FDA.

CALCIUM HYDROXIDE • Slaked Lime. Calcium Hydrate. Limewater. Lye. An alkali, a white powder with a slightly bitter taste. Used as a firming agent for various fruit products, as an egg preservative, in water treatment, and for dehairing hides. Used in cream depilatories; also in mortar, plaster, cement, pesticides, and fireproofing. Employed as a topical astringent and alkali in cosmetics solutions or lotions. Accidental ingestion can cause burns of the throat and esophagus; also death from shock and asphyxia due to swelling of the glottis and infection. Calcium hydroxide can also cause burns of the skin and eyes. The final report to the FDA of the Select Committee on GRAS Substances stated in 1980 that it should continue its GRAS status with no limitations other than good manufacturing practices. The FDA's data bank, PAFA (see page 10), has fully up-to-date toxicology information available on this food additive.

CALCIUM HYPOCHLORITE • A germicide and sterilizing agent, the active ingredient of chlorinated lime, used in the curd washing of cottage cheese, in sugar refining, as an oxidizing and bleaching agent, and as an algae killer, bactericide, deodorant, disinfectant, and fungicide. Sterilizes fruits and vegetables by washing in a 50 percent solution. Under various names, dilute hypochlorite is found in homes as laundry bleach and household bleach. Occasionally cases of poisoning occur when people mix household hypochlorite solution with various other household chemicals, which causes the release of poisonous chlorine gas. As with other corrosive agents, calcium hypochlorite's toxicity depends upon its concentration. It is highly corrosive to skin and mucous membranes. Ingestion may cause pain and inflammation of the mouth, pharynx, esophagus, and stomach, with erosion particularly of the mucous membranes of the stomach.

CALCIUM HYPOPHOSPHITE • Crystals of powder, slightly acid in solution and practically insoluble in alcohol. It is a corrosion inhibitor and has been used as a dietary supplement in veterinary medicine. The final report to the FDA of the Select Committee on GRAS Substances stated in 1980 that it should continue its GRAS status with no limitations other than good manufacturing practices. There is no reported use of the chemical and no toxicology information is available, according to the FDA.

CALCIUM 5'-INOSINATE • *See* Inosinate.

CALCIUM IODATE • White, odorless or nearly odorless powder used as a dough conditioner and oxidizing agent in bread, rolls, and buns. It is a nutritional source of iodine in foods, such as table salt, and used also in a topical disinfectant and as a deodorant. Low toxicity, but may cause allergic reactions. The FDA has not yet done a search of the toxicology literature concerning this additive.

CALCIUM IODOBEHENATE • Dietary supplement used in animal feed as an iodine source (*see*). GRAS.

CALCIUM LACTATE • White, almost odorless crystals or powder used as a buffer. A constituent of baking powders and confections; also used in dentifrices and as a yeast food and dough conditioner. In medical use, given for calcium deficiency; may cause gastrointestinal and cardiac disturbances. The final report to the FDA of the Select Committee on GRAS Substances stated in 1980 that it should continue its GRAS status with no limitations other than good manufacturing practices. The FDA is currently searching the toxicology literature concerning this additive.

CALCIUM LACTOBIONATE • A firming agent in pudding mixes. Although allowed as a food additive, there is no current reported use of the chemical, and therefore, although toxicology information may be available, it is not being updated by the FDA. *See* Calcium Lactate.

CALCIUM LIGNOSULFONATE • Made from calcium and sodium salts and woody material, it is used as a dispersing agent and stabilizer for pesticides used on bananas. There is no reported use of this chemical and no toxicology information is available, according to the FDA. *See* Calcium Sources.

CALCIUM METASILICATE • White power, insoluble in water, used as an absorbent, antacid, filler for paper coatings, and as a food additive. Use in food restricted to 5 percent in baking powder and 2 percent in table salt. Irritating dust.

CALCIUM OLEATE • Oleic Acid, Calcium Salt. Yellowish crystals, soluble in benzene. Grease-thickening agent and emulsifying agent. There is no reported use of the chemical and no toxicology information is available.

CALCIUM ORTHOPHOSPHATE • Buffer and neutralizing agent used in noncarbonated beverages. No known toxicity.

CALCIUM OXIDE • Quicklime. Burnt Lime. A hard, white or grayish white, odorless mass or powder that is used as a yeast food and dough conditioner for bread, rolls, and buns. It is also an alkali for neutralizing dairy products (including ice cream mixes, sour cream, and butter) and confections and is used in the processing of tripe. Industrial uses are for bricks, plaster, mortar, stucco, dehairing hides, fungicides, insecticides, and for clarification of beet and cane sugar juices. A strong caustic, it may severely damage skin and mucous membranes. *See* Calcium Sources. The final report to the FDA of the Select Committee on GRAS Substances stated in 1980 that it should continue its GRAS status with no limitations other than good manufacturing practices. The FDA's data bank, PAFA (see page 10), has fully up-to-date toxicology information available on this food additive.

CALCIUM PANTOTHENATE • Pantothenic Acid, Calcium Salt. A B-complex vitamin, pantothenate is a white, odorless powder with a sweetish taste and bitter aftertaste. Pantothenic acid occurs everywhere in plant and animal tissue, and the richest common source is liver; jelly of the queen bee contains six times as much. Rice bran and molasses are other good sources. Acid derivatives sold commercially are synthesized. *See d-*Pantothenamide. Biochemical defects from lack of calcium pantothenate may exist undetected for some time but eventually manifest themselves as tissue failures. The calcium chloride double salt of calcium pantothenate has been cleared for use in foods for special dietary uses. Moderately toxic by ingestion. The final report to the FDA of the Select Committee on GRAS Substances stated in 1980 that it should continue its GRAS status with no limitations other than good manufacturing practices. The FDA's data bank, PAFA (see page 10), has fully up-to-date toxicology information available on this food additive.

CALCIUM PEROXIDE • White or yellowish, odorless, almost tasteless powder that is derived from an interaction of a calcium salt and sodium peroxide with subsequent crystallization. Used in bakery products as a dough conditioner, bleaching of oils, modification of starches, and as a seed disinfectant. Irritating to the skin. Toxicology literature search has not been done concerning this additive, according to the FDA.

CALCIUM PHOSPHATE • Dibasic, Monobasic, and Tribasic. White, odorless powders used as yeast foods, dough conditioners, and firming agents. *Tribasic* is an anticaking agent used in table salt, powdered sugar, malted milk powder, condiments, puddings, meat, dry-curing mixtures, cereal flours, and vanilla powder. It is tasteless. Used as a gastric antacid mineral supplement, and a clarifying agent for sugars and syrups. *Dibasic* is used to improve bread, rolls, buns, cereal flours; a carrier for bleaching; used as a mineral supplement in cereals, in dental products, and in fertilizers. *Monobasic* is used in bread, rolls, buns, artificially sweetened fruit jelly, canned potatoes, canned sweet peppers, canned tomatoes, and as a jelling ingredient. Employed as a fertilizer, as an acidulant, in baking powders, and in wheat flours as a mineral supplement. Skin and eye irritant. The final report to the FDA of the Select Committee on GRAS Substances stated in 1980 that it should continue its GRAS status with no limitations other than good manufacturing practices. The FDA is searching the toxicology literature concerning this additive.

CALCIUM PHYTATE • Used as a sequestrant (*see*). When three hundred milligrams per kilogram of body weight was fed to rats as a diet supplement, it successfully provided calcium for bone deposition and the animals remained healthy. The final report to the FDA of the Select Committee on GRAS Substances stated in 1980 that it should continue its GRAS status with no limitations other than good manufacturing practices. There is no reported use of the chemical and no toxicology information is available, according to the FDA.

CALCIUM PROPIONATE • Propanoic Acid, Calcium Salt. White crystals or crystalline solid with the faint odor of propionic acid. A mold and rope inhibitor in breads and rolls and poultry stuffing, it is used in processed cheese, chocolate products, cakes, cupcakes, and artificially sweetened fruit jelly. It is used as a preservative in cosmetics and as an antifungal medication for the skin. GRAS. The FDA's data bank, PAFA (see page 10), has fully up-to-date toxicology information available on this food additive.

CALCIUM PYROPHOSPHATE • A fine white, odorless, tasteless powder used as a nutrient, an abrasive in dentifrices, a buffer, and as a neutralizing agent in foodstuffs. No known toxicity. The final report to the FDA of the Select Committee on GRAS Substances stated in 1980 that it should continue its GRAS status with no limitations other than good manufacturing practices. *See* Calcium Sources.

CALCIUM RESINATE • Yellowish white powder or lumps used to dilute the color of eggshells. No residue is permitted. It is also used in waterproofing and in paper, perfumes, and coatings for fabrics.

CALCIUM 5'-RIBONUCLEOTIDES • Flavor potentiators (*see*) in odorless, white crystals or powder with a characteristic taste. *See* Inosinate.

CALCIUM SACCHARIN • *See* Saccharin.

CALCIUM SALTS • Acetate, Chloride, Citrate, Diacetate, Gluconate, Phosphate (monobasic), Phytate, Sulfate. Emulsifier salts used in evaporated milk and frozen desserts. Also in enriched bread. Firming agent in potatoes and canned tomatoes. May be gastric irritants, but they have little oral toxicity. *See* Calcium Sulfate and Calcium Phosphate. GRAS.

CALCIUM SALTS OF FATTY ACIDS • Used as binders and anticaking agents in foods. The FDA's data bank, PAFA (see page 10), has not yet done a search of the toxicology literature concerning these additives.

CALCIUM SALTS OF PARTIALLY DIMERIZED ROSIN • Used as a coating on free citrus fruits. *See* Calcium Salts.

CALCIUM SILICATE • Okenite. An anticaking agent, white or slightly cream-colored, free-flowing powder. It is used up to 5 percent in baking powder and 2 percent in table salts. Absorbs water. Used in face powders because it has extremely fine particles and good water absorption. Also used as a coloring agent. Constituent of lime glass and cement, used in road construction. Practically nontoxic orally, except inhalation may cause irritation of the respiratory tract. On the FDA list of additives that need further study for mutagenic, teratogenic, subacute, and reproductive effects. The final report to the FDA of the Select Committee on GRAS Substances stated in 1980 that it should continue its GRAS status with no limitations other than good manufacturing practices. The FDA's data bank, PAFA (see page 10), has fully up-to-date toxicology information available on this food additive.

CALCIUM SORBATE • A preservative and fungus preventative used in beverages, baked goods, chocolate syrups, soda-fountain syrups, fresh fruit cocktail, tangerine puree (sherbet base), salads (potato, macaroni, cole slaw, gelatin), cheesecake, pie fillings, cake, cheese in consumer-size packages, and artificially sweetened jellies and preserves. No known toxicity. The final report to the FDA of the Select Committee on GRAS Substances stated in 1980 that it should continue its GRAS status with no limitations other than good manufacturing practices. There is no reported use of the chemical and no toxicology information is available, according to the FDA data bank.

CALCIUM SOURCES (harmless calcium salts) • Carbonate, Citrate, Glycerophosphate Oxide, Phosphate, Pyrophosphate, Sulfate (*see all*). Calcium is a mineral supplement for breakfast cereals, white corn meal, infant dietary formula, enriched flour, enriched bromated flour (*see* Bromates), enriched macaroni, noodle products, self-rising flours, enriched farina, cornmeal and corn grits, and enriched bread and rolls. Calcium is a major mineral in the body. It is incompletely absorbed from the gastrointestinal tract when in the diet, so its absorption is enhanced by calcium normally present in intestinal secretions. Vitamin D is also required for efficient absorption of calcium. Recommended daily requirements for adult females is 1.5 grams, for adult males, 1.2 grams, and for children, 0.8 gram. Calcium and phosphorus are the major constituents of teeth and bones. The ratio of calcium to phosphorus in cow's milk is approximately 1.2 to 1. In human milk the ratio is 2 to 1. The final report to the FDA of the Select Committee on GRAS Substances stated in 1980 that it should continue its GRAS status with no limitations other than good manufacturing practices.

CALCIUM STEARATE • Prepared from lime water (*see*), it is an emulsifier, a coloring agent, and is used in waterproofing. It is used as an emulsifier in hair-grooming products and in paints and printing ink. Nontoxic. The final report to the FDA of the Select Committee on GRAS Substances stated in 1980 that it should continue its GRAS status with no limitations other than good manufacturing practices. The FDA data bank, PAFA (see page 10), has not yet searched the toxicology literature concerning this additive.

CALCIUM STEAROYL LACTYLATE • *See* Calcium Stearoyl-2-Lactylate.

CALCIUM STEAROYL-2-LACTYLATE • The calcium salt of the stearic acid ester of lactyl lactate. A free-flowing, white-powder dough conditioner in yeast-leavened bakery products and prepared mixes for yeast-leavened bakery products. Also a whipping agent in dried, liquid, and frozen egg whites. On the FDA list of additives requiring further safety information since 1980. The FDA's data bank, PAFA, has fully up-to-date toxicology information available on this food additive.

CALCIUM SULFATE • Plaster of Paris. A fine, white to slightly yellow, odorless, tasteless powder used as a firming agent and yeast food and dough conditioner. Utilized in brewing and other fermentation industries, in Spanish-type sherry, as a jelling ingredient, in cereal flours, as a carrier for bleaching agent, in bread, rolls, and buns, in blue cheese and Gorgonzola cheese, artificially sweetened fruit, jelly, canned potatoes, canned sweet peppers, and canned tomatoes. Used also in creamed cottage cheese as an alkali. Also used in toothpaste and tooth powders as an abrasive and firming agent. Also used as a coloring agent in cosmetics. Employed industrially in cement, wall plaster, and insecticides. Because it absorbs moisture and hardens quickly, its ingestion may result in intestinal obstruction. Mixed with flour, it has been used to kill rodents. GRAS. The FDA's data bank, PAFA (see page 10), has fully up-to-date toxicology information available on this food additive.

CALCIUM SULPHIDE • A yellow powder formed by heating gypsum with charcoal at 1,000°F. Employed in depilatories. Used in acne preparations. Also used as a food preservative and in luminous paints. It can cause allergic reactions.

CALCIUM TARTRATE • White crystals, soluble in acids, derived from cream of tartar. Used as a food preservative and antacid. No known toxicity.

CALENDULA • Dried flowers of pot marigolds grown in gardens everywhere. Used as a natural flavoring agent. *See* Marigold, Pot, for foods in which it's used. Formerly used to soothe inflammation of skin and mucous membranes, now used in "natural" creams, oils, and powders for babies. No known toxicity. GRAS.

CALORIE • A unit used to express the heat output of an organism and the fuel or energy value of food. The amount of heat required to raise the temperature of one gram of water from 14.5 to 15.5°C at atmospheric pressure.

CALUMBA ROOT • Flavoring used in alcoholic beverages only. There is no reported use of the chemical and no toxicology information is available, according to the FDA data bank.

CAMOMILE • *See* Chamomile.

2-CAMPHANOL • *See* Borneol.

CAMPHENE • A synthetic spice and nutmeg flavoring agent for beverages, ice cream, ices, candy, and baked goods. Occurs naturally in calamus oil, citronella, ginger, lemon oil, mandarin oil, myrtle, petitgrain oil, and juniper berries. May be mutagenic. The FDA's data bank, PAFA (see page 10), has fully up-to-date toxicology information available on this food additive.

CAMPHOR OIL • Japanese White Oil. Camphor Tree. Distilled from trees at least fifty years old grown in China, Japan, Formosa, Brazil, and Sumatra. Camphor tree is used in spice flavorings for beverages, baked goods, and condiments. Used in emollient creams, hair tonics, eye lotions, preshave lotions, aftershave lotions, and skin fresheners as a preservative and to give a cool feeling to the skin. It is also used in horn-rimmed glasses, as a drug preservative, in embalming fluid, in the manufacture of explosives, in lacquers, as a moth repellent, and topically in liniments, cold medications, and anesthetics. It can cause contact dermatitis. In 1980, the FDA banned camphorated oil as a liniment for colds and sore muscles because of reports of poisonings through skin absorption and because of accidental ingestion. A New Jersey pharmacist had collected case reports and testified before the Advisory Review Panel on Over-the-Counter Drugs of the FDA in 1980. Camphor is readily absorbed through all sites of administration. Ingestion of two grams generally produces dangerous effects in an adult. Ingestion by pregnant women has caused fetal deaths. As of this writing, nothing new to report. The FDA data bank, PAFA, has not yet searched the toxicology literature concerning this additive.

CANANGA OIL • A natural flavor extract obtained by distillation from the flowers of the tree. Light to deep yellow liquid with a harsh floral odor. Used in cola, fruit, spice, and ginger ale flavorings for beverages, ice cream, ices, candy, baked goods. May cause allergic reactions. No known toxicity. GRAS. The FDA data bank, PAFA (see page 10), has not yet searched the toxicology literature concerning this additive.

CANDELILLA WAX • Obtained from candelilla plants. Brownish to yellow brown, hard, brittle, easily pulverized, partially insoluble in water. Hardens other waxes. Used as a coating for foods. GRAS. The FDA data bank, PAFA, has not yet searched the toxicology literature concerning this additive.

CANDIDA LIPOLYTICA • Derived from *Candida lypolytica,* used as a production aid in citric acid. No known toxicity.

CANDIDIA GUILLIERMONDII • Derived from *Candidia guilliermondii,* it is used as a production aid in citric acid. No known toxicity.

CANE SUGAR • *See* Sucrose.

CANOLA • A low erucic-acid rapeseed oil (*see*) used in salad oils because it contains 50 percent less saturated oils than other popular oils.

CANTHAXANTHIN • A color additive derived from edible mushrooms, crustaceans, trout, salmon, and tropical birds. It produces a pink color when used in foods. FAO/WHO said that up to twenty-five milligrams per kilogram of body weight is acceptable. Permanently listed in 1969 for human food, and permanently listed in 1985 in chicken feed to enhance the yellow color of chicken skin. It is exempt from certification. Oral intake may cause loss of night vision. The FDA data bank, PAFA, has fully up-to-date toxicology information available concerning this additive.

CAPERS • A natural flavoring from the spiny shrub. The picked flower bud is used as a condiment for sauces and salads. GRAS. The FDA data bank, PAFA (see page 10), has not yet searched the toxicology literature concerning this additive.

CAPRALDEHYDE • *See* Decanal.

CAPRIC ACID • Obtained from a large group of American plants. Solid crystalline mass with a rancid odor used in the manufacture of artificial fruit flavors. Also used to flavor lipsticks. No known toxicity. *See* Decanoic Acid.

CAPRIC ALDEHYDE • *See* Decanal.

CAPRINALDEHYDE • *See* Decanal.

CAPROALDEHYDE • *See* Hexanal.

CAPROIC ACID • Hexanoic Acid. A synthetic flavoring that occurs naturally in apples, butter acids, cocoa, grapes, oil of lavender, oil of lavandin, raspberries, strawberries, and tea. Used in butter, butterscotch, fruit, rum, and cheese flavorings. Used also in the manufacture of "hexyl" derivatives such as 4-hexylresorcinol (*see*). No known toxicity. The final report to the FDA of the Select Committee on GRAS Substances stated in 1980 that it should continue its GRAS status with no limitations other than good manufacturing practices.

CAPRYL BETAINE • *See* Caprylic Acid and Betaine.

CAPRYLAMINE OXIDE • *See* Caprylic Acid and Capric Acid.

CAPRYLIC ACID • An oil liquid made by the oxidation of octanol (*see*) for use in perfumery. Occurs naturally as a fatty acid in sweat, fusel oil, in the milk of cows and goats, and in palm and coconut oil. Cleared for use as a synthetic flavoring. No known toxicity. The final report to the FDA of the Select Committee on GRAS Substances stated in 1980 that it should continue its GRAS status with no limitations other than good manufacturing practices.

CAPRYLIC ALCOHOL • *See* 1-Octanol.

CAPSICUM • African Chilies. Cayenne Pepper. Tabasco Pepper. The dried fruit of a tropical plant used as a natural spice and ginger ale flavoring for beverages, ice cream, ices, candy, baked goods, chewing gum, meats, and sauces. The oleoresin form is used in sausage, spice, ginger ale, and cinnamon flavorings for beverages, ice cream, ices, candy, baked goods, chewing gum, meats, and condiments. Used internally as a digestive stimulant. Irritating to the mucous membranes, it can produce severe diarrhea and gastritis. May cause a "hot" sensation and sweating. *See* Cayenne Pepper for toxicity. GRAS. The FDA data bank, PAFA (see page 10), has not yet searched the toxicology literature concerning this additive.

CAPSORUBIN • Coloring from paprika (*see*).

CAPTAN • Agrosol. Merpan. Orthocide. Osocide. Vanguard. Vanicide. White- to creamy-colored powder, practically insoluble in water, derived from tetrahydrophthalmide and trichloromethylmercaptan. Used to treat seeds, to preserve fruit, and as a fungicide on almonds, animal feed, apples, beans, beef, beets, broccoli, cabbage, carrots, corn, garlic, kale, lettuce, peaches, peas, pork, potatoes, raisins, spinach, and strawberries. The FDA permits residues of up to 50 ppm in raisins and 100 ppm on corn seed for cattle and hog feed. The fungicide is less toxic than most, but in large doses can cause diarrhea and weight loss. A skin and lung irritant and a suspected cause of human birth defects. Pregnant women should avoid exposure to it. Also suspected of causing cancer. Moderately toxic to humans by ingestion.

CARAMEL • A chemically ill-defined group of materials produced by heating carbohydrates. Burnt sugar with a pleasant, slightly bitter taste. Made by heating sugar or glucose and adding small quantities of alkali or a trace mineral acid during heating. Caramel color prepared by ammonia process has been associated with blood toxicity in rats. Because of this, the joint FAO/WHO Expert Committee on Food Additives temporarily removed the acceptable daily intake for ammonia-made caramel. It was found to inhibit the metabolism of B_6 in rabbits. Caramel is widely used as a brown coloring in ice cream, baked goods, soft drinks, confections. As a flavoring, it is used in strawberry, butter, butterscotch, caramel, chocolate, cocoa, cola, fruit, cherry, grape, birch beer, liquor, rum, brandy, maple, black walnut, walnut, root beer, spice, ginger, ginger ale, vanilla, and cream soda beverages (2,200 ppm); in ice cream, candy, baked goods, and syrups (2,800 ppm); and in meats (2,100 ppm). Used as a coloring in cosmetics and a soothing agent in skin lotions. The FDA has given caramel priority for testing for its mutagenic, teratogenic, subacute, and reproductive effects as a food additive. Sulfite ammonia caramels tested on humans produced soft to liquid stools and increased bowel movements. The final report to the FDA of the Select Committee on GRAS Substances stated in 1980 that it should continue its GRAS status with no limitations other than good manufacturing practices. Permanently listed in 1963 as a coloring. Certification not required. The FDA data bank, PAFA (see page 10), has fully up-to-date toxicology information available concerning this additive.

CARAMEL COLOR III • Used as a color additive in beers and a variety of foods. Beer is the most important single source of this additive in the diet, although consumption of dark beers has been decreasing in recent years. The joint FAO/WHO Expert Committee on Food Additives has established an ADI (*see*) of 200 mg/kg/day. The safety of caramel color III has been questioned during recent years following feeding studies in the rat that showed reduced white cells and lymphocyte counts. In recent studies at Hazelton Laboratories America, Madison, Wisconsin, rats given caramel color III had soft feces and lower food and fluid consumption. No other toxicity was noted.

CARAWAY SEED AND OIL • The dried ripe seeds of a plant common to Europe and Asia and cultivated in England, Russia, and the U.S. A volatile, colorless to pale yellow liquid, it is used in liquor flavorings for beverages, ice cream, baked goods, and condiments; also used as a spice in baking. The oil is used in grape licorice, anisette, kümmel, liver, sausage, mint, caraway, and rye flavorings for beverages, ice cream, ices, candy, baked goods, chewing gum, meats, condiments, and liquors. The oil is used to perfume soap. Can cause contact dermatitis. A mild carminative, from one to two grams breaks up intestinal gas. Moderately toxic by ingestion and skin contact. A skin irritant. May be mutagenic. GRAS. The FDA data bank, PAFA, has not yet searched the toxicology literature concerning this additive.

CARAZOLOL • Conducton. Suacron. A beta-blocker drug that is used to counteract high blood pressure, chest pain, and irregular heartbeat in humans. It is used in the treatment of stress in pigs. See page 5.

CARBADOX • An antibacterial used in animal feed for swine. FDA tolerance for residues in swine is zero.

CARBADOX • Mecadox. Fortigro. An antibacterial used in animal feed for swine. The Expert Committee on Food Additives of the World Health Organization would not set an ADI or NOEL (*see both*) for this drug since it is a cancer-causing agent. FDA tolerance for carbadox residues in swine is zero. In 1994, twenty-five cows at a Wisconsin farm were given swine feed containing carbadox. The FDA monitored milk, infant formula, and cheese to determine if any carbadox was found. The FDA said there were no detectable levels of the antibacterial.

CARBAMATE • A compound based on carbamic acid which is used only in the form of its numerous derivatives and salts. Carbamates are used in pesticides. Among the carbamate pesticides are aldicarb, 4-benzothienyl-N-methyl carbamate, bufencarb (BUX), carbaryl, carbofuran, isolan, 2-isopropyl phenyl-N-methyl carbamate, 3-isopropyl phenylmethyl carbamate, maneb, propoxur, thiram, Zectran, zineb, and ziram. Carbamic acid, which is colorless and odorless, causes depression of bone marrow and degeneration of the brain, nausea, vomiting. It is moderately toxic by many routes.

N-CARBAMOYL ARSANILIC ACID • White, nearly odorless powder added to animal feed as a growth stimulant. It is an arsenic (*see*) compound that is on the Community Right-To-Know List. Poison by ingestion. Has caused tumors in laboratory animals.

CARBARSONE • An antiamebic and antihistomonad used in turkey and chicken feed. FDA residue tolerance is 0.025 percent to 0.0375 percent in the feed, 2 ppm in residue in edible byproducts of chickens and turkeys, and 0.5 ppm as residue in muscle meat of chickens and turkeys and in eggs.

CARBARYL • Sevin. Pesticide used on corn and other vegetables and fruits. Causes nausea, vomiting, diarrhea, lung damage, blurred vision, excessive salivation, muscle twitching, cyanosis, convulsions, coma, and death. It is a poison via oral and skin absorption. It is an eye and skin irritant. Absorption through skin is slow. It does not accumulate in the tissues and is much less toxic than parathion (*see*). FDA residue tolerances are: for pineapple bran for feed, 20 ppm; as residues in or on pineapples, 2 ppm; as residue in eggs, 0.25 ppm; as residue in fat, meat, meat byproducts from layer chickens, 0.05 ppm; as residues in kidney and liver of cattle, goats, horses, sheep, and swine, 1 ppm; as residue in fat, meat, and meat byproducts of cattle, swine, goats, horses, and shrimp, 0.1 ppm; as a residue in various raw agricultural products, 0.2–100 ppm.

CARBETHOXY MALATHION • Malathion. Vegru Malatox. Vetiol. Zithiol. Malacide. Carbophos. A brown to yellow liquid used as an insecticide on animal feed, citrus pulp, grapes, nonmedicated cattle-feed concentrate blocks, packaging material, and safflower oil. FDA permits a residue of up to 12 ppm in grapes, 0.6 ppm in safflower oil, 50 ppm in dehydrated citrus pulp, 10 ppm in nonmedicated cattle-feed concentrate blocks. A human poison by ingestion. May be mutagenic. Has caused allergic skin reactions. It can interfere with nerve transmission.

CARBOFURAN • A pesticide used in animal feed. FDA residue tolerances are: in various raw agricultural commodities, 2 ppm; on dried grape pomace, 6 ppm; soybean soap-stock, 6 ppm; in raisin waste, 6 ppm; peanut soap-stock, 24 ppm.

CARBOHYDRASE, ASPERGILLUS • An enzyme from fermentation of *Aspergillus oryzae* used as a production aid and tenderizing agent in alcoholic beverages, ale, bakery products, beer, dairy products, meats, poultry, and starch syrups. The FDA says that solutions of water and this enzyme applied or injected into raw meat cuts shall not result in a gain of more than 3 percent above the weight of the untreated product. When heated to decomposition, it emits acrid smoke and irritating fumes. The FDA data bank, PAFA (see page 18), has not yet searched the toxicology literature concerning this additive.

CARBOHYDRASE, RHIZOPUS • A production aid derived from *Rhizopus oryzae* used in processing dextrose (*see*). When heated to decomposition, it emits acrid smoke and irritating fumes. There is no reported use of the chemical and no toxicology information is available, according to the FDA.

CARBOHYDRASE and CELLULASE • Derived from *Aspergillus niger,* this enzyme permits easy shucking of clams and peeling of shrimp. The FDA permits use at a level not in excess of the amount reasonably required to accomplish the intended effect. When heated to decomposition, it emits acrid smoke and irritating fumes. There is no reported use of the chemical and no toxicology information is available, according to the FDA.

CARBOHYDRASE ENZYME DERIVED FROM ASPERGILLUS NIGER • *See* Carbohydrase and Cellulose.

CARBOHYDRASE AND PROTEASE • An enzyme from the controlled fermentation of *Bacillus licheniformis,* it is a brown powder or liquid used in beer, alcoholic beverages, candy, dextrose, fish meal, nutritive sweeteners, protein hydrolysates, and starch syrups. When heated to decomposition, it emits acrid smoke and irritating fumes. GRAS.

CARBOMYCIN • Deltamycin. An animal antibiotic used on chicken. It is also used in combination with oxytetracycline (*see*). The FDA allows no residue in cooked edible tissues of chicken. Poison by subcutaneous route. Moderately toxic by vein and injection into the muscle. When heated to decomposition, it emits toxic fumes.

CARBON BLACK • Several forms of artificially prepared carbon or charcoal, including animal charcoal, furnace black, channel (gas) black, lampblack, activated charcoal. Animal charcoal is used as a black coloring in confectionery. Activated charcoal is used as an antidote for ingested poisons, and as an adsorbent in diarrhea. The others have industrial uses. Carbon black, which was not subject to certification (*see* Certified) by the FDA, was reevaluated and then banned in 1976. It was found in tests to contain a cancer-causing byproduct that was released during dye manufacture. It can no longer be used in candies such as licorice and jelly beans or in drugs or cosmetics.

CARBON DIOXIDE • Colorless, odorless, noncombustible gas with a faint acid taste. Used as a pressure-dispensing agent in gassed creams. Also used in the carbonation of beverages and as dry ice for refrigeration in the frozen-food industry. Used onstage to produce harmless smoke or fumes. May cause shortness of breath, vomiting, high blood pressure, and disorientation if inhaled in sufficient amounts. GRAS. The FDA data bank, PAFA (see page 10), has fully up-to-date toxicology information available concerning this additive.

CARBON DISULFIDE • A clear, colorless liquid used as a fumigant for cereal grains. Extremely hazardous. A human poison by ingestion. Mildly toxic to humans by inhalation.

CARBON TETRACHLORIDE • Carbon Tet. Tetrachloromethane. Perchloromethane. A colorless, clear, heavy, nonflammable liquid obtained from carbon disulfide and chlorine. It is used as a fumigant on cereal grains. Poisonous by inhalation, ingestion, or skin absorption. Acute poisoning causes nausea, diarrhea, headache, stupor, kidney damage, and can be fatal. Chronic poisoning involves liver damage, but can also cause kidney damage. It has caused cancer in animals. Because it is so toxic, the FDA banned its use in products for the home in 1970. It is still used as a fumigant for grains and in industry.

CARBONATE, POTASSIUM • *See* Potassium Carbonate.

CARBONATE, SODIUM • *See* Sodium Carbonate.

CARBONYL IRON • Iron that has been processed with carbon and oxygen. Used as a coloring. *See* Iron Salts. The final report to the FDA of the Select Committee on GRAS Substances stated in 1980 that there is no available evidence that it is a hazard to the public when used as it is now and it should continue its GRAS status with limitations on the amounts that can be added to food.

CARBOPHENOTHION • A pesticide used on citrus meal fed to cattle. FDA tolerance is 10 ppm. *See* Organophosphates.

CARBOXINE • Vitavax. Carboxin. A fungicide used on barley, beans, corn, oats, peanut hulls, rice, sorghum, and wheat for animal feeds. Poison by ingestion. Moderately toxic by skin contact.

CARBOXYMETHYL CELLULOSE • Sodium. Made from cotton byproducts, it occurs as a white powder or in granules. A synthetic gum, it is used as a stabilizer in ice cream, beverages, and other foods. It is employed in bath preparations, beauty masks, dentifrices, hair-grooming aids, hand creams, rouge, shampoos, and shaving creams. As an emulsifier, stabilizer, and foaming agent, it is a barrier agent (*see*). It is used medicinally as a laxative or antacid. It has been shown to cause cancer in animals when ingested. Its toxicity on the skin is unknown. The final report to the FDA of the Select Committee on GRAS Substances stated in 1980 that it should continue its GRAS status with no limitations other than good manufacturing practices. The FDA data bank, PAFA (see page 10), has a toxicology literature search in progress concerning this chemical.

CARDAMON OIL • Grains of Paradise. A natural flavoring and aromatic agent from the dried ripe seeds of trees common to India, Ceylon, and Guatemala. Used in butter, chocolate, liquor, spice, and vanilla flavorings for beverages, ice cream, ices, candy, baked goods (1,700 ppm), meats, and condiments. The seed oil is used in chocolate, cocoa, coffee, cherry liquor, liver, sausage, root beer, sarsaparilla, cardamon, ginger ale, vanilla, and cream soda flavorings for beverages, ice cream, ices, candy, baked goods, chewing gum, liquor, pickles, curry powder, and condiments. Used also in perfumes and soaps. As a medicine, it breaks up intestinal gas. May be mutagenic. The FDA has not yet done a toxicology literature search on this additive.

CARMINE • Extract of Cochineal. A crimson pigment derived from a Mexican and Central American species of a scaly female insect that feeds on various cacti. Carmine and cochineal *extracts* are permanently listed, but cochineal alone is not authorized for use. The colorings once used in red apple sauce, confections, baked goods, meats, and spices have been withdrawn by the FDA. Carmine was involved in an outbreak of salmonellosis (an intestinal infection) that killed one infant in a Boston hospital and made twenty-two patients seriously ill. Carmine, used in a diagnostic solution to test the digestive organs, was found to be the infecting agent. Also used in cosmetics. The FDA has not yet done a toxicology literature search on this additive.

CARMINIC ACID • Natural Red No. 4. Used in mascaras, liquid rouge, paste rouge, and red eye shadows. It is the glucosidal coloring matter from a scaly insect (*see* Carmine). Color is deep red in water and violet to yellow in acids. May cause allergic reactions. Not subject to certification by the FDA.

CARNAUBA WAX • The exudate from the leaves of the Brazilian wax palm tree used as a candy glaze and polish. The crude wax is yellow or dirty green, brittle, and very hard. It is used in many polishes and varnishes, and when mixed with other waxes, it makes them harder and gives them more luster. Used as a texturizer in foundation makeups, mascara, cream rouge, lipsticks, liquid powders, depilatories, and deodorant sticks. It rarely causes allergic reactions. It is on the FDA list for further study for mutagenic, teratogenic, subacute, and reproductive effects. The final report to the FDA of the Select Committee on GRAS Substances stated in 1980 that there were insufficient biological and other studies upon which to base an evaluation of it when it is used as a food ingredient. GRAS. An FDA toxicology literature search was in progress at this writing.

L-CARNITINE • Levocarnitine Carnitor. Vitacarn. A B-vitamin factor found in muscle, liver, and meat extracts. Used for patients born with systemic carnitine deficiency. It is a thyroid inhibitor. It enables fatty acids to produce energy in persons who are carnitine deficient. Potential adverse reactions include nausea, vomiting, cramps, diarrhea, and body odor. The FDA has not yet done a toxicology literature search concerning this additive.

CAROB BEAN • *See* Locust Bean Gum.

b-CAROPHYLLENE • A synthetic spice flavoring. Occurs naturally in cloves, black currant buds, yarrow herb, grapefruit, allspice, and black pepper. The liquid smells like oil of cloves and turpentine. Used in beverages, ice cream, ices, candy, baked goods, chewing gum, and condiments. A skin irritant. The FDA data bank, PAFA (see page 10), has fully up-to-date toxicology information available on this additive.

CAROPHYLLENE ALCOHOL • A flavoring that occurs in essential oils, especially in clove oil. Colorless, oily, with a clovelike odor. Used as a synthetic mushroom flavoring for baked goods and condiments. The FDA data bank, PAFA, has fully up-to-date toxicology information available on this additive.

CAROTENE • Provitamin A. Beta-carotene. Found in all plants and many animal tissues, it is the chief yellow coloring matter of carrots, butter, and egg yolk. Extracted as red crystals or crystalline powder, it is used as a vegetable dye in butter, margarine, shortening, skimmed milk, buttermilk, and cottage cheese. It is also used to manufacture vitamin A and is a nutrient added to skimmed milk, vegetable shortening, and margarine at the rate of 5,000 to 13,000 IU (International Units) per pound. Insoluble in water, acids, and alkalis. Too much carotene in the blood (exceeding 200 micrograms per 100 milliliters of blood) can lead to carotenemia—a pale yellow-red pigmentation of the skin that may be mistaken for jaundice. It is a benign condition that withdrawal of carotene from the diet cures. The final report to the FDA of the Select Committee on GRAS Substances stated in 1980 that it should continue its GRAS status with no limitations other than good manufacturing practices. Beta-carotene has been permanently listed as a coloring since 1964. The FDA data bank, PAFA (see page 10), has fully up-to-date toxicology information available on this additive.

CAROTENOID • Any of several pigments, most of which are yellow, orange, or red. They occur widely in plants and animals.

CARRAGEENAN • Chondrus Extract. Irish Moss. A stabilizer and emulsifier, seaweedlike in odor, derived from Irish moss, used in oils in cosmetics and foods. It is used as an emulsifier in chocolate products, chocolate-flavored drinks, chocolate milk, gassed cream (pressure-dispensed whipped cream), syrups for frozen products, confections, evaporated milk, cheese spreads and cheese foods, ice cream, frozen custard, sherbets, ices, French dressing, artificially sweetened jellies and jams. Completely soluble in hot water and not coagulated by acids. Salts of carrageenan, such as calcium, ammonium, potassium, or sodium, are used as a demulcent to soothe mucous membrane irritation. Carrageenan stimulated the formation of fibrous tissue when subcutaneously injected into the guinea pig. When a single dose of it dissolved in saline was injected under the skin of the rat, it caused sarcomas after approximately two years. Its cancer-causing ability may be that of a foreign-body irritant because upon administration to rats and mice at high levels in their diet, it did not appear to induce tumors, although survival of the animals for this period was not good. The final report to the FDA of the Select Committee on GRAS Substances stated in 1980 that while no available evidence on it demonstrates a hazard to the public at current use levels, uncertainties exist, requiring additional studies. The FDA continued GRAS status while tests were being completed and evaluated. As of this writing, nothing has been reported. The FDA data bank, PAFA (see page 10), has not yet done a toxicology literature search.

CARROT JUICE POWDER • *See* Carrot Oil.

CARROT OIL • Either of two oils from the seeds of carrots. A light yellow essential oil that has a spicy odor and is used in liqueurs, flavorings, and perfumes. It is used as a violet, fruit, rum, and spice flavoring for beverages, ice cream, ices, candy, baked goods, gelatin desserts, puddings, condiments, and soups. Rich in vitamin A, it is also used as a coloring and has been permanently listed since 1964. A skin irritant. When heated to decomposition, it emits acrid smoke and irritating fumes. GRAS. The FDA data bank, PAFA, has fully up-to-date toxicology information available on this additive.

CARROT SEED EXTRACT • Extract of the seeds of *Daucus carota sativa. See* Carrot Oil.

CARVACROL • A colorless to pale yellow liquid with a pungent, spicy odor, related to thymol but more toxic. It is found naturally in oil of origanum, dittany-of-crete oil, oregano, lavage oil, marjoram, and savory. It is a synthetic flavoring used in citrus, fruit, mint, and spice flavorings for beverages, ice cream, ices, candy, baked goods, and condiments. It is used as a disinfectant and is corrosive; one gram by mouth can cause respiratory and circulatory depression and cardiac failure leading to death. The FDA data bank, PAFA (see page 10), has fully up-to-date toxicology information available on this additive.

CARVACRYL ETHYL ETHER • A synthetic spice flavoring agent for beverages, ice cream, ices, candy, and baked goods. Found naturally in caraway and grapefruit. The FDA data bank, PAFA, has fully up-to-date toxicology information available on this additive.

CARVEOL • A synthetic mint, spearmint, spice, and caraway flavoring agent for beverages, ice cream, ices, candy, and baked goods. Found naturally in caraway and grape, baked fruit. The FDA data bank, PAFA, has fully up-to-date toxicology information available on this additive.

CARVOL • *See d*-Carvone.

4-CARVOMENTHENOL • A synthetic citrus and spice flavoring for beverages, ice cream, ices, candy, and baked goods. Occurs naturally in cardamon oil, juniper berries. The FDA data bank, PAFA, has fully up-to-date toxicology information available on this additive.

(*d*- or *l*-) CARVONE • Oil of Caraway. *d*-Carvone is usually prepared by distillation from caraway seed and dill seed oil. It is colorless to light yellow with an odor of caraway. *l*-Carvone occurs in several essential oils. It may be isolated from spearmint oil or synthesized commercially from *d*-limonene. It is colorless to pale yellow with the odor of spearmint. Carvol is a synthetic liquor, mint, and spice flavoring agent for beverages, ice cream, ices, candy, and baked goods. Used also in perfumery and soaps. It breaks up intestinal gas and is used as a stimulant. The FDA data bank, PAFA (see page 10), has fully up-to-date toxicology information available on this additive. GRAS.

CARVYL ACETATE • A synthetic mint flavoring for beverages, ice cream, ices, candy, and baked goods. The FDA data bank, PAFA, has fully up-to-date toxicology information available on this additive.

CARVYL PROPIONATE • A synthetic mint flavoring for beverages, ice cream, ices, candy, and baked goods. The FDA data bank, PAFA, has fully up-to-date toxicology information available on this additive.

CARVYLOPHYLLENE ACETATE • A general fixative that occurs in many essential oils, especially in clove oil. Colorless, oily, with a clovelike odor. Used for beverages, ice cream, ices, candy, baked goods, and chewing gum. Practically insoluble in alcohol. No known toxicity.

CASCARA, BITTERLESS EXTRACT • A natural flavoring derived from the dried bark of a plant grown from northern Idaho to northern California. Cathartic. Used in butter, maple, caramel, and vanilla flavorings for beverages, ice cream, ices, and baked goods. Also used as a laxative. The freshly dried bark causes vomiting, so it must be dried for a year before use, when the side effect has disappeared. It has a bitter taste and its laxative effect is due to its ability to irritate the mucosa of the large intestine. The FDA data bank, PAFA, has not yet done a toxicology search on this additive.

CASCARILLA BARK • A natural flavoring agent obtained from the bark of a tree grown in Haiti, the Bahamas, and Cuba. The *dried extract* is added to smoking tobacco for flavoring and used in bitters and spice flavorings for beverages. The *oil,* obtained by distillation, is light yellow to amber, with a spicy odor. It is used in cola, fruit, root beer, and spice flavorings for beverages, ice cream, ices, candy, baked goods, and condiments. No known toxicity. GRAS. The FDA data bank, PAFA (see page 10), has not yet done a toxicology search on this additive.

CASEIN • Ammonium Caseinate. Calcium Caseinate. Potassium Caseinate. Sodium Caseinate. The principal protein of cow's milk. It is a white, water-absorbing powder without noticeable odor. Used as a texturizer for ice cream, frozen custard, ice milk, fruit sherbets, and in special diet preparations. Also used in protective cream and as the "protein" in hair preparations to make the hair thicker and more manageable. It is also used to make depilatories less irritating, as a film-former in beauty masks, and as an emulsifier in many cosmetics. Nontoxic. The final report to the FDA of the Select Committee on GRAS Substances stated in 1980 that it should continue its GRAS status with no limitations other than good manufacturing practices. The FDA has a toxicology literature search now in progress.

CASHOO EXTRACT • *See* Catechu Extract.

CASSIA BARK • Padang or Batavia. GRAS. *See* Cassia Bark, Chinese.

CASSIA BARK, CHINESE • A natural flavoring extract from cultivated trees. Used in cola, root beer, and spice flavorings for beverages, ice cream, candy, and baked goods. The *bark oil* is used in berry, chocolate, lemon, coffee, cola, cherry, peach, rum, peppermint, pecan, root beer, cassia, ginger ale, and cinnamon flavorings for beverages, ice cream, ices, candy, baked goods, chewing gum, meats, and condiments. The *buds* are used in spice flavorings for beverages. Cassia bark can cause inflammation and erosion of the gastrointestinal tract. GRAS.

CASSIA OIL • Cloves. Chinese Oil of Cinnamon. Darker, less agreeable, and heavier than true cinnamon. Obtained from a tropical Asian tree, it is used in bitters, fruit, liquor, meat, root beer, sarsaparilla, and spice flavorings for beverages, ice cream, candy, and baked goods (3,000 ppm). It is also used in perfumes, poultices, and as a laxative. It can cause irritation and allergy, such as a stuffy nose.

CASSIE, ABSOLUTE • A natural flavoring from the flowers of the acacia plant. Used in blackberry, violet, vermouth, and fruit flavorings for beverages, ice cream, ices, candy, baked goods, and gelatin desserts. No known toxicity. The FDA data bank, PAFA (see page 10), has not yet done a toxicology search on this additive.

CASSIS • *See* Currant Buds, Absolute.

CASTOR OIL • Palm Christi Oil. Tang Tang Oil. Ricinus Oil. Palm Cristi Oil. The seed of the castor oil plant. After the oil is expressed from the beans, a residual castor pomace remains, which contains a potent allergen. This may be incorporated in fertilizer, which is the main source of exposure, but people who live near a castor-bean processing factory may also be sensitized. A flavoring, pale yellow and viscous, it has a slight acrid, sometimes nauseating taste. Used in butter and nut flavorings for beverages, ice cream, ices, candy, and baked goods. Also an antisticking agent in hard-candy products, and a component of protective coatings, a drying oil, and a releasing agent (*see*). The raw material is a constituent of embalming fluid, and a cathartic. It is also used in bath oils, nail-polish removers, solid perfumes, face masks, shaving creams, lipsticks, and many men's hairdressings. It is also used as a plasticizer in nail polish. It forms a tough, shiny film when dried. More than 50 percent of the lipsticks in the United States use a substantial amount of castor oil. Ingestion of large amounts may cause pelvic congestion and induce abortions. Soothing to the skin. The FDA data bank, PAFA (see page 10), has fully up-to-date toxicology information available.

CASTOREUM EXTRACT • Castor. Used in perfumes as a fixative (*see*). A creamy, orange-brown substance with a strong penetrating odor and bitter taste that consists of the dried perineal glands of the beaver and their secretion. The glands and secretions are taken from the area between the vulva and anus in the female beaver and from the scrotum and anus in the male beaver. Professional trappers use castor to scent bait. The FDA data bank, PAFA, has not yet done a toxicology search on this additive.

CATALASE • An enzyme from bovine liver used in milk, for making cheese, and for the elimination of peroxide. It is used also in combination with glucose oxidase for treatment of food wrappers to prevent oxidative deterioration of food. The FDA data bank, PAFA (see page 10), has not yet done a toxicology search on this additive.

CATALYST • A substance that causes or speeds up a chemical reaction but does not itself change.

CATECHU EXTRACT • Black Cutch Extract. Cachou Extract. Cashoo Extract. Pegu Catechu Extract. A preparation from the heartwood of the *Acacia catechu* (*see* Acacia) grown in India, Sri Lanka, and Jamaica. Used in bitters, fruit, and rum flavorings for beverages, ice cream, ices, candy, baked goods, and chewing gum. Used also in toilet preparations and for brown and black colorings. The powder is used in fruit, rum, and spice flavorings for beverages, ice cream, candy, baked goods, and chewing gum. Incompatible with iron compounds, gelatin, limewater, and zinc. Used as an astringent in diarrhea. May cause allergic reactions. The FDA data bank, PAFA (see page 10), has not yet done a toxicology search on this additive.

CAYENNE PEPPER • Red Pepper. A condiment made from the pungent fruit of the plant. Used in sausage and pepper flavorings for beverages, ice cream, ices, candy, meats, soups, and condiments. Reported to retard growth of Mexicans, South Americans, and Spaniards who eat a great deal of these peppers. Rats fed the ingredient of pepper that makes it hot, a reddish brown liquid called capsaicin, used in flavorings and pickles, were stunted in growth. A report by F. M. Gannett of the Eppley Institute for Research, University of Nebraska Medical Center, Omaha, at the 1988 American Chemical Society meeting, Toronto, Canada, said that capsaicin is not a low-level mutagen as earlier believed but is actually antimutagenic.

CEDAR • Cedarwood Oil. The oil from white, red, or various cedars obtained by distillation from fresh leaves and branches. A colorless to yellow liquid, it is used in fruit and spice flavorings for beverages, ice cream, ices, candy, baked goods, chewing gum, and liquors. It is often used in perfumes, soaps, and sachets for its warm woodsy scent. Used frequently as a substitute for oil of lavender. There is usually a strong camphor odor that repels insects. Cedar oil can be a photosensitizer, causing skin reactions when the skin is exposed to light. Similar toxicity to camphor oil (*see*). The FDA data bank, PAFA (see page 10), has not yet done a toxicology search on this additive.

CEDARWOOD OIL • *See* Cedar.

CEDRO OIL • *See* Lemon Oil.

CEDRYL ACETATE • Colorless liquid having a light cedar odor. Used in fragrances. The FDA data bank, PAFA (see page 10), has fully up-to-date toxicology information available concerning this additive.

CEFTIOFUR • An animal drug used in beef. The FDA limits residues to 3 ppm in muscle, 9 ppm in kidney, 6 ppm in liver, and 12 ppm in fat of cattle. When heated to decomposition, it emits acrid smoke and irritating fumes.

CELERY SEED • A yellowish to greenish brown liquid, having a pleasant aromatic odor, distilled from the dried ripe fruit of the plant grown in southern Europe. Celery seed is used in sausage and celery flavorings for beverages (1,000 ppm), baked goods, condiments (2,500 ppm), soups, meats, and pickles. *Celery seed solid extract* is used in celery, meat, and spice flavorings for beverages, ice cream, ices, candy, baked goods, condiments, and maple syrup. *Celery seed oil* is used in fruit, honey, maple, sausage, nut, root beer, spice, vanilla, and cream soda flavorings for beverages, ice cream, ices, candy, baked goods, chewing gum, meats, soup, pickles, and condiments. Celery seed may cause a sensitivity to light. GRAS. The FDA data bank, PAFA (see page 10), has not yet done a toxicology search on this additive.

CELLULASE ENZYME • Derived from *Aspergillus niger*. An enzyme for removal of visceral mass in lamb processing and shell from shrimp.

CELLULOSE • Chief constituent of the fiber of plants. Cotton contains about 90 percent cellulose. It is the basic material for cellulose gums (*see*). Used as an emulsifier in cosmetic creams. The FDA data bank, PAFA, is now searching the toxicology literature concerning this additive.

CELLULOSE GUMS • Any of several fibrous substances consisting of the chief part of the cell walls of plants. *Cellulose acetate,* obtained by treating cellulose with food-starch modifier, is insoluble in water, alcohol, and ether. Used in the manufacture of rubber and celluloid substitutes, airplane dopes, varnishes, and lacquer. *Ethylcellulose* is a film-former in lipstick. *Methylcellulose* (Methocel) and *hydroxyethylcellulose* (Cellosize) are used as emulsifiers in hand creams and lotions. They are resistant to bacterial decomposition and give uniform viscosity to products. No known toxicity. The final report to the FDA of the Select Committee on GRAS Substances stated in 1980 that it should continue its GRAS status for packaging only with no limitations other than good manufacturing practices.

CENTAURY (CENTRUIUM) HERB • Flavoring in alcoholic beverages only. The FDA data bank, PAFA (see page 10), has not yet done a toxicology search on this additive.

CEPHARPIRIN • An animal drug used in beef and milk. The FDA limits residue to 0.02 ppm in milk and 0.1 ppm in uncooked edible tissues of dairy cattle. Moderately toxic by injection into the vein. When heated to decomposition, it emits toxic fumes.

CERESIN • Ceresine. Earth Wax. Used in protective creams. It is a white or yellow hard, brittle wax made by purifying ozokerite (*see*), found in Ukraine, Utah, and Texas. It is used as a substitute for beeswax and paraffin (*see both*); it is also used to wax paper and cloth, as a polish, and in dentistry for taking wax impressions. May cause allergic reactions.

CERTIFIED • Each batch of coal tar or petrochemical colors, with the exception of those used in food and cosmetic dyes, must be certified by the FDA as "harmless and suitable for use." The manufacturer must submit samples of every batch for testing, and the lot test number accompanies the colors through all subsequent packaging.

CETONE D • *See* Methyl *b*-Naphthyl Ketone.

CETONE V • *See* Allyl *a*-Ionone.

CETYL • Means derived from cetyl alcohol (*see*).

CETYL ALCOHOL • An emollient and emulsion stabilizer used in many foods and cosmetics preparations including baby lotion, brilliantine hairdressings, deodorants and antiperspirants, cream depilatories, eyelash creams and oils, foundation creams, hair lacquers, hair straighteners, hand lotions, lipsticks, liquid powders, mascaras, nail-polish removers, nail whiteners, cream rouge, and shampoos. Cetyl alcohol is waxy, crystalline solid found in spermaceti (*see*). It has a low toxicity for both skin and ingestion and is sometimes used as a laxative. Can cause hives.

CETYL ARACHIDATE • An ester produced by the reaction of cetyl alcohol and arachidic acid. The acid is found in fish oils and vegetables, particularly peanut oil. A fatty compound used as an emulsifier. Nontoxic.

CETYL ESTERS • Synthetic spermaceti (*see*).

CETYLIC ACID • *See* Palmitic Acid.

CEYLON CINNAMON • *See* Cinnamon.

CEYLON CINNAMON LEAF OIL • *See* Cinnamon Leaf Oil.

CHACONINE • An alkaloid in plants of the Solanaceae family such as potatoes and tomatoes. In laboratory animals, it caused birth defects, but the World Health Organization said that the amount in potatoes is not significant.

CHAMOMILE • Roman, German, and Hungarian Chamomile. The daisy-like white and yellow heads of these flowers provide a coloring agent known as apigenin. The essential oil distilled from the flower heads is pale blue and is added to shampoos to impart the odor of chamomile. Powdered flowers are used to bring out a bright yellow color in the hair. Also used in rinses and skin fresheners. *Roman chamomile* is used in berry, fruit, vermouth, maple, spice and vanilla flavorings, and *English chamomile* is used in chocolate, fruit, and liquor flavorings for beverages, ice cream, ices, candy, and baked goods. *Roman chamomile oil* is used in chocolate, fruit, vermouth, and spice flavorings for beverages, ice cream, ices, candy, baked goods, gelatin desserts, and liquors. *Hungarian chamomile oil* is used in chocolate, fruit, and liquor flavorings for beverages, ice cream, ices, candy, baked goods, chewing gum, and liquors. Chamomile contains sesquiterpene lactones that may cause allergic contact dermatitis and stomach upsets. GRAS. The FDA says there is no reported use of the chemical and no toxicology information is available.

CHAR SMOKE FLAVOR • The FDA data bank, PAFA (see page 10), has not yet done a toxicology search on this additive.

CHECKERBERRY EXTRACT • *See* Wintergreen Oil.

CHECKERBERRY OIL • *See* Wintergreen Oil.

CHELATING AGENT • Any compound, usually one that binds and precipitates metals such as ethylenediamine tetraacetic acid (EDTA), that removes trace metals. *See* Sequestering Agent.

CHEMICALS USED IN WASHING FRUITS AND VEGETABLES • Polyacrylamide, potassium bromide, sodium dodecylbenzenesulfonate, sodium hypochlorite, sodium 2-ethyl-1-hexylsulfate, sodium *n*-alkylbenzene sulfonate, sodium mono- and dimethyl-naphthalene sulfonates; alkylene oxide adducts of alkyl alcohols and phosphate esters of alkylene oxides. Adducts of alkyl alcohol mixtures. Use of such chemicals followed by rinsing to remove residues. Some individual chemicals remain in limited amounts in wash water, according to the FDA.

CHERRY BARK (WILD) EXTRACT • A natural flavoring extracted from the pits of sweet and sour cherries used in cherry flavoring for beverages, ice cream, and ices. GRAS. The FDA data bank, PAFA (see page 10), has not yet done a toxicology search on this additive.

CHERRY LAUREL LEAVES • *Prunus laurocerasus.* A flavoring. There is no reported use of the chemical and no toxicology information is available, according to the FDA.

CHERRY PIT OIL • A natural flavoring and fragrance extracted from the pits of sweet and sour cherries. Also a cherry flavoring for beverages, ice cream, and condiments. The FDA data bank, PAFA, has not yet done a toxicology search on this additive.

CHERRY PLUM • Source of purplish red color. *See* Anthocyanins.

CHERVIL • A natural flavoring extracted from an aromatic Eurasian plant and used in spice flavorings for beverages, ice cream, ices, candy, baked goods, and condiments. A chewing gum base. GRAS. There is no reported use of the chemical and no toxicology information is available.

CHESTNUT LEAVES • *Castanea*. Nuts from an American or European tree used as a remedy for piles and backaches. An astringent, the bark and leaves were used to make a tonic that was also reportedly useful in the treatment of upper-respiratory ailments such as coughs, particularly whooping cough. The bark of Spanish chestnut contains tannins (*see* Tannic Acid). The FDA's data bank, PAFA, has not yet done a search on this additive.

CHEWING GUM BASE • Chicle, chiquibal, crown gum, gutta hang kang, massaranduba balata, massaranduba chocolate, nispero lechi caspi, pendare, perillo, rosidinha, Venezuelan chicle, liche devaca, Niger gutta, tuno, chilte, natural rubber, glycerol ester of tall oil resin.

CHICLE • The gummy, milky resin obtained from trees grown in Mexico and Central America. Rubberlike and quite soft at moderate temperatures. Used in the manufacture of chewing gum, insulation, and waterproofing. The FDA data bank, PAFA, has fully up-to-date toxicology information available on this additive.

CHICORY EXTRACT • A natural flavor extract from a plant, usually with blue flowers and leaves. Used in butter, caramel, chocolate, coffee, maple, nut, root beer, sarsaparilla, vanilla, wintergreen, and birch beer flavorings for beverages, ice cream, ices, candy, and baked goods. The root of the plant is dried, roasted, and ground for mixing with coffee. The FDA data bank, PAFA, has not yet done a toxicology literature search on this additive.

CHILTE • A chewing gum base component of vegetable origin. No known toxicity. The FDA data bank, PAFA (see page 10), has fully up-to-date toxicology information available on this additive.

CHINA BARK EXTRACT • *See* Quillaja Extract.

CHINESE CINNAMON • *See* Cinnamon.

CHINESE CINNAMON LEAF OIL • *See* Cinnamon Leaf Oil.

CHIQUIBUL • *Manilkara zapotilla*. The FDA data bank, PAFA, has not yet searched the toxicology literature for this additive.

CHIRATA (CHIRETTA, EAST INDIAN BOLONONG) and HERB EXTRACT • Flavoring used in alcoholic beverages only. The FDA data bank, PAFA (see page 10), has not yet done a toxicology literature search on this additive.

CHIVES • A member of the onion family, native to Eurasia. The leaves are used for a seasoning. GRAS. The FDA data bank, PAFA, has not yet done a toxicology literature search on this additive.

CHLORAMPHENICOL • An antibiotic used on beef, pork, and lamb. In the EPA Genetic Toxicology Program (*see*). Poison by intraperitoneal, intravenous, and subcutaneous routes. Moderately toxic by ingestion. A human carcinogen that causes leukemia, aplastic anemia, and other bone-marrow changes by ingestion.

CHLORDANE • An organochlorine pesticide introduced in 1945 that was among the first to be developed for insect control. Because of its persistence in the environment, most of its uses were suspended by order of the EPA in 1975. Several specified uses are still permitted, including pest control on pineapple, strawberries, and Florida citrus crops. It can also be used to remedy a number of other pest-control problems that plague certain areas of the U.S. Chlordane causes cancer of the liver in mice. It is less toxic than other similar pesticides, but acute exposure stimulates the central nervous system. It has also been implicated in acute blood dyscrasia (abnormalities) such as aplastic anemia. Can be absorbed through the skin.

CHLORDIMEFORM • Colorless crystals derived from ethyl formate and ammonia, it is a fumigant, an insecticide, and a miticide. It also kills insect eggs. It is sold for use on cotton and vegetable crops. It is less toxic than organophosphates and is biodegradable. It is used in dried apple pomace and cottonseed hulls. In dried prunes as a residue resulting from application to growing plums. In animal feed the tolerance is up to 25 ppm. In prunes it is 15 ppm.

CHLORETHEPHON • Water-absorbing needles from benzene used as a plant-growth regulator, present as residues in animal feed, barley, raisin waste, sugarcane molasses, and wheat-milling fractions (except flour). The FDA permits a residue of 5 ppm in barley and wheat-milling fractions (except flour), 1.5 ppm in sugarcane molasses, and 65 ppm in raisin waste when used for animal feed. Moderately toxic by ingestion. Mildly toxic by skin contact. May be irritating to exposed skin and eyes or if inhaled.

CHLORHEXIDINE DIHYDROCHLORIDE • A veterinarian drug used for cattle. The FDA tolerance residue in edible tissue of calves is zero.

CHLORIMURON • A pesticide and herbicide used in soybeans, peanuts, peanut hulls. FDA tolerance residues are from 0.02 to 0.05 ppm.

CHLORINE DIOXIDE • Flour bleacher and oxidizing agent. A yellow to reddish yellow gas with an unpleasant odor, highly irritating and corrosive to the skin and mucous membranes of the respiratory tract. Reacts violently with organic materials. It can kill. The FDA data bank, PAFA (see page 10), has not yet done a toxicology literature search on this additive.

CHLORINE GAS • Flour-bleaching and aging and oxidizing agent. Also used in water purification. Found in the earth's crust, it is a greenish yellow gas with a suffocating odor. A powerful irritant, dangerous to inhale, and lethal. Thirty ppm will cause coughing. The chlorine used in drinking water often contains carcinogenic carbon tetrachloride, a contaminant formed during production. Chlorination has also been found to sometimes form undesirable "ring" compounds in water, such as toluene, xylene, and the suspected carcinogen styrene—they have been observed in both drinking-water and waste-water plants in the Midwest. The FDA data bank, PAFA, was, as of this writing, doing a toxicology literature search on this gas.

CHLORITE • *See* Calcium Hypochlorite.

4-CHLORO-1-BUTANOL • Tetramethylene Chlorohydrin. An animal drug used in cows to treat mastitis, but the FDA does not permit any residue in milk. Moderately toxic by ingestion and may be mutagenic.

CHLOROACETIC ACID • Used in packaging adhesives and as a preservative. Not permitted in alcoholic beverages or foods. In the EPA Genetic Toxicology Program and considered an extremely hazardous substance.

CHLOROPHENAMIDINE • Acaron. Fundex. A pesticide used in animal feed. FDA residue tolerance of 15 ppm in dried prunes, 25 ppm in dried apple pomace, and 10 ppm in cottonseed hulls when used for animal feed. Poison by ingestion, skin contact, and injection. Possible cancer-causing agent and mutagen. Eye and skin irritant.

1-(4-CHLOROPHENOXY)-3,3-DIMETHYL-1-(1,2,3-TRIAZOL-1-YL)-2-BUTAN-2-ONE • Amiral. MEB 6447. Triadimefon. A fungicide used on barley (except flour) and wheat (except flour). FDA residue tolerance is 4 ppm in barley and wheat, milled fractions (except flour). Poisonous by ingestion.

1-(4-CHLOROPHENOXY)-3-3-DIMETHYL-1-(IH-1,2,4-TRIAZOL-1-YL)-2-BUTANONE • A fungicide used in animal feed. FDA residue tolerances are: residues on grape pomace, 3 ppm; on apple pomace, 4 ppm; on raisin waste, 7 ppm.

2(m-CHLOROPHENOXY) PROPIONIC ACID • A growth regulator used in pineapple bran. FDA residue tolerance is 3 ppm.

1-(4-CHLOROPHENYL)-3-(2,6-DIFLUOROBENZOYL)UREA • Difluon. Dimilin. An insecticide used in animal feed, soybean hulls, and soybean soapstock when used for animal feed. EPA Genetic Toxicology Program (*see*). Moderately toxic by skin contact. Mildly toxic by ingestion. May be mutagenic.

_p_-CHLOROPHENYL-2,4,5-TRICHLOROPHENYL SULFONE • Tetradifon. Akaritox. A pesticide. FDA residue tolerance is 120 ppm in dried hops, 10 ppm in dried figs, and 8 ppm in dried tea. Moderately toxic by ingestion. Mildly toxic by skin contact. May cause birth defects.

CHLOROPHYLL • The green coloring matter of plants, which plays an essential part in photosynthesis. Used in antiperspirants, dentifrices, deodorants, and mouthwashes as a deodorizing agent. It imparts a greenish color to certain fats and oils, notably olive oil and soybean. Can cause a sensitivity to light. The FDA data bank, PAFA (see page 10), has not yet done a toxicology literature search for this additive.

CHLORPENTAFLUOROETHANE • Alone or with carbon dioxide. Used as propellant and aerating agent in food. *See* Pentane. The FDA data bank, PAFA (see page 18), has fully up-to-date toxicology information available.

CHLORPROMAZINE • Ormazine. Thorazine. Thor-Pram. An antipsychotic and antinausea medication introduced in the 1950s, it is also used for intractable hiccups and mild alcohol withdrawal. It is used to tranquilize pigs on their way to market. See page 5. Potential adverse reactions to the medication in humans include a drop in white blood cells, sedation, uncontrolled movements, Parkinsonism-like symptoms, dizziness, a drop in blood pressure when rising from a seated or prone position, vision changes, dry mouth, constipation, urine retention, male breast enlargement, inhibited ejaculation, liver dysfunction, weight gain, increased appetite, fever, photosensitivity, irregular heartbeat, and sweating. Tardive dyskinesia (*see*) may occur after prolonged used. Alcohol and other central nervous system depressants may increase central nervous system depression. Drugs used to treat Parkinsonism and antidepressants may increase chlorpromazine's nerve-suppressing activity. Blood pressure medications that act on the brain may be less effective. Oral blood thinners may be less effective, and propranolol can increase the levels of both propranolol and chlorpromazine. Contraindicated in central nervous system depression, bone marrow suppression, brain damage, Reye's syndrome, and coma. Also contraindicated with use of spinal or epidural anesthetic or adrenergic blocking agents (*see*); in the elderly, contraindicated in patients with liver disease, hardening of the arteries, or cardiovascular disease, or respiratory disorders, glaucoma, and enlarged prostate, and in acutely ill or dehydrated children. The ingested drug may take effect in thirty to sixty minutes and may last up to three weeks after stopping the drug.

CHLORPYRIFOS • 0,0-Dimethyl-0-(3,5,6-Trichloro-2-Pyridyl)Phosphorothioate. Dursban. Lorsban. White granular powder used as an insecticide and acaricide on corn and other vegetables. Poison by ingestion. A skin irritant. FDA residue tolerance is 90 ppm in barley milling fractions (except flour), 130 ppm in oat milling fractions (except flour), 90 ppm in sorghum milling fractions (except flour), 30 ppm in rice milling fractions (except flour), 30 ppm in wheat milling fractions (except flour). Limitations as above when used for animal feed.

CHLORSULON • Curatrem. An animal drug used to treat worms.

CHLORTETRACYCLINE • Aureomycin. Biomycin. Biomitsin. A preservative, an antibiotic, used in a dip for uncooked poultry. One of the reasons for increased resistance to antibiotics in patients is believed to be the widespread use of antibiotics in food animals. In 1969, the British restricted the veterinary use of antibiotics. In 1972, the FDA-appointed committee to study the use of antibiotics in animals recommended curbs on use. Many strains of bacteria are known to be resistant to tetracycline. The use of this antibiotic has caused permanent discoloration of the permanent teeth in children given the drug prior to the eruption of the second teeth. The drug can also cause skin rash, gastrointestinal upsets, and inflammations in the ano-genital area.

CHOLECALCIFEROL • Vitamin D$_3$. White crystals used as a dietary supplement and nutrient in breakfast cereals, grain products, margarine, milk, milk products, and pasta. Poison by ingestion and may cause birth defects. GRAS.

CHOLESTEROL • A fat-soluble, crystalline steroid alcohol (*see*) occurring in all animal fats and oils, nervous tissue, egg yolk, and blood. Used as an emulsifier and lubricant in brilliantine hairdressings, eye creams, shampoos, and other cosmetics products. It is important in metabolism but has been implicated as contributing to hardening of the arteries and subsequently heart attacks. Nontoxic to the skin.

CHOLIC ACID • A colorless or white crystalline powder that occurs in the bile of most vertebrates and is used as an emulsifying agent in dried egg whites and as a choleretic to regulate the secretion of bile. Bitter taste; sweetish aftertaste. No known toxicity. The final report to the FDA of the Select Committee on GRAS Substances stated in 1980 that it should continue its GRAS status with no limitations other than good manufacturing practices. There is no reported use of the chemical and no toxicology information is available.

CHOLINE • A syrupy liquid included in the B complex. It is a base widely distributed among plant and animal products. It is either free or in combination with lecithin. It is essential in the metabolism of fat, especially in the liver, and it is used in the form of salts to treat liver disease. It is also used to feed animals, especially poultry.

CHOLINE BITARTRATE • A dietary supplement included in the B complex and found in the form of a thick, syrupy liquid in most animal tissue. It is necessary to nerve function and fat metabolism and can be manufactured in the body but not at a sufficient rate to meet health requirements. Dietary choline protects against poor growth, fatty liver, and renal damage in many animals. Choline deficiency has not been demonstrated in man, but the National Academy of Sciences lists five hundred to nine hundred milligrams per day as sufficient for the average man. The final report to the FDA of the Select Committee on GRAS Substances stated in 1980 that it should continue its GRAS status with no limitations other than good manufacturing practices. The FDA data bank, PAFA (see page 10), has fully up-to-date toxicology information.

CHOLINE CHLORIDE • Ferric Choline Citrate. A dietary supplement with the same function as choline bitartrate (*see*). The final report to the FDA of the Select Committee on GRAS Substances stated in 1980 that it should continue its GRAS status with no limitations other than good manufacturing practices. The FDA data bank, PAFA, was, as of this writing, conducting a search of the toxicology literature concerning this additive.

CHOLINE HYDROCHLORIDE • Colorless to white, water-absorbing crystals used as a fungicide on various feeds. On the Community Right-to-Know List (*see*). Moderately toxic to humans by ingestion. May be mutagenic.

CHONDRUS • *See* Carrageenan.

CHYMOSIN ENZYME • Prepared from *E. coli* K-12. Used as a stabilizer and thickener. GRAS.

CINCHONA EXTRACT • The extract of the bark of various species of cinchona cultivated in Java, India, and South America. A natural flavoring, *red cinchona bark* is used in bitters, fruit, rum, vermouth, and spice flavorings for beverages, ice cream, ices, candy, liquors, and bitters (1,000 ppm). *Yellow cinchona bark* is a natural flavoring from the bark of a species of South American tree used in bitters, fruit, and vermouth flavorings for liquors and bitters. The yellow extract is used as a bitters flavoring for beverages. Quinine is derived from it. May rarely cause allergies. The FDA data bank, PAFA (see page 10), has not yet conducted a toxicology literature search for this additive.

CINENE • *See* d-Limonene.

CINEOLE • The FDA data bank, PAFA, has up-to-date toxicology information available on this additive. *See* Eucalyptol.

CINNAMAL • *See* Cinnamaldehyde.

CINNAMALDEHYDE • Cinnamic Aldehyde. A synthetic yellowish, oily liquid with a strong odor of cinnamon isolated from a wood-rotting fungus. Occurs naturally in cassia bark extract, cinnamon bark, and root oils. Used in cola, apple, cherry, liquor, rum, nut, pecan, spice, cinnamon, vanilla, and cream soda flavorings for beverages, ice cream, ices, candy, baked goods, chewing gum (4,900 ppm), condiments, and meats. Also used in the perfume industry and to flavor mouthwash and toothpaste. Also to scent powder and hair tonic. It is irritating to the skin and mucous membranes, especially if undiluted. Can cause inflammation and erosion of the gastrointestinal tract. One of the most common allergens. GRAS. The FDA data bank, PAFA, has up-to-date toxicology information available on this additive.

CINNAMALDEHYDE ETHYLENE GLYCOL ACETAL • Spice, cassia, cinnamon, and clove flavoring agent for beverages, ice cream, ices, candy, baked goods, chewing gum, and condiments. The FDA data bank, PAFA, has up-to-date information available on this additive. *See* Cinnamaldehyde for toxicity.

CINNAMEIN • *See* Benzyl Cinnamate.

CINNAMIC ACID • A cherry, honey, spice, cassia, and cinnamon flavoring agent for beverages, ice cream, ices, candy, baked goods, and chewing gum. Also used in suntan lotions and perfumes. Occurs in storax, balsam Peru, cinnamon leaves, and coca leaves. Usually isolated from wood-rotting fungus. Used mainly in the perfume industry. It may cause allergic skin rashes. The FDA data bank, PAFA (see page 10), has up-to-date toxicology information available.

CINNAMIC ALCOHOL • Fragrance ingredient. One of the most common allergens in fragrances and flavorings. Used in mouthwashes, toilet soaps, toothpastes, and sanitary napkins. *See* Cinnamaldehyde.

CINNAMIC ALDEHYDE • Found in cinnamon oil, cassia oil, cinnamon powder, patchouli oil, flavoring agents, toilet soaps, and perfumes. It cross-reacts with balsam of Peru and benzoin. May cause depigmentation and hives.

CINNAMON (CEYLON, CHINESE, SAIGON) • Obtained from the dried bark of cultivated trees. *See* Cinnamaldehyde for toxicity. Used in bitters, cola, apple, plum, vermouth, sausage, eggnog, cinnamon, and vanilla flavorings for beverages, ice cream, ices, candy (4,000 ppm), baked goods (1,900 ppm), condiments, meats, and apple butter. Used to flavor toothpaste and mouthwash and to scent hair tonic and powder. Extracts have been used to break up intestinal gas and to treat diarrhea, but can be irritating to the gastrointestinal system. GRAS. The FDA data bank, PAFA (see page 10), has not yet done a toxicology literature search.

CINNAMON BARK • Extract and Oil. From the dried bark of cultivated trees, the *extract* is used in cola, eggnog, root beer, cinnamon, and ginger ale flavorings for beverages, ice cream, baked goods, condiments, and meats. The *oil* is used in berry, cola, cherry, rum, root beer, cinnamon, and ginger ale flavorings for beverages, condiments, and meats. Can be a skin sensitizer in humans and cause mild sensitivity to light. The FDA data bank, PAFA, has not yet done a toxicology literature search on this additive.

CINNAMON LEAF OIL • Oil of Cassia. Chinese Cinnamon. Yellowish to brown volatile oil from the leaves and twigs of cultivated trees. About 80 to 90 percent cinnamal. It has the characteristic odor and taste of cassia cinnamon and darkens and thickens upon aging or exposure to air. Used in cola, apricot, rum, root beer, cinnamon and ginger ale flavorings for beverages, ice cream, ices, candy, baked goods, chewing gum, gelatin desserts, condiments, pickles, and sliced fruits. Cinnamon oil is used to scent perfumes and as a flavoring in dentifrices. Can cause contact dermatitis. The FDA data bank, PAFA, has not yet done a toxicology literature search.

CINNAMYL ACETATE • A synthetic flavoring, colorless to yellow liquid with a sweet floral odor. Occurs naturally in cassia bark. Used in apricot, cherry, grape, peach, pineapple, cinnamon, and vanilla flavorings for beverages, ice cream, ices, candy, baked goods, chewing gum, and condiments. Can cause allergic reactions. The FDA data bank, PAFA (see page 10), has fully up-to-date toxicology information available.

CINNAMYL ALCOHOL • A synthetic flavoring, white to slightly yellow liquid with a balsamic odor. Occurs in storax, balsam Peru, cinnamon leaves, and hyacinth oil. Used in raspberry, strawberry, apricot, peach, plum, prune, grape, liquor, brandy, nut, black walnut, spice, and cinnamon flavorings for beverages, ice cream, ices, candy, baked goods, chewing gum, gelatin desserts, and brandy. Used also in synthetic perfumes and in deodorants. Can cause allergic reactions. The FDA data bank, PAFA, has fully up-to-date toxicology information available.

CINNAMYL ANTHRANILATE • A synthetic flavoring agent and fragrance ingredient used since the 1940s as an imitation grape or cherry flavor. It is used as a fragrance in soaps, detergents, creams, lotions, and perfumes. U.S. sales equaled more than two thousand pounds in 1976. The National Cancer Institute reported on December 20, 1980, that it caused liver cancer in male and female mice and caused both kidney and pancreatic cancers in male rats in feeding studies. Earlier studies showed it increased lung tumors in mice. The FDA banned the use of it in food in 1982. Most companies voluntarily stopped using it in cosmetics after publication of the NCI information. It has not been banned.

CINNAMYL BENZOATE • A synthetic butter, caramel, and fruit flavoring agent for beverages, ice cream, ices, candy, baked goods, condiments, and chewing gum. The FDA data bank, PAFA (see page 10), has fully up-to-date toxicology information available.

CINNAMYL BUTYRATE • A synthetic citrus orange and fruit flavoring for beverages, ice cream, ices, candy, baked goods, and chewing gum. The FDA data bank, PAFA, has fully up-to-date toxicology information available.

CINNAMYL CINNAMATE • A synthetic fruit flavoring agent for beverages, ice cream, ices, candy, and baked goods. The FDA data bank, PAFA, has fully up-to-date toxicology information available.

CINNAMYL FORMATE • Formic Acid. A synthetic flavoring, colorless to yellow liquid with a faint cinnamon odor. Used in banana, cherry, pear, and spice flavorings for beverages, ice cream, ices, candy, baked goods, and chewing gum. The FDA data bank, PAFA, has fully up-to-date toxicology information available. *See* Formic Acid for toxicity.

CINNAMYL ISOBUTYRATE • A synthetic strawberry, citrus, apple, banana, grape, peach, pear, and pineapple flavoring agent for beverages, ice cream, ices, candy, baked goods, gelatin desserts, chewing gum, and toppings. The FDA data bank, PAFA, has fully up-to-date toxicology information available.

CINNAMYL ISOVALERATE • A synthetic flavoring, colorless to yellow liquid with a spicy, fruity-floral odor. Used in strawberry, chocolate, apple, apricot, cherry, grape, maple nut, nut, spice, peach, pineapple, and plum flavorings for beverages, ice cream, ices, candy, baked goods, chewing gum, and gelatin desserts. The FDA data bank, PAFA (see page 10), has fully up-to-date toxicology information available.

CINNAMYL PHENYLACETATE • A synthetic flavoring, colorless to yellow liquid with a fruity-floral odor. Used in berry, apple, chocolate, currant, grape, peach, pear, and pineapple flavorings for beverages, ice cream, ices, candy, and baked goods. The FDA data bank, PAFA, has fully up-to-date toxicology information available.

CINNAMYL PROPIONATE • A synthetic flavoring, colorless to yellow liquid with a fruity-floral odor. Used in berry, apple, chocolate, currant, grape, peach, pear, and pineapple flavorings for beverages, ice cream, ices, candy, baked goods, chewing gum, and gelatin desserts. The FDA data bank, PAFA, has fully up-to-date toxicology information available.

CINNCLOVAL • *See* Cinnamaldehyde Ethylene Glycol Acetal.

CINOXATE • *See* Cinnamic Acid.

CIRE D'ABEILLE ABSOLUTE • *See* Beeswax, Bleached.

CITRAL • A light, oily liquid that occurs naturally in grapefruit, orange, peach, ginger, grapefruit oil, oil of lemon, and oil of lime. Either isolated from citral oils or made synthetically. Used in strawberry, lemon, lime, orange, apple, cherry, grape, spice, ginger, and vanilla flavorings for beverages, ice cream, ices, candy, baked goods, and chewing gum. Used in perfumes, soaps, and colognes for its lemon and verbena scents. Also used in the synthesis of vitamin A. Causes discoloration of white soaps. Found also in detergents and furniture polish. The compound has been reported to inhibit wound healing and tumor rejection in animals. Vitamin A counteracts its toxicity, but in commercial products to which pure citral has been added, vitamin A may not be present. The FDA data bank, PAFA (see page 10), has fully up-to-date toxicology information available. GRAS.

CITRAL DIMETHYL ACETAL • A synthetic citrus, lemon, and fruit flavoring agent for beverages, ices, candy, and condiments. The FDA data bank, PAFA, has fully up-to-date toxicology information available.

CITRATE, CALCIUM • *See* Calcium Citrate.

CITRATE, ISOPROPYL • *See* Isopropyl Citrate.

CITRATE, MONOGLYCERIDE • *See* Monoglyceride Citrate.

CITRATE, SODIUM • *See* Sodium Citrate.

CITRATE, STEARYL • *See* Stearyl Citrate.

CITRATE SALTS • Softening agent for cheese spreads; emulsifier salts to blend pasteurized processed cheeses and cheese foods. Citrates may interfere with the results of laboratory tests including tests for pancreatic function, abnormal liver function, and blood alkalinity-acidity.

CITRIC ACID • One of the most widely used acids in the cosmetics industry, it is derived from citrus fruit by fermentation of crude sugars. It is also extracted from citrus fruits and occurs naturally in coffee and peaches. It is a flavoring for beverages (2,500 ppm), ice cream, ices, candy (4,300 ppm), baked goods, and chewing gum (3,600 ppm). Citric acid is used to neutralize lye employed in peeling vegetables, as an adjuster of acid-alkalinity in fruit juices, wines, jams, jellies, jelly candies, canned fruit, carbonated beverages, frozen fruit, canned vegetables, frozen dairy products, cheese spreads, sherbet, confections, canned figs, dried egg white, mayonnaise, salad dressing, fruit butter, preserves, and fresh beef blood. Employed in curing meats, for firming peppers, potatoes, tomatoes, and lima beans, and to prevent off-flavors in fried potatoes. Removes trace metals and brightens color in various commercial products. Employed as a preservative, sequestering agent (*see*) to adjust acid-alkali balance; as a foam inhibitor and plasticizer in cosmetics; and as an astringent alone or in astringent compounds. Among the cosmetics products in which it is frequently found are freckle and nail bleaches, bath preparations, skin fresheners, cleansing creams, depilatories, eye lotions, hair colorings, hair rinses, and hair-waving preparations. The clear, crystalline, water-absorbing chemicals are also used to prevent scurvy, a deficiency disease, and as a refreshing drink with water and sugar added. It has been used to dissolve urinary bladder stones. No known toxicity. The final report to the FDA of the Select Committee on GRAS Substances stated in 1980 that it should continue its GRAS status with no limitations other than good manufacturing practices. The FDA data bank, PAFA (see page 10), has fully up-to-date toxicology information available.

CITRIDIC ACID • *See* Aconitic Acid.

CITROFLEX A-4 • *See* Tributyl Acetylcitrate.

CITRONELLA OIL • A natural food-flavoring extract from fresh grass grown in Asia. It consists of about 60 percent geraniol (*see*), 15 percent citronellol (*see*), and 10 to 15 percent camphene (*see*). Almost colorless with a pleasant odor. Used in citrus, fruit, and ginger ale flavorings for beverages, ice cream, ices, candy, and baked goods. Used in perfumes, toilet waters, and perfumed cosmetics; also an insect repellent. May cause allergic reactions such as stuffy nose, hay fever, asthma, and skin rash when used in cosmetics. When ingested, can cause vomiting, cyanosis, convulsions, damage to intestinal mucosa, and when taken in sufficient amounts, death. The FDA data bank, PAFA, has not yet done a search of the toxicology literature. GRAS.

CITRONELLAL • A synthetic flavoring agent. The chief constituent of citronella oil (*see*). Also found in lemon and lemongrass oils. Colorless liquid with an intense lemon-rose odor. Used in citrus, lemon, cherry, and spice flavorings for beverages, ice cream, ices, candy, baked goods, chewing gum, and gelatin desserts. A milk irritant. The FDA data bank, PAFA (see page 10), has fully up-to-date toxicology information available. *See* Citronella Oil for toxicity.

CITRONELLOL • A synthetic flavoring. Obtained from citronellal, geraniol, geranium rose oil, or citronella oil (*see all*). Colorless liquid with a roselike odor. The *d* form is more oily and is the major ingredient of rhodinol (*see*). Used in berry, citrus, cola, fruit, rose, and floral flavorings for beverages, ice cream, ices, candy, baked goods, chewing gum, and gelatin desserts. Used in perfumes. A mild irritant. The FDA data bank, PAFA, has fully up-to-date toxicology information available. *See* Citronella Oil.

CITRONELLOXY ACETALDEHYDE • A synthetic floral, rose, and fruit flavoring agent for beverages, ice cream, ices, candy, and baked goods. The FDA data bank, PAFA, has fully up-to-date toxicology information available. *See* Citronella Oil for toxicity.

CITRONELLYL ACETATE • A synthetic flavoring agent, colorless liquid with a fruity odor. Used in lemon, rose, apricot, banana, grape, pear, and raisin flavorings for beverages, ice cream, ices, candy, baked goods, chewing gum, and gelatin desserts. A major ingredient of rhodinyl acetate (*see*). The FDA data bank, PAFA, has fully up-to-date toxicology information available.

CITRONELLYL BUTYRATE • A synthetic flavoring agent, colorless liquid with a strong fruit-rose odor. Used in cola, floral, rose, apple, pineapple, plum, prune, and honey flavorings for beverages, ice cream, ices, candy, baked goods, chewing gum, and gelatin desserts. A major ingredient of rhodinyl acetate (*see*). The FDA data bank, PAFA (see page 10), has fully up-to-date toxicology information available.

CITRONELLYL FORMATE • Formic Acid. A synthetic flavoring agent, colorless liquid with a strong fruity odor. Used in orange, apple, apricot, peach, plum, and honey flavorings for beverages, ice cream, ices, candy, baked goods. A major ingredient of rhodinyl acetate (*see*). *See* Formic Acid for toxicity. The FDA data bank, PAFA, has fully up-to-date toxicology information available.

CITRONELLYL ISOBUTYRATE • A synthetic flavoring agent, colorless liquid with a rose-fruit odor. Used in raspberry, strawberry, floral, rose, and grape flavorings for beverages, ice cream, ices, candy, baked goods, and gelatin desserts. A major ingredient of rhodinyl acetate (*see*). The FDA data bank, PAFA, has fully up-to-date toxicology information available.

CITRONELLYL PHENYLACETATE • A synthetic butter, caramel, rose, fruit, and honey flavoring agent for beverages, ice cream, ices, candy, and baked goods. A major ingredient of rhodinyl acetate (*see*). The FDA data bank, PAFA, has fully up-to-date toxicology information available.

CITRONELLYL PROPIONATE • A synthetic flavoring agent, colorless liquid with a rose-fruit odor. Used in lemon and fruit flavorings for beverages, ice cream, ices, candy, baked goods, and chewing gum. A major ingredient of rhodinyl acetate (*see*). The FDA data bank, PAFA, has fully up-to-date toxicology information available.

CITRONELLYL VALERATE • A synthetic flavoring agent for beverages, ice cream, ices, candy, and baked goods. The FDA data bank, PAFA (see page 10), has fully up-to-date toxicology information available.

CITRUS BIOFLAVONOIDS • Vitamin P complex nutrient supplement up to one gram per day. Occur naturally in plant colorings and in the tonka bean; also in lemon juice. High concentrates can be obtained from all citrus fruits, rose hips, and black currants. Commercial methods extract rinds of oranges, tangerines, lemons, limes, kumquats, and grapefruit. P vitamin is related to healthy blood vessels and skin. At one time it was thought to prevent colds. Any health claim for bioflavonoids renders the product illegal, according to FDA rules.

CITRUS PEEL EXTRACT • A natural flavor extract from the peel or rind of grapefruit, lemon, lime, orange, and tangerine. Color, odor, and taste characteristic of source. Used as flavoring agents in bitters, lemon, lime, orange, vermouth, beer, and ginger ale flavorings for beverages, ice cream, ices, candy, and baked goods. The FDA data bank, PAFA, has not yet done a search of the toxicology literature for this additive. GRAS.

CITRUS OILS • Eugenol. Eucalyptol. Anethole, a-Irone, Orris, and Menthol (*see all*). Used in flavoring food products and cosmetics and as odorants in special soaps.

CITRUS RED NO. 2 • Monoazo. Used only for coloring orange skins that are not intended for processing, and that meet minimum maturity standards established by or under laws of the states in which the oranges are grown. Used to color Florida but not California oranges. Oranges colored with Citrus Red No. 2 are not supposed to bear more than 2 ppm of the color additive calculated on the weight of the whole fruit. Citrus Red No. 2 toxicity is far from determined even though, theoretically, consumers would not ingest the dye because they peel the orange before eating. The 2-naphthol constituent of the dye if ingested in quantity can cause eye lens clouding, kidney damage, vomiting, and circulatory collapse. May cause allergic reactions and cross-react with clothing, hair dyes, and with sulfanilamides. Application to the skin can cause peeling, and deaths have been reported after application to the skin. The FDA data bank, PAFA (see page 10), has fully up-to-date toxicology information available. *See* FD and C Colors.

CIVET, ABSOLUTE • Flavoring derived from the unctuous secretions from the receptacles between the anus and genitalia of both the male and female civet cat. Semisolid, yellowish to brown mass with an unpleasant odor. Used in raspberry, butter, caramel, grape, and rum flavorings for beverages, ice cream, ices, candy, baked goods, gelatin desserts, and chewing gum. A fixative in perfumery. The FDA data bank, PAFA, has not yet done a toxicology literature search for this additive.

CLARIFICATION • Removal from liquid of small amounts of suspended matter; for example, the removal of particles and traces of copper and iron from vinegar and certain beverages.

CLARIFYING AGENT • A substance that removes from liquids small amounts of suspended matter. Butyl alcohol, for instance, is a clarifying agent for clear shampoos.

CLARY • Clary Sage. A well-known spice in food and beverages. A fixative (*see*) for perfumes. A natural extract of an aromatic herb grown in southern Europe and cultivated widely in England. The herb is a vermouth and spice flavoring agent in vermouth (500 ppm). Clary oil is used in butter, black cherry, grape, licorice, vermouth, wine, root beer, birch beer, spice, vanilla, and cream soda flavorings for beverages, ice cream, ices, candy, baked goods, condiments, and vermouth. The FDA data bank, PAFA (see page 10), has not yet done a toxicology search on this additive.

CLAYS • China Clay. Kaolin. Used to clarify liquids (*see* Clarification) and as a filler for paper. Also used in the manufacture of porcelain and pottery, as an emollient, and as a poultice and gastrointestinal adsorbent. Nontoxic. The final report to the FDA of the Select Committee on GRAS Substances stated in 1980 that it should continue its GRAS status with no limitations other than good manufacturing practices. The FDA data bank, PAFA, has fully up-to-date toxicology information available.

CLOPROSTENOL • Estrumate. An animal drug used to treat infertility in sows and to synchronize estrus in cows.

CLOPYRALID • An herbicide used in animal feed. FDA residue limits are 12 ppm in barley, oats, and wheat (except in their flours) when used for animal feed.

CLOVE BUD EXTRACT • A natural flavor extract from the pungent, fragrant, reddish brown dried flower buds of a tropical tree. Used in berry, fruit, meat, root beer, and spice flavorings for beverages, ice cream, candy, baked goods, condiments, and meats. Cloves are also used as a dental analgesic and germicide. They may cause intestinal upsets. Rats poisoned with clove oil have shown paralysis of hind legs and jaws, with prostration and eventually death. The FDA gave toxicity studies of clove additives top priority in 1980. As of this writing, nothing new has been reported. The FDA data bank, PAFA (see page 10), has fully up-to-date toxicology information available. GRAS.

CLOVE BUD OIL • The volatile, colorless or pale yellow oil obtained by steam distillation from the dried flower buds of a tropical tree. A characteristic clove odor and taste. Used in raspberry, coffee, cola, banana, cherry, peach, plum, rum, sausage, eggnog, pecan, and root beer flavorings for beverages, ice cream, ices, candy, baked goods, chewing gum (1,800 ppm), gelatin desserts, meats, liquors, spiced fruit (830 ppm), jelly, and condiments. Used as an antiseptic and flavoring in tooth powders, as a scent in hair tonics, to flavor postage-stamp glue, and as a toothache treatment. It is 82 to 87 percent eugenol (*see*) and has the characteristic clove oil odor and taste. It is strongly irritating to the skin and can cause allergic skin rashes. Its use in perfumes and cosmetics is frowned upon, although in very diluted forms it is innocuous. The final report to the FDA of the Select Committee on GRAS Substances stated in 1980 that it should continue its GRAS status with no limitations other than good manufacturing practices. The FDA data bank, PAFA (see page 10), has not yet done a toxicology literature search for this additive.

CLOVE BUD OLEORESIN • A natural resinous, viscous flavoring extract from the tree that produces clove buds. Used in fruit, meat, and spice flavorings for meat. The FDA data bank, PAFA, has not yet done a toxicology search for this additive. *See* Clove Bud Extract for toxicity.

CLOVE LEAF OIL • The volatile, pale yellow oil obtained by steam distillation of the leaves of the tropical tree that produces clove buds. Used in loganberry, cherry, root beer, sarsaparilla, and cinnamon flavorings for beverages, ice cream, ices, candy, baked goods, chewing gum, gelatin desserts, meats, pickles, apple butter, and condiments. *See* Clove Bud Extract for toxicity. The final report to the FDA of the Select Committee on GRAS Substances stated in 1980 that it should continue its GRAS status with no limitations other than good manufacturing practices. The FDA data bank, PAFA, has not yet done a toxicology search for this additive.

CLOVE STEM OIL • The volatile, yellow to light brown oil obtained by steam distillation from the dried stems of the tropical tree that produces clove buds. Characteristic odor and taste of cloves. Used in berry, cherry, root beer, ginger ale, and ginger beer flavorings for beverages, ice cream, ices, candy, baked goods, and condiments. *See* Clove Bud Extract for toxicity. The final report to the FDA of the Select Committee on GRAS Substances stated in 1980 that it should continue its GRAS status with no limitations other than good manufacturing practices.

CLOVER • An herb, a natural flavoring extract from a plant characterized by three leaves and flower in dense heads. Used in fruit flavorings for beverages, ice cream, ices, candy, and baked goods. May cause sensitivity to light. GRAS. There is no reported use of the chemical and no toxicology information is available, according to the FDA.

CLOVER BLOSSOM EXTRACT • Trifolium Extract. The extract of the flowers of *Trifolium pratense*. Used in fruit flavorings. May cause sensitivity to light. There is no reported use of the chemical and no toxicology information is available, according to the FDA.

CLOVERLEAF OIL • Eugenia Caryophyllus Leaf Oil. The volatile oil obtained by steam distillation of the leaves of *Eugenia caryophyllus*. It consists mostly of eugenol (*see*). The FDA data bank, PAFA (see page 10), has not yet done a toxicology literature search on this additive.

CLOVES • *Eugenia caryophyllata*. An evergreen tree, the clove is native to the Spice Islands and the Philippines and is cultivated in India, South America, the West Indies, and other tropical areas. The oldest medical use was in China, where it was taken for various ailments as early as 240 B.C. Medicinally, herbalists use cloves to treat flatulence, diarrhea, and liver, stomach, and bowel ailments. It is also used as a stimulant for nerves. Clove oil is still sold in modern drugstores as a treatment for toothaches. Clove tea with mace is used in a tea for nausea. In 1992, the FDA proposed a ban on clove oil in astringent (*see*) drug products because it has not been shown to be safe and effective for its stated claims. The FDA data bank, PAFA, has not yet done a toxicology literature search on this additive.

CLOXACILLIN • Alcloxa. Apo-Cloxi. Austrastaph. Bactopen. Cloxapen. Novocloxin. Orbenin. Orbenin Injection. Tegopen. A penicillin antibiotic introduced in 1962 for systemic infections caused by penicillinase-producing staphylococci (*see* Staphybiotic). It is used in cattle. The FDA says residues in meat of cattle should not exceed 0.01 ppm. In humans, it may cause lung problems, nausea, vomiting, gastric distress, diarrhea, hypersensitivity including potentially fatal allergic reaction, liver problems, and overgrowth of nonsusceptible organisms.

COAL TAR • Used in adhesives, creosotes, insecticides, phenols, woodworking, preservation of food, synthetic flavors, and dyes to make colors used in cosmetics, including hair dyes. Thick liquid or semisolid tar obtained from bituminous coal, it contains many constituents including benzene, xylenes, naphthalene, pyridine, quinolineoline, phenol, and cresol. The main concern about coal-tar derivatives is that they cause cancer in animals, but they are also frequent sources of allergic reactions, particularly skin rashes and hives.

COBALT SOURCES • Carbonate, Chloride, Gluconate, and Sulfate. Cobalt is a metal occurring in the earth's crust; gray, hard, and magnetic. All here are used as a mineral supplement at the rate of one milligram per day. It is used as a nutrient in animal feed. Excess administration can result in an overproduction of red blood cells and gastrointestinal upset. In the 1960s, it was discovered that cobalt salts added to beer to maintain the head caused serious heart problems in beer drinkers. Cobalt sulfate has been banned. GRAS.

COCA LEAF EXTRACT (DECOCAINIZED) • Flavoring from the dried leaves of cocaine-containing plants grown in Bolivia, Brazil, Peru, and Java. Used in bitters and cola flavoring for beverages, ice cream, ices, and candy. Once a central nervous system stimulant. The FDA data bank, PAFA (see page 10), has not yet done a toxicology literature search on this additive. GRAS.

COCCIDIOSIS • A group of diseases due to coccidia, one-celled animals that cause serious infections in many species of animals. It is rare in humans except in persons suffering from AIDS.

COCCIDIOSTAT • A drug generally added to animal feed to partially inhibit or delay the development of coccidiosis (*see*).

COCHINEAL • The FDA data bank, PAFA, has fully up-to-date toxicology information available on this additive. It is no longer authorized for use. *See* Carmine.

COCOA • A powder prepared from the roasted and cured kernels of ripe seeds of *Theobroma cacao* and other species of *Theobroma*. A brownish powder with a chocolate odor, it is used as a flavoring. May cause wheezing, rash, and other symptoms of allergy, particularly in children.

COCOA BUTTER SUBSTITUTE FROM COCONUT OIL, PALM KERNEL OIL OR BOTH • The FDA data bank, PAFA (see page 10), says there is no reported use of the additives and no toxicology information is available.

COCOA BUTTER SUBSTITUTE FROM PALM OIL • The FDA data bank, PAFA, is conducting a toxicology literature search, as of this writing.

COCOA EXTRACT • Extract of *Theobroma cacao*. The FDA data bank, PAFA, has not yet done a toxicology literature search on this additive. *See* Cocoa.

COCOAMPHOCARBOXYPROPIONIC ACID • *See* Coconut Oil.

COCOAMPHODIACETATE • Widely used in cosmetics in the manufacture of toilet soaps, creams, lubricants, chocolate, and suppositories. *See* Coconut Oil.

COCOAMPHODIPRIOPIONATE • *See* Coconut Oil.

COCONUT ACIDS • *See* Coconut Oil.

COCONUT ALCOHOLS • *See* Coconut Oil.

COCONUT OIL • The white, semisolid, highly saturated fat expressed from the kernels of the coconut. Used in chocolate, candies, in baking instead of lard, and in self-basting turkeys. A saturated fat that is not recommended for those worried about fat-clogged arteries. No known toxicity. Used in the manufacture of baby soaps, shampoos, shaving lathers, cuticle removers, preshaving lotions, hairdressings, soaps, ointment bases, and massage creams. Stable when exposed to air. Lathers readily and is a fine skin cleaner. Usually blended with other fats. May cause allergic skin rashes. The final report to the FDA of the Select Committee on GRAS Substances stated in 1980 that it should continue its GRAS status with no limitations other than good manufacturing practices. The FDA data bank, PAFA (see page 10), is conducting a toxicology literature search concerning this additive, as of this writing.

COD-LIVER OIL • The fixed oil expressed from fresh livers used in skin ointments and special skin creams to promote healing. Pale yellow with a bland, slightly fishy odor. Contains vitamins A and D, which promote healing of wounds and abscesses. No known toxicity.

COFFEE • Coffee beans. Dry, unroasted seeds of *Coffea arabica*. Contains caffeine (*see*). An essential oil used as a flavoring. GRAS. The FDA data bank, PAFA (see page 10), is conducting a toxicology literature search, as of this writing.

COGNAC OIL • Wine Yeast Oil. The volatile oil obtained from distillation of wine, with the characteristic aroma of cognac. *Green cognac oil* is used as a flavoring for beverages, ice cream, ices, candy, baked goods, chewing gum, liquors, and condiments. *White cognac oil,* which has the same constituents as green oil, is used in berry, cherry, grape, brandy, and rum flavorings for beverages, ice cream, ices, candy, baked goods, and gelatin desserts. No known toxicity. GRAS. The FDA data bank, PAFA, has not yet done a toxicology literature search on this additive.

COLLAGEN • Protein substance found in connective tissue. In cosmetics, it is usually derived from animal tissue. Allergic reactions are not infrequent. The FDA data bank, PAFA, has fully up-to-date toxicology information available.

COLLOIDAL SILICON DIOXIDE • Practically insoluble in water. A free-flowing agent in salt, seasoned salt, and sodium bicarbonate. Also included in vitamin products, dietary products, spices, meat-curing compounds, flavoring powders, dehydrated honey, dehydrated molasses, and dehydrated nondiastatic malt. Percentages range from 1 percent in salt to 2 percent in dehydrated products. Prolonged inhalation of the silicon dust can cause fibrosis of the lungs. Increases susceptibility to tuberculosis. Chemically and biologically inert when ingested. *See* Silicon Dioxide.

COLORING • More than 90 percent of the food colorings now in use are manufactured, frequently from coal-tar colors. The coal-tar derivatives need to be certified, which means that batches of the dyes are chemically tested and approved by the FDA. As more and more food colors are banned, interest has grown in color derived from natural sources such as carotene (*see*) from carrots, which is used to color margarine, and beet juice, which provides a red color for some foods. *See* FD and C Colors for information on the synthetics now in use.

COLORS • *See* FD and C Colors.

COMMUNITY RIGHT-TO-KNOW LIST • Manufacturers that employ toxic chemicals while making products must respond, under the law, to inquiries from employees and citizens in the area. Cyanide, which is used in the manufacture of pesticides and some food additives, is an example of a chemical on this list compiled by the U.S. Environmental Protection Agency.

CONCRETE • A semisolid mixture of essential oil and fatty, waxy material that is obtained by the solvent extraction of flowers or plants followed by solvent removal.

CONDENSED ANIMAL PROTEIN HYDROLYSATE • A feed used for poultry and cattle.

CONTACT DERMATITIS • *See* Allergic Contact Dermatitis.

COPAIBA OIL • Jesuits' Balsam. From steam distillation of South American balsam, *Copaifera l.* It is a yellow liquid with an aromatic odor and slightly bitter taste. It is used as a flavoring agent in various food. The FDA data bank, PAFA (see page 10), has not as yet done a toxicology literature search on this additive.

COPALS, MANILA • A resin obtained as a fossil or as an exudate from various species of tropical plants. Must be heated in alcohol or other solvents. May cause allergic reactions, particularly skin rashes. Although allowed as a food additive, there is no current reported use of the chemical, and therefore, although toxicology information may be available, it is not being updated by the FDA.

COPOLYMER • Result of polymerization (*see* Polymer) that includes at least two different molecules, each of which is capable of polymerizing alone. Together they form a new, distinct molecule. They are used in the manufacture of nail enamels and face masks.

COPOLYMER CONDENSATES OF ETHYLENE OXIDE AND PROPYLENE OXIDE • Stabilizers in flavor concentrates, processing and wetting agents in yeast-leavened bakery products, dough conditioners, surfactants, defoaming agents, and nutrient supplements in animal feed. No known toxicity.

COPPER • Gluconate, Sulfate. One of the earliest known metals. An essential nutrient for all mammals. Naturally occurring or experimentally produced copper deficiency in animals leads to a variety of abnormalities including anemia, skeletal defects, and muscle degeneration. Copper deficiency is extremely rare in man. The body of an adult contains from 75 to 150 milligrams of copper. Concentrations are highest in the brain, liver, and heart. A copper intake of two milligrams per day appears to maintain a balance in adults. An ordinary diet provides two to five milligrams daily. Copper is nontoxic, but soluble copper salts, notably copper sulfate, are highly irritating to the skin and mucous membranes and, when ingested, cause serious vomiting. Copper salts include copper carbonate, chloride, gluconate, hydroxide, orthophosphate, oxide, pyrophosphate, and sulfate. The final report to the FDA of the Select Committee on GRAS Substances stated in 1980 that it should continue its GRAS status with no limitations other than good manufacturing practices. The FDA data bank, PAFA (see page 10), has not yet done a toxicology literature search for this additive.

COPRA OIL • From the kernel of the fruit of the coconut palm, *Cocos nucifera.* Fatty solid or liquid with a sweet, nutty taste. Used as a coating agent, emulsifying agent, and as a texturizer in baked goods, candy, desserts, and margarine. Nontoxic. GRAS.

CORIANDER OIL • The colorless or pale yellow volatile oil from the dried ripe fruit of a plant grown in Asia and Europe. Used as a flavoring agent in raspberry, bitters, fruit, meat, spice, ginger ale, and vanilla flavorings for beverages, ice cream, ices, candy, baked goods (880 ppm), chewing gum, meats (1,300 ppm), liquors (1,000 ppm), and condiments. Used to flavor dentifrices. The *oil* is used in blackberry, raspberry, chocolate, coffee, cola, fruit, liquor, sausage, root beer, spice, ginger ale, and vanilla flavorings for beverages, ice cream, ices, candy, baked goods, chewing gum, condiments, meats, and liquors. Can cause allergic reactions, particularly of the skin. Coriander is used as a weak medication (up to one gram) to break up intestinal gas. GRAS. The FDA data bank, PAFA, has not yet done a toxicology literature search on this additive.

CORK, OAK • Flavoring in alcoholic beverages only. The FDA data bank, PAFA (see page 10), has not yet done a toxicology literature search on this additive.

CORN • Corn Sugar. Dextrose. Used in maple, nut, and root beer flavorings for beverages, ice cream, ices, candy, and baked goods. The *oil* is used in emollient creams and toothpastes. The *syrup* is used as a texturizer and carrying agent in cosmetics. It is also used for envelopes, stamps, sticker tapes, ale, aspirin, bacon, baking mixes, powders, beers, bourbon, breads, cheeses, cereals, chop suey, chow mein, confectioners' sugar, cream puffs, fish products, ginger ale, hams, jellies, processed meats, peanut butters, canned peas, plastic food wrappers, sherbets, whiskeys, and American wines. It may also be found in capsules, lozenges, ointments, suppositories, vitamins, fritters, Fritos, frostings, canned or frozen fruit, graham crackers, gravies, grits, gum, monosodium glutamate, Nescafé, oleomargarine, pablum, paper, peanut butter, tortillas, vinegar, yeasts, bologna, baking powders, bath powders, frying fats, fruit juices, and laxatives. May cause allergic reactions including skin rashes and asthma.

CORN ACID • *See* Corn Oil.

CORN COB MEAL • The milled powder prepared from the cobs of *Zea mays*.

CORN DEXTRIN • Dextri-Maltose. A white or yellow powder obtained by enzymatic action of barley malt on corn flours, used as a modifier or thickening agent in milk and milk products. Nontoxic. The final report to the FDA of the Select Committee on GRAS Substances stated in 1980 that it should continue its GRAS status with no limitations other than good manufacturing practices.

CORN ENDOSPERM OIL • Used in chicken feed to enhance yellow color of chicken skin and eggs. Permanently listed since 1967.

CORN FLOUR • A finely ground powder. Used in face and bath powder. *See* Corn Oil.

CORN GERM EXTRACT • The extract of the germ of *Zea mays*.

CORN GLUTEN • A nutrient supplement for various foods.

CORN OIL • Light yellow, clear, oily liquid used as a coating agent, emulsifying agent, and texturizer in bakery products, margarine, mayonnaise, and salad oil. Also used in emollient creams and toothpastes. Obtained as a byproduct by wet-milling of the grain for use in the manufacture of corn starch, dextrins, and yellow oil. It has a faint characteristic odor and taste and thickens upon exposure to air. Human skin irritant and allergen. Has caused birth defects in experimental animals. GRAS.

CORN POPPY EXTRACT • The extract obtained from the petals of the *Papaver rhoeas*.

CORN SILK • Used as a natural flavoring extract in baked goods, baking mixes, beverages, soft candies, and frozen dairy desserts. The final report to the

FDA of the Select Committee on GRAS Substances stated in 1980 that there were insufficient biological and other studies upon which to base an evaluation when it is used as a food ingredient. It remains GRAS. The FDA data bank, PAFA (see page 10), has not yet done a toxicology search for this additive.

CORN SUGAR • *See* Corn Syrup.

CORN SYRUP • Corn Sugar. Dextrose. A sweet syrup prepared from cornstarch. Used in maple, nut, and root beer flavorings for beverages, ice cream, ices, candy, and baked goods. Also used for envelopes, stamps, sticking tapes, aspirin, and many food products including bacon, baking mixes, powders, beer, bourbon, breads, cereals, pastries, candy, carbonated beverages, catsups, cheeses, chop suey, chow mein, confectioners' sugar, cream puffs, fish products, ginger ale, hams, jellies, processed meats, peanut butter, canned peas, plastic food wraps, sherbet, whiskey, and American wines. May cause allergic reactions. The final report to the FDA of the Select Committee on GRAS Substances stated in 1980 that there is no available evidence that it is a hazard to the public when used as it is now and it should continue in GRAS status with no limitations on amounts that can be added to food. The FDA data bank, PAFA (see page 10), has fully up-to-date toxicology information available.

CORNSTARCH • Many containers are powdered with cornstarch to prevent sticking. The dietetic grade is marketed as Maizena and Mondamin. It is an absorbent dusting powder and a demulcent for irritated colons. May cause allergic reactions, including skin rashes and asthma. The final report to the FDA of the Select Committee on GRAS Substances stated in 1980 that it should continue its GRAS status with no limitations other than good manufacturing practices.

CORPS PRALINE • *See* Maltol.

COSTMARY • Virgin Mary. A natural flavoring derived from an herb native to Asia. Its yellow aromatic flowers are shaped like buttons. Used as a pot herb and salad plant. Infrequently used today as a flavoring in beer and ale. Regarded as sacred to the Virgin Mary. There is no reported use of the chemical and no toxicology information is available, according to the FDA.

COSTUS ROOT OIL • The volatile oil is obtained by steam distillation from dried roots of an herb. Light yellow to brown, viscous liquid with a persistent violetlike odor. A natural fruit and vanilla flavoring for beverages, ice cream, ices, candy, baked goods, chewing gum, and gelatin desserts. The FDA data bank, PAFA (see page 10), has fully up-to-date toxicology information available.

COTTONSEED FLOUR • Cooked, partly defatted, and toasted flour used for pale yellow coloring. Sometimes used to make gin. It is permanently listed as a coloring. It is known to cause allergies, and because it is used in a wide variety of products without notice, it may be hard to avoid. More often, exposure to the allergens arises from the use of *cottonseed meal,* which may be found in fertilizers and in feed for cattle, hogs, poultry, and dogs. Symptoms usually result from inhalation, but allergic reactions can also occur from ingesting cottonseed meal used in pan-greasing compounds and in foods such as some fried cakes, fig bars, and cookies. The FDA data bank, PAFA (see page 10), has fully up-to-date toxicology information available.

COTTONSEED OIL • The fixed oil from the seeds of the cultivated varieties of the plant. Pale yellow, oily, odorless liquid used in the manufacture of soaps, creams, baby creams, nail-polish removers, and lubricants. The oil is used in most salad oils, oleomargarines, mayonnaises, salad dressings. Lard compounds and lard substitutes are made with cottonseed oil. Sardines may be packed in it. Most commercial fried products such as potato chips and doughnuts are fried in cottonseed oil, and restaurants use it for cooking. Candies, particularly chocolates, often contain this oil and it is used to polish fruits at stands. It is used in baby creams, soaps, creams, nail-polish removers, and lubricants. It is also used in cotton wadding or batting in cushions, comforters, mattresses, and upholstery, and in varnishes, fertilizers, and animal feeds. Known to cause many allergic reactions, but because of its wide use in cosmetics, foods, and other products, it is hard to avoid.

COUCHGRASS • *See* Dog Grass Extract.

COUMAPHOS • Agridip. Asunthol. Baymix 50. Used in animal feed as an insecticide and to counteract worms. Poison by ingestion, skin contact, inhalation, and injection. May be a mutagen.

COUMARIN • Tonka Bean. Cumarin. A fragrant ingredient of tonka beans, sweet woodruff, cramp bark, and many other plants. It is made synthetically as well. Used in over 300 products in the United States, including acne preparations, antiseptics, deodorants, "skin fresheners," hair dyes, and shampoos. It has been widely used as a fragrance in soaps, detergents, perfumes, and sunscreens. May produce allergic contact dermatitis (*see*) and photosensitivity (*see*). It has anti–blood clotting effects, and anticlotting agents are derived from it. Coumarin is prohibited in foods because it is toxic by ingestion and carcinogenic. No known toxicity on the skin.

COUMARONE-INDENE RESIN • Coating for fruit. FDA limits it to 200 ppm on fresh-weight basis. The FDA data bank, PAFA, has fully up-to-date toxicology information available.

CRANBERRY JUICE CONCENTRATE • Bright red coloring from the juice of the red acid berry, produced by any of several plants of the genus *Vaccinium* grown in the U.S. and Europe. Food manufacturers may substitute this natural coloring for the synthetic reds that were banned. No known toxicity.

CRANBERRY POMACE • Source of natural red coloring. *See* Anthocyanins.

CREAM OF TARTAR • A white crystalline salt in tartars from wine making, prepared especially from argols and also synthetically from tartaric acid (*see*). Has a pleasant acid taste. Used as a thickening agent and in certain treatments of metals.

CREOSOL • *See* 2-Methoxy-4-Methylphenol.

CREOSOTE • Obtained from wood or tar, either almost colorless or yellowish. Used locally as an antiseptic, internally as an expectorant. It has a smoky odor and a caustic, burning taste. Large doses internally may cause stomach irritation, heart problems, and death. It is also used as a mild insect repellent.

***p*-CRESOL** • A synthetic nut and vanilla flavoring agent. Obtained from coal tar. It occurs naturally in tea and is used for beverages, ice cream, ices, candy, and baked goods. It is more powerful than phenol and less toxic. Phenol is an extremely toxic acid obtained from coal tar that has many industrial uses, including as a disinfectant for toilets and as an anesthetic. The FDA data bank, PAFA (see page 10), has fully up-to-date toxicology information available.

4-CRESOL • *See p*-Cresol.

o-**CRESYL ACETATE** • *See o*-Tolyl Acetate.

p-**CRESYL ACETATE** • *See p*-Tolyl Acetate.

CRETAN DITTANY • *See* Dittany of Crete.

CROCETIN • Yellow coloring from saffron (*see*).

CROCUS EXTRACT • *See* Saffron.

CROSS-REACTIVITY • When the body mistakes one compound for another of similar chemical composition.

CRUFOMATE • An antiworm insecticide from petroleum used on cattle, goats, and sheep. FDA residue tolerance is 1 ppm in meat, fat, and byproducts.

CRYOLITE (SODIUM ALUMINUM FLUORIDE) • A mineral used as an insecticide. The FDA tolerance on fruits and vegetables is 0.7 ppm.

CRYPTOXANTHIN • A natural yellow coloring from corn and marigolds. *See* Xanthophyll.

CUBEBS • *Piper cubeba.* Tailed Pepper. Java Pepper. The mature, unripe, sun-dried fruit of a perennial vine grown in South Asia, Java, Sumatra, the Indies, and Sri Lanka. It has a strong, spicy odor and is used in fruit flavoring for beverages (800 ppm). The *volatile oil* is obtained by steam distillation from the fruit and is colorless to light green with a characteristic spicy odor and a slightly acrid taste. It is used in berry, fruit, and ginger flavorings for beverages, ice cream, ices, candy, baked goods, meats, and condiments. Java pepper was formerly used to stimulate healing of mucous membranes. The fruit has been used as a stimulant and diuretic and is sometimes smoked in cigarettes. The FDA data bank, PAFA, has not yet done a toxicology literature search for the oil. The cubeb alone is not reportedly used and therefore no information is available.

CUCUMBER JUICE • From the succulent fruit of the vine and used as an astringent by many "natural" cosmetics fans. It has a pleasant aroma and imparts a cool feeling to the skin. Nontoxic.

CUMALDEHYDE • *See* Cuminaldehyde.

CUMENEALDEHYDE • Colorless liquid with a floral odor used as a flavoring agent in various foods. Moderately toxic by ingestion. Narcotic in high doses. The FDA data bank, PAFA (see page 10), has fully up-to-date toxicology information available.

CUMIN • Cummin. A natural flavoring obtained from the seeds of an Old World plant. Used in spice and sausage flavorings for baked goods (2,500 ppm), condiments (3,900 ppm), and meats. A *volatile oil,* light yellow to brown, with a strong, disagreeable odor, is distilled from the plant. It is used in berry, fruit, sausage, and spice flavorings for beverages, ice cream, ices, candy, chewing gum, baked goods, meats, pickles, and condiments. Moderately toxic by ingestion and skin contact. A skin irritant. May be mutagenic. GRAS. The FDA data bank, PAFA, has not done a toxicology literature search on this additive.

CUMINAL • *See* Cuminaldehyde.

CUMINALDEHYDE • It is a constituent of eucalyptus, myrrh, cassia, cumin, and other essential oils, but is often made synthetically. Colorless to yellowish, oily, with a strong, lasting odor. It is used as a synthetic flavoring in berry, fruit, and spice flavorings for beverages, ice cream, ices, candy, baked goods, chewing gum, and condiments. Used in perfumery. No known toxicity.

CUMINIC ALDEHYDE • *See* Cuminaldehyde.

CUPRIC ACETATE • The copper salt of acetic acid and copper (*see both*).

CUPRIC CHLORIDE • Copper Chloride. A copper salt used in hair dye. A yellow to brown, water-absorbing powder that is soluble in diluted acids. It is also used in pigments for glass and ceramics and as a feed additive, disinfectant, and wood preservative. Irritating to the skin and mucous membranes. Irritating when ingested, causing vomiting. *See* Copper.

CUPRIC OXIDE • *See* Copper.

CUPRIC SULFATE • Copper sulfate occurs in nature as hydrocyanite. Grayish white to greenish white crystals. Used as an agricultural fungicide, herbicide, and in the preparation of azo dyes (*see*). Used in hair dyes as a coloring. Irritating if ingested. No known toxicity on the skin and used medicinally as a skin fungicide. *See* Copper.

CUPROUS IODIDE • The final report to the FDA of the Select Committee on GRAS Substances stated in 1980 that it should continue its GRAS status with no limitations other than good manufacturing practices. There is no reported use of the chemical and no toxicology information is available. *See* Iodine Sources.

CURACAO PEEL EXTRACT • A natural flavoring extracted from a plant native to the Caribbean island. Used in orange and liquor flavorings for beverages (1,700 ppm). GRAS.

CURACAO PEEL OIL • A natural flavoring extracted from a plant native to the Caribbean island. Used in berry, lime, and liquor flavorings for beverages, ice cream, ices, candy, and baked goods. No known toxicity.

CURCUMIN • The orange-yellow colorant derived from turmeric (*see*) and used as a natural food coloring. It does not require certification because it is a natural product, but the Expert Committee on Food Additives of the FDA recommended that the acceptable daily intake of curcumin (and turmeric) be limited to 0.5 milligrams per kilogram of body weight. Moderately toxic by injection. A skin irritant.

CURING AGENTS • These include salt, nitrites (*see*), and other compounds used to stabilize color, give flavor, and/or preserve.

CURRANT BUDS, ABSOLUTE • A natural flavoring from a variety of small raisins grown principally in Greece. Used in fruit, berry, and raspberry flavorings for beverages, ice cream, ices, candy, and baked goods. No known toxicity. The FDA data bank, PAFA (see page 10), has not yet done a toxicology literature search for this additive.

CURRANTE BLACK, BUDS AND LEAVES • *See* Currant Buds, Absolute.

CUSPARIA BARK • Essential oil from the bark of angostura used as a flavoring. *See* Angostura. GRAS.

CYANAMIDE • Water-absorbing crystals used as a fumigant for uncooked bacon, cereal flours, cereals that are cooked before being eaten, cocoa, uncooked ham, and uncooked sausage. FDA residue tolerances are 125 ppm in cereal flours,

90 ppm in cereals that are cooked before being eaten, 50 ppm in uncooked bacon, ham, and sausage, and 200 ppm in cocoa. The vapor is intensely irritating to lungs. After mild exposure, symptoms may be worsened by ingestion of alcohol.

CYANIDE • Prussic Acid. Hydrocyanic Acid. An inorganic salt, it is one of the most rapid poisons known. Poisoning may occur when any compound releases cyanide. Cyanide is used as a fungistat, insecticide, and rodenticide and is in metal polishes, especially for silver, and in electroplating solutions, art materials, photographic processes, and metallurgy.

CYANO-, CYAN- • From the Greek *kaynos,* meaning a dark blue. The prefix is commonly used to signify compounds containing the cyanide group *CN*. If the cyanide is not released from the compound, its presence is presumed not harmful.

CYANO(4-FLURO-3-PHENOXYPHENYL)METHYL-3-(2,2 DICHLOROETHENYL)-2,2-DIMETHYL-PROPANECARBOXYLATE • An insecticide used in animal feed. *See* Cyanamide.

CYANOCOBALAMIN • *See* Vitamin B$_{12}$.

CYANODITHIOIMIDOCARBONATE, DISODIUM • Bacteria-killing component in the processing of sugarcane. Many organic cyano compounds are decomposed in the body to yield highly toxic cyanide.

CYCLAMATES • Sodium and Calcium. Artificial sweetening agent about thirty times as sweet as refined sugar, removed from the food market on September 1, 1969, because they were found to cause bladder cancer in rats. At that time 175 million Americans were swallowing cyclamates in significant doses in many products ranging from chewing gum to soft drinks.

CYCLAMEN ALDEHYDE • Colorless liquid with a strong floral odor used as a flavoring agent in various food products. Moderately toxic by ingestion. A human skin irritant. GRAS.

CYCLAMIC ACID • Fairly strong acid with a sweet taste. It is the acid from which cyclamates were derived (*see*).

CYCLODEXTRINS • Enzymatically modified starches shaped like doughnuts. The cavity of the molecule repels water and organic compounds can fill the cavity. As a result, caffeine can be removed from tea and coffee, bitter components can be removed from citrus fruits, and flavor oils can be extracted from onion and garlic and other plants. Cyclodextrins can be recovered and reused.

CYCLOHEXANE • Hexamethylene. A hydrocarbon (*see*) solvent widely used in industry in the manufacture of nylon, for cellulose fats, oils, waxes, and resins, and in paint and varnish removers, glass substitutes, and fungicides. Colorless liquid with a pungent odor. It is also used to dilute colors in food. Poison by intravenous route. Moderately toxic by ingestion. A systemic irritant by inhalation and ingestion. A skin irritant. May cause mutations. The FDA data bank, PAFA (see page 10), has fully up-to-date toxicology information available.

CYCLOHEXANE ETHYL ACETATE • A synthetic fruit and honey flavoring for beverages, ice cream, ices, candy, and baked goods. *See* Cyclohexaneacetic Acid for toxicity. The FDA data bank, PAFA, has fully up-to-date toxicology information available.

CYCLOHEXANEACETIC ACID • A synthetic butter and fruit flavoring for beverages, ice cream, ices, candy, and baked goods. Cyclohexane in high concentrations may act as a narcotic and skin irritant. The FDA data bank, PAFA, has fully up-to-date toxicology information available.

CYCLOHEXYL ANTHRANILATE • A synthetic apple, banana, and grape flavoring for beverages, ice cream, ices, candy, baked goods, and gelatin desserts. Some cyclohexyl compounds are irritating to the skin. The FDA data bank, PAFA, has fully up-to-date toxicology information available.

CYCLOHEXYL CINNAMATE • A synthetic apple, apricot, peach, and prune flavoring for beverages, ice cream, ices, candy, and baked goods. Some cyclohexyl compounds are irritating to the skin. The FDA data bank, PAFA (see page 10), has fully up-to-date toxicology information available.

CYCLOHEXYL FORMATE • Formic Acid. A synthetic cherry flavoring for beverages, ice cream, ices, candy, and baked goods. Some cyclohexyl compounds are irritating to the skin. The FDA data bank, PAFA, has fully up-to-date toxicology information available.

CYCLOHEXYL ISOVALERATE • A synthetic strawberry and apple flavoring for beverages, ice cream, ices, candy, and baked goods. Some cyclohexyl compounds are irritating to the skin. The FDA data bank, PAFA, has fully up-to-date toxicology information available.

CYCLOHEXYL PROPIONATE • A synthetic fruit flavoring for beverages, ice cream, ices, candy, and baked goods. Some cyclohexyl compounds are irritating to the skin. The FDA data bank, PAFA, has fully up-to-date toxicology information available.

CYCLOPENADECANOLIDE • *See* Pentadecalactone.

CYFLUTHRIN • An insecticide used in cattle, goats, hogs, and sheep. The FDA limit for residues in meat is 0.05 ppm. Residues in milk, 0.1 ppm.

CYHEXATIN • An insecticide used in animal feed. FDA residue in apple pomace and citrus pulp is 8 ppm.

o-**CYMEN-3-OL** • *See p*-Cymene.

p-**CYMENE** • A synthetic flavoring, a volatile hydrocarbon solvent that occurs naturally in star anise, coriander, cumin, mace oil, oil of mandarin, and origanum oil. Used in fragrances; also in citrus and spice flavorings for beverages, ice cream, candies, and baked goods. Its ingestion pure may cause a burning sensation in the mouth and nausea, salivation, headache, giddiness, vertigo, confusion, and coma. Contact with the pure liquid may cause blisters of the skin and inflammation of mucous membranes. The FDA data bank, PAFA (see page 10), has fully up-to-date toxicology information available.

CYMOL • *See p*-Cymene.

CYMOPHENOL • *See* Carvacrol.

CYNARON • *See* Acimeton.

CYROMAZINE • A pesticide used in poultry feed. The FDA tolerance residue in fat, meat, and meat byproducts of poultry are 0.05 ppm; 0.25 ppm as residue in eggs.

CYSTEINE • L-Form. An essential amino acid (*see*), it is derived from hair and used in hair products and creams. Soluble in water, it is used in bakery products as a nutrient. It has been used to promote wound healing. On the list of FDA additives to be studied. As of this writing, no new evaluation has been made public. GRAS. The FDA data bank, PAFA (see page 10), has fully up-to-date toxicology information available.

CYSTINE • A nonessential amino acid (*see*) found in urine and in horsehair. Colorless, practically odorless, white crystals, it is used as a nutrient supplement and in emollients. On the FDA list for further study. May have reproductive effects. As of this writing, no new evaluation has been made public. GRAS. The FDA data bank, PAFA, has fully up-to-date toxicology information available.

D

2,4-D • (2,4-Dichlorophenoxy)acetic acid. Prepared from phenol and chloroacetic acid (*see both*), it is an herbicide that belongs to the same class as dioxin (*see*) and is widely used by home gardeners and farmers. The FDA permits it as a residue in milled fractions (except flour) derived from barley, oats, rye, and wheat to be ingested as food or to be converted into food or feed. The FDA tolerances for residues are 2 ppm in milled fractions, 1 ppm in potable water in the western United States, and 5 ppm in processed feeds using sugarcane bagasse or molasses. 2,4-D does not cause acute toxicity, but its long-term effects are a matter of controversy and it has been linked to cancer. An excess of non-Hodgkin's lymphoma among farmers has been strongly associated with its use. It does cause eye irritation and gastrointestinal upsets.

DAILY VALUE (DV) • Substituted for the percentage of U.S. Recommended Dietary Allowances (*see*). It is a guideline based on the daily needs of the general population. The percentages are supposed to help you compare the nutrients in a particular food with dietary recommendations that help reduce risk for some chronic diseases.

DALAPON • 2,2-Dichloropropanoic acid. Used as an herbicide in citrus pulp for cattle feed. FDA tolerance is 20 ppm.

DAMIANA LEAVES • The dried leaves of a plant of California and Texas used as a flavoring. Formerly used as a tonic and aphrodisiac. The FDA data bank, PAFA, has not yet done a toxicology literature search on this additive.

DAMMAR • Resin used to produce a gloss and adhesion in nail lacquer. It is a yellowish white, semitransparent exudate from a plant grown in the East Indies and the Philippines. Comes in varying degrees of hardness. It has a bitter taste. Also used for preserving animal and vegetable specimens for science laboratories. May cause allergic contact dermatitis. The FDA data bank, PAFA (see page 10), has not yet done a toxicology literature search for this additive.

DANDELION LEAF AND ROOT • Lion's Tooth. Used as a skin-refreshing bath additive. Obtained from *Taraxacum* plants, which grow abundantly in the U.S. The common dandelion weed eaten as a salad green was used by the Indians for heartburn. Rich in vitamins A and C, it is also used as a flavoring. Dandelion coffee is made from the dried roots of the plant. The *root extract* is used in bitters, butter, caramel, floral, fruit, root beer, and vanilla flavorings for beverages, ice cream, ices, candy, and baked goods. The *fluid extract* is used in butter, caramel, fruit, maple, and vanilla flavorings for beverages, ice cream, ices, candy, and baked goods. The FDA's data bank, PAFA (see page 10), has not yet done a toxicology search on this additive. GRAS.

DAUCUS CAROTA • *See* Carrot Oil.

DAVANA OIL • A plant extract used in fruit flavorings for beverages, ice cream, ices, candy, baked goods, and chewing gum. The FDA's data bank, PAFA, has not yet done a toxicology search on this additive.

DDVP • *See* Dichlorvos.

o-**DECALACTONE** • A synthetic flavoring agent. Occurs naturally in butter, cream, and milk. Colorless with a fruity odor. Used in coconut and fruit flavorings for beverages, ice cream, ices, candy, baked goods, oleomargarine (10 ppm), and toppings. The FDA data bank, PAFA, has fully up-to-date toxicology information available on this additive.

γ-**DECALACTONE** • A synthetic flavoring agent, colorless, with a fruity odor, used in citrus, orange, coconut, and fruit flavorings for beverages, ice cream, ices, candy, baked goods, and gelatin desserts. The FDA data bank, PAFA, has fully up-to-date toxicology information available on this additive.

DECANAL • A synthetic flavoring agent. Occurs naturally in sweet orange peel, sweet mandarin oil, grapefruit oil, orris, and coriander. Colorless to light yellow with a definite fatlike odor that becomes florallike when diluted. Used in berry, citrus, lemon, orange, fruit, and honey flavorings for beverages, ice cream, ices, candy, baked goods, chewing gum, and gelatin desserts. Moderately toxic by ingestion. A severe skin irritant. The FDA data bank, PAFA (see page 10), has fully up-to-date toxicology information available on this additive. GRAS.

DECANAL DIMETHYL ACETAL • A synthetic flavoring agent. Occurs naturally in anise, butter acid, oil of lemon, and oil of lime. Used in butter, coconut, fruit, liquor, whiskey, and cheese flavorings for beverages, ice cream, ices, candy, baked goods, chewing gum, and gelatin desserts. No known toxicity. The FDA data bank, PAFA, has fully up-to-date toxicology information available on this additive. GRAS.

DECANOIC ACID • A synthetic flavoring agent that occurs naturally in anise, butter acids, oil of lemon, and oil of lime and is used to flavor butter, coconut, fruit, liquor, and cheese flavorings for beverages, ice cream, ices, candy, baked goods, chewing gum, gelatin desserts, puddings, and shortenings. Poisonous by intravenous route. A skin irritant. May be mutagenic. The FDA data bank, PAFA, has fully up-to-date toxicology information available on this additive.

1-DECANOL • A synthetic flavoring agent. Occurs naturally in orange and ambrette seed. Used in butter, lemon, orange, coconut, and fruit flavorings for beverages, ice cream, ices, candy, baked goods, and chewing gum. The FDA data bank, PAFA, has fully up-to-date toxicology information available on this additive.

DECANYL ACETATE • *See* Decyl Acetate.

2-DECENAL • A synthetic fruit flavoring for beverages, ice cream, ices, candy, and baked goods. Moderately toxic by skin contact and mildly toxic by ingestion. A severe skin irritant. The FDA data bank, PAFA (see page 10), has fully up-to-date toxicology information available on this additive.

DECENALDEHYDE • *See* 2-Decenal.

DECOQUINATE • Decox. An animal antifungal drug used in beef, chicken, and goat. FDA residue limits are 2 ppm in uncooked edible tissues other than muscle, and 1 ppm in skeletal muscle of chickens, cattle, and goats.

DECYL ACETATE • A synthetic berry, orange, apple, peach, plum, and honey flavoring agent for beverages, ice cream, ices, candy, baked goods, and chewing gum. No known toxicity.

DECYL ALCOHOL • An intermediate (*see*) for surface-active agents, an antifoam agent, and a fixative in perfumes. Occurs naturally in sweet orange and ambrette seed. Derived commercially from liquid paraffin wax (*see*). Colorless to light yellow liquid. Used also for synthetic lubricants and as a synthetic fruit flavoring. Moderately toxic by skin contact. Mildly toxic by ingestion, inhalation, and possibly other routes. Has caused tumors in animals. A severe human skin and eye irritant.

DECYL BENZENE SODIUM SULFONATE • Defoaming agent and dispersing aid used on fresh citrus fruit. Poison by intravenous route. Moderately toxic by ingestion. A severe eye irritant.

DECYL BUTYRATE • A synthetic citrus and fruit flavoring agent for beverages, ice cream, ices, candy, and baked goods. No known toxicity.

DECYL PROPIONATE • A synthetic citrus and fruit flavoring agent for beverages, ice cream, ices, candy, and baked goods. No known toxicity.

DECYLIC ACID • *See* Decanoic Acid.

DECYLIC ALCOHOL • *See* 1-Decanol.

DEERTONGUE • Liatris. Vanilla plant. The extract of *Trilisa odoratissima* found from Virginia to Florida and Louisiana. Contains the volatile oil coumarin (*see*). Used in perfumery and to make tobacco smell better. The FDA's data bank, PAFA (see page 10), has not yet done a toxicology search on this additive.

DEFATTED • Meaning the fat has been partly or totally removed from a product. If partly removed, there is no minimum percentage set by the Food and Drug Administration.

DEFATTED COTTONSEED OIL • From cottonseed flour (*see*) with the fat removed.

DEFOAMING AGENT • Antifoamer. Foam Inhibitor. Any number of surfactants (*see*), such as liquid glycerides (*see*), which are used to control the amount of foam produced in the processing of baked goods, coffee, whiteners, candies, milk products, jams, jellies, and fruit juices. They remove the head from processed drinks, such as orange and pineapple juice. Among the defoamers used are dimethylpolysiloxane, polyoxyethylene 40 monostearate, polysorbate 60, propylene glycol alginate, silicon dioxide, sorbitan monostearate, aluminum stearate, butyl stearate, fatty acids, hydroxylated lecithin, isopropyl alcohol, magnesium stearate, mineral oil, petrolatum, petroleum waxes, polyethylene glycol, polysorbate 80, potassium stearate, hydrogenated tallow alcohol, sodium polyacrylate, synthetic petroleum wax, oleic acid from tall oil and fatty acids.

DEHYDRATED • With the water removed.

DEHYDRATED BEETS • Used for coloring and flavoring. The FDA data bank, PAFA (see page 10), has fully up-to-date toxicology information available.

DEHYDROACETIC ACID • DHA. Sodium Dehydroacetate. A weak acid that forms a white, odorless powder with an acrid taste. Used as a preservative in cut or peeled squash. Used as an antienzyme agent in toothpaste to prevent tooth decay and as a preservative for foods and shampoos. Also used as a fungi- and bacteria-destroying agent in cosmetics. The presence of organic matter decreases its effectiveness. Not irritating or allergy causing, but it is a kidney-blocking agent and can impair kidney function. Large doses can cause vomiting, imbalance, and convulsions. The FDA data bank, PAFA (see page 10), has fully up-to-date toxicology information available.

DELANEY AMENDMENT • Written by Congressman James Delaney, the amendment was part of the 1958 law requested by the Food and Drug Administration. The law stated that food and chemical manufacturers had to test additives before they were put on the market and the results had to be submitted to the FDA. Delaney's amendment specifically states that no additive may be permitted in any amount if tests show that it produces cancer when fed to man or animals or by other appropriate tests. Ever since it was enacted, the food and chemical industries have tried to get it repealed. By the time you read this, they may have succeeded.

DELAYED HYPERSENSITIVITY • Manifested primarily as contact dermatitis due to chemicals such as neomycin sulfate or to parabens (*see both*), a common preservative in food products. Certain multiple allergic reactions to chemicals added to food, directly or indirectly, may also cause delayed hypersensitivity, especially the antibiotics.

DELTAMETHRIN • A pesticide that contains cyanide used for tomato products. The FDA permits a residue of 1 ppm.

DEMETON-S • An organophosphate (*see*) pesticide used in animal feed. FDA residue limits of 5 ppm in dehydrated sugar-beet pulp when used for animal feed. Poison by ingestion and other routes.

DEMULCENT • A soothing, usually thick, oily or creamy substance used to relieve pain in inflamed or irritated mucous surfaces. The gum acacia, for instance, is used as a demulcent.

DENATURANT • A substance that changes another substance's natural qualities or characteristics. For example, denatonium benzoate is added to the alcoholic content in cosmetics to make it undrinkable.

DERMATITIS • Inflammation of the skin.

DESOXYCHOLIC ACID • An emulsifying agent, white, crystalline, powdered, almost insoluble in water. Used in dried egg whites up to 0.1 percent. No known toxicity. The final report to the FDA of the Select Committee on GRAS Substances stated in 1980 that it should continue its GRAS status with no limitations other than good manufacturing practices. Moderately toxic by ingestion. Has caused tumors in animals. There is no reported use of the chemical and no toxicology information is available.

DEXTRAN • A term applied to polysaccharides produced by bacteria growing on sugar. Used as a foam stabilizer for beer, in soft-center confections, and as a substitute for barley malt. It has also been used as a plasma expander for emergency treatment of shock. Has caused cancer in rats. The final report to the

FDA of the Select Committee on GRAS Substances stated in 1980 that there is no available evidence that it is a hazard to the public when used as it is now and it should continue its GRAS status with limitations on amounts that can be added to food. The FDA's data bank, PAFA (see page 10), has not yet done a toxicology search on this additive.

DEXTRIN • British Gum. Starch Gum. White or yellow powder produced from starch and used as a foam stabilizer for beer, a diluting agent for dry extracts and pills, in polishing cereals, for preparing emulsions and dry bandages, for thickening industrial dye pastes, and in matches, fireworks, and explosives. Also used as a thickener in cream and liquid cosmetics. May cause an allergic reaction. The final report to the FDA of the Select Committee on GRAS Substances stated in 1980 that it should continue its GRAS status with no limitations other than good manufacturing practices. The FDA data bank, PAFA, has fully up-to-date toxicology information available.

DEXTROSE • The final report to the FDA of the Select Committee on GRAS Substances stated in 1980 that there is no available evidence that it is a hazard to the public when used as it is now and it should continue its GRAS status with no limitations other than good manufacturing practices. The FDA data bank, PAFA, has fully up-to-date toxicology information available. *See* Corn Syrup.

DHC • *See* Dihydrochalcones.

DI-(BUTAN-3-ONE-YL) SULFIDE • Used in the manufacture of flavorings. The FDA data bank, PAFA, has fully up-to-date toxicology information available for this additive.

1,2-(DI[1'-ETHOXY]ETHOXY) PROPANE • A gas. *See* Propane. The FDA data bank, PAFA (see page 10), has fully up-to-date toxicology information available for this additive.

DI (2-ETHYLHEXYL) ADIPATE • Light-colored, oily liquid used as a plasticizer, usually in processing polyvinyl and other polymers. The FDA data bank, PAFA (see page 10), is, as of this writing, conducting a search of the toxicology literature concerning this additive.

DI (2-ETHYLHEXYL) PHTHALATE • A light-colored, odorless liquid used as a plasticizer for many resins. The FDA data bank, PAFA, is, as of this writing, conducting a search of the toxicology literature concerning this additive.

DI-(2-ETHYLHEXYL)SODIUM SULFOSUCCINATE • White, waxy solid widely used as an emulsifier and as a processing aid. Used in beverage mixes, cocoa, eggs, fruit-juice drinks, gelatin desserts, hog carcasses, milk, molasses, and poultry. FDA limits from 9 ppm in finished foods to 25 ppm in molasses.

DIACETIN • A mixture of the diesters (*see*) of glycerin (*see*) and acetic acid (*see*) used as a plasticizer, softening agent, or as a solvent for cellulose derivatives, resins, and shellacs. No known toxicity.

DIACETYL • It occurs naturally in cheese, cocoa, pears, coffee, raspberries, strawberries, and cooked chicken, but is usually prepared by a special fermentation of glucose. It is a yellowish green liquid. Also used as a carrier of aroma of butter, vinegar, and coffee. Also used in blueberry, raspberry, strawberry, butter, buttermilk, butterscotch, caramel, chocolate, coffee, fruit, cheese, cherry, liquor, rum, wine, nut, almond, spice, ginger ale, vanilla, and cream soda flavorings for beverages, ice cream, ices, candy, baked goods, gelatin desserts, chewing gum, and shortening. Cleared by the U.S. Department of Agriculture (Meat Inspection Division) to flavor oleomargarine in "amount sufficient for the purpose." Diacetyl compounds have been associated with cancer when ingested by experimental animals. GRAS. The FDA data bank, PAFA (see page 10), has fully up-to-date toxicology information available.

DIACETYL TARTARIC OF MONOGLYCERIDES and DIGLYCERIDES • An emulsifying agent used to improve volume and uniformity in bakery products up to 20 percent by weight of the combination of such a preparation and the shortening. The final report to the FDA of the Select Committee on GRAS Substances stated in 1980 that it should continue its GRAS status with no limitations other than good manufacturing practices.

DIALIFOR • Torak. An insecticide used in animal feed, apple pomace, dried citrus pulp, dried grape pomace, raisin waste, and raisins. FDA allows tolerances of up to 2 ppm in raisins, 40 ppm in dried apple pomace, 20 ppm in dried grape pomace, 115 ppm in dried citrus pulp, and 10 ppm in raisin waste when used for animal feed. Poison by ingestion and skin contact. Had adverse reproductive effects in experimental animals.

DIALLYL POLYSULFIDES • Used in the manufacture of flavors. The FDA data bank, PAFA (see page 10), has fully up-to-date toxicology information available.

DIALLYL TRISULFIDES • Used in the manufacture of flavors. The FDA data bank, PAFA, has fully up-to-date toxicology information available.

DIAMINOZIDE • Alar. Butanedioic Acid. Mono(2,2-Dimethyl hydrazide). This apple-growth regulator was a particular focus of alarm in 1988 and 1989 when its residues were reported to be hazardous to children. The FDA residue tolerances were 10 ppm in dried tomato pomace, 90 ppm in residues of peanut meal, both for animal feed; 0.2 ppm in fat, meat, or meat byproducts of cattle, goats, hogs, poultry, and sheep; 0.02 ppm residues in milk; 0.2 ppm as residues in eggs; 20 ppm as residues in apples; and 30 ppm as residues in cherries, nectarines, and peaches. Probable human carcinogen. Causes multiple tumors in animals. Diaminozide was removed from the market in 1989 and is now permitted only for use on flower beds.

DIAMMONIUM PHOSPHATE • Used in animal feed as a source of nonprotein nitrogen and phosphorus for ruminants.

1,4-DIANILINOANTHRAQUINONE • *See* Coal Tar.

DIASMOL • *See* 1,3-Nonanediol Acetate (mixed esters).

DIASTASE • A mixture of enzymes from malt. It converts at least fifty times its weight of potato starch into sugars in thirty minutes. Used to convert starch into sugar. In 1992 diastase and diastase malt aluminum hydroxide were shown not to be safe and effective as claimed in OTC digestive-aid products and the FDA banned the compounds for that purpose. The FDA data bank, PAFA (see page 10), has fully up-to-date toxicology information available and diastase is still permitted as a food-processing agent.

DIATOMACEOUS EARTH • Kieselguhr. A porous and relatively pure form of silica formed from fossil remains of diatoms—one-celled algae with shells. Inert when ingested. Used in dentifrices, as a clarifying agent, and as an absorbent for liquids because it can absorb about four times its weight in water. Used as a buffer for acid-proofing food packaging and as an insecticide. Also used in nail polishes and face powders. The dust can cause lung damage after long exposure to high concentrations. The final report to the FDA of the Select Committee on GRAS Substances stated in 1980 that it should continue its GRAS status with no limitations other than good manufacturing practices. There is no reported use of the chemical and no toxicology information is available.

DIAZIDE • Alfa-Tox. Liquid with a faint esterlike odor widely used as an insecticide in animal feed. FDA permits 1 percent to 2 percent in animal feed. Poison by ingestion, skin contact, and other routes except for inhalation, during which is it mildly toxic. Human systemic effects by ingestion include changes in movement, muscle weakness, and sweating. Caused birth defects in animals. It is a severe skin and eye irritant in humans and emits toxic fumes when heated.

DIAZO- • A compound containing two nitrogen atoms, such as diazolidinyl urea (*see*), one of the newer preservatives, or diazepam, a popular muscle relaxant.

DIAZOLIDINYL UREA • Oxymethurea. 1,3-Bis(hydroxymethl) urea. Crystals from alcohol, very soluble in water. Used in the textile industry in cotton; also as a pesticide and in cosmetics as an antiseptic. May release formaldehyde (*see*).

DIBENZYL ETHER • A synthetic fruit and spice flavoring agent for beverages, ice cream, ices, candy, baked goods, and chewing gum. The Flavor and Extract Manufacturers Association evaluated the safety of this additive. High-dose female rats had increased liver weights. A no-effect level was achieved at 196 mg/kg/day. In a 60-kg human (about 132 pounds), this would be equivalent to approximately 11.8 grams a day. The FDA data bank, PAFA (see page 10), has fully up-to-date toxicology information available for this additive.

a,a-DIBROMO-a-CYANOACETAMIDE • An antimicrobial agent used in beets and sugarcane. FDA limits are up to 10 ppm and not less than 2 ppm based on weight of raw sugarcane or raw beets. Poison by ingestion. A severe skin and eye irritant. Cyanide and its compounds are on the Community Right-To-Know List.

2,2-DIBROMO-3-NITRILOPROPIONAMIDE • Preservative used alone for control of microorganisms in raw sugar in cane and beet sugar mills (2–10 ppm). The FDA data bank, PAFA, has fully up-to-date toxicology information available for this additive.

4,4-DIBUTYL-y-BUTYROLACTONE • A synthetic butter, coconut, and nut flavoring agent for ice cream, candy, ices, and baked goods. The FDA data bank, PAFA (see page 10), has fully up-to-date toxicology information available for this additive.

DIBUTYL SEBACATE • Sebacic Acid. A synthetic fruit flavoring usually obtained from castor oil and used for beverages, ice cream, and baked goods. Also used for sealing food packages. Used in fruit-fragrance cosmetics. Mildly toxic by ingestion. Oral doses in rats cause reproductive effects. The FDA data bank, PAFA, has fully up-to-date toxicology information available for this additive.

DIBUTYL SULFIDE • *See* Butyl Sulfide.

DIBUTYLENE TETRAFURFURAL • Derived from bran, rice hulls, or corn cobs, it is used in the manufacture of medicinals and as a solvent and flavoring in cosmetics and food. Toxic when absorbed by the skin. Irritating to the eye.

DICHLORODIFLUOROMETHANE • Colorless, odorless gas used to freeze foods by direct contact and for chilling cocktail glasses. Narcotic in high doses. In EPA Genetic Toxicology Program (*see*). The FDA data bank, PAFA, has fully up-to-date toxicology information available for this additive.

1,2-DICHLOROETHANE • Colorless, clear liquid with a pleasant odor and sweet taste. A human poison by ingestion. The World Health Organization Committee found it causes birth defects and that it causes cancer in mice and rats when administered orally. The committee's opinion was that 1,2-dichloroethane should not be used in food. *See* Ethylene Dichloride.

DICHLOROMETHANE • *See* Methylene Chloride.

DICHLOROPHENOXYACETIC ACID • A widely used herbicide on milled barley, oats, rye, and wheat (except their milled flour fractions) and sugarcane. FDA residue limits are up to 5 ppm in sugarcane molasses, 2 ppm in milled fractions (except flour) in barley, oats, and wheat, and 0.1 in potable water. Poison by ingestion and other routes. Moderately toxic by skin contact. A suspected human cancer-causing agent. Human systemic effects by ingestion include sleepiness, convulsions, coma, and nausea or vomiting. Can cause liver and kidney injury. A skin and severe eye irritant. Human mutagenic data. Experimental reproductive effects. When heated to decomposition, it emits toxic fumes.

3-(3,4-DICHLOROPHENYL)-1,1-DIMETHYL UREA • Marmer. Telvar Diuron Weed Killer. Vonduron. A widely used herbicide employed on animal feed. FDA limitation of 4 ppm in dried citrus pulp when used for livestock feed. In EPA Genetic Toxicology Program (*see*). Chlorophenol compounds are on the Community Right-To-Know List (*see*). Caused tumors and birth defects in laboratory animals.

a,a-DICHLOROPRIONIC ACID, SODIUM SALT • *See* Dichloropropionic Acid.

DICHLOROPROPIONANILIDE • Propanil. Supernox. An herbicide used on animal feed, rice, rice bran, rice hulls, and rice polishings. FDA limitations are 10 ppm in rice bran, rice hulls, and rice polishings when used for animal feed. In EPA Genetic Toxicology Program (*see*). Poison by ingestion. Mildly toxic by skin contact.

DICHLOROPROPIONIC ACID • Basinex. Crisapon. Revenge. Unipon. An herbicide used in animal feed, citrus pulp, and potable water. FDA residue allowances are 0.2 ppm in potable water and 20 ppm in citrus pulp used as animal feed. Moderately toxic by ingestion. Corrosive. A skin irritant.

DICHLORVOS • Dimethyl Dichlorovinyl Phosphate. Apavap. Chlorvinphos. DDVF. VPON. 2,2-Dichlorovinyl. An organophosphate (*see*) insecticide with contact and vapor action. It has been widely used for control of agricultural, industrial, and domestic pests since the 1950s. It is used in pet flea collars and flea sprays. DDVP is available in oil solutions, emulsifiable concentration, and aerosol formulations. Its topical (skin) application has been approved for beef and dairy cattle, goats, sheep, swine, and chickens to control fleas, flies, and mites. It is also used in tomato greenhouses and applied to mushrooms, lettuce, and radishes. Aerosols and strips are used domestically for control of ants, bedbugs, ticks, cockroaches, and other pests. Nerve gases used in wars include organophosphates. It is suspected of causing cancer and birth defects. Heat decomposition causes highly toxic fumes. As of this writing, the EPA is moving to have the use of dichlorvos on food packaging banned because it poses "more than a negligible risk." It is in at least 350 other products, and it may take years to get this pesticide off the market.

DICYCLOHEXYL DISULFIDE • *See* Sulfides.

DIESTER • A compound containing two ester groupings. An ester is formed from an alcohol and an acid by eliminating water. It is usually employed in fragrant liquids for artificial fruit perfumes and flavors.

DIETARY FOOD SUPPLEMENT • Any food product to which enough vitamins and minerals have been added to furnish more than 50 percent of the recommended daily allowance in a single serving, according to the FDA. Such foods must, of course, have ingredients identified on the label.

DIETHANOLAMINE • Colorless liquid or crystalline alcohol. It is used as a solvent, emulsifying agent, and detergent. Also employed in emollients for its softening properties and as a dispersing agent and humectant in other cosmetic products. It may be irritating to the skin and mucous membranes. *See* Ethanolamines.

DIETHYL ACETALDEHYDE • Ethyl Butyraldehyde. A flavoring agent used in many foods. Moderately toxic by ingestion. A skin irritant.

DIETHYL ACETIC ACID • Colorless, volatile liquid with a rancid odor used as a flavoring in a variety of foods. Moderately toxic by ingestion and skin contact.

DIETHYL ASPARTATE • The diester of ethyl alcohol and aspartic acid (*see both*).

DIETHYL DICARBONATE • Viscous liquid with a fruity odor used as a fermentation inhibitor and fungicide. Prohibited in the U.S. but permitted in wine in other countries. Poison by ingestion.

DIETHYL GLUTAMATE • *See* Glutamate.

DIETHYL MALATE • Malic Acid. A synthetic apple and rum flavoring agent for beverages, ice cream, ices, candy, baked goods, gelatin, and puddings. The FDA data bank, PAFA, has fully up-to-date toxicology information available for this additive.

DIETHYL MALONATE • A synthetic berry, fruit, apple, grape, peach, and pear flavoring for beverages, ice cream, ices, candy, and baked goods. The FDA data bank, PAFA (see page 10), has fully up-to-date toxicology information available for this additive.

DIETHYL PALMITOYL ASPARTATE • *See* Aspartic Acid.

DIETHYL-*o*-PHTHALATE • Clear, colorless liquid used as a plasticizer in packaging material. Moderately toxic by ingestion. Has caused adverse effects in experimental animals.

DIETHYL PYROCARBONATE (DEP) • A fermentation inhibitor in still wines, beer, and orange juice added before or during bottling at a level not to exceed 200 to 500 ppm. DEP was widely used because it supposedly did its job of preserving and then decomposed within twenty-four hours. However, instead of disappearing, it reacted with the ammonia in beverages to form urethane, according to University of Stockholm researchers. They said that DEP caused urethane concentrations of 0.1 to 0.2 mg per liter in orange juice and approximately 1 mg per liter in white wine and beer. Since 1943 urethane has been identified as a cancer-causing agent. The FDA had not required listing of DEP on the label and therefore did not know how many beverages were actually treated with this additive. The FDA banned the use of DEP in 1976.

DIETHYL SEBACATE • Sebacic Acid. A synthetic butter, coconut, apple, melon, peach, and nut flavoring for beverages, ice cream, ices, candy, baked goods, chewing gum, and gelatin desserts. Mildly toxic by ingestion. A skin irritant. The FDA data bank, PAFA (see page 10), has fully up-to-date toxicology information available for this additive.

DIETHYL SUCCINATE • A synthetic raspberry, butter, orange, and grape flavoring for beverages, ice cream, ices, candy, and baked goods. No known toxicity. The FDA data bank, PAFA, has fully up-to-date toxicology information available for this additive.

DIETHYL TARTRATE • The FDA data bank, PAFA, has fully up-to-date toxicology information available for this additive. *See* Tartaric Acid.

DIETHYLAMINOETHANOL • Colorless, water-absorbing liquid with the properties of ammonia and alcohol. Toxic by ingestion. Used to obtain fatty-acid derivatives, as an emulsifying agent, and as a curing agent for resin. The FDA data bank, PAFA (see page 10), has fully up-to-date toxicology information available for this additive.

DIETHYLENE GLYCOL DISTEARATE • White, waxlike solid with a faint fatty odor. Used as an emulsifying agent for oils, solvents, and waxes, as a lubricating agent for paper and cardboard, and as a thickening agent. Although allowed as a food additive, there is no current reported use of the chemical, and therefore, although toxicology information may be available, it is not being updated, according to the FDA.

DIETHYLENETRIAMINE • Yellow liquid with an ammonia odor, strongly alkaline. Used as a solvent. There is no reported use of the chemical and no toxicology information is available.

DIETHYLPYRAZINE • Derived from ethyl bromide or chloride, it is used as a corrosion inhibitor and insecticide. The FDA data bank, PAFA, has fully up-to-date toxicology information available for this additive.

DIETHYLSTILBESTROL (DES) • Stilbestrol. A synthetic estrogen fed to cattle and poultry to fatten them. A proven carcinogen, hormonal in nature, according to the FDA, which has given top priority to the study of the safety of DES. The FDA stipulates a zero tolerance for the compound after a proper withdrawal period. In 1971, three Harvard scientists linked DES to a rare form of vaginal cancer in the daughters of women who had taken DES during pregnancy. An estimated 100,000 to 150,000 head of cattle containing residues of the hormone are apparently getting to market. The European Common Market and Sweden have forbidden the use of DES in cattle.

2,5-DIETHYLTETRAHYDROFURAN • A solvent used in processing resins. The FDA data bank, PAFA, has fully up-to-date toxicology information available for this additive.

DIFURURYL ETHER • Used in the manufacture of food additives. The FDA data bank, PAFA (see page 10), has fully up-to-date toxicology information available for this additive.

DIGLYCERIDES • Emulsifiers. *See* Glycerides.

DIHYDROANETHOLE • *See p*-Propyl Anisole.

DIHYDROCARVEOL • A synthetic flavoring agent occurring naturally in black pepper. A colorless, oily liquid with a spearmint odor, it is used in liquor, mint, spice, and caraway flavorings for beverages, ice cream, ices, candy, baked goods, and alcoholic beverages. A moderate skin and eye irritant. The FDA data bank, PAFA, has fully up-to-date toxicology information available for this additive.

DIHYDROCARVONE • Colorless liquid with a spearmintlike odor used as a flavoring agent in various foods. Moderately toxic when injected under the skin. The FDA data bank, PAFA, has fully up-to-date toxicology information available for this additive.

DIHYDROCHALCONES (DHC) • A new class of intensely sweet compounds—about fifteen hundred times sweeter than sugar—obtained by a simple chemical modification of naturally occurring bioflavonoids (*see*). Hydrogenation (*see*) of naringin and neohesperidin (the predominant bitter constituents in grapefruit and Seville orange rind) provides the intensely sweet dihydrochalcones. DHCs are seemingly safe. There have not been any reports, thus far, of side effects in either multigenerational feeding studies or in long-term feeding trials. The disadvantage is that they cannot be easily reproduced in the laboratory, so supplies are dependent upon natural sources. A more serious problem is that the intense, pleasant sweetness of DHCs is slow in onset, with considerable lingering taste, which renders them unsuitable for many food uses. Approval to use DHCs in toothpaste and chewing gum is pending. Food scientists are now trying to find derivatives and analogues of DHCs to overcome the slow onset and lingering factor in the natural compounds.

DIHYDROCHOLESTEROL • *See* Cholesterol.

DIHYDROCHOLESTERYL OCTYLDECAOATE • *See* Cholesterol and Stearic Acid.

DIHYDROCOUMARIN • A synthetic flavoring agent occurring naturally in tonka bean, oil of lavender, and sweet clovers. Used in butter, caramel, coconut, floral, fruit, cherry, liquor, rum, nut, root beer, spice, cinnamon, vanilla, cream soda, and tonka flavorings for beverages, ice cream, ices, candy, baked goods, chewing gum, gelatin desserts, and puddings. Prolonged feeding has revealed a possible trend toward liver injury. The FDA data bank, PAFA (see page 10), has fully up-to-date toxicology information available for this additive.

5,6-DIHYDROL-2-(2,6-XYLIDINO)-4H1,3-THIAZINE • Bay. Xylazine. An animal drug used in meat. Poison by ingestion.

5,7-DIHYDRO-2-METHYLTHIENO(3,4-D)PYRIMIDINE • Derived from organic matter, used in the manufacture of food additives. The FDA data bank, PAFA, has fully up-to-date toxicology information available for this additive.

2,3-DIHYDRO-3-OXO-BENZISOSULFONAZOLE • See Saccharin.

1,2-DIHYDROPRYRIDAZINE-3,6-DIONE • A pesticide used on potato chips. FDA residue tolerance is 160 ppm. Moderately toxic by ingestion. Can cause chronic liver damage and acute central nervous system effects. Being studied as a possible cancer-causing agent.

DIHYDROSTREPTOMYCIN • An antibiotic used in beef and milk. FDA residue tolerance is zero in uncooked edible tissues of calves and in milk. May cause birth defects in humans. May be a mutagen.

DIHYDROXYACETOPHENONE • Light tan crystals that absorb ultraviolet light. It is used in plastics, dyes, fungicides, and plant-growth promoters. The FDA data bank, PAFA, has fully up-to-date toxicology information available for this additive.

DIISOBUTYL ADIPATE • Diba. Isobutyl Adipate. A plasticizer used in packaging materials. Mildly toxic by ingestion.

DIISO PRO PANO LAMINE • DIPA. White, crystalline solid that is used as an emulsifying agent for polishes, textile specialities, leather compounds, insecticides, cutting oils, and water paints. See Propyl Alcohol.

2,3-DIKETOBUTANE • See Diacetyl.

DILAURYL CITRATE • See Fatty Alcohols and Citric Acid.

DILAURYL THIODIPROPIONATE • An antioxidant. White crystalline flakes with a sweet odor, in general food use to extend shelf life. In fat or oil up to 0.02 percent. The final report to the FDA of the Select Committee on GRAS Substances stated in 1980 that there is no available evidence that it is a hazard to the public when used as it is now and it should continue its GRAS status with no limitations other than good manufacturing practices. There is no reported use of the chemical and no toxicology information is available.

DILINOLEATE • Dimer Acid. Widely used as an emulsifier, it is derived from linoleic acid (see).

DILINOLEIC ACID • See Linoleic Acid.

DILL • Anethum graveolens. A natural flavoring agent from a European herb bearing a seedlike fruit. Used in sausage and spice flavorings for baked goods (4,800 ppm), meats, and pickles (8,200 ppm). Also used in medicine. Can cause sensitivity to light. The final report to the FDA of the Select Committee on GRAS Substances stated in 1980 that it should continue its GRAS status with no limitations other than good manufacturing practices. The FDA data bank, PAFA (see page 10), is, as of this writing, conducting a search of the toxicology literature concerning this additive.

DILL OIL • The volatile oil obtained from the crushed, dried seeds or fruits of the herb. Slightly yellow, with a caraway odor and flavor. Used in strawberry, fruit, sausage, and dill flavorings for beverages, ice cream, ices, baked goods, gelatin desserts, chewing gum, meat, liquors, pickles, and condiments. The final report to the FDA of the Select Committee on GRAS Substances stated in 1980 that it should continue its GRAS status with no limitations other than good manufacturing practices. The FDA data bank, PAFA, has fully up-to-date toxicology information available for this additive. *See* Dill for toxicity.

DILLSEED • Indian Dill. The volatile oil from a variety of dill herbs. Obtained by steam distillation. Light yellow, with a harsh carawaylike odor. Used in rye flavorings for baked goods, condiments, and meats. The final report to the FDA of the Select Committee on GRAS Substances stated in 1980 that it should continue its GRAS status with no limitations other than good manufacturing practices. The FDA data bank, PAFA, is, as of this writing, conducting a search of the toxicology literature concerning this additive.

DILUENT • Any component of a color additive mixture that is not itself a color additive and has been intentionally mixed in to facilitate the uses of the mixture in coloring cosmetics or in coloring the human body, food, and drugs. The diluent may serve another function in cosmetics, as, for example, an emulsifier or stabilizer. Ethylcellulose is an example.

DIMETHICONE • *See* Dimethyl Polysiloxane.

3,4-DIMETHOXY-1-VINYLBENZENE • *See* Benzene and Vinyl.

***m*-DIMETHOXYBENZENE** • Resorcinol. A synthetic fruit, nut, and vanilla flavoring for beverages, ice cream, ices, candy, and baked goods. Used on the skin as a bactericidal and fungicidal ointment. Has the same toxicity as phenol (extremely toxic), but causes more severe convulsions. The FDA data bank, PAFA (see page 10), has fully up-to-date toxicology information available for this additive.

***p*-DIMETHOXYBENZENE** • A synthetic raspberry, fruit, nut, hazelnut, root beer, and vanilla flavoring agent for beverages, ice cream, ices, candy, and baked goods. The FDA data bank, PAFA, has fully up-to-date toxicology information available for this additive. See previous entry for toxicity.

3,4-DIMETHOXYBENZENECARBONAL • *See* Veratraldehyde.

1,1-DIMETHOXYETHANE • *See* Ethylene Glycol.

2,6-DIMETHOXYPHENOL • *See* Phenol.

1-([2,5-DIMETHOXYPHENYL]AZO)-2-NAPHTHOL • A coloring used on oranges with an FDA limit of 2 ppm by weight calculated on the basis of the whole fruit. Causes cancer in animals and is under International Agency for Research on Cancer review.

3-(DIMETHOXYPHOSPHINYLOXY)*n*-METHYL-cis-CROTONAMIDE • Apadrin. Bilobran. A reddish brown solid with a mild odor widely used as an insecticide in tomato products. The FDA residue tolerance is 2 ppm in concentrated tomato products. In the EPA Genetic Toxicology Program (*see*). The EPA considers it extremely hazardous. It is poisonous by ingestion, inhalation, and skin contact.

1,4-DIMETHYL-4-ACETYL-1-CYCLOHEXENE • Prepared from acetylaldehyde and methanol (*see both*), it is used in processing food additives. The FDA data bank, PAFA, has fully up-to-date toxicology information available for this additive.

DIMETHYL BENZYL CARBINOL AND CARBINYL • Flavoring agents used in various foods. Moderately toxic by ingestion. *See a,a*-Dimethylphenethyl Alcohol.

DIMETHYL DIALKYL AMMONIUM CHLORIDE • *See* Quaternary Ammonium Compounds. The FDA data bank, PAFA, has fully up-to-date toxicology information available for this additive.

DIMETHYL-0-(1,2-DIBROMO-2,2-DICHLOROETHYL)PHOSPHATE • Widely used insecticide on various foods. Poison by ingestion and inhalation. Moderately toxic by skin injection. *See* Organophosphates.

DIMETHYL DICARBONATE • A fungicide and yeast inhibitor used in wine. Limited to 200 ppm in wine. There is no reported use of the chemical and no toxicology information is available.

DIMETHYL DICHLOROVINYL PHOSPHATE • *See* Dichlorvos.

DIMETHYL ETHER RESORCINOL • A benzene derivative, originally obtained from certain resins but now usually synthesized. *See* m-Dimethoxybenzene.

DIMETHYL ETHERPROTOCATECHUALDEHYDE • *See* Verataldehyde.

2,6-DIMETHYL-5-HEPTENAL • A synthetic fruit flavoring for beverages, ice cream, ices, candy, baked goods, gelatin desserts, and chewing gum. The FDA data bank, PAFA (see page 10), has fully up-to-date toxicology information available for this additive.

3,7-DIMETHYL-7-HYDROXYOCTANAL • *See* Hydroxycitronellal.

DIMETHYL KETONE • *See* Diacetyl.

DIMETHYL-3-METHYL-4-NITROPHENYLPHOSPHOROTHIONATE • Accothion. A widely used insecticide on wheat gluten. FDA tolerance for residue is 30 ppm in wheat gluten. In the EPA Genetic Toxicology Program and on the EPA Extremely Hazardous List (*see both*). Poisonous by ingestion, inhalation, and other routes. Moderately toxic by skin contact. Human systemic effects upon ingestion include overactivity, diarrhea, nausea or vomiting, and shortness of breath.

0,0-DIMETHYL METHYLCARBAMOYLMETHYL PHOSPHORODITHIOATE • A widely used insecticide in animal feed, citrus pulp. FDA residue limits are 5 ppm for dried citrus pulp when used for animal feed. Poison by ingestion, skin contact, and other routes. May cause cancer and birth defects.

N′,N′-DIMETHYL-N-[(METHYLCARBAMOYL)OXY]-1-METHYLTHIOOXAMIMIDIC ACID • Widely used insecticide in animal feed, pineapple bran, and pineapples. Residue limitations of 6 ppm in pineapple bran when used for animal feed. Poison by ingestion and inhalation. Moderately toxic by skin contact. On the EPA Extremely Hazardous Substances List.

3,7-DIMETHYL-(E)-2,6-OCTADIEN-1-OL • *See* Geraniol.

2-cis-3,7-DIMETHYL-2,6-OCTADIEN-1-OL • *See* Nerol.

3,7-DIMETHYL-1,6-OCTADIEN-3-OL • *See* Linalool.

3,7-DIMETHYL-2,6-OCTADIENAL • Pale yellow liquid with a strong lemon odor used as a flavoring agent in baked goods, candy, and ice cream. Mildly toxic by ingestion. A human skin irritant. *See* Citral.

3,7-DIMETHYL-1-OCTANOL • A synthetic flavoring, colorless, with a sweet roselike odor. Used in floral, rose, and fruit flavorings for beverages, ice cream, ices, candy, and baked goods. The FDA data bank, PAFA, has fully up-to-date toxicology information available for this additive.

2,6-DIMETHYL-1-OCTEN-8-OL • *See* Rhodinol.

DIMETHYL POLYSILOXANE • Dimethicone. Antifoam A. An antifoaming agent for use in processing foods in "amounts reasonably required to inhibit foaming." Used as a chewing gum base, in molasses, soft drinks, sugar distillation, skimmed milk, wine fermentation, syrups, soups, rendered fats, and curing solutions. Not to exceed 10 ppm in nonalcoholic beverages. Zero tolerance in milk; 250 ppm in salt for cooking; and 10 ppm in foods ready for consumption. Used to combat flatulence. Low toxicity. The FDA data bank, PAFA, has fully up-to-date toxicology information available for this additive.

DIMETHYL PYRAZINE • Flavoring agent with a nutty or potatolike taste and coffee odor used in various foods. Moderately toxic by ingestion and is an experimental mutagen. GRAS. The FDA data bank, PAFA (see page 10), has fully up-to-date toxicology information available for this additive.

2,5-DIMETHYL PYRROLE • A colorless to yellow, oily liquid that was used as a flavoring agent in various foods. GRAS. Although allowed as a food additive, there is no current reported use of the chemical, and therefore, although toxicology information may be available, it is not being updated, according to the FDA.

DIMETHYL RESORCINOL • See m-Dimethoxybenzene.

DIMETHYL SUCCINATE • Succinic Acid. A synthetic fruit flavoring agent for beverages, ice cream, ices, candy, baked goods, and chewing gum. The FDA data bank, PAFA, has fully up-to-date toxicology information available for this additive.

DIMETHYL SULFATE • Sulfuric Acid. Dimethyl Ester. Colorless, oily liquid used as a methylating agent (to add methyl) in the manufacture of cosmetic dyes, perfumes, and flavorings. Methyl salicylate (see) is an example. Extremely hazardous, dimethyl sulfate has delayed lethal qualities. Liquid produces severe blistering, necrosis of the skin. Sufficient skin absorption can result in serious poisoning. Vapors hurt the eyes. Ingestion can cause paralysis, coma, prostration, kidney damage, and death.

DIMETHYL SULFIDE • See Methyl Sulfide.

0,0-DIMETHYL-0-(3,5,6-TRICHLORO-2-PYRIDYL)PHOSPHOROTHIOATE • See Chlorpyrifos.

1,1-DIMETHYL-3-(a,a,a-TRIFLUORO-m-TOLYL)UREA • Cottonex. Herbicide used in animal feed. FDA limit of 0.2 ppm in sugarcane when used for animal feed. In EPA Genetic Toxicology Program (see) and under review by the International Agency for Research on Cancer (IARC) (see). Moderately toxic by ingestion. May be mutagenic.

2,4-DIMETHYLACETOPHENONE • Colorless liquid with the odor of mimosa, it is used as a synthetic grape, vanilla, and cream soda flavoring agent for beverages, ice cream, ices, candy, baked goods, and liquor. It is also used in perfumery. The FDA data bank, PAFA (see page 10), has fully up-to-date toxicology information available for this additive.

DIMETHYLAMINE • A gas with an ammonia odor derived from ammonia and methanol. It was used in the processing of food additives, pesticides, surfactants, and many other products. There is no reported use of the chemical and no toxicology information is available.

2,4-DIMETHYLBENZALDEHYDE • See Benzaldehyde.

2,3-DIMETHYLBENZOFURAN • *See* Furfural and Benzene.

DIMETHYLBENZYL ALCOHOL • A constituent of the essential oil from *Curcuma long* and related plants. It smells like menthol. It is used as a flavoring and scent. The FDA data bank, PAFA (see page 10), has fully up-to-date toxicology information available for this additive.

a,a-**DIMETHYLBENZYL ISOBUTYRATE** • A synthetic fruit flavoring agent for beverages, ice cream, ices, candy, and baked goods. The FDA data bank, PAFA, has fully up-to-date toxicology information available for this additive.

DIMETHYLGLYOXAL • *See* Diacetyl.

DIMETHYLKETOL • *See* Acetoin.

DIMETHYLOCTADECYLBENZYLAMMONIUM CHLORIDE • Quaternol 1. Varisoft SDC. An antimicrobial agent used in beets, sugarcane, and raw sugarcane juice. FDA residue limits are 1.5–6.0 ppm and 0.05 ppm based on weight of raw sugarcane or raw beets. Moderately toxic by ingestion. A human skin irritant and severe eye irritant.

DIMETHYLOCTANOL • Pelargol. Colorless liquid with a sweet rose odor used as a flavoring agent in bakery products, beverages, chewing gum, confections, ice cream, and pickles. Moderately toxic by skin contact. The FDA data bank, PAFA (see page 10), has fully up-to-date toxicology information available for this additive.

a,a-**DIMETHYLPHENETHYL ACETATE** • Acetic Acid. A colorless liquid with a floral-fruity odor. A synthetic cherry and honey flavoring agent for beverages, ice cream, ices, candy, baked goods, and chewing gum. The FDA data bank, PAFA, has fully up-to-date toxicology information available for this additive.

a,a-**DIMETHYLPHENETHYL ALCOHOL** • A synthetic fruit flavoring agent for beverages, ice cream, ices, candy, chewing gum, jellies, gelatin desserts, and baked goods. The FDA data bank, PAFA, has fully up-to-date toxicology information available for this additive.

a,a-**DIMETHYLPHENETHYL BUTYRATE** • Butyric Acid. A synthetic fruit flavoring agent for beverages, ice cream, ices, candy, and baked goods. The FDA data bank, PAFA (see page 10), has fully up-to-date toxicology information available for this additive.

a,a-**DIMETHYLPHENETHYL FORMATE** • Formic Acid. A synthetic spice flavoring agent for beverages, ice cream, ices, and candy. The FDA data bank, PAFA, has fully up-to-date toxicology information available for this additive.

2,6-DINITRO-N,N-DIPROPYL-4-(TRIFLUOROMETHYL)BENZENEAMINE • Agreflan. Crisalin. Widely used herbicide on barley, carrots, peppermint oil, soybeans, spearmint oil, and wheat. Residue tolerance set by FDA is 2 ppm in peppermint oil and spearmint oil. EPA Genetic Toxicology Program. Community Right-To-Know List (*see both*). Moderately toxic by ingestion. Caused cancer, tumors, and birth defects in experimental animals.

2,7-DINITROSOS-1-NAPHTHOL • Used in the manufacture of dyes. *See* Coal Tar.

DINKUM OIL • *See* Eucalyptus Oil.

2,6-DINTRO-3-METHOXY-1-METHYL-4-TERT-BUTYL-BENZENE • *See* Musk.

2,4-DINTRO-6-OCTYLPHENYL CROTONATE + 2,6-DINTRO-4-OCTYL-PHENYL CROTONATE • Fungicide residue on dried apple pomace as a result of application to growing apples. FDA residue tolerance of 0.3 ppm. Derived from crotonic acid, which is obtained from crotonaldehyde, which is used in chemical warfare.

DIOCTYL- • Containing two octyl groups. Octyl is obtained from octane, a liquid paraffin found in petroleum.

DIOCTYL ADIPATE • *See* Adipic Acid.

DIOCTYL DILINOLEATE • *See* Linoleic Acid.

DIOCTYL MALEATE • *See* Malic Acid.

DIOCTYL SODIUM SULFOSUCCINATE • Docusate Sodium. A waxlike solid that is very soluble in water. It is used as a dispersing and solubilizing agent in foods, drugs, and cosmetics. In foods and beverages it is used in gums, cocoa, and various hard-to-wet materials. Also a wetting agent in the cleaning of fruits, vegetables, and leafy plant material. Used in nonalcoholic beverages and sherbets at a rate not to exceed 0.5 percent of the weight of such ingredients. Finished cocoa beverages can have 75 ppm in the finished products. It is stool softener in laxatives. Eye irritation may result from use in eye preparations. The FDA data bank, PAFA (see page 10), has fully up-to-date toxicology information available for this additive.

DIOXATHION • A widely used pesticide in animal feed and dehydrated citrus pulp. Poisonous by ingestion. *See* Organophosphates.

DIOXIN • The commonly used name for TCDD. 2,3,7,8-tetrachlorodibenzo-p-dioxin. It is a halogenated aromatic hydrocarbon and causes mutagenic and carcinogenic changes in animals. It is a byproduct of agent orange (2,4-D and 2,4,5-T; *see both*). It is the most toxic of the chlorine-containing dioxin compounds. The long-term human consequences of exposure to this compound are controversial, but it certainly would be wise to avoid exposure to it. It is a suspected cancer-causing agent.

DIOXYMETHYLENE PROTOCATECHUICALDEHYDE • *See* Piperonal.

DIPA • The abbreviation for *diisopropanolamine* (*see*).

DIPENTENE • *See* Limonene.

DIPHENYL ETHER • Colorless crystals with the odor of geranium. Used in perfumery. Toxic by inhalation. Also an intermediate in processing. The FDA data bank, PAFA, has fully up-to-date toxicology information available for this additive.

DIPHENYL KETONE • *See* Benzophenones.

1,3-DIPHENYL-2-PROPANONE • A synthetic fruit, honey, and nut flavoring for beverages, ice cream, ices, candy, and baked goods. The FDA data bank, PAFA, has fully up-to-date toxicology information available for this additive.

DIPHENYLAMINE • Big Dipper. An insecticide used on various products. Poison by ingestion. Has caused birth defects in experimental animals.

DIPOTASSIUM EDTA • *See* Ethylenediamine Tetraacetic Acid.

DIPOTASSIUM GLYCYRRHIZATE • The dipotassium salt of glycyrrhizic acid (*see*).

DIPOTASSIUM PERSULFATE • White, odorless crystals used as a defoaming agent and a dispersant (*see both*) in fresh citrus fruit and in poultry. Moderately toxic and a skin irritant.

DIPOTASSIUM PHOSPHATE • A sequestrant. A white grain, very soluble in water. Used as a buffering agent to control the degree of acidity in solutions. It is used in the preparation of powdered nondairy coffee creams and in cheeses up to 3 percent by weight of cheese. It is used medicinally as a saline cathartic. No known toxicity. GRAS.

DIPROPYL DISULFIDE • A synthetic flavoring agent. Colorless, insoluble in water. Occurs naturally in onion. Used in imitation of onion flavoring for pickle products and in baked goods. No known toxicity.

DIPROPYL KETONE • See 4-Heptanone.

DIPROPYL TRISULFIDE • See Sulfides.

DIQUAT DIBROMIDE • Yellow crystals used as an herbicide in animal feed, potable water, potato chips, potato wastes, and processed potatoes. FDA residue tolerance is 0.01 ppm in potable water, 0.5 ppm in processed potatoes including potato chips, and 1 ppm in dried potato wastes when used for animal feed. EPA Genetic Toxicology Program (*see*). Poison by ingestion and other routes. Poisoning complications include vomiting, mucosal ulcers, diarrhea, and other intestinal tract problems. Heart damage and irregular beats occur in severe poisonings. Causes birth defects in experimental animals. A skin and eye irritant.

DISODIUM ADENOSINE TRIPHOSPHATE • A preservative derived from adenylic acid. See Adenosine Triphosphate.

DISODIUM CITRATE • White granular powder or crystals used as a buffer, nutrient for cultured buttermilk, and as a sequestrant (*see*). It is used in cured beef, carbonated beverages, nondairy creamers, cured meat food products, margarine, evaporated milk, oleomargarine, and cured and fresh pork. FDA says it is not to exceed 500 ppm or 1.8 mg/square inch of surface. Moderately toxic if injected under the skin. See Sodium Citrate.

DISODIUM CYANODITHIOMIDOCARBONATE • Bacteria-killing component in the processing of sugarcane. Any substance that releases the cyanide ion can cause poisoning. Sodium cyanide is one of the swiftest poisons known. The FDA data bank, PAFA (see page 10), has fully up-to-date toxicology information available for this additive.

DISODIUM EDTA • White crystalline powder, soluble in water, used as a food preservative and sequestering agent. Promotes color retention in frozen white potatoes (100 ppm), canned potatoes (110 ppm), cooked chickpeas (165 ppm), dried banana cereal (315 ppm), canned strawberry pie filling (500 ppm), gefilte fish (50 ppm), and salad dressing (75 ppm). See Ethylenediamine Tetraacetic Acid (EDTA).

DISODIUM EDTA-COPPER • Copper Versenate. Used as a sequestering agent. See Ethylenediamine Tetraacetic Acid for toxicity.

DISODIUM ETHYLENE-1,2-DISODIUM ETHYLENE-1,2-BISDITHIOCARBA-MATE • Chem Bam. Spring-Bak. An antimicrobial agent used on beets and sugarcane. FDA limits use to 3 ppm based on weight of raw sugarcane or raw beets. EPA Genetic Toxicology Program (*see*). Poison by ingestion. Caused birth defects and mutations in experimental animals.

DISODIUM GUANYLATE • A flavor intensifier believed to be more effective than sodium inosinate and sodium glutamate. It is the disodium salt of 5′-guanylic acid, widely distributed in nature as a precursor of RNA and DNA. Can be isolated from certain mushrooms and is used in canned vegetables. The FDA data bank, PAFA (see page 10), has fully up-to-date toxicology information available for this additive.

DISODIUM INDIGO-5,5-DISULFONATE • Blue No. 2. Acid Blue W. Blue-brown powder used as a color additive on various products. EPA Genetic Toxicology Program (*see*). Moderately toxic by ingestion. Caused tumors in experimental animals. *See* FD and C Colors.

DISODIUM 5′-INOSINATE • Flavor potentiator (*see*), odorless, colorless or white crystal or powder, with a characteristic taste. Used in canned vegetables. The FDA data bank, PAFA (see page 10), has fully up-to-date toxicology information available for this additive. *See* Inosinate.

DISODIUM PHOSPHATE (DIBASIC) • A sequestrant (*see*) used in evaporated milk up to 0.1 percent by weight of finished product; in macaroni and noodle products at not less than 0.5 percent nor more than 1 percent. It is used as an emulsifier up to 3 percent by weight in specified cheeses. Cleared by the U.S. Department of Agriculture's Meat Inspection Department to prevent cooked-out juices in cured hams, pork shoulders and loins, canned hams, chopped hams, and bacon (5 percent in the pickling and 5 percent injected into the product). Used as a buffer to adjust acidity in chocolate products, beverages, sauces, toppings, and enriched farina. Incompatible with alkaloids. It is a mild saline cathartic and has been used in phosphorous-deficiency treatment. It may cause mild irritation to the skin and mucous membranes and can cause purging. GRAS.

DISODIUM PYROPHOSPHATE • Sodium Pyrophosphate. An emulsifier and texturizer used to decrease the loss of fluid from a compound. It is GRAS for use in foods as a sequestrant. *See* Sodium Pyrophosphate.

DISODIUM SUCCINATE • *See* Succinic Acid and Sodium.

DISOYAMINE • *See* Soybean Oil.

DISPERSANT • A dispersing agent, such as polyphosphate, for promoting the formation and stabilization of a dispersion of one substance in another. An emulsion, for instance, would consist of a dispersed substance and the medium in which it is dispersed.

DISTARCH PHOSPHATE • A combination of starch and sodium metaphosphate. It is a water softener, sequestering agent, and texturizer. A modified starch once commonly used in baby foods. It is used in dandruff shampoos. The final report to the FDA of the Select Committee on GRAS Substances stated in 1980 that there is no available evidence that it is a hazard to the public when used as it is now and it should continue its GRAS status with no limitations other than good manufacturing practices.

DISTARCH PROPANOL • A modified starch. The final report to the FDA of the Select Committee on GRAS Substances stated in 1980 that while there is no available evidence demonstrating a hazard to the public at current use levels, uncertainties exist, requiring that additional studies be conducted. The FDA allowed GRAS status to continue while tests were being completed and evaluated. Since 1980, however, nothing new has been reported.

DISTEARYL THIODIPROPIONATE • Antioxidant used in packaging materials. FDA limits it to 0.005 percent migrating from food packages.

DISTILLATE • The volatile material recovered by condensing the vapors of an extract or fruit material that is heated to its boiling point in a still.

DISTILLED • The result of evaporation and subsequent condensation of a liquid, as when water is boiled and the steam is condensed.

DISTILLED ACETYLATED MONOGLYCERIDES • Food emulsifiers and binders in nutrient capsules and tablets to make them palatable; also food-coating agents. Per the FDA, use is "at level not in excess of the amount reasonably required to produce the intended effect." Cleared by the USDA Meat Inspection Department as an emulsifier for shortening. No known toxicity.

DITTANY OF CRETE • *Origanum dictamnus*. A natural flavoring extracted from a small herb grown in Crete. Employed in spice flavorings for beverages and baked goods. There is no reported use of the chemical and no toxicology information is available.

DIURON • A preemergent herbicide in dried citrus pulp used as animal feed as a result of application during growing. Repeated doses produce anemia in rats.

o-DODECALACTONE • A synthetic flavoring. Occurs naturally in butter, cream, and milk. Used in butter, fruit, and pear flavorings for candy, baked goods, oleomargarine, and toppings. Not to exceed 20 ppm in oleomargarine. The FDA data bank, PAFA, has fully up-to-date toxicology information available for this additive.

γ-DODECALACTONE • A synthetic flavoring, colorless, with a coconut odor that becomes butterlike in low concentrations. Used in butter, butterscotch, coconut, fruit, maple, and nut flavorings for beverages, ice cream, ices, candy, baked goods, gelatin desserts, puddings, and jellies. The FDA data bank, PAFA (see page 10), has fully up-to-date toxicology information available for this additive.

1-DODECANAL • Lauryl Aldehyde. Found in pine needles, lime, orange, and other essential oils, it is colorless to light yellow with a fatty odor. It is used as a flavoring agent in various products. Mildly toxic by ingestion.

DODECANOIC ACID • *See* Lauric Acid.

DODECYL ALCOHOL • *See* Fatty Alcohols.

DODECYL GALLATE • An antioxidant. Although allowed as a food additive, there is no current reported use of the chemical, and therefore, although toxicology information may be available, it is not being updated, according to the FDA. *See* Fatty Alcohols.

a-(p-DODECYL PHENYL)-1,1-DIMETHYL UREA • A pesticide.

N-DODECYL SARCOSINE SODIUM SALT • Antifogging agent, antistatic agent used in packaging material. When heated to decomposition, it emits toxic fumes.

DODECYLBENZENESULFONIC ACID • A detergent used to sanitize glass containers for holding milk. FDA permits a residue of less than 400 ppm in solution. May cause skin irritation. If swallowed, will cause vomiting.

DOG GRASS EXTRACT • A natural flavoring extract used in maple flavoring for beverages, ice cream, ices, candy, and baked goods. Derives its name from the fact that it is eaten by sick dogs. The FDA's data bank, PAFA (see page 10), has not yet done a toxicology search on this additive. GRAS.

DOWCO 179 • *See* Chlorpyrifos.

DRACO RUBIN EXTRACT • *See* Dragon's Blood Extract.

DRAGON'S BLOOD EXTRACT • *Daemonorops* spp. The resinous secretion of the fruit of trees grown in Sumatra, Borneo, and India. Almost odorless and tasteless and available in the form of red sticks, pieces, or cakes. Makes a bright crimson powder. Used in bitters flavoring for beverages. Also used to color lacquers and varnishes. There is no reported use of the chemical and no toxicology information is available.

DRIED SORGHUM GRAIN SYRUP • A corn syrup substitute produced from the starch of sorghum grain. *See* Sorghum.

DRIED YEAST • A dietary source of folic acid. Used to enrich farina, cornmeal, corn grits, and bakery products. Dried yeast is cleared for use in food provided the total folic acid content of the yeast does not exceed 0.04 milligrams per gram of yeast. Nontoxic.

DRY MILK, NONFAT • *See* Nonfat Dry Milk.

DRYING AGENTS • *See* Rosin.

DULCAMARA EXTRACT • Bittersweet Nightshade. Extract of the dried stems of *Solanum dulcamara*. Belonging to the family of the nightshades, it is used as a preservative. The ripe berries are used for pies and jams. The unripened berries are deadly. It is made into an ointment by herbalists to treat skin cancers and burns. It induces sweating. *See also* Horse Nettle.

DULSE • A natural flavoring extract from red seaweed. Used as a food condiment. No known toxicity. GRAS.

DV • Abbreviation for *daily value* (*see*).

E

EARTH WAX • General name for ozokerite, ceresin, and montan waxes. *See* Waxes.

ECZEMA • Inflammation of the skin.

EDTA • *See* Ethylenediamine Tetraacetic Acid.

EGG • Particularly associated with eczema in children. May also cause reactions ranging from hives to anaphylaxis. Eggs may also be found in root beer, soups, sausage, coffee, and in cosmetics.

EICOSAPENTAENOIC ACID (EPA) • Found in fish oil (*see*), it reduces production of thromboxane, a clotting agent in the blood, thus making the platelets less "sticky."

ELAIDIC ACID • *See* Oleic Acid.

ELDER FLOWERS • *Sambucus canadensis.* A natural flavoring from the small white flowers of a shrub or small tree. Used in fruit, wine, and spice flavorings for beverages, ice cream, ices, candy, baked goods, and wine. The leaves and bark can cause nausea, vomiting, and diarrhea. The FDA's data bank, PAFA (see page 10), has not yet done a toxicology search on this additive. GRAS.

ELDER TREE LEAVES • Flavoring for use in alcoholic beverages only. There is no reported use of the chemical and no toxicology information is available. *See* Elder Flowers.

ELDERBERRY JUICE POWDER • Dried powder from the juice of the edible berry of a North American elder tree. Used for red coloring. Nontoxic.

ELECAMPANE RHIZOME AND ROOTS • Flavoring in alcoholic beverages only. From a large, coarse European herb having yellow ray flowers. There is no reported use of the chemical and no toxicology information is available.

ELEMI • A soft, yellowish, fragrant plastic resin from several Asiatic and Philippine trees. Slightly soluble in water but readily soluble in alcohol. An oily resin derived from the tropical trees. The *gum* is used in fruit flavoring for beverages, ice cream, ices, candy, and baked goods. The *oil* is used in citrus, fruit, vermouth, and spice flavorings for beverages, ice cream, ices, candy, baked goods, and soups. Used for gloss and adhesion in nail lacquer and to scent soaps and colognes. The resins are used industrially for making varnishes and inks. The FDA's data bank, PAFA (see page 10), has not yet done a toxicology search on this additive.

EMULSIFIERS • Widely used additives to stabilize a mixture and to ensure consistency. They make chocolate more mixable with milk and keep puddings from separating. One of the most widely used emulsifiers is lecithin (*see*) and another is polysorbate 60 (*see*). Di- and monoglycerides (*see both*) are also used in many products. Among common emulsifiers in cosmetics are stearic acid soaps such as potassium and sodium stearates.

EMULSIFYING OIL • Soluble Oil. An oil that when mixed with water produces a milky emulsion. Sodium sulfonate is an example.

EMULSIFYING WAX • Waxes that are treated so that they mix more easily.

EMULSION • What is formed when two or more nonmixable liquids are shaken so thoroughly together that the mixture continues to appear to be homogenized. Most oils form emulsions with water.

ENANTHIC ACID • Used in peeling solutions for fruits and vegetables. *See* Heptanoic Acid.

ENDOSULFAN • Thiodan. Brown crystals made from methane and benzene, it is related to the long-banned but still environmentally present pesticide DDT. Endosulfan is used as an insecticide on fruits and vegetables and on growing tea. It is used especially on tomatoes, carrots, lettuce, and spinach. FDA residue limit on dried tea is 24 ppm. It is toxic by ingestion, inhalation, and skin absorption. Emerging evidence indicates that this insecticide and other chemicals that imitate the human reproductive hormone estrogen may be associated with instances of breast cancer, although definite proof is lacking.

ENDOTHAL • Aquathol. Endothall. An herbicide in potable water. FDA residue tolerance is 0.2 ppm in potable water. Poisonous by ingestion. Irritating to skin, eyes, and mucous membranes. Causes diarrhea.

ENZYMATICALLY HYDROLYZED PROTEIN • Enzymes are used to break down protein in solution. The final report to the FDA of the Select Committee on GRAS Substances stated in 1980 that it should continue its GRAS status with no limitations other than good manufacturing practices.

ENZYME • Any of a unique class of proteins that catalyze a broad spectrum of biochemical reactions. Enzymes are formed in living cells. One enzyme can cause a chemical process that no other enzyme can. Among the enzymes used in foods are those produced by *Aspergillus niger* and *Aspergillus oryzae* for bakery products and, for milk clotting, *Endothis parasitica* or *Bacillus cerus*. The FDA's data bank, PAFA (see page 10), has not yet done a toxicology search on these additives.

ENZYME-MODIFIED FATS • Enzymes such as lipase are used to break down fats and used in the manufacture of cheese and similar foods and as a flavoring. No known toxicity.

ENZYME-MODIFIED SOY PROTEIN • A foaming agent in soda water. No known toxicity.

EPA EXTREMELY HAZARDOUS SUBSTANCES LIST • A list of highly toxic chemicals cited by the Environmental Protection Agency.

EPICHLOROHYDRIN • A colorless liquid with an odor resembling chloroform. It is soluble in water but mixes readily with alcohol and ether. A modifier for food starches that the FDA permits up to a level of 0.3 percent in starch. Used as a solvent for cosmetic resins (*see*) and in the manufacture of varnishes, lacquers, and cements for celluloid articles. A strong skin irritant and sensitizer. Daily administration of one milligram per kilogram of body weight to skin killed all of a group of rats in four days, indicating a cumulative potential. A thirty-minute exposure to air concentrations of 8,300 ppm was lethal to mice. Poisoned animals showed cyanosis, muscular relaxation or paralysis, convulsions, and death. There may be fifty thousand workers exposed to epichlorohydrin, according to OSHA. A two-year study of workers who had been exposed to the substance for six months or more before January 1966 showed an increase in the incidence of cancer. Chronic exposure is known to cause kidney damage in humans. Germany regulates it as a known carcinogen. FDA residue tolerances are less than 0.1 percent with propylene and less than 5 ppm in modified food starch. There is no reported use of the chemical and no toxicology information is available.

1,8-EPOXY-*p*-MENTHANE • *See* Eucalyptol.

EQUISETIC ACID • *See* Aconitic Acid.

ERGOCALCIFEROL • Vitamin D_2.

ERIGERON CANADENSIS • *See* Erigeron Oil.

ERIGERON OIL • *Erigeron canadensis*. Horseweed. Fleabane Oil. Derived from the leaves and tops of a plant grown in the northern and central United States. Used in fruit and spice flavorings for beverages, ice cream, ices, candy, baked goods, and sauces. There is no reported use of the chemical and no toxicology information is available.

ERIODICTYON CALIFORNIUM • *See* Yerba Santa Fluid Extract.

ERURIC ACID • Docosenoic Acid. An acid found in rapeseed, mustard seed, and wallflower seeds. It constitutes 40 to 50 percent of fatty acids of nasturtium seeds. No known toxicity.

ERYTHROBIC ACID • Isoascorbic Acid. Antioxidant. White, slightly yellow crystals that darken on exposure to light. Isoascorbic acid contains one-twentieth the vitamin capacity of ascorbic acid (*see*). Antioxidant used in pickling brine at a rate of 7.5 ounces per 100 gallons; in meat products at the rate of 0.75 ounce per 100 pounds; in beverages; baked goods; and cured cuts and cured pulverized products to accelerate color fixing in curing, to 0.75 ounce per 100 pounds. Nontoxic. The final report to the FDA of the Select Committee on GRAS Substances stated in 1980 that it should continue its GRAS status with no limitations other than good manufacturing practices. The FDA data bank, PAFA (see page 10), has fully up-to-date toxicology information available for this additive.

ERYTHROMYCIN • An antibacterial obtained from the strains of *Streptomyces erythreus* found in the soil. Used to treat a wide range of bacterial infections in humans. It is used as a drug for beef, chicken, eggs, pork, and turkey. FDA tolerances are 0.1 ppm in uncooked edible tissues of swine; zero in uncooked edible tissues of beef cattle and milk; 0.025 ppm in uncooked eggs; and 0.125 ppm in uncooked edible tissues of chickens and turkeys. EPA Genetic Toxicology Program (*see*). Moderately toxic by ingestion. The use of antibiotics in animal feed is highly controversial because it could lead to resistance to the antibiotic in humans as well as allergic reactions.

ERYTHROSINE • Sodium or potassium salt of tetraiodofluorescein, a coal-tar derivative. A brown powder that becomes red in solution. FD and C Red No. 3 is an example. *See* Coal Tar for toxicity.

ERYTHROXYLON COCA • *See* Coca Leaf Extract (Decocainized).

ESCHERICHIA COLI • A gram-negative (*see*) bacteria commonly found in fecal matter and in the human intestines. Certain strains may cause intestinal and urinary tract infections.

ESSENCE • An extract of a substance that retains its fundamental or most desirable properties in concentrated form, such as a fragrance or flavoring.

ESSENTIAL OIL • The oily liquid obtained from plants through a variety of processes. The essential oil usually has the taste and smell of the original plant. Essential oils are called volatile because most of them are easily vaporized. The only theories for calling such oils "essential" are (1) the oils were believed essential to life and (2) they were the "essence" of the plant. The use of essential oils as preservatives is ancient. A large number of oils have antiseptic, germicidal, and preservative action; however, they are primarily used for fragrances and flavorings. No known toxicity when used on the skin. A teaspoon may cause illness in an adult, and less than an ounce may kill.

ESTER • A compound formed from an alcohol and an acid by elimination of water, as ethyl acetate (*see*). Usually, fragrant liquids used for artificial fruit perfumes and flavors. Esterification of rosin, for example, reduces its allergy-causing properties. Toxicity depends on the ester.

ESTERASE-LIPASE • Derived from *Mucor miehei*. An enzyme used as a flavor enhancer in cheese, fats, oils, and milk products. There is no reported use of the chemical and no toxicology information is available.

ESTRADIOL • Oestradiol. Estrace. Estinyl. Estra-L. Estraderm. depGynogen. Depo-Estradiol. Dura-Estrin. E-Cypionate. Estro-Cyp. Estrofem. Estroject-LA. Estronol-LA. Delestrogen. Dioval. Duragen 10. Estraval. Menaval. Valergen. Most potent of the natural estrogenic female hormones. In animals it is implanted in steers and heifers and lambs. It is also implanted in combination with testosterone or progesterone, two other powerful sex hormones. The FDA permits zero tolerance in meat. Estradiol is given to humans by skin patch, tablets, injection, or vaginal cream to treat menopausal symptoms, the effects of a hysterectomy, primary ovarian failure, atrophic vaginitis, postpartum breast engorgement, and inoperable prostate cancer. Potential adverse reactions include nausea, vomiting, depression, high blood pressure, dizziness, migraine, libido changes, water retention, increased risk of stroke, blood clots of the lung, and heart attack. May also worsen nearsightedness, cause intolerance of contact lenses, and lead to loss of appetite, increased appetite, excessive thirst, pancreatitis, bloating, and abdominal cramps. Women may have breakthrough bleeding, altered menstrual flow, painful or absent menstruation, enlargement of benign tumors of the uterus, cervical erosion, abnormal secretions, and vaginal candidiasis. In men there may be enlargement of the breast, testicular atrophy, and impotence. In both sexes there may be jaundice, high blood sugar, high calcium in the blood, folic acid deficiency, dark spots appearing on the skin, hives, acne, oily skin, hairiness or loss of hair, leg cramps, and hemorrhages into the skin. Contraindicated in persons with blood-clot disorders, cancer of the breast, reproductive organs, or genitals, in those with undiagnosed abnormal genital bleeding, and in pregnancy. Should be used with caution in those with high blood pressure, asthma, mental depression, bone disease, blood problems, gallbladder disease, migraine, seizures, diabetes, absences of menstruation, heart failure, liver or kidney dysfunction, and a family history of breast or genital tract cancer. Estradiol's use as an implant in animals is unnecessary and should be outlawed.

ESTRADIOL BENZOATE • *See* Estradiol.

ESTRADIOL-3-BENZOATE • White or slightly brownish, crystalline hormone powder used as a growth promoter in beef and lamb. FDA tolerances are set at 120 parts per trillion in muscle; 480 ppt in fat; 360 ppt in kidney; 240 ppt in liver of heifers, steers, and calves. Tolerance of 120 ppm in muscles and 600 ppm in fat, kidney, and liver of lambs. Has caused cancer in experimental animals as well as birth defects. It is an estrogen used in human medication for birth control and postmenopausal symptoms and does cause side effects. *See* Estradiol.

ESTRADIOL MONOPALMITATE • An estrogen used to promote growth in chickens. It has a zero tolerance in chickens for market. *See* Estradiol.

ESTRAGOLE • A colorless to light yellow, oily liquid occurring naturally in anise, star anise, basil, estragon oil, and pimento oil. Used as a synthetic fruit, licorice, anise, and spice flavoring for beverages, ice cream, ices, candy, baked goods, chewing gum, and condiments. The FDA data bank, PAFA (see page 10), has fully up-to-date toxicology information available for this additive. GRAS.

ESTRAGON • Tarragon. A flavoring agent from the oil of leaves of a plant native to Eurasia and used in fruit, licorice, liquor, root beer, and spice flavorings for beverages, ice cream, ices, candy, baked goods, meats, liquor, and condiments. GRAS.

ESTROGEN • *See* Estradiol.

ETHANAL • *See* Acetaldehyde and Heptanal.

1,2-ETHANEDITHIOL • Derived from ethylene glycol, it is used as a chelating agent (*see*). The vapors cause a severe headache and nausea. The FDA data bank, PAFA, has fully up-to-date toxicology information available for this additive.

ETHANOIC ACID • *See* Acetic Acid.

ETHANOL • Ethyl Alcohol. Rubbing Alcohol. Ordinary Alcohol. Used as a solvent in candy, candy glaze, beverages, ice cream, ices, baked goods, liquors, sauses, and gelatin desserts. An antibacterial used in mouthwashes, nail enamel, astringents, liquid lip rouge, and many other cosmetics products. Clear, colorless, and very flammable, it is made by the fermentation of starch, sugar, and other carbohydrates. Used medicinally as a topical antiseptic, sedative, and blood-vessel dilator. Ingestion of large amounts may cause nausea, vomiting, impaired perception, stupor, coma, and death. When it is deliberately denatured (*see* Denaturant), it is poisonous. GRAS.

ETHANOLAMINE DITHIODIGLYCOATE • *See* Ethanolamines.

ETHANOLAMINE THIOGLYCOLATE • *See* Ethanolamines.

ETHANOLAMINES • Three compounds—monoethanolamine, diethanolamine, and triethanolamine—with low melting points, colorless, and solid that readily absorb water and form viscous liquids and are soluble both in water and alcohol. They have an ammonia smell and are strong bases. Used in cold permanent-wave lotions as a preservative. Also form soaps with fatty acids (*see*) and are widely used as detergents and emulsifying agents. Large quantities are required for a lethal oral dose in mice (2,140 milligrams per kilogram of body weight). They have been used medicinally as sclerosal agents for varicose veins. Can be irritating to skin if very alkaline.

ETHANTHALDEHYDE • *See* Heptanal.

ETHANTHIC ALCOHOL • *See* Heptyl Alcohol.

ETHANTHYL ALCOHOL • *See* Heptyl Alcohol.

ETHEPHON • A pesticide used in raisin-water waste for use in animal feed. FDA residue tolerance is 65 ppm.

ETHER • An organic compound. Acetic ether (*see* Ethyl Acetate) is used in nail polishes as a solvent. Water-insoluble, fat-insoluble liquid with a characteristic odor. It is obtained chiefly by the distillation of alcohol with sulfuric acid and is used chiefly as a solvent. A mild skin irritant. Inhalation or ingestion causes central nervous system depression.

ETHION • An insecticide to kill mites. In fat of cattle it is permitted to 2.5 ppm; in meat and byproducts of cattle as a residue, 0.75 ppm; in milk, zero; and in animal feed from 4 to 10 ppm. It inhibits nerve signals. *See* Organophosphates.

ETHOPABATE • Odorless, white to pink crystals used as an animal drug in chickens to combat bacteria. FDA limits residue to 1.5 ppm in uncooked liver and kidney, 0.5 ppm in uncooked muscles of chickens.

ETHOVAN • *See* Ethyl Vanillin.

2-(1-[ETHOXY IMINO]BUTYL)-5-(2-[ETHYL THIO]PROPYL)-3-HYDROXY-2-CYCLOHEXENE-1-ONE • An herbicide used in animal feed, flaxseed meal, potato pomace, sunflower meal, tomato products (concentrated), and peanut soap-stock. FDA limitations of residue: 24 ppm in tomato products, concentrated; 15 ppm in cottonseed soap-stock; 7 ppm in flaxseed meal; 75 ppm in peanut soap-stock; and 20 ppm in sunflower meal used for animal feed.

p-**ETHOXYBENZALDEHYDE** • A synthetic fruit and vanilla flavoring for beverages, ice cream, ices, candy, and baked goods. The FDA data bank, PAFA (see page 10), has fully up-to-date toxicology information available for this additive.

ETHOXYLATE • An ethyl (*see*) and oxygen compound is added to an additive to make it less or more soluble in water, depending upon the mixture. Ethoxylate acts as an emulsifier.

ETHOXYLATED MONO- AND DIGLYCERIDES • Dough conditioners in bread used to increase the volume of the loaf (not to exceed 0.5 percent of flour used). Also used as an emulsifier in pan-release agents for yeast-leavened bakery products. *See* Glycerides.

ETHOXYQUIN • 1,2-Dihydro-6-Ethoxy-2,2,4-Trimethylquinoline. An antioxidant (*see*) to preserve color in chili powder, paprika, and ground chili at levels not to exceed 100 ppm. The residues for edible products of animals are restricted to 5 ppm in or on the uncooked fat of meat from animals except poultry; 3 ppm in or on the uncooked liver and fat of poultry; and 0.5 ppm in or on the uncooked muscle meat of animals. *See* Coal Tar for toxicity. The FDA data bank, PAFA (see page 10), has fully up-to-date toxicology information available for this additive. *See also* Santoquin.

ETHYL • Signifies a hydrocarbon derived from natural gas.

ETHYL ABIETATE • Amber-colored, thick liquid made from ethyl chloride and rosin. It is used in lacquers and coatings. Skin irritant. Although allowed as a food additive, there is no current reported use of the chemical, and therefore, although toxicology information may be available, it is not being updated, according to the FDA.

ETHYL ACETATE • A colorless liquid with a pleasant fruity odor that occurs naturally in apples, bananas, grape juice, pineapple, raspberries, and strawberries. It is employed as a synthetic flavoring agent in blackberry, raspberry, strawberry, butter, lemon, apple, banana, cherry, grape, peach, pineapple, brandy, muscatel, rum, whiskey, mint, almond, and cream soda flavorings for beverages, ice cream, ices, candy, baked goods, chewing gum, gelatins, puddings, and liquor. A useful solvent in nail enamels and nail-polish remover. Also an artificial fruit essence for perfumes. It is a mild local irritant and central nervous system depressant. The vapors are irritating, and prolonged inhalation may cause kidney and liver damage. Irritating to the skin. Its fat-solvent action produces drying and cracking and sets the stage for secondary infections. The FDA data bank, PAFA, has fully up-to-date toxicology information available for this additive. GRAS.

ETHYL ACETOACETATE • Acetoacetic Ester. A synthetic flavoring that occurs naturally in strawberries. Pleasant odor. Used in loganberry, strawberry, apple, apricot, cherry, peach, liquor, and muscatel flavorings for beverages, ice cream, ices, candy, baked goods, chewing gum, and gelatin desserts. Moderately irritating to skin and mucous membranes. The FDA data bank, PAFA (see page 10), has fully up-to-date toxicology information available for this additive.

ETHYL ACETONE • *See* 2-Pentanone.

ETHYL 2-ACETYL-3-PHENYLPROPIONATE • A synthetic fruit flavoring for beverages, ice cream, ices, candy, baked goods, chewing gum, and gelatin desserts. The FDA data bank, PAFA, has fully up-to-date toxicology information available for this additive.

ETHYL ACONITATE • Aconitic Acid. A synthetic fruit, liquor, and rum flavoring for beverages, ice cream, ices, candy, baked goods, and gelatin desserts. The FDA data bank, PAFA, has fully up-to-date toxicology information available for this additive.

ETHYL ACRYLATE • A synthetic flavoring agent that occurs naturally in pineapple and raspberries. Used in fruit, liquor, and rum flavorings for beverages, ice cream, ices, candy, baked goods, and chewing gum. Also used in the manufacture of water-resistant paint, paper coating, and leather finishes. Highly irritating to the eyes, skin, and mucous membranes and may cause lethargy and convulsions if the concentrated vapor is inhaled. The final report to the FDA of the Select Committee on GRAS Substances stated in 1980 that it should continue its GRAS status with no limitations other than good manufacturing practices. The FDA data bank, PAFA, has fully up-to-date toxicology information available for this additive.

ETHYL ALCOHOL • Contains ethanol (*see*), grain alcohol, and neutral spirits and is used as a solvent in candy glaze, beverages, ices, ice cream, candy, baked goods, liquors, sauces, gelatin desserts, and pizza crusts. It is rapidly absorbed through the gastric and intestinal mucosa. If ingested within a few minutes, the fatal dose in adults is considered one and one-half to two pints of whiskey (40 to 55 percent ethyl alcohol). It was approved in 1976 for use in pizza crusts to extend handling and storage life. The FDA's data bank, PAFA (see page 10), has not yet done a toxicology search on this additive.

ETHYL *p*-ANISATE • A synthetic flavoring agent, colorless to lightly yellow liquid with a light fruity smell. Used in berry, fruit, grape, licorice, anise, liquor, rum, and vanilla flavorings for beverages, ice cream, ices, candy, and baked goods. The FDA data bank, PAFA, has fully up-to-date toxicology information available for this additive.

ETHYL ANTHRANILATE • A synthetic flavoring agent soluble in alcohol and propylene glycol. Clear, colorless-to-amber liquid with an odor of orange blossoms. Used in berry, mandarin, orange, floral, jasmine, neroli, fruit, grape, peach, and raisin flavorings for beverages, ice cream, ices, candy, baked goods, gelatin desserts, and chewing gum. Used in perfumery. The FDA data bank, PAFA, has fully up-to-date toxicology information available for this additive.

ETHYL ASPARTATE • The ester of ethyl alcohol and aspartic acid (*see both*).

ETHYL BENZENECARBOXYLATE • *See* Ethyl Benzoate.

ETHYL BENZOATE • Essence de Niobe. Ethyl Benzenecarboxylate. An artificial fruit essence almost insoluble in water, with a pleasant odor. Used in currant, strawberry, fruit, cherry, grape, liquor, nut, walnut, vanilla, and raspberry flavorings for beverages, ice cream, ices, candy, baked goods, chewing gum, gelatin desserts, and liquors. The FDA data bank, PAFA (see page 10), has fully up-to-date toxicology information available for this additive.

ETHYL BENZOYLACETATE • A synthetic fruit flavoring agent for beverages, ice cream, ices, candy, and baked goods. It becomes yellow when exposed to light. Pleasant odor. The FDA data bank, PAFA, has fully up-to-date toxicology information available for this additive.

ETHYL BENZYL ACETOACETATE • *See* Ethyl 2-Acetyl-3-Phenylpropionate.

ETHYL BENZYL BUTYRATE • A synthetic fruit flavoring for beverages, ice cream, ices, candy, and baked goods. Although allowed as a food additive, there is no current reported use of the chemical, and therefore, although toxicology information may be available, it is not being updated, according to the FDA.

ETHYL BUTYL ACETATE • A synthetic fruit flavoring for beverages, ice cream, ices, and candy. The FDA data bank, PAFA, has fully up-to-date toxicology information available for this additive.

ETHYL BUTYRATE • Butyric Acid. Pineapple Oil. Colorless, with a pineapple odor. It occurs naturally in apples and strawberries. In alcoholic solution it is known as pineapple oil. Used in blueberry, raspberry, strawberry, butter, caramel, cream, orange, banana, cherry, grape, peach, pineapple, rum, walnut, and eggnog flavorings for beverages, ice cream, ices, candy, baked goods, gelatins, puddings, and chewing gum (1,400 ppm). Mildly toxic by ingestion. A skin irritant. The FDA data bank, PAFA (see page 10), has fully up-to-date toxicology information available for this additive. GRAS.

ETHYL CAPRATE • *See* Cognac Oil.

ETHYL CAPROATE • Colorless to yellowish liquid, pleasant odor, soluble in alcohol and ether. Used in artificial fruit essences. *See* Cognac Oil.

ETHYL CAPRYLATE • *See* Cognac Oil.

ETHYL CARBONATE • Carbonic Acid Diethyl Ester. Pleasant odor. Practically insoluble in water. Solvent for nail enamels. No known toxicity.

ETHYL CARVACROL • *See* Carvacryl Ethyl Ether.

ETHYL CELLULOSE • Cellulose Ether. White granules prepared from wood pulp or chemical cotton and used as a binder and filler in dry vitamin preparations up to 35 percent, in chewing gum up to 0.025 percent, and in confectionery up to 0.012 percent. Also used in the manufacture of plastics and lacquers. Binding, dispersing, and emulsifying agent used in cosmetics, particularly nail polishes and liquid lip rouge. Also used as a diluent (*see*). Not susceptible to bacterial or fungal decomposition. No known toxicity.

ETHYL CINNAMATE • Cinnamic Acid. An almost colorless, oily liquid with a faint cinnamon odor. Used as a synthetic flavoring in raspberry, strawberry, cherry, grape, peach, plum, spice, cinnamon, and vanilla flavorings for beverages, ice cream, ices, candy, baked goods, chewing gum, and gelatin desserts. Also used as a fixative for perfumes; also to scent heavy oriental and floral perfumes in soaps, toilet waters, face powders, and perfumes. Insoluble in water. No known toxicity for the skin. Moderately toxic by ingestion. The FDA data bank, PAFA (see page 10), has fully up-to-date toxicology information available for this additive.

ETHYL CITRATE • A bitter, oily sequestrant used in dried egg whites. No known toxicity. *See* Sequestering Agent.

ETHYL CYCLOHEXANEPROPIONATE • A synthetic pineapple flavoring agent for beverages, ice cream, ices, candy, and baked goods. The FDA data bank, PAFA, has fully up-to-date toxicology information available for this additive.

ETHYL DECANOATE • Decanoic Acid. A synthetic flavoring occurring naturally in green and white cognac oils. Used in strawberry, cherry, grape, pineapple, liquor, brandy, cognac, and rum flavorings for beverages, ice cream, ices, candy, baked goods, gelatin desserts, and liquors. The FDA data bank, PAFA (see page 10), has fully up-to-date toxicology information available for this additive.

ETHYL DIHYDROXYPROPYL • PABA. The ester of ethyl alcohol and *p*-dihydroxypropyl aminobenzoic acid. *See* Ethyl Alcohol and Para-Aminobenzoic Acid.

ETHYL DIISOPROPYLCINNAMATE • *See* Cinnamic Acid.

2-ETHYL-3,5(6)-DIMETHYLPYRAZINE • A colorless to slightly yellow liquid with the smell of roasted cocoa used as a flavoring agent in various products. GRAS.

ETHYL DODECANOATE • *See* Ethyl Laurate.

O,O-ETHYL-S-2(ETHYL THIO)ETHYL PHOSPHORODITHIOATE • Widely used insecticide on animal feed, pineapples, and dehydrated sugar-beet pulp. FDA limitation of 5 ppm in dehydrated sugar-beet pulp and pineapple bran when used for animal feed. Poisonous by ingestion, inhalation, and skin contact. May cause mutations. EPA considers it extremely hazardous and it is on the EPA Genetic Toxicology Program (*see*).

ETHYL FORMATE • Formic Acid. A colorless, flammable liquid with a distinct odor occurring naturally in apples and coffee extract. Used as a yeast and mold inhibitor and as a fumigant for bulk and packaged raisins and dried currants; fungicide for cashew nuts, cereals, tobacco, and dried fruits. Also a synthetic flavoring agent for blueberry, raspberry, strawberry, butter, butterscotch, apple, apricot, banana, cherry, grape, peach, plum, pineapple, tutti-frutti, brandy, rum, sherry, and whiskey flavorings for beverages, ice cream, ices, candy, baked goods, liquor, gelatin, and chewing gum. Irritating to the skin and mucous membranes, and in high concentrations it is narcotic. The final report to the FDA of the Select Committee on GRAS Substances stated in 1980 that it should continue its GRAS status with no limitations other than good manufacturing practices. *See* Formic Acid for further toxicity. The FDA data bank, PAFA (see page 10), has not yet done a search of the toxicology literature concerning this additive.

ETHYL FORMIC ACID • *See* Propionic Acid.

ETHYL 2-FURANPROPIONATE • A synthetic raspberry, apple, cherry, and pineapple flavoring agent for beverages, ice cream, ices, candy, and baked goods. The FDA data bank, PAFA, has fully up-to-date toxicology information available for this additive.

ETHYL FURYLPROPIONATE • *See* Ethyl 2-Furanpropionate.

ETHYL GLUTAMATE • The ester of ethyl alcohol and glutamic acid. *See* Glutamate.

4-ETHYL GUAIACOL • A synthetic coffee and fruit flavoring agent for beverages, ice cream, ices, and gelatin desserts. The FDA data bank, PAFA, has fully up-to-date toxicology information available for this additive.

ETHYL HEPTANOATE • A synthetic flavoring agent, colorless, with a fruity, winelike odor and taste, and a burning aftertaste. Used in blueberry, strawberry, butter, butterscotch, coconut, apple, cherry, grape, melon, peach, pineapple, plum, vanilla, cheese, nut, rum, brandy, and cognac flavorings for beverages, ice cream, ices, candy, baked goods, gelatin desserts, chewing gum, and liqueurs. The FDA data bank, PAFA, has fully up-to-date toxicology information available for this additive.

2-ETHYL-2-HEPTENAL • A synthetic pineapple flavoring agent for beverages and candy. The FDA data bank, PAFA (see page 10), has fully up-to-date toxicology information available for this additive.

ETHYL HEXADECANOATE • *See* Ethyl Palmitate.

ETHYL 2,4-HEXADIENOATE • *See* Ethyl Sorbate.

ETHYL HEXANEDIOL • *See* Sorbic Acid.

ETHYL HEXANOATE • A synthetic flavoring agent that occurs naturally in apples, pineapples, and strawberries. Used in fruit, rum, nut, and cheese flavorings for beverages, ice cream, ices, candy, baked goods, chewing gum, gelatin desserts, and jelly. The FDA data bank, PAFA, has fully up-to-date toxicology information available for this additive.

ETHYL 3-HYDROXYBUTYRATE • Used as a stabilizer and antioxidant. The FDA data bank, PAFA, has fully up-to-date toxicology information available for this additive.

ETHYL HYDROXYMETHYL OLEYL OXAZOLINE • A synthetic wax. No known toxicity.

ETHYL a-HYDROXYPROPIONATE • *See* Ethyl Lactate.

ETHYL ISOBUTYRATE • Isobutyric Acid. A synthetic strawberry, fruit, cherry, and butter flavoring agent for flavorings for beverages, ice cream, ices, candy, baked goods, gelatin desserts, and toppings. The FDA data bank, PAFA (see page 10), has fully up-to-date toxicology information available for this additive.

ETHYL ISOVALERATE • Colorless, oily liquid with a fruity odor derived from ethanol and valerate. A synthetic flavoring used in alcoholic solution for pineapple flavoring for beverages, ice cream, ices, candy, baked goods, chewing gum, and gelatin desserts. Used in essential oils and perfumery. The FDA data bank, PAFA, has fully up-to-date toxicology information available for this additive. *See* Valeric Acid.

ETHYL LACTATE • Colorless liquid with a mild odor. Derived from lactic acid with ethanol. Used as a solvent for nitrocellulose, lacquers, resins, and enamels. Used in strawberry, butter, butterscotch, coconut, grape, rum, maple, cheese, and nut flavorings for beverages, ice cream, ices, candy, baked goods, chewing gum (3,100 ppm), gelatin desserts, syrup, and brandy (1,000 ppm). The FDA data bank, PAFA, has fully up-to-date toxicology information available for this additive. *See* Lactic Acid.

ETHYL LAURATE • The ester of ethyl alcohol and lauric acid used as a synthetic flavoring agent. It is a colorless oil with a light, fruity odor. Insoluble in water, very soluble in alcohol. Used in berry, coconut, fruit, grape, liquor, cognac, rum, nut, spice, nutmeg, and cheese flavorings for beverages, ice cream, ices, candy, baked goods, chewing gum, and liqueurs. It is also used as a solvent. The FDA data bank, PAFA (see page 10), has fully up-to-date toxicology information available for this additive.

ETHYL LEVULINATE • Levulinic Acid. Colorless liquid soluble in water. Used as a solvent for cellulose acetate and starch and flavorings. A synthetic apple flavoring for beverages, ice cream, ices, candy, and baked goods. The FDA data bank, PAFA, has fully up-to-date toxicology information available for this additive. *See* Levulinic Acid.

ETHYL LINOLEATE • Prepared from sunflower seed oil, it is used in the vitamin industry.

ETHYL MALATE • *See* Diethyl Malate.

ETHYL MALONATE • Colorless liquid, sweet ester odor. Insoluble in water. Used in certain pigments and flavoring. No known toxicity.

ETHYL MALTOL • White crystalline powder with a sweet fruity taste, it is used as a flavoring agent and processing aid in chocolate, desserts, and wine. Moderately toxic by injection. The FDA data bank, PAFA, has fully up-to-date toxicology information available for this additive.

4-ETHYL-2-METHOXYPHENOL • *See* 4-Ethyl Guaiacol.

ETHYL trans-2-METHYL-2-BUTENOATE • *See* Ethyl Tiglate.

ETHYL 3-METHYLBUTYRATE • A synthetic fruit flavoring agent for beverages, ice cream, ices, and candy. The FDA data bank, PAFA (see page 10), has fully up-to-date toxicology information available for this additive.

ETHYL METHYLENE PHOSPHORODITHIOATE • A widely used insecticide in animal feed. FDA allows residue tolerance of up to 10 ppm in dried tea, 4 ppm in raisins, and 10 ppm in dried citrus pulp when used for animal feed. Extremely hazardous substance. Poison by ingestion and skin contact. Human systemic effects by ingestion include paralysis, motor activity changes, fever, and interference with nerve transmission.

ETHYL METHYLPHENYLGLYCIDATE • Strawberry Aldehyde. Colorless to yellowish liquid having a strong odor suggestive of strawberry. A synthetic berry, loganberry, raspberry, strawberry, coconut, fruit, cherry, grape, pineapple, liquor, and wine flavoring for beverages, ice cream, ices, candy, baked goods, gelatin, pudding, and chewing gum. Used in perfumery. Caused growth retardation in rats, particularly males, and testicular atrophy. Females showed paralysis of hindquarters and deterioration of muscles. GRAS. The FDA data bank, PAFA, has fully up-to-date toxicology information available for this additive.

2-ETHYL-3-METHYLPYRAZINE • Colorless to slightly yellow liquid with a strong raw-potato odor. Used as a flavoring agent in various foods. GRAS. The FDA data bank, PAFA (see page 10), has fully up-to-date toxicology information available for this additive.

ETHYL MYRISTATE • The ester of ethyl alcohol and myristic acid (*see both*). A synthetic coconut, fruit, honey, and cognac flavoring agent for beverages, ice cream, ices, candy, baked goods, and liqueurs. The FDA data bank, PAFA, has fully up-to-date toxicology information available for this additive.

ETHYL NITRITE • Sweet Spirit of Niter. Spirit of Nitrous Ether. A synthetic flavoring agent, a colorless or yellowish liquid with a characteristic odor and a burning, sweetish taste. Used in strawberry, cherry, pineapple, liquor, brandy, and rum flavorings for beverages, ice cream, ices, candy, baked goods, chewing gum, syrups, and icings. It may cause hemoglobinemia, in which oxygen is diminished in the red blood cells, low blood pressure, and when it is in high concentration, narcosis. The FDA data bank, PAFA, has fully up-to-date toxicology information available for this additive.

ETHYL NONANOATE • Nonanoic Acid. A synthetic fruit and rum flavoring agent for beverages, ice cream, ices, candy, baked goods, gelatin desserts, chewing gum, icings, and liqueurs. Mildly toxic by ingestion. A skin irritant. The FDA data bank, PAFA, has fully up-to-date toxicology information available for this additive.

ETHYL 2-NONYNOATE • A synthetic berry, fruit, and melon flavoring agent for beverages, ice cream, ices, candy, and baked goods. The FDA data bank, PAFA, has fully up-to-date toxicology information available for this additive.

ETHYL OCTANOATE • Octanoic Acid. A synthetic flavoring agent that occurs naturally in both cognac-green and cognac-white oils. Used in strawberry, butter, citrus, apple, pineapple, rum, nut, and cheese flavorings for beverages, ice cream, ices, candy, baked goods, gelatin desserts, and chewing gum. Mildly toxic by ingestion. A skin irritant. The FDA data bank, PAFA, has fully up-to-date toxicology information available for this additive.

ETHYL OCTYNE CARBONATE • *See* Ethyl 2-Nonynoate.

ETHYL OLEATE • Oleic Acid. A synthetic flavoring agent, yellowish, oily, insoluble in water. Used in butter and fruit flavorings for beverages, ice cream, ices, candy, baked goods, gelatin desserts, and puddings. An ingredient in nail-polish remover. It is made from carbon, hydrogen, oxygen, and oleic acid (*see*). The FDA data bank, PAFA, has fully up-to-date toxicology information available for this additive.

ETHYL 3-OXOBUTANOATE • *See* Ethyl Acetoacetate.

ETHYL OXYHYDRATE • *See* Rum Ether.

ETHYL PALMITATE • Ethyl Hexadecanoate. The ester of ethyl alcohol and palmitic acid (*see both*). A synthetic flavoring agent, colorless or nearly colorless liquid, with a pleasant odor. Used in butter, honey, apricot, and cherry flavorings for beverages, ice cream, ices, candy, and baked goods. The FDA data bank, PAFA (see page 10), has fully up-to-date toxicology information available for this additive.

ETHYL PERSATE • Persic Oil Acid, Ethyl Ester. The ethyl ester of the fatty acids derived from either apricot kernel oil or peach kernel oil. *See* Apricot and Peach Kernel Oil.

ETHYL PHENYLACETATE • Phenylacetic Acid. A fixative for perfumes, colorless or nearly colorless liquid, with a sweet honey-rose odor. Also a synthetic flavoring agent in honey, butter, apricot, and cherry flavorings for beverages, ice cream, ices, candy, baked goods, and syrups. Moderately toxic by ingestion. The FDA data bank, PAFA, has fully up-to-date toxicology information available for this additive.

ETHYL PHENYLACRYLATE • *See* Ethyl Cinnamate.

ETHYL 3-PHENYLBUTYRATE • A synthetic berry, strawberry, fruit, and cherry flavoring agent for beverages, ice cream, ices, candy, baked goods, and gelatin desserts. No known toxicity.

ETHYL 4-PHENYLBUTYRATE • A synthetic fruit flavoring agent for beverages and candy. The FDA data bank, PAFA (see page 10), has fully up-to-date toxicology information available for this additive.

ETHYL PHENYLGLYCIDATE • Colorless liquid with a strong strawberry odor used as a flavoring agent. Moderately toxic by ingestion. May be mutagenic. The FDA data bank, PAFA, has fully up-to-date toxicology information available for this additive.

ETHYL 3-PHENYLPROPIONATE • A synthetic fruit flavoring agent for beverages, ice cream, ices, candy, and baked goods. No known toxicity. The FDA data bank, PAFA, has fully up-to-date toxicology information available for this additive. *See* Ethyl Cinnamate.

ETHYL 1-PROPENE-1,2,3-TRICARBOXYLATE • *See* Ethyl Aconitate.

ETHYL PROPIONATE • Propionic Acid. A synthetic flavoring agent, colorless, transparent liquid, with a fruit odor. Occurs naturally in apples. Used in butter, fruit, and rum flavorings for beverages, ice cream, gelatin desserts, baked goods, and chewing gum (1,100 ppm). Moderately toxic by ingestion. A skin irritant. The FDA data bank, PAFA, has fully up-to-date toxicology information available for this additive.

ETHYL PYRUVATE • Pyruvic Acid. A synthetic chocolate, fruit, rum, maple, and spice flavoring agent for beverages, ice cream, ices, candy, and baked goods. The FDA data bank, PAFA, has fully up-to-date toxicology information available for this additive.

ETHYL SALICYLATE • Salicylic Ether. Used in the manufacture of artificial perfumes. Occurs naturally in strawberries and has a pleasant odor. Used as a synthetic flavoring agent in fruit, root beer, sassafras, and wintergreen flavorings for beverages, ice cream, ices, candy, baked goods, chewing gum, gelatins, and puddings. At one time it was given medically to rheumatics. May interact with harmful results with medications such as anticoagulants, antidepressants, and medications for cancer such as Methotrexate. May cause allergic reaction in persons allergic to salicylates (*see*). At one time it was used to treat rheumatics. The FDA data bank, PAFA (see page 10), has fully up-to-date toxicology information available for this additive.

ETHYL SEBACATE • *See* Diethyl Sebacate.

ETHYL SORBATE • A synthetic fruit flavoring agent for beverages, ice cream, ices, candy, and baked goods. The FDA data bank, PAFA, has fully up-to-date toxicology information available for this additive.

ETHYL STEARATE • The ester of ethyl alcohol and stearic acid (*see both*).

ETHYL TETRADECANOATE • *See* Ethyl Myristate.

ETHYL TIGLATE • Tiglic Acid. A synthetic raspberry, strawberry, pineapple, and rum flavoring agent for beverages, ice cream, ices, candy, and liquor. The FDA data bank, PAFA (see page 10), has fully up-to-date toxicology information available for this additive.

ETHYL 10-UNDECENOATE • A synthetic coconut, fruit, cognac, and nut flavoring agent for beverages, ice cream, ices, candy, baked goods, and liquor. The FDA data bank, PAFA, has fully up-to-date toxicology information available for this additive.

ETHYL UROCANATE • The ester of ethyl alcohol and urocanic acid. *See* Imidazole.

ETHYL VALERATE • Valeric Acid. A synthetic butter, apple, apricot, peach, and nut flavoring agent for beverages, ice cream, ices, candy, baked goods, gelatin desserts, and chewing gum. The FDA data bank, PAFA, has fully up-to-date toxicology information available for this additive.

ETHYL VANILLIN • An ingredient in perfumes. Colorless flakes with an odor and flavor stronger than vanilla. Used as a synthetic flavoring agent in raspberry, strawberry, butter, butterscotch, caramel, rum, butter, chocolate, cocoa, citrus, coconut, macaroon, cola, fruit, cherry, grape, honey, liquor, muscatel, rum, maple, nut, pecan, root beer, vanilla, and cream soda for beverages, ice cream, ices, candy, baked goods, gelatin desserts, puddings, chewing gum, imitation vanilla extract (28,000 ppm), liquor, icings, and toppings. Caused mild skin irritation in humans. In rats, it produced a reduction in growth rate and heart, kidney, liver, lung, spleen, and stomach injuries. GRAS. The FDA data bank, PAFA (see page 10), has fully up-to-date toxicology information available for this additive.

ETHYLACETIC ACID • *See* Butyric Acid.

2-ETHYLBUTRYIC ACID • A synthetic fruit, nut, and walnut flavoring agent for beverages, ice cream, ices, candy, and baked goods. No known toxicity.

ETHYLENE • The sixth highest volume chemical produced in the United States, it is a colorless gas with a sweet odor and taste. It is derived from heat cracking hydrocarbon gases or fluid removal from of ethanol. It is used to make chemical compounds, including those used to make plastics, refrigerants, anesthetics, and orchard sprays to accelerate fruit ripening. It is highly flammable and potentially explosive. It can asphyxiate.

ETHYLENE BRASSYLATE • *See* Eruric Acid.

1,2-ETHYLENE DIBROMIDE • A colorless, nonflammable liquid with a sweetish odor, derived from bromine and ethylene. Used as a scavenger for lead in gasoline, as a fumigant and general solvent, and in waterproofing products. A cancer-causing agent, toxic by inhalation, ingestion, and skin absorption; a strong irritant to eyes and skin.

ETHYLENE GLYCOL • A slightly viscous liquid with a sweet taste. Absorbs twice its weight in water. Used as an antifreeze and humectant (*see*); also as a solvent. Toxic when ingested, causing central nervous system depression, vomiting, drowsiness, coma, respiratory failure, kidney damage, and possibly death.

ETHYLENE DICHLORIDE (EDC) • Dutch Liquid. 1,2-Dichloroethane. Ethylene Chloride. The halogenate aliphatic hydrocarbon derived from the action of chlorine on ethylene. It is used in the manufacture of vinyl chloride (*see*). A colorless, heavy liquid with a sweet odor, it is widely used as a fumigant for cereal grains, corn grits, cracked rice, and fermented malt beverages; as a solvent for fats, waxes, spices, and resins; as a lead scavenger in antiknock gasolines; in paint, varnish, and finish removers; as a wetting agent; as a penetrating agent; in organic synthesis; and in the making of polyvinyl chloride (PVC) (*see*). EDC is also used as an ingredient in cosmetics and as a food additive. It is one of the highest-volume chemicals produced. It can be highly toxic whether taken into the body by ingestion, inhalation, or skin absorption. It is irritating to the mucous membranes. In cancer testing, the National Cancer Institute found this compound caused stomach cancer, vascularized cancers of multiple organs, and cancers beneath the skin in male rats. Female rats exposed to EDC developed mammary cancers—in some high-dose animals as early as the twentieth week of the study. The chemical also caused breast cancers as well as uterine cancers in female mice and respiratory tract cancers in both sexes. Deaths due to liver and kidney injury following ingestion of large amounts (thirty to seventy grams) have been reported. Clouding of the eyes, hemorrhages, and destruction of the adrenal cortex have been reported in humans and dogs. Annual production in the United States is now estimated at about 10 billion pounds—the sixteenth largest of all chemicals. EDC has been found in human milk and in the exhaled breath of nursing mothers who were exposed to the chemical. FDA tolerances for residues are 125 ppm in cereal grain and 25 ppm in fermented malt beverages. On the Community Right-To-Know List and under International Agency for Research on Cancer (IARC) review (*see both*). Human poison by ingestion. Skin irritant. Implicated in worker sterility. The World Health Organization Committee found it causes birth defects and that it causes cancer in mice and rats when administered orally. The committee expressed the opinion that this solvent (1,2-dichloroethane) should not be used in food.

ETHYLENE DIOLEAMIDE • *See* Fatty Acids.

ETHYLENE DISTEARAMIDE • *See* Fatty Acids.

ETHYLENE OXIDE • A fumigant used on ground spices and other processed natural seasonings. A colorless gas, liquid at 12°C. Derived from the oxidation of ethylene in air or oxygen with silver catalyst. Irritant to the eyes and skin. A suspected human carcinogen. On the Community Right-To-Know List and under IARC review (*see both*).

ETHYLENE OXIDE–METHYL FORMATE MIXTURE • A mold and yeast control agent in dried and glacéed fruits. Ethylene oxide is highly irritating to the mucous membranes and eyes. High concentrations may cause pulmonary edema. Inhalation of methyl formate vapor produces nasal and eye irritation, retching, narcosis, and death from pulmonary irritation. Exposure to 1 percent vapor for two and a half hours or 5 percent vapor for one-half hour is lethal.

ETHYLENE OXIDE POLYMER • Used as a stabilizer in fermented malt beer (300 ppm by weight). *See* Ethylene Oxide and Polymer.

ETHYLENE UREA • *See* Urea.

ETHYLENEBUTYRALDEHYDE • A synthetic chocolate flavoring agent for beverages, ice cream, ices, candy, and baked goods. No known toxicity.

ETHYLENEDIAMINE • Colorless, clear, thick, and strongly alkaline. A component of a bacteria-killing component in processing sugarcane. Also used as a solvent for casein, albumin, and shellac. Has been used as a urinary acidifier. It can cause sensitization leading to asthma and allergic skin rashes.

ETHYLENEDIAMINE TETRAACETIC ACID (EDTA) • An important compound in cosmetics used primarily as a sequestering agent (*see*). EDTA salts are used in crabmeat (cooked and canned) to retard struvite (crystal) formation and promote color retention. It is also used in nonstandardized dressings. It may be irritating to the skin and mucous membranes and cause allergies such as asthma and skin rashes. Also used as a sequestrant in carbonated beverages. When ingested, it may cause errors in a number of laboratory tests, including those for calcium, carbon dioxide, nitrogen, and muscular activity. It is on the FDA list of food additives to be studied for toxicity. It can cause kidney damage. The trisodium salt of EDTA was fed to rats and mice for nearly two years. According to a summary of the report, "although a variety of tumors occurred among test and control animals of both species, the test did not indicate that any of the tumors observed in the test animals were attributed to EDTA." The tests were part of the National Cancer Institute's Carcinogenesis Bioassay Program. The FDA data bank, PAFA (see page 10), has fully up-to-date toxicology information available for this additive.

trans-1,2-ETHYLENEDICARBOXYLIC ACID • *See* Fumaric Acid.

ETHYLPARABEN • *See* Propylparaben.

EUBATUS, RUBUS • *See* Blackberry Bark Extract.

EUCALYPTOL • Eucalyptus Oil. A chief constituent of eucalyptus and cajeput oils. Occurs naturally in allspice, star anise, bay, calamus, and peppermint oil. Eucalyptus oil is 70 to 80 percent active eucalyptol. Eucalyptol is used in mint flavorings for beverages, ice cream, ices, candy, baked goods, and chewing gum. An antiseptic, antispasmodic, and expectorant. Used to flavor toothpaste and mouthwash and to cover up malodors in depilatories. It is not used in hypoallergenic cosmetics. Fatalities followed ingestion of doses as small as three to five milliliters (about a teaspoon), and recovery has occurred after doses as large as twenty to thirty milliliters (about four to five teaspoons). Symptoms of poisoning are epigastric burning with nausea, weakness, water retention, and delirium. The FDA data bank, PAFA (see page 10), has fully up-to-date toxicology information available for this additive.

EUCALYPTUS EXTRACT • *See* Eucalyptus Oil.

EUCALYPTUS GLOBULUS LEAVES • A flavoring. *See* Eucalyptus Oil.

EUCALYPTUS OIL • Dinkum Oil. The colorless to pale yellow volatile liquid from the fresh leaves of the eucalyptus tree. It is 70 to 80 percent eucalyptol and has a spicy, cool taste and a characteristic aromatic, somewhat camphorlike odor. Used in fruit, mint, root beer, spice, and ginger ale flavorings for beverages, ice cream, ices, candy, baked goods, chewing gum, and liquor. Has been used as an expectorant, vermifuge, and local antiseptic. Fatalities have followed doses as small as three to five milliliters (about equal to a teaspoon), and about one milliliter has caused coma. Symptoms include epigastric burning with nausea. Symptoms have been reported to occur as long as two hours after ingestion. The FDA data bank, PAFA, has not yet done a search of the toxicology literature concerning this additive.

EUCHEUMA COTTONI EXTRACT • Eucheuma Spinosum Extract. A stabilizing and thickening agent in foods. Used in dairy products to suspend particles and for gelling. No known toxicity. *See* Hydrogenation and Carrageenan.

EUGENOL • An ingredient in perfumes and dentifrices obtained from clove oil. Occurs naturally in allspice, basil, bay leaves, calamus, pimento, and laurel leaves. It has a spicy, pungent taste. Used as a fixative in perfumes. Darkens and thickens upon exposure to air. Used as a defoamer in yeast production, in the manufacture of vanilla, and in perfumery. It is a synthetic fruit, nut, and spice flavoring for beverages, ice cream, ices, candy, baked goods, chewing gum, gelatin desserts, meats (2,000 ppm), and condiments. Eugenol also acts as a local antiseptic. When ingested, may cause vomiting and gastric irritation. Because of its potential as an allergen, it is left out of hypoallergenic cosmetics. Toxicity is similar to phenol, which is highly toxic. Death in laboratory animals given eugenol is due to vascular collapse. GRAS. The FDA data bank, PAFA (see page 10), has fully up-to-date toxicology information available for this additive.

EUGENYL ACETATE • Acetic Acid. A synthetic berry, fruit, mint, spice, and vanilla flavoring agent for beverages, ice cream, ices, candy, baked goods, chewing gum, and condiments. The FDA data bank, PAFA, has fully up-to-date toxicology information available for this additive.

EUGENYL BENZOATE • A synthetic fruit and spice flavoring agent for beverages, ice cream, ices, candy, and baked goods. The FDA data bank, PAFA, has fully up-to-date toxicology information available for this additive.

EUGENYL FORMATE • Formic Acid. A synthetic spice flavoring agent used in condiments. The FDA data bank, PAFA (see page 10), has fully up-to-date toxicology information available for this additive. *See* Formic Acid for toxicity.

EUGENYL METHYL ETHER • A synthetic raspberry, strawberry, fruit, spice, clove, and ginger flavoring agent for beverages, ice cream, ices, candy, baked goods, and jellies. The FDA data bank, PAFA, has fully up-to-date toxicology information available for this additive.

EVERNIA FURFURACEA • *See* Oak Moss, Absolute.

EVERNIA PRUNASTIC • *See* Oak Moss, Absolute.

EXALTOLIDE • *See* Pentadecalactone.

EXCITOTOXICOLOGY • The study of chemicals that overstimulate and damage nerves. Glutamate (*see*) is considered an excitoxin.

EXCITOTOXIN • *See* Excitotoxicology.

EXTRACT • The solution that results from passing alcohol or an alcohol-water mixture through a substance. Examples of extracts would be the alcohol-water mixture of vanillin, orange, or lemon extracts found among the spices and flavorings on the supermarket shelf. Extracts are not as strong as essential oils (*see*).

EYE ALLERGY • There are many forms of allergy of the eye. The mucous membranes of the eye may be involved in allergic rhinitis. Such allergic conjunctivitis may also occur by itself without irritation of the nose. Another form, spring "pinkeye," is probably due to allergens in the air. Dust, mold spores, foods, and eye medications may all cause conjunctivitis. There is also a less severe, chronic form of allergic conjunctivitis. Symptoms include prolonged photophobia, itching, burning, and a feeling of dryness. There may be a watery discharge, and finding the source of allergy is often difficult.

F

FAMPHUR • 0,0-Dimethyl 0-P (Dimethylsulfo/amoyl)Phenyl Phosphoro-thioate. An insecticide to combat grubs in animal feed. The FDA residue tolerance is 0.1 ppm in meat, fat, and meat byproducts of cattle.

FARNESOL • A flavoring agent that occurs naturally in ambrette seed, star anise, cassia, linden flowers, oils of musk seed, citronella, rose, and balsam. Used in berry, apricot, banana, cherry, melon, peach, citrus, fruit, raspberry, and strawberry flavorings for beverages, ice cream, ices, candy, baked goods, and gelatin desserts. Used in perfumery to emphasize the odor of sweet floral perfumes such as lilac. Mildly toxic when ingested. Causes mutations in laboratory animals. The FDA data bank, PAFA (see page 10), has fully up-to-date toxicology information available for this additive.

FASEB • Abbreviation for the Federation of American Societies for Experimental Biology, members of which evaluate studies for the FDA.

FAT • The most concentrated source of food energy and very necessary to health. Fat deposits provide insulation and protection for body structure as well as storing energy. Food fats are carriers of fat-soluble vitamins and include certain essential unsaturated fatty acids (see). Saturated fats contain only single-bond carbon linkages and are the least active chemically. They are usually solid at room temperature. Most animal fats are saturated. The common saturated fats are acetic, butyric, caproic, caprylic, capric, lauric, myristic, palmitic, stearic, arachidic, and behenic. Butterfat, coconut oil, and peanut oil are high in saturated fats. Unsaturated fats contain one or more double-bond carbon linkages and are usually liquid at room temperature. Vegetable oils and fish oils most frequently contain unsaturated fats. Among the unsaturated fats are caproleic, lauroleic, myristoleic, palmitoleic, oleic, petroselinic, vaccenic, linolenic, elaesosearic, gadoleic, arachidonic, and erucic.

FAT FREE • Less than 0.5 grams per serving.

FATIGUE • Everyone's nose becomes "fatigued" when smelling a certain odor. No matter how much you like a fragrance, you can only smell it for a short interval. It is nature's way of protecting humans from overstimulation of the olfactory sense.

FATTY ACIDS • One of any mixture of liquid and solid acids, capric, caprylic, lauric, myristic, oleic, palmitic, and stearic. In combination with glycerin they form fat. Necessary for normal growth and skin. In foods they are used as emulsifiers, binders, and lubricants, and as defoamer components in the processing of beet sugar and yeast. Polyglycerol esters of fatty acids are prepared from edible fats, oils, corn, cottonseed, palm, fruit, peanut, safflower, soybean oils, lard, and tallow. Used as emulsifiers and defoaming agents in beet sugar and yeast production, and as lubricant binders and components in the manufacture of other food additives. Fatty acid salts (one or more of the aluminum, ammonium, calcium, magnesium, potassium, and sodium salts of all the above fatty acids) are used as emulsifiers, binders, and anticaking agents. A free fatty acid (FFA) is the uncombined fatty acid present in a fat. Some raw oils may contain as much as 3 percent FFA. These are removed in the refining process, and refined fats and oils ready for use as foods usually have extremely low FFA content. *See* Stearic Acid. No known toxicity.

FATTY ALCOHOLS • Cetyl, Stearyl, Lauryl, Myristyl. Solid alcohols made from acids and widely used in cosmetics. Cetyl and stearyl alcohols form an occlusive film to keep skin moisture from evaporating, and they impart a velvety feel to the skin. Lauryl and myristyl are used in detergents and creams. In foods, synthetic fatty alcohols include hexyl, octyl, decyl, lauryl, myristyl, cetyl, and stearyl alcohols. They are used as substitutes for the corresponding naturally derived fatty alcohols. Very low toxicity.

FD AND C COLORS • Food, Drug, and Cosmetic Colors. A color additive is any dye, pigment, or other substance capable of coloring a food, drug, or cosmetic, on any part of the human body. In 1900, there were more than eighty dyes used to color food. There were no regulations, and the same dye used to color clothes could be used to color candy. In 1906, the first comprehensive legislation for food colors was passed. Only seven colors, when tested, were shown to be composed of known ingredients that demonstrated no harmful effects. Those colors were orange, erythrosin, ponceau 3R, amaranth, indigotin, naphthol yellow, and light green. A voluntary system of certification for batches of color dyes was set up. In 1938, new legislation was passed, superseding the 1906 act. The colors were given numbers instead of chemical names, and every batch had to be certified. Fifteen food colors were in use at the time. In 1950, children were made ill by certain coloring used in candy and popcorn. These incidents led to the delisting of FD and C Orange No. 1 and Orange No. 2 and FD and C Red No. 32. Since that time, because of experimental evidence of possible harm, Red 1 and Yellow 1,2,3, and 4 have also been delisted. Violet 1 was removed in 1973. In 1976, one of the most widely used of all colors, FD and C Red No. 2, was removed because it was found to cause tumors in rats. In 1976, Red No. 4 was banned for coloring maraschino cherries (its last use), and carbon black was also banned, because both contain cancer-causing agents.

Earlier, in 1960, scientific investigations were required by law to determine the suitability of all colors in use for permanent listing. Citrus Red No. 2 (limited to 2 ppm) for coloring orange skins has been permanently listed. Blue No. 1, Red No. 3, Yellow No. 5, and Red No. 40 are permanently listed without any restrictions. In 1959, the Food and Drug Administration approved the use of "lakes," in which the dyes have been mixed with alumina hydrate to make them insoluble. *See* FD and C Lakes.

The other food coloring additives remained on the "temporary list." The provisional list permitted colors then in use to continue on a provisional, or interim, basis pending completion of studies to determine whether the colors should be permanently approved or terminated. FD and C Red No. 3 (erythrosin) is permanently listed for use in food and ingested drugs and provisionally listed for cosmetics and externally applied drugs. It is used in foods such as gelatins, cake mixes, ice cream, fruit cocktail cherries, bakery goods, and sausage casings.

The FDA postponed the closing date for the provisionally listed color additives—FD and C Red No. 3, D&C Red No. 33, and D&C Red No. 36—to May 2, 1988, to allow additional time to study "complex scientific and legal questions about the colors before deciding to approve or terminate their use in food, drugs and cosmetics." The agency asked for sixty days to consider the impact of the October 1987 U.S. Court of Appeals ruling that there is no exception to the Delaney Amendment (see), which says that cancer-causing agents may not be added to food. On July 13, 1988, the Public Citizen Health Research Group announced that the FDA agreed to revoke by July 15, 1988, the permanent listing of four color additives used in drugs and cosmetics—D&C Red No. 8, D&C Red No. 9, D&C Red No. 19, and D&C Orange No. 17. In a unanimous decision in October 1987, the U.S. Court of Appeals for the District of Columbia said the FDA lacked legal authority to approve two of the colors, D&C Orange No. 17 and D&C Red No. 19, since they had been found to induce cancer in laboratory animals. The Supreme Court ruled against an appeal on April 18, 1988. Meanwhile, Public Citizen also brought a similar suit, challenging the use of D&C Red No. 8 and D&C Red No. 9, which was before the U.S. Circuit Court of Appeals in Philadelphia. Under an agreement between the FDA and Public Citizen, the case was sent back to the FDA, and the agency delisted these colors as well as D&C Orange No. 17 and D&C Red No. 19. Other countries as well as the World Health Organization maintain there are inconsistencies in safety data and in the banning of some colors, which, in turn, affects international commerce. As of this writing, there is still a great deal of confusion about the colors, with the FDA maintaining that the cancer risk is minimal—as low as one in a billion—for the colors, while groups such as Nader's Public Citizen maintain that *any* cancer risk for a food additive is unacceptable. In 1990, the lakes of Red No. 3 were removed for all uses from the approved list. The color itself was also removed in 1990 for cosmetic and external drug use. It is still, as of this writing, approved for food and ingested drugs.

FD AND C BLUE NO. 1 • Brilliant Blue FD and C. A coal-tar derivative, triphenylmethane, it is used as a coloring in bottled soft drinks, gelatin desserts, ice cream, ices, dry drink powders, candy, confections, bakery products, cereals, and puddings. It is also used for hair colorings, face powders, and other cosmetics. May cause allergic reactions. On the FDA permanent list of color additives. Rated 1A—that is, completely acceptable for nonfood use—by the World Health Organization. However, it produces malignant tumors at the site of injection and by ingestion in the rat. The FDA data bank, PAFA (see page 10), has fully up-to-date toxicology information available for this additive. *See* FD and C Colors.

FD AND C BLUE NO. 1 ALUMINUM LAKE • Aluminum salt of certified FD and C Blue No. 1 (*see*). *See* FD and C Colors and FD and C Lakes.

FD AND C BLUE NO. 2 • Indigotin. Indigo Carmine. A dark blue powder, a coal-tar derivative, triphenylmethane; almost always contains sodium chloride or sulfate. Easily faded by light. Used in bottled soft drinks, bakery products, cereals, candy, confections, and dry drink powders. It is also used in mint-flavored jelly, frozen desserts, candy, confections, and rinses and as a dye in kidney tests and for testing milk. It is a sensitizer in the allergic. On the provisional list of approved color additives. Produces malignant tumors at the site of injection when introduced under the skin of rats. The World Health Organization gives it a toxicology rating of B—available data not entirely sufficient to meet requirements for food use. Permanently listed for foods and drugs in 1987. The FDA data bank, PAFA (see page 10), has fully up-to-date toxicology information available for this additive. *See* FD and C Colors.

FD AND C CITRUS RED NO. 2 • Found in 1960 to damage internal organs and to be a weak cancer-causing agent. Used to color orange skins. The World Health Organization said the color has been shown to cause cancer and that toxicological data available were inadequate to allow the determination of a safe limit; they recommended that it not be used as a food color. The FDA ruled on October 28, 1971, that the results of several rodent studies and one dog study using both oral and injected Citrus Red No. 2 showed either no adverse effect or no adverse-effect levels. No abnormalities in urinary bladders were reported. The FDA noted that a paper presented in 1965 by the University of Otega Medical School reported a significant level of urinary bladder cancers in rodents fed the dye for up to twenty-four months. The FDA said that since slides of the tissues in photographs were not yet available for examination, and since there has been no confirmation of the studies, the listing of Citrus Red No. 2 should remain unchanged until the Otega results can be confirmed by examination. *See* FD and C Colors.

FD AND C GREEN NO. 1 • Guinea Green B. A dull, dark green powder used as a coloring in bottled soft drinks. The certified color industry did not apply for the extension of this color because of the small demand for its use, so it was automatically deleted from the list of color additives in 1966. Rated E by the World Health Organization, meaning it was found to be harmful and not to be used in food. *See* FD and C Colors.

FD AND C GREEN NO. 2 • Light Green S.F. Yellow. Coloring used in bottled soft drinks. Because of lack of demand for this color, the certified color industry did not petition for extension and it was automatically deleted in 1966. It produces tumors at the site of injection under the skin of rats. *See* FD and C Colors.

FD AND C GREEN NO. 3 • Fast Green. Permanently listed for use in food, drugs, and cosmetics, except in the area of the eye, by the FDA in 1983. Used as a coloring in mint-flavored jelly, frozen desserts, gelatin desserts, candy, confections, baking products, and cereals. Has been suspected of being a sensitizer in the allergic. On the FDA permanent list of approved color additives. Produces malignant tumors at the site of injection when introduced under the skin of rats.

The World Health Organization gives it a toxicology rating of 1A, meaning that it is completely acceptable. The FDA data bank, PAFA (see page 10), has fully up-to-date toxicology information available for this additive. *See* FD and C Colors.

FD AND C LAKES • Aluminum or Calcium Lakes. Lakes are pigments prepared by combining FD and C colors with a form of aluminum or calcium, which makes the colors insoluble. Aluminum and calcium lakes are used in confection and candy products and for dyeing eggshells and other products that are adversely affected by water. *See* FD and C Colors for toxicity.

FD AND C RED NO. 2 • Amaranth. Formerly one of the most widely used cosmetic and food colorings. A dark, reddish brown powder that turns bright red when mixed with fluid. A monoazo color, it was used in lipsticks, rouges, and other cosmetics as well as in cereals, maraschino cherries, and desserts. The safety of this dye was questioned by American scientists for more than twenty years. Two Russian scientists found that FD and C Red No. 2 prevented some pregnancies and caused some stillbirths in rats. The FDA ordered manufacturers using the color to submit data on all food, drug, and cosmetics products containing it. Controversial tests at the FDA's National Center for Toxicological Research in Arkansas showed that in high doses Red No. 2 caused a statistically significant increase in a variety of cancers in female rats. The dye was banned by the FDA in January 1976.

FD AND C RED NO. 3 • Erythrosin. Bluish Pink. A coal-tar derivative, a xanthene color, used in toothpaste and in canned fruit cocktail, ice cream, cereals, puddings, fruit salad, sherbets, gelatin desserts, cherry pie mix (up to 0.01 percent), candy, confections, and in mixes with maraschino cherries. Has been determined a carcinogen. It was reported in 1981 by NIH researchers that Red No. 3 may interfere with transmission of nerve impulses in the brain. It contains iodine and has been shown to affect the thyroid glands of laboratory animals, but not of humans. Children who eat large amounts of artificially colored cherries, gelatin desserts, and other FD and C Red No. 3–colored products could be at risk. *See* FD and C Colors. The FDA was supposed to permanently list this color in 1988 but has postponed the ruling "to allow the agency additional time to study complex scientific and legal questions about the color before deciding to approve or terminate its use in food." The FDA data bank, PAFA (see page 10), has fully up-to-date toxicology information available for this additive.

FD AND C RED NO. 3 ALUMINUM LAKE • The aluminum salt of certified FD and C Red No. 3 (*see*). *See* FD and C Colors and FD and C Lakes.

FD AND C RED NO. 4 • A monoazo color and coal tar. Used in mouthwashes, bath salts, and hair rinses. It was banned in food by the FDA in 1964 when it was shown to damage the adrenal glands and bladders of dogs. The agency relented and gave it a provisional license for use in maraschino cherries. It was banned in all food in 1976 because it was shown to cause urinary bladder polyps and atrophy of the adrenal glands in animals. It was also banned in orally taken drugs but is still permitted in cosmetics for external use only. *See* FD and C Colors.

FD AND C RED NO. 20 • Permanently listed by the FDA in 1983 for general use in drugs and cosmetics (except in areas around the eye).

FD AND C RED NO. 22 • Permanently listed by the FDA in 1983 for general use in drugs and cosmetics (except in areas around the eye).

FD AND C RED NO. 40 • Allura Red AC. Newest color. Used widely in the cosmetics industry. Approved in 1971. Allied Chemical has an exclusive patent on it. It is substituted for FD and C Red No. 4 in many cosmetic, food, and drug products. Permanently listed because unlike the producers of "temporary" colors, this producer supplied reproductive data. However, many American scientists feel that the safety of Red No. 40 is far from established, particularly because all the tests were conducted by the manufacturer, and therefore, the dye should not have received a permanent safety rating. The National Cancer Institute reported that p-credine, a chemical used in the preparation of Red No. 40, was carcinogenic in animals. In rats, a high (3,800–8,350 mg/kg) oral dose of the coloring caused adverse reproductive effects. The FDA permanently listed Red No. 40 for use in foods and ingested drugs but only temporarily listed it for cosmetics and externally applied drugs. The FDA data bank, PAFA (see page 18), has fully up-to-date toxicology information available for this additive. *See* Azo Dyes and FD and C Colors.

FD AND C VIOLET NO. 1 • Used as a coloring matter in gelatin desserts, ice cream, sherbets, carbonated beverages, dry drink powders, candy, confections, bakery products, cereals, puddings, and for the Department of Agriculture's meat stamp. A Canadian study in 1962 showed the dye caused cancer in 50 percent of the rats fed the dye in food. The FDA did not consider this valid evidence since the exact nature of the dye used could not be determined and all records and specimens were lost and not available for study. Furthermore, previous and subsequent studies have not confirmed evidence of Violet 1 causing cancer in rats. However, a two-year study with dogs did show noncancerous lesions on the dogs' ears after being fed Violet 1. The FDA again felt the study was not adequate but that the ear lesions did not appear to be dye-related and that perhaps two years might be too short a period to determine their eventual outcome. The FDA ruled on October 28, 1971, that Violet 1 should remain provisionally listed pending the outcome of a new dog study to be started as soon as possible and to last seven years. The FDA finally banned the use of Violet 1 in 1973. In 1976, however, the U.S. Department of Agriculture found that Violet 1 was still being used as a "denaturant" on carcasses, meats, and food products. The USDA ruled that any such mixing of Violet 1 with any substance intended for food use will cause the final product to be "adulterated." *See* FD and C Colors.

FD AND C YELLOW NO. 5 • Tartrazine. A coal-tar derivative, it is a pyrazole color used in prepared breakfast cereals, imitation strawberry jelly, bottled soft drinks, gelatin desserts, ice cream, sherbets, dry drink powders, candy, confections, bakery products, spaghetti, and puddings. Also used as a coloring in hair rinses, hair-waving fluids, and in bath salts. Causes allergic reactions in persons sensitive to aspirin. The certified color industry petitioned for permanent listing of this color in February 1966 with no limitations other than good manufacturing practice. However, in February 1966, the FDA proposed the listing of this color with a maximum rate of use of 300 ppm in food. The color industry objected to the limitations. Yellow No. 5 was thereafter permanently listed as a color additive without restrictions. Rated 1A by the World Health Organization—acceptable in food. It is estimated that half the aspirin-sensitive people plus 47,000 to 94,000 others in the nation are sensitive to this dye. It is used in about 60 percent of both over-the-counter and prescription drugs. Efforts were made to ban this color in over-the-counter pain relievers, antihistamines, oral decongestants, and prescription anti-inflammatory drugs. Aspirin-sensitive patients have been reported to develop life-threatening asthmatic symptoms upon ingestion of Yellow No. 5. Since 1981, it is supposed to be listed on the label if it is used. The FDA data bank, PAFA (see page 10), has fully up-to-date toxicology information available for this additive. *See* FD and C Colors.

FD AND C YELLOW NO. 5 ALUMINUM LAKE • *See* FD and C Yellow No. 5, FD and C Colors, and FD and C Lakes.

FD AND C YELLOW NO. 6 • Monoazo. Sunset Yellow FCF. A coal-tar, monoazo color used in carbonated beverages, bakery products, candy, confectionery products, gelatin desserts, and dry drink powders. It is also used in hair rinses as well as other cosmetics. It is not used in products that contain fats and oils. Since there is evidence that it causes allergic reactions, alcoholic beverages that contain it must list it on the label according to the Bureau of Alcohol. Rated 1A by the World Health Organization—acceptable in foods. Permanently listed December 22, 1986. In 1989, a ruling went into effect that it had to be listed on labels because of its ability to induce allergic reactions. The FDA data bank, PAFA, has fully up-to-date toxicology information available for this additive. *See* FD and C Colors.

FD AND C YELLOW NO. 6 ALUMINUM LAKE • The FDA data bank, PAFA, has fully up-to-date toxicology information available for this additive. *See* FD and C Yellow No. 6, FD and C Colors, and FD and C Lakes.

FECULOSE STARCH ACETATE • *See* Modified Starch.

FENAMIPHOS • A worm killer used in animal feeds, pineapples, and raisins. FDA's residue tolerances are 25 ppm in citrus oil, 0.3 ppm in raisins, 5 ppm in dried apple pomace, 2.5 ppm in citrus molasses, 10 ppm in pineapple bran, and 3 ppm in raisin waste when used for animal feed. EPA considers it extremely hazardous. Poison by ingestion, inhalation, and skin contact.

FENARIMOL • White, odorless crystals used as a fungicide in animal feed and apples. Limited to 0.2 ppm in wet and dry apple pomace when used for animal feed. The FDA residue tolerance for meat and meat byproducts of cattle, goats, hogs, or sheep is 0.01 ppm. As a residue in fat, kidney, and livers of cattle, sheep, hogs, goats, and poultry, it is 0.1; in eggs, 0.01; in milk, 0.003. Moderately toxic by ingestion. Caused mutations in experimental animals.

FENBENDAZOLE • Panacur. Animal drug used to combat worms in animal feed and in beef and pork. Tolerance of residues in liver of cattle is 0.8 ppm, 5 ppm in swine muscle, and 20 ppm in swine kidney and skin. Can cause mutations.

FENCHOL • *See* Fenchyl Alcohol.

***d*-FENCHONE** • A synthetic flavoring occurring naturally in common fennel (*see*). An oily liquid with a camphor smell, it is practically insoluble in water. Used in berry, liquor, and spice flavorings for beverages, ice cream, ices, candy, baked goods, and liquors. Used medically as a counterirritant. The FDA data bank, PAFA (see page 10), has fully up-to-date toxicology information available for this additive.

FENCHYL ALCOHOL • A synthetic berry, lime, and spice flavoring agent for beverages, ice cream, ices, candy, and baked goods. No known toxicity.

FENNEL • Common. Sweet. One of the earliest known herbs from the tall, beautiful shrub. The fennel flowers appear in June and are bright yellow with a characteristic fennel taste. *Common fennel* is used as a sausage and spice flavoring for beverages, baked goods, meats, and condiments. *Sweet fennel* has the same uses and is also included in ice cream, ices, and candy. *Sweet fennel oil* is used in raspberry, fruit, licorice, anise, rye, sausage, root beer, sarsaparilla, spice, wintergreen, and birch beer flavorings for beverages, ice cream, ices, candy, baked goods, gelatin desserts, condiments, meats, and liquors. Compresses of *fennel tea* are used by organic cosmeticians to soothe inflamed eyelids and watery eyes. May cause allergic reactions. The FDA data bank, PAFA (see page 10), has not yet done a search of the toxicology literature concerning this additive. GRAS.

FENOXAPROP-ETHYL • Acclaim. Furore. Puma. Whip. A selective postemergent herbicide to control grassy weeds in broad-leaved crops and turf grass. The FDA limits residue to 0.05 ppm on cottonseed, peanuts, peanut hulls, rice grain, and soybeans. The tolerance limit in meat and meat byproducts and fat of cattle, goats, hogs, and sheep is also 0.05 ppm, and in milk is 0.02 ppm.

FENPROSTALENE • Bovilene. An animal drug used to treat beef. FDA residue limit is 20 ppb in liver, from 10 to 30 ppm in uncooked edible parts, and 100 ppb at injection site in cattle. A prostaglandin used to induce abortion in feedlot heifers and for estrus control in beef and nonlactating dairy cattle.

FENTHION • Mercaptophos. Widely used insecticide in fish, meat, and sauces. FDA limits residues in grass, alfalfa, and rice as well as in fat, meat, and meat byproducts of hogs and poultry, and in milk, to 1 ppm. EPA Genetic Toxicology Program (*see*). A human poison by any route. Caused tumors and birth defects in experimental animals. *See* Organophosphates.

FENUGREEK SEED • Greek Hay. An annual herb grown in southern Europe, North Africa, and India. The seeds are used in making curry. *Fenugreek* is a butter, butterscotch, maple, black walnut, and spice flavoring for beverages, ice cream, ices, candy, baked goods, syrups, meats, and condiments. The *extract* (*see*) is a butter, butterscotch, caramel, chocolate, coffee, fruit, maple, meat, black walnut, walnut, root beer, spice, and vanilla flavoring agent for beverages, ice cream, ices, pickles, liquors, and icings. The *oleoresin* (*see*) is a fruit, maple, and nut flavoring agent for beverages, ice cream, ices, candy, baked goods, puddings, and syrups. It is also used in hair tonic, supposedly to prevent baldness; also added to powders, poultices, and ointments. The FDA data bank, PAFA (see page 10), has not yet done a search of the toxicology literature concerning this additive. GRAS.

FENVALERATE • Sumifly. An insecticide used in animal feed, sunflower seeds, and tomatoes. Insecticide residue tolerance of 0.05 ppm on all food items. Limitation of 20 ppm in animal feed. Cyanide and its compounds are on the

Community Right-To-Know List. Poison by ingestion. Moderately toxic by skin contact. Highly toxic to fish and bees. Corrosive and causes eye damage. A skin irritant.

FERMENTATION-DERIVED MILK-CLOTTING ENZYME • Used in the production of cheese as permitted by Standards of Identity (*see*).

FERRIC CHLORIDE • Flavoring agent for various foods. EPA Genetic Toxicology Program (*see*). Withdrawn as a coloring agent. Moderately toxic by ingestion. Corrosive. Causes adverse reproductive effects in experimental animals. The FDA data bank, PAFA (see page 10), has not yet done a search of the toxicology literature concerning this additive. GRAS as a nutrient.

FERRIC CHOLINE CITRATE • *See* Iron Salts.

FERRIC CITRATE • White crystals, odorless with a metallic taste. Used as a nutrient supplement in various foods. There is no reported use of the chemical and no toxicology information is available.

FERRIC ORTHOPHOSPHATE • *See* Iron Salts.

FERRIC PHOSPHATE • A dietary supplement used in egg substitutes, pasta products, and rice products. The final report to the FDA of the Select Committee on GRAS Substances stated in 1980 that there is no available evidence that it is a hazard to the public when used as it is now and it should continue its GRAS status with limitations on the amounts that can be added to food. The FDA data bank, PAFA (see page 10), has not yet done a search of the toxicology literature concerning this additive. *See* Iron Salts.

FERRIC PYROPHOSPHATE • The FDA data bank, PAFA, has not yet done a search of the toxicology literature concerning this additive. *See* Iron Salts. GRAS.

FERRIC SODIUM PYROPHOSPHATE • A nutrient supplement. The final report to the FDA of the Select Committee on GRAS Substances stated in 1980 that there is no available evidence that it is a hazard to the public when used as it is now and it should continue its GRAS status with limitations on the amounts that can be added to food. There is no reported use of the chemical and no toxicology information is available. *See* Iron Salts.

FERRIC SULFATE • A flavoring agent. The FDA data bank, PAFA, has not yet done a search of the toxicology literature concerning this additive. *See* Iron Salts.

FERROCHOLINATE • Greenish brown solid used as a nutrient supplement. *See* Iron Salts.

FERROCYANIDE SALTS • Salts of ferrocyanic acid obtained by the reaction of a cyanide with an iron sulfate. Used as a coloring. The FDA data bank, PAFA (see page 10), has not yet done a search of the toxicology literature concerning this additive.

FERROUS ASCORBATE • Blue-violet solid used as a nutrient supplement. There is no reported use of the chemical and no toxicology information is available. *See* Iron Salts.

FERROUS CARBONATE • A nutrient supplement. There is no reported use of the chemical and no toxicology information is available. *See* Iron Salts.

FERROUS CITRATE • A nutrient supplement. There is no reported use of the chemical and no toxicology information is available. *See* Iron Salts.

FERROUS FUMARATE • Dietary supplement. The FDA data bank, PAFA, has not yet done a search of the toxicology literature concerning this additive. *See* Iron Salts.

FERROUS GLUCONATE • Gluconic Acid, Iron Salt. Iron Gluconate. Ferronicum. Used as a food coloring, it is a yellowish gray. It is also used as a flavoring agent and to treat iron-deficiency anemia. It may cause gastrointestinal disturbances. When painted on mouse skin in 2,600-milligram doses per kilogram of body weight, it caused tumors. It is permanently listed as a coloring for ripe olives only. GRAS.

FERROUS LACTATE • Lactic Acid. Iron Salt. Iron Lactate. Greenish white crystals that have a slightly peculiar odor. It is derived from the interaction of calcium lactate with ferrous sulfate, or the direct action of the lactic acid on iron filings. It is used as a food additive and dietary supplement. Causes tumors when injected under the skin of mice. There is no reported use of the chemical and no toxicology information is available. GRAS.

FERROUS SULFATE • Green or Iron Vitriol. Pale bluish green, odorless crystals, efflorescent in dry air. An astringent and deodorant. Once used in hair dyes. No longer authorized for use. A source of iron used medicinally. The FDA data bank, PAFA (see page 10), has not yet done a search of the toxicology literature concerning this additive. *See* Iron Salts. GRAS.

FERROUS SULFATE HEPTAHYDRATE • Pale green crystals or granules used as clarifying agent, dietary supplement, nutrient supplement, processing aid, or stabilizer in baking mixes, cereals, infant foods, pasta products, and wine. Moderately toxic by ingestion. Causes mutations in rats. *See* Iron Salts. Withdrawn by the FDA as a coloring agent for food.

FERULA ASAFOETIDA • *See* Asafoetida Extract.

FIBER • Commonly termed "bulk"—the indigestible carbohydrates, including cellulose, hemicellulose, and gums. Fiber is added to food to reduce calorie content, as a thickening agent, and as a stabilizer. If an apple a day keeps the doctor away, it may be because of the fiber content. Scientists have suspected that the high intestinal cancer rate in the United States may be linked to the 80 percent decrease of consumption of fiber in the average diet during the past century. Essentially, three classes of fiber are found in the fruit, leaves, stems, seeds, flowers, and roots of different plants. The first class is the insoluble cellulose found in the plant-cell wall. Some of the other polysaccharides constitute a second class and are also found in the cell wall (hemicellulose and pectic polymers), in the endosperm of seeds (mucilages), or in the plant's surface (gums). The third class, the lignins, are noncarbohydrates that infiltrate and contribute to the death of the plant cell, which then becomes part of the woody reinforcing plant structure.

Enzymes from a number of the more than four hundred kinds of bacteria in the human colon are capable of digesting many components of plant fiber. Doctors have found that the water-holding capacity of some fibers may be helpful in treating colon disease. The fibers' bile-absorption properties might be used in modifying cholesterol metabolism. Plant fibers are also capable of binding trace metals and bile acids. These properties modify the action of the gut contents. Fibers pass through the gut somewhat like a sponge, probably altering metabolism in the intestine. The fibers appear to protect intestinal cells by removing foreign substances, such as carcinogens produced by charbroiling. Increased fiber consumption has been recommended for relief of some symptoms of diverticular disease, irritable bowel syndrome, and constipation.

FICIN • An enzyme occurring in the latex of tropical trees. A buff-colored powder with an acrid odor. Absorbs water. Concentrated and used as a meat tenderizer. Ten to twenty times more powerful than papain tenderizers. Used to clot milk, as a protein digestant in the brewing industry, and as a chill-proofing agent in beer. Also used in making cheese as a substitute for rennet in the coagulation of milk, and used for removing casings from sausages. Can cause irritation to the skin, eyes, and mucous membranes, and in large doses can cause purging. The FDA data bank, PAFA (see page 10), has not yet done a search of the toxicology literature concerning this additive.

FIELD POPPY EXTRACT • Extract of the petals of *Papaver rhoeas* used in coloring and as an odorant.

FILLED MILK • A combination of skim milk and vegetable oil to replace milk fat. Usually has the same amount of protein and calories as whole milk. Used as a milk substitute. It often contains the high-cholesterol fatty acids (*see*) of coconut oil. Nontoxic.

FINOCHIO • *See* Fennel.

FIR NEEDLE OIL • Fir Oil. Pine. Balsam. An essential oil obtained by the steam distillation of needles and twigs of several varieties of pine trees native to both Canada and Siberia. Used as a scent in perfumes and as a flavoring agent. The FDA data bank, PAFA, has not yet done a search of the toxicology literature concerning this additive.

FISH GLYCERIDES • *See* Fish Oil and Glycerin.

FISH OIL • A fatty oil from fish or marine mammals used in soap manufacturing. Rich in omega-3 fatty acids that were reported in the 1980s to reduce fats in the blood and thus is believed to reduce the risk of coronary artery disease. The final report to the FDA of the Select Committee on GRAS Substances stated in 1980 that it should continue its GRAS status for food packaging with no limitations other than good manufacturing practices. The FDA data bank, PAFA (see page 10), has not yet done a search of the toxicology literature concerning this additive.

FISH PROTEIN CONCENTRATE • Dietary supplement. No known toxicity.

FIXATIVE • A chemical that reduces the tendency of an odor or flavor to vaporize, making the odor or flavor last longer. An example is musk (*see*), which is used in perfume, and undecyl aldehyde as a fixative for citrus flavors.

FLAVONOIDS • A large group of compounds widely distributed throughout nature. They include quercetin, present in onion skins, and anthocyanins, the major commercially used group. *See* Bioflavonoids.

FLAVOR ENHANCERS • *See* Flavor Potentiators.

FLAVOR POTENTIATORS • One of the newest and fastest-growing categories of additives, potentiators enhance the total seasoning effect, generally without contributing any taste or odor of their own. They are effective in minute doses—in parts per million or even less. A potentiator produces no identifiable effect itself but exaggerates one's response. They alter the response of the sensory nerve endings on the tongue and in the nose. The first true potentiators in the United States were the 5'-nucleotides, which are derived from a natural seasoning long in use in Japan: small flakes of dry bonito (a tunalike fish). These are often added to modify and improve the flavor of soups, and from bonito a 5'-nucleotide, disodium inosinate (*see*), has been isolated and identified as a flavor potentiator. Another 5'-nucleotide is disodium guanylate (*see*), one of the newer additives on the market, which gives one a sensation of "fullness" and "increased viscosity" when eating. The product is advertised as being able to give diners a sense of "full-bodied flavor" when ingesting a food containing it.

FLAVORING COMPOUND • A flavoring composed of two or more substances. The substances may be natural or synthetic, and they are usually closely guarded secrets. Normally, a flavoring compound is complete; that is, it is added to a food without any additional flavorings being necessary. A strawberry flavoring compound, for example, may contain twenty-eight separate ingredients before it is complete.

FLAVORINGS • More than two thousand flavorings are added to foods, of which approximately five hundred are natural and the rest synthetic. This is the largest category of additive. Lemon and orange are examples of natural flavorings, while benzaldehyde and methyl salicylate (*see both*) are examples from the laboratory.

FLAXSEED • The seed of the flax plant may be "hidden" in cereals and milk of cows fed flaxseed. It is also in flaxseed tea and the laxative Flaxolyn. It is a frequent allergen when ingested, inhaled, or put in direct contact. Flaxseeds are the source of linseed oil. Among other hidden sources are dog food, wave-setting preparations, shampoos, hair tonics, depilatories, patent leather, insulating materials, rugs and some cloths, Roman meal, cough remedies, and muffins.

FLEABANE OIL • Oil of Canada Fleabane. Erigeron Oil. The pale yellow volatile oil from a fresh flowering herb. It takes its name from its supposed ability to drive away fleas. Used in fruit and spice flavorings for beverages, ice cream, ices, candy, baked goods, and sauce. No known toxicity.

FLUAZIFOP-BUTYL • An herbicide used on animal feed. FDA permits a residue of from 0.2 to 1.0 ppm on various feeds.

FLUCYTHRINATE • An herbicide used on animal feed. FDA tolerance is 10 ppm for apple pomace, 0.2 on cottonseed oil, 0.1 ppm in cottonseed and corn grain, 2 on cabbage, 3 on corn forage, and 0.2 on sugar bagasse.

FLUORIDE • An acid salt used in toothpaste to prevent tooth decay. *See* Fluorine Sources.

FLUORINE SOURCES • Calcium Fluoride, Hydrofluorosillic Acid, Potassium Fluoride, Sodium Fluoride, and Sodium Silicofluoride. All have been used in the fluoridation of water. Fluorides cross the placental barrier and the effects on the fetus are unknown. New clinical evidence shows that kidney disturbance is sometimes due to the amount of fluoride fluoridation contributes to the blood. A National Research Council's committee on Health Effects of Ingested Fluoride concluded in 1993 that fluoridated coater at present levels is safe. It has "no effect" on kidneys, the gastrointestinal tract, fertility, or birth defects.

4′-FLUORO-4(4-[2-PYRIDYL]-1*p* IPERAZINYL)BUTYROPHENONE • Azaperone. Suicalm. A sedative and tranquilizer used on animals. Poison by ingestion.

FLURIDONE • An herbicide. The FDA tolerance is 0.05 ppm for residue in fish, crayfish, milk, eggs, and in fat, meat, and meat byproducts of cattle, goats, or hogs. Limit is 0.1 ppm as a residue in kidney and liver of cattle, hogs, or goats, and 0.1–1.0 ppm as residue in or on various fruits and vegetables.

FOAM INHIBITOR • An antifoaming agent, such as dimethyl polysiloxane (*see*), used in chewing gum bases, soft drinks, and fruit juices to keep them from foaming. *See* Defoaming Agents.

FOAM STABILIZERS • Used in soft drinks and brewing. *See* Vegetable Gums.

FOAMING AGENT • Used to help whipped topping peak when it is being whipped with cold milk. A commonly added foaming agent is sodium caseinate (*see*).

FOLIC ACID • A yellowish orange compound and member of the vitamin B complex, used as a nutrient. Used in cosmetic emollients. Occurs naturally in liver, kidney, mushrooms, and green leaves. Aids in cell formation, especially red blood cells. The FDA data bank, PAFA (see page 10), has fully up-to-date toxicology information available for this additive.

FOOD RED 6 • Formerly Ext. FD and C Red No. 15, FD and C Red No. 1, and Ponceau 3R. One of the first approved certified coal-tar colors. Food Red 6 was delisted as a food additive as possibly harmful. Dark red powder, it changes to cherry red in solution. *See* FD and C Colors.

FORMALDEHYDE • Paraformaldehyde. Preservative in defoaming agents and in animal feeds. A colorless gas obtained by the oxidation of methyl alcohol and generally used in watery solution. Formaldehyde is generally known as a disinfectant, germicide, fungicide, defoamer, and preservative, and it is used in embalming fluid. One ounce taken by mouth causes death within two hours. Skin reaction after exposure. It is a highly reactive chemical that is damaging to the hereditary substances in the cells of several species. It causes lung cancer in rats and has a number of other harmful biological consequences. Researchers from the Division of Cancer Cause and Prevention of the National Cancer Institute recommended in April 1983 that since formaldehyde is involved in DNA damage and inhibits its repair, since it potentiates the toxicity of X rays in human lung cells, and since it may act in concert with other chemical agents to produce mutagenic and carcinogenic effects, it should be "further investigated." The question is whether we ingest any formaldehyde when we ingest the animals that ate the feed and the products that had undergone "defoaming" by formaldehyde. The ADI (*see*) set for formaldehyde is 3 mg/kg of body weight. Researchers at Italy's University of Milano studied the health risk from consumption of cheese made using formaldehyde (Grana Padano) and concluded there was no appreciable health risk. The FDA data bank, PAFA (see page 10), has fully up-to-date toxicology information available for this additive.

FORMALIN • Fungicide in water of salmon, trout, largemouth bass, catfish, and bluegills. *See* Formaldehyde.

FORMESAFEN SODIUM • A pesticide used on soybeans. FDA tolerance is 0.05 ppm on soybeans.

FORMETANATE HYDROCHLORIDE • A pesticide in citrus molasses resulting from application to growing fruit. The FDA tolerance is 10 ppm in citrus molasses and 8 ppm on growing fruit.

FORMIC ACID • Colorless, pungent, highly corrosive, it occurs naturally in apples and other fruit. Used as a decalcifier and for dehairing hides. Chronic absorption is known to cause albuminuria—protein in the urine. It caused cancer when administered orally in rats, mice, and hamsters in doses from thirty-one to forty-nine milligrams per kilogram of body weight. Used as a preservative for silage. Silage is not supposed to be fed to livestock within 4 weeks of treatment. FDA residue tolerance is 2.25 percent of silage on a dry basis and 0.45 percent when direct cut. The FDA data bank, PAFA, has fully up-to-date toxicology information available for this additive.

FORMIC ETHER • See Ethyl Formate.

FORTIFIED • Fortification of food refers to the addition of nutrients such as vitamin C to breakfast drinks and vitamin D to milk. It actually increases the nutritional values of the original food.

FRANKINCENSE • Aromatic gum resin obtained from African and Asian trees and used chiefly as incense. For food use, see Olibanum Extract.

FREE • Product contains none or only insignificant amounts of a substance.

FRESH • A food that has not been heat-processed or frozen and supposedly contains no preservatives.

FOS • Abbreviation for Fructooligosaccharides (see).

FRUCTOOLIGOSACCHARIDES • FOS. Sugars that occur naturally in plants such as tomatoes, onions and bananas. They are not digestible in the stomach and travel unabsorbed to the intestine. They promote the growth of beneficial bacteria in the intestines such as those used to culture yogurt. They are now used in poultry feed to enhance growth and reduce intestinal pathogens. Applications have been made to use them as a food additive for human foods.

FRUCTOSE • A sugar occurring naturally in large numbers of fruits and in honey. It is the sweetest of the foodstuffs. It is also used as a medicine, preservative, common sugar, and to prevent sandiness in ice cream. Researchers at the General Clinical Research Center at the University of Colorado School of Medicine in Denver report that fructose is absorbed in the gastrointestinal tract more slowly than sugars like sucrose, which contain glucose. As a result, even though the body converts some fructose to glucose, 80 to 90 percent of the sugar is absorbed intact, and there is only a slight increase in blood glucose levels immediately after consumption. Fructose can be up to two times sweeter than sucrose. Recent advances in enzyme technology have made it possible to produce fructose on a commercial scale. It caused tumors in mice when injected under the skin in 5,000-mg doses per kilogram of body weight.

FRUIT JUICE • Used to color foods consistent with good manufacturing practices. Permanently listed. The FDA data bank, PAFA (see page 10), has fully up-to-date toxicology information available for this additive.

FULLER'S EARTH • A white or brown naturally occurring earthy substance. A nonplastic variety of kaolin (see) containing an aluminum magnesium silicate. Used as an absorbent and to decolorize fats and oils. Used in dry shampoos, hair colorings, beauty masks, and as a dusting powder; also used for lubricants and soaps. No longer permitted in cosmetics. The FDA data bank, PAFA, has fully up-to-date toxicology information available for this additive.

FUMARIC ACID • White, odorless, derived from many plants, and essential to vegetable and animal tissue respiration; prepared industrially. An acidulant used as a leavening agent and a dry acid for dessert powders and confections (up to 3 percent). Also as apple, peach, and vanilla flavoring agent for beverages, baked goods (1,300 ppm), and gelatin desserts (3,600 ppm). Used in baked goods as an antioxidant and as a substitute for tartaric acid (*see*). The FDA data bank, PAFA, has fully up-to-date toxicology information available for this additive. GRAS.

FUMIGANTS • Chemicals and gases used to kill pests on crops. Among those approved for use by the FDA are carbon tetrachloride with either carbon disulfide or ethylene chloride, with or without pentane; or methyl bromide. Also carbon disulfide, carbon tetrachloride, ethylene dichloride, and ethyl bromide. All are highly toxic and should be applied only by experts in their use.

FUNGAFLOR • Imazalil. Fungicide used in animal feed. Poison by ingestion and has caused adverse reproductive effects in experimental animals.

FURADAN • White, crystalline solid widely used as an insecticide in animal feed. Limitation in animal feed is from 2 ppm in grape pomace to 24 ppm in peanut soap-stock fatty acids. Insecticide residue tolerance of 2 ppm in raisins. Extremely hazardous substance, it is on the EPA Genetic Toxicology Program (*see*). Poisonous by inhalation, ingestion, and skin contact. Causes birth defects in experimental animals.

2-FURALDEHYDE • *See* Furfural.

2-FURANACROLEIN • *See* Furyl Acrolein.

FURCELLERAN • Sodium, Calcium, Potassium, and Ammonium. Extracted from red seaweed grown in northern-European waters. The processed gum is a white, odorless powder soluble in water as an emulsifier, stabilizer, and thickener in foods. It is a natural colloid and gelling agent. Also used in puddings, ice cream, and jams, in products for diabetics, as a carrier for food preservatives, and in bactericides. It is also used in over-the-counter drugs for weight reducing and toothpastes. Since 1980, on the FDA list of additives to be studied for mutagenic, teratogenic, subacute, and reproductive effects. The FDA data bank, PAFA (see page 10), claims to have fully up-to-date toxicology information available for this additive, but no action has been taken.

FURFURAL • Artificial Ant Oil. A colorless liquid with a peculiar odor. Occurs naturally in angelica root, apples, coffee, peaches, and skim milk. Used as a solvent, insecticide, fungicide, to decolor resins, and as a synthetic flavoring in butterscotch, butter, caramel, coffee, fruit, brandy, rum, rye, molasses, nut, and cassia flavorings for beverages, ice cream, ices, candy, gelatin, desserts, syrups (the biggest user; up to 30 ppm), and spirits. Darkens when exposed to air. It irritates mucous membranes and acts on the central nervous system. Causes tearing and inflammation of the eyes and throat. Ingestion or absorption of 0.06 grams produces persistent headache. Used continually, it leads to nervous disturbances and eye disorders (including photosensitivity).

FURFURYL ACETATE • Acetic Acid. A synthetic raspberry, fruit, and ginger ale flavoring for beverages, ice cream, ices, candy, baked goods, and chewing gum. No known toxicity.

FURFURYL ALCOHOL • A synthetic flavoring obtained mainly from corncobs and roasted coffee beans. Has a faint burning odor and a bitter taste. Used in butter, butterscotch, caramel, coffee, fruit, and brandy flavorings for beverages, ice cream, ices, candy, baked goods, gelatin desserts, and icings. It is poisonous.

FURFURYL MERCAPTAN • A synthetic fruit, liquor, rum, nut, chocolate, and spice flavoring agent that occurs naturally in coffee and is used for beverages, ice cream, ices, candy, and baked goods. No known toxicity.

2-FURFURYLIDENE BUTYRALDEHYDE • A synthetic fruit, liquor, rum, nut, and spice flavoring agent for beverages, ice cream, ices, candy, and baked goods. No known toxicity.

FURYL ACETONE • See (2-Furyl)-2-Propanone.

FURYL ACROLEIN • A synthetic coffee, fruit, cassia, and cinnamon flavoring agent for beverages, ice cream, ices, candy, baked goods, gelatin desserts, and puddings. No known toxicity.

4-(2-FURYL)-3-BUTEN-2-ONE • A synthetic nut, almond, and spice flavoring agent for beverages, ice cream, ices, candy, baked goods, and gelatin desserts. No known toxicity.

(2-FURYL)-2-PROPANONE • A synthetic fruit flavoring agent for ice cream, ices, candy, and baked goods. No known toxicity.

FUSEL OIL (REFINED) • A synthetic flavoring that occurs naturally in cognac oil. It is also a product of carbohydrate fermentation to produce ethyl alcohol (see) and varies widely in composition. Used in grape, brandy, cordial, rum, rye, scotch, whiskey, and wine flavorings for beverages, ice cream, ices, candy, baked goods, chewing gum, gelatin desserts, puddings, and liquor. Commercial amyl alcohol (see), its major ingredient, is more toxic than ethyl alcohol, and as little as thirty milligrams has caused death. Smaller amounts have caused methemoglobinuria (blood cells in the urine) and kidney damage.

G

g • Abbreviation for gram (see).

a-GALACTOSIDASE • Derived from Mortierella vinaceae, it is an enzyme used in sugar beet production.

GALANGAL ROOT • East Indian Root. Chinese Ginger. The pungent aromatic oil of the galangal root is a bitters, vermouth, spice, and ginger ale flavoring agent for beverages. The extract is a bitters, fruit, liquor, spice, and ginger ale flavoring agent for beverages, ice cream, ices, candy, baked goods, bitters, and liquors. Related to true ginger, it was formerly used in cooking and in medicine to treat colic. No known toxicity. GRAS.

GALBANUM OIL • A yellowish to green or brown aromatic bitter gum resin from an Asiatic plant used as incense. The oil is a fruit, nut, and spice flavoring for beverages, ice cream, ices, candy, baked goods, and condiments. Has been used medicinally to break up intestinal gas and as an expectorant. No known toxicity.

GALLIC ACID • *See* Propyl Gallate.

GALLOTANNIC ACID • *See* Tannic Acid.

GAMBIR CATECHU • *See* Catechu Extract.

GAMBIR GUM • *See* Catechu Extract.

GARDEN ROSEMARY OIL • *See* Rosemary Extract.

GARDENOL • *See* a-Methylbenzyl Acetate.

GARLIC EXTRACT • An extract from *Allium sativum,* a yellowish liquid with a strong odor used in fruit and garlic flavorings. Is being tested as an antibiotic and has been used to counteract intestinal worms. GRAS.

GARLIC OIL • Yellow liquid with a strong odor, obtained from the crushed bulbs or cloves of the plant. Used in fruit and garlic flavorings for beverages, ice cream, ices, candy, baked goods, chewing gum, and condiments. Has been used medicinally to combat intestinal worms. Reevaluated and found to be GRAS by the FDA's committee of experts in 1976.

GAS • A combustion product from the controlled combustion in air of butane, propane, or natural gas. It is used for removing or displacing oxygen in the processing, storage, or packaging of citrus products, vegetable fats, vegetable oils, coffee, and wine. No known toxicity when used in packaging.

GEL • A semisolid, apparently homogenous substance that may be elastic and jellylike (gelatin) or more or less rigid (silica gel) and that is formed in various ways such as by coagulation or evaporation.

GELATINS • Gelatin is a protein obtained by boiling skin, tendons, ligaments, or bones with water. It is colorless or slightly yellow, tasteless, and absorbs five to ten times its weight of cold water. Used as a food thickener and stabilizer and a base for fruit gelatins and puddings. Employed medicinally to treat malnutrition and brittle fingernails. Used in protein shampoos because it sticks to the hair and gives it "more body," in peelable face masks, and as a fingernail strengthener. No known toxicity.

GELLAN GUM • Used as a stabilizer in various foods.

GENET, ABSOLUTE • A natural flavoring from flowers used in fruit and honey flavorings for beverages, ice cream, ices, candy, baked goods, and chewing gum. The extract is a raspberry and fruit flavoring for beverages. No known toxicity.

GENETIC TOXICOLOGY PROGRAM • The U.S. Environmental Protection Agency has certain chemicals under study to determine their effects on genes, the parts of the cell that carry inherited characteristics. Damage to the mechanisms of genes can lead to birth defects and cancer, as well as other illnesses.

GENTAMYCIN SULFATE • Garamycin Sulfate. An antibiotic used to treat pork and turkey. FDA residue limitations are 0.1 ppm in turkey and 0.1 in swine muscle. This drug is also used to treat serious infections in humans, and theoretically, resistance to the drug could build up by eating treated pork or turkey. Allergic reactions to the drug in the meat could also occur.

GENTIAN ROOT EXTRACT • The yellow or pale bitter root of central- and southern-European plants used in angostura, chocolate, cola, fruit, vermouth, maple, root beer, and vanilla flavorings for beverages, ice cream, ices, candy, and liquors. It has been used as a bitter tonic. No known toxicity.

GERANIAL • *See* Citral.

GERANIALDEHYDE • *See* Citral.

GERANIOL • Used in perfumery to compound artificial attar of roses and artificial orange blossom oil. Also used in depilatories to mask odors. Oily sweet, with a rose odor, it occurs naturally in apples, bay leaves, cherries, grapefruit, ginger, lavender, and a number of other essential oils. A synthetic flavoring agent that occurs naturally in apples, bay leaves, cherries, coriander, grapefruit, oranges, tea, ginger, mace oil, and the oils of lavender, lavandin, lemon, lime, mandarin, and petitgrain. A berry, lemon, rose, apple, cherry, peach, honey, root beer, cassia, cinnamon, ginger ale, and nutmeg flavoring for beverages, ice cream, ices, candy, baked goods, chewing gum, and toppings. Geraniol is omitted from hypoallergenic cosmetics. Can cause allergic reactions. No specific toxicity information is available, but deaths have been reported from ingestion of unknown amounts of citronella oil (*see*), which is 93 percent geraniol; gastric mucosa was found to be severely damaged. GRAS.

GERANIUM • An essential oil used as flavoring. The FDA data bank, PAFA (see page 10), has not yet done a search of the toxicology literature concerning this additive. *See* Geranium Rose Oil. GRAS.

GERANIUM ROSE OIL • A synthetic flavoring agent that occurs naturally in geranium herbs and rose petals. Used in strawberry, lemon, cola, geranium, rose, violet, cherry, honey, rum, brandy, cognac, nut, vanilla, spice, and ginger ale flavorings for beverages, ice cream, ices, candy, baked goods, gelatin desserts, chewing gum, and jelly. A geranium root derivative has been used as an astringent and to treat chronic diarrhea in dogs. A teaspoon may cause illness in an adult, and less than an ounce may kill. May affect those allergic to geraniums. The FDA data bank, PAFA, has not yet done a search of the toxicology literature concerning this additive.

GERANYL ACETATE • Geraniol Acetate. Clear, colorless liquid with the odor of lavender, it is a constituent of several essential oils. Used in berry, lemon, orange, floral, apple, grape, peach, pear, honey, spice, and ginger ale flavorings for beverages, ice cream, ices, candy, baked goods, gelatin desserts, chewing gum, and syrup. It is obtained from geraniol (*see*). The FDA data bank, PAFA, has fully up-to-date toxicology information available for this additive. GRAS.

GERANYL ACETOACETATE • A synthetic fruit flavoring agent for beverages, ice cream, ices, candy, and baked goods. The FDA data bank, PAFA, has fully up-to-date toxicology information available for this additive.

GERANYL BENZOATE • Benzoic Acid. A synthetic flavoring agent, slightly yellowish liquid, with a floral odor. Used in floral and fruit flavorings for beverages, ice cream, ices, baked goods, and candy. The FDA data bank, PAFA (see page 10), has fully up-to-date toxicology information available for this additive.

GERANYL BUTYRATE • Geraniol Butyrate. Colorless liquid that occurs in several essential oils, it is used in perfumes. It is used in berry, citrus, fruit, apple, cherry, pear, and pineapple flavorings for beverages, ice cream, ices, candy, baked goods, chewing gum, and gelatin desserts. Used as a synthetic attar of rose. The FDA data bank, PAFA, has fully up-to-date toxicology information available for this additive. *See* Geraniol.

GERANYL FORMATE • Geraniol Formate. Colorless liquid with a roselike odor, insoluble in alcohol, it occurs in several essential oils. Used in perfumes and soaps as a synthetic neroli bigarade oil (*see*). A fresh leafy, rose odor, it is used in berry, citrus, apple, apricot, and peach flavorings for beverages, ice cream, ices, candy, baked goods, gelatins, chewing gum, and puddings. The FDA data bank, PAFA, has fully up-to-date toxicology information available for this additive. *See* Geraniol.

GERANYL HEXANOATE • Hexanoic Acid. A synthetic citrus and pineapple flavoring agent for beverages, ice cream, ices, candy, and baked goods. The FDA data bank, PAFA, has fully up-to-date toxicology information available for this additive.

GERANYL ISOBUTYRIC ACID • Isobutyric Acid. A synthetic floral, rose, apple, pear, and pineapple flavoring agent for beverages, ice cream, ices, candy, baked goods, chewing gum, gelatin desserts, and puddings. The FDA data bank, PAFA, has fully up-to-date toxicology information available for this additive.

GERANYL ISOVALERATE • A synthetic berry, lime, apple, peach, and pineapple flavoring agent for beverages, ice cream, ices, candy, and baked goods. The FDA data bank, PAFA (see page 10), has fully up-to-date toxicology information available for this additive.

GERANYL PHENYLACETATE • Phenylacetic Acid. A synthetic flavoring, yellow liquid with a honey-rose odor. Used in fruit flavorings for beverages, ice cream, ices, candy, baked goods, and chewing gum. The FDA data bank, PAFA, has fully up-to-date toxicology information available for this additive.

GERANYL PROPIONATE • Geraniol Propionate. Colorless liquid with a roselike odor, it is soluble in most oils and is used in perfumery. A synthetic flavoring used in berry, geranium, apple, pear, pineapple, and honey flavorings for beverages, ice cream, ices, candy, baked goods, chewing gum, and gelatin desserts. The FDA data bank, PAFA (see page 10), has fully up-to-date toxicology information available for this additive.

GERMANDER • *Teuerium chamaedrys* or *Teucrium polium*. Flavoring in alcoholic beverages only. An American plant. There is no reported use of the chemical and no toxicology information is available. *See* Sage.

GHATTI GUM • Indian Gum. The gummy exudate from the stems of a plant abundant in India and Ceylon. Used as an emulsifier and in butter, butterscotch, and fruit flavorings for beverages. Has caused an occasional allergy, but when ingested in large amounts, it has not caused obvious distress. The FDA's reevaluation in 1976 found the gum was GRAS if used at the rate of 0.2 percent for alcoholic beverages and 0.1 percent for all other food categories. In pharmaceutical preparations one part ghatti usually replaces two parts acacia (*see*). The final report to the FDA of the Select Committee on GRAS Substances stated in 1980 that there is no evidence in the available information that it is a hazard to the public when used as it is now and it should continue its GRAS status with limitations on the amount that can be added to food. The FDA data bank, PAFA, has fully up-to-date toxicology information available for this additive.

GIBBERELLIC ACID AND ITS SALTS • Used for malt beverages and distilled spirits. A plant growth-promoting hormone synthesized in 1978. Mildly toxic by ingestion. Caused tumors in experimental animals. The FDA data bank, PAFA (see page 10), has fully up-to-date toxicology information available for this additive.

GIGARTINA EXTRACTS • A stabilizer from red algae of the sea. *See* Algae, Red. *See* Carrageenan.

GINGER • *Zingiber officinale.* Derived from the rootlike stem of plants cultivated in all tropical countries, it is used in apple, plum, sausage, eggnog, pumpkin, ginger, ginger ale, and ginger beer flavorings for beverages, ice cream, ices, baked goods (2,500 ppm), and meats. The *extract* is used for cola, sausage, root beer, ginger, ginger ale, and ginger beer flavorings for beverages, ice cream, ices, candy, baked goods, chewing gum, meats, and condiments. The *oleoresin,* which is a ginger flavoring, is used in root beer and ginger ale for the same products. Ginger has been used to break up intestinal gas and colic. GRAS. The FDA data bank, PAFA, has not yet done a search of the toxicology literature concerning this additive.

GINGER OIL • Obtained from the dried rhizomes of *Zingiber officinale,* it is used in flavorings for beverages, ice cream, ices, candy, baked goods, chewing gum, meats, and condiments. It is also used in perfumes. Employed medicinally to break up intestinal gas. A skin irritant. Has been shown to be mutagenic in rabbits. GRAS. The FDA data bank, PAFA (see page 10), has not yet done a search of the toxicology literature concerning this additive.

GINSENG • Root of the ginseng plant grown in China, Korea, and the United States. It produces a resin, a sugar starch, glue, and volatile oil. Ginseng is used as a flavoring and has a sweetish, licoricelike taste and is widely used in oriental medicines as an aromatic bitter. It is used in American cosmetics as a demulcent (*see*). No known toxicity.

GLUCAMINE • An organic compound that is prepared from glucose (*see*).

GLUCITOL • Sorbitol. Sorbol. White crystalline powder with a sweet taste used as an anticaking agent, curing agent, drying agent, emulsifier, firming agent, flavoring agent, formulation aid, free-flowing agent, humectant, lubricant, nutritive sweetener, pickling agent, releasing agent, sequestrant, stabilizer, surface finishing agent, texturizing agent, and thickener. Used in baked goods, baking mixes, low-calorie beverages, hard and soft candy, chewing gum, chocolate, cough drops, frankfurters, frozen dairy desserts, jams, jellies, sausage, and shredded coconut. GRAS. Limitation of 99 percent in hard candy and cough drops, 75 percent in chewing gum, 98 percent in soft candy, 30 percent in nonstandardized jams and jellies, 30 percent in baked goods, 17 percent in frozen dairy desserts, 12 percent in all other foods. Mildly toxic by ingestion. Human systemic effects by ingestion include diarrhea. *See also* Sorbitol.

GLUCOAMYLASE • An enzyme used to break down sugars in food processing. No known toxicity.

GLUCODELTA LACTONE • White crystalline powder used as an acidifier, binder, curing agent, leavening agent, pH control agent, pickling agent, and sequestering agent (*see*). Used in meat mixes, dessert mixes, frankfurters,

Genoa salami, and sausages. GRAS. The FDA data bank, PAFA (see page 10), has fully up-to-date toxicology information available for this additive.

GLUCOMANNAN • A powder extracted from the roots of the konjac plant. The promoters claim that the powder, taken in a capsule before meals, absorbs liquid and swells in the stomach to form a gel and reduces hunger. The FDA was asked to approve it as GRAS but refused to do so unless scientific data were submitted.

GLUCONATE • Calcium and Sodium. A sequestering agent (*see*) derived from glucose, a sugar. Odorless, tasteless. Used as a buffer for confections and a firming agent for tomatoes and apple slices. Sodium gluconate is also used as a nutrient and dietary supplement. The final report to the FDA of the Select Committee on GRAS Substances stated in 1980 that it should continue its GRAS status with no limitations other than good manufacturing practices.

GLUCONIC ACID • A light, amber liquid with the faint odor of vinegar, produced from corn. It is water soluble and used as a dietary supplement and as a sequestering agent (*see*). The magnesium salt of gluconic acid has been used as an antispasmodic. There is no reported use of the chemical and no toxicology information is available. GRAS.

GLUCONO-DELTA-LACTONE • An acid with a sweet taste; fine, white, odorless. It is used as a leavening agent in jelly powders and soft-drink powders where dry food acid is desired. Used in the dairy industry to prevent milkstone, and by breweries to prevent beer stone, and is also a component of many cleaning compounds. Cleared by the U.S. Department of Agriculture's Meat Inspection Division for use at eight ounces for each hundred pounds of cured, pulverized meat or meat food product to speed up the color-fixing process and to reduce the time required for smoking. The FDA data bank, PAFA (see page 10), has fully up-to-date toxicology information available for this additive.

GLUCOSE • Occurs naturally in blood, grape, and corn sugars. A source of energy for plants and animals. Sweeter than sucrose (*see*), glucose syrup is used to flavor sausage, hamburger, meat loaf, luncheon meat, and chopped or pressed ham. It is also used as an extender in maple syrup. It is used medicinally for nutritional purposes and in the treatment of diabetic coma. Used to soothe the skin and as a filler in cosmetics. No known toxicity in cosmetics, but confectioners frequently suffer erosions and fissures around their nails, and the nails loosen and sometimes fall off.

***d*-GLUCOSE** • Corn sugar. See Glucose.

GLUCOSE GLUTAMATE • Used as a humectant in hand creams and lotions, it occurs naturally in animal blood, grape, and corn sugars and is a source of energy for plants and animals. It is sweeter than sucrose. Glucose syrup is used in to flavor sausage, hamburger, and other processed meats. Also used as an extender in maple syrup and medicinally as a nutrient. Glutamate is the salt of glutamic acid and is used to enhance natural food flavors. The FDA asked for further studies as to its potential mutagenic, teratogenic, subacute, and reproductive effects in 1980. Since then, the FDA has not reported any action.

GLUCURONIC ACID • A carbohydrate that is widely distributed in the animal kingdom.

GLUTAMATE • Ammonium and monopotassium salt of glutamic acid (*see*). Used to enhance natural flavors, to improve the taste of tobacco, and to impart meat flavor to foods. It is used as an antioxidant in cosmetics to prevent spoilage. It is being studied by the FDA for mutagenic, teratogenic, subacute, and reproductive effects. The final report to the FDA of the Select Committee on GRAS Substances stated in 1980 that there is no available evidence that it is a hazard to the public when used as it is now and it should continue its GRAS status with limitations on the amount that can be added to food.

GLUTAMIC ACID • A white, practically odorless, free-flowing, crystalline powder, a nonessential amino acid (*see*) usually manufactured from vegetable protein. A salt substitute, it has been used to treat epilepsy and to correct stomach acids. It is used to enhance food flavors and to add meat flavor to foods. Glutamic acid with hydrochloride (*see* Hydrochloric Acid) is used to improve the taste of beer. It is also employed as an antioxidant in cosmetics and as a softener in permanent-wave solutions to help protect against hair damage. It is being studied by the FDA for mutagenic, teratogenic, subacute, and reproductive effects. The final report to the FDA of the Select Committee on GRAS Substances stated in 1980 that there is no available evidence that it is a hazard to the public when used as it is now and it should continue its GRAS status with limitations on the amount that can be added to food. The FDA data bank, PAFA (see page 10), has fully up-to-date toxicology information available for this additive.

GLUTAMINE • A nonessential amino acid (*see*) used as a medicine, dietary supplement, and as a culture medium. Mildly toxic by ingestion. Caused adverse reproductive effects in experimental animals. The FDA data bank, PAFA, has fully up-to-date toxicology information available for this additive.

GLUTARAL • *See* Glutaraldehyde and Glutaric Acid.

GLUTARALDEHYDE • A food flavoring. An amino acid (*see*) that occurs in green sugar beets. It has a faint agreeable odor and is used as a fixing agent for enzymes added to foods. It is used as a flavor enhancer in foods. Also used in creams and emollients. Poisonous by ingestion. Caused birth defects in experimental animals. A severe human skin irritant. The FDA data bank, PAFA, has fully up-to-date toxicology information available for this additive. *See* Glutaric Acid.

GLUTARIC ACID • Pentanedioic Acid. A crystalline fatty acid that occurs in green sugar beets, meat, and in crude wood. Very soluble in alcohol and ether. Widely used in oriental medicine as an aromatic bitter, it is used in American cosmetics as a demulcent (*see*). No known toxicity.

GLUTEN • A mixture of proteins from wheat flour, obtained as an extremely sticky, yellowish gray mass by making a dough and then washing out the starch. It consists almost entirely of two proteins, gliadin and glutelin, the exact proportions of which depend upon the variety of wheat. Contributes to the porous and spongy structure of bread. There is no toxicology information available.

GLY- • The abbreviation for glycine (*see*).

(MONO)GLYCERIDE CITRATE • Aids the action of and helps dissolve antioxidant formulations for oils and fats, such as shortenings for cooking. No known toxicity.

GLYCERIDES • Monoglycerides, Diglycerides, and Monosodium Glycerides of Edible Fats and Oils. Any of a large class of compounds that are esters (*see*) of the sweet alcohol glycerin. They are also made synthetically. Emulsifying and defoaming agents. Used in bakery products to maintain "softness," in beverages, ice cream, ices, ice milk, milk, chewing gum base, shortening, lard, oleomargarine, confections, sweet chocolate, chocolate, rendered animal fat, and whipped toppings. The diglycerides are on the FDA list of food additives to be studied for possible mutagenic, teratogenic, subacute, and reproductive effects. The glycerides are also used in cosmetic creams as texturizers, emulsifiers, and emollients. The final report to the FDA of the Select Committee on GRAS Substances stated in 1980 that it should continue its GRAS status with no limitations other than good manufacturing practices.

GLYCERIN • Glycerol. Any byproduct of soap manufacture, an oily fluid obtained by adding alkalies (*see*) to fats and fixed oils. A sweet (about 0.6 times as cane sugar), warm-tasting substance. Used as a humectant in tobacco and in marshmallows, pastilles, and jellylike candies; as a solvent for colors and flavors; as a bodying agent in combination with gelatins and edible gums; as a plasticizer in edible coatings for meat and cheese. It is used, too, in beverages, confectionery, baked goods, chewing gum, gelatin desserts, meat products, soda-fountain fudge. Also used in perfumery. A solvent, humectant, and emollient in many cosmetics, it absorbs moisture from the air and, therefore, helps keep moisture in creams and other products, even if the consumer leaves the cap off the container. Also helps the products to spread better. Among the many products containing glycerin are cream rouge, face packs and masks, freckle lotions, hand creams and lotions, hair lacquer, liquid face powder, mouthwashes, protective creams, skin fresheners, and toothpastes. In concentrated solutions it is irritating to the mucous membranes, but as used, nontoxic, nonirritating, nonallergenic. Contact with a strong oxidizing agent such as chromium trioxide, potassium chlorate, or potassium permanganate (*see*) may produce an explosion. The final report to the FDA of the Select Committee on GRAS Substances stated in 1980 that it should continue its GRAS status with no limitations other than good manufacturing practices. The FDA data bank, PAFA (see page 10), is, as of this writing, conducting a search of the toxicology literature concerning this additive.

GLYCEROL • *See* Glycerin.

GLYCEROL ESTER OF WOOD ROSIN • Made from refined, pale yellow-colored wood rosin and food-grade glycerin (*see*). A hard, pale amber-colored resin, it is used as a chewing gum base and as a beverage stabilizer. No known toxicity.

GLYCEROL TRIBUTYRATE • *See* (tri-) Butyrin.

GLYCERYL ABIETATE • A density adjuster for citrus oil used in the preparation of alcoholic beverages and still and carbonated fruit drinks. Also cleared as a plasticizing material in chewing gum base. No known toxicity.

GLYCERYL BEHENATE • Used to form tablets. There is no reported use of the chemical and no toxicology information is available. GRAS. *See* Behenic Acid.

GLYCERYL CAPRATE • The monoester of glycerin and caprylic acid (*see both*).

GLYCERYL CAPRYLATE • *See* Glycerin and Caprylic Acid.

GLYCERYL CAPRYLATE/CAPRATE • A mixture of caprylic acid and capric acid (*see both*).

GLYCERYL COCONATE • *See* Glycerin and Coconut Oil.

GLYCERYL DILAURATE • *See* Glycerin and Lauric Acid.

GLYCERYL DIOLEATE • The diester of glycerin and oleic acid (*see both*).

GLYCERYL DISTEARATE • The diester of glycerin and stearic acid (*see both*).

GLYCERYL HYDROSTEARATE • *See* Glyceryl Monostearate.

GLYCERYL HYDROXYSTEARATE • The monoester of glycerin and hydroxy-stearic acid (*see both*).

GLYCERYL ISOSTEARATE • *See* Glyceryl Monostearate.

GLYCERYL-LACTO ESTERS OF FATTY ACIDS • *See* Glycerin and Fatty Acids. The FDA data bank, PAFA (see page 10), has fully up-to-date toxicology information available for this additive.

GLYCERYL LACTOOLEATE AND LACTOPALMITATE OF FATTY ACIDS • Food emulsifiers used in shortening where free and combined lactic acid does not exceed 1.75 percent of shortening plus additive. They add calories but are considered nontoxic. The final report to the FDA of the Select Committee on GRAS Substances stated in 1980 that it should continue its GRAS status with no limitations other than good manufacturing practices. There is no reported use of the chemical and no toxicology information is available.

GLYCERYL LANOLATE • The monoester of glycerin and lanolin (*see both*).

GLYCERYL LINOLEATE • The monoester of glycerin and linoleic acid (*see both*).

GLYCERYL MONO- AND DIESTERS • Manufactured by reacting edible glycerides with ethylene oxide. These are used as defoamers in yeast production. No known toxicity. The final report to the FDA of the Select Committee on GRAS Substances stated in 1980 that it should continue its GRAS status with no limitations other than good manufacturing practices.

GLYCERYL MONOSTEARATE • An emulsifying and dispersing agent used in oleomargarine, shortenings, and other food products as well as in baby creams, face masks, foundation cake makeup, liquid powders, hair conditioners, hand lotions, mascara, and nail whiteners. It is a mixture of two glyceryls, a white, waxlike solid, or beads, and is soluble in hot organic solvents such as alcohol. Lethal when injected in large doses into mice. The FDA data bank, PAFA (see page 10), is, as of this writing, conducting a search of the toxicology literature concerning this additive.

GLYCERYL MYRISTATE • *See* Glycerin and Myristic Acid.

GLYCERYL OLEATE • *See* Glycerin and Oleic Acid.

GLYCERYL PABA • The ester of glycine and para-aminobenzoic acid (*see both*).

GLYCERYL PALMITATE LACTATE • The lactic acid ester (*see*) of glyceryl palmitate.

GLYCERYL RICINOLEATE • *See* Glycerin.

GLYCERYL SESQUIOLEATE • *See* Glycerin.

GLYCERYL STARCH • *See* Starch and Glycerin.

GLYCERYL STEARATE • An emulsifier. *See* Glycerin.

GLYCERYL TRIACETATE • The FDA data bank, PAFA (see page 10), has fully up-to-date toxicology information available for this additive. *See* Triacetin. GRAS.

GLYCERYL TRIBUTYRATE • *See* Tributyrin.

GLYCERYL TRIMYRISTATE • *See* Glycerin and Myristic Acid.

GLYCERYL TRIUNDECANOATE • The triester of glycerin and undecylenic acid (*see both*).

GLYCINE • An amino acid (*see*) classified as nonessential. Made up of sweet-tasting crystals, it is used as a dietary supplement and as a gastric antacid. Used with saccharin to mask its aftertaste. Mildly toxic by ingestion. Used as a texturizer in cosmetics. The FDA data bank, PAFA (see page 10), has fully up-to-date toxicology information available for this additive.

GLYCOCHOLIC ACID • A product of mixing cholic acid and glycine, it is the chief ingredient of bile in vegetarian animals. It is used as an emulsifying agent for dried egg whites up to 0.1 percent. No known toxicity. The final report to the FDA of the Select Committee on GRAS Substances stated in 1980 that it should continue its GRAS status with no limitations other than good manufacturing practices. There is no reported use of the chemical and no toxicology information is available.

GLYCOFUROL • The ethoxylated ether of tetrahydrofurfuryl alcohol. *See* Furfural.

GLYCOGEN • Distributed throughout cell protoplasm, it is an animal starch found especially in liver and muscle. Used as a violet dye and in biochemical research. No known toxicity.

GLYCOL DISTEARATE • Alcohol from glycol. *See* Glycols.

GLYCOL STEARATE SE • An emulsifier. *See* Glycols and Stearic Acid.

GLYCOLIC ACID • Contained in sugarcane juice, it is an odorless, slightly water-absorbing acid used to control the acid/alkali balance in cosmetics and whenever a cheap organic acid is needed. It is also used in copper brightening, decontamination procedures, and in dyeing. It is a mild irritant to the skin and mucous membranes. The final report to the FDA of the Select Committee on GRAS Substances stated in 1980 that it should continue its GRAS status with no limitations other than good manufacturing practices.

GLYCOLS • Propylene Glycol. Glycerin, Ethylene Glycol, Carbitol. Diethylene Glycol. *Glycol* literally means "glycerin" plus "alcohol." A group of syrupy alcohols derived from hydrocarbons (*see*) and used in foods as emulsifiers and in chewing gum bases and in cosmetics as humectants. The FDA cautions manufacturers that glycols may cause adverse reactions in users. Propylene glycol and glycerin (*see both*) are considered safe. Other glycols in low concentrations may be harmless for external application, but ethylene glycol, carbitol, and diethylene glycol are hazardous in concentrations exceeding 5 percent even in preparations for use on small areas of the body. Therefore, in sunscreen lotions and protective creams where the area of application is extensive, they should not be used at all. Wetting agents (*see*) increase the absorption of glycols and therefore their toxicity.

GLYCOPHEN • Promidione. Rovral. A fungicide used in animal feed, ginseng (dried), grape pomace (dried), raisin waste, raisins, and soap-stock. FDA residue tolerance of 300 ppm in raisins, 4 in dried ginseng, and 225 ppm in dried grape pomace and raisin waste for animal feed. Moderately toxic by ingestion.

GLYCYRRHETINIC ACID • Used as a flavoring, to soothe skin, and as a carrier. Prepared from licorice root, it is soluble in chloroform, alcohol, and acetic acid (*see*). It has been used medicinally to treat a disease of the adrenal gland. No known toxicity when used in cosmetics.

GLYCYRRHETINYL STEARATE • The stearic acid ester of glycyrrhetinic acid (*see*).

GLYCYRRHIZA AND GLYCYRRHIZA EXTRACT • The FDA data bank, PAFA (see page 10), has not yet done a search of the toxicology literature concerning this additive. GRAS. *See* Glycyrrhizin, Ammoniated.

GLYCYRRHIZIC ACID • Used as a flavoring, coloring, and to soothe the skin in cosmetics. Extracted from licorice, the crystalline material is soluble in hot water and alcohol. *See* Glycyrrhetinic Acid.

GLYCYRRHIZIN, AMMONIATED • Licorice. Product of dried root from the Mediterranean region used in licorice, anise, root beer, wintergreen, and birch beer flavorings for beverages, ice cream, ices, candy, and baked goods. Also used as a demulcent and expectorant and as a drug vehicle. The final report to the FDA of the Select Committee on GRAS Substances stated in 1980 that it should continue its GRAS status with limitations on amounts that can be added to food. Cases have been reported of avid licorice eaters who develop high blood pressure. The FDA data bank, PAFA, has not yet done a search of the toxicology literature concerning this additive. *See* Licorice.

GLYOXYLIC ACID • Used as a coloring. Syrup or crystals that occur in unripe fruit, young leaves, and baby sugar beets. Maladorous and strongly corrosive. Forms a thick syrup, very soluble in water, sparingly soluble in alcohol. It absorbs water from the air and condenses with urea to form allantoin (*see*) and gives a nice blue color with sulfuric acid. It is a skin irritant.

GLYPHOSATE • A broad-spectrum, postemergent herbicide used in animal feed. FDA residues allowed are 0.4 ppm in dried citrus pulp, 20 ppm in soybean hulls, and 30 ppm in sugarcane molasses.

GRADE • Grading and inspection assure purity, wholesomeness, and appearance. The USDA has established grades for more than three hundred food products. Grading for most products is done voluntarily at the manufacturer's request (and expense) by a USDA inspector, and a USDA grade symbol may then appear on the package; lack of a symbol does not mean substandard product. Unfortunately, these grades lack continuity among product categories (Grade AA is the highest grade for eggs; Grade A is the highest for milk). Meat and poultry, however, whether fresh or processed and packaged, must be inspected and carry an inspection stamp.

GRAINS OF PARADISE • Pungent aromatic seeds of a tropical African plant of the ginger family. It is a natural flavoring used in fruit, ginger, ginger ale, and

---

pepper flavorings for beverages, ice cream, ices, and candy. No known toxicity. GRAS. The FDA data bank, PAFA (see page 10), has not yet done a search of the toxicology literature concerning this additive.

GRAM (g) • A metric unit of weight. There are about twenty-eight grams in one ounce. Food labels list fat, protein, carbohydrate, and fiber in grams per serving.

GRAM-NEGATIVE, -POSITIVE • Classification of bacteria according to whether or not they accept a stain named after Hans Gram, a Danish bacteriologist. Different life processes and vulnerabilities of germs are reflected by their gram-positive or gram-negative characteristics. An antibiotic may be effective against certain gram-positive germs and have no effect on gram-negative ones and vice versa.

GRAMINIS • *See* Dog Grass Extract.

GRAPE COLOR EXTRACT • The extract of the pulp of *Vitis vinifera* used as a coloring. Permanently listed since 1981. The FDA data bank, PAFA (see page 10), has fully up-to-date toxicology information available for this additive.

GRAPE JUICE • The liquid expressed from fresh grapes used as a coloring.

GRAPE POMACE • Source of natural red and blue colorings. Also used as an animal feed. *See* Anthocyanins.

GRAPE-SEED OIL • An ingredient in fragrances obtained by expression from the fresh peel of the grape. The yellow, sometimes reddish liquid is also used in fruit flavorings. No known toxicity.

GRAPEFRUIT OIL • The yellow, sometimes reddish liquid is an ingredient in fragrances obtained by expression from the fresh peel of the grapefruit. Used in lemon, lime, orange, and peach flavorings for beverages, ice cream, ices, candy, baked goods, gelatin desserts, chewing gum (1,500 ppm), and toppings. An experimental tumor-causing agent. A skin irritant. GRAS. The FDA data bank, PAFA, has not yet done a search of the toxicology literature concerning this additive.

GRAPESKIN EXTRACT • Enocianina. A purple-red liquid extracted from the residue of grapes pressed for use in grape juice and wine. Used for coloring in still and carbonated drinks and ales, beverage bases, and alcoholic beverages. Regarding the spraying of grapes, specifications by the FDA restrict pesticide residues to not more than 10 ppm of lead and not more than 1 ppm of arsenic. The FDA data bank, PAFA (see page 10), has fully up-to-date toxicology information available for this additive.

GRAS • The Generally Recognized as Safe list was established in 1958 by Congress. Those substances that had been added to food over a long time, which under conditions of their intended use were generally recognized as safe by qualified scientists, would be exempt from premarket clearance. Congress had acted on a very marginal response—on the basis of returns from those scientists sent questionnaires. Only 355 out of 900 responded, and only about 100 of those responses had substantive comments. Three items were removed from the originally published list. Since then, developments in science and in consumer awareness have brought to light the inadequacies of the testing of food additives and, ironically, the complete lack of testing of the GRAS list. President Nixon directed the FDA to reevaluate items on the GRAS list. The reevaluation was completed and a number of items were moved from the list. Although there were a number of others on the list, some of them top priority, to be studied in 1980, nothing has been reported by the FDA on their status since then.

GREEN • *See* FD and C Green (Nos. 1,2,3).

GREEN BEAN EXTRACT • The extract of the unripe beans of domesticated species of *Phaseolus*.

GROUND LIMESTONE • Used as a flavoring. The FDA data bank, PAFA (see page 10), has not yet done a search of the toxicology literature concerning this additive. GRAS.

GROUNDSEL EXTRACT • Extract of *Senecio vulgaris*, a North American maritime shrub or tree.

GUAIAC WOOD OIL • Yellow to amber, semisolid mass with a floral odor. Soluble in alcohol. Derived from steam distillation of guaiac wood. A *gum resin* used in fruit and rum flavorings for beverages, ice cream, ices, candy, and baked goods. The *oil* is a raspberry, strawberry, rose, fruit, honey, ginger, and ginger ale flavoring for beverages, ice cream, candy, baked goods, gelatin desserts, and chewing gum. Formerly used to treat rheumatism. Used as a perfume fixative and modifier, soap odorant, and in fragrances. The FDA data bank, PAFA, has not yet done a search of the toxicology literature concerning this additive.

GUAIACYL ACETATE • A synthetic berry flavoring for beverages, ice cream, ices, candy, gelatin, chewing gum, and baked goods. The FDA data bank, PAFA, has fully up-to-date toxicology information available for this additive.

GUAIACYL PHENYLACETATE • A synthetic berry, coffee, honey, tobacco, and smoke flavoring agent for beverages, ice cream, ices, candy, baked goods and toppings. The FDA data bank, PAFA (see page 10), has fully up-to-date toxicology information available for this additive.

GUAIOL • An alcohol from guaiac wood, *Guaiacum santum*. The FDA data bank, PAFA, has fully up-to-date toxicology information available for this additive.

GUANIDOETHYL CELLULOSE • *See* Guaiac Wood Oil.

GUANYLIC ACID SODIUM SALT • Disodium Guanylate. A flavor enhancer used in canned foods, poultry, sauces, snack items, and soups. Mildly toxic by ingestion. Has caused mutations in experimental animals.

GUAR GUM • Guar Flour. From ground nutritive seed tissue of plants cultivated in India, it has five to eight times the thickening power of starch. A free-flowing powder, it is used as a stabilizer for frozen fruit, icings, glazes, and fruit drinks and as a thickener for hot and cold drinks. Also a binder for meats, confections, baked goods, cheese spreads, cream cheese, ice cream, ices, French dressing, and salad dressing. Keeps tablet formulations from disintegrating and is used in cosmetic emulsions, toothpastes, lotions, and creams. Employed also as a bulk laxative, appetite suppressant, and to treat peptic ulcers. The FDA's reevaluation in 1976 found guar gum to be GRAS if used as a stabilizer, thickener, and firming agent at 0.35 percent in baked goods, 1.2 percent in breakfast cereals; 2 percent in fats and oils, 1.2 percent in gravies, 1 percent in sweet sauces, toppings, and syrups, and 2 percent in processed vegetables and vegetable juices. In large amounts, it may cause nausea, flatulence, or abdominal cramps. The final report to the FDA of the Select Committee on GRAS Substances stated in 1980 that there is no available evidence that it is a hazard to the public when used as it is now and it should continue its GRAS status with limitations on amounts that can be added to food. The FDA data bank, PAFA, has fully up-to-date toxicology information available for this additive.

GUARANA GUM • The dried paste consisting mainly of crushed seed from a plant grown in Brazil. Contains about 4 percent caffeine. Used in cola flavorings for beverages and candy. The FDA data bank, PAFA (see page 10), has not yet done a search of the toxicology literature concerning this additive. *See* Caffeine for toxicity.

GUARANINE • *See* Caffeine.

GUAVA • Extracted from the fruit of a small shrubby American tree widely cultivated in warm regions. The fruit is sweet, sometimes acid, globular, and yellow. It is used to flavor jelly. The FDA data bank, PAFA, has not yet done a search of the toxicology literature concerning this additive. GRAS.

GUINEA GREEN B • *See* FD and C Green No. 1.

GUM • True plant gums are the dried exudates from various plants obtained when the bark is cut or other injury is suffered. Gums are soluble in hot or cold water and are sticky. Today, the term *gum,* both for natural and synthetic sources, usually refers to resins. Gums are also used as emulsifiers, stabilizers, and suspending agents. No known toxicity.

GUM ACACIA • *See* Acacia.

GUM ARABIC • Acacia Gum. The exudate from acacia trees grown in the Sudan used in face masks, hairsprays, setting lotions, rouge, and powders for compacts. Serves as an emulsifier, stabilizer, and gelling agent. It may cause allergic reactions such as hay fever, dermatitis, gastrointestinal distress, and asthma. GRAS.

GUM BENJAMIN • *See* Benzoin.

GUM BENZOIN • Used as a preservative in creams and ointments and as a skin protective. It is the balsamic resin from benzoin grown in Thailand, Cambodia, Sumatra, and Cochin China. Also used to glaze confections. No known toxicity.

GUM DAMMAR • *See* Dammar.

GUM GHATTI • *See* Ghatti Gum.

GUM GLUTEN • Used as a stabilizer in macaroni products. *See* Gluten.

GUM GUAIAC • Resin from the wood of the guaiacum used widely as an antioxidant in edible fats or oils, beverages, rendered animal fat, or a combination of such fats and vegetable fats. It is also used in cosmetic creams and lotions. Brown or greenish brown. Formerly used in treatment of rheumatism. No known toxicity. The final report to the FDA of the Select Committee on GRAS Substances stated in 1980 that it should continue its GRAS status with no limitations other than good manufacturing practices.

GUM KARAYA • Sterculia Gum. Used in hairsprays, beauty masks, setting lotions, depilatories, rouge, powder for compacts, shaving creams, denture adhesive powder, hand lotions, and toothpastes. It is the dried exudate of a tree native to India. Karaya came into wide use during World War I as a cheaper substitute for gum tragacanth (*see*). Karaya swells in water and alcohol, but does not dissolve. It is used in finger wave lotions, which dry quickly and are not sticky.

Because of its high viscosity at low concentrations, its ability to produce highly stable emulsions, and its resistance to acids, it is widely used in frozen food products. In 1971, however, the FDA put this additive on the list of chemicals to be studied for teratogenic, mutagenic, subacute, and reproductive effects. It can cause allergic reactions such as hay fever, dermatitis, gastrointestinal diseases, and asthma. It is omitted from hypoallergenic cosmetics. GRAS.

GUM ROSIN • *See* Rosins.

GUM SUMATRA • *See* Gum Benzoin.

GUM TRAGACANTH • The dried gummy exudate from plants found in Iran, Asia Minor, and Syria. A thickener and stabilizer, odorless, and with a gluelike taste. Used in fruit jelly, ornamental icings, fruit, sherbets, water ices, salad dressing, French dressing, confections, and candy. An emulsifier used in brilliantines, shaving creams, toothpastes, face packs, foundation creams, hairsprays, mascara, depilatories, compact powder, rouge, dentifrices, setting lotions, eye makeup, and hand lotions. Also employed in compounding drugs and pastes. One of the oldest known natural emulsifiers, its history predates the Christian era by hundreds of years; it has been recognized in the U.S. Pharmacopoeia since 1829. It has a long shelf life and is resistant to acids. Aside from occasional allergic reactions, it can be ingested in large amounts with little harm except for diarrhea, gas, or constipation. When reevaluated, it was found to be GRAS in the following percentages: 0.2 for baked goods; 0.7 percent in condiments and relishes; 1.3 in fats and oils; 0.8 percent in gravies and sauces; 0.2 percent in meat products; 0.2 percent in processed fruits; and 0.1 percent in all other categories. GRAS.

GUTHION • Azinphos-methyl. A pesticide used to combat mites. It inhibits nerve transmission. *See* Organophosphates.

H

HALOFUGINONE HYDROBROMIDE • An animal antibiotic used in broiler-chicken feed. The FDA's residue limitation is 0.3 ppm in uncooked chicken liver and 0.1 in uncooked edible tissue of chicken.

HALOXON • Galloxon. An antiworm medicine for animals. FDA residue tolerance is 0.1 ppm in edible tissues of cattle, sheep, and goats.

HAW BARK • Black Extract. Extract of the fruit of a hawthorn shrub or tree. Used in butter, caramel, cola, maple, and walnut flavorings for beverages, ice cream, ices, candy, and baked goods. Has been used as a uterine antispasmodic. The FDA data bank, PAFA (see page 10), has not yet done a search of the toxicology literature concerning this additive.

HAZELNUT OIL • The oil obtained from the various species of the hazelnut tree, genus *Corylus*.

HCL • The abbreviation for *hydrochloride*.

HEATHER EXTRACT • An extract of *Calluna vulgaris,* also called ling extract.

HECTORITE • An emulsifier and extender. A clay consisting of silicate of magnesium and lithium, it is used in the chill-proofing of beer. The dust can be irritating to the lungs. No known toxicity of the skin.

HEDEOMA OIL • *See* Pennyroyal Oil.

HELIOTROPIN • Piperonal. Used in cherry and vanilla flavors. A purple diazo dye used in perfumery and soaps. Consists of colorless, lustrous crystals that have a heliotrope odor. Usually made from the oxidation of piperic acid. Ingestion of large amounts may cause central nervous system depression. Applications to the skin may cause allergic reactions and skin irritations. Not recommended for use in cosmetics or perfumes.

HELIOTROPINE • *See* Heliotropin.

HELIOTROPYL ACETATE • *See* Piperonyl Acetate.

HELIUM • This colorless, odorless, tasteless gas is used as propellant for foods packed in pressurized containers. No known toxicity. The final report to the FDA of the Select Committee on GRAS Substances stated in 1980 that it should continue its GRAS status with no limitations other than good manufacturing practices. There is no reported use of the chemical and no toxicology information is available.

HEMICELLULOSE • Used in feed as a source of metabolizable energy. It is in the cell walls of all plants and of some seaweeds and contains a variety of sugars. Nontoxic.

HEMLOCK OIL • Spruce Oil. A natural flavoring extract from North American or Asian nonpoisonous hemlock. Used in fruit, root beer, and spice flavorings for beverages, ice cream, ices, candy, baked goods, gelatin desserts, puddings, and chewing gum. There is no reported use of the chemical and no toxicology information is available.

HENDECANAL • *See* Undecanal.

HENDECEN-9-OL • *See* 9-Undecanal.

10-HENDECENYL ACETATE • *See* 10-Undecen-1-yl Acetate.

2,4-HEPTADIENAL • Slightly yellow liquid used as a flavoring agent in various foods. Poisonous by skin contact. Moderately toxic by ingestion. Severe skin irritant. The FDA data bank, PAFA (see page 10), has fully up-to-date toxicology information available for this additive.

y-**HEPTALACTONE** • A synthetic coconut, nut, and vanilla flavoring for beverages, ice cream, ices, candy, and baked goods. The FDA data bank, PAFA, has fully up-to-date toxicology information available for this additive.

HEPTALDEHYDE • *See* Heptanal.

HEPTANAL • Heptaldehyde. Oily, colorless liquid with a penetrating fruit odor made from castor oil. A synthetic flavoring agent used in citrus, apple, melon, cognac, rum, and almond flavorings for beverages, ice cream, ices, candy, baked goods, and liqueurs. Used in perfumery. Mildly toxic by ingestion. The FDA data bank, PAFA (see page 10), has fully up-to-date toxicology information available for this additive.

HEPTANAL DIMETHYL ACETAL • A synthetic fruit, melon, and mushroom flavoring agent for beverages, ice cream, ices, candy, baked goods, chewing gum, and condiments. The FDA data bank, PAFA, has fully up-to-date toxicology information available for this additive.

HEPTANAL GLYCERYL ACETAL • A synthetic mushroom flavoring for beverages, ice cream, ices, candy, and baked goods. The FDA data bank, PAFA, has fully up-to-date toxicology information available for this additive.

2,3-HEPTANEDIONE • A synthetic raspberry, strawberry, butter, fruit, rum, nut, and cheese flavoring agent for beverages, ice cream, ices, candy, baked goods, and chewing gum. The FDA data bank, PAFA, has fully up-to-date toxicology information available for this additive.

HEPTANOIC ACID • Enanthic Acid. Found in various fusel oils and in rancid oils, it has the faint odor of tallow. It is made from grapes and is a fatty acid used chiefly in making esters (*see*) for flavoring materials. The FDA data bank, PAFA, has fully up-to-date toxicology information available for this additive.

2-HEPTANOL • A synthetic flavoring agent, liquid and miscible with alcohol and ether. The FDA data bank, PAFA (see page 10), has fully up-to-date toxicology information available for this additive. *See* Heptyl Alcohol for use.

2-HEPTANONE • A synthetic flavoring agent, liquid, with a penetrating odor, used to give a "peppery" smell to such cheeses as Roquefort. Found naturally in oil of cloves and in cinnamon bark oil. Used in berry, butter, fruit, and cheese flavorings for beverages, ice cream, ices, candy, baked goods, chewing gum, and condiments (25 ppm). Used also in perfumery as a constituent of artificial carnation oils. The lethal concentration in air for rats is 4,000 ppm. In high doses it is narcotic and a suspected irritant to human mucous membranes. The FDA data bank, PAFA, has fully up-to-date toxicology information available for this additive.

3-HEPTANONE • A synthetic melon flavoring agent for beverages, ice cream, ices, candy, and baked goods. *See* 2-Heptanone, which is a similar compound. The FDA data bank, PAFA, has fully up-to-date toxicology information available for this additive.

4-HEPTANONE • A synthetic strawberry and fruit flavoring agent for beverages, ice cream, ices, candy, baked goods, and gelatin desserts. *See* 2-Heptanone, which is a similar compound. The FDA data bank, PAFA, has fully up-to-date toxicology information available for this additive.

HEPTYL ACETATE • A synthetic berry, banana, melon, pear, and pineapple flavoring agent for beverages, ice cream, ices, candy, and baked goods. No known toxicity. The FDA data bank, PAFA (see page 10), has fully up-to-date toxicology information available for this additive. *See* 2-Heptanone.

HEPTYL ALCOHOL • 1-Heptanol. Colorless, fragrant liquid miscible with alcohol. A synthetic flavoring agent with a fatty, citrus odor, used in fruit flavorings for beverages, ice cream, ices, candy, and baked goods. Moderately toxic by ingestion and skin contact. Used in perfumery. The FDA data bank, PAFA, has fully up-to-date toxicology information available for this additive. *See* 2-Heptanone.

HEPTYL ALDEHYDE • *See* Heptanal.

HEPTYL BUTYRATE • Butyric Acid. A synthetic raspberry, floral, violet, apricot, melon, and plum flavoring agent for beverages, ice cream, ices, candy, baked goods. The FDA data bank, PAFA, has fully up-to-date toxicology information available for this additive.

γ-**HEPTYL BUTYROLACTONE** • *See* *γ*-Undecalactone.

HEPTYL CINNAMATE • A synthetic cinnamon flavoring. The FDA data bank, PAFA, has fully up-to-date toxicology information available for this additive.

HEPTYL FORMATE • Used in artificial fruit essences. A skin irritant. The FDA data bank, PAFA (see page 10), has fully up-to-date toxicology information available for this additive. *See* 2-Heptanone.

HEPTYL HEPTANOATE • Colorless liquid with fruity odor used in artificial fruit essences. *See* 2-Heptanone.

HEPTYL ISOBUTYRATE • A synthetic coconut, apricot, peach, pineapple, and plum flavoring agent for beverages, ice cream, ices, candy, and baked goods. No known toxicity.

HEPTYL PELARGONATE • Liquid with pleasant odor used in flavors and perfumes. *See* 2-Heptanone.

***n*-HEPTYLIC ACID** • *See* Heptanoic Acid.

HEPTYLPARABEN • A preservative. The FDA data bank, PAFA, has fully up-to-date toxicology information available for this additive. *See* Parabens.

HERB ROBERT EXTRACT • Extract of the entire plant *Geranium robertianum*. *See* Geranium Rose Oil.

HESPERIDIN • A natural bioflavonoid (*see*). Fine needles from citrus fruit peel. Used as a synthetic sweetener. The FDA data bank, PAFA, has not yet done a search of the toxicology literature concerning this additive.

HEXACHLOROPHENE • An antibacterial used in animal products. Its use is restricted by the FDA. In 1969 scientists reported microscopically visible brain damage in rats from small concentrations of this chemical. The company that had the patent on hexachlorophene, the Swiss-based Givaudan Corporation, sold the chemical only to those companies that could demonstrate a safe and effective use for it. However, when the patent ran out, it was sold for many purposes. It is still used in small amounts in some cosmetic products for humans.

1-HEXADECANOIC ACID • *See* Palmitic Acid.

1-HEXADECANOL • Cetyl Alcohol. A synthetic chocolate flavoring agent for ice cream, ices, and candy. Moderately toxic by ingestion. An eye and skin irritant. The FDA data bank, PAFA (see page 10), has fully up-to-date toxicology information available for this additive.

ω-6-HEXADECENLACTONE • Ambrettolide. 6-Hexadecenolide. A synthetic fruit flavoring agent for beverages, ice cream, ices, candy, baked goods, gelatin desserts, and chewing gum. The FDA data bank, PAFA, has fully up-to-date toxicology information available for this additive.

6-HEXADECENOLIDE • *See* ω-6-Hexadecenlactone.

HEXADECYLIC ACID • *See* Palmitic Acid.

2,4-HEXADIENOATE • *See* Allyl Sorbate.

HEXAHYDROPYRIDENE • *See* Piperidine.

HEXAHYDROTHYMOL • *See* Menthol.

HEXAKIS • A pesticide to kill mites in animal feeds. The residue tolerances set by the FDA range from 20 ppm in raisin waste to 100 ppm in dried grape pomace. A corrosive skin and eye irritant.

***y*-HEXALACTONE** • A synthetic butter, fruit, honey, and vanilla flavoring for beverages, ice cream, ices, candy, baked goods, chewing gum, and gelatin desserts. The FDA data bank, PAFA (see page 10), has fully up-to-date toxicology information available for this additive.

HEXALDEHYDE • *See* Hexanal.

HEXAMETHYLENETETRAMINE (HMT) • Methenamine. Odorless powder or crystals used in adhesives, coatings, as a stabilizer for lubricating and insulating oils, as a urinary antibacterial, and as a urinary antiseptic for animals. It is used in the production of provolone cheese. Studies at Italy's University of Milano concluded there was no appreciable health risk from ingestion of cheese made with this additive.

HEXANAL • Hexaldehyde. Hexoic Aldehyde. A synthetic flavoring agent occurring naturally in apples, coffee, cooked chicken, strawberries, tea, and tobacco leaves (oils). Used in butter, fruit, honey, and rum flavorings for beverages, ice cream, ices, candy, baked goods, chewing gum, and gelatin desserts. The FDA data bank, PAFA (see page 10), has fully up-to-date toxicology information available for this additive.

1-HEXANAL • *See* Hexyl Alcohol.

2,3-HEXANDIONE • A synthetic strawberry, butter, citrus, banana, pineapple, rum, and cheese flavoring agent for beverages, ice cream, ices, candy, and baked goods. No known toxicity.

HEXANE • A colorless volatile liquid derived from distillation of petroleum and used as a solvent for spice oleoresins (*see*). Also used in low-temperature thermometers instead of mercury, usually with a blue or red dye. It is a mild central nervous system depressant that may be irritating to the respiratory tract. The FDA data bank, PAFA, has fully up-to-date toxicology information available for this additive.

HEXANEDIOIC ACID • *See* Adipic Acid.

1,2,6-HEXANETRIOL • An alcohol used as a solvent. No known skin toxicity.

HEXANOIC ACID • A synthetic flavoring agent that occurs naturally in apples, butter acids, cocoa, grapes, oil of lavender, oil of lavandin, raspberries, strawberries, and tea. Used in butter, butterscotch, chocolate, berries, strawberries, and tea. Used in butter, butterscotch, chocolate, berries, fruit, rum, pecan, and cheese flavorings for beverages, ice cream, ices, candy, baked goods, chewing gum, and condiments. Moderately toxic by ingestion and skin contact. Severe eye irritant. Has caused mutations in laboratory animals. The FDA data bank, PAFA (see page 10), has fully up-to-date toxicology information available for this additive.

HEXANOL • Hexyl Alcohol. Used as an antiseptic and preservative in cosmetics, it occurs as the acetate (*see*) in seeds and fruits of *Heracleum sphondylium* and *Umbelliferae*. Colorless liquid slightly soluble in water, it is miscible with alcohol. The FDA data bank, PAFA, has fully up-to-date toxicology information available for this additive.

HEXAZINONE • A weed killer used in various plant products. Moderately toxic by ingestion and mildly toxic by skin contact. Has caused adverse reproductive effects in laboratory animals.

2-HEXEN-1-OL • A synthetic flavoring that occurs naturally in grapes; similar compound to 3-Hexen-1-ol (*see*). Used in fruit and mint flavorings for beverages, ice cream, ices, candy, and baked goods. The FDA data bank, PAFA, has fully up-to-date toxicology information available for this additive.

3-HEXEN-1-OL • Leaf Alcohol. Blatteralkohol. A colorless liquid with a fruity odor, it is a flavoring that occurs naturally in leaves of odoriferous plants and grapefruit, raspberries, and tea. Strong odor. Used in fruit and mint flavorings for beverages, ice cream, ices, candy, and baked goods. The FDA data bank, PAFA, has fully up-to-date toxicology information available for this additive.

2-HEXEN-1-YL ACETATE • A synthetic fruit flavoring agent for beverages, ice cream, ices, candy, and baked goods. The FDA data bank, PAFA (see page 10), has fully up-to-date toxicology information available for this additive.

2-HEXENAL • A synthetic berry and fruit flavoring agent that occurs naturally in apples and strawberries and is used for beverages, ice cream, ices, candy, and baked goods. No known toxicity.

cis-3-HEXENAL • A synthetic fruit flavoring agent for beverages, ice cream, ices, and candy. No known toxicity.

2-HEXENOIC ACID • *See* Methyl Hexenoate.

cis-3-HEXENYL 2-METHYL BUTYRATE • Colorless liquid with a strong fruity odor used as a flavoring in various foods. The FDA data bank, PAFA, has fully up-to-date toxicology information available for this additive.

HEXOIC ACID • *See* Caproic Acid.

HEXOIC ALDEHYDE • A synthetic berry, apple, pear, and pineapple flavoring agent for beverages, ice cream, ices, candy, baked goods, and chewing gum.

HEXONE • Colorless liquid with a fruity odor used as a favoring agent in various foods. Moderately toxic by ingestion. Mildly toxic by inhalation. Very irritating to the skin, eyes, and mucous membranes. A human systemic irritant by inhalation. Narcotic in high concentration.

HEXYL ACETATE • Acetic Acid. Hexyl Ester. A synthetic berry, apple, pear, and pineapple flavoring agent for beverages, ice cream, ices, candy, baked goods, and chewing gum. Mildly toxic by ingestion. The FDA data bank, PAFA (see page 10), has fully up-to-date toxicology information available for this additive.

2-HEXYL-4-ACETOXYTETRAHYDROFURAN • A synthetic fruit flavoring agent for beverages, ice cream, ices, candy, and baked goods. Although allowed as a food additive, there is no current reported use of the chemical, and therefore, although toxicology information may be available, it is not being updated, according to the FDA.

HEXYL ALCOHOL • 1-Hexanal. A synthetic flavoring agent that occurs naturally in apples, oil of lavender, strawberries, and tea. Used in berry, coconut, and fruit flavorings for beverages, ice cream, ices, candy, baked goods, chewing gum, and gelatin desserts. Also used in antiseptics and in perfumery. The FDA data bank, PAFA, has fully up-to-date toxicology information available for this additive. *See* Hexanol.

HEXYL-2-BUTENOATE • Colorless liquid with a fruity odor used as a flavoring in various foods. The FDA data bank, PAFA (see page 10), has fully up-to-date toxicology information available for this additive. GRAS.

HEXYL CINNAMALDEHYDE • Yellow liquid with a jasmine odor used as a flavoring agent in various foods. Moderately toxic by ingestion. A skin irritant.

The FDA data bank, PAFA, has fully up-to-date toxicology information available for this additive.

a-HEXYL CINNAMALDEHYDE • A synthetic flavoring, pale yellow liquid with a jasminelike odor. Used in berry, fruit, and honey flavorings for beverages, ice cream, ices, candy, baked goods, and gelatin desserts.

HEXYL ESTER • *See* Hexyl Acetate.

HEXYL FORMATE • Formic Acid. A synthetic raspberry and fruit flavoring agent for beverages, ice cream, ices, candy, and baked goods. The FDA data bank, PAFA, has fully up-to-date toxicology information available for this additive. *See* Formic Acid for toxicity.

HEXYL 2-FUROATE • A synthetic coffee, maple, and mushroom flavoring agent for candy and condiments. The FDA data bank, PAFA, has fully up-to-date toxicology information available for this additive.

HEXYL HEXANOATE • Hexanoic Acid. A synthetic fruit flavoring agent for beverages, ice cream, ices, candy, and baked goods. The FDA data bank, PAFA, has fully up-to-date toxicology information available for this additive.

HEXYL ISOVALERATE • A colorless liquid with a fruity odor used as a flavoring in various foods. The FDA data bank, PAFA (see page 10), has fully up-to-date toxicology information available for this additive.

2-HEXYL-5(OR 6)-KETO-1,4-DIOXANE • A synthetic cream flavoring agent for beverages, ice cream, ices, candy, and baked goods. No known toxicity.

HEXYL LAURATE • *See* Lauric Acid.

HEXYL 2-METHYL BUTYRATE • Colorless liquid; strong fresh-green, fruity odor used as a flavoring agent. The FDA data bank, PAFA, has fully up-to-date toxicology information available for this additive.

HEXYL OCTANOATE • Octanoic Acid. A synthetic fruit flavoring agent for beverages and puddings. The FDA data bank, PAFA, has fully up-to-date toxicology information available for this additive.

HEXYL PROPIONATE • Propionic Acid. A synthetic fruit flavoring agent for beverages, ice cream, ices, candy, and baked goods. The FDA data bank, PAFA, has fully up-to-date toxicology information available for this additive.

HEXYLENE GLYCOL DIACETATE • *See* 1,3-Nonanediol Acetate.

2-HEXYLIDENE CYCLOPENTANONE • A synthetic fruit flavoring agent for beverages, ice cream, ices, candy, and baked goods. No known toxicity.

4-HEXYLRESORCINOL • Used in mouthwashes and sunburn creams. A heavy, pale yellow liquid that becomes solid upon standing at room temperature. It has a pungent odor and a sharp astringent taste and has been used medicinally as an antiworm medicine and antiseptic. It can cause severe gastrointestinal irritation; bowel, liver, and heart damage have been reported. Concentrated solutions can cause burns of the skin and mucous membranes.

HEXYTHIAZOX • A white, odorless, crystalline pesticide used to kill mites on pears. FDA residue tolerance is 0.3 ppm.

HICKORY BARK EXTRACT • A natural flavoring extract from the hickory nut tree used in butter, caramel, rum, maple, nut, spice, tobacco, and smoke flavorings for beverages, ice cream, ices, candy, baked goods, condiments, and liquors. There is no reported use of the chemical and no toxicology information is available. GRAS.

HICKORY SMOKE CONDENSATE (HSC) • A food flavoring popular in the U.S. Available data have suggested that this additive has tumor-initiating and -promoting potential. Researchers at Japan's Nagoya City University Medical School gave rats a diet containing 5 percent HSC, and the animals developed precancerous lesions. No effect was observed at lower doses. The FDA data bank, PAFA (see page 10), has not yet done a search of the toxicology literature concerning this additive.

HIGH-AMYLOSE CORNSTARCH • Cornstarch that has been treated with enzymes to make it sweeter.

HIGH-FRUCTOSE CORN SYRUP • Corn syrup (*see*) that has been treated with enzymes to make it sweeter. Used in beverages, candy, frozen desserts, dairy drinks, canned fruits, processed ham, hamburger, ice cream, luncheon meat, meat loaf, poultry, and sausage.

HINOKITIOL • The organic compound distilled from the leaves of arborvitae, it is a pale yellow oil with a camphor smell and is used in perfumery and flavoring. Low toxicity.

HIPBERRY EXTRACT • *See* Rose Hips Extract.

HISTAMINE • A chemical released by mast cells and considered responsible for much of the swelling and itching characteristics of hay fever and other allergies.

HISTIDINE • L and DL forms. An essential amino acid (*see*) used as a nutrient. It is a building block of protein. Soluble in water. (L-Histidine is the natural form.) It is used in cosmetic creams. Since 1980 histidine has been on the FDA list of additives that need further study. GRAS. The FDA data bank, PAFA (see page 10), has fully up-to-date toxicology information available for this additive.

HONEY • Used as a coloring, flavoring, and emollient in cosmetics. Formerly used in hair bleaches. The common, sweet, viscous material manufactured in the sacs of various kinds of bees from the nectar of flowers. The flavor and color depend upon the plants from which the nectar was taken.

HONEYDEW MELON JUICE • Liquid expressed from fresh honeydew.

HONEYSUCKLE • The common fragrant tubular flowers, filled with honey, which are used in perfumes. No known toxicity.

HOPS • *Humulus lupulus.* Used in beer brewing and in fruit and root beer flavorings for beverages. Derived from the carefully dried pineconelike fruit of the hop plant grown in Europe, Asia, and North America. Light yellow or greenish, it is an oily liquid with a bitter taste and aromatic odor. A *solid extract* is used in bitters, fruit, and root beer flavorings for beverages, ice cream, ices, candy, and baked goods. *Hops oil* is used in raspberry, grape, whiskey, and spice flavorings for beverages, ice cream, ices, candy, baked goods, chewing gum, and condiments. Hops at one time were thought to be a sedative. The FDA data bank, PAFA (see page 10), has not yet done a search of the toxicology literature concerning this additive.

HOPS OIL • *See* Hops.

HOREHOUND EXTRACT • Hoarhound. A flavoring extracted from a mint-like plant cultivated in Europe, Asia, and the United States, *Marrubium vulgare.* It has a bitter taste and is used in maple, nut, and root beer flavorings for beverages, ice cream, ices, candy, and baked goods. It is also a bitter tonic and expectorant. The FDA data bank, PAFA, has not yet done a search of the toxicology literature concerning this additive. GRAS.

HORMONES • A hormone is a chemical produced by a gland and secreted into the bloodstream, affecting the function of distant cells or organs. U.S. beef producers have been using growth hormones, powerful chemicals from the pituitary gland at the base of the brain, to increase the weight of cattle from 10 to 20 percent for the same amount of feed. Diethylstilbestrol, another hormone, an estrogen, was used by beef and poultry producers to increase the weight of meat, for which they are paid by the pound. The FDA has tried to ban diethylstilbestrol for that purpose because it has been shown to be carcinogenic, but spot checks have shown that it is still present in some meat and poultry products. In 1988, the twelve-nation European Community put a ban on American beef because of the use of growth hormones in raising cattle for meat. The American position is that the growth hormones approved for cattle by the Department of Agriculture are not harmful to humans. Environmentalists who testified in favor of the European legislators have maintained that such hormones create tumors and genetic deformities in children. Hormones are still being used in feed and by implantation in cattle, chickens, and turkeys, as you can determine by checking listings, including those for estradiol, mibolerone, testosterone propionate, and trenbolone.

HORSE CHESTNUT • The seeds of *Aeschylus hippocastanum.* A tonic, natural astringent for the skin, and fever-reducing substance that contains tannic acid (*see*). No known toxicity.

HORSE NETTLE • Solanum. Bull Nettle. Radical Weed. Air-dried ripe fruit of *Solanum carolinense,* a South American nightshade plant. It is also grown in Florida. It is used as a sedative and anticonvulsant.

HORSEMINT LEAVES EXTRACT • *Monarda* spp. A flavoring extract from any of several coarse, aromatic plants grown from New York to Florida and from Texas to Wisconsin. Used in fruit flavorings for beverages (600 ppm). Formerly used as an aromatic stimulant and to break up intestinal gas. There is no reported use of the chemical and no toxicology information is available. GRAS.

HORSERADISH EXTRACT • Scurvy Grass. *Armoracia lapathifolia.* A condiment ingredient utilizing the grated root from the tall, coarse, white-flowered herb native to Europe. Often combined with vinegar or other ingredients. Contains ascorbic acid (*see*) and acts as an antiseptic in cosmetics. The FDA data bank, PAFA (see page 10), has not yet done a search of the toxicology literature concerning this additive. GRAS.

HOUSELEEK EXTRACT • Extract of the common houseleek *Sempervivum tectorum.* Old herbal remedy for soothing the skin.

HPP • Hydrolyzed Plant Protein. *See* Hydrolyzed Vegetable Protein.

HUMECTANT • A substance used to preserve the moisture content of materials, such as confections and tobacco. Glycerin, propylene glycol, and sorbitol (*see all*) are widely used humectants. *See* individual substances for toxicity.

HUMULUS • A hop plant, a herbaceous vine with palmate leaves and pistillate flowers. No known toxicity.

HVP • *See* Hydrolyzed Vegetable Protein.

HYACINTH, ABSOLUTE • *Hyacinthus orientalis.* The extract of the common fragrant flower, used as a flavoring for chewing gum and in perfumes and soaps. Dark green liquid with a penetrating odor, the juice of the hyacinth is irritating to the skin and can cause allergic reactions. The bulb can cause severe gastrointestinal symptoms. The FDA data bank, PAFA (see page 10), has not yet done a search of the toxicology literature concerning this additive.

HYACINTHIN • *See* Phenylacetaldehyde.

HYBRID SAFFLOWER OIL • The oil derived from the seeds of a genetic strain that contains mostly oleic acid triglyceride as distinct from safflower oil.

HYDRATED • Combined with water.

HYDRATED ALUMINA • *See* Aluminum Hydroxide.

HYDRATED SILICA • An anticaking agent to keep loose powders free-flowing. *See* Silica and Hydrated.

HYDRATROPALDEHYDE • *See* 2-Phenylpropionaldehyde.

HYDRATROPALDEHYDE DIMETHYL ACETAL • *See* 2-Phenylpropionaldehyde Dimethyl Acetal.

HYDRAZINE • Colorless fuming liquid used as a solvent and catalyst for inorganic materials. Used in steam in contact with food. FDA allows zero residue. A reducing agent (*see*) and chlorine scavenger, it is a highly toxic chemical. It is a cancer-causing agent, and direct liquid contact with skin or eyes may produce severe burns. Vapors are highly irritating to the nose and throat and may cause injury to the lungs, liver, and kidneys. Although allowed as a food additive, there is no current reported use of the chemical, and therefore, although toxicology information may be available, it is not being updated, according to the FDA.

a-HYDRO-OMEGA-HYDROXY-POLY(OXYETHYLENE)POLY(OXYPROPYLENE) (51-57 MOLES)POLY(OXYETHYLENE) BLOCK COPOLYMERS, (MOL WT. 14,000) • Dough conditioner. FDA tolerance is 0.5 percent of flour used. *See* Copolymer Condensates of Ethylene Oxide and Propylene Oxide.

a-HYDRO-OMEGA-HYDROXY-POLY(OXYETHYLENE)POLY(OXYPROPYLENE) (55-61 MOLES)POLY(OXYETHYLENE) BLOCK COPOLYMERS, (MOL WT. 9,760–13,200) • Solubilizer and stabilizer in flavor concentrations. FDA permits use according to general manufacturing principles. *See* Copolymer Condensates of Ethylene Oxide and Propylene Oxide.

a-HYDRO-OMEGA-HYDROXY-POLY(OXYETHYLENE)POLY(OXYPROPYLENE) (53-59 MOLES)POLY(OXYETHYLENE)(14-16 MOLES) BLOCK COPOLYMER, (MOL WT. 3,500–4,125) • A solubilizing and dispersing agent in combination with dioctyl sodium sulfosuccinate (*see*). FDA tolerance is 10 ppm total in finished beverage or fruit drink. See Copolymer Condensates of Ethylene Oxide and Propylene Oxide.

HYDROBIOTIC FEED • *See* Verxite Granules and Verxite Grits.

HYDROCARBONS • A large class of organic compounds containing only carbon and hydrogen. Petroleum, natural gas, coal, and bitumens are common hydrocarbon products. Hydrocarbons also include mineral oils, paraffin wax, and ozokerite (*see all*).

HYDROCHLORIC ACID • An acid used as a modifier for food starch, in the manufacture of sodium glutamate (*see*) and gelatin, for the conversion of corn-starch to syrup (0.012 percent), and to adjust the pH (acid-alkalinity balance) in the brewing industry (0.02 percent). Also used as a solvent. A clear, colorless or slightly yellowish, corrosive liquid, it is a water solution of hydrogen chloride of varying concentrations. Used in hair bleaches to speed up oxidation in rinses and to remove color. Inhalation of the fumes causes choking and inflammation of the respiratory tract. Ingestion may corrode the mucous membranes, esoph-agus, and stomach and cause diarrhea. Circulatory collapse and death can occur. GRAS. The FDA data bank, PAFA (see page 10), is, as of this writing, conducting a search of the toxicology literature concerning this additive.

HYDROCHLOROFLUORCARBON 22, 142b, 152a • Propellants and refrig-erants derived from chlorofluorocarbon; any of several compounds comprised of carbon, fluorine, chlorine, and hydrogen. Though safer than many propellant gases, their use has diminished because of suspected effects on stratospheric ozone.

HYDROCINNAMALDEHYDE • Colorless to slightly yellow liquid with a strong hyacinth odor used as a flavoring agent in various foods. A human skin irritant.

HYDROCINNAMIC ALCOHOL • Colorless, thick liquid with a sweet hyacinth odor used as a flavoring agent in various foods. Moderately toxic by ingestion. Mildly toxic by skin contact.

HYDROCINNAMYL ACETATE • Colorless liquid with a spicy, floral odor used as a flavoring agent in various foods. Mildly toxic by ingestion.

HYDROCORTISONE SODIUM SUCCINATE • A-Hydrocort. Solu-Cortef. An adrenal gland hormone used to decrease severe inflammation. Used to treat cows, and the FDA permits up to 10 ppb in milk. The drug also suppresses the immune response. Has caused adverse reproductive effects in laboratory animals.

HYDROGEN CYANIDE • A colorless gas or liquid with a characteristic odor. In veterinary preparations used to treat mastitis, inflammation of the udders. As a fumigant, the FDA residue tolerances are 200 ppm in cocoa, 125 ppm in cereal flours, 90 ppm in cereals cooked before eaten, and 50 ppm in uncooked ham, bacon, and sausage. In humans, high concentrations may cause shortness of breath, paralysis, unconsciousness, convulsions, and respiratory arrest. Chronic exposure over long periods may cause fatigue and weakness. Exposure to 150 ppm from thirty minutes to an hour may endanger life. Death may result from a few minutes exposure to 300 ppm. Average fatal dose is 50 to 60 mg. The compressed gas is used for exterminating rodents and insects. Must be handled by specially trained experts.

HYDROGEN PEROXIDE • A bleaching and oxidizing agent, a detergent, and an antiseptic. Used in skin bleaches, hair bleaches, cold creams, mouth-washes, toothpastes, and in cold permanent waves. An unstable compound readily broken down into water and oxygen, it is made from barium peroxide and diluted phosphoric acid. Generally recognized as safe as a preservative and germ killer in milk and cheese as well as in cosmetics. Bleaches tripe and butter; used in the treatment of eggs before drying and in cheddar and Swiss cheeses. A 3 percent solution is used medicinally as an antiseptic and germicide. A strong oxidizer, undiluted it can cause burns of the skin and mucous membranes. In 1980, the Japanese notified the World Health Organization that hydrogen peroxide was suspect as a cancer-causing agent. It was widely used in Japanese fish cakes. The noodles were dipped in dilute hydrogen peroxide for disinfecting. The fish meat and raw flour were also mixed with hydrogen peroxide. In laboratory rats, it was discovered that in the sixty-fifth week, the lining of the duodenum was thickened but no cancers occurred. The Japanese Welfare Ministry decided that hydrogen peroxide is safe for food when it is entirely decomposed and that the food should not contain any residual. The FDA data bank, PAFA (see page 10), is, as of this writing, conducting a search of the toxicology literature concerning this additive.

HYDROGEN SULFIDE • Colorless gas with a terrible odor. It is derived from sulfuric acid as a byproduct of petroleum refining. Highly flammable. Toxic by inhalation. Strong irritant to the eyes. Used as a source of sulfur and hydrogen in the manufacture of food additives. The FDA data bank, PAFA, has fully up-to-date toxicology information available for this additive.

HYDROGENATED CORN SYRUP • Used in cat and dog food as a humectant (*see*). *Also see* Corn Syrup.

HYDROGENATED HONEY • *See* hydrogenation and honey.

HYDROGENATED MENHADEN OIL • Obtained along the west coast of North America from the menhaden fish, which is somewhat larger than herring. The oil contains myristic acid, palmitic acid, and linoleic acid (*see all*). Used as a substitute for linseed oil. Hydrogenated menhaden oil is used as a substitute for tallow. GRAS.

HYDROGENATED OIL • Oil that is partially converted from naturally polyunsaturated fats to saturated. Makes liquid oils partially solid. May adversely affect the levels of fat in the blood and has been linked to colon cancer in some reports. *See* Hydrogenation.

HYDROGENATED PEANUT OIL • *See* Hydrogenation and Peanut Oil.

HYDROGENATED SOY GLYCERIDE • *See* Soybean Oil and Hydrogenation.

HYDROGENATED SOYBEAN OIL • *See* Soybean Oil and Hydrogenation.

HYDROGENATED SPERM OIL • Used to coat bakery pans so products will not stick. *See* Sperm Oil.

HYDROGENATED STARCH HYDROLYSATE • The end product of the hydrogenation of corn syrup. *See* Hydrogenation and Corn Syrup.

HYDROGENATED TALLOW • A component used in the production of beet sugar and yeast to inhibit foaming. *See* Hydrogenation. No known toxicity. The final report to the FDA of the Select Committee on GRAS Substances stated in 1980 that it should continue its GRAS status with no limitations other than good manufacturing practices.

HYDROGENATED TALLOW ACID • *See* Hydrogenated Tallow.

HYDROGENATED TALLOW ALCOHOL • *See* Hydrogenated Tallow, which has the same uses. The final report to the FDA of the Select Committee on GRAS Substances stated in 1980 that it should continue its GRAS status with no limitations other than good manufacturing practices.

HYDROGENATED TALLOW BETAINE • *See* Hydrogenated Tallow and Betaine.

HYDROGENATED TALLOW GLYCERIDE • *See* Hydrogenated Tallow and Glycerides.

HYDROGENATED TALLOWTRIMONIUM CHLORIDE • *See* Quaternary Ammonium Compounds.

HYDROGENATED VEGETABLE GLYCERIDE • An emollient to prevent the skin from losing moisture. *See* Vegetable Oils and Hydrogenation.

HYDROGENATION • The process of adding hydrogen gas under high pressure to liquid oils. It is the most widely used chemical process in the edible-fat industry. Used in the manufacture of petrol (from coal), margarine, and shortening. Used primarily in the cosmetics and food industries to convert liquid oils to semisolid fats at room temperature (Crisco, for example). Reduces the amount of acid in the compound and improves color. Usually, the higher the amount of hydrogenation, the lower the unsaturation in the fat and the less possibility of flavor degradation or spoilage due to oxidation. Hydrogenated oils still contain some unsaturated components that are susceptible to rancidity. Therefore, the addition of antioxidants is still necessary.

HYDROLYSIS • Decomposition that changes a compound into other compounds by taking up the elements of water. For example, hydrolysis of salt into an acid and a base or hydrolysis of an ester into an alcohol and an acid.

HYDROLYZED • Subject to hydrolysis or turned partly into water. *Hydrolysis* is derived from the Greek *hydro,* meaning "water," and *lysis,* meaning "a setting free." It occurs as a chemical process in which the decomposition of a compound is brought about by water, resolving it into a simpler compound. Hydrolysis also occurs in the digestion of foods. The proteins in the stomach react with water in an enzyme reaction to form peptones and amino acids (*see*).

HYDROLYZED CASEIN • *See* Casein and Hydrolyzed.

HYDROLYZED KERATIN • The widely used hydrolysate of keratin, a protein obtained from hair, wool, horn, nails, claws, beaks, membranes of egg shells, and nerve tissues. The hydrolysate is derived by acid, enzyme, or other forms of hydrolysis. The word *animal* was removed from this ingredient name. Used in dietary protein supplements.

HYDROLYZED LEATHER MEAL • Used in swine feed up to 1 percent of weight.

HYDROLYZED MILK PROTEIN • *See* Acid-Hydrolyzed Proteins.

HYDROLYZED PLANT PROTEIN • Used as a flavoring. *See* Hydrolyzed Vegetable Protein.

HYDROLYZED PROTEIN • The word *animal* was removed from this ingredient's name. Used in gels and in animal feed. *See* Proteins and Hydrolyzed.

HYDROLYZED SOY PROTEIN • *See* Soybean and Hydrolyzed.

HYDROLYZED VEGETABLE PROTEIN • HPP. HVP. The hydrolysate (liquefied product) of vegetable protein derived by acid, enzyme, or other method of hydrolysis. A flavor enhancer used in soup, beef, and stew. High salt and glutamate content with low-quality protein. On the GRAS list, but the Select Committee of the Federation of American Societies for Experimental Biology (FASEB) advised the FDA that hydrolyzed vegetable protein contains dicarboxylic amino acid (a building block of the protein that affects growth) when used at present levels in strained and junior baby foods. They said that the effects of this substance on children should be studied further. The effects on adults of vegetable and animal protein hydrolysates demonstrate "no current hazard," but the FASEB voiced uncertainties about future consumption levels for those products and recommended further studies.

HYDROLYZED YEAST • The hydrolysate of yeast (liquefaction) derived from acid, enzyme, or other method of hydrolysis.

HYDROLYZED YEAST PROTEIN • *See* Hydrolyzed Yeast.

HYDROQUINONE • Used in bleach and freckle creams and in suntan lotions. A white crystalline phenol (*see*) that occurs naturally but is usually manufactured in the laboratory. Hydroquinone combines rapidly with oxygen and becomes brown when exposed to air. Death has occurred from the ingestion of as little as five grams. Ingestion of as little as one gram (one-thirtieth of an ounce) has caused nausea, vomiting, ringing in the ears, delirium, a sense of suffocation, and collapse. Industrial workers exposed to the chemical have suffered clouding of the eye lens. Application to the skin may cause allergic reactions. It can cause depigmentation in a 2 percent solution. When injected into the abdomen of mice in 28-mg doses per kilogram of body weight, it caused bladder cancer, but other studies in which animals were fed the chemical did not show it to induce cancer. However, it did cause atrophy of the liver and aplastic anemia. The FDA data bank, PAFA (see page 10), has fully up-to-date toxicology information available for this additive.

HYDROQUINONE DIMETHYL ETHER • White flakes with a sweet clover odor used as a fixative in foods, perfumes, dyes, cosmetics, and especially in suntan preparations. *See* Hydroquinone.

3-HYDROXY-2-BUTANONE • The FDA data bank, PAFA (see page 10), has fully up-to-date toxicology information available for this additive. *See* Acetoin.

2-HYDROXY-*p*-CYMENE • *See* Carvacrol.

(Z)-4-HYDROXY-6-DODECENOIC ACID LACTONE • One of the newer synthetic flavorings. The FDA data bank, PAFA, has not yet done a search of the toxicology literature concerning this additive.

5-HYDROXY-4-OCTANONE • A synthetic butter, butterscotch, fruit, cheese, and nut flavoring agent for beverages, ice cream, ices, candy, and baked goods. No known toxicity.

HYDROXY PROPYLMETHYL CELLULOSE CARBONATE • Prepared from wood pulp or cotton by treatment with methyl chloride. Used as a substitute for water-soluble gums, to render paper greaseproof, and as a thickener. The final report to the FDA of the Select Committee on GRAS Substances stated in 1980 that it should continue its GRAS status with limitations on amounts that can be added to food.

p-HYDROXYANISOLE • *See* Guaiacol.

HYDROXYANTHROQUINONEAMINOPROPYL METHYL MORPHOLIUMIUN METHOSULFATE • A solvent for resins and waxes; an antioxidant and plasticizer. May be irritating to the skin.

o-HYDROXYBENZALDEHYDE • *See* Salicylaldehyde.

p-HYDROXYBENZOATE • *See* Propylparaben.

o-HYDROXYBENZOIC ACID • *See* Salicylic Acid.

p-HYDROXYBENZOIC ACID • Prepared from *p*-bromophenol. Used as a preservative and fungicide. *See* Benzoic Acid for toxicity.

p-HYDROXYBENZYL ACETONE • *See* 4-(*p*-Hydroxyphenyl)-2-Butanone.

p-HYDROXYBENZYL ISOTHIOCYANATE • A derivative of mustard oil used in flavoring. The final report to the FDA of the Select Committee on GRAS Substances stated in 1980 that it should continue its GRAS status with no limitations other than good manufacturing practices.

2-HYDROXYCAMPHANE • *See* Borneol.

HYDROXYCITRONELLAL • Colorless liquid obtained by the addition of citronellol. Used as a fixative and a fragrance in perfumery for its sweet lilylike odor. It can cause allergic reactions. The FDA data bank, PAFA (see page 10), has fully up-to-date toxicology information available for this additive.

HYDROXYCITRONELLAL DIETHYL ACETAL • A synthetic citrus and fruit flavoring agent for beverages, ice cream, ices, candy, and baked goods. The FDA data bank, PAFA, has fully up-to-date toxicology information available for this additive.

HYDROXYCITRONELLAL DIMETHYL ACETAL • A synthetic flavoring agent, a colorless liquid with a light floral odor. Used in fruit and cherry flavorings for beverages, ice cream, ices, candy, and baked goods. The FDA data bank, PAFA (see page 10), has fully up-to-date toxicology information available for this additive.

HYDROXYCITRONELLOL • A synthetic lemon, floral, and cherry flavoring agent for beverages, ice cream, ices, candy, baked goods, gelatin desserts, and chewing gum. The FDA data bank, PAFA, has fully up-to-date toxicology information available for this additive.

HYDROXYLAMINE HCL • An antioxidant for fatty acids and soaps, sodium nitrite (*see*). May be slightly irritating to skin, eyes, and mucous membranes and may cause a depletion of oxygen in the blood when ingested. In the body it is reportedly decomposed to sodium nitrite.

HYDROXYLATE • The process in which an atom of hydrogen and an atom of oxygen are introduced into a compound to make the compound more soluble.

HYDROXYLATED LECITHIN • An emulsifier and antioxidant used in baked goods, ice cream, and margarine. According to the Food and Agricultural Organization/World Health Organization Expert Committee on Food Additives, the safety of hydroxylated lecithin (*see* Lecithin) has not been adequately established. It has been cleared by the FDA for use as a food emulsifier. The FDA data bank, PAFA, has fully up-to-date toxicology information available for this additive.

HYDROXYLATION • The process in which an atom of hydrogen and an atom of oxygen are introduced into a compound to make that compound more soluble.

HYDROXYMETHYLCELLULOSE • Thickener and bodying agent derived from plants. Used to thicken cosmetics and as a setting aid in hair products. *See* Carboxymethyl Cellulose.

HYDROXYOCTACOSANYL HYDROXYSTEARATE • *See* Stearic Acid and Hydroxylation.

4-(*p*-HYDROXYPHENYL)-2-BUTANONE • A synthetic fruit flavoring for beverages, ice cream, ices, candy, baked goods, gelatin desserts, and chewing gum. The FDA data bank, PAFA (see page 10), has fully up-to-date toxicology information available for this additive.

HYDROXYPHENYL GLYCINEAMIDE • Derived from the nonessential amino acid glycine (*see*). Used as a buffering agent and as a violet scent.

HYDROXYPROLINE • L-Proline. The hydroxylated (*see*) amino acid used to add "protein" to cosmetics. There is no reported use of the chemical and no toxicology information is available.

HYDROXYPROPYL CELLULOSE • A thickener. The FDA data bank, PAFA (see page 10), has fully up-to-date toxicology information available for this additive. *See* Hydroxymethylcellulose.

HYDROXYPROPYL GUAR • Guar Gum. 2-Hydroxypropyl Ether. *See* Guar Gum.

HYDROXYPROPYL METHYLCELLULOSE • An emulsifier used in food except standards of identity foods, which do not provide for such use. The FDA data bank, PAFA, has fully up-to-date toxicology information available for this additive. *See* Cellulose Gums and Standards of Identity.

HYDROXYPROPYL STARCH, HYDROXYPROPYL STARCH OXIDIZED, AND HYDROXYPROPYL DISTARCHPHOSPHATE • These are all modified starches. The final report to the FDA of the Select Committee on GRAS Substances stated in 1980 that while no available evidence on these starches demonstrates a hazard to the public when they are used at levels that are now current and in the manner now practiced, uncertainties exist requiring that additional studies be conducted. In 1980, the FDA said GRAS status would continue while tests were being completed and evaluated. Nothing new has been reported by the FDA since then.

HYDROXYPROPYLAMINE NITRITE • *See* Nitrite.

HYDROXYQUINOLINE SULFATE • Was used as a component of a cottage-cheese coagulant but has been banned by the FDA.

HYDROXYSTEARIC ACID • *See* Stearic Acid.

HYDROXYSTEARMIDE MEA • A mixture of ethanolamide of hydroxy-stearic acid. *See* Stearic Acid.

HYDROXYSTEARYL METHYLGLUCAMINE • An amino sugar. *See* Glucose.

HYGROMYCIN • A broad-spectrum antibiotic from *Streptomyces hygroscopicus* used in animal feed. The FDA allows zero residue in eggs of poultry and in uncooked edible tissues and byproducts of swine and poultry.

HYPERICUM • Hypericin. Blue-black needles obtained from pyridine (*see*). The solutions are red or green with a red cast. Small amounts seem to be a tranquilizer and have been used as an antidepressant in medicine. It can produce a sensitivity to light.

HYPERSENSITIVITY • The condition in persons previously exposed to an antigen in which tissue damage results from an immune reaction to a further dose of the antigen. Classically, four types of hypersensitivity are recognized, but the term is often used to mean the type of allergy associated with hay fever and asthma.

HYPNONE • *See* Acetophenone.

HYPO • Prefix from the Greek meaning "under" or "below," as in hypoacidity—acidity in a lesser degree than is usual or normal.

HYPOPHOSPHORIC ACID • Crystals used in baking powder, sodium salt. No known toxicity.

HYSSOP EXTRACT • Extract of *Hyssopus officinalis*. A synthetic flavoring from the aromatic herb. Used in bitters. The *extract* is a liquor flavoring for beverages, ice cream, and ice. The *oil* is a liquor and spice flavoring. The FDA data bank, PAFA (see page 10), has not yet done a search of the toxicology literature concerning this additive. GRAS.

I

ICELAND MOSS EXTRACT • The extract of *Lichen islandicus*. A water-soluble gum that gels on cooling. Used to flavor alcoholic beverages, as a food additive, and in cosmetic gels. There is no reported use of the chemical and no toxicology information is available.

IgE • Antibodies that are responsible for the majority of allergic reactions. Medical scientists feel that, if their efforts succeed in suppressing IgE formation, they will have a method of not only more effectively treating allergies but also of preventing many of them from occurring. *See also* Antibody.

IGF-I • Abbreviation for insulinlike growth factor; it is a natural protein required for normal growth. It is associated with the use of recombinant bovine somatotropin (*see*). Allegations have been made that milk from treated cows may cause breast cancer. The consumption of dietary IGF-I in milk, the FDA maintains, plays no role in inducing or promoting any human disease, including breast cancer.

IMAZALIL • An antifungal used on dried citrus pulp for animal feed. FDA residue tolerance is 25 ppm in the pulp and 0.01 to 0.50 ppm in cattle fats, swine, sheep, and milk.

IMAZETHAPYR • An herbicide used on soybeans. FDA residue tolerance is 0.1 ppm.

IMIDAZOLE • Glyoxaline. White crystalline base made by the action of ammonia and formaldehyde on glyoxal. It is used as a biological control of pests and as an antihistamine.

IMIDAZOLINE • A derivative of imidazole (*see*); also called *glyoxalidine*.

IMIDAZOLIDINYL UREA • A bactericidal preservative with a low toxicity in animals. Sensitivity reactions have been reported in humans.

IMITATION • A flavor containing any portion of nonnatural materials. For instance, unless a strawberry flavoring is made entirely from strawberries, it must be called imitation. When a processor fails to use all the standard ingredients in mayonnaise, he must call it salad dressing. *Imitation* means that the product contains fewer vitamins, minerals, or the other nutrients than the food it resembles. With reference to a fragrance, it means containing all or some portion of nonnatural materials.

IMITATION MILK • Contains no milk derivative. Usually contains water, sugar, and vegetable fat. A source of protein (such as soybean) with various additive flavorings. Imitation milk contains 1 percent protein compared to 3.5 percent in whole cow's milk.

IMMORTELLE EXTRACT • *Erythrina micopteryx.* A natural flavoring extract from a red-flowered tropical tree. The name derives from the French *immortel*—"immortal" or "everlasting." Used in raspberry, fruit, and liquor flavoring for beverages, ice cream, ices, baked goods, candy, gelatin desserts, and chewing gum. GRAS. The FDA data bank, PAFA (see page 10), has not yet done a search of the toxicology literature concerning this additive.

IMPERATORIA • *Peucedanum ostruthium.* A flavoring from a tropical grass used in malt beer. There is no reported use of the chemical and no toxicology information is available.

INDIAN CRESS EXTRACT • The extract obtained from the flowers of *Tropaeolum majus.*

INDIAN GUM • *See* Ghatti Gum.

INDIAN TRAGACANTH • *See* Karaya Gum.

INDIGO • Probably the oldest known dye. Prepared from various *Indigofera* plants native to Bengal, Java, and Guatemala. Dark blue powder with a coppery luster. No known skin irritation.

INDIGO CARMINE • *See* FD and C Blue No. 2.

INDOLE • A white, lustrous, flaky substance with an unpleasant odor, occurring naturally in jasmine oil and orange flowers and used as a synthetic flavoring agent in raspberry, strawberry, bitters, chocolate, orange, coffee, violet, fruit, nut, and cheese flavorings for beverages, ice cream, ices, candy, baked goods, and gelatin desserts. Also used in perfumes. It can be extracted from coal tar and feces; in highly diluted solutions, the odor is pleasant. The lethal dose in dogs is sixty milligrams per kilogram of body weight. Moderately toxic by ingestion and skin contact. Has caused tumors and cancer in laboratory animals. The FDA data bank, PAFA (see page 10), has fully up-to-date toxicology information available for this additive.

INOSINATE • A salt of inosinic acid used to intensify flavor, as with sodium glutamate (*see*). Inosinic acid is prepared from meat extract; also from dried sardines. No known toxicity.

INOSITOL • A dietary supplement of the vitamin B family used in emollients. Found in plant and animal tissues. Isolated commercially from corn. A fine, white, crystalline powder, it is odorless with a sweet taste. Stable in air. No known toxicity. The final report to the FDA of the Select Committee on GRAS Substances stated in 1980 that it should continue its GRAS status with no limitations other than good manufacturing practices. The FDA data bank, PAFA, has fully up-to-date toxicology information available for this additive.

INSOLUBLE GLUCOSE ISAMASE ENZYME PREPARATIONS • GRAS. *See* Enzyme.

INTERMEDIATE • A chemical substance found as part of a necessary step between one organic compound and another, as in the production of dyes, pharmaceuticals, or other artificial products that develop properties only upon oxidation. Used frequently for artificial colors.

INTERNATIONAL AGENCY FOR RESEARCH ON CANCER (IARC) • A United Nations organization that gathers information on suspected environmental carcinogens and summarizes available data with appropriate references. Included in these reviews are synonyms, physical and chemical properties, uses and occurrence, and biological data relevant to the evaluation of the risk of cancer to humans. The more than forty monographs in the series contain an evaluation of about nine hundred materials.

INVERT SUGAR • Inversol. Colorose. A mixture of 50 percent glucose and 50 percent fructose. It is sweeter than sucrose. Commercially produced by "inversion" of sucrose. Honey is mostly invert sugar. Invert sugar is used in confectionery and in brewing. Like glycerin (*see*) it holds in moisture and prevents drying out. Used medicinally in intravenous solutions. No known toxicity. The final report to the FDA of the Select Committee on GRAS Substances stated in 1980 that there is no available evidence that it is a hazard to the public when used as it is now and it should continue its GRAS status with limitations on amounts that can be added to food. The FDA data bank, PAFA (see page 10), has fully up-to-date toxicology information available for this additive.

INVERTASE FROM *SACCHAROMYCES CEREVISIAE* • An enzyme used in processing. The FDA data bank, PAFA, has not yet done a search of the toxicology literature concerning this additive.

IODINE SOURCES • Calcium Iodate, Cuprous Iodide, Potassium Iodate, and Potassium Iodide. Discovered in 1811 and classed among the rarer earth elements, it is found in the earth's crust as bluish black scales. Nearly two hundred products contain this chemical. They are prescription and over-the-counter medications. Iodine is an integral part of the thyroid hormones, which have important metabolic roles, and is an essential nutrient for humans. Iodine deficiency leads to thyroid enlargement or goiter. Nutritionists have found that the most efficient way to add iodine to the diet is through the use of iodized salt. The FDA has ordered all table salts to specify whether the product contains iodide. However, many commercially prepared food items do not contain iodized salt. Iodized salt contains up to 0.01 percent; dietary supplements contain 0.16 percent. Cuprous and potassium iodides are used in table salts; potassium iodide is in some drinking water; and potassium iodate is used in animal feeds. Dietary iodine is absorbed from the intestinal tract, and the main human sources are from food and water. Seafoods are good sources, and dairy products may be good sources if the cows eat enriched grain. Adult daily iodine requirement is believed to be 110 to 150 milligrams. Growing children and pregnant or lactating women may need more. Iodine compounds are used in expectorants and thinners, particularly in the treatment of asthma and in contrast media for X rays and fluoroscopy. They can produce a diffuse red, pimply rash, hives, asthma, and sometimes, anaphylactic shock. Iodine is also used as an antiseptic and germicide in cosmetics.

IONONE • Used as a scent in perfumery and as a flavoring agent in foods, it occurs naturally in *Boronia,* an Australian shrub. Colorless to pale yellow with an odor reminiscent of cedarwood or violets. It may cause allergic reactions. The FDA data bank, PAFA (see page 10), has fully up-to-date toxicology information available for this additive.

IPRODIONE • Glycophene. A fungicide used on cattle, goats, hogs, chickens, sheep, and eggs. FDA residue tolerance on animal feed ranges from 10 to 300 ppm.

IRIS FLORENTINA • *See* Orris.

IRISH MOSS • Emulsifier for frozen desserts, dressings, fruits, jelly, and preserves. *See* Carrageenan.

IRON • It is an essential mineral element and occurs widely in foods, especially organ meats such as liver, red meats, poultry, and leafy vegetables. The principal foods to which iron or iron salts are added are enriched cereals, some beverages including milk, poultry stuffing, cornmeal, corn grits, and bread. *Iron ammonium citrate* is an anticaking agent in salt. *Iron-choline citrate* is cleared for use as a source of iron in foods for special dietary use. *Iron peptonate,* a combination of oxide and peptone, is made soluble by the presence of sodium citrate and is used in the treatment of iron-deficiency anemia. The recommended daily allowance for children and adults is from 0.2 milligram to 1 milligram and 18 milligrams per day for pregnant women. Iron is potentially toxic in all forms.

IRON CAPRYLATE, IRON LINOLEATE, IRON NAPHTHENATE, AND IRON TALLATE • All are used in packaging. Iron naphthenate was said by the Select Committee on GRAS Substances to have so little known about it that there was nothing upon which to base an evaluation when it is used as a food ingredient. As for the others, the final report to the FDA of the Select Committee on GRAS Substances stated in 1980 that they should continue their GRAS status with no limitations other than good manufacturing practices. There is no reported use of iron caprylate, iron naphthenate, or iron linoleate, and no toxicology information is available.

IRON-CHOLINE CITRATE COMPLEX • *See* Iron and Citrate Salts.

IRON OXIDE • Any of several natural or synthetic oxides of iron (iron combined with oxygen) varying in color from red-brown or black-orange to yellow. Used for dyeing eggshells and for pet food. There is no reported use of the chemical and no toxicology information is available. *See* Iron for toxicity.

IRON SALTS • Iron Sources. Ferric Choline Citrate; Ferric Orthophosphate; Ferric Phosphate; Ferric Sodium Pyrophosphate; Ferrous Fumarate; Ferrous Gluconate; Ferrous Lactate; and Ferrous Sulfate. *Ferric phosphate* is widely used as a food supplement, particularly in bread enrichment. *Ferric pyrophosphate* is a grayish blue powder used in ceramics. *Ferric sodium pyrophosphate* is used in prepared breakfast cereals, poultry stuffing, enriched flours, self-rising flours, farina, cornmeal, corn grits, bread, and rolls. The final report to the FDA of the Select Committee on GRAS Substances stated in 1980 that there is no available evidence that it is a hazard to the public when used as it is now and should continue as GRAS with limitations on amounts that can be added to food. It may cause gastrointestinal disturbances. *Ferrous lactate* is greenish white with a sweet iron taste. It is affected by air and light. It is also used to treat anemia. The final report to the FDA of the Select Committee on GRAS Substances stated in 1980 that there is no evidence that ferrous lactate is hazardous and therefore it should continue as GRAS with limitations. *Ferrous sulfate* is blue-green and odorless and oxidized in air and is used as a wood preservative, weed killer, and to treat anemia. Large quantities can cause gastrointestinal disturbances. For *ferric choline citrate, see* Choline Chloride. Among other irons used are ferrous gluconate, ferrous fumarate, sodium ferric EDTA, sodium ferricitropyrophosphate, ferrous citrate, and ferrous ascorbate. Iron salts are used in cosmetics mainly for coloring and as astringents.

a-IRONE • A synthetic flavoring derived from the violet family and usually isolated from irises and orris oil. A light yellow, viscous liquid, it gives off the delicate fragrance of violets when put in alcohol. It is also used to flavor dentifrices and in perfumery. *See* Orris for toxicity.

IRRADIATED ENZYMES • Used to control insects. FDA requires that the dose not exceed ten kilograys.

IRRADIATED ERGOSTEROL • *See* Vitamin D_2.

IRRADIATED FOOD • To control pests in any food or to inhibit maturation of fresh food. FDA regulations say the dose cannot exceed one kilogray.

IRRADIATED PORK • For control of *Trichinella spiralis*. FDA says minimum dose is 0.3 kilograys. Maximum dose, 1 kilogray.

IRRADIATED POULTRY • To control pathogens in fresh or frozen uncooked poultry. FDA says dose must not exceed thirty kilograys.

IRRADIATED SPICES, HERBS, AND SEASONINGS • To control insects and/or microorganisms. FDA says dose is not to exceed thirty kilograys.

IRRADIATED YEAST • A nutrient in enriched farina, a source of vitamin D.

ISO- • Greek for "equal." In chemistry, it is a prefix added to the name of one compound to denote another composed of the same kinds and numbers of atoms but different from each other in structural arrangement.

ISOAMYL ACETATE • A synthetic flavoring agent that occurs naturally in bananas and pears. Colorless, pearlike odor and taste, it is used in raspberry, strawberry, butter, caramel, coconut, cola, apple, banana, cherry, grape, peach, pea, pineapple, rum, cream soda, and vanilla flavorings for beverages, ice cream, ices, candy, baked goods, chewing gum (2,700 ppm), and gelatin desserts. Also used in perfuming shoe polish, among other industrial uses. Exposure to 950 ppm for one hour has caused headache, fatigue, shoulder pain, and irritation of the mucous membranes. The FDA data bank, PAFA (see page 10), has fully up-to-date toxicology information available for this additive.

ISOAMYL ACETOACETATE • A synthetic fruit and apple flavoring for beverages, ice cream, ices, candy, and baked goods. The FDA data bank, PAFA, has fully up-to-date toxicology information available for this additive.

ISOAMYL ALCOHOL • A synthetic flavoring agent that occurs naturally in apples, cognac, lemons, peppermint, raspberry, strawberry, and tea. Used in chocolate, apple, banana, brandy, and rum flavorings for beverages, ice cream, ices, candy, baked goods, gelatin desserts, chewing gum, and brandy. A central nervous system depressant. Vapor exposures have caused marked irritation of the eyes, nose, and throat, and headache. Amyl alcohols are highly toxic, and ingestion has caused human deaths from respiratory failure. Isoamyl alcohol may cause heart, lung, and kidney damage. The FDA data bank, PAFA, has fully up-to-date toxicology information available for this additive.

ISOAMYL BENZOATE • A synthetic berry, apple, cherry, plum, prune, liquor, rum, and maple flavoring agent for beverages, ice cream, ices, candy, gelatin desserts, baked goods, and chewing gum. Also used in perfumery and cosmetics. The FDA data bank, PAFA, has fully up-to-date toxicology information available for this additive.

ISOAMYL CINNAMATE • A synthetic strawberry, butter, caramel, chocolate, cocoa, fruit, peach, pineapple, and honey flavoring agent for beverages, ice cream, candy, and baked goods. The FDA data bank, PAFA, has fully up-to-date toxicology information available for this additive.

ISOAMYL FORMATE • Formic Acid. A synthetic flavoring agent, colorless, liquid, with a fruity smell. Used in strawberry, apple, apricot, banana, peach, and pineapple flavorings for beverages, ice cream, candy, baked goods, gelatin desserts, and chewing gum. The FDA data bank, PAFA (see page 10), has fully up-to-date toxicology information available for this additive. *See* Formic Acid for toxicity.

ISOAMYL 2-FURANBUTYRATE • A synthetic chocolate, coffee, fruit, and whiskey flavoring agent for beverages, ice cream, ices, candy, baked goods, and gelatin. The FDA data bank, PAFA, has fully up-to-date toxicology information available for this additive.

ISOAMYL 2-FURANPROPIONATE • A synthetic chocolate, coffee, fruit, and whiskey flavoring agent for beverages, ice cream, ices, candy, and baked goods. The FDA data bank, PAFA, has fully up-to-date toxicology information available for this additive.

a-**ISOAMYL FURFURYLACETATE** • *See* Isoamyl 2-Furanpropionate.

a-**ISOAMYL FURFURYLPROPIONATE** • *See* Isoamyl 2-Furanbutyrate.

ISOAMYL ISOBUTYRATE • A synthetic fruit and banana flavoring agent for beverages, ice cream, ices, candy, baked goods, gelatin desserts, puddings, and chewing gum (2,000 ppm). Used in manufacture of artificial rum and fruit essences. The FDA data bank, PAFA, has fully up-to-date toxicology information available for this additive.

ISOAMYL ISOVALERATE • A synthetic flavoring agent, clear, colorless, liquid, with an apple odor. Occurs naturally in bananas and peaches. Used in raspberry, strawberry, apple, apricot, banana, cherry, peach, pineapple, honey, rum, walnut, vanilla, and cream soda flavoring for beverages, ice cream, ices, candy, baked goods, gelatin desserts, puddings, jellies, liqueurs, and chewing gum. No known toxicity.

ISOAMYL LAURATE • The ester of isoamyl alcohol and lauric acid (*see both*) used as a synthetic fruit flavoring for beverages, ice cream, ices, candy, and baked goods. The FDA data bank, PAFA (see page 10), has fully up-to-date toxicology information available for this additive.

ISOAMYL NONANOATE • A synthetic chocolate, fruit, and liquor flavoring agent for beverages, ice cream, ices, candy, baked goods, and gelatin desserts. The FDA data bank, PAFA, has fully up-to-date toxicology information available for this additive.

ISOAMYL OCTANOATE • A synthetic chocolate, fruit, and liquor flavoring agent for beverages, ice cream, ices, candy, baked goods, and gelatin desserts. The FDA data bank, PAFA, has fully up-to-date toxicology information available for this additive.

ISOAMYL PHENYLACETATE • A synthetic butter, chocolate, cocoa, peach, honey, licorice, and anise flavoring agent for beverages, ice cream, ices, candy, baked goods, toppings, and gelatin desserts. The FDA data bank, PAFA, has fully up-to-date toxicology information available for this additive.

ISOAMYL PYRUVATE • A synthetic flavoring agent, a colorless liquid with a pleasant odor. Used in root beer and fruit flavorings for beverages, ice cream, ices, candy, and baked goods. Also used in perfumery and soaps. The FDA data bank, PAFA (see page 10), has fully up-to-date toxicology information available for this additive. *See* Salicylic Acid for toxicity.

ISOASCORBIC ACID • Preservative. GRAS. *See* Erythrobic Acid.

ISOBORNEOL • A synthetic fruit and spice flavoring agent for beverages, ice cream, ices, candy, baked goods, and chewing gum. The FDA data bank, PAFA, has fully up-to-date toxicology information available for this additive. *See* Borneol for toxicity.

ISOBORNYL ACETATE • A synthetic pine odor in bath preparations. Also used as a synthetic fruit flavoring for beverages, ice cream, ices, candy, baked goods, and gelatin. The FDA data bank, PAFA, has fully up-to-date toxicology information available for this additive.

ISOBUTANE • A propellant. There is no reported use of the chemical and no toxicology information is available. GRAS. *See* Butane.

ISOBUTYL ACETATE • The ester of isobutyl alcohol and acetic acid used as a synthetic flavoring agent. A clear, colorless liquid with a fruity odor. Used in raspberry, strawberry, butter, banana, and grape flavorings for beverages, ice cream, ices, candy, baked goods, gelatin desserts, chewing gum, and icings. It may be mildly irritating to mucous membranes, and in high concentrations it is narcotic. The FDA data bank, PAFA, has fully up-to-date toxicology information available for this additive.

ISOBUTYL ACETOACETATE • A synthetic berry and fruit flavoring agent for beverages, ice cream, ices, candy, and baked goods. The FDA data bank, PAFA (see page 10), has fully up-to-date toxicology information available for this additive. *See* Isobutyl Acetate for toxicity.

ISOBUTYL ALCOHOL • Present in fusel oil; also produced by fermentation of carbohydrates. Colorless liquid with an odor of amyl alcohol, it is used in the manufacture of synthetic fruit flavorings and as a solvent. It is mildly irritating to skin and mucous membranes and, in high concentrations, narcotic. The FDA data bank, PAFA, has fully up-to-date toxicology information available for this additive.

ISOBUTYL ANTHRANILATE • A synthetic mandarin, cherry, and grape flavoring agent for beverages, ice cream, ices, candy, baked goods, and chewing gum (1,700 ppm). The FDA data bank, PAFA, has fully up-to-date toxicology information available for this additive.

ISOBUTYL BENZOATE • A synthetic berry, cherry, plum, and pineapple flavoring agent for beverages, ice cream, ices, candy, and baked goods. The FDA data bank, PAFA, has fully up-to-date toxicology information available for this additive.

ISOBUTYL BUTYRATE • A synthetic berry, apple, banana, pineapple, liquor, and rum flavoring agent for beverages, ice cream, ices, candy, puddings, liquors, and baked goods. The FDA data bank, PAFA (see page 10), has fully up-to-date toxicology information available for this additive.

2(4)-ISOBUTYL-4(2)-DIMETHYLDIHYDRO-4H-1,3,5-DIMETHYLDIHYDRO-4H-1,3,5-DITHIAZINE • A newer synthetic flavoring. The FDA data bank, PAFA, has not yet done a search of the toxicology literature concerning this additive.

ISOBUTYL 2-FURANPROPIONATE • A synthetic berry and pineapple flavoring agent for beverages, ice cream, ices, gelatin desserts, chewing gum, and ices. The FDA data bank, PAFA, has fully up-to-date toxicology information available for this additive.

ISOBUTYL HEXANOATE • A synthetic apple and pineapple flavoring agent for beverages, ice cream, ices, chewing gums, and baked goods. The FDA data bank, PAFA, has fully up-to-date toxicology information available for this additive.

ISOBUTYL ISOBUTYRATE • A synthetic strawberry, butter, fruit, banana, and liquor flavoring agent for beverages, ice cream, ices, candy, gelatin desserts, puddings, liquors, and baked goods. The FDA data bank, PAFA, has fully up-to-date toxicology information available for this additive.

ISOBUTYL PABA • *See* Propylparaben.

ISOBUTYL PALMITATE • *See* Palmitic Acid.

ISOBUTYL PARABEN • *See* Parabens.

ISOBUTYL PELARGONATE • The ester of isobutyl alcohol and pelargonic acid (*see both*).

ISOBUTYL PHENYLACETATE • A synthetic butter, caramel, chocolate, fruit, honey, and nut flavoring agent for beverages, ice cream, ices, candy, puddings, maraschino cherries, and baked goods. The FDA data bank, PAFA, has fully up-to-date toxicology information available for this additive.

ISOBUTYL PROPIONATE • A synthetic strawberry, butter, peach, and rum flavoring agent for beverages, ice cream, candy, and baked goods. Used in the manufacture of fruit essences. The FDA data bank, PAFA (see page 10), has fully up-to-date toxicology information available for this additive.

ISOBUTYL SALICYLATE • A synthetic flavoring agent, a colorless liquid with an orchid odor. Used in fruit and root beer flavorings for beverages, ice cream, ices, candy, and baked goods. The FDA data bank, PAFA, has fully up-to-date toxicology information available for this additive. *See* Salicylic Acid for toxicity.

ISOBUTYL STEARATE • The ester of isobutyl alcohol and stearic acid. *See* Fatty Alcohols. Used in waterproof coatings, polishes, face creams, rouges, ointments, soaps, dyes, and lubricants. No known toxicity.

ISOBUTYLENE RESIN, POLYISOBUTYLENE • A component of chewing gum base.

ISOBUTYLENE/ISOPYRENE COPOLYMER • A copolymer of isobutylene and isopyrene monomers derived from petroleum and used as resins. A chewing gum base. Isobutylene is used to produce antioxidants for foods, food supplements, and packaging. Vapors may cause asphyxiation.

ISOBUTYLENE/MALEIC ANHYDRIDE COPOLYMER • A copolymer of isobutylene and maleic anhydride monomers derived from petroleum and used as a resin. Strong irritant.

a-**ISOBUTYLPHENETHYL ALCOHOL** • A synthetic butter, caramel, chocolate, fruit, and spice flavoring agent for beverages, ice cream, ices, candy, baked goods, liqueurs, and chocolate. The FDA data bank, PAFA (see page 10), has fully up-to-date toxicology information available for this additive. *See* Isoamyl Alcohol for toxicity.

ISOBUTYRALDEHYDE • A synthetic flavoring agent that occurs naturally in soy sauce, tea, tobacco, and coffee. It has a pungent odor. Used in berry, butter, caramel, fruit, liquor, and wine flavorings for beverages, ice cream, ices, candy, baked goods, and liquor. The FDA data bank, PAFA, has fully up-to-date toxicology information available for this additive.

ISOBUTYRIC ACID • A synthetic flavoring agent that occurs naturally in bay, bay leaves, parsley, and strawberries. It has a pungent odor. Used in butter, butterscotch, fruit, liquor, rum, cheese, nut, vanilla, and cream soda flavorings for beverages, ice cream, ices, candy, baked goods, chewing gum, and margarine. It is a mild irritant. A pungent liquid that smells like butyric acid (*see*). The FDA data bank, PAFA (see page 10), has fully up-to-date toxicology information available for this additive.

ISOCETYL ALCOHOL • *See* Cetyl Alcohol.

ISOCETYL ISODECANOATE • *See* Cetyl Alcohol.

ISOCETYL PALMITATE • *See* Cetyl Alcohol and Palmitic Acid.

ISOCETYL STEARATE • *See* Cetyl Alcohol and Stearic Acid.

ISOCETYL STEAROYL STEARATE • The ester of isocetyl alcohol, stearic alcohol, and stearic acid. *See* Fatty Acids.

ISOEUGENOL • An aromatic liquid phenol oil obtained from eugenol (*see*) by mixing with an alkali. A synthetic flavoring agent, pale yellow, viscous, with a floral odor. Occurs naturally in mace oil. Used in mint, fruit, spice, cinnamon, and clove flavorings for beverages, ice cream, ices, baked goods, chewing gum (1,000 ppm), and condiments. Used in the manufacture of vanillin (*see*). Moderately toxic by ingestion. Has caused mutations in experimental animals. The FDA data bank, PAFA, has fully up-to-date toxicology information available for this additive.

ISOEUGENOL ACETATE • *See* Acetylisoeugenol.

ISOEUGENYL ACETATE • A synthetic berry, fruit, and spice flavoring agent for beverages, ice cream, ices, candy, baked goods, and chewing gum. The FDA data bank, PAFA (see page 10), has fully up-to-date toxicology information available for this additive.

ISOEUGENYL ETHYL ETHER • A synthetic flavoring agent, white, crystalline, with a spicy, clovelike odor. Used in fruit and vanilla flavorings for beverages, ice cream, ices, candy, and baked goods. The FDA data bank, PAFA, has fully up-to-date toxicology information available for this additive.

ISOEUGENYL FORMATE • A synthetic spice flavoring agent used in condiments. The FDA data bank, PAFA, has fully up-to-date toxicology information available for this additive. *See* Formic Acid for toxicity.

ISOEUGENYL METHYL ETHER • A synthetic raspberry, strawberry, cherry, and clove flavoring agent for beverages, ices, ice cream, candy, baked goods, gelatin desserts, and chewing gum. The FDA data bank, PAFA (see page 10), has fully up-to-date toxicology information available for this additive.

ISOEUGENYL PHENYLACETATE • A synthetic fruit, honey, and spice flavoring agent for beverages, ice cream, ices, candy, and baked goods. The FDA data bank, PAFA, has fully up-to-date toxicology information available for this additive.

ISOJASMONE • *See* Jasmone.

ISOLATE • A substance that is freed from chemical contaminants.

ISOLEUCINE • L and D Forms. An essential amino acid not synthesized within the human body. Isolated commercially from beet sugar, it is a building block of protein. The FDA asked for further study of this nutrient in 1980. The FDA data bank, PAFA, has fully up-to-date toxicology information available for this additive. GRAS.

ISOMALT • Palatinit. A free-flowing crystalline sweetener that resembles sucrose. It is actually produced from sugar. The enzymes of the digestive system are unable to break down isomalt. It is only two calories per gram and reportedly has no aftertaste and is heat stable.

ISONONYL ISONONANOATE • The ester (*see*) produced by the reaction of nonyl alcohol with nonanoic acid. Used in fruit flavorings for lipsticks and mouthwashes. Occurs in cocoa, oil of lavender. No known toxicity.

ISOPARAFFINIC PETROLEUM HYDROCARBONS, SYNTHETIC • Coating agent, in insecticide formulations, used on eggs, fruits, pickles, vegetables, wine, and vinegar. *See* Paraffin Wax.

ISOPHORONE • White, watery liquid that is irritating to skin and eyes. It is used in solvents for polyvinyl and nitrocellulose resins, and in pesticides. The FDA data bank, PAFA (see page 10), has fully up-to-date toxicology information available for this additive.

ISOPROPANOL • *See* Isopropyl Alcohol.

ISOPROPANOLAMINE • An emulsifying agent with a light ammonia odor that is soluble in water. It is used as a plasticizer and in insecticides as well as in cosmetic creams. No known toxicity.

ISOPROPYL ALCOHOL • Isopropanol. An antibacterial, solvent, and denaturant (*see*). Solvent for the spice oleoresins. Used in hair-color rinses, body rubs, hand lotions, aftershave lotions, and many other cosmetics. It is prepared from propylene, which is obtained in the cracking of petroleum. Also used in antifreeze compositions and as a solvent for gums, shellac, and essential oils. Ingestion or inhalation of large quantities of the vapor may cause flushing, headache, dizziness, mental depression, nausea, vomiting, narcosis, anesthesia, and coma. The fatal ingested dose is around a fluid ounce. The

FDA data bank, PAFA, has fully up-to-date toxicology information available for this additive.

ISOPROPYL CITRATE • A sequestrant and antioxidant agent used in oleomargarine and salad oils. The final report to the FDA of the Select Committee on GRAS Substances stated in 1980 that it should continue its GRAS status with no limitations other than good manufacturing practices. When heated to decomposition, it emits acrid smoke and irritating fumes. The FDA data bank, PAFA (see page 10), has fully up-to-date toxicology information available for this additive.

ISOPROPYL FORMATE • Formic Acid. A synthetic berry and melon flavoring agent for beverages, ice cream, candy, and baked goods. The FDA data bank, PAFA, has fully up-to-date toxicology information available for this additive. See Formic Acid for toxicity.

ISOPROPYL HEXANOATE • A synthetic pineapple flavoring agent for beverages, ice cream, ices, candy, and baked goods. The FDA data bank, PAFA, has fully up-to-date toxicology information available for this additive.

ISOPROPYL ISOBUTYRATE • A synthetic pineapple flavoring agent for beverages, ice cream, ices, candy, and baked goods. The FDA data bank, PAFA, has fully up-to-date toxicology information available for this additive.

ISOPROPYL ISOSTEARATE • See Stearic Acid and Propylene Glycol.

ISOPROPYL ISOVALERATE • A synthetic pineapple and nut flavoring agent for beverages, ice cream, ices, candy, and baked goods. The FDA data bank, PAFA, has fully up-to-date toxicology information available for this additive.

ISOPROPYL PHENYLACETATE • A synthetic butter, caramel, and honey flavoring agent for beverages, ice cream, ices, candy, and baked goods. The FDA data bank, PAFA (see page 10), has fully up-to-date toxicology information available for this additive.

ISOSAFROEUGENOL • White crystalline powder with a vanilla odor used as a flavoring agent in various foods. Moderately toxic by ingestion.

ISOSTEARIC ACID • A saturated fatty acid that has the same uses as stearic acid and oleic acids (see both).

ISOTHIOUREA • Antifungal agent used on citrus fruit. Prohibited from direct addition or use in human food.

ISOVALERIC ACID • Occurs in valerian, hop oil, tobacco, and other plants. Colorless liquid with a disagreeable taste and odor used in flavors and perfumes. A poison by skin contact. Moderately toxic by ingestion. A corrosive skin and eye irritant. The FDA data bank, PAFA, has fully up-to-date toxicology information available for this additive. See Valeric Acid.

ISOVALERIC ACID, ALLYL ESTER, BENZYL ESTER, BUTYL ESTER, ETHYL ESTER • Flavoring agents in various foods. The allyl ester is under International Agency for Research on Cancer (IARC) review. The allyl form is poisonous by ingestion. The others are mildly toxic by ingestion. Moderately toxic by skin contact. Skin irritants.

ISOVINYL FORMATE • Formic Acid. A synthetic fruit flavoring agent for beverages, ice cream, ices, candy, and baked goods. See Formic Acid for toxicity.

ISOVINYL PROPIONATE • See Isovinyl Formate.

IVA • *Achillea moschata jacq.* A flavoring for alcoholic beverages only from a small American ground pine that smells like skin. There is no reported use of the chemical and no toxicology information is available.

IVERMECTIN • Mectizan. Hyvermectin. A drug used to treat river blindness in humans, it is used to treat worms in animals, especially cattle, swine, and reindeer. FDA limits residues to 15 ppb in cattle and reindeer liver, and 20 ppb in swine liver. Poison by injection under the skin. Potential adverse human effects include dizziness, fever, headache, tender swollen glands, rash, and fatigue.

J

JAGUAR GUM • *See* Guar Gum.

JAMBUL OLEORESIN • Java Plum. *Syzygium jambolanum.* Used medically as an antidiarrheal medication. Used as a flavoring in foods. The FDA data bank, PAFA (see page 10), has not yet done a search of the toxicology literature concerning this additive.

JAPAN WAX • Japan Tallow. Sumac Wax. Vegetable Wax. A fat squeezed from the fruit of a tree grown in Japan and China. Pale yellow, flat cakes, disks, or squares, with a fatlike rancid odor and taste. Used as a substitute for beeswax in cosmetics and in food packaging; also in floor waxes and polishes. It is related to poison ivy and may cause allergic contact dermatitis. The final report to the FDA of the Select Committee on GRAS Substances stated in 1980 that there were insufficient biological and other studies upon which to base an evaluation when it is used as a food ingredient. It remains GRAS for packaging. There is no reported use of the chemical and no toxicology information is available.

JASMINE • Oil and Spiritus (alcoholic solution). The *oil* is extracted from a tropical shrub with extremely fragrant white flowers and is used in raspberry, strawberry, floral, and cherry flavorings for beverages, ice cream, ices, candy, baked goods, gelatin desserts, chewing gum, and jelly. The *spiritus* is used in blackberry, strawberry, and fruit flavorings for beverages, ice cream, ices, candy, baked goods, gelatin, and cherries. Used in perfumes. May cause allergic reactions. GRAS. The FDA data bank, PAFA (see page 10), has not yet done a search of the toxicology literature concerning this additive.

JASMINE ABSOLUTE • Oil of jasmine obtained by extraction with volatile or nonvolatile solvents. Sometimes called the "natural perfume" because the oil is not subjected to heat and distilled oils. *See* Absolute. May cause allergic reactions. The FDA data bank, PAFA, has not yet done a search of the toxicology literature concerning this additive.

JASMONYL • *See* 1,3-Nonanediol Acetate.

JASMONE • Derived from the oil of jasmine flowers, it is used in flavorings and perfumery.

JELUTONG • *Dyera costulata hook.* Any of several trees with a milky white exudate. Resembles chicle and is used chiefly in waterproofing and in chewing gum. The FDA data bank, PAFA, has fully up-to-date toxicology information available for this additive.

JOJOBA OIL • The oil extracted from the beanlike seeds of the desert shrub *Simondsia chinensis*. A liquid wax used as a lubricant and as a substitute for sperm oil, carnauba wax and beeswax. Mexicans and Indians have long used the bean's oily wax as a hair conditioner and skin lubricant. United States companies are now promoting the ingredient in shampoos, moisturizers, sun screens, and conditioners as a treatment for "crow's feet," wrinkles, stretch marks, and dry skin. May cause allergic reactions.

JUNIPER • Extract, Oil, and Berries. A flavoring from the dried ripe fruit of trees grown in northern Europe, Asia, and North America. The greenish yellow *extract* is used in liquor, root beer, sarsaparilla, wintergreen, and birch beer flavorings for beverages, ice cream, ices, candy, and baked goods. The *oil* is used in berry, cola, pineapple, gin, rum, whiskey, root beer, ginger, and meat flavorings for beverages, ice cream, ices, candy, baked goods, gelatin desserts, chewing gum, meats, and liquors. The *berries* are used in gin flavoring for condiments and liquors. Juniper is also used in fumigating and was formerly a diuretic for reducing body water. The oil is mildly toxic by ingestion; a human skin irritant and allergen, and if taken internally, a severe kidney irritation similar to that caused by turpentine may result. GRAS. The FDA data bank, PAFA, has not yet done a search of the toxicology literature concerning this additive.

K

KABAT • Altosid. Methoprene. Amber liquid used as an insect growth regulator in animal feed, dried apples, apricots, barley cereal, beef, corn cereal, cornmeal, grits, hominy, macaroni, oat cereal, dried peaches, potable water, dried prunes, raisins, rice cereal, rye cereal, spices, wheat cereal, and wheat flour. The FDA's insect growth regulator residue tolerance is 10 ppm in the grains and rice and dried fruits. Exempt from the tolerance is potable water. Moderately toxic by skin contact. Mildly toxic by ingestion. Has caused mutations in laboratory animals.

KADAYA • *See* Karaya Gum.

KAOLIN • China Clay. Used as an anticaking agent in food. Aids in the covering ability of face powder and in absorbing oil secreted by the skin. Used in baby powder, bath powder, face masks, foundation cake makeup, liquid powder, face powder, dry rouge, and emollients. Originally obtained from Kaoling Hill in Kiangsi Province in southeast China. Essentially a hydrated aluminum silicate (*see*). It is a white or yellowish white mass or powder, insoluble in water and absorbent. Used medicinally to treat intestinal disorders, but in large doses it may cause obstructions, perforations, or granuloma (tumor) formation. It is also used in the manufacture of porcelain, pottery, bricks, and color lakes (*see* FD and C Lakes). No known toxicity for the skin. The final report to the FDA of the Select Committee on GRAS Substances stated in 1980 that it should continue its GRAS status with no limitations other than good manufacturing practices. *See* Clays.

KARAYA GUM • Kaday. Katilo. Kullo. Kuteera. Sterculia. Indian Traga-canth. Mucara. The exudate of a tree found in India. The finely ground white powder is used in gelatins and in gumdrops, prepared ices, ice cream, and as a filler for lemon custard. Also a citrus and spice flavoring agent for beverages, ice cream, ices (1,300 ppm), candy, meats, baked goods, toppings (3,500 ppm), and emulsions (18,000 ppm). Used instead of the more expensive gum traga-canth (*see*) and in bulk laxatives. Reevaluated by the FDA in 1976 and found to be GRAS in the following percentages: 0.3 for frozen dairy desserts and mixes; 0.02 percent for milk products; 0.9 percent for soft candy; and 0.002 for all other food categories. The FDA data bank, PAFA (see page 10), has fully up-to-date toxicology information available for this additive.

KATILO • *See* Karaya Gum.

KAUTSCHIN • *See* Limonene.

KELP • Recovered from the giant Pacific marine plant *Macrocystis pyriferae*. Used as a seasoning and to provide iodine in the diet. It has many minerals that are associated with seawater and, as a result, is high in sodium. The Japanese report that kelp reduced normal thyroid function, probably because of its iodine content. The FDA has also reported that high levels of arsenic have been found in people who eat a lot of kelp as a vegetable. The final report to the FDA of the Select Committee on GRAS Substances stated in 1980 that it should con-tinue its GRAS status with no limitations other than good manufacturing prac-tices. The FDA data bank, PAFA (see page 10), has not yet done a search of the toxicology literature concerning this additive.

KETONAROME • *See* Methylcyclopentenolone.

KETONE C-7 • *See* 2-Heptanone.

2-KETOPROPIONALDEHYDE • *See* Pyruvaldehyde.

a-KETOPROPIONALDEHYDE • *See* Pyruvic Acid.

KIDNEY BEAN EXTRACT • Extract of *Phaseolus vulgaris*. The beans were used as a nutrient and a laxative by the American Indians. No known toxicity.

KOLA NUT EXTRACT • Guru Nut. A natural extract from the brownish seed, about the size of a chestnut, produced by trees in Africa, the West Indies, and Brazil. Contains caffeine (*see*). Used in butter, caramel, chocolate, cocoa, coffee, cola, walnut, and root beer flavorings for beverages, ice cream, ices, candy, and baked goods. Has been used to treat epilepsy. GRAS. The FDA data bank, PAFA, has not yet done a search of the toxicology literature concerning this additive.

KOSHER • Parve. U. Hebrew word meaning "proper" or "fit," used espe-cially for food prepared according to Orthodox dietary and religious laws. For-bidden are pork, horseflesh, shellfish, and parts of beef and lamb. All meat and poultry must be killed by a Jew trained in the prescribed ritual, then soaked or salted to remove all blood. Milk and its products must not be eaten with meat. The notifications on packages meaning the product has been prepared under dietary laws are *U* or *Parve*.

KRAMERIA EXTRACT • Rhatany Extract. A synthetic flavoring derived from the dried root of either of two American shrubs. Used in raspberry, bitters, fruit, and rum flavorings. Used in cosmetics as an astringent. Low oral toxicity.

Large doses may produce gastric distress. Can cause tumors and death after injection, but not after ingestion.

KULLO • *See* Karaya Gum.

KUTEERA • *See* Karaya Gum.

L

LABDANUM • Absolute, Oil, and Oleoresin. A synthetic musk flavoring agent. It is a volatile oil obtained by steam distillation from gum extracted from various rockrose shrubs. Golden yellow, viscous, with a strong balsamic odor and a bitter taste. The *absolute* is used in raspberry, fruit, and vanilla flavorings for beverages, ice cream, ices, candy, baked goods, gelatin desserts, and chewing gum. The *oil* is used in fruit and spice flavorings for beverages, ice cream, ices, candy, and baked goods. The *oleoresin* (*see*) is used in fruit and vanilla flavorings for beverages, ice cream, ices, candy, and baked goods. Also used in perfumes, especially as a fixative. Mildly toxic by ingestion. A skin irritant. The FDA data bank, PAFA (see page 10), has not yet done a search of the toxicology literature concerning this additive.

LABRADOR TEA EXTRACT • Hudson Bay Tea. Marsh Tea. The extract of the dried flowering plant or young shoots of *Ledum palustre* or *Ledum groelandicum*, a tall, resinous evergreen shrub found in bogs and swamps and moist meadows. Brewed like tea, it has a pleasing odor and is stimulating. It was used by the Indians and settlers as a tonic supposed to purify blood. It was also employed to treat wounds. The *Ledum palustre* contains, among other things, tannin and valeric acid (*see both*). No known toxicity.

LACTASE ENZYME PREPARATION FROM *KLYVEROMYCES LACTIS* • An enzyme that breaks down lactose (*see*). There is no reported use of the chemical and no toxicology information is available. GRAS.

LACTIC ACID • Butyl Lactate. Ethyl Lactate. Odorless, colorless, usually a syrupy product normally present in blood and muscle tissue as a product of the metabolism of glucose and glycogen. Present in sour milk, beer, sauerkraut, pickles, and other food products made by bacterial fermentation. It is produced commercially by fermentation of whey, cornstarch, potatoes, and molasses. Used as an acidulant in beverages, candy, olives, dried egg whites, cottage cheese, confections, bread, rolls, buns, cheese products, frozen desserts, sherbets, ices, fruit jelly, butter, preserves, jams (sufficient amounts may be added to compensate for a deficiency of fruit acidity), and in the brewing industry. Also used in infant-feeding formulas. Used in blackberry, butter, butterscotch, lime, chocolate, fruit, walnut, spice, and cheese flavorings for beverages, ice cream, ices, candy, baked goods, gelatins, puddings, chewing gum, toppings, pickles, and olives (24,000 ppm). Also used in skin fresheners. It is caustic in concentrated solutions when taken internally or applied to the skin. In cosmetic products, it may cause stinging in sensitive people, particularly in fair-skinned women. The final report to the FDA of the Select Committee on GRAS Substances stated in 1980 that it should continue its GRAS status with no limitations other than good manufacturing practices. The FDA data bank, PAFA (see page 10), has fully up-to-date toxicology information available for this additive.

LACTIC YEASTS • Obtained from milk. *See* Lactic Acid.

LACTOFEN • A pesticide used on soybeans. FDA tolerance is 0.05 ppm.

LACTOFLAVIN • *See* Riboflavin.

LACTOSE • Milk Sugar. Saccharum Lactin. D-Lactose. A slightly sweet-tasting, colorless sugar present in the milk of mammals (humans have 6.7 percent and cows 4.3 percent). Occurs as a white powder or crystalline mass as a byproduct of the cheese industry. Produced from whey (*see*). It is inexpensive and is widely used in the food industry as a culture medium, such as in souring milk, and as a humectant (*see*) and nutrient in infant or debilitated-patient formulas. Also used as a medical diuretic and laxative. Used widely as a base in eye lotions. Stable in air but readily absorbs odors. It is generally nontoxic but was found to cause tumors when injected under the skin of mice in 50-mg doses per kilogram of body weight. The FDA data bank, PAFA (see page 10), has not yet done a search of the toxicology literature concerning this additive.

LACTYLIC ESTERS OF FATTY ACIDS • Emulsifiers used in food products. The FDA data bank, PAFA, has fully up-to-date toxicology information available for this additive. *See* Ester and Fatty Acids.

LACTYLIC STEARATE • Salt of stearic acid (*see*) used as a dough conditioner to add volume and to keep baked products soft; it makes bread less sticky. *See* Stearic Acid for toxicity.

LADY'S-MANTLE EXTRACT • From the dried leaves and flowering shoots of *Alchemilla vulgaris*. A common European herb covered with spreading hairs, it has been used for centuries by herbalists to concoct love potions.

LAKES, COLOR • A lake is an organic pigment prepared by precipitating a soluble color with a form of aluminum, calcium, barium, potassium, strontium, or zirconium, which then makes the colors insoluble. Not all colors are suitable for making lakes.

LAMINARIA • Seaweed from which algin is extracted. *See* Alginates. GRAS.

LANALOOL • Synthetic flavoring. GRAS.

LANOLIN • Wool Fat. Wool Wax. A product of the oil glands of sheep. Used as a chewing gum base component. Used in lipstick, liquid powder, mascara, nail-polish remover, protective oil, rouge, eye shadow, foundation creams, foundation cake makeup, hair conditioners, eye creams, cold creams, brilliantine hairdressings, ointment bases, and emollients. A water-absorbing base material and a natural emulsifier, it absorbs and holds water to the skin. Chemically a wax instead of a fat. Contains about 25 to 30 percent water. Advertisers have found that the words *contains lanolin* help to sell a product and have promoted it as being able to "penetrate the skin better than other oils," although there is little scientific proof of this. Lanolin has been found to be a common skin sensitizer causing allergic contact skin rashes. It will not prevent or cure wrinkles and will not stop hair loss. It is not used in pure form today because of its allergy-causing potential. Products derived from it are less likely to cause allergic reactions. The FDA data bank, PAFA (see page 10), has fully up-to-date toxicology information available for this additive.

LANOLIN ALCOHOLS • Sterols, triterpene, alcohols. Aliphatic alcohols. Derived from lanolin (*see*), lanolin alcohols are available commercially as solid waxy materials that are yellow to amber in color or as pale to golden yellow liquids. They are widely used as emulsifiers and emollients in hand creams and lotions, and while less likely to cause an allergic reaction than lanolin, they still may do so in certain sensitive individuals.

LANTANA • *See* Oregano.

LARCH GUM • Larch Turpentine. Venice Turpentine. Oleoresin (*see*) from *Larix decidua,* grown in middle and southern Europe. A yellow, sometimes greenish, tenacious, thick liquid with a pleasant, aromatic odor, it has a hot, somewhat bitter taste. It becomes hard and brittle on prolonged exposure. It is used as a stabilizer, thickener, and texturizer. No known toxicity.

LARD AND LARD OILS • Pork Fat and Oils. It is the purified internal fat from the abdomen of the hog. It is a soft, white, unctuous mass, with a slight characteristic odor and a bland taste. It is used in packaging and in chewing gum bases. Easily absorbed by the skin, it is used as a lubricant, emollient, and base in shaving creams, soaps, and various cosmetic creams. Insoluble in water. When lard was fed to laboratory animals in doses of from 2 to 25 percent of the diet, the male mice had a shortened life span and increased osteoarthritis. This was thought to be due to the large amounts of fat and not specifically to lard. The final report to the FDA of the Select Committee on GRAS Substances stated in 1980 that it should continue its GRAS status with no limitations other than good manufacturing practices. There is no reported use of the chemical and no toxicology information is available.

LARD GLYCERIDE • *See* Lard and Lard Oils.

LARIXINIC ACID • *See* Maltol.

LASALOCID • An antibiotic used in beef, chicken, and lamb. Tolerance residue of 0.3 ppm in chicken skin, 0.7 ppm in cattle liver, and 1.2 ppm in sheep muscle. Poison by ingestion and injection. An eye and skin irritant.

LASSO • *See* Alachlor.

LATEX • Synthetic Rubber. Component of chewing gum base. The milky, usually white juice or exudate of plants obtained by tapping. Used in beauty masks for its coating ability and in balloons, condoms, and gloves. Any of various gums, resins, fats, or waxes in an emulsion of water and synthetic rubber or plastic are now considered latex. Ingredients of latex compounds can be poisonous, depending upon which plant products are used. Can cause skin rash. In May 1991, the FDA cautioned doctors and manufacturers about potential allergic reactions to latex products. Allergic reactions caused the deaths of four patients undergoing medical procedures involving an inflatable latex cuff. The FDA also reported fifty cases of life-threatening allergic reactions involving latex gloves and, in other instances, contact with rubber dental devices, balloons, and racquetball handles.

LAUREL BERRIES • *Laurus nobilis.* The fresh berries and leaf extract of the laurel tree. The *berries* are used as a flavoring for beverages, and the *leaf extract* is a spice flavoring for vegetables. There is no reported use of the chemical and no toxicology information is available. *See* Laurel Leaf Oil. GRAS.

LAUREL GALLATE • An antioxidant, the laurel ester of gallic acid. *See* Propyl Gallate.

LAUREL LEAF OIL • Derived from steam distillation of the leaves of *Laurus nobilis,* it is a yellow liquid with a spicy odor used as a flavoring agent. Moderately toxic by ingestion. A skin irritant. GRAS.

LAURIC ACID • Dodecanoic Acid. A common constituent of vegetable fats, especially coconut oil and laurel oil. A white, glossy powder, insoluble in water, used in the manufacture of miscellaneous flavors for beverages, ice cream, candy, baked goods, gelatins, and puddings. Its derivatives are widely used as a base in the manufacture of soaps, detergents, and lauryl alcohol (*see* Fatty Alcohols) because of their foaming properties. Has a slight odor of bay and makes large, copious bubbles when in soap. A mild irritant but not a sensitizer. The FDA data bank, PAFA (see page 10), has fully up-to-date toxicology information available for this additive.

LAURIC ALDEHYDE • The FDA data bank, PAFA, has fully up-to-date toxicology information available for this additive. *See* Lauric Acid.

LAUROAMPHOACETATE • A preservative. *See* Imidazol.

LAUROAMPHODIACETATE • A preservative. *See* Imidazol.

LAUROAMPHODIPROPIONATE • *See* Propionic Acid and Lauric Acid.

LAUROAMPHODIPROPIONIC ACID • A preservative. *See* Lauric Acid and Propionic Acid.

LAUROAMPHOHDROXYPROPYLSULFONATE • *See* Imidazol.

LAUROAMPHOPROPIONATE • *See* Lauric Acid and Propionic Acid.

LAUROSTEARIC ACID • *See* Lauric Acid.

LAURYL ACETATE • Dodecyl Acetate. Colorless liquid with fruity odor used in flavoring. The FDA data bank, PAFA (see page 10), has fully up-to-date toxicology information available for this additive.

LAURYL ALCOHOL, SYNTHETIC • The FDA data bank, PAFA, has fully up-to-date toxicology information available for this additive. *See* Fatty Alcohols.

LAVANDIN OIL • A flavoring from a hybrid related to the lavender plant; pale yellow liquid with a camphor-lavender smell. Used in berry and citrus flavorings for beverages, ice cream, ices, candy, baked goods, and chewing gum. Used in soaps and perfumes. A skin irritant. GRAS. The FDA data bank, PAFA, has not yet done a search of the toxicology literature concerning this additive.

LAVENDER OIL • *Lavandula officinalis.* The colorless liquid extracted from the fresh, flowery tops of the plant. Smells like lavender and is used in ginger ale flavoring for beverages. *Lavender absolute* is a fruit flavoring for beverages, ice cream, ices, candy, and baked goods. *Lavender concrete* is a fruit flavoring for beverages, ice cream, ices, candy, and baked goods. Lavender was once used to break up stomach gas. Used in skin fresheners, powders, shaving preparations, mouthwashes, dentifrices, and perfumes. It can cause allergic reactions and has been found to cause adverse skin reactions when the skin is exposed to sunlight. GRAS.

LEAF ALCOHOL • *See* 3-Hexen-1-Ol.

LEATHER MEAL, HYDROLYZED • Used in feed. FDA tolerance, 1 percent by weight of feed.

LEAVENING • From the Latin *levare,* "to raise." A substance, such as yeast, that produces fermentation in dough or liquid. Leavening lightens or enlivens, such as baking soda when it produces a gas that lightens dough or batter.

LECHEA CASPI or DE VACA • A genus of herbs that have branched stems and minute purplish flowers. The FDA data bank, PAFA (see page 10), has fully up-to-date toxicology information available for this additive.

LECITHIN • From the Greek, meaning "egg yolk." A natural antioxidant and emollient composed of units of choline, phosphoric acid, fatty acids, and glycerin (*see all*). Commercially isolated from eggs, soybeans, corn, and egg yolk and used as an antioxidant in prepared breakfast cereals, candy, sweet chocolate, bread, rolls, buns, and oleomargarine. Egg yolk is 8 to 9 percent lecithin. Hydroxylated lecithin is a defoaming component in yeast and beet-sugar production. Lecithin with or without phosphatides (components of fat) is an emulsifier for sweet chocolate, milk chocolate, bakery products, frozen desserts, oleomargarine, rendered animal fat, or a combination of vegetable-animal fats. Also used in eye creams, lipsticks, liquid powders, hand creams and lotions, soaps, and many other cosmetics. Also a natural spreading agent. Nontoxic. The final report to the FDA of the Select Committee on GRAS Substances stated in 1980 that it should continue its GRAS status with no limitations other than good manufacturing practices. The FDA data bank, PAFA (see page 10), has fully up-to-date toxicology information available for this additive.

LEEK OIL • *Sempervivum tectorium.* Native to the mountains of Europe and to the Greek islands, its longevity led to its being named *sempervivum,* which translated means "ever alive." It is used as a flavoring. It has been used to treat shingles, gout, and to get rid of bugs. Its pulp was applied to the skin for rashes and inflammation, and to remove warts and calluses. The juice was used to reduce fever and to treat insect stings. The juice mixed with honey was prescribed for thrush, a fungal infection of the mouth, and an ointment made from the plant was used to treat ulcers, burns, scalds, and inflammation. The FDA data bank, PAFA, has not yet done a search of the toxicology literature concerning this additive.

LEMON • Extract and Oil. The common fresh fruit. The *extract* is used in lemon flavorings for beverages, ice cream, ices, candy, baked goods, and icings. *Lemon oil* is a blueberry, loganberry, strawberry, butter, grapefruit, lemon, lime, orange, cola, coconut, honey, wine, rum, root beer, and ginger ale flavoring for beverages, ice cream, ices, candy, baked goods, gelatin desserts, chewing gum (1,900 ppm), condiments, meats, syrups, icings, and cereals. Lemon oil is suspected of being a cancer-causing agent. GRAS. The FDA data bank, PAFA (see page 10), has fully up-to-date toxicology information available for this additive.

LEMON BALM • Sweet Balm. Garden Balm. Used in perfumes and as a soothing facial treatment. An Old World mint cultivated for its lemon-flavored, fragrant leaves. Often considered a weed, it has been used by herbalists as a medicine and to flavor foods and medicines. It reputedly imparts long life. Also used to treat earache and toothache. Nontoxic.

LEMON EXTRACT • *See* Lemon Oil.

LEMON JUICE • *See* Lemon.

LEMON OIL • Cedro Oil. Used in perfumes and food flavorings, it is the volatile oil expressed from the fresh peel. A pale to deep yellow, it has the characteristic odor and taste of the outer part of fresh lemon peel. It can cause an allergic reaction and has been suspected of being a co-agent cause of cancer. The FDA data bank, PAFA, has not yet done a search of the toxicology literature concerning this additive.

LEMON OIL, TERPENELESS • A lemon fruit, ginger, and ginger ale flavoring agent for beverages, ice cream, ices, candy, baked goods, gelatin desserts, chewing gum, and toppings. Terpene, which is removed to improve flavor, is a class of unsaturated hydrocarbons. The FDA data bank, PAFA (see page 10), has not yet done a search of the toxicology literature concerning this additive. *See* Lemon for toxicity.

LEMON PEEL • From the outer rind, the extract is used as a flavor in medicines, beverages, confectionery, and cooking. The FDA data bank, PAFA, has not yet done a search of the toxicology literature concerning this additive. *See* Lemon for toxicity.

LEMON VERBENA EXTRACT • Extract of *Lippia citriodoral*. The FDA data bank, PAFA, has not yet done a search of the toxicology literature concerning this additive. *See* Lemongrass Oil.

LEMONGRASS OIL • Indian Oil of Verbena. Used in perfumes, especially those added to soap. It is the volatile oil distilled from the leaves of lemon grasses. A yellowish or reddish brown liquid, it has a strong odor of verbena. Also used in insect repellent. Used in lemon and fruit flavorings for beverages, ice cream, ices, candy, baked goods, gelatin desserts, and chewing gum. Death reported when taken internally, and autopsy showed the lining of the intestines was severely damaged.

LEUCINE • L and DL forms. An essential amino acid (*see*) for human nutrition not manufactured in the body. It is isolated commercially from gluten, casein, and keratin (*see all*). It has a sweet taste. It has caused birth defects in experimental animals. The FDA data bank, PAFA, has fully up-to-date toxicology information available for this additive. GRAS.

LEVAMISOLE • Ergamisol. A drug that appears to restore depressed immune function. Used as an animal drug and in animal feed to fight parasites in beef, lamb, and pork. FDA limitations are 0.1 ppm in cattle, sheep, and swine. Poisonous by ingestion and other routes. Human systemic effects by ingestion include coma, skin rash and irritation, and fever. There was a great deal of controversy over the pricing of this drug in 1992, when it was revealed that while veterinary drug cost $14, for the human cancer patient, the cost was up to $1,500. The company that produces the drug explained that it backed fourteen hundred studies involving forty thousand patients, and that this was factored into the cost of the drug for humans.

LEVULINIC ACID • Crystals used as intermediates for plasticizers, solvents, resins, flavors, and pharmaceuticals. The FDA data bank, PAFA (see page 10), has fully up-to-date toxicology information available for this additive.

LEVULOSE • *See* Fructose.

LICORICE • Liquorice. Glycyrrhizin. Monoammonium Glycyrrhizinate. Ammoniated Glycyrrhizin. Extract, Extract Powder, and Root. A black substance derived from a plant, *Glycyrrhiza glabra,* "sweet root," belonging to the Leguminosae and cultured from southern Europe to Central Asia. It is used in fruit, licorice, anise, maple, and root beer flavorings for beverages, ice cream, ices, candy (29,000 ppm), baked goods, gelatin, chewing gum, and syrups. *Licorice root* is used in licorice and root beer flavorings for beverages, candy, baked goods, chewing gum (3,200 ppm), tobacco, and medicines. Some people known to have eaten licorice candy regularly and generously had raised blood pressure, headaches, and muscle weakness. It can cause asthma, intestinal upsets, and contact dermatitis. No known skin toxicity. Tentatively affirmed as GRAS in 1983. The FDA data bank, PAFA (see page 10), has not yet done a search of the toxicology literature concerning this additive.

LIGHT GREEN • *See* FD and C Green No. 2.

LIGNIN • Binding agent in animal feed from plant fibers. There is no reported use of the chemical and no toxicology information is available.

LIME OIL • A natural flavoring extracted from the fruit of a tropical tree. Colorless to greenish. Used in grapefruit, lemon, lemon-lime, lime, orange, cola, fruit, rum, nut, and ginger flavorings for beverages, ice cream, ices, candy, baked goods, gelatin desserts, chewing gum (3,100 ppm), and condiments. Terpeneless (*see* Lemon Oil, Terpeneless) lime oil is used in lemon, lime, lemon-lime, cola, pineapple, ginger, and ginger ale flavorings for beverages, ice cream, ices, candy, baked goods, gelatin desserts, chewing gum, and syrups. Also used in perfumery and as an antiseptic. A source of vitamin C. Can cause an adverse reaction when skin applied with lime oil is exposed to sunlight. The FDA data bank, PAFA, is, as of this writing, conducting a search of the toxicology literature concerning this additive.

LIME WATER • Calcium hydroxide (*see*) solution. Clear, colorless, and odorless, it is strongly alkaline. It is used to prepare many food additives, such as emulsifiers and waterproofing compounds. *See* Calcium Stearate, for example.

LIMESTONE, GROUND • Flavoring agent. GRAS.

LIMONENE • D, L, and DL forms. A synthetic flavoring agent that occurs naturally in star anise, buchu leaves, caraway, celery, oranges, coriander, cumin, cardamon, sweet fennel, common fennel, mace, marigold, oil of lavandin, oil of lemon, oil of mandarin, peppermint, petitgrain oil, pimento oil, orange leaf (absolute), orange peel (sweet oil), origanum oil, black pepper, peels of citrus, macrocarpa bunge, and hops oil. Used in lime, fruit, and spice flavorings for beverages, ice cream, ices, candy, baked goods, gelatin desserts, and chewing gum. A skin irritant and sensitizer. GRAS. It caused loss of weight and tumors in some experimental animals, and therefore, the WHO Committee on Food Additives recommended its used be reduced and restricted to seventy-five nanograms per kilogram of body weight per day. For D and L limonene, the FDA data bank, PAFA (see page 10), has fully up-to-date toxicology information available. For the DL form, although allowed as a food additive, there is no current reported use of the chemical, and therefore, although toxicology information may be available, it is not being updated, according to the FDA.

LINALOE WOOD OIL • Bois de Rose Oil. A natural flavoring agent that is the colorless to yellow, volatile essential oil distilled from a Mexican tree. It has a pleasant flowery scent and is soluble in most fixed oils. Used in berry, citrus, fruit, liquor, and ginger flavorings for beverages, ice cream, ices, candy, baked goods, and liquors. Also used in perfumes. May cause allergic reactions.

LINALOOL • A synthetic flavoring that occurs naturally in basil, bois de rose oil, cassia, coriander, cocoa, grapefruit, grapefruit oil, oranges, peaches, tea, bay and bay-leaf extract, ginger, lavender, laurel leaves, and other oils. Used in flavorings such as blueberry, chocolate, and lemon. Used in perfumes and soaps instead of bergamot or French lavender. It is a fragrant, colorless liquid. May cause allergic reactions and is mildly toxic by ingestion. The FDA data bank, PAFA (see page 10), has fully up-to-date toxicology information available for this additive.

LINALYL ACETATE • A colorless, fragrant liquid, slightly soluble in water. It is the most valuable constituent of bergamot and lavender oils, which are used in perfumery. It occurs naturally in basil, jasmine oil, lavandin oil, lavender oil, and lemon oil. It has a strong floral scent. Colorless, it is used in berry, citrus, peach, pear, and ginger flavorings for beverages, ice cream, ices, candy, baked goods, gelatin desserts, and chewing gum. The FDA data bank, PAFA, has fully up-to-date toxicology information available for this additive. GRAS.

LINALYL ANTHRANILATE • A synthetic berry, citrus, fruit, and grape flavoring agent for beverages, ice cream, ices, candy, and baked goods. The FDA data bank, PAFA, has fully up-to-date toxicology information available for this additive.

LINALYL BENZOATE • A synthetic flavoring, brownish yellow, with a rose-like odor. Used in berry, citrus, fruit, and peach flavoring agents for beverages, ice cream, ices, candy, gelatin desserts, and baked goods. The FDA data bank, PAFA, has fully up-to-date toxicology information available for this additive.

LINALYL CINNAMATE • A synthetic loganberry, floral, rose, fruit, grape, and honey flavoring agent for beverages, ice cream, ices, candy, and baked goods. The FDA data bank, PAFA (see page 10), has fully up-to-date toxicology information available for this additive.

LINALYL FORMATE • Formic Acid. A synthetic flavoring agent that occurs naturally in oil of lavandin. Used in berry, apple, apricot, peach, and pineapple flavorings for beverages, ice cream, ices, candy, and baked goods. The FDA data bank, PAFA, has fully up-to-date toxicology information available for this additive. *See* Formic Acid for toxicity.

LINALYL HEXANOATE • A synthetic fruit flavoring agent for beverages, ice cream, ices, candy, and baked goods. The FDA data bank, PAFA, has fully up-to-date toxicology information available for this additive.

LINALYL ISOBUTRYATE • A synthetic flavoring, colorless to slightly yellow, with a fruity odor. Used in berry, citrus, fruit, banana, black currant, cherry, pear, pineapple, plum, nut, and spice flavorings for beverages, ice cream, ices, candy, and baked goods. The FDA data bank, PAFA, has fully up-to-date toxicology information available for this additive.

LINALYL ISOVALERATE • A synthetic flavoring, colorless to slightly yellow, with a fruity odor. Used in loganberry, apple, apricot, peach, pear, and plum flavorings for beverages, ice cream, ices, candy, gelatin desserts, and baked goods. The FDA data bank, PAFA, has fully up-to-date toxicology information available for this additive.

LINALYL OCTANOATE • A synthetic citrus, rose and apple, pineapple, and honey flavoring agent for beverages, ice cream, ices, candy, gelatin desserts, and baked goods. The FDA data bank, PAFA (see page 10), has fully up-to-date toxicology information available for this additive.

LINALYL PROPIONATE • A synthetic currant, orange, banana, pear, and pineapple flavoring agent for beverages, ice cream, ices, candy, and baked goods. The FDA data bank, PAFA, has fully up-to-date toxicology information available for this additive.

LINCOMYCIN • Lincocin. An antibacterial introduced in 1965, it is used to treat respiratory tract, skin, soft-tissue, gynecologic, and urinary tract infections, osteomyelitis, and blood poisoning caused by streptococci, pneumococci, and staphylococci. FDA tolerance for residues are 15 ppm; for edible tissues of chickens and swine, 0.1 ppm. Potential adverse reactions may include blood problems, dizziness, headache, low blood pressure, sore tongue, ringing in the ears, nausea, vomiting, severe colitis, persistent diarrhea, abdominal cramps, itching around the anus, vaginitis, jaundice, rashes, hives, pain at injection site, and serious allergic reactions. Antidiarrheal medicines reduce oral absorption of lincomycin. Lincomycin may reduce the effectiveness of drugs to treat myasthenia gravis.

LINDEN FLOWERS • *Tilia glabra vent.* A natural flavoring extract from the flowers of the tree grown in Europe and the U.S. Used in raspberry and vermouth flavorings for beverages (2,000 ppm). Also used in fragrances. The FDA data bank, PAFA, has not yet done a search of the toxicology literature concerning this additive. GRAS.

LINOLEAMIDE • A releasing agent that prevents food from sticking to containers. *See* Linoleic Acid.

LINOLEIC ACID • An essential fatty acid (*see*) prepared from edible fats and oils. Component of vitamin F and a major constituent of many vegetable oils, for example, cottonseed and soybean. Used in emulsifiers and vitamins. Large doses can cause nausea and vomiting. When given in large doses to rats, weight loss and progressive secondary anemia developed. No known skin toxicity and, in fact, may have emollient properties. The final report to the FDA of the Select Committee on GRAS Substances stated in 1980 that it should continue its GRAS status with no limitations other than good manufacturing practices. The FDA data bank, PAFA (see page 10), has not yet done a search of the toxicology literature concerning this additive.

LINSEED OIL • Golden amber or brown oil with a peculiar odor and bland taste. Used in paints, varnishes, as a film, in printing inks, and for its protein. *See* Flaxseed.

LIPASE • Any class of enzymes that break down fat to glycerol and fatty acids (*see both*). It is used in the manufacture of cheeses. The FDA data bank,

PAFA, has not yet done a search of the toxicology literature concerning this additive.

LOAEL • Lowest-Observable-Adverse-Effect-Level used to signify the lowest dose of a substance that causes an adverse effect in an experimental animal. *See also* NOEL.

LOCUST BEAN GUM • Saint John's Bread. Carob Bean Gum. A thickener and stabilizer in cosmetics and foods. Also used in depilatories. A natural flavor extract from the seed of the carob tree cultivated in the Mediterranean area. The history of the carob tree dates back more than two thousand years to when the ancient Egyptians used locust bean gum as an adhesive in mummy binding. It is alleged that the "locust" (through confusion of the locusts with carob) and wild honey that sustained John the Baptist in the wilderness was from this plant, thus the name Saint John's bread. The carob pods are used as feed for stock today because of their high protein content. They are also eaten by some health food enthusiasts for the same purpose. They are also used as a thickener and stabilizer (*see* Gum). Carob bean extract is used in raspberry, bitters, butter, butterscotch, caramel, chocolate, cherry, brandy, wine, maple, root beer, spice, vanilla, cream soda, and grape flavorings for beverages, ice cream, ices, candy, baked goods, gelatin desserts (600 ppm), icings, and toppings (1,000 ppm). A University of Minnesota pediatric cardiologist reported in 1981 that locust bean may lower blood cholesterol levels. Dr. James Zavoral and associates found that twenty-eight adults and children with histories of familial hypercholesterolemia were fed foods rich in locust bean gum. Some of those included breads, cookies, crackers, and Tater Tots. After four weeks on the special diets, their cholesterol dropped 10 percent, and after six weeks, 20 percent. The final report to the FDA of the Select Committee on GRAS Substances stated in 1980 that it should continue its GRAS status with limitations on amounts that can be added to food.

LOVAGE • Smallage. *Levisticum officinale.* Flavoring obtained from the root of an aromatic herb native to southern Europe and grown in monastery gardens centuries ago for medicine and food flavoring. It has a hot, sharp, biting taste. The yellow-brown oil is extracted from the root or other parts of the herb. It has a reputation for improving health and inciting love; Czechoslovakian girls reportedly wear it in a bag around their necks when dating boys. It supposedly has deodorant properties when added to bathwater. Used in bitters, maple, and walnut flavorings for beverages, ice cream, ices, candy, baked goods, chewing gum, and table syrups. The *extract* is used in berry, butter, butterscotch, caramel, coffee, fruit, maple, meat, black walnut, and spice flavorings for the same foods as above, plus condiments and icings. The *oil,* yellow-brown and aromatic, is used in butter, butterscotch, caramel, coffee, fruit, licorice, liquor, maple, nut, walnut, and spice flavorings for the same foods as is the extract. The FDA data bank, PAFA (see page 10), has not yet done a search of the toxicology literature concerning this additive.

LOW CALORIE • Fewer than forty calories per serving.

LOW CHOLESTEROL • Twenty milligrams or less per serving.

LOW FAT • Three grams or less per serving.

LOW SATURATED FAT • One gram or less per serving.

LOW SODIUM • 140 milligrams or less per serving.

LUNGMOSS • Lungwort. *Sticta pulmonacea ach.* Any of several plants once thought helpful in pulmonary diseases. Used as a flavoring in foods. There is no reported use of the chemical and no toxicology information is available.

LUPULIN EXTRACT • Lupine. Hops. Extract of *Lupinus albus.* The seed has been used as a food since earliest times. A natural flavoring agent from a plant (*Humulus lupulus*) grown in Europe, Asia, and North America. Used in beer brewing. Formerly used as aromatic bitters and as a sedative. At one time veterinary usage was recommended for treatment of nymphomania. It produces a light blue dye. GRAS. The FDA data bank, PAFA (see page 10), has not yet done a search of the toxicology literature concerning this additive.

LUTEIN • *See* Xanthophyll.

LYCOPENE • Red crystals, insoluble in water. The main pigment of tomato, paprika, and rose hips. No known toxicity.

LYSINE • L form. An essential amino acid (*see*) isolated from casein, fibrin, or blood. It is used for food enrichment for wheat-based foods. Lysine improves protein quality and results in improved growth and tissue synthesis. Employed in the fortification of specialty bread and cereal mixes up to 0.25 percent to 0.5 percent of the weight of flour. On the FDA list for further study since 1980. GRAS. The FDA data bank, PAFA, has not yet done a search of the toxicology literature concerning this additive.

L-LYSINE • *See* Lysine.

LYSOZYME • Found in animal tissue and used in cheese production to inhibit the growth of *Clostridium tyrobutyricum.* The use level is less than 40 mg of lysozyme per liter of cheese milk, resulting in a concentration of less than 400 mg of lysozyme per kilogram of cheese. In studies related to allergenic effects, the reactions produced by egg-white lysozyme in humans were less severe than those seen with other proteins, such as albumin, that have a long history of use as food components. On the basis of available data, the WHO Committee on food additives concluded that the low additional intake of lysozyme via cheese was not a hazard to consumer health, provided that the enzyme use complied with specifications.

M

MACE • Oil and Oleoresin. Obtained by steam distillation from the ripe, dried seed of the nutmeg. Colorless to pale yellow, with the taste and odor of nutmeg. Used in bitters, meat, and spice flavorings for beverages, ice cream, ices, baked goods, condiments, and meats (2,000 ppm). The *oil* is used in chocolate, cocoa, coconut, cola, fruit, nut, spice, and ginger ale flavorings for beverages, ice cream, ices, candy, baked goods, chewing gum, condiments, and meats. The *oleoresin* (*see*) is used in sausage and spice flavorings for baked goods, condiments, meats, and pickles. *See* Nutmeg for toxicity. The final report to the FDA of the Select Committee on GRAS Substances stated in 1980 that while no available evidence demonstrates a hazard to the public at current use levels, uncertainties exist, requiring additional studies. In 1980 the FDA continued GRAS status while tests were being completed and evaluated. The FDA data bank, PAFA (see page 10), has not yet done a search of the toxicology literature concerning this additive.

MADURAMICIN AMMONIUM • Cygro. An antiparasite medication used in chicken feed to prevent infection. FDA residue tolerances in chicken are 0.24 ppm in muscle, 0.72 ppm in liver, and 0.48 ppm in fat. When used as a medication to treat infection, the residue tolerances are the same as in uncooked chicken.

MAGNESIA • Slightly alkaline white powder taken from any one of several ores, such as periclase. Named after Magnesia, an ancient city in Asia Minor. An antacid. No known toxicity.

MAGNESIUM • Magnesium Acetate, Magnesium Phosphate, Magnesium Sulfate, Magnesium Silicate, Magnesium Carbonate, Magnesium Chloride, Magnesium Cyclamate, Magnesium Stearate, and Magnesium Hydroxide. A silver-white, light, malleable metal that occurs abundantly in nature and is widely used in combination with various chemicals as a powder. *Magnesium acetate* is used as a buffer and neutralizer in nonalcoholic beverages. GRAS. *Magnesium phosphate,* a white, odorless powder, and *magnesium sulfate,* are used as mineral supplements for food. Recommended daily allowances, according to the National Academy of Sciences, are 40 milligrams for infants, 100 to 300 milligrams for children, and 350 milligrams for adult males and females. Magnesium sulfate is also used as a corrective in the brewing industry and for fertilizers. *Magnesium silicate,* a fine, white, odorless and tasteless powder, is used in table salt and vanilla powder as an anticaking agent. In table salt it is limited to 2 percent. *Magnesium carbonate* is used as an alkali for sour cream, butter, ice cream, cacao products, and canned peas. It is also used as a drying agent and an anticaking agent. Magnesium carbonate is also used as a perfume carrier and coloring agent. Used in baby powder, bath powder, tooth powders, face masks, liquid powders, face powders, and dry rouge. It is a silver-white, crystalline salt that occurs in nature as magnetite or dolomite. Can be prepared artificially and is also used in paint, printing ink, table salt, and as an antacid. Nontoxic to the intact skin but may cause irritation when applied to abraded skin. *Magnesium chloride* is used as a buffer and neutralizer in nonalcoholic beverages and for color retention and as a firming agent in canned peas. GRAS. *Magnesium citrate* is a buffer and neutralizer in nonalcoholic beverages. *Magnesium cyclamate* was banned in 1969 as an artificial sweetener. *Magnesium hydroxide* is used as an alkali in dentifrices and skin creams, in canned peas, and as a drying agent and color-retention agent for improved gelling in the manufacture of cheese. Slightly alkaline, crystalline compound obtained by hydration of magnesia (*see*) or by precipitation of seawater by lime. Toxic when inhaled. Harmless to skin and in fact soothes it. *Magnesium stearate,* a soft, white powder, tasteless, odorless and insoluble in water, is used as a dietary supplement, in food packaging, and as an emulsifying agent in cosmetics. Magnesium was reevaluated by the FDA in 1976 as not harmful as presently used at current levels. However, the World Health Organization Food Committee recommends further study of magnesium silicate because kidney damage in dogs has been reported upon ingestion. Magnesium carbonate, chloride, sulfate, stearate, phosphate, and silicate are all GRAS according to the final report to the FDA of the Select Committee on GRAS Substances and they should continue their GRAS status with no limitations other than good manufacturing practices.

MAGNESIUM CAPRATE • There is no reported use of the chemical and no toxicology information is available.

MAGNESIUM CAPRYLATE • There is no reported use of the chemical and no toxicology information is available.

MAGNESIUM CARBONATE • The FDA data bank, PAFA (see page 10), is, as of this writing, conducting a search of the toxicology literature concerning this additive. *See* Magnesium.

MAGNESIUM CHLORIDE • The FDA data bank, PAFA, is, as of this writing, conducting a search of the toxicology literature concerning this additive. *See* Magnesium.

MAGNESIUM FUMARATE • There is no reported use of the chemical and no toxicology information is available.

MAGNESIUM GLUCONATE • A buffering agent in soda water. The FDA data bank, PAFA, is, as of this writing, conducting a search of the toxicology literature concerning this additive. *See* Magnesium.

MAGNESIUM GLYCEROPHOSPHATE • There is no reported use of the chemical and no toxicology information is available.

MAGNESIUM HYDROXIDE • The FDA data bank, PAFA (see page 10), is, as of this writing, conducting a search of the toxicology literature concerning this additive. *See* Magnesium.

MAGNESIUM LACTATE • Buffering and neutralizing agent in cacao products and canned peas. *See* Magnesium.

MAGNESIUM LAURATE • There is no reported use of the chemical and no toxicology information is available.

MAGNESIUM MYRISTATE • There is no reported use of the chemical and no toxicology information is available.

MAGNESIUM OLEATE • There is no reported use of the chemical and no toxicology information is available.

MAGNESIUM OXIDE • Magnesia. White, odorless powder used as an alkali, anticaking agent, firming agent, free-flow agent, lubricant, neutralizing agent, nutrient, pH control agent, and releasing agent. It is used as a neutralizer in frozen dairy products, butter, cacao products, and canned peas. Inhalation can cause fever in humans. Has caused tumors in hamsters. The FDA data bank, PAFA (see page 10), is, as of this writing, conducting a search of the toxicology literature concerning this additive. *See* Magnesium.

MAGNESIUM PALMITATE • There is no reported use of the chemical and no toxicology information is available.

MAGNESIUM PHOSPHATE • The FDA data bank, PAFA, has fully up-to-date toxicology information available for this additive. *See* Magnesium.

MAGNESIUM PHOSPHIDE • A fumigant used in animal feed and on processed foods. FDA residue tolerance is 0.01 ppm in processed foods and 0.1 ppm in animal feeds. A poison. Moderately toxic by inhalation. *See* Magnesium.

MAGNESIUM SALTS OF FATTY ACIDS • The FDA data bank, PAFA, has not yet done a search of the toxicology literature concerning these additives. *See* Magnesium and Fatty Acids.

MAGNESIUM SILICATE • The FDA data bank, PAFA (see page 10), has fully up-to-date toxicology information available for this additive. *See* Magnesium.

MAGNESIUM STEARATE • The FDA data bank, PAFA, is, as of this writing, conducting a search of the toxicology literature concerning this additive. *See* Magnesium.

MAGNESIUM SULFATE • The FDA data bank, PAFA, has fully up-to-date toxicology information available for this additive. *See* Magnesium.

MAIDENHAIR FERN • Venus Hair. Extract of the leaves of the fern *Adiantum capillus-veneris*. Used as a flavoring in alcoholic beverages only and in herbal creams to soothe irritated skin. There is no reported use of the chemical and no toxicology information is available.

MALATHION • Yellow liquid derived from diethyl maleate and dimethyl-dithiophosphoric acid. It is an insecticide against such pests as aphids, the leaf-cutter bee, and the Mediterranean fruit fly. Toxic when absorbed through the skin and can damage transmission of nerve signals. In dehydrated citrus pulp for animal feed, the FDA allows a tolerance of 50 ppm. In nonmedicated cattle-feed concentrate blocks, the residue tolerance, from application of the pesticide to paper used in packaging, is 10 ppm.

MALEIC ACID • Colorless crystals with a bad taste. Toxic by ingestion. Used as a preservative for oils and fats. The FDA data bank, PAFA (see page 10), has not yet done a search of the toxicology literature concerning this additive.

MALEIC HYDRAZIDE • Regulates the growth of unwanted "suckers" on about 90 percent of the U.S. tobacco crop. It is also applied to 10 to 15 percent of domestic potatoes and onions to prevent sprouting after harvest. It is highly toxic to humans and has produced central nervous system disturbances and liver damage in experimental animals. It has led to liver and other tumors in some mice. However, other studies, including one done for the National Cancer Institute, published in 1969, show no carcinogenic effects from it. It has produced genetic damage in plant and animal systems, a fact that often signals a cancer-causing effect. The FDA residue tolerance for potato chips is 160 ppm from use as a preharvest pesticide.

MALIC ACID • A colorless, crystalline compound with a strong acid taste that occurs naturally in a wide variety of fruits, including apples and cherries. A flavoring agent and aid in aging wine. It has a strong acid taste. Used as an alkali in frozen dairy products, beverages, baked goods, confections, fruit, butter, and jelly and jam preserves "in amount sufficient to compensate for the deficiency of fruit in artificially sweetened fruit." An alkali and antioxidant in cosmetics and ingredient of hair lacquer. Irritating to the skin and can cause allergic reactions when used in hair lacquers. The final report to the FDA of the Select Committee on GRAS Substances stated in 1980 that it should continue its GRAS status with no limitations other than good manufacturing practices.

MALLOW EXTRACT • From the herb family. A moderate purplish red that is paler than magenta rose. Used in coloring and also as a source of pectin (*see*). No known toxicity.

MALT EXTRACT • Extracted from barley that has been allowed to germinate, then heated to destroy vitality and dried. It contains sugars, proteins, and salts from barley. The extract is mixed with water and allowed to solidify. It is used as a nutrient and as a texturizer in cured meat and poultry. FDA limitations are 2.5 percent in cured meat. It is also widely used in the brewing industry. GRAS. The FDA data bank, PAFA (see page 10), has fully up-to-date toxicology information available for this additive.

MALTITOL • Obtained by hydrogenation from maltose (*see*).

MALTODEXTRIN • The sugar obtained by hydrolysis of starch. A combination of maltol (*see*) and dextrin (*see*) used as a texturizer and flavor enhancer in candies, particularly chocolate. No known toxicity. The final report to the FDA of the Select Committee on GRAS Substances stated in 1980 that it should continue its GRAS status with no limitations other than good manufacturing practices. The FDA data bank, PAFA, has fully up-to-date toxicology information available for this additive.

MALTOL • A white, crystalline powder with a butterscotch odor, found in the bark of young larch trees, pine seeds, chicory, wood tars, and in roasted malt. It imparts a "freshly baked" odor and flavor to bread and cakes. Used as a synthetic chocolate, coffee, fruit, maple, nut, and vanilla flavoring agent for beverages, ice cream, ices, candy, baked goods, gelatin desserts, chewing gum, and jelly. The FDA data bank, PAFA, has fully up-to-date toxicology information available for this additive.

MALTOSE • Malt Sugar. Colorless crystals derived from malt extract and used as a nutrient, sweetener, culture medium, and stabilizer. It is soluble in water and used as a sweetener for diabetics and in brewing. It is nontoxic but has been reported to cause tumors when injected under the skin of mice in doses of five hundred milligrams per kilogram of body weight. There is no reported use of the chemical and no toxicology information is available.

MANDARIN OIL • Obtained by expression of the peel of a ripe mandarin orange, *Citrus reticulata blanco.* Clear, dark orange to reddish yellow, with a pleasant orangelike odor. It is an orange, tangerine, cherry, and grape flavoring for beverages, ice cream, ices, candy, baked goods, chewing gum, and gelatin desserts. GRAS. The FDA data bank, PAFA (see page 10), has not yet done a search of the toxicology literature concerning this additive.

MANGANESE CHLORIDE • The FDA data bank, PAFA (see page 10), has not yet done a search of the toxicology literature concerning this additive. *See* Manganese Sources.

MANGANESE CITRATE • There is no reported use of the chemical and no toxicology information is available.

MANGANESE GLUCONATE • The FDA data bank, PAFA, has not yet done a search of the toxicology literature concerning this additive. *See* Manganese Sources.

MANGANESE GLYCEROPHOSPHATE • There is no reported use of the chemical and no toxicology information is available.

MANGANESE HYPOPHOSPHITE • Used as a dietary supplement. There is no toxicology information available.

MANGANESE SOURCES • Manganese Acetate, Manganese Carbonate, Manganese Chloride, Manganese Citrate, Manganese Gluconate, Manganese Sulfate, Manganese Glycerophosphate, Manganese Hypophosphite, and Manganese Oxide. A mineral supplement first isolated in 1774, it occurs in minerals and in minute quantities in animals, plants, and in water. Many forms are used in dyeing. Manganous salts are activators of enzymes and are necessary to the development of strong bones. They are used as nutrients and as dairy substitutes. Toxicity occurs by inhalation. Symptoms include languor, sleepiness, wakefulness, emotional disturbances, and Parkinson-like symptoms. *Manganese chloride, citrate, glycerophosphate,* and *hypophosphite* are all considered GRAS according to the final report of the Select Committee on GRAS Substances and should continue their GRAS status as nutrients with no limitations other than good manufacturing practices. However, according to the Select Committee, not enough is known about *manganese oxide* to evaluate it as a food ingredient.

MANGANESE SULFATE • The FDA data bank, PAFA (see page 10), has not yet done a search of the toxicology literature concerning this additive. *See* Manganese Sources.

MANGANOUS OXIDE • A dietary supplement derived by reduction of the dioxide in hydrogen or by heating the carbonate without air. It is also used in ceramics, paints, bleaching tallow, animal feeds, and fertilizers. GRAS. There is no reported use of the chemical and no toxicology information is available.

MANNITOL • Widespread in plants but mostly prepared from seaweed, it is a white, crystalline solid, odorless and sweet tasting. It is used as a texturizer in chewing gum and candy up to 5 percent. It has been used as a sweetener in "sugar-free" products but has calories and carbohydrates. Used as a dusting or antisticking agent in a number of food products. A humectant in hand creams and lotions and used in hair-grooming products as an emulsifier and antioxidant. It is under study by the FDA because it can cause gastrointestinal disturbances. It may worsen kidney disease. In 1982, the FDA reported that it does not cause cancer in rats. GRAS. The FDA data bank, PAFA, is, as of this writing, conducting a search of the toxicology literature concerning this additive.

MANNOSE • A carbohydrate occurring in some plants. It has a sweet taste.

MAPLE, MOUNTAIN • Flavoring. No known toxicity.

MARGARINE • Oleomargarine. A butter substitute made from animal or vegetable fats or oils. If oils are used, they are "hardened" into fats by hydrogenation (*see*). Skimmed milk, water, salt, coloring matter (*see* Carotene), artificial flavors, lecithin (*see*), and small amounts of vitamins are usually added. By federal regulations, margarine contains at least 80 percent fat. No known toxicity.

MARIGOLD, POT • A natural plant extract. The oil is used in various flavorings for beverages, ice cream, ices, candy, and baked goods. The FDA data bank, PAFA (see page 10), has not yet done a search of the toxicology literature concerning this additive. *See* Tagetes. GRAS.

MARJORAM, POT • Sweet Marjoram. *Marjorana onites.* The natural extract of the flowers and leaves of two varieties of the fragrant marjoram plant. The *oleoresin* (*see*) is used in sausage and spice flavorings for condiments and meats. The *seed* is used in sausage and spice flavorings for meats (3,500 ppm) and condiments. *Sweet marjoram* is used in sausage and spice flavorings for beverages, baked goods (2,000 ppm), condiments, meats, and soups. The *sweet oil* is used in vermouth, wine, and spice flavorings for beverages, ice creams, ices, candy, baked goods, and condiments. Also used in hair preparations, perfumes, and soaps. Can irritate the skin. The redness, itching, and warmth experienced when marjoram is applied to the skin are caused by the local dilation of the blood vessels or by local reflex. May produce allergic reactions. Essential oils such as marjoram are believed to penetrate the skin easily and produce systemic effects. GRAS.

MARSHMALLOW ROOT • *See* Althea Root.

MASSARANDUBA CHOCOLATE • *Manilkara solimoesensis gilly.* The FDA data bank, PAFA (see page 10), has fully up-to-date toxicology information available for this additive.

MATÉ EXTRACT • Paraguay Tea Extract. St. Bartholomew's Tea. Jesuits' Tea. A natural flavoring extract from small gourds grown in South America where maté is a stimulant beverage. Among its constituents are caffeine, purines, and tannins. The FDA data bank, PAFA, has not yet done a search of the toxicology literature concerning this additive. *See* Caffeine and Tannic Acid for toxicity. GRAS.

MATRICARIA EXTRACT • Wild Chamomile Extract. Extract of the flower heads of *Matricaria chamomilla.* Used internally as a soothing tea and tonic and externally as a soothing medication for contusions and other inflammation. *See* Tannic Acid. GRAS.

MATRICARIA OIL • Camomile Oil. Wild Chamomile Extract. The volatile oil distilled from the dried flower heads of *Matricaria chamomilla.* Used internally as a tonic and soothing tea and externally as a soothing medication for contusions and other inflammation. *See* Matricaria Extract.

MATURING AGENTS • *See* Bleaching Agents.

MAYONNAISE • The common salad dressing. Semisolid, made with eggs, vegetable oil, and vinegar or lemon juice.

MELAMINE • Cyanuramide. Used in the manufacture of paper and paperboard for packaging materials. An experimental cancer-causing and tumor-causing agent. Moderately toxic by ingestion. An eye, skin, and mucous membrane irritant. Causes skin rash in humans.

MELENGESTROL ACETATE • A progesterone used to treat animals and to suppress ovulation when added to animal feed. Residue limit is zero according to the FDA.

MELISSA • *See* Balm Oil. GRAS.

MELONAL • *See* 2,6-Dimethyl-5-Heptenal.

MENADIONE • Vitamin K$_3$. Not permitted as a dietary supplement in prenatal supplements or any others for humans. However, menadione is permitted as a nutritional supplement in chicken, swine, and turkey feed for prevention of vitamin K deficiency. Used as a preservative in emollients. A synthetic with properties of vitamin K. Bright yellow crystals that are insoluble in water. They are used medically to prevent blood clotting and in food to prevent souring of milk products. Can be irritating to mucous membranes, respiratory passages, and the skin.

MENHADEN OIL • Pogy Oil. Mossbunker oil. Obtained along the coast of Africa from the menhaden fish, which are a little larger than herring. The fish glycerides of menhaden are reddish and have a strong fishy odor. Used in soaps and creams. There is no reported use of the chemical and no toxicology information is available.

MENTHA ARVENSIS, OIL • From *Mentha arvensis,* it is a colorless to yellow liquid with a minty odor used as a flavoring agent. GRAS. Has caused reproductive problems in experimental animals.

p-MENTHA-1,8-DIEN-7-OL • A synthetic citrus, fruit, mint, and vanilla flavoring agent for beverages, ice cream, ices, candy, and baked goods. It is found naturally in caraway. Can cause skin irritation. The FDA data bank, PAFA (see page 10), has fully up-to-date toxicology information available for this additive.

MENTHADIENOL • Although allowed as a food additive, there is no current reported use of the chemical, and therefore, although toxicology information may be available, it is not being updated, according to the FDA.

MENTHOL • A flavoring agent that can be obtained naturally from peppermint or other mint oils and can be made synthetically by hydrogenation (*see*) of thymol (*see*). Used in butter, caramel, fruit, peppermint, and spearmint flavorings for beverages, ice cream, ices, candy, baked goods, chewing gum (1,100 ppm), and liquor. Also used in perfumes, emollient creams, hair tonics, mouthwashes, shaving creams, preshave lotions, aftershave lotions, body rubs, liniments, and skin fresheners. It gives that "cool" feeling to the skin after use. It is a local anesthetic. It is nontoxic in low doses, but in concentrations of 3 percent or more it is an irritant that can, if continued long, induce changes in all layers of the mucous membranes. It can also cause severe abdominal pain, nausea, vomiting, vertigo, and coma when ingested in its concentrated form. The lethal dose in rats is two grams per kilogram of body weight. GRAS. The FDA data bank, PAFA (see page 10), has fully up-to-date toxicology information available for this additive.

MENTHONE • A synthetic flavoring agent that occurs naturally in raspberries and peppermint oil. Bitter, with a slight peppermint taste. Used in fruit and mint flavorings for beverages, ice cream, ices, candy, baked goods, and chewing gum. May cause gastric distress. The FDA data bank, PAFA, has fully up-to-date toxicology information available for this additive.

MENTHYL ACETATE • A natural flavoring agent in peppermint oil. Colorless, with a mint odor. Used in fruit, mint, and spice flavorings for beverages, ice cream, ices, candy, baked goods, and chewing gum; also in perfumes and toilet waters. Mildly toxic by ingestion. A skin irritant. The FDA data bank, PAFA (see page 10), has fully up-to-date toxicology information available for this additive. GRAS.

N-(MERCAPTO METHYL)PHTALIMIDE • Phosphamidon. An organophosphate insecticide limited by the FDA to 0.2 ppm as a residue in meat byproducts of cattle. *See* Organophosphates for toxicity.

METALAXYL • A fungicide used in animal feed, dried hops, potato chips, processed potatoes, soybean meal, sugar beet molasses, processed tomatoes, and wheat milling fractions. FDA limits residues to 7 ppm in citrus oil, 4 ppm in processed potatoes including potato chips, and 3 ppm in processed tomatoes.

METALDEHYDE • A polymer of acetaldehyde (see) used as a slug and snail poison on strawberries at the time of harvest. FDA residue tolerance is zero. Ingestion may cause severe abdominal pain, nausea, vomiting, diarrhea, fever, convulsions, and coma.

METHANE ARSONIC ACID • Used in or on cottonseed hulls used for animal feed. See Arsenic.

METHANE DICHLORIDE • Colorless, volatile liquid with the odor of chloroform used to dilute color and extract chemicals. It is used to decaffeinate coffee, fruits, hops, spices, and vegetables. FDA permits residues of 30 ppm in spice oleoresins, 2.2 percent in hops extract, and 10 ppm in decaffeinated coffee. Moderately toxic by ingestion. An experimental cancer-causing and tumor-causing agent. Human systemic effects by ingestion and inhalation include numbness, altered sleep, convulsions, euphoria, and changes in cardiac rate. It causes birth defects in experimental animals and may be mutagenic in humans. It is an eye and severe skin irritant.

METHANETHIOL • Methyl Mercaptan. A pesticide and fungicide isolated from the roots of a plant. Occurs in the "sour" gas of west Texas, in coal tar, and in petroleum. Produced in the intestinal tract by action of bacteria. Found in urine after ingestion of asparagus. Its odor may cause nausea and it may be narcotic in high concentrations.

METHANOL • Methyl Alcohol. Wood Alcohol. Wood Spirit. A solvent and denaturant obtained by the destructive distillation of wood. Flammable, poisonous liquid with a nauseating odor. Better solvent than ethyl alcohol. It is used primarily in antifreeze compounds, paints, cements, inks, varnishes, shellacs, wood strippers, windshield-wiper solvents, automotive radiators, and as a solvent for dyes. It is also used in the fuel Sterno, in home heating-oil extenders, as an octane booster in gasoline, and as a fuel for soldering torches. It is a softening agent for plastics and the raw material for making formaldehyde. In the food industry, it is used to extract hops and spices. It is on the Community-Right-To-Know List (see). Methanol is highly toxic and readily absorbed from all routes of exposure. It possesses narcotic properties. Toxic effects are primarily on the nervous system. Symptoms include headache, dizziness, confusion, abdominal pain, lung problems, weakness, and coma. Ingestion can cause blindness and death. Lesser exposure causes blurring of vision, headache, and GI disturbances. It is also a fire hazard. If you must use a product containing methanol, make sure you do so either outdoors or in a well-ventilated area. Use gloves.

METHILANIN • See Acimeton.

METHIONINE • An essential amino acid (see) that occurs in protein. Used as a dietary substance. It is attracted to fat, and Rutgers University researchers have patented a process to impregnate a carrier material with methionine for use in deep-frying cooking oil to impart a "fresh" potato or potato chip flavor to snack foods, soups, or salad dressings. Used as a texturizer in cosmetic creams. Methionine is mildly toxic by injection and has caused birth defects in experimental animals. On the FDA list of additives requiring further study since 1980. The FDA data bank, PAFA (see page 10), has fully up-to-date toxicology information available for this additive. GRAS.

METHOPRENE • A growth inhibitor that mimics juvenile hormone in insects. It is used in animal feed or mineral blocks for cattle. The FDA residue tolerances are 22.7 to 45.4 mg per 100 body weight each much; 0.05 ppm as residues in eggs and milk; 0.1 ppm as residues in meat and meat byproducts of cattle, goats, hogs, and sheep; 0.3 ppm as residues in fat of cattle, goats, hogs, and sheep; 0.05 ppm as residues in fat and meat of poultry.

2-METHOXY-3,6-DICHLOROBENZOIC ACID • Banex. An herbicide used in animal feed and on sugarcane. The FDA residue tolerance is 2 ppm on sugarcane molasses and 2 ppm in sugarcane molasses when used for animal feed. In the EPA Genetic Toxicology Program (*see*). Moderately toxic by ingestion.

4-METHOXY-2-METHYL-2-BUTANETHIOL • The FDA data bank, PAFA, has not yet done a search of the toxicology literature concerning this additive.

p-**METHOXY-A-METHYLCINNAMALDEHYDE** • A flavoring. The FDA data bank, PAFA, has fully up-to-date toxicology information available for this additive.

2-METHOXY-4-METHYLPHENOL • Creosol. A synthetic flavoring that occurs naturally in cassia and is used in fruit, rum, nut, and clove flavorings for beverages, ice cream, ices, candy, baked goods, and liqueurs. About the same toxicity as phenol, a highly caustic, poisonous compound derived from benzene. The FDA data bank, PAFA, has fully up-to-date toxicology information available for this additive.

2-METHOXY-3(5)-METHYLPYRAZINE • A colorless liquid with the odor of roasted hazelnuts used as a flavoring agent in various foods. GRAS. The FDA data bank, PAFA, has fully up-to-date toxicology information available for this additive.

1-METHOXY-4-PROPENYLBENZENE • *See* Anethole.

2-METHOXY-4-PROPENYLPHENOL • The FDA data bank, PAFA, has fully up-to-date toxicology information available for this additive. *See* Isoeugenol.

p-**METHOXYACETOPHENONE** • *p*-Acetanisole. Crystalline solid with a pleasant odor. Soluble in alcohol and fixed oils and derived from the interaction of anisole and acetyl chloride with aluminum chloride and carbon disulfide. Used in perfumery as a synthetic floral odor and in flavoring.

4-METHOXYACETOPHENONE • Colorless to pale yellow solid with a hawthorn odor used as a flavoring agent in various foods. Moderately toxic by ingestion. Human systemic effects by inhalation; caused increased pulse rate. A skin irritant.

0-METHOXYBENZALDEHYDE • A synthetic flavoring agent that occurs naturally in cassia oil and is used in spice and cinnamon flavorings for beverages, baked goods, and chewing gum. No known toxicity.

p-**METHOXYBENZALDEHYDE** • Anisaldehyde. A synthetic flavoring agent that occurs naturally in hawthorn, fennel, oil of anise, star anise, and Tahiti vanilla beans. Used in raspberry, strawberry, butter, caramel, chocolate, apricot, cherry, peach, licorice, anise, nut, black walnut, walnut, spice, and vanilla flavorings for beverages, ice cream, ices, candy, baked goods, gelatin desserts, and chewing gum. No known toxicity.

METHOXYBENZENE • *See* Anisole.

p-**METHOXYBENZYL ACETATE** • *See* Anisyl Acetate.

p-**METHOXYBENZYL ALCOHOL** • See Anisyl Alcohol.

p-**METHOXYBENZYL FORMATE** • *See* Anisyl Formate.

1-METHOXYCARBONYL-1-PROPEN-2-YL DIMETHYL PHOSPHATE • Mevinphos. An organophosphate pesticide in dehydrated parsley as a result of application to the growing crop. FDA residue tolerance is 4 ppm. *See* Organophosphates for toxicity.

p-**METHOXYCINNAMALDEHYDE** • A flavoring. The FDA data bank, PAFA (see page 10), has fully up-to-date toxicology information available for this additive.

METHOXYETHANOL • *See* Ethanol.

4-*p*-METHOXYPHENYL-2-BUTANONE • A flavoring agent used in foods, it has a pale yellow color and a sweet floral odor. The FDA data bank, PAFA (see page 18), has fully up-to-date toxicology information available for this additive.

1-(*p*-METHOXYPHENYL)-1-PENTEN-3-ONE • A synthetic butter, cream, fruit, maple, nut, and vanilla flavoring agent for beverages, ice cream, ices, candy, and baked goods. No known toxicity.

1-(*p*-METHOXYPHENYL)-2-PROPANONE • A synthetic flavoring agent that occurs naturally in star anise. Used in fruit and vanilla flavorings for beverages, ice cream, ices, candy, and baked goods. No known toxicity.

3-L-METHOXYPROPANE-1,2-DIOL • A synthetic flavoring. The FDA data bank, PAFA, has not yet done a search of the toxicology literature concerning this additive.

2-METHOXYPYRAZINE • A colorless to yellow liquid with a nutty, cocoa-like odor used as a flavoring in a variety of foods. Skin and eye irritant. The FDA data bank, PAFA (see page 10), has fully up-to-date toxicology information available for this additive. GRAS.

p-**METHOXYTOLUENE** • *See* *p*-Methyl Anisole.

4-METHOXYTOLUENE-2,5-DIAMINE HCL • A colorless liquid used in perfumery and flavorings. *See* Toluene.

METHYL ABIETATE • *See* Abietic Acid.

METHYL ACETAMIDE • *See* Methyl Acetate.

METHYL ACETATE • Acetic Acid. Colorless liquid that occurs naturally in coffee, with a pleasant apple odor. Used in perfume to emphasize floral scents, especially that of rose, and in toilet waters having a lavender odor. Also occurs naturally in peppermint oil. A flavoring used in fruit, rum, and nut flavorings for beverages, ice cream, ices, candy, baked goods, gelatin desserts, puddings, and liquor. Used as a solvent for many resins and oils. May be irritating to the respiratory tract and, in high concentrations, may be narcotic. Since it has an effective fat-solvent drying effect on skin, it may cause skin problems such as chafing and cracking. The FDA data bank, PAFA (see page 10), has fully up-to-date toxicology information available for this additive.

METHYL ACRYLATE • 2-Propanoic Acid, Methyl Ester. Derived from ethylene chlorohydrin, it is transparent and elastic. Used to coat paper and plastic film. Can be highly irritating to the eyes, skin, and mucous membranes. Convulsions occur if vapors are inhaled in high concentrations. GRAS for packaging. The final report to the FDA of the Select Committee on GRAS Substances stated in 1980 that there were insufficient biological and other studies upon which to base an evaluation of it when used as a food ingredient. There is no reported use of the chemical and no toxicology information is available.

METHYL ALCOHOL • Solvent for spice oleoresins and in hops extract for beer. Clear, colorless liquid derived from carbon monoxide and hydrogen under pressure. Toxic by ingestion. Can cause blindness. Used in the manufacture of formaldehyde, acetic acid, and other compounds. Used to denature (*see* Denaturant) alcohol. FDA tolerance for residues on spices is less than 50 ppm or less than 2.2 percent by weight. The FDA data bank, PAFA (see page 10), has fully up-to-date toxicology information available for this additive.

METHYL AMYL KETONE • *See* 2-Heptanone.

METHYL ANISATE • Anisic Acid. A synthetic fruit, melon, liquor, root beer, and spice flavoring agent for beverages, ice cream, ices, candy, and baked goods. The FDA data bank, PAFA, has fully up-to-date toxicology information available for this additive.

p-**METHYL ANISOLE** • The FDA data bank, PAFA, has fully up-to-date toxicology information available for this additive. *See* Ylang-Ylang Oil.

METHYL ANTHRANILATE • Occurs naturally in neroli, ylang-ylang, bergamot, jasmine, and other essential oils. Colorless to pale yellow liquid with a bluish fluorescence and a grapelike odor. It is made synthetically from coal tar (*see*). Used in loganberry, strawberry, orange, floral, rose, violet, cherry, grape, melon, liquor, wine, and honey flavorings for beverages, ice cream, ices, candy, baked goods, chewing gum (2,200 ppm), and liquors. Used as an "orange" scent for ointments, in the manufacture of synthetic perfumes, and in suntan lotions. Can irritate the skin. GRAS. The FDA data bank, PAFA (see page 10), has fully up-to-date toxicology information available for this additive.

N-METHYL ANTHRANILIC ACID, METHYL ESTER • *See* Methyl Anthranilate.

METHYL BENZOATE • Essence of oil of Niobe. Made from methanol and benzoic acid (*see both*). Colorless, transparent liquid with a pleasant fruity odor. Used in fruit, rum, liquor, nut, spice, and vanilla flavorings for beverages, ice cream, ices, candy, and baked goods. Also used in perfumes. The FDA data bank, PAFA (see page 10), has fully up-to-date toxicology information available for this additive.

METHYL-5-BENZOYL BENZIMIDAZOLE-2-CARBAMATE • Vermirax. Telmin. Mebendazole. An antiworm medicine for animals. In the EPA Genetic Toxicology Program. Poison by ingestion. Causes mutations in animals.

METHYL BROMIDE • Prepared from the action of hydrobromic acid on methanol (*see*), it is used as a fumigant in warehouses and for extracting oils from nuts, seeds, and flowers. Inhalation causes dizziness, headache, vomiting, abdominal pain, mental confusion, convulsions, pulmonary edema, coma, and death. Chronic exposure can cause central nervous system depression or kidney injury. FDA tolerance for various crops is from 5 to 200 ppm.

METHYL-1-(BUTYL CARBAMOYL)2-BENZIMIDAZOLYLCARBAMATE • BBC. Benylate. Benomyl. A fungicide used on apples, apricots, bananas, cherries, mangoes, nectarines, peaches, pears, pineapples, plums, raisins, tomato products (concentrated). FDA residue tolerances are 50 ppm in raisins and concentrated tomato products; 125 ppm in dried grape pomace and raisin waste; 70 ppm in dried apple pomace; 50 ppm in dried citrus pulp; 20 ppm in rice hulls. In EPA Genetic Toxicology Program. Poison by ingestion. A human skin irritant. May cause birth defects.

METHYL *p*-tert-BUTYPHENYLACETATE • A synthetic chocolate, fruit, and honey flavoring for beverages, ice cream, ices, candy, and baked goods. The FDA data bank, PAFA, has fully up-to-date toxicology information available for this additive.

METHYL BUTYRATE • A synthetic flavoring agent that occurs naturally in apples. Colorless. Used in fruit and rum flavorings for beverages, ice cream, candy, and baked goods. The FDA data bank, PAFA (see page 10), has fully up-to-date toxicology information available for this additive.

METHYL CHLORIDE • Chloromethane. Colorless gas or colorless liquid with a sweet taste, it is used as a spray for pesticides in food storage and processing areas. It is not supposed to contact fatty foods. Poisonous, it can cause severe injury to liver and kidney.

METHYL CINNAMATE • White crystals, strawberrylike odor, and soluble in alcohol. Derived by heating methanol, cinnamic acid, and sulfuric acid. A synthetic strawberry, butter, cream, cherry, grape, peach, plum, and vanilla flavoring agent for beverages, ice cream, ices, candy, baked goods, chewing gum, and condiments. Used also in perfumes. The FDA data bank, PAFA (see page 10), has fully up-to-date toxicology information available for this additive. *See* Cinnamic Acid.

METHYL DISULFIDE • A synthetic onion flavoring agent for baked goods, condiments, and pickle products. No known toxicity.

METHYL ESTER OF FATTY ACIDS • Produced from edible fats and oils. Used in dehydrating grapes to produce raisins. FDA tolerance is less than 3 percent of weight or less than 200 ppm in raisins *See* Esters and Fatty Acids.

METHYL ESTER OF ROSIN PARTIALLY HYDROGENATED • Used as a constituent of chewing gum base. *See* Rosin and Hydrogenation.

METHYL ESTERS OF HIGHER FATTY ACIDS • Used in animal feed. No known toxicity.

METHYL ETHYL CELLULOSE • A foaming, aerating, and emulsifying agent prepared from wood pulp or chemical cotton. Used in vegetable-fat whipped topping as an emulsifying agent. Used as a bulk laxative but absorbed from the bowel. For toxicity, *see* Sodium Carboxymethyl Cellulose.

METHYL FORMATE • Colorless liquid with a sweet odor used as a fumigant in raisins and dried currants. FDA residue tolerance of 250 ppm as formic acid (*see*) in raisins and dried currants.

METHYL GLUCOSIDE OF FATTY ACIDS OF EDIBLE COCONUT OIL • Used in the manufacture of beet sugar and as an aid in crystallization of sucrose and dextrose. No known toxicity except that coconut is thought to contribute to cholesterol clogging of the arteries. The FDA data bank, PAFA (see page 10), has fully up-to-date toxicology information available for this additive.

METHYL HEPTANOATE • A synthetic berry, grape, peach, and pineapple flavoring agent for beverages, ice cream, ices, candy, and baked goods. The FDA data bank, PAFA, has fully up-to-date toxicology information available for this additive.

6-METHYL-5-HEPTEN-2-ONE • Methyl Heptenone. A synthetic flavoring agent that occurs naturally in oil of lavender and oil of lemon. Used in berry, citrus, banana, melon, pear, peach, and pineapple flavorings for beverages, ice cream, ices, candy, baked goods, and gelatin desserts. Moderately toxic by ingestion. A skin irritant. The FDA data bank, PAFA, has fully up-to-date toxicology information available for this additive.

METHYL HEPTENONE • *See* 6-Methyl-5-Hepten-2-One.

METHYL HEXENOATE • A synthetic pineapple flavoring agent for beverages, ice cream, ices, candy, and baked goods. The FDA data bank, PAFA, has fully up-to-date toxicology information available for this additive.

METHYL-*p*-HYDROXYBENZOATE • Methylparaben. A preservative in beverages, baked goods, candy, and artificially sweetened jellies and preserves. Methylparaben may cause allergic skin reaction. On the FDA list of additives requiring further study. GRAS. The FDA data bank, PAFA (see page 10), has not yet done a search of the toxicology literature concerning this additive.

METHYL ISOBUTYL KETONE • A synthetic fruit flavoring agent for beverages, ice cream, ices, candy, and baked goods. Used as solvent for cellulose and lacquer. Similar in toxicity to methyl ethyl ketone, which is irritating to the eyes and mucous membranes, but likely more toxic. Causes intestinal upsets and central nervous system depression.

METHYL ISOBUTYRATE • A synthetic fruit flavoring agent for beverages, ice cream, ices, candy, and baked goods. The FDA data bank, PAFA, has fully up-to-date toxicology information available for this additive.

1-METHYL-4-ISOPROPYLCYCLOHEXADIENE-1,3 • A colorless liquid with a lemony odor, it used as a flavoring agent in various foods. Moderately toxic by ingestion.

METHYL LAURATE • The ester of methyl alcohol and lauric acid. Derived from coconut oil. A synthetic flavoring agent for beverages, ice cream, ices, candy, and baked goods. It is also used in detergents, emulsifiers, wetting agents, stabilizers, resins, lubricants, and plasticizers. The FDA data bank, PAFA (see page 10), has fully up-to-date toxicology information available for this additive.

METHYL LINOLEATE • The ester of methyl alcohol and linoleic acid, it is a colorless oil derived from safflower oil and used in detergents, emulsifiers, wetting agents, stabilizers, resins, lubricants, and plasticizers. The FDA data bank, PAFA, has fully up-to-date toxicology information available for this additive.

METHYL MERCAPTAN • A synthetic flavoring agent that occurs naturally in caseinate, cheese, skim milk, coffee, and cooked beef. Used in coffee flavorings for beverages, ice cream, ices, candy, and baked goods. The FDA data bank, PAFA, has fully up-to-date toxicology information available for this additive. *See* Methanethiol for toxicity.

METHYL-2-METHYL BUTYRATE • Colorless liquid with a sweet applelike odor used as a flavoring agent in various foods. No known toxicity.

METHYL MYRISTATE • The FDA data bank, PAFA, has fully up-to-date toxicology information available for this additive. *See* Myristic Acid.

METHYL b-NAPHTHYL KETONE • Orange Crystals. 2' Acetonaphthone. A synthetic flavoring agent used in berry, strawberry, citrus, fruit, grape, and vanilla flavorings for beverages, ice cream, ices, candy, baked goods, gelatin desserts, and chewing gum. *See* Methyl Isobutyl Ketone for toxicity.

METHYL NONANOATE • A synthetic berry, citrus, pineapple, honey, and cognac flavoring agent for beverages, ice cream, ices, candy, and baked goods. The FDA data bank, PAFA (see page 10), has fully up-to-date toxicology information available for this additive.

METHYL 2-NONENOATE • A synthetic berry and melon flavoring agent for beverages, ice cream, ices, candy, and baked goods. The FDA data bank, PAFA, has fully up-to-date toxicology information available for this additive.

METHYL 2-NONYNOATE • A synthetic berry, floral, violet, fruit, and banana flavoring agent for beverages, ice cream, ices, candy, gelatin desserts, baked goods, and condiments. No known toxicity.

METHYL OCTANOATE • A synthetic flavoring agent that occurs naturally in pineapple. Used in pineapple and berry flavorings for beverages, ice cream, ices, candy, and baked goods. The FDA data bank, PAFA, has fully up-to-date toxicology information available for this additive.

METHYL 2-OCTYNOATE • A synthetic flavoring agent used in berry, raspberry, strawberry, floral, violet, fruit, peach, liquor, and muscatel flavorings for beverages, ice cream, ices, candy, baked goods, gelatin desserts, chewing gum, and jellies. The FDA data bank, PAFA, has fully up-to-date toxicology information available for this additive.

METHYL PARABEN • Methyl-*p*-hydroxybenzoate.

METHYL PELARGONATE • Nonanoic Acid, Methyl Ester. The ester of ethyl alcohol and pelargonic acid used in perfume and flavorings. No known toxicity.

4-METHYL-2-PENTANONE • A synthetic fruit flavoring for beverages, ice cream, ices, candy, and baked goods. The FDA data bank, PAFA (see page 10), has fully up-to-date toxicology information available for this additive.

2-METHYL-4-PHENYL-2-BUTYL ACETATE • A synthetic fruit and tea flavoring agent for beverages, ice creams, ices, candy, and baked goods. No known toxicity.

3-METHYL-3-PHENYL GLYCIDIC ACID, ETHYL ESTER • A synthetic strawberry flavoring. GRAS.

METHYL PHENYLACETATE • Colorless liquid with a honeylike odor used in strawberry, chocolate, peach, and honey flavorings for beverages, ice cream, ices, baked goods, candy, gelatin desserts, chewing gum, and syrup. Also used in perfumery. Moderately toxic by ingestion and skin contact. The FDA data bank, PAFA, has fully up-to-date toxicology information available for this additive. *See* Phenyl Acetate.

2-METHYL-4-PHENYLBUTYRALDEHYDE • A synthetic nut flavoring agent for beverages, ice cream, ices, candy, and baked goods. The FDA data bank, PAFA, has fully up-to-date toxicology information available for this additive.

3-METHYL-2-PHENYLBUTYRATE • A synthetic fruit flavoring for beverages, ice cream, ices, and candy. The FDA data bank, PAFA, has fully up-to-date toxicology information available for this additive.

METHYL-4-PHENYLBUTYRATE • A synthetic strawberry, fruit, and honey flavoring agent for beverages, ice cream, ices, candy, and baked goods. The FDA data bank, PAFA (see page 10), has fully up-to-date toxicology information available for this additive.

METHYL PIPERAZINE • Colorless liquid that absorbs water. Used as a surfactant (*see*).

METHYL PREDNISOLONE • Medrol. Meprolone. A-methaPred. Solu-Medrol. A hormone secreted by the adrenal gland that affects carbohydrate and protein metabolism. It was introduced as a medication in 1957 to treat severe inflammation or for immunosuppression or to decrease residual damage following spinal-cord trauma. Used to treat cows. FDA limits residue to 10 ppb in milk. Most adverse reactions are the result of dose or length of time of administration. Should be taken with food or milk to reduce GI irritation. Potential adverse reactions include euphoria, insomnia, psychotic behavior, high blood pressure, swelling, cataracts, glaucoma, peptic ulcer, GI irritation, increased appetite, high blood sugar, growth suppression in children, delayed wound healing, acne, skin eruptions, muscle weakness, pancreatitis, hairiness, decreased immunity, and acute adrenal gland insufficiency. When withdrawn, there may be rebound inflammation, fatigue, weakness, joint pain, fever, dizziness, lethargy, depression, fainting, a drop in blood pressure upon arising from a seated or prone position, shortness of breath, loss of appetite, and high blood sugar. Sudden withdrawal may be fatal. Contraindicated in systemic fungal infections. Should be used cautiously in patients with GI ulceration or kidney disease, high blood pressure, diabetes, chicken pox, osteoporosis, Cushing's syndrome, blood clotting disorders, seizures, myasthenia gravis, congestive heart failure, tuberculosis, herpes, and emotional instability.

METHYL SALICYLATE • Salicylic Acid. Oil of Wintergreen. Found naturally in sweet birch, cassia, and wintergreen. Used in strawberry, grape, mint, walnut, root beer, sarsaparilla, spice, wintergreen, birch beer, and vanilla flavorings for beverages, ice cream, ices, candy, baked goods, chewing gum (8,400 ppm), and syrup. The volatile oil is obtained by maceration. Used in perfumery and as a counterirritant, local anesthetic, disinfectant in cosmetics, and as an ultraviolet absorber in sunburn lotions. Toxic by ingestion. Use in foods restricted by the FDA. Lethal dose 30 cc in adults, 10 ml in children. The FDA proposed that liniments and other liquid preparations containing more than 5 percent methyl salicylate be marketed in special child-resistant containers. The FDA data bank, PAFA (see page 10), has fully up-to-date toxicology information available for this additive.

METHYL SILICONE • Prepared by hydrolyzing (*see* Hydrolyzed) dimethyl-dichlorosilane or its esters, it is used to help compounds resist oxidation. No known toxicity. *See* Silicones.

METHYL SULFIDE • A synthetic flavoring agent that occurs naturally in caseinate, cheese, coffee, coffee extract, and skim milk. Disagreeable odor. Used in chocolate, cocoa, fruit, and molasses flavorings for beverages, ice cream, ices, candy, baked goods, gelatin desserts, and syrups. Used also as a solvent for minerals. No known toxicity.

METHYL 9-UNDECENOATE • A synthetic citrus and honey flavoring agent for beverages, ice cream, ices, candy, and baked goods. The FDA data bank, PAFA, has fully up-to-date toxicology information available for this additive.

METHYL 2-UNDECYNOATE • A synthetic floral and violet flavoring agent for beverages, ice cream, ices, candy, and baked goods. The FDA data bank, PAFA, has fully up-to-date toxicology information available for this additive.

METHYL VALERATE • A synthetic flavoring agent that occurs naturally in pineapple. Used in fruit flavorings for beverages, ice cream, ices, candy, and baked goods. The FDA data bank, PAFA, has fully up-to-date toxicology information available for this additive.

2-METHYL VALERIC ACID • A synthetic chocolate flavoring agent for candy. The FDA data bank, PAFA (see page 10), has fully up-to-date toxicology information available for this additive.

METHYLACETALDEHYDE • *See* Propionaldehyde.

METHYLACETIC ACID • *See* Propionic Acid.

4-METHYLACETOPHENONE • Colorless liquid with a fruit odor, it is used as a flavoring agent in various foods. Moderately toxic by ingestion. A human skin irritant. The FDA data bank, PAFA, has fully up-to-date toxicology information available for this additive.

METHYLACETOPYRONONE • White, crystalline powder used as a preservative in various foods. Poison by ingestion. Causes tumors in experimental animals. GRAS.

2-METHYLALLYL BUTYRATE • A synthetic pineapple flavoring for beverages, ice cream, ices, candy, and baked goods. The FDA data bank, PAFA, has fully up-to-date toxicology information available for this additive. *See* Butyric Acid.

o-METHYLANISOLE • A synthetic fruit and nut flavoring for beverages, ice cream, ices, candy, and baked goods. The FDA data bank, PAFA, has fully up-to-date toxicology information available for this additive.

p-METHYLANISOLE • A synthetic berry, maple, black walnut, walnut, and spice flavoring agent for beverages, ice cream, ices, candy, baked goods, gelatin desserts, puddings, condiments, and syrups. The FDA data bank, PAFA, has fully up-to-date toxicology information available for this additive.

METHYLBENZENE ACETATE • A colorless liquid with a honey or jasmine odor, it is used as a flavoring agent in a variety of foods. Moderately toxic by ingestion and skin contact.

METHYLBENZOCARBOXYLATE • Colorless liquid with a fragrant odor used as a flavoring agent in various foods. Moderately toxic by ingestion. Mildly toxic by skin contact.

METHYLBENZYL ACETATE • A synthetic flavoring agent, colorless, with a gardenia odor. Used in cherry and fruit flavorings for beverages, ice cream, ices, candy, baked goods, gelatin desserts, and chewing gum. The FDA data bank, PAFA, has fully up-to-date toxicology information available for this additive. *See* Methyl Acetate for toxicity.

a-**METHYLBENZYL ACETATE** • Acetic Acid. A synthetic berry and fruit flavoring agent for beverages, ice cream, ices, candy, baked goods, chewing gum, and toppings. The FDA data bank, PAFA, has fully up-to-date toxicology information available for this additive. *See* Methyl Acetate for toxicity.

a-**METHYLBENZYL ALCOHOL** • A synthetic flavoring agent, colorless, with a hyacinth odor. Used in strawberry, rose, fruit, and honey flavorings for beverages, ice cream, ices, candy, baked goods, gelatin desserts, and chewing gum. Methyl alcohol is wood alcohol, a widely used solvent in paints, varnishes, and paint removers. Readily absorbed from the gastrointestinal tract; as little as two teaspoonfuls is considered toxic if ingested. The fatal does lies between two and eight ounces. The FDA data bank, PAFA (see page 10), has fully up-to-date toxicology information available for this additive.

a-**METHYLBENZYL BUTYRATE** • A synthetic berry and fruit flavoring agent for beverages, ice cream, ices, candy, and baked goods. The FDA data bank, PAFA, has fully up-to-date toxicology information available for this additive.

a-**METHYLBENZYL ISOBUTYRATE** • A synthetic fruit flavoring agent for beverages, ice cream, ices, candy, and baked goods. No known toxicity.

a-**METHYLBENZYL FORMATE** • Formic Acid. A synthetic fruit and berry flavoring agent for beverages, ice cream, ices, candy, and baked goods. *See* Formic Acid for toxicity.

1-(3-METHYL)BUTYL BENZOATE • Amyl Benzoate. Isopentyl Benzoate. Used as a flavoring agent in various foods. Mildly toxic by ingestion. A skin irritant.

2-METHYLBUTYL ISOVALERATE • *See* Valeric Acid.

2-METHYLBUTYRALDEHYDE • A synthetic flavoring agent that occurs naturally in coffee and tea. Used in chocolate and fruit flavoring for beverages, ice cream, ices, candy, and baked goods. No known toxicity.

3-METHYLBUTYRALDEHYDE • A synthetic flavoring agent that occurs naturally in coffee extract, oil of lavender, and peppermint oil. Used in butter, chocolate, cocoa, fruit, and nut flavorings for beverages, ice cream, ices, candy, baked goods, and gelatin desserts. The FDA data bank, PAFA, has fully up-to-date toxicology information available for this additive.

2-METHYLBUTYRIC ACID • A synthetic fruit flavoring agent for beverages, ice cream, ices, and candy. The FDA data bank, PAFA (see page 10), has fully up-to-date toxicology information available for this additive.

METHYLCELLULOSE • Cellulose, Methyl Ether. A binder, thickener, dispersing and emulsifying agent, it is prepared from wood pulp or chemical cotton by treatment with alcohol. Swells in water. Soluble in cold water and insoluble in hot. The commercial product has a methoxyl content of 29 percent. It is used as a bodying agent for beverages and canned fruits sweetened with artificial sweeteners; a thickener for kosher food products; a bulking agent for low-calorie crackers; a binder in nonwheat baked goods for nonallergic diets; a beer-foam stabilizer; a condiment carrier; in food products for diabetics and low-calorie dietetic products; an edible film for food products; a leavening agent for prepared mixes; a clarifier for vinegar and beverages; and in imitation jellies and jams, processed cheese, confectionery, and toppings. It is also used in wave-setting lotions, foam stabilizers, bath oils, and other cosmetic products. It is a bulk laxative. Ingestion of large doses may cause flatulence, distension of the abdomen, or intestinal obstruction, and it may also affect the absorption of minerals or other drugs. A dose injected into the abdomen of rats causes cancer. Nontoxic on the skin. The final report to the FDA of the Select Committee on GRAS Substances stated in 1980 that there is no available evidence that it is a hazard to the public when used as it is now and it should continue its GRAS status with limitations on the amounts that can be added to foods. *See also* Carboxymethyl Cellulose.

METHYLCHLOROPINDOL • Coccidiostat. An antibiotic drug for animals used on beef and in feed as well as cereal grains, chicken, fruits, goat, lamb, milk, pork, turkey, and vegetables. FDA limits it to 0.2 ppm in cereal grains, vegetables, and fruits; 15 ppm in uncooked liver and kidney; 5 ppm in uncooked muscle of chickens and turkeys.

6-METHYLCOUMARIN • A synthetic flavoring agent, white needles from benzene with a coconut odor. Used in butter, caramel, coconut, fruit, nut, root beer, and vanilla flavorings for beverages, ice cream, ices, candy, baked goods, gelatin desserts, puddings, and chewing gum. Moderately toxic by ingestion. Unlike methylcoumarin, which is listed as GRAS by the Flavor Extract Manufacturers Association, coumarin, once widely used in foods, is banned. Prolonged feeding of coumarin causes liver injury. The FDA data bank, PAFA (see page 10), has fully up-to-date toxicology information available for this additive.

METHYLCYCLOPENTENOLONE • A synthetic flavoring agent used in berry, butter, butterscotch, caramel, maple, hazelnut, pecan, walnut, fruit, and vanilla flavorings for beverages, ice cream, ices, candy, baked goods, chewing gum, gelatin desserts, and syrups. No known toxicity.

METHYLENE CHLORIDE • Dichloromethane. Methane Dichloride. Methylene Dichloride. Aerothene NM. Solaestine. Freon 30. Somethine. F-30. A colorless gas that compresses into a colorless liquid of pleasant odor and sweet taste. It is widely used as a degreaser, solvent for spices, waxes, oils, paint, and varnish thinner, and as a cleanser in many industries and work settings; in aerosols, including pesticides; in refrigeration and air-conditioning equipment; in coffee decaffeination and spice extraction processes; and in paint and varnish removers. It is considered the best liquid paint remover and is a component in aerosol propellants in many formulations including cosmetics, pesticides, paints, and lubricants. Methylene chloride is nonflammable and a good grease remover and therefore products may contain high percentages of the chemical. For instance, paint strippers are usually 40 to 80 percent methylene chloride. Some labeled "nonflammable" are almost 100 percent. Spray paints may contain up to 33 percent of the chemical. High concentrations are narcotic. Methylene chloride enters your body when you breathe it in the air. Once it enters the body, it generates carbon monoxide, which interferes with the blood's ability to pick up and deliver oxygen. The body responds to lack of oxygen by working the heart harder. People with angina (chest pains) from coronary artery disease are extremely sensitive to carbon monoxide and may have increased chest pains from exposure to methylene chloride, even below the legal exposure limit (100 parts per million over an eight-hour workshift). No one is watching how consumers use the products. The use of a paint remover in a poorly ventilated setting has led to fatalities, according to a report in the November 8, 1990, issue of the *American Journal of Emergency Medicine.* Since smoking increases the carbon monoxide level in the blood, smokers are doubly affected. Small amounts can also be absorbed through the skin. Damage to the liver, kidney, and central nervous system can occur, and persistent postrecovery symptoms after inhalation include headache, nervousness, insomnia, and tremor. It is also a skin irritant. Methylene chloride is considered to have "poor warning properties" since most people cannot smell it until it reaches a hazardous level (100–500 ppm). If you can smell it, you may be overexposed. Methylene chloride causes cancer in animals and is considered a potential cancer-causing agent in humans. The World Health Organization's Food Additive Committee said that epidemiological studies have not shown any carcinogenic effect of dichloromethane after occupational exposure. However, the committee noted that the ability to detect excess risk in these studies was limited. On the basis of the available data, the Committee concluded that the use of dichloromethane as an extraction solvent in food processing should be limited to use for spice oleoresins and the decaffeination of tea and coffee and for food additives in which previous specifications drawn up by the Committee included residues of dichloromethane. FDA residue tolerances are 30 ppm in spice oleoresins; less than 10 ppm in decaffeinated roasted coffee and decaffeinated instant coffee; and 2.2 percent as a residue in hops extract added before or during cooking of beer.

5-METHYLFURFURAL • A synthetic honey, maple, and meat flavoring for beverages, ice cream, ices, candy, and baked goods. The FDA data bank, PAFA, has fully up-to-date toxicology information available for this additive.

2-METHYLOCTANAL • A synthetic citrus flavoring agent for beverages, ice cream, ices, candy, and baked goods. The FDA data bank, PAFA (see page 10), has fully up-to-date toxicology information available for this additive.

METHYLPARABEN • Methyl *p*-Hydroxybenzoate. Preservative in jelly and preserves. Used in bubble baths, cold creams, eyeliners, and liquid makeup. It is an antimicrobial and preservative made of small, odorless, colorless crystals that have a burning taste. FDA residue tolerance in milk from cows treated with mastitis formulations is zero. Nontoxic in small amounts but can cause allergic skin reactions. *See* Methyl-*p*-Hydroxybenzoate. GRAS.

2-METHYLPENTANOIC ACID • *See* 2-Methyl Valeric Acid.

***b*-METHYLPHENETHYL ALCOHOL** • A synthetic berry, rose, melon, and honey flavoring agent for beverages, ice cream, ices, candy, and baked goods.

The FDA data bank, PAFA (see page 10), has fully up-to-date toxicology information available for this additive.

METHYLPHENYL ETHER • *See* Anisole.

METHYLPROTOCATECHUIC ALDEHYDE • *See* Vanillin.

4-METHYLQUINOLINE • A synthetic butter, caramel, fruit, honey, and nut flavoring agent for beverages, ice cream, ices, candy, and baked goods. No known toxicity.

2-METHYLRESORCINOL • Orcin. An aromatic compound with white crystalline prisms derived from lichen and used in medicine and as a reagent for sugars and starches. *See* Resorcinol.

METHYLTHEOBROMINE • *See* Caffeine.

2-METHYLUNDECANAL • A synthetic flavoring agent, colorless, with a fatty odor. Used in a variety of foods. The FDA data bank, PAFA (see page 10), has fully up-to-date toxicology information available for this additive.

METOLACHLOR • An odorless, preemergent herbicide. FDA residue tolerances are 0.02 ppm in cattle, goat, sheep, and hog fat and meat byproducts and in eggs; 0.05 ppm as residue in cattle, goat, hog, and sheep liver; 0.1 ppm as residue in corn grain and cottonseed; 0.3 ppm as residue in sorghum grain; 0.2 ppm as residue in soybean; 2 ppm as residue in or on sorghum forage and fodder; and 8 ppm as residue in or on corn forage or fodder.

METOSERPATE HYDROCHLORIDE • An animal drug used in chickens. FDA limits residue to 0.02 ppm in chicken. Crystals from benzene and cyclohexane, used as a sedative. Poisonous by ingestion.

METSULFURON METHYL • A pre- and postemergent herbicide. FDA tolerances for residues in or on grain, green forage, hay, straw of barley and wheat are 0.05 to 20 ppm.

MEXICAN SAGE • *See* Oregano.

mg • Abbreviation for *milligram* (*see*).

MIBOLERONE • Crystalline solid used as an animal feed drug. A male hormone, it is used in dog food to increase growth. Caused adverse reproductive effects and birth defects in experimental animals.

MICROCAPSULES • Used for flavoring oils, these tiny vessels contain gelatin, arabinogalactin, silicon dioxide, glutaraldehyde, and octyl alcohol (*see all*).

MICROCRYSTALLINE CELLULOSE • Used in frozen desserts. GRAS but limited in standardized products. *See* Cellulose.

MICROPARTICULATED PROTEIN PRODUCT • Thickener and texturizer in frozen dessert products. May not be used to replace milk fat in standardized frozen desserts. GRAS. There is no reported use of the chemical and no toxicology information is available.

MILFOIL • *See* Yarrow.

MILK • Milk may be a hidden ingredient in cream of rice, macaroni, filled candy bars, Ovaltine, junket, prepared flours, frankfurters, and other sausages. Some people are allergic to milk. *See also* Nonfat Dry Milk.

MILK-CLOTTING ENZYME FROM *BACILLUS CEREUS* • Used to clot milk in cheese making. There is no reported use of the chemical and no toxicology information is available.

MILK-CLOTTING ENZYME FROM *ENTOTHIA PARASITICA, MUCOR MIEHEI, OR MUCOR PUSILLUS* • Used to clot milk for making cheese. The FDA data bank, PAFA (see page 10), has not yet done a search of the toxicology literature concerning this additive.

MILLET EXTRACT • An extract of the seeds of *Panicum miliaceum.*

MILLIGRAM (mg) • A metric unit of weight equal to one-thousandth of a gram. Food labels list cholesterol and sodium in milligrams per serving.

MILO STARCH • *See* Modified Starch. The final report to the FDA of the Select Committee on GRAS Substances stated in 1980 that it should continue its GRAS status with no limitations other than good manufacturing practices.

MIMOSA, ABSOLUTE • *Acacia decurrens.* Reddish yellow solid with a long-lasting, pleasant odor resembling ylang-ylang, used in perfumes. Derived from trees, shrubs, and herbs native to tropical and warm regions. Mimosa droops and closes its leaves when touched. A natural flavoring agent used in raspberry and fruit flavorings for beverages, ice cream, ices, candy, and baked goods. Also used in tanning. May produce allergic skin reactions. The FDA data bank, PAFA (see page 10), has not yet done a search of the toxicology literature concerning this additive.

MINERAL OIL • White Oil. It is a mixture of refined liquid hydrocarbons (*see*) derived from petroleum. Colorless, transparent, odorless, and tasteless. It is used as a defoaming component in the processing of beet sugar and yeast; as a coating for fresh fruits and vegetables; and a lubricant and binder for capsules and tablets supplying small amounts of flavor, spice condiments, and vitamins. Also employed as a lubricant in food-processing equipment; a dough-divider oil; a pan oil; and a lubricant in meatpacking plants. It is also used in confectionery as a sealant. It is also employed in baby creams, baby lotions, bay oil, brilliantine hairdressings, cleansing creams, cold creams, emollients, moisturizing creams, eye creams, foundation creams and makeup, hair conditioners, hand lotions, lipsticks, mascaras, rouge, shaving creams, compact powders, makeup removers, and suntan creams, oils, and ointments. Also a cosmetic lubricant, protective agent, and binder. When heated, it smells like petroleum. It stays on top of the skin and leaves a shiny protective surface. May inhibit absorption of digestive fats and has a mild laxative effect. A human cancer-causing agent by inhalation. Causes birth defects if inhaled by humans and also causes testicular tumors in the fetus. An eye irritant. FDA tolerances include 200 ppm in dried fruits and vegetables from use as a releasing agent in drying pans; less than 0.095 percent in meat from use as a hot-melt coating; less than 0.10 percent in egg white solids; and less than 0.06 percent as a releasing agent, binder, and/or lubricant in or on capsules or tablets containing concentrates of flavors, spices, condiments, and nutrients intended for addition to food. The FDA data bank, PAFA (see page 10), has fully up-to-date toxicology information available for this additive.

MIXED CARBOHYDRASE AND PROTEASE ENZYME PRODUCTS • Enzymes. GRAS. *See* Enzyme.

MOCA • Bis Amine. Curalin M. Packaging adhesive prohibited from indirect addition to human food. International Agency for Research on Cancer (IARC) review (*see*). EPA Genetic Toxicology Program and Community

Right-To-Know List (*see both*). Moderately toxic by ingestion. Caused cancer and tumors in experimental animals.

MODIFIED SEA SALT • Salts derived from seawater with a reduced sodium chloride content.

MODIFIED STARCH • Ordinary starch that has been altered chemically to modify such properties as thickening or jelling. Babies have difficulty in digesting starch in its original form. Modified starch is used in baby food on the theory that it is easier to digest. Questions about safety have arisen because babies do not have the resistance of adults to chemicals. Among chemicals used to modify starch are propylene oxide, succinic anhydride, 1-octenyl succinic anhydride, aluminum sulfate, and sodium hydroxide (*see all*). On the FDA top-priority list for reevaluation since 1980. Nothing new reported by the FDA since.

MOENOMYCIN • Bambermycin. Menomycin. An antibiotic produced by *Streptomyces roseoflavus* used as an animal-feed drug for poultry, calves, and swine. An eye and skin irritant. Moderately toxic by ingestion.

MOLASSES EXTRACT • Extract of sugarcane, a thick, brown, viscid syrup. Separated from raw sugar in the successive processes of sugar manufacture and graded according to its quality. It is a natural flavoring agent for candy, baked goods, ice cream, and medicines. The FDA data bank, PAFA (see page 10), has not yet done a search of the toxicology literature concerning this additive.

MOLYBDATE ORANGE • A solution of lead chromate, lead molybdate, and lead sulfate. Used in printing inks. Toxic by ingestion.

MOLYBDENUM • A dietary supplement. The dark gray powdered mineral is a trace element in animal and plant metabolism. Resembles chromium and tungsten in many of its properties. Low order of toxicity.

MONARDA **SPECIES** • *See* Horsemint Leaves Extract.

MONESIN • Antibiotic isolated from *Streptomyces cinnamonensis*. Used in feed to combat parasites and fungus infections. FDA residue limits are 0.05 ppm in edible tissues of cattle; 1.5 ppm in muscle tissue of chicken and turkey; 3 ppm as residue in skin with fat of chicken and turkey; and 4.5 ppm as residue in liver of chicken. Used as a medicated block for cattle; in liquid feed for cattle; in goat feed.

MONO- AND DIGLYCERIDES OF FATS OR OILS • Mono- and diglycerides of edible fat-forming acids, used as emulsifiers in oleomargarine. GRAS. The FDA data bank, PAFA (see page 10), has fully up-to-date toxicology information available for this additive. *See* Glycerides.

4-MONOAMINOPHOSPHATIDE • *See* Lecithin.

4-MONOAMMONIUM GLUTAMATE • The FDA data bank, PAFA (see page 10), has not yet done a search of the toxicology literature concerning this additive. GRAS. *See* Glutamate.

MONOAZO COLOR • A dye made from diazonium and phenol, both coaltar derivatives (*see* Coal Tar).

MONOCALCIUM PHOSPHATE • Buffer and neutralizing agent in self-rising cereal flours or meals. GRAS. *See* Calcium Phosphate.

MONOGLYCERIDE CITRATE • Helps dissolve antioxidant formulations that retard rancidity in oils and fats. The final report to the FDA of the Select

Committee on GRAS Substances stated in 1980 that there were insufficient biological and other studies upon which to evaluate it when it is used as a food ingredient.

MONOGLYCERIDES OF FATTY ACIDS • Stabilizers in shortenings. *See* Fatty Acids. No known toxicity.

MONOGLYCEROL CITRATE • A preservative. *See* Glycerin.

MONOISOPROPYL CITRATE • A sequestrant and plasticizer and antioxidant aid used in fats, lard, meat, oleomargarine, packaging materials, sausage, and shortening. GRAS. There is no reported use of the chemical and no toxicology information is available. *See* Isopropyl Citrate.

MONOMER • A molecule that by repetition in a long chain builds up a large structure or polymer (*see*). Ethylene, the gas, for instance, is the monomer of polyethylene (*see*).

MONOPOTASSIUM GLUTAMATE • Flavor enhancer and salt substitute used on meat. EPA Genetic Toxicology Program (*see*). Mildly toxic by ingestion. Human systemic effects by ingestion: headache. The FDA data bank, PAFA (see page 10), has not yet done a search of the toxicology literature concerning this additive. *See* Glutamate.

MONOSACCHARIDE LACTATE CONDENSATE • The condensation product of sodium lactate and the sugars glucose, fructose, ribose, glucosamine, and deoxyribose.

MONOSODIUM GLUTAMATE (MSG) • Accent. Zest. The monosodium salt of glutamic acid (*see*), one of the amino acids. Occurs naturally in seaweed, sea tangles, soybeans, and sugar beets. Used to intensify meat and spice flavorings in meats, condiments, pickles, soups, candy, and baked goods. Believed responsible for the so-called "Chinese-restaurant syndrome" in which diners suffer from chest pain, headache, and numbness after eating a Chinese meal. Causes brain damage in young rodents and brain damage effects in rats, rabbits, chicks, and monkeys. Baby-food processors removed MSG from baby-food products. Depression, irritability, and other mood changes have been reported. On the FDA list of additives needing further study for mutagenic, teratogenic, subacute, and reproductive effects. Studies have shown that MSG administered to animals during the neonatal period resulted in reproductive dysfunction when both males and females became adults. Females treated with MSG had fewer pregnancies and smaller litters, while males showed reduced fertility. The final report to the FDA of the Select Committee on GRAS Substances stated in 1980 that while no available evidence on it demonstrates a hazard to the public at current use levels, uncertainties exist, requiring additional studies. GRAS status has continued since 1980 while tests were being completed and evaluated. The FDA data bank, PAFA (see page 10), has fully up-to-date toxicology information available for this additive.

MONOSODIUM METHYLARSONATE • Arsonate Liquid. Weed-E-Rad. An herbicide used on animal feed and cottonseed hulls. FDA residue limit is 0.9 ppm in cottonseed hulls when used for animal feed. Arsenic and its compounds are on the Community Right-To-Know List and in the EPA Genetic Toxicology Program (*see both*). Moderately toxic by ingestion. A skin and eye irritant.

MONOPOTASSIUM PHOSPHATE • A derivative of edible fat. Used as an emulsifying agent in food products and as a buffer in prepared cereal. Cleared by the USDA's Meat Inspection Department to decrease the amounts of cooked-out juices in canned hams, pork shoulders, pork loins, chopped hams, and bacon. Monosodium phosphate is a urinary acidifier but has no known toxicity. The final report to the FDA of the Select Committee on GRAS Substances stated in 1980 that it should continue its GRAS status with no limitations other than good manufacturing practices.

MONOSODIUM PHOSPHATE • Used as an emulsifier for cheeses, frozen eggs, and jellies. The FDA's tolerance is set at less than 5 percent. In medicine it is used as a laxative. GRAS.

MONOSODIUM PHOSPHATE DERIVATIVES OF DIGLYCERIDES • Derived from edible fats or oils or edible fat-forming fatty acids and used as emulsifiers. GRAS.

MONOSTARCH PHOSPHATE • A modified starch (*see*). The final report to the FDA of the Select Committee on GRAS Substances stated in 1980 that there is no available evidence that it is a hazard to the public when used as it is now and it should continue its GRAS status with limitations on amounts that can be added to food.

MONOUNSATURATED FATS • The saturation of fat refers to the chemical structure of its fatty acids. Saturated fats, which are hard at room temperature—lard, suet, and butter fat are examples—consist primarily of fatty acids that contain a full load of hydrogen atoms. Monounsaturated fatty acids, however, can accept two additional hydrogen atoms. Fats that contain primarily monounsaturated fatty acids are liquid at room temperature but may become thickened when refrigerated. Polyunsaturated fats, which are liquid at room temperature, remain so even in the refrigerator and consist mainly of fatty acids that can hold four or more additional hydrogen atoms. Examples of polyunsaturated fats are safflower and corn oil. Examples of monounsaturated fats are olive oil, rapeseed oil, cashews, and avocados. Once thought to be neutral, monounsaturated fats may be beneficial for blood cholesterol levels. This concept evolved from epidemiological studies of populations who have a diet high in monounsaturates and a lower artery-disease rate than populations eating a high saturated-fat diet. Some even suggest that monounsaturates may be even better than polyunsaturates in preventing heart disease. Monounsaturates are normally manufactured by the body and are believed to be less likely to have some of the side effects thought to occur with polyunsaturates.

MORANTEL • Paratect. Suiminth. A worm medicine used to treat cattle that leaves residues in beef and milk. FDA limits residues to 1.2 ppm to 4.8 ppm in cattle and 0.4 ppm in milk.

MORELLONE • *See* 3-Benzyl-4-Heptanone.

MORPHOLINE • Salt Fatty Acid. Coating on fresh fruits and vegetables. Broad industrial uses. Used as a surfactant (*see*) and an emulsifier in cosmetics. Prepared by taking the water out of diethanolamine (*see*). A mobile, water-absorbing liquid that mixes with water. It has a strong ammonia odor. A cheap solvent for resins, waxes, and dyes. Also used as a corrosion inhibitor, antioxidant, plasticizer, viscosity improver, insecticide, fungicide, local anesthetic, and antiseptic. A strong alkali, irritating to the eyes, skin, and mucous membranes. It may cause kidney and liver injury and can produce sloughing of the skin. Although allowed as a food additive, there is no current reported use of the chemical, and therefore, although toxicology information may be available, it is not being updated, according to the FDA.

MORPHOLINE STEARATE • A coating and preservative. *See* Morpholine.

MOSCHUS MOSCHIFERUS • *See* Musk.

MOUNTAIN ASH EXTRACT • The extract from the berries of a European tree or shrub, *Sorbus aucuparia*. High in vitamin C, it has been used by herbalists to cure and prevent scurvy and to treat nausea. Used in cosmetics as an antioxidant. No known toxicity.

MOUNTAIN MAPLE EXTRACT • Extract from a tall shrub or bushy tree found in the eastern United States. Used in chocolate, malt, and maple flavorings for beverages, ice cream, ices, candy, and baked goods. The FDA data bank, PAFA (see page 10), has not yet done a search of the toxicology literature concerning this additive.

MSG • *See* Monosodium Glutamate.

MUCOUS MEMBRANES • The thin layers of tissues that line the respiratory tract, including the nose, and the intestinal tract and are kept moist by a sticky substance called mucus. These membranes are also found in other parts of the body that communiciate with air.

MUGWORT • The extract of the flowering herb *Artemisia absinthium*. *See* Wormwood and Sesquiterpene Lactones.

MUIRA PUAMA EXTRACT • A wood extract used as an aromatic resin and fat. No known toxicity.

MULBERRY EXTRACT • An extract of the dried leaves of various species of *Morus,* which produces a purplish black dye.

MULLEIN FLOWERS • The flowers from common mullein, *Verbascum thapsus.* Used as a flavoring in alcoholic beverages only and in henna hair coloring. There is no reported use of the chemical and no toxicology information is available.

MUSHROOM EXTRACT • The extract of various species of mushrooms, used as an oil and plasticizer.

MUSK • It is the dried secretion from preputial follicles of the northern-Asian small hornless deer, which has musk in its glands. Musk is a brown, unctuous, smelly substance associated with attracting the opposite sex and is promoted by stores for such purposes. As *musk ambrette* it is used in fruit, cherry, maple, mint, nut, black walnut, pecan, spice, and vanilla flavorings for beverages, ice cream, ices, candy, baked goods, gelatin desserts, pudding, and chewing gum. Musk ambrette, as a synthetic fixative, is widely used as a fragrance agent in perfumes, soaps, detergents, creams, lotions, and dentifrices in the U.S. at an estimated one hundred thousand pounds per year. It reportedly damages the myelin, the covering of nerve fibers. It can cause photosensitivity (*see*) and contact dermatitis. The problem is mostly with aftershave lotions. (*Musk tetralin,* in use for twenty years as a fragrance ingredient, was identified as a neurotoxin and removed from the market in 1978.) Musk ambrette has been generally recognized as safe as a food additive by the FDA. As *musk tonquin* it is used in fruit, maple, and molasses flavorings for beverages, ice cream, ices, candy, baked goods, and syrups. As *musk ketone* it is used in chewing gum and candy. At one time musk was a stimulant and nerve sedative in medicine. Can cause allergic reactions. GRAS.

MUSTARD • Black, Brown, and Red. Pulverized, dried, ripe seeds of the mustard plant (*Brassica nigra*) grown in Europe and Asia and naturalized in the U.S. Used in mustard and spice flavorings for condiments (5,200 ppm) and meats (2,300 ppm). Used as an emetic. Used in soaps, liniments, and lubricants. It has an intensely pungent odor that can be irritating. It is a strong skin blisterer. Can cause allergic reactions. May cause a sensitivity to light. On the FDA list of products to be studied for possible mutagenic, teratogenic, subacute, and reproductive effects. The final report to the FDA of the Select Committee on GRAS Substances stated in 1980 that it should continue its GRAS status with no limitations other than good manufacturing practices. The FDA data bank, PAFA (see page 10), has not yet done a search of the toxicology literature concerning this additive.

MUSTARD • Yellow and White. The pulverized, dried, ripe seeds of the mustard plant (*Brassica alba*) grown in Europe and Asia and naturalized in the U.S. Used in sausage and spice flavorings for beverages, baked goods, condiments (8,200 ppm), meats, and pickles (3,800 ppm). Used as an emetic. The final report to the FDA of the Select Committee on GRAS Substances stated in 1980 that it should continue its GRAS status with no limitations other than good manufacturing practices. *See* Mustard, Black, Brown, and Red for toxicity.

MUSTARD OIL • *See* Allyl Isothiocyanate.

MUTAGENIC • Having the power to cause mutations. A mutation is a sudden change in the character of a gene that is perpetuated in subsequent divisions of the cells in which it occurs. It can be induced by the application of such stimuli as radiation, certain food chemicals, or pesticides. Certain food additives such as caffeine have been found to "break" chromosomes.

MYCLOBUTANIL • A systemic fungicide used on fruits. FDA limits residue to 5 ppm in apple or grape pomace for feed; 10 ppm in grapes and raisins; 25 ppm in raisin waste; 0.05 ppm in meat, fat, and meat byproducts of cattle, goats, hogs, poultry, and sheep; 0.3 ppm in liver of cattle, goats, hogs, poultry, and sheep; and 0.02 ppm in eggs.

MYRCENE • A synthetic flavoring agent that occurs naturally in galbanum oil, pimenta oil, orange peel, palma rosa oil, and hops oil. Pleasant aroma. Used in fruit, root beer, and coriander flavorings for beverages, ice cream, ices, candy, and baked goods. A moderate skin and eye irritant. Found to cause birth defects in experimental animals. The FDA data bank, PAFA (see page 10), has fully up-to-date toxicology information available for this additive.

MYRISTALDEHYDE • A synthetic citrus and fruit flavoring agent for beverages, ice cream, ices, candy, baked goods, and gelatin desserts. The FDA data bank, PAFA, has fully up-to-date toxicology information available for this additive. *See* Nutmeg for toxicity.

MYRISTIC ACID • Used in shampoos, shaving soaps, and creams. A solid organic acid that occurs naturally in butter acids (such as nutmeg, which is 80 percent butter), oil of lovage, coconut oil, mace oil, cire d'abeille in palm-seed fats, and in most animal and vegetable fats. Used in butter, butterscotch, chocolate, cocoa, and fruit flavorings for beverages, ice cream, ices, candy, baked goods, and gelatin desserts. A human skin irritant. Causes mutations in laboratory animals. The FDA data bank, PAFA, has fully up-to-date toxicology information available for this additive.

MYRISTIC FRAGRANS HOUTT • *See* Mace and Nutmeg.

MYRISTYL ALCOHOL • The FDA data bank, PAFA (see page 10), has fully up-to-date toxicology information available for this additive. *See* Fatty Alcohols.

MYROXYLON • *See* Balsam Peru.

MYRRH • Used in perfumes, dentifrices, and skin topics. One of the gifts of the Magi, it is a yellowish to reddish brown, aromatic bitter gum resin that is obtained from various trees, especially from East Africa and Arabia. Used by the ancients as an ingredient of incense and perfumes and as a remedy for localized skin problems. The gum is used in fruit, liquor, tobacco, and smoke flavorings for beverages, baked goods, ice cream, ices, candy, chewing gum, and soups. The oil is used in honey and liquor flavorings for beverages, ice cream, ices, candy, and baked goods. The gum resin has been used to break up intestinal gas and as a topical stimulant. The FDA data bank, PAFA, has not yet done a search of the toxicology literature concerning this additive.

MYRTLE LEAVES • The extract of the leaves of *Myrtus communis,* a European shrub used in alcoholic beverages only. There is no reported use of the chemical and no toxicology information is available.

MYRTRIMONIUM BROMIDE • *See* Quaternary Ammonium Compounds.

N

NAPHTHA • Obtained from the distillation of petroleum, coal tar, and shale oil. It is a common diluent (*see*) found in nail lacquer. *Naphtha* is an imprecise term because various fractions of petroleum may be called that. Among the common naphthas that are used as solvents are coal tar/naphtha and petroleum/naphtha. Naphthas are used as solvents for asphalts, road tars, pitches, paints, dry-cleaning fluids, in cleansing compounds, in engraving and lithography, rubber cements, and naphtha soaps. Causes upper-respiratory-tract irritation. Although allowed as a food additive, there is no current reported use of the chemical, and therefore, although toxicology information may be available, it is not being updated, according to the FDA.

NAPHTHALENE • A coal tar (*see*) derivative. Used to manufacture dyes, solvents, fungicides, smokeless powder, lubricants, as a moth repellent, and as a topical and internal antiseptic. It has been used as a dusting powder to combat insects on animals. Naphthalene can enter your body through inhalation, skin absorption, ingestion, and eye and skin contact. It may produce damage to the eyes, liver, kidneys, skin, red blood cells, and the central nervous system. Has reportedly caused anemia in infants exposed to clothing and blankets stored in naphthalene mothballs. Can cause allergic contact dermatitis in adults and children.

2-NAPHTHALENTHIOL • Derived from naphthalene (*see*), it has a disagreeable odor. It is used in the manufacture of food additives. The FDA data bank, PAFA (see page 10), has fully up-to-date toxicology information available on this food additive.

NAPHTHYL ANTHRANILATE • A synthetic fruit and grape flavoring agent for beverages, ice cream, ices, baked goods, and candy. The FDA data bank, PAFA, has fully up-to-date toxicology information available on this food additive.

b-NAPHTHYL ETHYL ETHER • White crystals with an orange-blossom odor, used in perfumes, soaps, and flavoring. The FDA data bank, PAFA, has fully up-to-date toxicology information available on this food additive. *See* Nerol.

b-NAPHTHYL METHYL ETHER • White crystals with a menthol odor. Used to perfume soaps. A synthetic berry, fruit, honey, and nut flavoring agent for beverages, ice cream, ices, chewing gum, candy, and baked goods. The FDA data bank, PAFA, has fully up-to-date toxicology information available on this food additive.

NARASIN • An antibiotic in broiler-chicken feed that is used to combat parasites and as a growth stimulant. It is derived from *Streptomyces aureofaciens.* *See* Antibiotics.

NARINGIN EXTRACT • Naringin is in the flowers, fruit, and rind of the grapefruit tree. Most abundant in immature fruit. Extracted from grapefruit peel. Used in bitters, grapefruit, and pineapple flavorings for beverages, ice cream, ices, and liquors. The FDA data bank, PAFA (see page 10), has not yet done a toxicology literature search on this food additive. GRAS.

NASTURTIUM EXTRACT • The extract of the leaves and stems of *Tropaaeolum majus*. A member of the mustard family, it has pungent and tasty leaves. It is rich in vitamins A and C and contains vitamins B and B_2. It is soothing to the skin and supposedly has blood-thinning factors and increases the flow of urine. No known toxicity.

NATAMYCIN • Pimaricin. Natacyn. Myprozine. A fungicide produced from *Streptomyces natalensis* from soil near Pietermaritzburg, South Africa. It is applied to surface cuts and to slices of cheese where standards permit to inhibit mold. FDA residue tolerance is 200 to 300 ppm. Used to treat fungal infections of the eye or eyelid in humans. Potential adverse reactions include swelling around the eyes and "black eyes" from blood gathering there. The FDA data bank, PAFA, has fully up-to-date toxicology information available on this food additive. *See* Antibiotics.

NATURAL • The Federal Trade Commission says that food advertised as "natural" may not contain synthetic or artificial ingredients and may not be more than minimally processed. For example, minimal processing includes such actions as washing or peeling fruits or vegetables; homogenizing milk; canning, bottling, and freezing food; baking bread; aging and roasting meats; and grinding nuts. It does not include processes that, in general, cannot be done in a home kitchen and involve certain types of chemicals or sophisticated technology. Chemically bleached foods, for example, will not qualify as minimally processed.

NATIONAL TOXICOLOGY PROGRAM (NTP) • Under the aegis of the National Institute of Environmental Health Sciences, the NTP tests chemicals for all federal agencies upon request. The program's staff also tests for cancer-causing agents.

N-BUTANE • *See* Butane.

NDGA • *See* Nordihydroguaiaretic Acid.

NEO-DHC • *See* Dihydrochalcones.

NEOFOLINONE • Occurs naturally in oil of lavender, orange leaf (absolute), palma rosa oil, rose, neroli, and oil of petitgrain. Used in citrus, honey, and neroli flavorings for beverages, ice cream, ices, candy, baked goods, chewing gum, gelatin desserts, and puddings. No known toxicity.

NEOHESPERIDINE DIHYDROCHALCONE • *See* Dihydrochalcones.

(*d*)-NEOMENTHOL • A flavoring agent that occurs naturally in Japanese mint oil. Used in mint flavorings for beverages, ice cream, candy, and baked goods. The FDA data bank, PAFA (see page 10), has fully up-to-date toxicology information available on this food additive. *See* Menthol for toxicity.

NEOMYCIN SULFATE • Biosol Veterinary. Otobiotic. Neomix. Sulfate. Bactine First Aid Antibiotic. Campho-Phenique Triple Antibiotic Ointment. Mycitracin Plus Pain Reliever. Mycifradin. Myciguent. Neosporin Ointment. Neosulf. Introduced in 1951, it is one of the most widely used antibiotics for humans. The oral form is used to treat infectious diarrhea caused by *Escherichia coli* (*see*). Among potential adverse reactions: headache, lethargy, ear problems, nausea, vomiting, kidney dysfunction, skin rashes, and hypersensitivity reactions. Interacts with Cephalothin, dimenhydrinate, oral anticoagulants (decreases vitamin K), IV loop diuretics, Cisplatin, methoxyflurane, and other aminoglycoside antibiotics. It is used as an animal drug to treat cattle. FDA residue limits are 0.25 ppm in calves and 0.15 ppm in milk.

NEQUINATE • An animal drug used to treat chickens. FDA residue limit is 0.1 ppm in chickens. A coccidiostat (*see*) added to chicken feed to inhibit or delay the onset of coccidiosis, a common and serious disease of many species that involves intestines and lungs. It has been reported in individuals with AIDS.

NEROL • A primary alcohol used in perfumes, especially in rose and orange-blossom scents. Occurs naturally in oil of lavender, orange leaf, palma rosa oil, rose, neroli, and oil of petitgrain. It is colorless, with the odor of rose. Used in citrus, neroli, and honey flavorings for beverages, ice cream, ices, candy, baked goods, gelatin desserts, puddings, and chewing gum. Similar to turpentine in toxicity. The FDA data bank, PAFA, has fully up-to-date toxicology information available on this food additive.

NEROLI BIGARADE OIL • Used chiefly in cologne and in perfumes. Named for the putative discoverer, Anna Maria de la Tremoille, princess of Nerole (1670). A fragrant, pale yellow essential oil obtained from the flowers of the sour orange tree, *Citrus aurantium*. It darkens upon standing. Used in berry, orange, cola, cherry, spice, and ginger ale flavorings for beverages, ice cream, ices, candy, baked goods, and chewing gum. The FDA data bank, PAFA, has not yet done a toxicology literature search on this food additive. GRAS.

NEROLIDOL • A sesquiterpene alcohol. A straw-colored liquid with an odor similiar to rose and apple. Occurs naturally in balsam Peru and oils of orange flower, neroli, sweet orange, and ylang-ylang. Also made synthetically. Used in perfumery and flavoring. The FDA data bank, PAFA, has fully up-to-date toxicology information available on this food additive. *See* Nerol.

NEROSOL • *See* Nerol.

NERYL ACETATE • A synthetic citrus, fruit, and neroli flavoring for beverages, ice cream, ices, candy, and baked goods. The FDA data bank, PAFA (see page 10), has fully up-to-date toxicology information available on this food additive.

NERYL BUTYRATE • A synthetic berry, chocolate, cocoa, citrus, and fruit flavoring agent for beverages, ice cream, ices, candy, and baked goods. The FDA data bank, PAFA, has fully up-to-date toxicology information available on this food additive.

NERYL FORMATE • Formic Acid. A synthetic berry, citrus, apple, peach, and pineapple flavoring agent for beverages, ice cream, ices, candy, and baked goods. The FDA data bank, PAFA, has fully up-to-date toxicology information available on this food additive. *See* Formic Acid for toxicity.

NERYL ISOBUTYRATE • A synthetic citrus and fruit flavoring agent for beverages, ice cream, ices, candy, and baked goods. The FDA data bank, PAFA, has fully up-to-date toxicology information available on this food additive.

NERYL ISOVALERATE • A synthetic berry, rose, and nut flavoring agent for beverages, ice cream, ices, candy, and baked goods. The FDA data bank, PAFA, has fully up-to-date toxicology information available on this food additive.

NERYL PROPIONATE • A synthetic berry and fruit flavoring agent for beverages, ice cream, ices, candy, and baked goods. The FDA data bank, PAFA, has fully up-to-date toxicology information available on this food additive.

NETSON • *See* Acimeton.

NETTLES • Used in hair tonics and shampoos. It is obtained from a troublesome weed with stingers. It has a long history and was used in folk medicine. Its flesh is rich in minerals and plant hormones, and it supposedly stimulates hair growth and shines and softens hair. Also used to make tomatoes resistant to spoilage, to encourage the growth of strawberries, and to stimulate the fermentation of humus.

NEUTRALIZING AGENT • A substance, such as ammonium bicarbonate or tartaric acid (*see both*), used to adjust the acidity or alkalinity of certain foods. *See* pH.

NIACIN • Nicotinic Acid. Nicotinamide. White or yellow crystalline powder, it is an essential nutrient that participates in many energy-yielding reactions and aids in the maintenance of a normal nervous system. It is a component of the vitamin B complex. Added to prepared breakfast cereals, peanut butter, baby cereals, enriched flours, macaroni, noodles, breads, rolls, cornmeal, corn grits, and farina. Niacin is present in significant amounts in liver, yeast, meat, legumes, and whole cereals. Recommended daily intake is eighteen to nineteen milligrams for men and thirteen to fifteen milligrams for women. The final report to the FDA of the Select Committee on GRAS Substances stated in 1980 that it should continue its GRAS status with no limitations other than good manufacturing practices. The FDA data bank, PAFA, has fully up-to-date toxicology information available on this food additive.

NIACINAMIDE • Nicotinamide. Vitamin B. Used as a skin stimulant. A white or yellow, crystalline, odorless powder used to treat pellagra, a vitamin-deficiency disease, and in the assay of enzymes for substrates. No known skin toxicity. The final report to the FDA of the Select Committee on GRAS Substances stated in 1980 that it should continue its GRAS status with no limitations other than good manufacturing practices. The FDA data bank, PAFA (see page 10), has fully up-to-date toxicology information available on this food additive.

NIACINAMIDE ASCORBATE • A complex of ascorbic acid (*see*) and niacinamide (*see*). Occurs as a practically odorless yellow powder that may gradually darken on exposure to air. Used as a dietary supplement. *See* Niacin.

NICARBAZIN • Nicoxin. Nicrazin. An animal drug used in chicken feed to inhibit or delay coccidiosis (*see*). FDA residue limit is 4 ppm in uncooked muscle, liver, skin, and neck of chickens.

NICKEL • Lustrous, white, hard metal that occurs in the earth that is used as a catalyst for the hydrogenation (*see*) of fat. Nickel may cause dermatitis in sensitive individuals, and ingestion of large amounts of the soluble salts may cause nausea, vomiting, and diarrhea. The final report to the FDA of the Select Committee on GRAS Substances stated in 1980 that it should continue its GRAS status with no limitations other than good manufacturing practices. The FDA data bank, PAFA (see page 10), is currently searching the toxicology literature concerning this additive.

NICKEL SULFATE • Occurs in the earth's crust as a salt of nickel. Obtained as green or blue crystals and used chiefly in nickel plating. Used in hair dyes and astringents. It has a sweet, astringent taste. Used as a mineral supplement up to one milligram per day. It acts as an irritant and causes vomiting when swallowed. Its systemic effects include blood-vessel, brain, and kidney damage and nervous depression. Frequently causes skin rash when used in cosmetics. The lethal dose varies widely. The dose in guinea pigs is sixty-two milligrams per kilogram.

NICOTINAMIDE • *See* Niacin.

NICOTINIC ACID • *See* Niacin.

NIGER GUTTA • *Ficus platyphylla del.* The coagulated latex from a tree that is mixed with chicle (*see*) to make chewing gum. The FDA data bank, PAFA, has fully up-to-date toxicology information available on this food additive.

NIOSH • National Institute of Occupational Safety and Health.

NISIN PREPARATION • Crystals from *Streptococcus lactis* used as a preservative and antimicrobial agent in cheese spreads. FDA limits residue to 250 ppm in the finished product. It is also used in canned vegetables and fruit. There is no reported use of the chemical and no toxicology information is available, according to the FDA's data bank, PAFA (see page 10).

NITER • *See* Nitrate.

NITRATE • Potassium and Sodium. *Potassium nitrate,* also known as salt-peter and niter, is used as a color fixative in cured meats. *Sodium nitrate,* also called Chile saltpeter, is used as a color fixative in cured meats. Both nitrates are used in matches and to improve the burning properties of tobacco. They combine with natural stomach saliva and food substances (secondary amines) to create nitrosamines, powerful cancer-causing agents. Nitrosamines have also been found in fish treated with nitrates. Researchers at the Michael Reese Medical Center's Department of Pathology in Chicago induced cancer in mice by giving single doses of nitrosamine (either 0.315 or 0.625 micrograms) for each gram of the animal's weight. (A microgram is one-millionth of a gram.) This is in contrast to the way other researchers have induced cancer in laboratory animals with nitrosamines, by using repeated small doses or single large doses. The tumors that developed were analogous to human liver tumors. Nitrosamines caused pancreatic cancer in hamsters similar to human pancreatic cancers. Nitrates have caused deaths from methemoglobinemia (it cuts off oxygen to the brain). Because nitrates are difficult to control in processing, they are being used less often. However, they are still employed in long-curing processes, such as for country hams as well as dried, cured, and fermented sausages. In the early seventies, baby-food manufacturers voluntarily removed nitrates from their products. The U.S. Department of Agriculture, which has jurisdiction over meats, and the FDA, which has jurisdiction over processed poultry, have asked manufacturers to show that the use of nitrates is safe. Efforts to ban nitrates have failed because manufacturers claim there is no good substitute for them.

Nitrates change into nitrites on exposure to air. Our major intake of nitrates in foodstuffs comes from vegetables, water supplies, or from nitrates used as additives in meat-curing. Nitrates are natural constituents of plants. They occur in small amounts in fruits but are high in certain vegetables—spinach, beets, radishes, eggplant, celery, lettuce, collards, and turnip greens—as high as more than 3,000 ppm. The two most important factors responsible for large accumulations of nitrates in vegetables are the high levels of fertilization with nitrate fertilizers and the tendency of the species to accumulate nitrate. The FDA data bank, PAFA (see page 10), has fully up-to-date toxicology information available on this food additive.

NITRITE • Potassium and Sodium. *Potassium nitrite* is used as a color fixative in the more than $125-billion-a-year cured-meat business. *Sodium nitrite* has the peculiar ability to react chemically with the myoglobin molecule and impart red-bloodedness to processed meats, to convey tanginess to the palate, and to resist the growth of *Clostridium botulinum* spores. It is used as a color fixative in cured meats, bacon, bologna, frankfurters, deviled ham, meat spread, potted meats, spiced ham, Vienna sausages, smoke-cured tuna fish products, and in smoke-cured shad and salmon. Nitrite combines with natural stomach and food chemicals (secondary amines) to create nitrosamines, powerful cancer-causing agents. The U.S. Department of Agriculture, which has jurisdiction over processed meats, and the FDA, which has jurisdiction over processed poultry, asked manufacturers to show that the use of nitrites was safe and that nitrosamines were not formed in the products as preliminary tests had showed in bacon. Processors claimed there was no chemical substitute for nitrite. They said alternative processing methods could be used, but the products would not look or taste the same. Baby-food manufacturers voluntarily removed nitrites from baby foods in the early seventies. The FDA found that adding vitamin C to processed meats prevents or at least retards the formation of nitrosamines. In May 1978, the USDA announced plans to require bacon manufacturers to reduce their use of nitrite from 150 to 120 ppm and to use preservatives that retard nitrosamine formation. Processors would have been required to keep nitrosamine levels to 10 ppm under the interim plan.

But in August 1978 a new concern about nitrite was raised. The USDA and the FDA issued a joint announcement that the substance had been directly linked to cancer by a Massachusetts Institute of Technology study. That work was later disputed. In 1982, amyl and butyl nitrites used by homosexual men were linked to Kaposi's sarcoma and other abnormalities of the immune system.

Researchers at Michael Reese Medical Center linked infinitesimal amounts of nitrite to cancer in young laboratory mice, especially in the liver and lungs. Dr. Koshlya Rijhsinghani and her colleagues gave single doses (either 0.315 or 0.625 micrograms) of nitrosamine for each gram of the animal's weight. This method differs from the way other researchers have induced cancer in mice with nitrosamines by repeated small doses or single large doses. Nitrosamines also produce cancer in hamsters similar to pancreatic cancers in humans.

In 1980, the FDA revoked its proposed phaseout because manufacturers said there was no adequate substitute for nitrites. In 1977, Germany banned nitrites and nitrates except in certain species of fish. However, a Committee on Nitrite and Alternative Curing Agents in Food, formed by the National Research Council in the United States, concluded that there was no single agent or process that could replace nitrite completely: "Several chemical and physical treatments appear to be comparable in inhibiting outgrowth of *Clostridium botulinum* spores in types of meat products, but none confers the color and flavor that consumers have come to expect in nitrite-cured meats." Until the all-purpose agent comes along or until consumer preference changes, the best compromise will probably be continued use of nitrite in conventional amounts with vitamins C and E added to block formation of nitrosamines, or the use of smaller amounts of nitrite in combination with biological acidification, irradiation, or the chemicals potassium sorbate, sodium hypophosphite, or fumarate esters, the committee said.

To reduce nitrosamines in bacon, the U.S. Department of Agriculture requires meat packers to add sodium ascorbate or sodium erythrobate (vitamin Cs) to the curing brine. This offers only a partial barrier because ascorbate is soluble in water and its activity in fat is limited. Vitamin E, however, inhibits nitrosation in fatty tissues. The Committee suggested that both C and E be added to provide more complete protection. The FDA data bank, PAFA (see page 10), has fully up-to-date toxicology information available on this food additive.

If you must eat nitrite-laced meats, include a food or drink high in vitamin C at the same time—for example, orange juice, grapefruit juice, cranberry juice, or lettuce.

NITRO- • A prefix denoting one atom of nitrogen and two of oxygen. *Nitro* also denotes a class of dyes derived from coal tars. Nitro dyes can be absorbed through the skin. When absorbed or ingested, they can cause a lack of oxygen in the blood. Chronic exposure may cause liver damage. *See* FD and C Colors.

3-NITRO-4-HYDROXYPHENYLARSONIC ACID • Roxarsone. Tufts of pale yellow needles used to control intestinal infections and to improve growth and feed efficiency. FDA residue limits are 0.5 ppm as arsenic in muscle meat and eggs of chickens; 2 ppm as arsenic in edible byproducts of turkey and swine; and 0.5 ppm as arsenic in muscle tissue and byproducts other than liver and kidney. *See* Arsenic.

NITROFURAZONE • Aldomycin. Furacillin. Coxistat. A once widely used antibiotic in animal feed for pigs and poultry. FDA withdrew permission for its use in 1991. A human sensitizer. International Agency for Research on Cancer (IARC) review and EPA Genetic Toxicology Program (*see both*). Potential adverse reactions include kidney toxicity, redness, itching, burning, water retention, severe blistering, and allergic skin rash.

3-([5-NITROFURFURYLIDENE]AMINO)2-OXAZOLIDONE • Bifuron. Corizium. Diafuron. Enterotoxon. Furazone. Furazolidone. Furoxone. A widely used antiprotozoal (*see*) drug in animals, particularly for pigs. It is also a human medication for diarrhea and enteritis caused by *Giardia lamblia* and *Vibrio cholerae*. Taken by mouth, it works inside the intestines to counteract cholera, colitis, and/or diarrhea caused by the bacteria. Potential adverse reactions include joint pain, fever, itching, skin rash or redness, nausea, vomiting, diarrhea, stomach pain, headache, and sore throat. Severe high blood pressure and other undesirable side effects may occur if combined with MAO inhibitors (certain antidepressants), ephedrine, or tricyclic antidepressants, or the ingestion of aged cheese, caviar, yeast or protein extracts, fava or broad beans, smoked or pickled meat, poultry or fish, fermented sausages (bologna, pepperoni, salami, summer sausage) or other fermented meat, or any overripe fruit. You should not drink dark beer, red wine, sherry, or liqueurs. If the human medication is taken, the above foods and drinks are to be avoided for at least two weeks after stopping furazolidone. The FDA says that residues must be zero in meat sent to market, but who can do adequate testing for its presence all the time?

NITROGEN • A gas that is 78 percent of the atmosphere by volume and essential to all living things. Odorless. Used as a preservative for cosmetics, in which it is nontoxic. In high concentrations, it can asphyxiate. Toxic concentration in humans is 90 ppm; in mice, 250 ppm. GRAS. The FDA data bank, PAFA (see page 10), has fully up-to-date toxicology information available on this food additive.

NITROGEN OXIDES • Nitrous Oxide (*see*), Nitric Oxide, Nitrogen Dioxide, Nitrogen Trioxide, Nitrogen Pentoxide. A bleaching agent for cereal flour, *nitrogen dioxide* is a deadly poison gas. Short exposure may cause little pain or discomfort, but several days later, fluid retention and inflammation of the lungs can cause death. About 200 ppm can be fatal. There is no reported use of the chemical and no toxicology information is available, according to the FDA's data bank, PAFA.

NITROMIDE WITH SULFANITRAN • A feed additive used in chicken feed. Both ingredients are antibacterials. FDA tolerance is zero residue for nitromide in uncooked edible chicken.

4-NITROPHENYLARSONIC ACID • Nitarsone. An animal-feed drug used to combat intestinal parasites chiefly affecting turkeys, chickens, and other birds. The FDA says the feed additive is not to be used in excess of the amount reasonably required to accomplish the intended effect. An arsenic compound, it is on the Community Right-To-Know List (*see*). Poison by ingestion.

NITROSYL CHLORIDE • Nonexplosive, corrosive, reddish yellow gas, intensely irritating to the eyes, skin, and mucosa. Used as a bleaching agent for cereal flour. Inhalation may cause pulmonary edema and hemorrhage. There is no reported use of the chemical and no toxicology information is available, according to the FDA's data bank, PAFA (see page 10).

NITROUS OXIDE • Laughing Gas. A whipping agent for whipped cosmetic creams and a propellant in pressurized cosmetic containers. Slightly sweetish odor and taste. Colorless. Used in rocket fuel. Less irritating than other nitrogen oxides but narcotic in high concentrations, and it can asphyxiate. GRAS.

NOAEL • No Observed Adverse Effect Level. See NOEL.

NOEL • Test results that show a given dose of a substance has a No-Observed-Effect Level or sometimes called a No-Observed-Adverse-Effect Level. The safety factor usually has a value of 100 in the case of a NOEL derived from long-term animal study, on the assumption that humans are ten times as sensitive as the test animal used and that there is a ten fold range of sensitivity within the human population.

NONADIENAL • Cucumber Aldehyde or Alcohol. A flavoring agent used in various foods. A moderate skin irritant. The FDA data bank, PAFA, has fully up-to-date toxicology information available on this food additive.

g-NONALACTONE • Aldehyde C-18. Prunolide. Coconut Aldehyde. A synthetic berry, coconut, fruit, and nut flavoring agent for beverages, ice cream, ices, candy, baked goods, gelatin desserts, chewing gum, and icings. The FDA data bank, PAFA, has fully up-to-date toxicology information available on this food additive.

NONALOL • *See* Nonyl Alcohol.

NONANAL • Pelargonic Aldehyde. Colorless liquid with an orange-rose odor. A synthetic flavoring that occurs naturally in lemon oil, rose, sweet orange oil, mandarin, lime, orris, and ginger. Used in lemon and fruit flavorings for beverages, ice cream, ices, candy, baked goods, chewing gum, and gelatin desserts. Used also in perfumery. A severe skin irritant. The FDA data bank, PAFA (see page 10), has fully up-to-date toxicology information available on this food additive. *See* Aldehyde, Aliphatic.

1,3-NONANEDIOL ACETATE • Colorless to slightly yellow mixture of isomers used in synthetic berry and fruit flavoring for beverages, ice cream, ices, candy, and baked goods. No known toxicity. *See* Nonanoic Acid and Acetic Acid.

NONANNOYL 4-HYDROXY-3-METHOXYBENZYLAMIDE • Perlargonyl Vanillylamide. A synthetic spice flavoring agent for candy, baked goods, and condiments. The FDA data bank, PAFA, has fully up-to-date toxicology information available on this food additive.

NONANOIC ACID • Pelargonic Acid. Nonoic acid. Nonglic Acid. A colorless, oily liquid that is insoluble in water, it occurs in the oil of pelargonium plants such as the geranium. Used in berry, fruit, nut, and spice flavorings for beverages, ice cream, ices, candy, baked goods, and shortenings. It is practically insoluble in water and is used in producing salts and in the manufacture of lacquers. Can be irritating to the skin. The FDA data bank, PAFA, has fully up-to-date toxicology information available on this food additive.

2-NONANOL • *See* Nonyl Alcohol.

3-NONANON-1-YL-ACETATE • A synthetic berry, rose, fruit, and cheese flavoring agent for beverages, ice cream, ices, candy, and baked goods. Although allowed as a food additive, there is no current reported use of the chemical, and therefore, although toxicology information may be available, the FDA is not updating it.

2-NONENAL • The FDA data bank, PAFA (see page 10), has fully up-to-date toxicology information available on this food additive. *See* Isoamyl Nonanoate.

NONFAT DRY MILK • The solid residue produced by removing the water from defatted cow's milk. Comparisons between whole and dry milk: 100 grams fluid whole milk contains 68 calories; 87 grams of water; 3.5 grams of protein; 3.5 grams of fat; 0.7 gram of ash; 4.9 grams of carbohydrate; 118 milligrams of calcium; 93 milligrams of phosphorous; 0.1 milligram of iron; 50 milligrams of sodium; 140 milligrams of potassium; 160 international units of vitamin A; 0.04 milligram of vitamin B_1; 0.17 milligram of B_2; 0.1 milligram of nicotinic acid; and 1 milligram of vitamin C. Total calories for one cup of milk is 166. Nonfat dry milk has 362 calories per 100 grams; 3.5 grams of water; 35.6 grams of protein; 1 gram of fat; 7.9 grams of ash; total carbohydrates, 52 grams; 1,300 milligrams of calcium; 1,030 milligrams of phosphorus; 0.6 milligrams of iron; 77 milligrams of sodium; 1,130 milligrams of potassium; 40 international units of vitamin A; 0.35 milligram of vitamin B_1; 196 milligrams of vitamin B_2; 1.1 milligrams of nicotinic acid; and 7 milligrams of vitamin C. The total calories for a tablespoon of dry nonfat milk is 28. *See* Milk.

NONNUTRITIVE SWEETENERS • Sugar substitutes that contain no calories. Saccharin and cyclamates (*see both*) are examples.

NONYL ACETATE • An ester produced by the reaction of nonyl alcohol and acetic acid (*see*). Pungent odor suggestive of mushrooms, but when diluted, it resembles the odor of gardenias. Insoluble in water. Used for beverages, ice cream, ices, candy, and baked goods. The FDA data bank, PAFA (see page 10), has fully up-to-date toxicology information available on this food additive.

NONYL ALCOHOL • Nonalol. A synthetic flavoring, colorless to yellow with a citronella-oil odor. Occurs in oil of orange. Used in butter, citrus, peach, and pineapple flavorings for beverages, ice cream, ices, candy, and chewing gum. Also used in the manufacture of artificial lemon oil. In experimental animals it has caused central nervous system and liver damage. The FDA data bank, PAFA, has fully up-to-date toxicology information available on this food additive.

NONYL CARBINOL • *See* 1-Decanol.

NONYL ISOVALERATE • A synthetic fruit and hazelnut flavoring agent for beverages, ice cream, ices, candy, and baked goods. The FDA data bank, PAFA, has fully up-to-date toxicology information available on this food additive.

y-NONYL LACTONE • Yellowish to almost colorless liquid with a coconut-like odor. Used in perfumery and flavors. *See* Nonyl Alcohol.

NONYL NONANOATE • Nonyl Pelargonate. Liquid with a floral odor used in flavors, perfumes, and organic synthesis. *See* Nonyl Alcohol.

NOOTKATONE • From a cypress tree grown in northwest Washington State and British Columbia. It is named after the Nootka people, who populated the area. It smells like cedar. It is used in flavorings and perfumes. The FDA data bank, PAFA (see page 10), has fully up-to-date toxicology information available on this food additive.

NOPINENE • *See* b-Pinene.

NORBIXIN • From the seeds of *Bixa zorellana,* used in a suspension of vegetable oil for coloring in food. *See* Annatto.

NORDIHYDROGUAIARETIC ACID • NDGA. An antioxidant used in brilliantines and other fat-based cosmetics. Occurs in resinous exudates of many plants. White or grayish white crystals. Lard containing 0.01 percent NDGA stored at room temperature for nineteen months in diffuse daylight showed no appreciable rancidity or color change. It was used as an antioxidant in prepared pie-crust mix, candy, lard, butter, ice cream, and pressure-dispensed whipped cream. Canada banned the additive in food in 1967 after it was shown to cause cysts and kidney damage in a large percentage of rats tested. The FDA removed it from the GRAS list of food additives in 1968 and prohibited its use in products over which it has control. The U.S. Department of Agriculture, which controls antioxidants in lard and animal shortenings, banned it in 1971.

NORFLURAZON • An herbicide used in hops and other feeds for animals. FDA tolerance limits are 1 ppm in dried citrus molasses, 3 ppm in citrus pulp, and 0.1 ppm in milk and fat, meat, and meat byproducts of cattle, goats, hogs, poultry, and sheep.

NORVALINE • A protein amino acid (*see*), soluble in hot water and insoluble in alcohol. *See* Valeric Acid.

NOTE • A distinct odor or flavor. *Top* note is the first note normally perceived when a flavor is smelled or tasted; usually volatile and gives "identity." *Middle* or *main* note is the substance of the flavor, the main characteristic. *Bottom* note is what is left when top and middle notes disappear. It is the residue when the aroma or flavoring evaporates.

NOVATONE • *See* Acetanisole.

NOVOBIOCIN • Albamycin. An antibiotic from *Streptomyces niveus,* it is used in animal feed for beef, chicken, duck, and turkey. FDA residue limits are 0.1 in milk, 1 ppm in cattle, chickens, turkeys, and ducks. Moderately toxic by ingestion.

NTP • Abbreviation for National Toxicology Program (*see*).

NUTMEG • A natural flavoring extracted from the dried ripe seed of *Myristica fragrans houtt.* Used in cola, vermouth, sausage, eggnog, and nutmeg flavorings for beverages, ice cream, ices, baked goods (2,000 ppm), condiments, meats, and pickles. The *oil* is used in loganberry, chocolate, lemon, cola, apple, grape, muscatel, rum, sausage, eggnog, pistachio, root beer, cinnamon, dill, ginger, mace, nutmeg, and vanilla flavorings for beverages, ice cream, ices, candy, baked goods, chewing gum, condiments, meats, syrups, and icings. In common household use since the Middle Ages, nutmeg is still a potentially toxic substance. Ingestion of as little as three whole seeds or five to fifteen grams of grated spice can cause flushing of the skin, irregular heart rhythm, absence of salivation, and central nervous system excitation, including euphoria and hallucinations. GRAS. The FDA data bank, PAFA (see page 10), has not yet done a toxicology literature search on this food additive.

NUTRASWEET • *See* Aspartame.

NYSTATIN • Mycostatin. Nadostine. Nilstat. Nystex. O-V Statin. Yellow to light tan powder with a cereallike odor. It is used in feed for poultry and pigs. FDA requires zero residue in eggs, swine, and poultry. Antifungal medication introduced in 1954. It is used in human medicine to treat oral, vaginal, and intestinal infections caused by *Candida albicans* (Moniliales) and other *Candida* species. In cream or ointment it is used to treat infant eczema, itching around the anus or vagina, and localized forms of candidiasis. Potential adverse reactions include nausea, vomiting, and diarrhea. Skin applications may cause occasional contact dermatitis from preservatives in some formulations. Nystatin is in the EPA Genetic Toxicology Program. Moderately toxic by ingestion. Causes birth defects in experimental animals.

O

OAK BARK EXTRACT • Oak Chip Extract. The extract from the white oak used in bitters and whiskey flavorings for beverages, ice cream, ices, candy, whiskey (1,000 ppm), and baked goods. Contains tannic acid (*see*) and is exceedingly astringent. In a wash, the Indians used it for sore eyes and as a tonic. Used in astringents in herbal cosmetics. The FDA data bank, PAFA (see page 10), has not yet done a toxicology literature search on this food additive.

OAK CHIP EXTRACT • *See* Oak Bark Extract.

OAKMOSS, ABSOLUTE • Any one of several lichens, *Evernia* spp., that grow on oak trees and yield a resin for use as a fixative (*see*) in perfumery. Stable green liquid with a long-lasting characteristic odor. Soluble in alcohol. Used in fruit, honey, and spice flavorings for beverages, ice cream, ices, candy, baked goods, gelatin desserts, condiments, and soups. A common allergen in aftershave lotions. The FDA data bank, PAFA, has not yet done a toxicology literature search on this food additive.

OAKWOOD, ENGLISH • *Quercus robur.* Used as a coloring. The FDA data bank, PAFA, has not yet done a toxicology literature search on this food additive.

OAT BRAN • The broken coat of oats, *Avena sativa. See* Oat Flour.

OAT EXTRACT • The extract of the seeds of oats, *Avena sativa. See* Oat Flour.

OAT FLOUR • Flour from the cereal grain that is an important crop grown in the temperate regions. Light yellowish or brown to weak greenish or yellow powder. Slight odor; starchy taste. Makes a bland ointment for cosmetic treatments, including soothing baths. No known toxicity.

OAT GUM • A plant extract used as a thickener and stabilizer in foods, such as pasteurized cheese spread and cream cheese, and in cosmetics. Also an antioxidant in butter, creams, and candy up to 1.5 percent. In foods, it can cause an allergic reaction, including diarrhea and intestinal gas. There is no reported use of the chemical and no toxicology information is available, according to the FDA's data bank, PAFA (see page 10).

OATMEAL • Meal obtained by grinding of oats from which the husks have been removed.

OCIMENE • A terpene obtained from sweet-basil oil. Used in flavors and perfumes. The FDA data bank, PAFA, has fully up-to-date toxicology information available on this food additive.

OCIMUM BASILICUM • *See* Basil Extract.

OCOTEA CYMBARUM OIL • An oil obtained by steam distillation from the wood of a Brazilian tree. Used chiefly as a source of safrole (*see*), a natural oil, and as a substitute for sassafras oil (*see* Sassafras Bark Extract). No known toxicity.

OCTADECANOIC ACID • Abracol S.L.G. Dermagine. Distearin. Orbon. Stearic Acid, Monoester With Glycerol. Pure white or cream-colored, waxlike solid used as a coating agent, emulsifier, lubricant, solvent, and texturizer in baked cooks, shortening, fruits, ice cream, nuts, peanut butter, puddings, and whipped toppings. *See* Stearic Acid.

1-OCTADECANOL • *See* Sterol.

9-OCTADECENOIC ACID • *See* Oleic Acid.

OCTAFLUOROCYCLOBUTANE • A nonflammable gas. A refrigerant and propellant and aerating agent in foamed or sprayed food products. Used alone or in combination with carbon dioxide or nitrous oxide (*see both*). Nontoxic when used alone.

OCTAHYDROCOUMARIN • One of the newer flavoring agents. The FDA data bank, PAFA (see page 10), has not yet done a toxicology literature search on this food additive. *See* Coumarin.

OCTALACTONE • D and G. *See* Lactic Acid. The FDA data bank, PAFA, has fully up-to-date toxicology information available on this food additive.

OCTANAL • Octanaldehyde. Found in many essential oils (*see*) including a number of citrus oils, it is a colorless to light yellow liquid with an orange odor. It is used as a flavoring agent in many foods. Mildly toxic by ingestion. The FDA data bank, PAFA, has fully up-to-date toxicology information available on this food additive.

OCTANOIC ACID • Colorless, oily liquid with a bad odor, derived from coconut. It is used as an antimicrobial agent in other food additives and as a defoaming agent, flavoring agent, and lubricant. It is used in baked goods, soft candies, cheese, fats, frozen dairy desserts, gelatins, meat products, oils, packaging materials, puddings, and snack foods. Mildly toxic by ingestion and a skin irritant, it has caused mutations in experimental animals. FDA residue limits are 0.0013 percent in baked goods; 0.04 percent in frozen dairy desserts; 0.005 percent in meat products and soft candies; 0.016 percent in snack foods; 0.001 percent in other food categories when used in accordance with good manufacturing practice. GRAS as an indirect additive. The FDA data bank, PAFA (see page 10), has fully up-to-date toxicology information available on this food additive.

1-OCTANOL • Caprylic Alcohol. Used in the manufacture of flavorings and perfumes. Colorless, viscous liquid, soluble in water, insoluble in oil. Occurs naturally in oil of lavender, oil of lemon, oil of lime, oil of lovage, orange peel, and coconut oil. It has a penetrating, aromatic scent. May cause skin rash.

3-OCTANOL • Colorless liquid with a strong nutty odor, it is used as a flavoring agent in various foods. It is a moderate skin and eye irritant. The FDA data bank, PAFA, has fully up-to-date toxicology information available on this food additive.

2-OCTANONE • A synthetic fruit and cheese flavoring agent for beverages, ice cream, ices, candy, and baked goods. The FDA data bank, PAFA, has fully up-to-date toxicology information available on this food additive.

3-OCTANONE • A synthetic flavoring that occurs naturally in oil of lavender. Used in citrus, coffee, peach, cheese, and spice flavorings for beverages, ice cream, ices, candy, and baked goods. No known toxicity.

OCTOXYNOL • Waxlike emulsifier, dispersing agent, and detergent derived from phenol (*see*) and used as a surfactant. The numbers from -1 to -70 after the additive signify the viscosity.

1-OCTEN-3-OL • A synthetic fruit and spice flavoring agent for beverages, ice cream, ices, candy, baked goods, condiments, and soups. The FDA data bank, PAFA (see page 10), has fully up-to-date toxicology information available on this food additive.

1-OCTENYL SUCCINIC ANHYDRIDE • A starch modifier incorporating up to 3 percent of the weight of the product. Limited to 2 percent in combination with aluminum sulfate (*see*). There is no reported use of the chemical and no toxicology information is available, according to the FDA's data bank, PAFA.

OCTODECANOIC ACID • *See* Stearic Acid.

OCTYL ACETATE • Acetic Acid, Octyl Ester. A colorless liquid with an orange-jasmine scent, it is used as a flavoring agent in various foods. Moderately toxic by ingestion. The FDA data bank, PAFA, has fully up-to-date toxicology information available on this food additive.

OCTYL ALCOHOL, SYNTHETIC • Caprylic Alcohol. Colorless, viscous liquid soluble in water and insoluble in oil. Used in the manufacture of perfumes and food additives. Occurs naturally in the oils of lavender, lemon, lime, lovage, orange peel, and coconut. It has a penetrating aromatic scent. Moderately toxic by ingestion. A skin irritant. Has caused mutations in experimental animals. There is no reported use of the chemical and no toxicology information is available, according to the FDA's data bank, PAFA.

_n_-OCTYL BICYCLOHEPTENE DICARBOXIMIDE • Dimethyl Carbate. Pyrodone. Octacide 264. A widely used insecticide in various foods. FDA residue tolerance is 10 ppm. Moderately toxic by ingestion and skin contact. Has caused adverse reproductive effects in experimental animals. Large doses may cause central nervous system stimulation followed by depression.

OCTYL BUTYRATE • Butyric Acid. A synthetic strawberry, butter, citrus, fruit, cherry, melon, peach, pineapple, pumpkin, and liquor flavoring agent for beverages, ice cream, ices, candy, and baked goods. The FDA data bank, PAFA (see page 10), has fully up-to-date toxicology information available on this food additive.

OCTYL FORMATE • Formic Acid. A synthetic flavoring, colorless with a fruity odor. Used in citrus and fruit flavorings for beverages, ice cream, ices, candy, and baked goods. The FDA data bank, PAFA, has fully up-to-date toxicology information available on this food additive. *See* Formic Acid for toxicity.

OCTYL GALLATE • A salt of gallic acid made from the tannins of nutgalls or from the *Penicillium glaucum* or *Aspergillus niger,* it is used as an antioxidant in margarine with a limit of 0.02 percent set by the FDA. Mildly toxic by ingestion. When heated to decomposition, it emits acrid smoke and irritating fumes. The FDA data bank, PAFA, has fully up-to-date toxicology information available on this food additive.

OCTYL HEPTANOATE • A synthetic citrus, coconut, and fruit flavoring for beverages, ice cream, ices, candy, and baked goods. The FDA data bank, PAFA (see page 10), has fully up-to-date toxicology information available on this food additive.

OCTYL ISOBUTYRATE • Isobutyric Acid. A synthetic citrus, fruit, melon, peach, liquor, and wine flavoring agent for beverages, ice cream, ices, candy, and baked goods. The FDA data bank, PAFA, has fully up-to-date toxicology information available on this food additive.

OCTYL ISOVALERATE • Isovaleric Acid. A synthetic berry, butter, citrus, apple, cherry, grape, honey, and nut flavoring agent for beverages, ice cream, ices, candy, and baked goods. The FDA data bank, PAFA, has fully up-to-date toxicology information available on this food additive.

OCTYL OCTANOATE • Octanoic Acid. A synthetic citrus, grape, and pineapple flavoring agent for beverages, ice cream, ices, candy, and baked goods. The FDA data bank, PAFA, has fully up-to-date toxicology information available on this food additive.

OCTYL PHENYLACETATE • Phenylacetic Acid. A synthetic berry, apple, banana, grape, peach, pear, and honey flavoring agent for beverages, ice cream, ices, candy, and baked goods. The FDA data bank, PAFA (see page 10), has fully up-to-date toxicology information available on this food additive.

OCTYL PROPIONATE • Propionic Acid. A synthetic berry, citrus, and melon flavoring agent for beverages, ice cream, ices, candy, and baked goods. The FDA data bank, PAFA, has fully up-to-date toxicology information available on this food additive.

1-OCTYL SUCCINIC ANHYDRIDE • Modifier for food starch. *See* Modified Starch.

ODORLESS LIGHT PETROLEUM HYDROCARBONS • Liquids with a faint odor used as coating agents, defoamers, and in insecticide formulations for beet sugar, eggs, fruits, pickles, vegetables, vinegar, and wine. *See* Petroleum.

OIL OF NIOBE • *See* Methyl Benzoate.

OIL OF SASSAFRAS • Used in dentifrices, perfumes, and soaps to correct disagreeable odors. It is 80 percent safrole. May produce allergic reactions in sensitive persons. It is illegal for use in foods.

OIL OF SASSAFRAS, SAFROLE FREE • This flavoring agent without the safrole is permitted in foods.

OLEAMIDE • An agent that prevents sticking to pans. *See* Oleic Acid.

OLEANDOMYCIN HYDROCHLORIDE • An antibiotic produced by *Streptomyces antibioticus* used in animal feed for chickens, swine, and turkeys. Moderately toxic by ingestion. FDA requires zero residue in chickens, turkeys, and swine for market.

OLEIC ACID • Obtained from various animal and vegetable fats and oils. Colorless. On exposure to air, it turns a yellow to brown color and develops a rancid odor. Used as a defoaming agent; as a synthetic butter, cheese, and spice flavoring agent for beverages, ice cream, ices, candy, baked goods, and condiments; as a lubricant and binder in various foods; and as a component in the manufacture of food additives. Used in preparations of soft soap, permanent-wave solutions, vanishing creams, brushless shave creams, cold creams, brilliantines, nail polish, toilet soaps, and lipsticks. Possesses better skin-penetrating properties than vegetable oils. Also employed in liquid makeup, liquid lip rouge, shampoos, and preshave lotions. Low oral toxicity but is mildly irritating to the skin. It caused tumors when injected under the skin of rabbits in 3,120-mg doses per kilogram of body weight and when painted on the skin of mice in 62-mg doses per kilogram of body weight. The final report to the FDA of the Select Committee on GRAS Substances stated in 1980 that it should continue its GRAS status as an additive and for packaging with no limitations other than good manufacturing practices. The FDA data bank, PAFA (see page 10), has fully up-to-date toxicology information available on this food additive.

OLEINIC ACID • *See* Oleic Acid.

OLEORESIN • A natural plant product consisting of essential oil and resin extracted from a substance, such as ginger, by means of alcohol, ether, or acetone. The solvent alcohol, for example, is percolated through the ginger. Although the oleoresin is similar to the spice from which it is derived, it is not identical because not all the substances in the spice are extracted. Oleoresins are usually more uniform and more potent than the original product. The normal use range of an oleoresin is from one-fifth to one-twentieth of the corresponding amount of the crude spice. Certain spices are extracted as oleoresins for color rather than for flavor. Examples of color-intensifying oleoresins are those from paprika and turmeric (*see both*).

OLESTRA • Sucrose Polyester. A fat substitute developed by Procter and Gamble that cannot be digested. It has no calories. It can supposedly replace conventional fats in french fries and baked desserts. However, it reportedly causes tumors and liver changes in animals.

OLIBANUM EXTRACT • Frankincense Extract. The extract of *Boswellia carterri* of various species. The volatile, distilled oil from the gum resin of a plant found in Ethiopia, Egypt, and Arabia. It was one of the gifts of the Magi. It is used in cola, fruit, and spice flavorings for beverages, ice cream, ices, candy, and baked goods. The FDA data bank, PAFA (see page 10), has not yet done a toxicology literature search on this food additive.

OLIVE OIL • A monounsaturated fat (*see*). Superior to mineral oils in penetrating power. Used in brilliantine hairdressings, emollients, eyelash oils, lipsticks, nail-polish removers, shampoos, soaps, face powders, hair colorings, and antiwrinkle and massage oils. It is a pale yellow or greenish fixed oil obtained from ripe olives grown around the Mediterranean Sea. May cause allergic reactions. Has been reported to be beneficial to blood cholesterol.

OMEGA-3 FATTY ACIDS • Found in fish oils, reported to lower fats in the blood and thus reduce the risk of coronary artery disease. *See* Fish Oil.

ONION EXTRACT • Extract of the bulbs of the onion *Allium cepa,* discovered in Asia. Used in meat, onion, and spice flavorings for beverages, ice cream, ices, baked goods, condiments, meats, and pickles. Skin irritant. When heated to decomposition, it emits acrid smoke and irritating fumes. GRAS. The FDA data bank, PAFA, has not yet done a toxicology literature search on this food additive.

OPOPANAX • Bisabol. An odorous, myrrh-type gum resin from a southern-European or African herb. Once used in medicine. Now used as a flavoring. The FDA data bank, PAFA, has not yet done a toxicology literature search on this food additive.

ORANGE B • Dull orange crystals derived from coal tar. Coloring for the casings of frankfurters and sausages. The color additive was limited to not more than 150 ppm by weight of finished food. In 1978, the FDA said use could result in exposure of consumers to beta-naphthylamine, a known cancer-causing agent. Although it was permanently listed by the FDA, the only manufacturer of it stopped making it. *See* FD and C Colors.

ORANGE BITTER, FLOWERS and PEEL • The essential oil is used as a flavoring. GRAS. The FDA data bank, PAFA (see page 10), has not yet done a toxicology literature search on this food additive.

ORANGE BLOSSOMS • Orange blossoms, absolute, is a natural flavoring derived from the fruit of the bitter-plant species. Used in citrus and fruit flavorings for beverages, ice cream, ices, candy, baked goods, and chewing gum. The *flowers* provide a natural flavoring extract for citrus and cola flavorings for beverages (2,000 ppm). The *orange leaf extract* is used as a natural fruit flavoring for beverages, ice cream, ices, and baked goods. *Orange peel bitter oil* is expressed from the fresh fruit and is used in orange and fruit flavorings for beverages, ice cream, ices, candy, gelatin desserts, chewing gum, and liquors. GRAS. The FDA data bank, PAFA, has not yet done a toxicology literature search on this food additive.

ORANGE CRYSTALS • *See* Methyl *b*-Naphthyl Ketone.

ORANGE FLOWER, BITTER OIL • *See* Nerol.

ORANGE LEAF • *See* Orange Blossoms.

ORANGE OIL • Sweet Orange Oil. Yellow to deep orange, highly volatile, unstable liquid with a characteristic orange taste and odor expressed from the fresh peel of the ripe fruit of the sweet-orange plant species. Once used as an expectorant, it is now employed in perfumery, soaps, and flavorings. Used in orange and fruit flavorings for beverages, ice cream, ices, candy, baked goods, gelatin desserts, and chewing gum. Inhalation or frequent contact with oil of orange may cause severe symptoms such as headache, dizziness, and shortness of breath. Perfumes, colognes, and toilet water containing oil of orange may cause allergic reaction in the hypersensitive. Omitted from hypoallergenic cosmetics. The FDA data bank, PAFA (see page 10), has not yet done a toxicology literature search on this food additive.

ORANGE PEEL, BITTER OIL • *See* Orange Blossoms.

ORANGE PEEL, SWEET EXTRACT • From the fresh rind of the fruit. Sweetish, fragrant odor; slightly bitter taste. Used in orange and ginger ale flavorings for beverages, ice cream, ices, candy, and baked goods. The FDA data bank, PAFA, has not yet done a toxicology literature search on this food additive.

ORANGE PEEL, SWEET OIL (TERPENELESS) • From the fresh rind of the fruit. Sweetish, fragrant odor; slightly bitter taste. Used in orange and fruit flavorings for beverages, ice cream, ices, candy, baked goods, gelatin desserts, and puddings. The FDA data bank, PAFA, has not yet done a toxicology literature search on this food additive.

ORANGE-SWEET, LEAF, FLOWER, PEEL • Used as a flavoring. *See* Orange Blossoms and Orange Oil. The FDA data bank, PAFA, has not yet done a toxicology literature search on this food additive.

OREGANO • Mexican Oregano. Mexican Sage. Origanum. The wild marjoram (*see*) plant, but spicier, ordinarily found in Eurasia. Used in loganberry, cherry, sausage, root beer, and spice flavorings for beverages, baked goods, condiments (2,800 ppm), and meats. *See* Origanum Oil for toxicity. GRAS. The FDA data bank, PAFA (see page 10), has not yet done a toxicology literature search on this food additive.

ORGANIC • There are no federal standards for the term, but it usually means produce grown without pesticides, herbicides, or synthetic fertilizers on land that has been free of such chemicals for one to seven years.

ORGANOPHOSPHATES • Compounds containing phosphorus that belong to several groups including:

• Phospholipids or phosphatides, which are widely distributed in plants and animals. Lecithin is an example.

• Esters of phosphinic and phosphonic acids, which are used as plasticizers, insecticides, resin modifiers, and flame retardants.

• Pyrophosphates, which are the basis for many insecticides that inhibit cholinesterase, an enzyme necessary for nerve transmission. Tetraethyl pyrophosphate (TEPP), which is highly toxic, was developed during World War II.

• The phosphoric esters of glycerol, glycol, and other fatty alcohols, which are used in fertilizers.

Organophosphates, pesticides, and insecticides can be extremely toxic. They can kill quickly or slowly depending on the degree of exposure. Most are easily absorbed through the skin, eyes, stomach, and lungs. Among the organophosphate pesticides in use are azinphosmethyl, carbophenothion, demeton, diazinon, dichlorvos, dicrotophos, dimethoate, endothion, EPN, fensulfothion, fenthion, Hinosan, methyl demeton, methyl parathion, mevinphos, mipafox, monocrotophos, naled, parathion, phorate, phosphamidon, Phostex, tetraethyl pyrophosphate (TEPP), thiometon, and trichlorfon.

Organophosphorus compounds are now being studied for delayed neurotoxicity. It can occur in factory workers exposed during the production of organophosphorus chemicals, which are used as plasticizers, lubricants, fire retardants, and pesticides.

ORIGAN • *See* Oregano.

ORIGANOL • *See* 4-Carvomenthenol.

ORIGANUM OIL • The volatile oil is obtained by steam distillation from a flowering herb. Yellowish red to dark brown, with a pungent odor. Used in vermouth, sausage, root beer, and spice flavorings for beverages, ice cream, ices, candy, baked goods, condiments, and meats. A teaspoonful can cause illness, and less than an ounce has killed adults. GRAS.

ORIZANOL • The ester of ferulic acid and terpene alcohol widely found in plants used in flavorings and perfumes. *See* Cinnamic Acid.

ORMETOPRIM • A feed additive. The FDA tolerance for residue in edible tissues of chickens, ducks, turkeys, salmonids, and catfish is 0.1 ppm.

ORRIS • Orris Root Oil. White Flag. Love Root. Made from the roots of the plant. Yellowish, semisolid, fragrant oil. Distilled for use in raspberry, blackberry, strawberry, violet, cherry, nut, and spice flavorings for beverages, ice cream, ices, candy, baked goods, gelatin desserts, chewing gum, and icings. It is also used in dusting powders, perfumes, dry shampoos, toothpaste, and sachets. Discontinued in the U.S. because of the frequent allergic reactions to orris, including infantile eczema, hay fever, stuffy nose, red eyes, and asthma. The FDA data bank, PAFA (see page 10), has not yet done a toxicology literature search on this food additive. *See* Orris Root Extract.

ORRIS ROOT EXTRACT • Obtained from dried orris root. Has an intense odor and is used in perfumery. Used in chocolate, fruit, nut, vanilla, and cream soda flavorings for beverages, ice cream, ices, candy, baked goods, gelatin desserts, and chewing gum. Causes frequent allergic reactions. The FDA data bank, PAFA, has not yet done a toxicology literature search on this food additive.

ORYZALIN • Surflan. Dirimal. An herbicide used in peppermint and spearmint. FDA limits it to 0.1 ppm in peppermint and spearmint oil.

OSMANTHUS ABSOLUTE • A widely distributed genus of evergreen shrubs or trees, family Oleaceae, with inconspicuous bisexual flowers and sometimes foliage resembling holly. Used in flavoring and perfumery. The FDA data bank, PAFA, has not yet done a toxicology literature search on this food additive.

OURICURY WAX • The hard brown wax exuded from the leaves of the Brazilian palm tree. Has the same properties and uses as carnauba wax (*see*).

OX BILE • Oxgall. Emulsifier from the fresh bile of male castrated bovines. Brownish green or dark green; viscous. Characteristic odor. Bitter, disagreeable taste. Used in dried egg whites up to 0.1 percent. No known toxicity. The final report to the FDA of the Select Committee on GRAS Substances stated in 1980 that it should continue its GRAS status with no limitations other than good manufacturing practices. There is no reported use of the chemical and no toxicology information is available, according to the FDA's data bank, PAFA (see page 10).

OXAZOLINE • A series of synthetic waxes that are versatile and miscible with most natural waxes and can be applied to the same uses.

OXFENDAZOLE • Crystals from chloroform and methanol, it is used in a suspension to kill worms in cattle. FDA tolerance is 0.8 ppm in cattle liver.

OXIDIZED POLYETHYLENE • The resin produced by exposing polyethylene (*see*) to air. It is used as a protective coating or component of protective coatings for fresh avocados, bananas, beets, coconuts, eggplant, garlic, grapefruit, lemons, limes, mangos, muskmelons, onions, oranges, papaya, peas (in pods), pineapple, plantain, pumpkin, rutabaga, squash (acorn), sweet potatoes, tangerines, turnips, watermelon, Brazil nuts, chestnuts, filberts, hazelnuts, pecans, and walnuts (all nuts in shells).

OXIDIZED TALLOW • A defoaming component used in yeast and beet-sugar production. *See* Tallow Flakes.

OXIDIZER • A substance that causes oxygen to combine with another substance. Oxygen and hydrogen peroxide are examples of oxidizers.

OXYFLUORFEN • Orange solid used as an herbicide in cottonseed oil, mint oil, and soybean oil. Limit of 0.25 ppm in the oils.

OXYSTEARIN • A mixture of the glycerides (*see*) of partially oxidized stearic acid (*see*) and other fatty acids (*see*). Occurs in animal fat and used chiefly in the manufacture of soaps, candles, cosmetics, suppositories, and pill coatings. Tan, waxy. Used as a crystallization inhibitor in cottonseed and soybean cooking. In salad oils up to 0.125 percent. Also used as a defoamer in the production of beet sugar and yeast. The Select Committee of the Federation of American Societies for Experimental Biology advising on food additives recommended further study of this additive. The final report to the FDA of the Select Committee on GRAS Substances stated in 1980 that while no available evidence on it demonstrates a hazard to the public at current use levels, uncertainties exist, requiring additional studies. GRAS status has continued since 1980 while tests were to be completed and evaluated. The FDA data bank, PAFA (see page 10), has fully up-to-date toxicology information available on this food additive.

OXYTETRACYCLINE • An antibiotic used in feed to increase growth and found in edible tissue of chickens and turkeys. FDA permits a residue in the birds of up to 3 ppm in liver and 1 ppm in uncooked muscle, fat, and skin. It is used in combination with carbomycin (*see*) in the drinking water of chickens. It is used in tablet form for cattle. Because it is an antimicrobial, it may cause sensitivity to light, nausea, inflammation of the mucous membranes of the mouth, and diarrhea. *See* Antibiotics.

OZOKERITE • Ceresin. A naturally occurring, waxlike mineral; a mixture of hydrocarbons. Colorless or white when pure; horrid odor. Upon refining, it yields a hard, white, microcrystalline wax known as ceresin (*see*). An emulsifier and thickening agent used in lipstick and cream rouge. No known toxicity.

OZONE • A colorless gas or dark blue liquid used as an antimicrobial in bottled water. Under the EPA Genetic Toxicology Program (*see*). Toxic effects are from inhalation.

P

PABA • *See* para-Aminobenzoic Acid.

PALATONE • *See* Maltol.

PALE CATECHU • *See* Catechu Extract.

PALM KERNEL OIL • The oil from the fruit of the oil palm *Elaeis guineensis,* a fatty solid with a sweet, nutty flavor. Used as a coating agent, emulsifying agent, and texturizer in confectionery products and margarine. GRAS.

PALM OIL • Palm Butter. Palm Tallow. Yellow-brown, buttery, edible solid at room temperature. Oil palms are native to Central Africa and Malaysia. A reddish yellow to dark dirty red. A fatty mass with a faint violet odor. Used as a shortening, as a substitute for tallow, and in making soaps and ointments. No known toxicity.

PALM OIL GLYCERIDE • *See* Palm Oil.

PALMA ROSA OIL • Geranium Oil. The volatile oil obtained by steam distillation from a variety of partially dried grass grown in East India and Java. Used in rose, fruit, and spice flavorings for beverages, ice cream, ices, candy, and baked goods. Believed as toxic as other essential oils, causing illness after ingestion of a teaspoonful and death after ingestion of an ounce. A skin irritant. GRAS.

PALMAMIDE MEA • A mixture of ethanolamides of the fatty acids derived from palm oil (*see*).

PALMITAMIDE • A substance that keeps food from sticking to a container. Used in packaging material. *See* Palmitic Acid.

PALMITIC ACID • A mixture of solid organic acids obtained from fats consisting chiefly of palmitic acid with varying amounts of stearic acid (*see*). It is white or faintly yellow and has a fatty odor and taste. Palmitic acid occurs naturally in allspice, anise, calamus oil, cascarilla bark, celery seed, butter acids, coffee, tea, and many animal fats and plant oils. It forms 40 percent of cow's milk. Obtained from palm oil, Japan wax, or Chinese vegetable tallow. No known toxicity to skin and hair provided no salts of oleic or lauric acids (*see both*) are present. Used in butter and cheese flavorings for seasoning preparations. Used as a texturizer in shampoos, shaving creams, and soaps. The FDA data bank, PAFA (see page 10), has fully up-to-date toxicology information available on this food additive.

PALMITOYL HYDROLYZED ANIMAL PROTEIN • *See* Hydrolyzed Protein.

PALMITOYL HYDROLYZED MILK PROTEIN • The condensation product of palmitic acid chloride and hydrolyzed milk protein. *See* Hydrolyzed and Milk.

PANCREATIC EXTRACT • Hi-Vegi-Lip. A preparation of pancreatic hormones used in disorders of the pancreas to aid digestion of starches, fats, and proteins. Potential adverse reactions include nausea and diarrhea. Should be used cautiously in persons allergic to pork. There is no reported use of the chemical and no toxicology information is available, according to the FDA's data bank, PAFA.

PANSY EXTRACT • The extract obtained from *Viola tricolor*. Flavoring in alcoholic beverages only. Also used as a coloring in cosmetics. There is no reported use of the chemical and no toxicology information is available, according to the FDA's data bank, PAFA (see page 10).

PANTHENOL • Dexpanthenol. Vitamin B Complex Factor. A viscous, slightly bitter liquid used as a medicinal supplement in foods to aid digestion and in liquid vitamins. Used in hair products and in emollients. It is good for human tissues. No known toxicity.

d-**PANTOTHENAMIDE** • Vitamin B Complex. Vitamin B_5. Made synthetically from the jelly of the queen bee, yeast, and molasses. Cleared as a source of pantothenic acid in foods for special dietary use. Pantothenic acid (common sources are liver, rice bran, and molasses) is essential for metabolism of carbohydrates, fats, and other important substances. Nerve damage has been observed in patients with low pantothenic acid. It helps release energy from carbohydrates in the breakdown of fats. Children and adults need from five to ten milligrams per day. *See* Calcium Pantothenate.

PANTOTHENIC ACID • Vitamin B_5. A necessity in human diets. It helps metabolize fats and proteins. Nontoxic.

d-**PANTOTHENYL ALCOHOL** • The final report to the FDA of the Select Committee on GRAS Substances stated in 1980 that it should continue its GRAS status with no limitations other than good manufacturing practices. There is no reported use of the chemical and no toxicology information is available, according to the FDA's data bank, PAFA (see page 10). *See* Calcium Pantothenate.

PANTOTHENYL ETHYL ETHER • The ethyl ether of the B vitamin panthenol (*see*).

PANTOTHENYL ETHYL ETHER ACETATE • The ester of acetic acid and the ethyl ether of the B vitamin panthenol (*see*).

PAPAIN • A proteinase enzyme for meat tenderizing. Prepared from papaya, a fruit, *Carica papaya,* grown in tropical countries. Used for clearing beverages. Added to enriched farina to reduce cooking time. Used medically to prevent adhesions. It is deactivated by cooking, but because of its protein-digesting ability it can dissolve necrotic material with disastrous results. The usual grade used in food digests about thirty-five times its weight of lean meat. It may cause allergic reactions. Has caused birth defects in experimental animals. The final report to the FDA of the Select Committee on GRAS Substances stated in 1980 that it should continue its GRAS status with no limitations other than good manufacturing practices. The FDA data bank, PAFA (see page 10), has fully up-to-date toxicology information available on this food additive.

PAPAYA • A fruit grown in tropical countries. It contains an enzyme, papain, used as a meat tenderizer and, medicinally, to prevent adhesions. It is deactivated by cooking. Because of its protein-digesting ability, it can dissolve necrotic (dead) material. It may cause allergic reactions. *See* Papain.

PAPRIKA • The finely ground pods of dried, ripe, sweet pepper, *Capsicum annuum*. The strong, reddish orange powder is used in sausage and spice flavorings for baked goods (1,900 ppm), condiments, meats (7,400 ppm), and soups (7,500 ppm). The *oleoresin* (*see*) is used in fruit, meat, and spice flavorings for beverages, ice cream, ices, candy, baked goods, condiments, and meats. Both paprika and paprika oleoresins are used as red coloring. Permanently listed since 1966 for use in foods consistent with good manufacturing practices. The FDA data bank, PAFA, has fully up-to-date toxicology information available on this food additive.

PARABENS • Butylparaben. Heptylparaben. Methylparaben. Propylparaben. Parahydroxybenzoate. The parabens are the most commonly used preservatives in the U.S. The parabens have a broad spectrum of antimicrobial activity, are safe to use—relatively nonirritating, nonsensitizing, and nonpoisonous—are stable over the pH (*see*) range in cosmetics, and are sufficiently soluble in water to be effective in liquids. The typical paraben preservative system contains 0.2 percent methyl- and 0.1 percent propylparaben. Methyl- and propylparaben are esters of parahydroxybenzoic acid. Neither occurs in nature. In foods, parabens function as preservatives that prevent the growth of molds and yeasts. They are used in baked goods, sugar substitutes, artificially sweetened jams, mincemeats, milk preparations, soft drinks, packaged fish, meat, poultry, jellies, fats, oils, and frozen dairy desserts. Methyl- and propylparabens are used at 1,000 ppm in tomato pulp, puree, catsup, pickles, and relishes. The only adverse effect of parabens reported was that methylparaben caused birth defects in offspring of mice and rats fed 550 milligrams per kilogram of body weight daily during pregnancy, and in hamsters fed 300 milligrams under the same conditions.

PARAFFIN WAX • A colorless, somewhat translucent, odorless mass with a greasy feel. Used as a defoaming component in yeast and sugar beet production. Not digested or absorbed in the intestines. Used to cover food products. Used in solid brilliantines, cold creams, wax depilatories, eyelash creams and oils, eyebrow pencils, lipsticks, liquefying creams, protective creams, and mascaras; also used for extracting perfumes from flowers. Obtained from the distillate of wood, coal, petroleum, or shale oil. Easily melts over boiling water. Cleared for use as a synthetic masticatory substance in chewing gum. Pure paraffin is harmless to the skin, but the presence of impurities may give rise to irritations and eczema. The FDA data bank, PAFA (see page 10), has fully up-to-date toxicology information available on this food additive.

PARAFORMALDEHYDE • Preservative used to control fungus in maple-tree tap holes (residue limit of 2 ppm of formaldehyde in maple syrup).

PARAQUAT • Defoliant and herbicide used in animal feed for goats, cattle, swine, and lambs. FDA limits residue to up to 0.2 ppm in dried hops, 3 in mint hay, 6 in sunflower seed hulls. Paraquat is in the EPA Genetic Toxicology Program (*see*). Poison by ingestion and skin contact. Causes ulceration of the digestive tract, diarrhea, vomiting, renal damage, jaundice, edema, hemorrhage, lung damage, and death from suffocation. When heated to decomposition, emits toxic fumes.

PARATHION • A deep brown to yellow liquid, it is an organophosphate (*see*) insecticide and acaricide. Highly toxic by skin contact, inhalation, or ingestion. It interferes with the transmission of nerve signals. Repeated exposure may, without warning, be increasingly hazardous. *See* Organophosphates.

PARIMIPHOS-METHYL • A pesticide used in rice and wheat. The residue tolerances set by the FDA are from 50 to 60 ppm.

PARMESAN CHEESE, REGGIANO CHEESE • A hard, dry cheese with a sharp flavor that is cured for several years. It is used as a flavoring. The FDA data bank, PAFA (see page 10), has not yet done a toxicology literature search on this food additive.

PARSLEY, LEAVES, OIL, and OLEORESIN • The aromatic *leaves* of the annual herb *Petroselinum* ssp., cultivated everywhere, are used in spice flavorings for beverages, meats, soups, baked goods, and condiments. Parsley *oil* is obtained by steam distillation of the ripe seeds of the herb. The *oleoresin* (*see*) is used in spice flavorings for condiments. Used as a preservative, perfume, and flavoring in cosmetics, it is obtained by steam distillation of the ripe seeds of the herb. Yellow to light brown with a harsh odor. Parsley may cause the skin to break out with a rash, redden, and swell when exposed to light. It may also cause an allergic reaction in the sensitive. GRAS. The FDA data bank, PAFA, has not yet done a toxicology literature search on this food additive.

PARSLEY SEED OIL • *See* Parsley, Leaves, Oil, and Oleoresin.

PARTIALLY DELACTOSED WHEY (PDW) • Used increasingly as a substitute for nonfat dry milk, which is more expensive. PDW is used in processed cheese foods and spreads. It is the result of the partial removal of lactose (*see*) from the milk ingredient whey (*see*).

PARTIALLY DEMINERALIZED AND DELACTOSED WHEY • Removal of some minerals as well as lactose from whey. *See* Partially Delactosed Whey.

PARVE • *See* Kosher.

PASSIONFLOWER • Extract of the various species of *Passiflora incarnata*. Indians used passionflower for swellings, relieving sore eyes, and to induce vomiting. It is used as a flavoring. It has been shown that an extract of the plant depresses the motor nerves of the spinal cord. The FDA data bank, PAFA (see page 10), has not yet done a toxicology literature search on this food additive.

PATCHOULI OIL • Patchouly Oil. It is the essential oil obtained from the leaves of an East Indian shrubby mint, *Pogostemon* spp. Yellowish to greenish brown liquid, with the pleasant fragrance of summer flowers. Used in cola, fruit, nut, and spice flavorings for beverages, ice cream, ices, candy, baked goods, and chewing gum. Used in perfume formulations to impart a long-lasting oriental aroma in soaps and cosmetics. May produce allergic reactions. The FDA data bank, PAFA, has not yet done a toxicology literature search on this food additive.

PEACH ALDEHYDE • *See* y-Undecalactone.

PEACH EXTRACT • *See* Peach Juice Extract.

PEACH JUICE EXTRACT • The liquid obtained from the pulp of the peach, *Prunus persica*. It is used as a natural flavoring and as an emollient. Nontoxic.

PEACH KERNEL OIL • Persic Oil. A light yellow liquid expressed from the seed. Smells like almonds. Used as a natural flavoring in conjunction with other natural flavorings. Used as an oil base in emollients, eyelash creams, and brilliantines. GRAS. There is no reported use of the chemical and no toxicology information is available, according to the FDA's data bank, PAFA (see page 10).

PEACH LEAVES • Flavoring for alcoholic beverages only. There is no reported use of the chemical and no toxicology information is available, according to the FDA's data bank, PAFA. *See* Peach Juice Extract.

PEANUT OIL • Arachis Oil. Greenish yellow, with a pleasant odor. Prepared by pressing shelled and skinned seeds of the peanut. A solvent in salad oil, shortening, mayonnaise, and confections. Also used in conjunction with natural flavorings. Peanut butter is about 50 percent peanut oil suspended in peanut fibers. Used in the manufacture of soaps, baby preparations, hair-grooming aids, nail driers, shampoos, and as a solvent for ointments and liniments; also in night creams and emollients. It is used as a substitute for almond and olive oils in cosmetic creams, brilliantines, antiwrinkle oils, and sunburn preparations. Has been reported to be a mild irritant in soap, but considered harmless to the skin. The oil acts as a mild cathartic and as a protective for the gastrointestinal tract when corrosive poisons have been swallowed. The final report to the FDA of the Select Committee on GRAS Substances stated in 1980 that it should continue its GRAS status with no limitations other than good manufacturing practices. The FDA data bank, PAFA (see page 10), has fully up-to-date toxicology information available on this food additive.

PEANUT STEARINE • The FDA data bank, PAFA, has not yet done a toxicology literature search on this food additive. *See* Peanut Oil. GRAS.

PEANUTAMIDE MEA • Loramine Wax. *See* Peanut Oil.

PEANUTAMIDE MIPA • A mixture of isopropanolamides of the fatty acids derived from peanut oil (*see*).

PECAN SHELL POWDER • A coloring agent used in cosmetics. Employed medicinally by the American Indians. It is the nut from a hickory of the southern central U.S. with rough bark and hard but brittle wood. Edible. No known toxicity.

PECTIN • Pectin is found in roots, stems, and fruits of plants and forms an integral part of such structures. It is a coarse or fine powder, practically odorless, with a gluey taste. Richest source of pectin is lemon or orange rind, which contains about 30 percent of this polysaccharide. Used as a stabilizer, thickener, and bodying agent for artificially sweetened beverages, syrups for frozen products, ice cream, ice milk, confections, fruit sherbets, water ices, French dressing, fruit jelly, preserves, and jams to compensate for a deficiency in natural pectin. Used in foods as a "cementing agent." Used in cosmetics as a gelling and thickening agent. Emulsifying agent used in place of various gums in toothpastes, hair-setting lotions, and protective creams. It is soothing and mildly acidic. Also used as an antidiarrheal medicine. No known toxicity. The final report to the FDA of the Select Committee on GRAS Substances stated in 1980 that it should continue its GRAS status with no limitations other than good manufacturing practices. The FDA data bank, PAFA (see page 10), is currently searching the toxicology literature concerning this additive.

PECTINASE • An enzyme used as a clarifying agent (*see*) in wine and juice. The FDA data bank, PAFA, has not yet done a toxicology literature search on this food additive.

PEGU CATECHU EXTRACT • *See* Catechu Extract.

PELARGONALDEHYDE • *See* Nonanal.

PELARGONIC ACID • Nonanoic Acid. A synthetic flavoring agent that occurs naturally in cocoa and oil of lavender. Used in berry, fruit, nut, and spice flavorings. A strong irritant.

PELARGONIC ALDEHYDE • *See* Pelargonic Acid.

PELARGONYL VANILLYLAMIDE • *See* Pelargonic Acid.

PENDARE • *Couma macrocarpa barb. Couma utilis.* A flavoring from tropical South American trees. *See* Coumarin. The FDA data bank, PAFA (see page 10), has fully up-to-date toxicology information available on this food additive.

PENDIMETHALIN • Prowl. Stomp. An herbicide. FDA tolerance is 0.1 ppm as a residue in or on corn fodder or forage, grain, potatoes, sorghum, soybeans, or sunflower seeds.

PENICILLINASE FROM *BACILLUS SUBTILIS* • An enzyme from a mold used in processing. There is no reported use of the chemical and no toxicology information is available, according to the FDA's data bank, PAFA.

PENICILLINS • Amoxicillin. Ampicillin. Azlocillin. Bacampicillin. Carbenicillin. Cloxacillin. Dicloxacillin. Methicillin. Mezlocillin. Nafcillin. Oxacillin. Penicillin G, V. Piperacillin. Ticarcillin. A group of beta-lactam antibiotics produced by several species of mold and/or semisynthetically. There are many kinds and they offer a broad clinical spectrum of activity. They act by inhibiting bacterial enzymes involved in making cell walls. Used to treat animal infections and in animal feed to prevent infections and to encourage growth, particularly in chickens, lamb, swine, turkey, pheasants, and quail. FDA limits residues to 0.05 ppm in cattle. Limitation of zero in chickens, pheasant, quail, swine, sheep, eggs, milk, and foods in which milk has been used. Limitation of 0.01 ppm in turkeys. In EPA Genetic Toxicology Program (*see*). Human reproductive effects by ingestion: abortion. Human systemic effects by intramuscular route: skin rash. Has been implicated in aplastic anemia.

PENNYROYAL OIL • Squaw Mint. Hedeoma. An extract of the flowering herb *Mentha pulegium.* Used since ancient days as a medicine, scent, flavoring, and food. Obtained from the dried flower tops and leaves, it contains tannin, which is soothing to the skin. Used in mint flavorings for beverages, ice cream, ices, candy, and baked goods. Formerly used as an aromatic perspirant, to stimulate menstrual flow, for flatulence, as an abortion inducer, and as a counteractant for painful menstruation. Brain damage has been reported following doses of less than one teaspoon. Nausea, vomiting, bleeding, circulatory collapse, confusion, restlessness, and delirium have been reported. The FDA data bank, PAFA (see page 10), has not yet done a toxicology literature search on this food additive.

PENTACHLOROPHENOL • Chlorophen. Santophen. Dark-colored flakes with a characteristic odor used as a preservative in packaging materials. FDA limit of 50 ppm in treated wood. International Agency for Research on Cancer (IARC) (*see*) review and on EPA Extremely Hazardous List, Community Right-To-Know List, and EPA Genetic Toxicology Program (*see all*). Human poison by ingestion. A suspected human cancer-causing agent. Causes birth defects in experimental animals. Skin irritant. Acute poisoning causes weakness with difficult breathing and changes in blood pressure and urinary output. Can cause death.

PENTADECALACTONE • Angelica Lactone. Exaltolide. It is obtained from the fruit and root of a plant grown in Europe and Asia. A synthetic berry, fruit, liquor, wine, nut, and vanilla flavoring agent for beverages, ice cream, ices, candy, baked goods, gelatin desserts, and alcoholic beverages. Used as a cosmetic fragrance. The FDA data bank, PAFA (see page 10), has fully up-to-date toxicology information available on this food additive.

PENTADECANOLIDE • *See* Pentadecalactone.

PENTADESMA BUTTER • Kanya Butter. The vegetable fat extracted from the nut of *Pentadesma butyracea*. *See* Shea Butter.

PENTAERYTHRITOL ESTER OF MALEIC ANHYDRIDE MODIFIED WOOD ROSIN • Coating on citrus fruit. Pentaerythritol is a resin made by treating acetaldehyde (*see*) with formaldehyde (*see*) in a solution of calcium hydroxide.

PENTAERYTHRITOL ESTER OF PARTIALLY HYDROGENATED WOOD ROSIN • Hard, amber-colored solid used as a coating for citrus fruits and in chewing gum bases.

PENTANAL • *See* Valeraldehyde.

PENTANE • The aliphatic hydrocarbon derived from petroleum. Used as a solvent. Narcotic in high doses.

2,3-PENTANEDIONE • A synthetic flavoring agent that occurs naturally in coffee. Used in strawberry, chocolate, butterscotch, butter, caramel, fruit, rum, and cheese flavorings for beverages, ice cream, ices, candy, baked goods, gelatin desserts, and puddings. No known toxicity.

2-PENTANETHIOL • *n*-Amyl Mercaptan. A liquid with a strong, unpleasant odor used in the manufacture of food additives. Mild irritant to skin and mucous membranes. May cause skin sensitization. The FDA data bank, PAFA, has not yet done a toxicology literature search on this food additive.

PENTANOIC ACID • *See* Valeric Acid.

1-PENTANOL • Pentyl Alcohol. *n*-Amyl Alcohol. Liquid with a mild, pleasant odor, slightly soluble in water. Used as a solvent. Irritating to the eyes and respiratory passages, and absorption may cause a lack of oxygen in the blood. The FDA data bank, PAFA (see page 10), has fully up-to-date toxicology information available on this food additive.

2-PENTANONE • A synthetic flavoring that occurs naturally in apples. Used in fruit flavorings for beverages, ice cream, ices, candy, and baked goods. Moderately toxic by ingestion. Mildly toxic by skin contact and inhalation. In humans, inhalation may cause headache, nausea, and irritation of the respiratory passages, eyes, and skin. The FDA data bank, PAFA, has fully up-to-date toxicology information available on this food additive.

4-PENTENOIC ACID • A synthetic butter and fruit flavoring agent for beverages, ice cream, ices, candy, baked goods, and margarine. The FDA data bank, PAFA (see page 10), has fully up-to-date toxicology information available on this food additive.

PENTYL ALCOHOL • *See* Amyl Alcohol.

PENTYL BUTYRATE • *See* Amyl Butyrate.

PEPPER, BLACK • A pungent product obtained from the dried, unripe berries of the East Indian pepper plant, *Piper nigrum*. Used in sausage and spice flavorings for beverages, baked goods, condiments, meats, soups, and pickles. Black pepper *oil* is used in meat and spice flavorings for beverages, ice cream, ices, candy, baked goods, condiments, and meats. Black pepper *oleoresin* (*see*) is used in sausage and pepper flavorings for beverages, ice cream, ices, candy, baked goods, condiments, and meats. Pepper was formerly used as a carminative to break up intestinal gas, to cause sweating, and as a gastric agent to promote gastric secretion. Has insecticidal properties. The FDA data bank, PAFA, has not yet done a toxicology literature search on this food additive.

PEPPER, RED • *See* Cayenne Pepper.

PEPPER, WHITE • The pungent product obtained from the undecorticated (with the outer covering intact) ripe berries of the pepper plant. Used in sausage and spice flavorings for beverages, baked goods, condiments, meats, and soups. White pepper *oil* is used in spice flavorings for baked goods. White pepper *oleoresin* (*see*) is used in spice flavorings for meats. *See* Pepper, Black.

PEPPER TREE OIL • *See* Schinus Molle Oil.

PEPPERMINT EXTRACT • *See* Peppermint Oil.

PEPPERMINT LEAVES • *See* Peppermint Oil.

PEPPERMINT OIL • It is the oil made from the dried leaves and tops of a plant common to Asian, European and American gardens, *Mentha piperita*. Used in chocolate, fruit, cordial, crème de menthe, peppermint, nut, and spice flavorings for beverages, ice cream, ices, candy (1,200 ppm), baked goods, gelatin desserts, chewing gum (8,300 ppm), meats, liquors, icings, and toppings. Peppermint has been used as a carminative to break up intestinal gas and as an antiseptic. Used in toothpaste and tooth powders, eye lotions, shaving lotions, and toilet waters. It can cause allergic reactions such as hay fever and skin rash. Two patients who consumed large quantities of peppermint candy over a long period developed irregular heart rhythms. GRAS. The FDA data bank, PAFA (see page 10), is currently searching the toxicology literature concerning this additive.

PEPSIN • A digestive enzyme found in gastric juice that helps break down protein. The product used to aid digestion is obtained from the glandular layer of the fresh stomach of a hog. Slightly acid taste and a mild odor. The FDA data bank, PAFA, has not yet done a toxicology literature search on this food additive.

PEPTONES • Secondary protein derivatives formed during digestion—the result of gastric and pancreatic juices acting upon protein. Peptones are used as a foam stabilizer for beer and as a processing aid in baked goods, confections, and frostings. Determined to be GRAS in 1982. The FDA data bank, PAFA (see page 10), has not yet done a toxicology literature search on this food additive.

PERACETIC ACID • Peroxyacetic Acid. A starch modifier prepared from acetaldehyde (*see*). It is 40 percent acetic acid and highly corrosive. Acrid odor; explodes violently on heating to 110 degrees. There is no reported use of the chemical and no toxicology information is available, according to the FDA's data bank, PAFA.

PERFLUOROHEXANE • Used to cool chickens.

PERILLA OIL • Light yellow oil derived from the seeds of *Perilla ocimodes,* grown in Japan and Korea. It is used as a substitute for linseed oil and as an edible oil in Asia. It is also used in the manufacture of varnishes.

PERILLALDEHYDE • Isolated from *Perilla arguta,* it is used as a sweet flavoring agent. The FDA data bank, PAFA, has fully up-to-date toxicology information available on this food additive.

PERLITE • A filtering aid that the final report to the FDA of the Select Committee on GRAS Substances stated in 1980 should continue its GRAS status with no limitations other than good manufacturing practices.

PEROXIDE • Benzoyl, Calcium, and Hydrogen. *Benzoyl peroxide* is used as a bleaching agent for flours, oils, and cheese. Has been used as a paste for treating poison ivy and for burns. May explode when heated. *Calcium peroxide* or *dioxide* is odorless, almost tasteless. Used as a dough conditioner and oxidizing agent for bread, rolls, and buns. Formerly used as an antiseptic. *Hydrogen peroxide* or *dioxide* is used as a bleaching and oxidizing agent, a modifier for food starch, and a preservative and bactericide for milk and cheese. Bitter taste. May decompose violently if traces of impurities are present. A strong oxidant that can injure skin and eyes. Chemists are cautioned to wear rubber gloves and goggles when handling it. Used in hair bleaches. May cause hair breakage and is an irritant. On the FDA list of additives to be studied for mutagenic, teratogenic, subacute, and reproductive effects.

PERSIC OIL • *See* Apricot and Peach Kernel Oil.

PERUVIAN BALSAM • *See* Balsam Peru. GRAS.

PETITGRAIN OIL • Used extensively in perfumes. It is the volatile oil obtained from the leaves and twigs and unripe fruit of the bitter-orange tree. Brownish to yellow with a bittersweet odor. Used in loganberry, violet, apple, banana, berry, grape, peach, pear, honey, muscatel, nut, ginger, and ginger ale flavorings for beverages, ice cream, ices, candy, baked goods, gelatin desserts, chewing gum, and condiments. Supposedly dissolves in sweat, and under the influence of sunlight becomes an irritant. May cause allergic skin reactions. GRAS. The FDA data bank, PAFA (see page 10), has not yet done a toxicology literature search on this food additive.

PETITGRAIN OIL (LEMON) • A fragrant essential oil from a variety of citrus trees. Used in citrus and fruit flavorings for beverages, ice cream, ices, candy, and baked goods. GRAS. The FDA data bank, PAFA, has not yet done a toxicology literature search on this food additive.

PETITGRAIN OIL (MANDARIN) • The fragrant essential oil from a variety of citrus tree. Used in orange, tangerine, and grape flavorings for beverages, ice cream, ices, candy, baked goods, and gelatin desserts. GRAS. The FDA data bank, PAFA, has not yet done a toxicology literature search on this food additive.

PETROLATUM • Crude or Mineral Oil. Vaseline. Petroleum Jelly. Paraffin Jelly. It is a purified mixture of semisolid hydrocarbons from petroleum. Yellowish to light amber or white, unctuous mass, practically odorless and tasteless, almost insoluble in water. A releasing agent and sealant for confections. A coating for fruits, vegetables, and cheese. A defoaming agent in yeast and beet-sugar production. Used in baking products, as a lubricant in meatpacking plants, and used in dried-egg albumin. Defoaming agent, lubricant, polishing agent, protective coating, release (nonstick) agent and sealing agent in bakery products, beet sugar, confectionery, egg-white solids, dehydrated fruits, and dehydrated vegetables. FDA limits petrolatum to 0.15 percent in bakery products, 0.2 percent in confectionery, 0.02 percent in dehydrated fruits and vegetables, 0.1 percent in egg white. May contain FDA-approved antioxidants. Petrolatum helps to soften and smooth the skin in the same way as any other emollient and is less expensive. The oily film helps prevent evaporation of moisture from the skin and protects the skin from irritation. However, petrolatum does cause allergic skin reactions in the hypersensitive. When ingested, it produces a mild laxative effect. Not absorbed but may inhibit digestion. It is generally nontoxic. The FDA data bank, PAFA (see page 10), has fully up-to-date toxicology information available on this food additive.

PETROLEUM • Hydrocarbons, Naphtha, Waxes. A highly complex mixture of paraffinic, naphthalenic, and aromatic hydrocarbons containing some sulfur and trace amounts of nitrogen and oxygen compounds. Believed to have originated from both plant and animal sources millions of years ago. By cracking petroleum into fractions, the gases butane, ethane, and propane are obtained, as well as naphtha, gasoline, kerosene, fuel oils, gas oil, lubricating oils, paraffin wax, and asphalt. A defoaming agent in processing beet sugar and yeast and a coating on cheese and raw fruits and vegetables. Used as a coating on eggshells; in froth-flotation cleaning of vegetables; as a float on fermentation fluids as in the manufacture of vinegar, wine, and pickle brine; as a component of pesticide formulations; in modified hops extract of beer; and in many other formulations. Formerly used for bronchitis, tapeworms, and externally for arthritis and skin problems. Many petroleum products are reported to be cancer-causing agents. Others, presumably those used on food, are inert. The FDA data bank, PAFA (see page 10), has fully up-to-date toxicology information available on this food additive.

PETROLEUM WAX • Used as a chewing gum base. The FDA data bank, PAFA, has fully up-to-date toxicology information available on this food additive. *See* Petroleum.

pH • The scale used to measure acidity and alkalinity. pH is the hydrogen (H) ion concentration of a solution; *p* stands for the power of hydrogen ion. The pH of a solution is measured on a scale of 14. A truly neutral solution, neither acidic nor alkaline, such as water, is 7. Acid is less than 7. Alkaline is more than 7.

The pH of blood is 7.3; vinegar is 2.3; lemon juice is 8.2; and lye is 13. Skin and hair are naturally acidic. Soap and detergents are alkaline.

***a*-PHELLANDRENE** • A synthetic flavoring agent that occurs naturally in all-spice, star anise, angelica root, bay, dill, sweet fennel, black pepper, peppermint oil, and pimenta. Isolated from the essential oils of the eucalyptus plant. Used in citrus and spice flavorings for beverages, ice cream, ices, candy, and baked goods. Can be irritating to, and is absorbed through, the skin. Ingestion can cause vomiting and diarrhea. The FDA data bank, PAFA, has fully up-to-date toxicology information available on this food additive.

PHENETHYL ALCOHOL • 2-Phenethyanol. It occurs naturally in oranges, raspberries, and tea. A synthetic fruit flavoring agent that is used in strawberry, butter, caramel, floral, fruit, and honey flavorings for beverages, ice cream, ices, candy, baked goods, chewing gum, and gelatin desserts. Practically all rose perfumes contain it. It is also used as a preservative in cosmetics. It is a sensitizer. It is a strong local anesthetic and has caused central nervous system injury in mice.

PHENETHYL ANTHRANILATES • A synthetic butter, caramel, fruit, honey, and grape flavoring agent for beverages, ice cream, ices, candy, and baked goods. *See* Coal Tar.

PHENETHYL BENZOATE • A synthetic fruit and honey flavoring agent for beverages, ice cream, ices, candy, chewing gum, and baked goods. *See* Coal Tar. The FDA data bank, PAFA (see page 10), has fully up-to-date toxicology information available on this food additive.

PHENETHYL BUTYRATE • A synthetic butter, strawberry, caramel, floral, apple, peach, pineapple, and honey flavoring agent for beverages, ice cream, ices, candy, and baked goods. The FDA data bank, PAFA, has fully up-to-date toxicology information available on this food additive. *See* Coal Tar.

PHENETHYL CINNAMATE • A synthetic fruit flavoring agent for beverages, ice cream, ices, candy, puddings, and baked goods. The FDA data bank, PAFA, has fully up-to-date toxicology information available on this food additive. *See* Coal Tar.

PHENETHYL FORMATE • Formic Acid. A synthetic berry, apple, apricot, banana, cherry, peach, pear, plum, and honey flavoring agent for beverages, ice cream, ices, candy, and baked goods. The FDA data bank, PAFA, has fully up-to-date toxicology information available on this food additive. *See* Coal Tar.

PHENETHYL ISOBUTYRATE • A synthetic flavoring agent, slightly yellow, with a rose odor. Used in strawberry, floral, rose, apple, peach, pineapple, honey, and cheese flavorings for beverages, ice cream, ices, candy, and baked goods. Mildly toxic by ingestion. *See* Coal Tar.

PHENETHYL ISOVALERATE • A synthetic apple, apricot, peach, pear, and pineapple flavoring agent for beverages, ice cream, ices, candy, baked goods, and chewing gum. Mildly toxic by ingestion. The FDA data bank, PAFA (see page 10), has fully up-to-date toxicology information available on this food additive. *See* Coal Tar.

2-PHENETHYL 2-METHYL BUTYRATE • Colorless liquid with a floral-fruity odor used as a flavoring agent in various foods. The FDA data bank, PAFA, has fully up-to-date toxicology information available on this food additive.

PHENETHYL PHENYLACETATE • A synthetic fruit and honey flavoring agent for beverages, ice cream, ices, candy, maraschino cherries, and baked goods. The FDA data bank, PAFA, has fully up-to-date toxicology information available on this food additive. *See* Coal Tar.

PHENETHYL PROPIONATE • A synthetic fruit and honey flavoring agent for beverages, ice cream, ices, candy, and baked goods. The FDA data bank, PAFA, has fully up-to-date toxicology information available on this food additive. *See* Coal Tar.

PHENETHYL SALICYLATE • A synthetic apricot and peach flavoring agent for beverages, ice cream, ices, candy, and baked goods. The FDA data bank, PAFA, has fully up-to-date toxicology information available on this food additive. *See* Coal Tar.

PHENETHYL SENECIOATE • A synthetic liquor and wine flavoring agent for beverages, ice cream, ices, candy, and alcoholic beverages. The FDA data bank, PAFA (see page 10), has fully up-to-date toxicology information available on this food additive. *See* Coal Tar.

PHENETHYL TIGLATE • A synthetic fruit and nut flavoring agent for beverages, ice cream, ices, candy, and baked goods. The FDA data bank, PAFA, has fully up-to-date toxicology information available on this food additive. *See* Coal Tar.

PHENOL • Obtained from coal tar (*see*), it is used in the manufacture of many food additives and processing aids. Ingestion of even small amounts of phenol may cause nausea, vomiting, circulatory collapse, paralysis, convulsions, coma, respiratory failure, and cardiac arrest. It is an antiseptic and general disinfectant. The FDA data bank, PAFA, has fully up-to-date toxicology information available on this food additive.

PHENOXYACETIC ACID • A synthetic fruit and honey flavoring agent for beverages, ice cream, ices, candy, and baked goods. Used to soften calluses and corns and other hard surfaces. A mild irritant. The FDA data bank, PAFA, has fully up-to-date toxicology information available on this food additive.

2-PHENOXYETHYL ISOBUTYRATE • A synthetic fruit flavoring, colorless, with a roselike odor. Used in beverages, ice cream, ices, candy, and baked goods. The FDA data bank, PAFA, has fully up-to-date toxicology information available on this food additive.

PHENYL ACETATE • A synthetic flavoring agent prepared from phenol and acetic chloride. Used in berry, butter, caramel, floral, rose, fruit, honey, and vanilla flavorings for beverages, ice cream, ices, candy, and baked goods. Phenol is highly toxic. Death from 1.5 grams has been reported.

4-PHENYL-2-BUTANOL • A synthetic fruit flavoring for beverages, ice cream, ices, candy, and baked goods. The FDA data bank, PAFA (see page 10), has fully up-to-date toxicology information available on this food additive.

4-PHENYL-3-BUTEN-2-OL • A synthetic fruit flavoring for beverages, ice cream, ices, candy, and baked goods. The FDA data bank, PAFA, has fully up-to-date toxicology information available on this food additive.

4-PHENYL-3-BUTEN-2-ONE • A synthetic chocolate, cocoa, fruit, cherry, nut, and vanilla flavoring agent for beverages, ice cream, ices, candy, baked goods, gelatin desserts, and shortenings. The FDA data bank, PAFA, has fully up-to-date toxicology information available on this food additive.

4-PHENYL-2-BUTYL ACETATE • A synthetic fruit and peach flavoring agent for beverages, ice cream, ices, candy, and baked goods. The FDA data bank, PAFA, has fully up-to-date toxicology information available on this food additive. *See* Acetic Acid for toxicity.

PHENYL DIMETHYL CARBONYL ISOBUTYRATE • *See a-a*-Dimethylbenzyl Isobutyrate.

PHENYL 2-FUROATE • A synthetic chocolate and mushroom flavoring agent for beverages, candy, and gelatin desserts. The FDA data bank, PAFA (see page 10), has fully up-to-date toxicology information available on this food additive.

1-PHENYL-3-METHYL-3-PENTANOL • A synthetic fruit flavoring agent for beverages, candy, and gelatin desserts. The FDA data bank, PAFA, has fully up-to-date toxicology information available on this food additive.

PHENYL PELARGONATE • Liquid, insoluble in water. Used in flavors, perfumes, bactericides, and fungicides.

1-PHENYL-1-PROPANOL • A synthetic fruit and honey flavoring agent for beverages, ice cream, ices, candy, and baked goods. The FDA data bank, PAFA, has fully up-to-date toxicology information available on this food additive.

3-PHENYL-1-PROPANOL • A synthetic flavoring that occurs naturally in tea. Used in strawberry, apricot, peach, plum, hazelnut, pistachio, cinnamon, and walnut flavorings for beverages, ice cream, ices, candy, baked goods, liqueurs, and chewing gum. The FDA data bank, PAFA, has fully up-to-date toxicology information available on this food additive.

PHENYLACETALDEHYDE • An oily, colorless liquid with a harsh odor. Upon dilution, emits the fragrance of lilacs and hyacinths. Derived from phenethyl alcohol. A synthetic raspberry, strawberry, apricot, cherry, peach, honey, and spice flavoring for beverages, ice cream, ices, candy, baked goods, and chewing gum. Used also in perfumes. Less irritating than formaldehyde (*see*), but a stronger central nervous system depressant. In addition, it sometimes produces fluid in the lungs upon ingestion. Because it is considered an irritant, it is not used in baby-cosmetic preparations. The FDA data bank, PAFA (see page 10), has fully up-to-date toxicology information available on this food additive.

PHENYLACETALDEHYDE 2,3-BUTYLENE GLYCOL ACETAL • A synthetic floral and fruit flavoring agent for candy. *See* Phenylacetaldehyde for toxicity.

PHENYLACETALDEHYDE DIMETHYL ACETAL • A colorless liquid with a strong odor used as a synthetic fruit, apricot, cherry, honey, and spice flavoring agent for beverages, ice cream, ices, candy, baked goods, and chewing gum. Moderately toxic by ingestion. The FDA data bank, PAFA (see page 10), has fully up-to-date toxicology information available on this food additive.

PHENYLACETALDEHYDE GLYCERYL ACETAL • A synthetic floral and fruit flavoring agent for beverages, candy, ice cream, and ices. *See* Phenylacetaldehyde and Acetic Acid for toxicity.

PHENYLACETIC ACID • A synthetic flavoring agent that occurs naturally in Japanese mint, oil of neroli, and black pepper. A glistening, white solid with a persistent, honeylike odor. Used in butter, chocolate, rose, honey, and vanilla flavorings for beverages, ice cream, ices, candy, baked goods, gelatin desserts, chewing gum, liquors, and syrups. Used as a starting material in the manufacture of perfumes and soaps. Also used in the manufacture of penicillin. Moderately toxic by ingestion. Causes birth defects in experimental animals. The FDA data bank, PAFA, has fully up-to-date toxicology information available on this food additive.

PHENYLALANINE • L form. An essential amino acid (*see*) considered essential for growth in normal human beings and not synthesized by the body. It is associated with phenylketonuria (PKU), an affliction that, if not detected soon after birth, leads to mental deterioration in children. Restricting phenylalanine in diets results in improvement. Whole egg contains 5.4 percent and skim milk 5.1 percent. Used to improve penetration of emollients. The FDA asked for further study of this amino acid as a food additive in 1980. The FDA data bank, PAFA, has fully up-to-date toxicology information available on this food additive.

2-PHENYLETHYL ISOVALERATE • *See* Phenethyl Isovalerate.

2-PHENYLPROPIONALDEHYDE • A synthetic berry, rose, apricot, cherry, peach, plum, and almond flavoring agent for beverages, ice cream, ices, candy, and baked goods. The FDA data bank, PAFA (see page 10), has fully up-to-date toxicology information available on this food additive.

3-PHENYLPROPIONALDEHYDE • A synthetic flavoring agent, slightly yellow, with a strong floral odor. Used in berry, rose, apricot, cherry, peach, plum, and almond flavorings for beverages, ice cream, ices, candy, and baked goods. The FDA data bank, PAFA, has fully up-to-date toxicology information available on this food additive.

2-PHENYLPROPIONALDEHYDE DIMETHYL ACETAL • A synthetic berry, floral, rose, fruit, honey, mushroom, nut, and spice flavoring agent for beverages, ice cream, ices, candy, baked goods, chewing gum, and condiments. The FDA data bank, PAFA, has fully up-to-date toxicology information available on this food additive. *See* Acetic Acid for toxicity.

3-PHENYLPROPYL ACETATE • A synthetic flavoring, colorless, with a spicy floral odor. Used in berry, fruit, and spice flavorings for beverages, ice cream, ices, candy, baked goods, chewing gum, and condiments. Propyl acetate may be irritating to skin and mucous membranes and narcotic in high concentrations. The FDA data bank, PAFA (see page 10), has fully up-to-date toxicology information available on this food additive.

2-PHENYLPROPYL BUTYRATE • A synthetic flavoring used in beverages, ice cream, ices, candy, and baked goods. No specific flavorings listed. The FDA data bank, PAFA, has fully up-to-date toxicology information available on this food additive.

3-PHENYLPROPYL CINNAMATE • A synthetic butter, caramel, chocolate, cocoa, coconut, grape, and spice flavoring agent for beverages, ice cream, ices, candy, and baked goods. The FDA data bank, PAFA, has fully up-to-date toxicology information available on this food additive.

3-PHENYLPROPYL FORMATE • Formic Acid. A synthetic currant, raspberry, butter, caramel, apricot, peach, and honey flavoring agent for beverages, ice cream, ices, candy, and baked goods. The FDA data bank, PAFA, has fully up-to-date toxicology information available on this food additive. *See* Formic Acid for toxicity.

3-PHENYLPROPYL HEXANOATE • A synthetic fruit flavoring for beverages, ice cream, ices, candy, and baked goods. No known toxicity.

2-PHENYLPROPYL ISOBUTYRATE • A synthetic fruit flavoring for beverages, ice cream, ices, and candy. No known toxicity.

3-PHENYLPROPYL ISOBUTYRATE • A synthetic apple, apricot, peach, pear, pineapple, and plum flavoring agent for beverages, ice cream, ices, candy, and baked goods. No known toxicity.

3-PHENYLPROPYL ISOVALERATE • A synthetic butter, caramel, apple, pear, and nut flavoring agent for beverages, ice cream, ices, candy, and baked goods. The FDA data bank, PAFA (see page 10), has fully up-to-date toxicology information available on this food additive.

3-PHENYLPROPYL PROPIONATE • A synthetic apricot flavoring for beverages, ice cream, ices, candy, and baked goods. The FDA data bank, PAFA, has fully up-to-date toxicology information available on this food additive.

2-3 (3-PHENYLPROPYL) TETRAHYDROFURAN • A synthetic fruit, honey, and maple flavoring agent for beverages, ice cream, ices, candy, gelatin, puddings, and chewing gum. The FDA data bank, PAFA, has fully up-to-date toxicology information available on this food additive.

PHORATE • Thimet. Vegfru. An insecticide used in animal feed. On EPA Extremely Hazardous Substances List and EPA Genetic Toxicology Program (*see both*). Poison by ingestion. Causes mutations in experimental animals and interferes with nerve signals.

PHOSALONE • An insecticide used to kill insects and mites. FDA residue tolerance resulting from application on dried apple pomace is 85 ppm; on dried prunes, 40 ppm; on raisins, 20 ppm; on dried citrus pulp, 12 ppm; on dried grape pomace, 45 ppm; and on tea, 8 ppm. *See* Organophosphates.

PHOSPHATE • A salt of ester of phosphoric acid (*see*). Used as an emulsifier and texturizer and sequestering agent (*see*) in foods. Sodium phosphate is used in evaporated milk up to 0.1 percent of weight. A carbonated beverage contains phosphoric acid. Without sufficient phosphate there is abnormal parathyroid (gland) function, bone metabolism, intestinal absorption, malnutrition, and kidney malfunction. Chemicals that interfere with phosphate action include detergents, mannitol (an alcohol used as a dietary supplement, the basis of dietetic sweets), vitamin D, and aluminum hydroxide (*see*), a leavening agent. Ingestion of large amounts of phosphates can cause kidney damage and may adversely affect the absorption of other minerals.

PHOSPHATE, AMMONIUM • Dibasic and Monobasic. *See* Ammonium Phosphate.

PHOSPHATE, CALCIUM, MONOBASIC and TRIBASIC • *See* Calcium Phosphate.

PHOSPHATE, CALCIUM HEXAMETA- • *See* Calcium Hexametaphosphate.

PHOSPHATE, POTASSIUM • Monobasic and Dibasic. *See* Potassium Phosphate.

PHOSPHATED DISTARCH PHOSPHATE • The final report to the FDA of the Select Committee on GRAS Substances stated in 1980 that there is no available evidence that it is a hazard to the public when used as it is now and it should continue its GRAS status with limitations on amounts that can be added to food. *See* Modified Starches.

PHOSPHOLIPIDS • Phosphatides. Complex fat substances found in all living cells. Lecithin is an example. It is used in hand creams and lotions. Phospholipids contain phosphoric acid and nitrogen and are soluble in the usual fat solvents, with the exception of acetone (*see*). They are used in moisturizers because they bind water and hold it in place. No known toxicity.

n-(PHOSPHONOMETHYL)GLYCINE • An herbicide used in animal feed, imported olives, palm oil, soybean oil, dried tea, and instant tea. FDA's residue allowances: 30 ppm in molasses, sugarcane; 0.1 ppm in palm oil; 0.1 ppm in olives; 1 ppm in dried tea; 4 ppm in instant tea. Moderately toxic by ingestion.

PHOSPHORIC ACID • A colorless, odorless solution made from phosphate rock. Mixes with water and alcohol. A sequestering agent (*see*) for rendered animal fat or a combination of such fat with vegetable fat. Also used as an acidulant and flavoring in soft drinks, jellies, frozen dairy products, bakery products, candy, cheese products, and in the brewing industry. It is also used as a sequestrant and antioxidant in hair tonics, nail polishes, and skin fresheners. Concentrated solutions are irritating to the skin and mucous membranes. The final report to the FDA of the Select Committee on GRAS Substances stated in 1980 that it should continue its GRAS status with no limitations other than good manufacturing practices. The FDA data bank, PAFA (see page 10), has fully up-to-date toxicology information available on this food additive.

PHOSPHOROUS CHLORIDE • Phosphate derivative used as a starch modifier and a chlorinating agent. Intensely irritating to the skin, eyes, and mucous membranes. Inhalation may cause fluid in the lungs. There is no reported use of the chemical and no toxicology information is available, according to the FDA's data bank, PAFA.

PHOSPHOROUS OXYCHLORIDE • Phosphoryl Chloride. Colorless, clear, strongly fuming vapors, used as a starch modifier and as a solvent and chlorinating agent. Inhalation may cause pulmonary edema.

PHOSPHOROUS SOURCES • Calcium Phosphate, Magnesium Phosphate, Potassium Glycerophosphate, and Sodium Phosphate. Mineral supplements for cereal products, particularly breakfast foods such as farina. They are also used in incendiary bombs and tracer bullets. Phosphorus was formerly used to treat rickets and degenerative disorders. *See* Phosphate.

PHOTOSENSITIVITY • A condition in which the application or ingestion of certain chemicals, such as propylparaben (*see*), causes skin problems—including rash, hyperpigmentation, and swelling—when the skin is exposed to sunlight.

PHTHALATES • Salts of phthalic acid (*see*) used to make food packaging. May be cancer-causing.

PHTHALIC ACID • Obtained by oxidation of various benzene derivatives, it can be isolated from the fungus *Gibberella fujikuroi*. It is used in the manufacture of plastics, dyes, and nail polishes. Moderately irritating to the skin and mucous membranes.

PHTHALIC ANHYDRIDE • White crystalline needles derived from naphthalene (*see*). Used as a hardener for resins and a plasticizer. Also used in many dyes, chlorinated products, insecticides, and polyesters. A skin irritant.

PHTHALIMIDOMETHYL-0,0-DIMETHYL PHOSPHORODITHIOATE • APPA. Kemolate. Prolate. Smidan. A widely used insecticide in cottonseed oil. FDA residue tolerance is 0.2 ppm in cottonseed. EPA Extremely Hazardous Substance List (*see*). A human poison by ingestion.

PHYTIC ACID • Occurs in nature in the seeds of cereal grains and is derived commercially from corn. It is used to chelate heavy metals, as a rust inhibitor, in metal cleaning, and in the treatment of hard water. Nontoxic, although those allergic to corn may have a reaction.

PICLORAM • Crystalline solid made from picolinic acid, it is used as an herbicide and defoliant. It is toxic by ingestion and inhalation. Its use has been restricted in the U.S. The FDA permits tolerances of 3 ppm in milled fractions (except flour) of barley, oats, and wheat resulting from application to the growing crop; 1 ppm in flour of barley and wheat; 0.2 ppm as residue in fat, meat byproducts, and meat of cattle, goats, hogs, and sheep; 0.05 ppm as residue in milk and eggs; and 0.5 as residue in oat, barley, and wheat grains.

PICRAMIC ACID • 4,6-Dinitro-2-Aminophenol. A red crystalline acid obtained from phenol (*see*) and used chiefly in making azo dyes (*see*). Highly toxic material. Readily absorbed through intact skin. Vapors absorbed through respiratory tract. Produces marked increase in metabolism and temperature, profuse sweating, collapse, and death. May cause skin rash, cataracts, and weight loss.

PILEWORT EXTRACT • An extract of *Ranunculus ficaria,* the coarse, hairy, perennial figwort of the eastern and central U.S. It was once used to treat tuberculosis. No known toxicity.

PIMARICIN • Natamycin. An antibiotic from *Streptomyces chattanoogensis* used as a fungicide and mold inhibitor in cheese and wine. It is used in human medicine to treat fungal infections of the eye or eyelid. Potential adverse reactions include swelling around the eyes. Moderately toxic by ingestion.

PIMENTA LEAF OIL • Jamaica Pepper. Allspice. Derived from the dried ripe fruit of the evergreen shrub grown in the West Indies and Central and South America. Used in raspberry, fruit, nut, and spice flavorings for beverages, ice cream, ices, candy, baked goods, gelatin desserts, chewing gum, condiments, and meat products. Moderately toxic by ingestion. A severe skin irritant. GRAS. The FDA data bank, PAFA (see page 10), has not yet done a toxicology literature search on this food additive.

PINE BARK, WHITE, SOLID EXTRACT • Extract from *Pinus strobus,* used as a flavoring. The FDA data bank, PAFA, has not yet done a toxicology literature search on this food additive.

PINE CONE EXTRACT • An extract from the cones of *Pinus sylvestris. See* Pine Needle Oil.

PINE MOUNTAIN OIL • *See* Pine Needle Oil and Pine Needle Dwarf Oil.

PINE NEEDLE DWARF OIL • Pine Mountain Oil. The volatile oil obtained by steam distillation from a variety of pine trees, *Pinus mugo turra* var. Colorless with a pleasant pine smell. Used in citrus, pineapple, and liquor flavorings for beverages, ice cream, ices, candy, and baked goods. The FDA data bank, PAFA (see page 10), has not yet done a toxicology literature search on this food additive.

PINE NEEDLE OIL • Pine Mountain Oil. An extract of various species of *Pinus* used as a natural flavoring in pineapple, citrus, and spice flavorings. Also used to scent bath products. Ingestion of large amounts can cause intestinal hemorrhages. The FDA data bank, PAFA, has not yet done a toxicology literature search on this food additive.

PINE SCOTCH OIL • Volatile oil obtained by steam distillation from the needles of a pine tree. Colorless or yellowish, with an odor of turpentine. Used in various flavorings for beverages, candy, and baked goods. The FDA data bank, PAFA, has not yet done a toxicology literature search on this food additive. *See* Turpentine for toxicity.

PINE TAR • A product obtained by distillation of pinewood. A blackish brown, viscous liquid, slightly soluble in water. Used as an antiseptic in skin diseases. May be irritating to the skin.

PINE TAR OIL • The extract from a variety of pine trees. A synthetic flavoring obtained from a species of pinewood. Used in licorice flavorings for ice cream, ices, and candy. Also used as a solvent, disinfectant, and deodorant. As a *pine tar,* it is used in hair tonics; also a solvent, disinfectant, and deodorant. As an *oil* from twigs and needles, it is used in pine bath-oil emulsions, bath salts, and perfumery. Irritating to the skin and mucous membranes. *Bornyl acetate,* a substance obtained from various pine needles, has a strong pine odor and is used in bath oils. It can cause nausea, vomiting, convulsions, and dizziness if ingested. In general, pine oil in concentrated form is an irritant to human skin and may cause allergic reactions. In small amounts it is nontoxic. The FDA data bank, PAFA (see page 10), has fully up-to-date toxicology information available on this food additive.

PINEAPPLE EXTRACT • *See* Pineapple Juice.

PINEAPPLE JUICE • The common juice from the tropical plant. Contains a protein-digesting and milk-clotting enzyme, bromelin (*see*). An antiinflammatory enzyme, it is used in cosmetic treatment creams. It is also used as a texturizer. No known toxicity.

a-PINENE • A synthetic flavoring agent that occurs naturally in angelica root oil, anise, star anise, asafetida oil, coriander, cumin, fennel, grapefruit, juniper berries, oils of lavender and lime, mandarin orange leaf, black pepper, peppermint, pimenta, and yarrow. It is the principal ingredient of turpentine (*see*). Used chiefly in the manufacture of camphor. Used in lemon and nutmeg flavorings for beverages, ice cream, ices, candy, baked goods, and condiments. Also used as a chewing gum base. Readily absorbed from the gastrointestinal tract, the skin, and the respiratory tract. It is a local irritant, central nervous system depressant, and an irritant to the bladder and kidney. Has caused benign skin tumors from chronic contact.

2-PINENE • *See a*-Pinene.

***b*-PINENE** • A synthetic flavoring that occurs naturally in black-currant buds, coriander, cumin, black pepper, and yarrow herb. Used in citrus flavorings for beverages, ice cream, ices, candy (600 ppm), and baked goods (600 ppm). Also cleared for use in chewing gum base. *See a*-Pinene for toxicity.

PINUS PUMILIO OIL • *See* Pine Needle Dwarf Oil.

PIPERIDINE • A synthetic flavoring that occurs naturally in black pepper. Used in beverages, candy, baked goods, meats, soups, and condiments. Soapy texture. Has been proposed for use as a tranquilizer and muscle relaxant. The FDA data bank, PAFA (see page 10), has fully up-to-date toxicology information available on this food additive.

PIPERINE • Celery Soda. A synthetic flavoring agent that occurs naturally in black pepper, it is used as a pungent brandy flavoring. It is also used as a nontoxic insecticide. Believed to be more toxic than the commercial pyrethrins. The FDA data bank, PAFA (see page 10), has fully up-to-date toxicology information available on this food additive.

PIPERITONE • A synthetic flavoring agent that occurs naturally in Japanese mint. Used in beverages, ice cream, ices, candy, and baked goods. Used to give dentifrices a minty flavor and to give perfumes their peppermint scent. The FDA data bank, PAFA, has fully up-to-date toxicology information available on this food additive.

PIPERONAL • Heliotropin. A synthetic flavoring and perfume agent that occurs naturally in vanilla and black pepper. White crystalline powder with a sweet floral odor. Used in strawberry, cola, cherry, rum, maple, nut, and vanilla flavorings in beverages, ice cream, ices, baked goods, gelatin puddings, and chewing gum. Used chiefly in perfumery. Ingestion of large amounts may cause central nervous system depression. Has been reported to cause skin rash. In lipsticks, said to produce marking of the skin. Not recommended by some cosmetic chemists because of its ability to produce skin irritation. The FDA data bank, PAFA, has fully up-to-date toxicology information available on this food additive.

PIPERONYL ACETATE • A synthetic fruit flavoring agent for beverages, ice cream, ices, candy, and baked goods. The FDA data bank, PAFA, has fully up-to-date toxicology information available on this food additive. *See* Piperonal for toxicity.

PIPERONYL ALDEHYDE • *See* Piperonal.

PIPERONYL BUTOXIDE • Butoxide. Pyburthrin. Butocide. A light brown liquid, a widely used insecticide in animal feed, dried foods, milled fractions derived from cereal grains, and packaging materials. It is used in combination with pyrethrins (*see*) in oil solutions, emulsions, powders, or aerosols. FDA permits residues of up to 10 ppm in milled fractions derived from cereal grains, in dried foods, and in animal feed. International Agency for Research on Cancer (IARC) review and on the Community Right-To-Know List. No evidence, as yet, that it is a cancer-causing agent, but it is poisonous by skin contact. Moderately toxic by ingestion. Large doses have caused vomiting and diarrhea in humans. Has shown adverse reproductive effects in experimental animals.

PIPERONYL ISOBUTYRATE • A synthetic fruit and cheese flavoring for beverages, ice cream, ices, candy, and baked goods. The FDA data bank, PAFA (see page 10), has fully up-to-date toxicology information available on this food additive. *See* Piperonal for toxicity.

PIPERONYL PIPERIDINE • *See* Piperine.

PIPSISSEWA LEAVES EXTRACT • Love-in-winter. Prince's Pine. Extracted from the leaves of an evergreen shrub. Used in root beer, sarsaparilla, wintergreen, and birch beer flavorings for beverages and candy. Its leaves have been used as an astringent, diuretic, and tonic. The Cree name means "to break up"—bladder stones, that is. GRAS. The FDA data bank, PAFA, has not yet done a toxicology literature search on this food additive.

PLANTAIN EXTRACT • The extract of various species of plantain. The starchy fruit is a staple item of diet throughout the tropics and is used for bladder infections by herbalists. It is a natural astringent and antiseptic with soothing and cooling effects on blemishes and burns.

PLANTAROME • *See* Yucca Extract.

PLUM EXTRACT • The extract of the fruit of the plum tree, *Prunus domestica*. The Indians boiled the wild plum and gargled with it to cure mouth sores.

POLOXALENE • Therabloat. Bloat Guard. An animal-feed drug derived from ethylene oxide and propylene oxide used to prevent bloat, an excessive accumulation of gas in the stomachs of cattle. Severe bloat can be fatal. No known toxicity.

POLOXAMER 331 • A thick liquid used as a dough conditioner, foam control agent, solubilizing agent in flavor concentrates, as a detergent, and in a wash for poultry. FDA limits it to equal weight in flavor concentrations and to 0.5 percent in poultry baths; 5 grams per hog in dehairing machines; and 0.5 percent by weight of flour. No known toxicity, but when heated to decomposition, it emits acrid smoke and irritating fumes.

POLY- • A prefix meaning "many."

POLYACRYLAMIDE • The polymer of acrylamide monomers, it is a white solid, water soluble, that is used as a thickening agent, suspending agent, and as an additive to adhesives. In modified form it is used to clarify (*see* Clarifying Agent) cane sugar. Used as a film former in the imprinting of soft-shell gelatin capsules. Used in washing fruits and vegetables. Used in the manufacture of plastics used in nail polishes. Highly toxic and irritating to the skin. Causes central nervous system paralysis. Can be absorbed through unbroken skin. There is no reported use of the chemical and no toxicology information is available, according to the FDA's data bank, PAFA (see page 10).

POLYACRYLIC ACID • The FDA data bank, PAFA, has fully up-to-date toxicology information available on this food additive. *See* Acrylic Resins.

POLYALKYL ACRYLATE • Used in the production of petroleum wax. *See* Petroleum.

POLYAMINO SUGAR CONDENSATE • The condensation product of the sugars fructose, galactose, glucose, lactose, maltose, mannose, rhamnose, ribose, or xylose, with a minute amount of amino acids such as alanine, arginine, aspartic acid, glutamic acid, glycine, histidine, hydroxyproline, isoleucine, leucine, lysine, methionine, phenylalanine, proline, pyroglutamic acid, serine, threonine, tyrosine, or valine. *See* Amino Acids.

POLYBUTENE • Indopol. Polybutylene. A plasticizer. A polymer (*see*) of one or more butylenes obtained from petroleum oils. Used in lubricating oil, adhesives, sealing tape, cable insulation, films, and coatings. May asphyxiate.

POLYDEXTROSE • A reduced-calorie bulking agent developed by Pfizer Inc. and approved for use in foods by the FDA in June 1981. The FDA says it is not a substitute for saccharin (*see*) nor a general sweetener but that it can replace sucrose (*see*) as a bulking agent in frozen desserts, cakes, and candies and reduce calories in some products as much as 50 percent. According to Pfizer, it is a one-calorie-per-gram bulking agent capable of replacing higher-calorie—four to nine calories per gram—ingredients such as sucrose, carbohydrates, and fats in many food products. The FDA data bank, PAFA (see page 10), has fully up-to-date toxicology information available on this food additive.

POLYETHOXYLATED ALKYLPHENOL • Dodecyl, Nonyl, and Octyl. Components of a commercial detergent for raw foods, followed by water rinsing. The only symptoms shown in animals poisoned with this substance is gastrointestinal irritation.

POLYETHYLENE • A polymer (*see*) of ethylene; a product of petroleum gas or dehydration of alcohol. One of a group of lightweight thermoplastics that have a good resistance to chemicals, low moisture absorption, and good insulating properties. Used as a chewing-gum base ingredient and as a film former and sheets for packaging. Also used as roughage replacement in feedlot rations for cattle. Used in hand lotions. No known skin toxicity, but implants of large amounts in rats caused cancer. Ingestion of large oral doses has produced kidney and liver damage.

POLYETHYLENE GLYCOL • 400–2,000 molecular weight. PEG. Defoaming agent in processed beet sugar and yeast. Used in hair straighteners, antiperspirants, baby products, fragrances, polish removers, hair tonics, lipsticks, and protective creams. It is a binder, plasticizing agent, solvent, and softener widely used for cosmetic cream bases and pharmaceutical ointments. Improves resistance to moisture and oxidation. The FDA data bank, PAFA (see page 10), has not yet done a toxicology literature search on this food additive.

POLYETHYLENE GLYCOL (600) DIOLEATE • Polyethylene glycol esters of mixed fatty acids from tall oil; polyethylene glycol (400 through 6,000). An agent in nonnutritive artificial sweeteners; a component of coatings and binders in tablet food; improves resistance to oxidation and moisture. The FDA data bank, PAFA, has not yet done a toxicology literature search on this food additive. *See* Polyols.

POLYGLYCERATE 60 • *See* Glycerides.

POLYGLYCEROL • Prepared from edible fats, oils, and esters of fatty acids. Derived from corn, cottonseed, palm, peanut, safflower, sesame, and soybean oils, lard, and tallow. Used as an emulsifier in cosmetics. No known toxicity.

POLYGLYCEROL ESTER • One of several partial or complete esters of saturated and unsaturated fatty acids with a variety of derivatives of polyglycerols ranging from diglycerol to triacontaglycerol. Prepared from edible fats, oils, and fatty acids, hydrogenated or nonhydrogenated (*see* Hydrogenation). Derived from corn, cottonseed, palm, peanut, safflower, sesame, and soybean oils, lard, and tallow. Used as lubricants, plasticizers, gelling agents, humectants, surface-active agents, dispersants, and emulsifiers in foods and cosmetic preparations. The FDA data bank, PAFA, has fully up-to-date toxicology information available on this food additive.

POLYGLYCERYL-4 COCOATE • *See* Coconut Oil and Polyglycerol.

POLYGLYCERYL-10 DECALINOLEATE • *See* Polyglycerol and Linoleic Acid.

POLYGLYCERYL-10 DECAOLEATE • *See* Oleic Acid and Polyglycerol.

POLYGLYCERYL-2 DIISOSTEATE • *See* Isostearic Acid and Polyglycerol.

POLYGLYCERYL-6 DIOLEATE • *See* Oleic Acid and Glycerin.

POLYGLYCERYL-6 DISTEARATE • *See* Stearic Acid and Glycerin.

POLYGLYCERYL-3 HYDROXYLAURYL ETHER • *See* Fatty Alcohols and Glycerin.

POLYGLYCERYL-4 ISOSTEARATE • *See* Isostearic Acid and Glycerin.

POLYGLYCERYL-2 LANOLIN ALCOHOL ETHER • *See* Lanolin and Glycerin.

POLYGLYCERYL-LAURYL ETHER • *See* Fatty Alcohols and Glycerin.

POLYGLYCERYL-3 OR -4 OLEATE • Oily liquid prepared by adding alcohol to coconut oil or other triglycerides with a polyglyceryl. Used in foods, drugs, and cosmetics as fat emulsifiers in conjunction with other emulsifiers to prepare creams, lotions, and other emulsion products. In addition, they may also be used as lubricants, plasticizers, gelling agents, and dispersants. No known toxicity.

POLYGLYCERYL-3 OR -4 OR -8 OLEATE • An ester of oleic acid and glycerin (*see both*).

POLYGLYCERYL-2 OR -4 OLEYL ETHER • The ether of oleyl alcohol and glycerin (*see both*).

POLYGLYCERYL-3-PEG-2 COCOAMIDE • *See* Coconut Oil and Glycerin.

POLYGLYCERYL-2-PEG-4 STEARATE • An ether of peg-4 stearate (*see*) and glycerin (*see*).

POLYGLYCERYL-2-SESQUIISOSTEARATE • A mixture of esters of isostearic acid and glycerin (*see both*).

POLYGLYCERYL-2-SESQUIOLEATE • A mixture of ester of oleic acid and glycerin (*see both*).

POLYGLYCERYL SORBITOL • A condensation product of glycerin and sorbitol (*see both*).

POLYGLYCERYL-3, -4, OR -8 STEARATE • An ester of stearic acid and glycerin (*see both*).

POLYGLYCERYL-10 TETRAOLEATE • An ester of oleic acid and glycerin (*see both*).

POLYGLYCERYL-2 TETRASTEARATE • *See* Stearic Acid and Glycerin.

POLYISOBUTENE • *See* Polybutene.

POLYISOBUTYLENE • Soft to hard, elastic, light, white solid, odorless and tasteless. Used as a chewing substance in gum. The FDA data bank, PAFA (see page 10), has fully up-to-date toxicology information available on this food additive. *See* Resin, Isobutylene.

POLYLIMONENE • A general fixative derived from citrus oils. It is used in candy (4,500 ppm), chewing gum, and baked goods (1,000 ppm). It can be a skin irritant and sensitizer. Although allowed as a food additive, there is no current reported use of the chemical, and therefore, although toxicology information may be available, the FDA is not updating it. *See* Limonene.

POLYMER • A substance or product formed by combining many small molecules (monomers). The result is essentially recurring long-chain structural units that have tensile strength, elasticity, and hardness. Examples of polymers (literally, "having many parts") are plastics, fibers, rubber, and human tissue.

POLYMIXIN B₄ • A generic term for antibiotics obtained from fermentation of various media by strains of *Bacillus polymyxa.* Used as a bactericide in yeast culture for beer. May cause renal irritation and damage.

POLYOLS • Alcohol compounds that absorb moisture. They have a low molecular weight: polyols with a weight above 1,000 are solids and less toxic than those whose weight is 600 or below. The latter are liquid, and although higher in toxicity, large doses are required to kill animals. Such deaths in animals have been found to be due to kidney damage. *See* Propylene Glycol and Polyethylene Glycol as examples.

POLYOXYALKALENE GLYCOL • Defoaming agent in beet sugar production. No known toxicity.

POLYOXYETHYLENE COMPOUNDS • Nonionic emulsifiers used in hand creams and lotions. Usually oily or waxy liquids. No known toxicity.

POLYOXYETHYLENE GLYCOL • Ester of edible cottonseed oil and fatty acids. Solubilizing agent in pickles. No known toxicity.

POLYOXYETHYLENE GLYCOL (600) MONORICINOLEATE • Defoaming component used in processing beet sugar and yeast. No known toxicity.

POLYOXYETHYLENE (40) MONOSTEARATE • Defoaming agent in processed foods; emulsifier for frozen desserts. Application to the skin of mice has been shown to cause skin tumors. The compound has been fed to animals and does not appear to produce tumors on its own, but there is a suggestion that it allows cancer-causing agents to penetrate more quickly. On the FDA list for further study for long- and short-term effects since 1980. The FDA data bank, PAFA (see page 10), has fully up-to-date toxicology information available on this food additive.

POLYOXYETHYLENE (20) SORBITAN MONOSTEARATE • Polysorbate 60. An emulsifier and flavor-dispersing agent in shortening and edible oils. Used in whipped vegetable-oil topping, cake, and cake mixes; caking icing or filling; sugar-type confection coatings; coconut spread; beverage mixes; confectionery; chicken bases; gelatin desserts; dressings made without egg yolks; solid-state, edible vegetable fat–water emulsions used in substitutes for milk or cream; dietary vitamin supplements; foaming agents in nonalcoholic beverage mixes to be added to alcoholic beverages; and a wetting and dispersing agent for powdered processed foods. The FDA asked for further study of this additive in 1980.

POLYOXYETHYLENE (20) SORBITAN MONOOLEATE • Emulsifier and defoamer in the production of beet sugar; a dietary vitamin and mineral supplement. Used in dill oil in spiced green beans, icing, frozen custard, iced milk,

fruit, and sherbet. The FDA asked for short-term, mutagenic, teratogenic, sub-acute, and reproductive effects in 1980 and has not reported any findings since.
POLYOXYETHYLENE (20) SORBITAN MONOPALMITATE • An emulsifier, flavor-dispersing agent, and defoaming agent. Used in whipped cream, beverages, confectionery, and soup. The FDA asked for further study of the safety of this additive in 1980 and has reported nothing about it since.
POLYOXYETHYLENE (20) SORBITAN TRISTEARATE • An emulsifier, defoaming agent, and flavor-dispersing agent. Used in cakes and cake mixes, including doughnuts, whipped mixes, whipped vegetable-oil toppings, cake icings and fillings, ice cream, frozen custard, ice milk, fruit sherbet, and nonstandardized frozen desserts; solid-state, edible vegetable fat–water emulsions used as substitutes for milk or cream in coffee; and a wetting and dispersing agent in processed powdered food. No known toxicity.
POLYOXYETHYLENE STEARATE • A mixture of stearate (*see* Stearic Acid) and ethylene oxide, it is a waxy solid once added to bread to make it "feel fresh." It was fed to rats as one-fourth of their diets and resulted in the formation of bladder stones, and subsequently a number of tumors. Banned in 1952.
POLYOXYPROPYLENE GLYCOL • Defoaming agent for yeast and beet sugar. No known toxicity.
POLYSORBATE 60 AND POLYSORBATE 80 • Both are emulsifiers that have been associated with the contaminant 1,4 dioxane, known to cause cancer in animals. The 60 is a condensate of sorbitol with stearic acid, and the 80 is a condensate of sorbitol and oleic acid (*see all*). The 60 is waxy, soluble in solvents, and is used as an emulsifier, stabilizer, wetting and dispersing agent for powdered processed foods, and a foaming agent for beverage mixes. It is added to chocolate coatings to prevent cocoa-butter substitutes from tasting greasy. It is found in frozen and gelatin desserts, cakes, cake mixes, doughnuts, and artificial chocolate coatings, nondairy whipped cream and creamers, powdered convenience foods, salad dressings made without egg yolks, and vitamin supplements. The 80 is a viscous liquid with a faint caramel odor and is used as an emulsifier, stabilizer, and humectant. It prevents oil from separating from nondairy whipped cream and helps nondairy coffee whiteners to dissolve. It is also found in baked goods, ice cream, frozen custard, shortenings, and vitamin and mineral supplements. FDA residue tolerances in various products are from less than 0.1 percent to 4.5 percent. Polysorbate 80 is also widely used in baby lotions, cold creams, cream deodorants, antiperspirants, suntan lotions, and in bath oil products. *Polysorbate 40* is also widely used as an emulsifier in cosmetic creams and lotions and as a stabilizer of essential oils in water. The FDA data bank, PAFA (see page 10), has fully up-to-date toxicology information available on these food additives.
POLYSORBATES • 1 through 85. These are widely used emulsifiers and stabilizers. For example, *polysorbate 20* is a viscous, oily liquid derived from lauric acid. It is an emulsifier used in cosmetic creams and lotions and a stabilizer of essential oils in water. It is used as a nonionic surfactant (*see*). The FDA data bank, PAFA, has fully up-to-date toxicology information available on these food additives.

POLYSTYRENE • Used in the manufacture of cosmetic resins. Reported to be an unintentional additive when tea and coffee are drunk from polystyrene cups. Colorless to yellowish, oily liquid with a penetrating odor. Obtained from ethylbenzene by removing the hydrogen or by chlorination. Sparingly soluble in water; soluble in alcohol. May be irritating to the eyes and mucous membranes and, in high concentrations, may be narcotic.

POLYUNSATURATED FATS • The saturation of fat refers to the chemical structure of its constituent fatty acids. Polyunsaturates are liquid at room temperature and consist mainly of fatty acids that can hold four or more additional hydrogen atoms. *See* Monounsaturated Fats.

POLYVINYL ACETATE • Used in chewing gum base. The FDA data bank, PAFA (see page 10), has fully up-to-date toxicology information available on this food additive.

POLYVINYL ALCOHOL • Synthetic resins used to dilute the color of eggshells and in lipstick, setting lotions, and various creams. A polymer is prepared from polyvinyl acetates by replacement of the acetate groups with the hydroxyl groups. Dry, unplasticized polyvinyl-alcohol powders are white to cream colored and have different viscosities. Solvent in hot and cold water but certain ones require alcohol-water mixtures. FDA requires no penetration of polyvinyl alcohol through eggshell. An experimental cancer-causing and tumor-inducing agent. International Agency for Research on Cancer (IARC) (*see*) review. Although allowed as a food additive, there is no current reported use of the chemical, and therefore, although toxicology information may be available, the FDA is not updating it.

POLYVINYL BUTYRAL • The condensation of polyvinyl alcohol and butyraldehyde (*see both*), it is a synthetic flavoring found in coffee and strawberry and is used in the manufacture of rubber and synthetic resins and plasticizers. May be an irritant and narcotic.

POLYVINYL CHLORIDE (PVC) • Chloroethylene Polymer. Derived from vinyl chloride (*see*), it consists of a white powder or colorless granules that are resistant to weather, moisture, acids, fats, petroleum products, and fungus. It is widely used for everything from plumbing to raincoats. The use of PVC as a plastic wrap for food, including meats, and for human blood, has alarmed some scientists. Human and animal blood can extract potentially harmful chemicals from the plastic. The chemicals are added to polyvinyl chloride to make it flexible, and they migrate from the plastic into the blood and into the meats in amounts directly proportional to the length of time of storage. The result can be contamination of the blood, causing lung shock, a condition in which the patient's blood circulation to the lungs is impeded. PVC is also used in cosmetics and toiletries in containers, nail enamels, and creams. PVC has caused tumors when injected under the skin of rats in doses of one hundred milligrams per kilogram of body weight.

POLYVINYL ETHYL ETHER • *See* Polyvinyl Alcohol.

POLYVINYL IMIDAZOLINIUM ACETATE • The polymer of vinyl imidazolinium aceta. *See* Polyvinylpyrrolidone.

POLYVINYL METHYL ETHER • *See* Polyvinyl Alcohol.

POLYVINYLPYRROLIDONE (PVP) • A faintly yellow, solid plastic resin resembling albumin. Used in dietary products. Also a clarifying agent in vinegar and wine. Limitation of six pounds per thousand gallons in wine. FDA requires that it be removed by filtration. The FDA residue tolerance is less than 10 ppm in beer from use as a clarifying agent; less than 40 ppm in vinegar and 60 ppm in wine from use as a clarifying agent; and less than 60 ppm as a tableting adjuvant in nonnutritive sweeteners and in flavor, vitamin, and mineral concentrates in tablet form. Ingestion may produce gas and fecal impaction or damage to lungs and kidneys. It may last in the system several months to a year. Strong circumstantial evidence indicates thesaurosis—foreign bodies in the lung—may be produced in susceptible individuals from concentrated exposure to PVP in hairsprays. Modest intravenous doses in rats caused them to develop tumors. The FDA data bank, PAFA (see page 10), has fully up-to-date toxicology information available on this food additive.

POMEGRANATE BARK EXTRACT • A flavoring from the dried bark, stem, or root of the tree *Punica granatum,* in the Mediterranean region and elsewhere. Contains about 20 percent tannic acid (*see*); rind of fruit contains 30 percent. Formerly used to expel tapeworms. Overdose can cause nausea, vomiting, and diarrhea. GRAS. The FDA data bank, PAFA, has not yet done a toxicology literature search on this food additive.

POPLAR EXTRACT • Balm of Gilead. Extract of the leaves and twigs of *Populus nigra.* In ancient times, the buds were mashed to make a soothing salve that was spread on sunburned areas, scalds, scratches, inflamed skin, and wounds. They were also simmered in lard for use as an ointment and for antiseptic purposes. The leaves and bark were steeped by American colonists to make a soothing tea. It supposedly helped allergies and soothed reddened eyes. Although allowed as a food additive, there is no current reported use of the chemical, and therefore, although toxicology information may be available, the FDA is not updating it.

POPPY SEED • The seed of the poppy, *Papaver somniferum.* Used as a natural spice for flavoring for baked goods (8,600 ppm). Also used in the manufacture of paints, varnishes, and soaps. GRAS. The FDA data bank, PAFA (see page 10), has not yet done a toxicology literature search on this food additive.

POT MARIGOLD • *See* Marigold, Pot. GRAS.

POT MARJORAM • *See* Marjoram, Pot. GRAS.

POTASSIUM • The healthy human body contains about nine grams of potassium. Most of it is found inside body cells. Potassium plays an important role in maintaining water balance and acid-base balance. It participates in the transmission of nerve impulses and in the transfer of messages from nerves to muscles. It also acts as a catalyst in carbohydrate and protein metabolism. Potassium is important for the maintenance of normal kidney function. It has a major effect on the heart and all the muscles of the body.

POTASSIUM ACETATE • Colorless, water-absorbing crystals or powder, odorless or with a faint acetic aroma and a salty taste. Used as a buffer and antimicrobial preservative. Very soluble in water. Also used medicinally to treat irregular heartbeat and as a diuretic. Although allowed as a food additive, there is no current reported use of the chemical, and therefore, although toxicology information may be available, the FDA is not updating it.

POTASSIUM ACID TARTRATE • The salt of tartaric acid. Colorless with a pleasant odor. An acid and buffer, it is the acid constituent of some baking powders. Used in effervescent beverages. It is also used in some confectionery products. Formerly a cathartic. The FDA data bank, PAFA (see page 10), has fully up-to-date toxicology information available on this food additive.

POTASSIUM ALGINATE • A stabilizer (see). GRAS. See Alginates.

POTASSIUM ALUM • See Alum.

POTASSIUM ASPARTAME • See Aspartame.

POTASSIUM ASPARTATE • The potassium salt of aspartic acid (see).

POTASSIUM BENZOATE • A preservative used in margarine and wine. FDA limits the amount to 0.1 percent or if used in combination with sorbic acid (see) to 0.2 percent in margarine and 0.1 percent in wine. There is no reported use of the chemical and no toxicology information is available, according to the FDA's data bank, PAFA. See Benzoic Acid.

POTASSIUM BICARBONATE • Carbonic Acid, Monopotassium Salt. Colorless, odorless, transparent crystals or powder, slightly alkaline, salty taste. Considered a miscellaneous and/or general-purpose food additive, it is present in fluids and tissues of the body as a product of normal metabolic processes. Soluble in water. It is used in baking, soft drinks, and in low-pH liquid detergents. The final report to the FDA of the Select Committee on GRAS Substances stated in 1980 that it should continue its GRAS status with no limitations other than good manufacturing practices. The FDA data bank, PAFA (see page 10), has fully up-to-date toxicology information available on this food additive.

POTASSIUM BISULFITE • Same uses as for sodium sulfite (see) in ale, beer, and fruit-pie mix. The final report to the FDA of the Select Committee on GRAS Substances stated in 1980 that there is no evidence in the available information that it is a hazard to the public when used as it is now and it should continue its GRAS status with limitations on the amounts that can be added to food. The FDA data bank, PAFA, has fully up-to-date toxicology information available on this food additive. See Sulfites.

POTASSIUM BROMATE • The compound is added as an improving agent in bread. The expected result is to obtain a fine spongelike quality with the action of oxygen. This method is used in Great Britain, the United States, and Japan. Legal allowance of potassium bromate is below 50 ppm in white flour and 75 ppm in whole wheat flour. Antiseptic and astringent in toothpaste, mouthwashes, and gargles as 3 to 5 percent solution. Colorless or white crystals. Very toxic when taken internally. Burns and skin irritation have been reported from its industrial uses. In toothpaste it has been reported to have caused inflammation and bleeding of gums. In 1980, the Ames Test (see) found it to be a mutagen. The World Health Organization Committee on Food Additives said in 1993 that new data about potassium bromate showed long-term toxicity and carcinogenicity including kidney tumors, tumors of the lining of the stomach, and thyroid tumors in rats and slightly increased kidney tumors in hamsters. On the basis of the new safety data and the new data on residual bromate in bread, the committee concluded the use of potassium bromate as a flour-treatment agent was not appropriate. The previous acceptable level of treatment of flours for bread-making was therefore withdrawn.

POTASSIUM BROMIDE • A preservative used in washing fruits and vegetables. Used medicinally as a sedative and antiepileptic. In large doses it can cause central nervous system depression. Prolonged intake may cause bromism. Bromism's main symptoms are headache, mental inertia, slow heartbeat, gastric distress, skin rash, acne, muscular weakness, and occasionally violent delirium. Bromides can cross the placental barrier and have caused skin rashes in the fetus. The FDA data bank, PAFA, has fully up-to-date toxicology information available on this food additive.

POTASSIUM CARBONATE • Salt of Tartar. Pearl Ash. Inorganic salt of potassium. Odorless, white powder soluble in water but practically insoluble in alcohol. Used as an alkali in combination with potassium hydroxide (*see*) for extracting color from annatto seed (*see*). Also used in confections and cocoa products. Used in freckle lotions, liquid shampoos, vanishing creams, setting lotions, and permanent-wave lotions; also in the manufacture of soap, glass, pottery, and to finish leather. Formerly employed as a diuretic to reduce body water and as an alkalizer. Irritating and caustic to human skin and may cause dermatitis of the scalp, forehead, and hands. The final report to the FDA of the Select Committee on GRAS Substances stated in 1980 that it should continue its GRAS status with no limitations other than good manufacturing practices. The FDA data bank, PAFA (see page 10), has fully up-to-date toxicology information available on this food additive.

POTASSIUM CASEINATE • The potassium salt of milk proteins used in ice cream, frozen custard, ice milk, and fruit sherbets. The FDA data bank, PAFA, has fully up-to-date toxicology information available on this food additive. *See* Casein.

POTASSIUM CHLORIDE • A colorless, crystalline, odorless powder with a salty taste. A yeast food used in the brewing industry to improve brewing and fermentation and in the jelling industry. Small intestinal ulcers may occur with oral administration. Large doses ingested can cause gastrointestinal irritation, purging, weakness, and circulatory collapse. Used as a substitute for sodium chloride (*see*) in low-sodium dietary foods. The final report to the FDA of the Select Committee on GRAS Substances stated in 1980 that it should continue its GRAS status with no limitations other than good manufacturing practices. The FDA data bank, PAFA (see page 10), is currently searching the toxicology literature concerning this additive.

POTASSIUM CITRATE • A transparent or white powder, odorless, with a cool, salty taste. Used as a buffer in confections and in artificially sweetened jellies and preserves. It is a urinary alkalizer and gastric antacid. No known toxicity. The final report to the FDA of the Select Committee on GRAS Substances stated in 1980 that it should continue its GRAS status with no limitations other than good manufacturing practices. The FDA data bank, PAFA, has fully up-to-date toxicology information available on this food additive.

POTASSIUM COCO HYDROLYZED PROTEIN • *See* Proteins.

POTASSIUM COCOATE • *See* Coconut Oil.

POTASSIUM CORNATE • The potassium salt of fatty acids derived from corn oil. *See* Corn Oil.

POTASSIUM GIBBERELLATE • The salt of gibberellic acid, a plant growth-promoting hormone. White crystalline powder that absorbs water. Used as an enzyme activator in fermented malt beverages. FDA limits it to 2 ppm in treated barley malt and 0.5 ppm in the finished beverage. The FDA data bank, PAFA (see page 10), has not yet done a toxicology literature search on this food additive.

POTASSIUM GLUCONATE • The potassium salt of gluconic acid (*see*) used as a buffering agent that helps keep soda water bubbling. Mildly toxic by ingestion. The final report to the FDA of the Select Committee on GRAS Substances stated in 1980 that it should continue its GRAS status with no limitations other than good manufacturing practices. There is no reported use of the chemical and no toxicology information is available, according to the FDA's data bank, PAFA.

POTASSIUM GLYCEROPHOSPHATE • Nutrient additive. *See* Glycerides. GRAS.

POTASSIUM HYDROXIDE • Caustic Potash. An alkali used to extract color from annatto seed, a peeling agent for tubers and fruits, also in cacao products. Occasionally used to prevent the growth of horns in calves. It is used as an emulsifier in hand lotions, as a cuticle softener, and as an alkali in liquid soaps, protective creams, shaving preparations, and cream rouges. Prepared industrially by electrolysis of potassium chloride (*see*). White or slightly yellow lumps. It may cause irritation of the skin in cuticle removers. Extremely corrosive, and ingestion may cause violent pain, bleeding, collapse, and death. When applied to the skin of mice, moderate dosages cause tumors. May cause skin rash and burning. Concentrations above 5 percent can destroy fingernails as well. Good-quality toilet soaps do not contain more than 0.25 percent free alkali. The FDA banned household products containing more than 10 percent potassium hydroxide. GRAS. The FDA data bank, PAFA (see page 10), has fully up-to-date toxicology information available on this food additive.

POTASSIUM HYPOPHOSPHATE • The final report to the FDA of the Select Committee on GRAS Substances stated in 1980 that it should continue its GRAS status with no limitations other than good manufacturing practices. There is no reported use of the chemical and no toxicology information is available, according to the FDA's data bank, PAFA. *See* Phosphate.

POTASSIUM IODATE • The FDA data bank, PAFA, has not yet done a toxicology literature search on this food additive. *See* Iodine Sources. GRAS.

POTASSIUM IODIDE • Potassium Salt. A dye remover and an antiseptic. Used in table salt as a source of dietary iodine. It is also in some drinking water. May cause allergic reactions. GRAS. The FDA data bank, PAFA, has not yet done a toxicology literature search on this food additive.

POTASSIUM LACTATE • Flavoring. There is no reported use of the chemical and no toxicology information is available, according to the FDA's data bank, PAFA (see page 10). *See* Lactic Acid. GRAS.

POTASSIUM LAURATE • The potassium salt of lauric acid (*see*). There is no reported use of the chemical and no toxicology information is available, according to the FDA's data bank, PAFA.

POTASSIUM LAURYL SULFATE • A water softener used in shampoos. *See* Sodium Lauryl Sulfate.

POTASSIUM METABISULFITE • Potassium Pyrosulfite. White or colorless, with an odor of sulfur dioxide (*see*), it is an antioxidant, preservative, and antifermentative in breweries and wineries. Should not be used in meats or foods recognized as sources of vitamin B_1. Also used for bleaching straw and as an antiseptic, preservative, antioxidant, and a developing agent in dyes. Low toxicity. The final report to the FDA of the Select Committee on GRAS Substances stated in 1980 that there is no available evidence that it is a hazard to the public when used as it is now and it should continue its GRAS status with limitations on the amounts that can be added to foods. The FDA data bank, PAFA, is currently searching the toxicology literature concerning this additive. *See* Sulfites.

POTASSIUM-*n*-METHYLDITHIO-CARBAMATE • A bacteria-killing component in controlling microorganisms in cane-sugar mills. Carbamates are used to prevent sprouting in potatoes and other products by stopping cell division, something we call mutations. Carbamate mutations may lead to birth defects and to cancer. The final report to the FDA of the Select Committee on GRAS Substances stated in 1980 that there is no available evidence that it is a hazard to the public when used as it is now and it should continue its GRAS status with limitations on the amounts that can be added to food. FDA residue tolerances are less than 3.5 ppm in sugarcane being processed, less than 4.1 ppm in terms of weight of raw cane or beets, and less than 200 ppm in cured cod roe. The FDA data bank, PAFA (see page 10), has fully up-to-date toxicology information available on this food additive.

POTASSIUM MYRISTATE • The potassium salt of myristic acid (*see*). The FDA data bank, PAFA, has not yet done a toxicology literature search on this food additive.

POTASSIUM NITRATE • The FDA data bank, PAFA, has not yet done a toxicology literature search on this food additive. *See* Nitrate.

POTASSIUM NITRITE • Although allowed as a food additive, there is no current reported use of the chemical, and therefore, although toxicology information may be available, the FDA is not updating it. *See* Nitrite.

POTASSIUM OCTOXYNOL-12 PHOSPHATE • The potassium salt of a mixture of esters of phosphoric acid and octoxynol (*see both*).

POTASSIUM PALMITATE • The potassium salt of palmitic acid (*see*). There is no reported use of the chemical and no toxicology information is available, according to the FDA's data bank, PAFA (see page 10).

POTASSIUM PERMANGANATE • Dark purple or bronzelike, odorless crystals with a sweet, antiseptic taste, used as a starch modifier. Dilute solutions are mildly irritating; highly concentrated solutions are caustic. The FDA data bank, PAFA, has not yet done a toxicology literature search on this food additive.

POTASSIUM PERSULFATE • White crystals, soluble in water or alcohol. Derived from potassium sulfate. Used as a flour-maturing agent, for modification of starch, and as an antiseptic. Sprayed on fresh citrus as a coating. Strong irritant. Although allowed as a food additive, there is no current reported use of the chemical, and therefore, although toxicology information may be available, the FDA is not updating it.

POTASSIUM PHOSPHATE • Monobasic, Dibasic, and Tribasic. Used as a yeast food in the brewing industry and in the production of champagne and other sparkling wines. Has been used medicinally as a urinary acidifier. No known toxicity. The final report to the FDA of the Select Committee on GRAS Substances stated in 1980 that it should continue its GRAS status with no limitations other than good manufacturing practices. The FDA data bank, PAFA (see page 10), is currently searching the toxicology literature concerning this additive.

POTASSIUM POLYMETAPHOSPHATE • The final report to the FDA of the Select Committee on GRAS Substances stated in 1980 that it should continue its GRAS status with no limitations other than good manufacturing practices. *See* Potassium Phosphate for uses.

POTASSIUM PYROPHOSPHATE • Colorless, deliquescent crystals or granules, used as a sequestering, peptizing, and dispersing agent and in soaps and detergents. Low toxicity. The final report to the FDA of the Select Committee on GRAS Substances stated in 1980 that it should continue its GRAS status with no limitations other than good manufacturing practices. The FDA data bank, PAFA, is currently searching the toxicology literature concerning this additive.

POTASSIUM SALTS OF FATTY ACIDS • In foods as binders, emulsifiers, and anticaking agents. *See* Fatty Acids.

POTASSIUM SILICATE • Soluble Potash Glass. Colorless or yellowish, translucent to transparent, glasslike particles. It is used for inorganic protective coatings, for phosphorous on television tubes, in detergents, as a catalyst, and in adhesives. Used as a binder in cosmetics and in soap manufacturing. Also used as a detergent and in the glass and ceramics industries. Usually very slowly soluble in cold water. No known toxicity. The final report to the FDA of the Select Committee on GRAS Substances stated in 1980 that it should continue its GRAS status with no limitations other than good manufacturing practices.

POTASSIUM SORBATE • Sorbic Acid Potassium Salt. White crystalline powder used as a preservative; a mold and yeast inhibitor; and a fungistat in beverages, baked goods, chocolate, and soda fountain syrups, fresh fruit cocktail, tangerine puree (sherbet base), salads (potato, macaroni, coleslaw, gelatin), cheesecake, pie fillings, cake, cheeses in consumer-size packages, and artificially sweetened jellies and preserves. Low oral toxicity but may cause irritation of the skin. GRAS. The FDA data bank, PAFA (see page 10), is currently searching the toxicology literature concerning this additive.

POTASSIUM STEARATE • Stearic Acid Potassium Salt. White powder with a fatty odor. Strongly alkaline. A defoaming agent in brewing. Also used in the manufacture of soap, hand creams, emulsified fragrances, lotions, and shaving creams. No known toxicity.

POTASSIUM SULFATE • Does not occur free in nature but is combined with sodium sulfate. Colorless or white crystalline powder, with a bitter taste. Used as a flavoring in foods. A water corrective used in the brewing industry. Used as a reagent (*see*) in cosmetics and as a salt substitute; also used as a fertilizer and a cathartic. Large doses can cause severe gastrointestinal bleeding. No known toxicity to the skin. GRAS. The FDA data bank, PAFA, has fully up-to-date toxicology information available on this food additive.

POTASSIUM SULFITE • *See* Sulfites.

POTASSIUM TRICHLOROISOCYANURATE • A sanitizer. *See* Arsenic.

POTASSIUM TRIPOLYPHOSPHATE • A white crystalline solid that is used in water-treating compounds, cleaners, and fertilizers; widely used as a sequestering agent (*see*) in processed foods. The final report to the FDA of the Select Committee on GRAS Substances stated in 1980 that it should continue its GRAS status with no limitations other than good manufacturing practices. The FDA data bank, PAFA (see page 10), is currently searching the toxicology literature concerning this additive.

POTATO STARCH • A flour prepared from potatoes ground to a pulp and washed of fibers. Swells in hot water to form a gel on cooling. A demulcent used in dusting powder; an emollient in dry shampoos and baby powders. With glycerin forms soothing, protective applications for eczema, skin rash, and chapped skin. May cause allergic skin reactions and stuffy nose in the hypersensitive. The final report to the FDA of the Select Committee on GRAS Substances stated in 1980 that it should continue its GRAS status with no limitations other than good manufacturing practices.

POTENTIATOR • A flavor ingredient with little flavor of its own that augments or alters the flavor response, such as sodium glutamate and sodium inosinate.

PPB • Abbreviation for *parts per billion*.

PPG • Abbreviation for *propylene glycol (see)*.

PPG BUTETH-260 THROUGH 5100 • Emulsifiers. *See* PPG Buteth-55.

PPG BUTETH ETHER-200 • Emulsifier. Polymer (*see*) prepared from butyl alcohol with propylene glycol (*see both*).

PPG-4-CETETH-1, -5, OR -10 • *See* Cetyl Alcohol.

PPG-8-CETETH-5, -10, OR -20 • *See* Cetyl Alcohol.

PPG-10-CETYL ETHER • *See* Cetyl Alcohol.

PPG-30 CETYL ETHER • A liquid nonionic surfactant (*see*). No known toxicity. *See* Cetyl Alcohol.

PPG-20-DECYLTETRADECETH-10 • *See* Decanoic Acid.

PPG-24 OR -66 GLYCERETH-24 OR -12 • *See* Glycerin.

PPG-27 AND -55 GLYCERYLETHER • *See* Glycerin and Propylene Glycol.

PPG-ISOCETYL ETHER • *See* Cetyl Alcohol.

PPG-3-ISOSTEARETH-9 • *See* Stearyl Alcohol and Propylene Glycol.

PPG-2, -5, -10, -20, OR -30 LANOLIN ALCOHOL ETHERS • *See* Lanolin Alcohol.

PPG-30 LANOLIN ETHER • Derived from lanolin alcohols (*see*).

PPG-9 LAURATE • *See* Lauric Acid.

PPG-20-METHYL GLUCOSE ETHER • *See* Propylene Glycol and Glucose.

PPG-3-MYRETH-11 • *See* Polyethylene Glycol and Myristic Acid.

PPG-4 MYRISTYL ETHER • *See* Fatty Alcohols.

PPG-10 OLEYL ETHER • *See* PPG-26 Oleate.

PPG-30 OR -50 OLEYL ETHER • *See* PPG-26 Oleate.

PPG-6-C12-18 PARETH • A mixture of synthetic alcohols. *See* Fatty Alcohols.

PPG-9-STEARETH-3 • *See* Stearyl Alcohol.

PPG-11 OR -15 STEARYL ETHER • *See* Propylene Glycol and Stearyl Alcohol.

PPM • Abbreviation for *parts per million.*

PRECIPITATE • To separate out from solution or suspension. A deposit of solid separated out from a solution or suspension as a result of a chemical or physical change, as by the action of a reagent (*see*).

PREDNISOLONE • Metacortandrolone. Cortalone. Delta-Cortef. Introduced in 1955, prednisolone is related chemically to cortisol. It is used to treat inflammation in cattle. FDA residue tolerance for milk is zero. It is used to treat severe inflammation, as an immunosuppressant, in the treatment of ulcerative colitis, and in proctitis in humans. Most adverse reactions are the result of dose or length of time of administration. Should be taken with food or milk to reduce GI irritation. Potential adverse reactions include euphoria, insomnia, psychotic behavior, high blood pressure, swelling, cataracts, glaucoma, peptic ulcer, GI irritation, increased appetite, high blood sugar, growth suppression in children, delayed wound healing, acne, skin eruptions, muscle weakness, pancreatitis, hairiness, decreased immunity, and acute adrenal gland insufficiency. When withdrawn, there may be rebound inflammation, fatigue, weakness, joint pain, fever, dizziness, lethargy, depression, fainting, a drop in blood pressure upon arising from a seated or prone position, shortness of breath, loss of appetite, and high blood sugar.

PREDNISONE • Deltacortisone. Introduced in 1955 and related chemically to cortisone, a hormone secreted by the adrenal gland, prednisone is widely used to treat severe inflammation, as an immunosuppressant, and to treat acute attacks of multiple sclerosis, arthritis, and irritable-bowel syndrome in humans. It is used to treat cattle and horses for inflammation. FDA has a zero limitation in milk. International Agency for Research on Cancer (IARC) (*see*) review. Most adverse reactions are the result of dose or length of time of administration. In humans, potential adverse reactions from medication include euphoria, insomnia, psychotic behavior, high blood pressure, swelling, cataracts, glaucoma, peptic ulcer, GI irritation, increased appetite, high blood sugar, growth suppression in children, delayed wound healing, acne, skin eruptions, muscle weakness, pancreatitis, hairiness, decreased immunity, irregular menstruation, male infertility, and acute adrenal gland insufficiency. When withdrawn, there may be rebound inflammation, fatigue, weakness, joint pain, fever, dizziness, lethargy, depression, fainting, a drop in blood pressure upon arising from a seated or prone position, shortness of breath, loss of appetite, and high blood sugar. Sudden withdrawal may be fatal. Contraindicated in systemic fungal infections. Should be used cautiously in patients with GI ulceration or kidney disease, high blood pressure, diabetes, chicken pox, or osteoporosis. Prednisone has been implicated in aplastic anemia and is an experimental tumor inducer.

PREDONIN • *See* Prednisone.

PREGELATINIZED STARCH • When starch and water are heated, the starch molecules burst and form a gelatin. The final report to the FDA of the Select Committee on GRAS Substances stated in 1980 that it should continue its GRAS status with no limitations other than good manufacturing practices.

PRESERVATIVES • About one hundred "antispoilants," which retard or prevent food from going "bad," are in common use. Preservatives for fatty products are called antioxidants. Preservatives used in bread are labeled mold or rope inhibitors. They include sodium propionate and calcium propionate (*see both*). Preservatives to prevent mold and fungus growth on citrus fruits are called fungicides. Among the most commonly used preservatives are sodium benzoate (*see*) to prevent the growth of microbes on cheese and syrups, sulfur dioxide (*see*) to inhibit discoloration in fruit juice concentrates, and nitrates and nitrites that are used to "cure" processed meats. In many instances a product might show no visible evidence of microbial contamination and yet contain actively growing, potentially harmful germs.

PRICKLY ASH BARK • A natural cola, maple, and root beer flavor extract from a prickly aromatic shrub or small tree, *Zanthoxylum* spp., bearing yellow flowers. Used in beverages, candy, and baked goods. GRAS. There is no reported use of the chemical and no toxicology information is available, according to the FDA's data bank, PAFA (see page 10).

PRIMATOL • Prometon. Aatrex. Zeazine. Weedex A. A widely used herbicide on cropland. Moderately toxic by ingestion. An experimental tumor inducer. Causes adverse reproductive effects in experimental animals. A skin and severe eye irritant.

PRIMULA EXTRACT • The extract of various species of *Primula* taken from the rhizome and roots of the primrose or cowslip. It has been used as an expectorant, diuretic, and worm medicine. In some sensitive persons, it may cause a rash.

PROCAINE PENICILLIN • An antibiotic used as an injection in animals. FDA tolerance in uncooked edible tissue of cattle is 0.05 ppm, and in uncooked edible tissue of turkey, 0.01 ppm. Zero tolerance in milk and uncooked edible tissue of chicken, pheasants, quail, swine, sheep, and eggs.

PROFENOFOS • A pesticide used in feed. FDA tolerances are 6 ppm in or on cottonseed hulls; 15 ppm in soap-stocks.

PROFLURALIN • Yellow-orange crystals used as an herbicide. FDA residue tolerances are 0.3 as a residue in or on soybean hay; 0.1 ppm in or on cottonseed, pod vegetables, and sunflower seeds; and 0.02 ppm as residue in or on eggs or milk, meat, fat, and meat byproducts of cattle, hogs, goats, poultry, and sheep.

PROGESTERONE • Corlutin. Cyclogest. Luteal Hormone. Synovex. Gesterol 50. Progestaject. A progestin drug that suppresses ovulation, possibly by inhibiting pituitary gonadotropin secretion. It forms a thick cervical mucus. Used to treat absent menstruation or abnormal uterine bleeding in humans. Used in beef and lamb to regulate reproductive cycles. Potential adverse reactions in humans include nausea, vomiting, depression, high blood pressure, dizziness, migraine, lethargy, blood clots, swelling, bloating, and abdominal cramps. May cause breakthrough bleeding, altered menstrual flow, painful or absent menstruation, enlargement of benign tumors of the uterus, cervical erosion, abnormal secretions, and vaginal candidiasis. There may be jaundice; high blood sugar; dark spots appearing on the skin; breast tenderness, enlargement, or secretion; and decreased libido. Contraindicated in persons with blood-clot disorders, cancer of the breast, undiagnosed abnormal vaginal bleeding, and in pregnancy. The FDA limits residues from progesterone treatment in animals to 3 ppb in muscle, 12 ppb in fat, 9 ppb in kidney, and 6 ppb in liver of steers and calves, and 3 ppb in muscle and 15 ppb for fat, kidney, and liver of lambs. International Agency for Research on Cancer (IARC) (*see*) review. A cancer and tumor inducer in experimental animals. May cause birth defects.

PROLINE • L Form. An amino acid (*see*) used as a food supplement but classified as nonessential. Usually isolated from wheat or gelatin. L-Proline is the naturally occurring form and DL-Proline is the synthetic. GRAS. The FDA data bank, PAFA (see page 10), has fully up-to-date toxicology information available on this food additive.

PROPANE • A gas heavier than air; odorless when pure. It is used as a fuel and refrigerant. Cleared for use in combination with octafluorocyclobutane in a spray propellant and as an aerating agent for foamed and sprayed foods. Cleared for use in a spray propellant and as an aerating agent for cosmetics in aerosols. May be narcotic in high concentrations. The final report to the FDA of the Select Committee on GRAS Substances stated in 1980 that it should continue its GRAS status with no limitations other than good manufacturing practices. There is no reported use of the chemical and no toxicology information is available, according to the FDA's data bank, PAFA.

1,2-PROPANEDIOL • *See* Propylene Glycol.

PROPANOIC ACID • *See* Propionic Acid.

PROPARGITE • A pesticide applied to growing crops to kill mites. FDA residue tolerance is 80 ppm in dried apple pomace and 40 ppm in dried citrus pulp and dried grape pulp. Less than 100 ppm can kill fish if it gets in water.

PROPAZINE • Propasin. Prozinex. An herbicide used on animal feed to control weeds. Moderately toxic by ingestion. Caused tumors in experimental animals.

PROPELLANT • A compressed gas used to expel the contents of containers in the form of aerosols. Chlorofluorocarbons were widely used because of their nonflammability. The strong possibility that they contribute to depletion of the ozone layer of the upper atmosphere has resulted in prohibition of their use for this purpose. Other propellants used are hydrocarbon gases, such as butane and propane, carbon dioxide, and nitrous oxide. The materials dispersed include shaving cream, whipping cream, and cosmetic preparations.

PROPETAMPHOS • A pesticide used as a spot, crack, and crevice treatment to kill parasites.

PROPIOMAZINE • Propionylpromethazine. A sedative and hypnotic used in human medicine. A tranquilizer used to treat stress in pigs. See page 5.

PROPIONALDEHYDE • Propanal. A synthetic flavoring agent that occurs naturally in apples and onions. Used in fruit flavorings for beverages, ice cream, ices, candy, and baked goods. Suffocating odor. May cause respiratory irritation. Moderately toxic by ingestion. The FDA data bank, PAFA (see page 10), has fully up-to-date toxicology information available on this food additive.

PROPIONIC ACID • Propanoic Acid. Occurs naturally in apples, strawberries, tea, and violet leaves. An oily liquid with a slightly pungent, rancid odor. Can be obtained from wood pulp, waste liquor, and by fermentation. Used in butter and fruit flavorings for beverages, ice cream, ices, candy, baked goods, and cheese flavorings for beverages, ice cream, ices, candy, baked goods, and cheese (600 ppm). Also used as an inhibitor and preservative to prevent mold in baked goods and processed cheeses. Also used in perfume bases and as a mold inhibitor, antioxidant, and preservative in cosmetics. Its salts have been used as antifungal agents to treat skin mold. May cause migraine in those susceptible to migraines, and contact with the chemical may cause skin irritations in bakery workers. Large oral dose in rats is lethal. GRAS. The FDA data bank, PAFA, has fully up-to-date toxicology information available on this food additive.

PROPYL ACETATE • Colorless liquid, soluble in water, derived from propane and acetate (*see both*). It has the odor of pears. A synthetic currant, raspberry, strawberry, apple, cherry, peach, pineapple, and rum flavoring agent for beverages, ice cream, ices, candy, and baked goods. Also used in the manufacture of perfumes and as a solvent for resins. It may be irritating to the skin and mucous membranes and narcotic in high doses. The FDA data bank, PAFA (see page 10), has fully up-to-date toxicology information available on this food additive.

PROPYL ALCOHOL • Obtained from natural gas and fusel oil. Alcoholic and slightly overpowering odor. Occurs naturally in cognac green oil, cognac white oil, and onion oil. A synthetic fruit flavoring for beverages, ice cream, ices, candy, and baked goods. Used instead of ethyl alcohol as a solvent for shellac, gums, resins, and oils; a denaturant (*see*) for alcohol in perfumery. Not a primary irritant, but because it dissolves fat, it has a drying effect on the skin and may lead to cracking, fissuring, and infections. No adverse effects have been reported from local application as a lotion, liniment, mouthwash, gargle, or sponge bath. Mildly irritating to the eyes and mucous membranes. Ingestion may cause symptoms similar to that of ethyl alcohol (*see*). The FDA data bank, PAFA, has fully up-to-date toxicology information available on this food additive.

p-PROPYL ANISOLE • A synthetic flavoring agent, colorless to pale yellow, with an anise odor. Used in licorice, root beer, spice, vanilla, wintergreen, and birch beer flavoring for beverages, ice cream, candy, and baked goods. Moderately toxic by ingestion. Caused mutations in experimental animals. The FDA data bank, PAFA (see page 10), has fully up-to-date toxicology information available on this food additive.

PROPYL BENZOATE • A synthetic fruit flavoring agent for beverages, ice cream, ices, candy, and baked goods. The FDA data bank, PAFA, has fully up-to-date toxicology information available on this food additive.

PROPYL BUTYRATE • Contains propyl alcohol and butyric acid. A synthetic strawberry, banana, pineapple, plum, tutti-frutti, liquor, and rum flavoring agent for beverages, ice cream, ices, candy, and baked goods. The FDA data bank, PAFA, has fully up-to-date toxicology information available on this food additive. *See* Propyl Alcohol and Butyric Acid for toxicity.

PROPYL CINNAMATE • Cinnamic Acid. A synthetic berry, floral, rose, apple, grape, and honey flavoring agent for beverages, ice cream, ices, candy, baked goods, and gelatins. The FDA data bank, PAFA, has fully up-to-date toxicology information available on this food additive.

PROPYL FORMATE • Formic Acid. A synthetic berry, apple, and rum flavoring agent for beverages, ice cream, ices, candy, and baked goods. The FDA data bank, PAFA, has fully up-to-date toxicology information available on this food additive. *See* Formic Acid for toxicity.

PROPYL 2-FURANACRYLATE • A synthetic coffee and honey flavoring agent for beverages and candy. The FDA data bank, PAFA, has fully up-to-date toxicology information available on this food additive.

PROPYL 2-FUROATE • A synthetic chocolate and mushroom flavoring agent for candy, baked goods, and condiments. The FDA data bank, PAFA (see page 10), has fully up-to-date toxicology information available on this food additive.

PROPYL GALLATE • A fine, white, odorless powder with a bitter taste used as an antioxidant for foods, fats, and oils and for potato flakes, mashed potatoes, and mayonnaise. Also used in lemon, lime, fruit, and spice flavorings for beverages, ice cream, ices, candy, baked goods, and gelatin desserts. Also used as an antioxidant in creams and lotions. Can cause stomach or skin irritation especially in people who suffer from asthma or are sensitive to aspirin. Reaffirmed as GRAS in the FDA's reevaluation in the following amounts: 0.02 percent maximum in fat or oil content of food; maximum of 0.015 percent in food prepared by the manufacturer. The FDA data bank, PAFA, has fully up-to-date toxicology information available on this food additive.

PROPYL HEPTANOATE • A synthetic berry, coffee, fruit, cognac, and rum flavoring agent for beverages, ice cream, ices, candy, liqueurs, and baked goods. The FDA data bank, PAFA, has fully up-to-date toxicology information available on this food additive.

PROPYL HEXANOATE • A synthetic pineapple flavoring agent for beverages, ice cream, ices, and candy. The FDA data bank, PAFA (see page 10), has fully up-to-date toxicology information available on this food additive.

PROPYL-*p*-HYDROXYBENZOATE • Propylparaben. A preservative used in beverages, candy, baked goods, and artificially sweetened jellies and preserves. Also used in fruit flavorings for beverages, ice cream, ices, candy, and baked goods. Less toxic than benzoic acid (*see*) or salicylic acid (*see*). Experimental animals showed no kidney or liver damage. On the FDA list for further study for short-term mutagenic, subacute, teratogenic, and reproductive effects. GRAS. The FDA data bank, PAFA, has not yet done a toxicology literature search on this food additive.

PROPYL ISOVALERATE • A synthetic strawberry, apple, banana, and peach flavoring agent for beverages, ice cream, ices, candy, and baked goods. The FDA data bank, PAFA, has fully up-to-date toxicology information available on this food additive.

PROPYL MERCAPTAN • A synthetic berry and onion flavoring agent for baked goods and pickles. The FDA data bank, PAFA, has fully up-to-date toxicology information available on this food additive.

PROPYL METHOXYBENZENE • *See p*-Propyl Anisole.

PROPYL PHENYLACETATE • A synthetic butter, caramel, rose, fruit, and honey flavoring agent for beverages, ice cream, ices, candy, and baked goods. The FDA data bank, PAFA, has fully up-to-date toxicology information available on this food additive. *See* Acetic Acid for toxicity.

PROPYL PROPIONATE • Propyl alcohol and propionic acid. A synthetic banana, cherry, melon, peach, prune, apple, plum, and rum flavoring agent for beverages, ice cream, ices, candy, and baked goods. Colorless, thick liquid prepared from glycerol (*see* Glycerin) used as an anticaking agent, antioxidant, dough conditioner, humectant, solvent, stabilizer, detergent, texturizer, thickener, and wetting agent. Used in alcoholic beverages, confections, flavorings, frostings, frozen dairy products, pork, nut products, poultry, seasonings, and wine. FDA limits it to 5 percent in alcoholic beverages; 24 percent in confections and frostings; 2.5 percent in frozen dairy products; 97 percent in seasonings and flavorings; 5 percent in nuts and nut products; and 2 percent in all other foods when used in accordance with good manufacturing practices. Limitation of 40 ppm in wine. EPA Genetic Toxicology Program. Caused birth defects in experimental animals. The FDA data bank, PAFA (see page 10), has fully up-to-date toxicology information available on this food additive.

PROPYLENE GLYCOL • 1,2-Propanediol. A clear, colorless, viscous liquid, slightly bitter tasting. In food, it is used in confectionery, chocolate products, ice cream emulsifiers, shredded coconut, beverages, baked goods, toppings, icings, and meat products to prevent discoloration during storage. Defoaming agent in processed beet sugar and yeast. Used in antifreeze in breweries and dairy establishments. It is the most common moisture-carrying vehicle other than water itself in cosmetics. It is being reduced and being replaced by safer glycols such as butylene and polyethylene glycol. Large oral doses in animals have been reported to cause central nervous system depression and slight kidney changes. The final report to the FDA of the Select Committee on GRAS Substances stated in 1980 that it should continue its GRAS status with no limitations other than good manufacturing practices. The FDA data bank, PAFA (see page 10), has fully up-to-date toxicology information available on this food additive.

PROPYLENE GLYCOL ALGINATE • Kelcloid. The propylene glycol ester of alginic acid (*see*), derived from seaweed. Used as a stabilizer, filler, and defoaming agent in food. Cleared for use in French dressing and salad dressing under the food standard regulations. Used as a stabilizer in ice cream, frozen custard, ice milk, fruit sherbet, and water ices, it is permitted up to 0.5 percent of the weight of the finished product. Can cause allergic reactions. The final report to the FDA of the Select Committee on GRAS Substances stated in 1980 that there is no available evidence that it is a hazard to the public when used as it is now and it should continue its GRAS status with limitations on amounts that can be added to food. The FDA data bank, PAFA, is currently searching the toxicology literature concerning this additive.

PROPYLENE GLYCOL MONOSTEARATE • Cream-colored wax that disperses in water and is soluble in hot alcohol. It is used as a lubricating agent and emulsifier; also a dough conditioner in baked goods. Employed as a stabilizer of essential oils. Slightly more toxic than propylene glycol (*see*) in animals and in large doses produces central nervous system depression and kidney injury. The final report to the FDA of the Select Committee on GRAS Substances stated in 1980 that it should continue its GRAS status with no limitations other than good manufacturing practices.

PROPYLENE OXIDE • Propene Oxide. Colorless, liquid starch modifier. FDA tolerance residues are less than 25 percent for treatment of starch; 700 ppm as propylene glycol in dried prunes and glacéed fruit; and 300 ppm in cocao gums and processed nut meats (except peanuts). There is no reported use of the chemical and no toxicology information is available, according to the FDA's data bank, PAFA (see page 10).

3-PROPYLIDENEPHTHALIDE • A synthetic fruit and spice flavoring agent for beverages, ice cream, ices, candy, and baked goods. No known toxicity.

PROPYLPARABEN • Propyl-*p*-Hydroxybenzoate. Developed in Europe, the esters of *p*-hydroxybenzoic acid are widely used in the cosmetics industry as preservatives and bacteria and fungus killers. They are active against a variety of organisms, are neutral, low in toxicity, slightly soluble, and active in all solutions, alkaline, neutral, or acid. Used in shampoos, baby preparations, foundation creams, beauty masks, dentifrices, eye lotions, hair-grooming aids, nail creams, and wave sets. Used medicinally to treat fungus infections. Can cause contact dermatitis. Less toxic than benzoic or salicylic acid (*see both*). GRAS.

PROPYLPARASEPT • *See* Propyl-*p*-Hydroxybenzoate.

a-PROPYLPHENETHYL ALCOHOL • A synthetic fruit flavoring agent for beverages, ice cream, ices, candy, and puddings. Toxicity similar to ethanol (*see*). The FDA data bank, PAFA (see page 10), has fully up-to-date toxicology information available on this food additive.

PROSTAGLANDINS • PGA. PGB. PGC. PGD. Taglandin F2-a. Lutalyse. A group of extremely potent hormonelike substances present in many tissues. There are more than sixteen known with effects such as dilating or constricting blood vessels, stimulation of intestinal or bronchial smooth muscle, uterine stimulation, and antagonism to hormones and influencing fat metabolism. Various prostaglandins in the body can cause fever, inflammation, and headaches. Prostaglandins or drugs that affect prostaglandins are used medically in humans to induce labor, prevent and treat peptic ulcers, control high blood pressure, in the treatment of bronchial asthma, and to induce delayed menstruation. They are used in animals to induce labor and to induce abortion.

PROTEASE • An enzyme used as a meat tenderizer and in sausage curing, dough conditioning, and beer-haze removal. The FDA data bank, PAFA, has not yet done a toxicology literature search on this food additive.

PROTECTIVE COATINGS • Antioxidants and preservatives that are used in goat cheeses and fresh fruits and vegetables to retard spoilage. The coatings may expose consumers to hidden antibiotics or coal-tar products. Among the coating additives used are anoxomer, calcium disodium and disodium EDTA, coumarone-indene resin, ethoxyquin, morpholine, natamycin, petroleum naphtha, polyacrylamide, synthetic paraffin and succinic derivatives, and terpene resin (*see all*). Citrus fruits, squash, grapes, sweet potatoes, asparagus, melons, papaya, plantain, turnips, watermelons, and nuts are commonly coated.

PROTEIN FATTY ACID CONDENSATES • *See* Amides.

PROTEIN HYDROLYSATES • Used as flavor enhancers, particularly in meat products. The FDA data bank, PAFA (see page 10), has not yet done a toxicology literature search on this food additive. *See* Proteins and Hydrolyzed.

PROTEINS • The chief nitrogen-containing constituents of plants and animals—the essential constituents of every living cell. They are complex but by weight contain about 50 percent carbon, about 20 percent oxygen, about 15 percent nitrogen, about 7 percent hydrogen, and some sulfur. Some also contain iron and phosphorous. Proteins are colorless, odorless, and generally tasteless. They vary in solubility. They readily undergo putrefaction, hydrolysis, and dilution with acids or alkalies. They are regarded as combinations of amino acids (*see*). Cosmetic manufacturers, particularly makers of hair products, claim "protein enrichment" is beneficial to the hair and skin. Hair, of course, is already dead. It does consist of a type of protein, keratin (*see*), but the surface of the hair is cornified tissue that cannot be revitalized. Such products will add body to thin hair and add gloss or luster, but so will other hair conditioners (*see*). As for face creams with protein, the lubricant is more beneficial than the protein. No known toxicity.

PROVITAMIN A • *See* Carotene.

PRUSSIATE OF SODA, YELLOW • Salt of hydrocyanic acid derived from ammonia. Anticaking agent in salt. Hydrocyanic acid is toxic by ingestion, inhalation, and skin absorption.

PSEUDOPINENE • A synthetic flavoring agent used in various foods. Mildly toxic by ingestion. *See a*-Pinene.

PSYLLIUM SEED HUSK • A stabilizer from the seed of the fleaseed plant used in frozen desserts up to 0.5 percent of the weight of the finished product. There is no reported use of the chemical and no toxicology information is available, according to the FDA's data bank, PAFA (see page 10).

PTEROYLGLUTAMIC ACID • Dietary supplement. Isolated from yeast.

PULEGONE • Found in oils of plants, principally the pennyroyal. Pleasant odor, midway between camphor and peppermint. Used in peppermint flavorings for beverages, ice cream, ices, candy, and baked goods. The FDA data bank, PAFA, has fully up-to-date toxicology information available on this food additive. *See* Pennyroyal Oil for toxicity.

PULPS • From wood, straw, bagasse, or other natural sources. A source of cellulose in food. The wood is treated with a mixture containing mainly sodium hydroxide (*see*). Treatment removes the fibrous lignin—the resinous substance that binds the fiber that lines the cells of wood. An indirect human food additive from packaging. The FDA's reevaluation in 1976 labeled pulps GRAS. There is no reported use of the chemical and no toxicology information is available, according to the FDA's data bank, PAFA (see page 10).

PYRANTEL TARTRATE • An antiworm medicine used in feed and as a veterinary medicine. The FDA's residue tolerance is 10 ppm in swine liver and kidney and 1 ppm in swine muscle.

PYRAZINE ETHANETHIOL • *See* Piperazine.

PYRETHRINS • Thick liquids from the pyrethrum flowers. Used in household insecticidal sprays and powders and deodorant sprays. Also used in paper bags for shipping cereals. Residues from packaging materials and equipment and storage areas may be only 1 ppm on dried foods, cereal grains, and dried prunes. Insecticides labeled nontoxic to human beings and pets usually contain pyrethrins.

PYRIDINE • Occurs naturally in coffee and coal tar. Disagreeable odor; sharp taste. Used in chocolate flavorings for beverages, ice cream, ices, candy, and baked goods. Also used as a solvent for organic liquids and compounds. Once used to treat asthma, but may cause central nervous system depression and irritation of the skin and respiratory tract. After prolonged administration, kidney and liver damage may result. Pyridine is absorbed from the respiratory and gastrointestinal tract. Small oral doses in humans have produced loss of appetite, nausea, fatigue, and mental depression. The FDA data bank, PAFA (see page 10), has fully up-to-date toxicology information available on this food additive.

PYRIDOXINE • *See* Pyridoxine Hydrochloride.

PYRIDOXINE DIOCTENOATE • Vitamin B_6 Hydrochloride. Texturizer. A colorless or white crystalline powder present in many foodstuffs. A coenzyme that helps in the metabolism of amino acids (*see*) and fats. Also soothing to the skin. Nontoxic.

PYRIDOXINE HYDROCHLORIDE • Vitamin B_6. A colorless or white crystalline powder added to evaporated milk base in infant foods. Present in many foodstuffs. Especially good sources are yeast, liver, and cereals. A coenzyme that helps in the metabolism of amino acids (see) and fat. Permits normal red blood cell formation. The final report to the FDA of the Select Committee on GRAS Substances stated in 1980 that it should continue its GRAS status with no limitations other than good manufacturing practices. The FDA data bank, PAFA, has not yet done a toxicology literature search on this food additive.

PYRIDOXINE TRIPALMITATE • Vitamin B_6 Tripalmitate. *See* Pyridoxine Hydrochloride.

PYRIDOXOL HYDROCHLORIDE • Vitamin B_6. Dietary supplement and nutrient used in baked goods, beverages and beverage bases, cereals, dairy products, meat products, plant-protein products, and snack foods.

PYROLIGNEOUS ACID AND EXTRACT • A yellow acid. Consists of 6 percent acetic acid (*see*) and small concentrations of creosote, methyl alcohol, and acetone (*see*). It is obtained by the destructive distillation of wood. Used as a synthetic flavoring in butter, butterscotch, caramel, rum, tobacco, smoke, and vanilla flavorings for beverages, ice cream, ices, candy, baked goods, puddings, and meats (300 ppm). The *extract* is used largely for smoking meats (300 ppm) and in smoke flavorings for baked goods (200 ppm) and alcoholic beverages. It is corrosive and may cause epigastric pain, vomiting, circulatory collapse, and death. The FDA data bank, PAFA (see page 10), has not yet done a toxicology literature search on this food additive.

PYROMUCIC ALDEHYDE • *See* Furfural.

PYROPHOSPHATE • Salt of pyrophosphoric acid. It increases the effectiveness of antioxidants in creams and ointments. In concentrated solutions it can be irritating to the skin and mucous membranes.

PYROPHYLLITE • Aluminum Silicate Monohydrate. Obtained naturally from clay or synthesized, it is used as an anticaking and coloring agent in powders. Used as a carrier or pelleting aid in animal feed. Nontoxic.

PYRORACEMIC ACID • *See* Pyruvic Acid.

PYRROLE • Colorless liquid with a mild, nutty odor used as a flavoring agent in various foods. GRAS when used at a level not in excess of the amount reasonably required to accomplish the intended effect. The FDA data bank, PAFA (see page 10), has fully up-to-date toxicology information available on this food additive.

PYRUVALDEHYDE • A synthetic flavoring, yellowish, with a pungent odor. Formed as an intermediate in the metabolism or fermentation of carbohydrates and lactic acid (*see*). Used in coffee, honey, and maple flavorings for beverages, ice cream, ices, candy, and baked goods. The FDA data bank, PAFA, has fully up-to-date toxicology information available on this food additive.

PYRUVIC ACID • An important intermediate in fermentation and metabolism, it occurs naturally in coffee and when sugar is metabolized in muscle. It is reduced to lactic acid (*see*) during exertion. Pyruvic acid is isolated from cane sugar. It is a synthetic flavoring used in coffee and rum flavorings for beverages, ice cream, ices, candy, chewing gum, and baked goods. Has been used as a paste in the treatment of deep burns. The FDA data bank, PAFA, has fully up-to-date toxicology information available on this food additive.

Q

QUACK GRASS • A couch grass, a pernicious weed in cultivated fields. *See* Dog Grass Extract.

QUASSIA EXTRACT • Bitter Ash. Bitterwood. Yellowish white to bright yellow chips. Bitter alkaloid obtained from the wood of *Quassia amara,* a tree bearing bright scarlet flowers grown in Jamaica, the Caribbean Islands, and South America. Named for a black slave who discovered its medicinal value in the mideighteenth century. Slight odor, bitter taste. Used in bitters, citrus, cherry, grape, liquor, root beer, sarsaparilla, and vanilla flavorings for beverages, baked goods, and liquors. In cosmetics, it is used chiefly as a denaturant for ethyl alcohol. Used to poison flies, to imitate hops, and as a bitter tonic and remedy for roundworms in children. Toxic to humans. The FDA data bank, PAFA (see page 10), has not yet done a toxicology literature search on this food additive.

QUATERNARY AMMONIUM COMPOUNDS • A wide variety of preservatives, surfactants, germicides, sanitizers, antiseptics, and deodorants. They are used in processing sugarcane and in beet sugar mills. Benzalkonium chloride (*see*) is one of the most popular. Quaternary ammonium compounds are synthetic derivatives of ammonia, a natural product that occurs in animal metabolism.

QUEBRACHO BARK EXTRACT • Extract of a native Argentine tree, used in fruit, rum, and vanilla flavorings for beverages, ice cream, candy, ices, and baked goods. Closely related to the tranquilizer reserpine. Once promoted as an aphrodisiac, it can cause low blood pressure, nausea, abdominal distress, weakness, and fatigue. The FDA data bank, PAFA (see page 10), has not yet done a toxicology literature search on this food additive.

QUERCITRON • The inner bark of a species of oak tree common in North America. Its active ingredient, isoquercitrin, is used in forming resins and in dark brown hair-dye shades mainly for dyeing artificial hairpieces. Allergic reactions have been reported. *See* Rutin.

QUERCUS ALBA • *See* Oak Bark Extract.

QUICK GRASS • Triticum. *See* Dog Grass Extract.

QUILLAIA • China Bark Extract. *See* Quillaja Extract.

QUILLAJA EXTRACT • Soapbark. Quillay Bark. Panama Bark. China Bark. The extract of the inner dried bark of a tree grown in South America, *Quillaja saponaria*. Used in fruit, root beer, and spice flavorings for beverages, ice cream, and candy. Formerly used to treat bronchitis and externally as a detergent and local irritant. The FDA data bank, PAFA, has not yet done a toxicology literature search on this food additive.

QUINCE SEED • The seed of a plant, *Cydonia* spp., grown in southern Asia and Europe for its fatty oil. Thick jelly produced by soaking seeds in water. Used in fruit flavorings for beverages, ice cream, ices, and baked goods. Used as a suspension in setting skin creams and lotions, as a thickening agent in depilatories, and as an emulsifier for fragrances, hand creams, lotions, rouges, and wave sets. Used medicinally as a demulcent. Has been largely replaced by cheaper substitutes. It may cause allergic reactions. GRAS. There is no reported use of the chemical and no toxicology information is available, according to the FDA's data bank, PAFA (see page 10).

QUININE BISULFATE • Most important alkaloid of cinchona extract (*see*) from trees that grow wild in South America and are cultivated in Java. Very bitter. Used in bitters flavoring for beverages and not to exceed 83 ppm in soda. Used to treat fever and as a local anesthetic and analgesic. No known toxicity. Although allowed as a food additive, there is no current reported use of the chemical, and therefore, although toxicology information may be available, the FDA is not updating it. *See* Quinine Extract.

QUININE EXTRACT • An extract of cinchona bark (*see* Cinchona Extract), which grows wild in South America. White crystalline powder, almost insoluble in water. It is used as a local anesthetic in hair tonics and sunscreen preparations. Used in bitters in limited amounts as flavoring for beverages. When taken internally, it reduces fever. It is also used as a flavoring agent in numerous over-the-counter cold and headache remedies as well as "bitter lemon" and tonic water, which may contain as much as five milligrams per hundred milliliters. Cinchonism, which may consist of nausea, vomiting, disturbances of vision, ringing in the ears, and nerve deafness, may occur from an overdose of quinine. If there is a sensitivity to quinine, such symptoms can result after ingesting tonic water. Quinine more commonly causes a rash. The World Health Organization Committee on Food Additives said the amount of quinine in drinks was not of concern to normal human beings, but that some consumers show an idiosyncratic, hyperreactivity to quinine, and therefore, its presence in foods and beverages should be noted.

QUININE HYDROCHLORIDE • A synthetic flavoring agent derived from cinchona bark (see Cinchona Extract) and used in bitters, citrus, and fruit flavorings for beverages. Some medical use as quinine sulfate (see). See Quinine Extract for toxicity.

QUININE SULFATE • A synthetic flavoring agent derived from cinchona bark (see Cinchona Extract) and used in bitters flavoring for beverages. Also used medicinally to treat malaria, as an analgesic, and as a local anesthetic. The FDA data bank, PAFA (see page 10), has fully up-to-date toxicology information available on this food additive.

QUINOLINE • A coal-tar derivative used in the manufacture of cosmetic dyes. Also a solvent for resins. Made either by the distillation of coal tar, bones, and alkaloids or by the interaction of aniline (see) with acetaldehyde and formaldehyde (see both). Absorbs water, has a weak base. Soluble in hot water. Also used as a preservative for anatomical specimens. See Coal Tar for toxicity. See also FD and C Colors. Although allowed as a food additive, there is no current reported use of the chemical, and therefore, although toxicology information may be available, the FDA is not updating it.

QUIZALOFOPETHYL • White crystals used as an herbicide in animal feed. FDA residue tolerances are 0.2 ppm in soybean hulls; 0.5 ppm in soybean meal; 1 ppm in soybean soap-stock; 0.5 on soybeans; 0.1 ppm in eggs; 0.05 ppm in milk fat; 0.02 ppm in meat of cattle, goats, hogs, and sheep; 0.05 ppm in fat, meat, and meat byproducts of cattle, goats, hogs, and sheep; and 1 ppm on cottonseed.

R

RACEMIC ACID • See Tartaric Acid.

RADISH EXTRACT • Extract of *Raphanus sativus.* The small seeds of the radish remain viable for years. Has been used as a food since ancient times. Used in herbal cosmetics.

RAISIN-SEED OIL • Dried grapes or berries used in lubricating creams. See Grape-Seed Oil.

RALGRO • Zeranol. Used to increase growth in beef and lamb. FDA limits residue to zero in cattle and sheep. Has adverse reproductive effects in experimental animals.

RAPESEED OIL, HYDROGENATED • Brownish yellow oil from a turniplike annual herb of European origin. Widely grown as a forage crop for sheep in the U.S. Canada sought clearance to sell rapeseed in the U.S. market, but it was barred because it contains erucic acid, which was cited in the early 1970s as a possible source of heart problems based on the results of tests on rats. New varieties of the seeds, canola, have been developed that have low erucic-acid levels. Now, rapeseed oil is used in American salad oils, peanut butter, and some cake mixes. A distinctly unpleasant odor. It is used chiefly as a lubricant, an illuminant, and in rubber substitutes; also used in soft soaps. Can cause acnelike skin eruptions. When rats were fed a diet high in rapeseed oil over a lifetime, they showed significantly greater degenerative changes in the liver and a higher incidence of kidney damage than animals fed other vegetable oils. GRAS. The FDA data bank, PAFA (see page 10), has fully up-to-date toxicology information available on this food additive.

RAPESEED OIL UNSAPONIFIABLES • The fraction of rapeseed oil (*see*) that is not changed into a fatty alcohol when it is saponified (heated with an alkali and an acid). GRAS except in infant formula.

RASPBERRY EXTRACT • *See* Raspberry Juice.

RASPBERRY JUICE • Juice from the fresh ripe fruit grown in Europe, Asia, the United States, and Canada. Used as a flavoring for lipsticks, food, and medicines. It has astringent properties.

RbST • Abbreviation for Recombinant Bovine Somatotropin. *See* Bovine Somatotropin and IGF-I.

RDA • *Recommended dietary allowances* of the Food and Nutrition Board, National Academy of Sciences, National Research Council.

REAGENT • A chemical that reacts or participates in a reaction; a substance that is used for the detection or determination of another substance by chemical or microscopical means. The various categories of reagents are colorimetric, to produce color-soluble compounds; fluxes, used to lower melting point; oxidizers, used in oxidation; precipitants, to produce insoluble compounds; reducers, used in reduction (*see*); and solvents, used to dissolve water-insoluble compounds.

RED • *See* FD and C Red Nos. 3, 4, 40, and Citrus Red No. 2.

RED ALGAE • Seaweed. GRAS. *See* Algae, Red.

RED PEPPER • Cayenne Pepper. A condiment made from the pungent fruit of the plant. Used in sausage and pepper flavorings. Also used as a stimulant in hair tonics, but may be an irritant and also cause allergic reactions.

RED RASPBERRY LEAF EXTRACT • An extract of the leaves of the red raspberry (*see* Raspberry Juice).

RED SAUNDERS • Red Sandalwood. Flavoring in alcoholic beverages only. No known toxicity.

REDUCED • Product has been nutritionally altered and contains at least 25 percent less of a nutrient such as fat or salt or 25 percent fewer calories than the regular product.

REDUCED-LACTOSE WHEY • GRAS. *See* Whey and Reducing Agent.

REDUCED-MINERALS WHEY • GRAS. *See* Whey and Reducing Agent.

REDUCING AGENT • A substance that decreases, deoxidizes, or concentrates the volume of another substance. For instance, a reducing agent is used to convert a metal oxide to the metal itself. It also means a substance that adds hydrogen agents to another, for example, when acetaldehyde is converted to alcohol in the final step of alcoholic fermentation. It is used in foods to keep metals from oxidizing and affecting the taste or color of fats, oils, salad dressings, and other foods containing minerals.

REDUCTION • The process of reducing by chemical or electrochemical means. The gain of one or more electrons by an ion or compound. It is the reverse of oxidation.

REGENERATED CELLULOSE • Miscellaneous use with resins. *See* Cellulose.

RELEASING AGENT • A compound such as butter or an oil that prevents a product from sticking to the sides of a container. Also refers to a chemical that permits easy removal of the meat of a clam or other crustacean.

RENNET • Rennin. Enzyme from the lining membranes of the stomach of suckling calves. Used for curdling milk in cheese-making and in junket. Sometimes used as a digestant. Reaffirmed GRAS in 1982. The FDA data bank, PAFA (see page 10), has fully up-to-date toxicology information available on this food additive.

RESIN, ACRYLAMIDE—ACRYLIC ACID • A clarifying agent in beet sugar and cane sugar juice. The acid is used in the synthesis of this acrylic resin. No known toxicity.

RESIN, COUMARONE—INDENE • A chewing gum base and protective coating for citrus fruits. Coumarone is derived from coal tar and is used with a mixture of indene chiefly in the synthesis of coumarone resins. No known toxicity.

RESIN, ISOBUTYLENE • Polyisobutylene. A chewing gum base made from the chemical used chiefly in manufacturing synthetic rubber. No known toxicity.

RESIN, METHACRYLIC AND DIVINYL BENZENE • A compound of fine particle size, weakly acidic. Used as an absorbent for vitamin B_{12} in nutritional-supplement-type products. No known toxicity.

RESIN, PETROLEUM HYDROCARBON • A chewing gum base synthesized from fuel oil. No known toxicity.

RESIN, TERPENE • Alpha and Beta Pinene. A chewing gum base and coating for fresh fruits and vegetables. Pinene has the same toxicity as turpentine (*see*).

RESINS • The brittle substance, usually translucent or transparent, formed from the hardened secretions of plants. Among the natural resins are dammar, elemi, and sandarac. Synthetic resins include polyvinyl acetate, various polyester resins, and sulfonamide resins. Resins have many uses in cosmetics. They contribute depth, gloss, flow adhesion, and water resistance. Toxicity depends upon ingredients used. *See* Gum.

RESORCINOL • A preservative, antiseptic, antifungal, astringent, and anti-itching agent, particularly in dandruff shampoos. Also used in hair dyes, lipsticks, and hair tonics. Also used in tanning, explosives, printing textiles, and the manufacture of resins. Obtained from various resins. Resorcinol's white crystals become pink on exposure to air. A sweetish taste. Irritating to the skin and mucous membranes. May cause allergic reactions, particularly of the skin. The FDA issued a notice in 1992 that resorcinol has not been shown to be safe and effective for stated claims in OTC products. The FDA data bank, PAFA (see page 10), has fully up-to-date toxicology information available on this food additive.

RETINOIDS • Derived from retinoic acid, vitamin A, it is used to treat acne and other skin disorders. *See* Vitamin A.

RETINOL • Vitamin A (see).

RETINYL PALMITATE • The ester of vitamin A and palmitic acid, sometimes mixed with vitamin D (see all).

RHAMNOSE • Occurs in poison sumac, Rhus toxicodendron. Combined with sugar in many other plants. It is used in the manufacture of food additives. The FDA data bank, PAFA, has not yet done a toxicology literature search on this food additive.

RHATANY ROOT • A flavoring. The dried root of Krameria triandra R. from Peru and Brazil. Used as a cosmetics astringent. See Krameria Extract. No known toxicity.

RHIZOPUS ORYZAE • An enzyme used in production of dextrose (sugar) from starch.

RHODENAL • See Citronellal.

RHODINOL • A synthetic flavoring agent isolated from geranium rose oil (see). It has the strong odor of rose and consists essentially of geraniol and citronellol (see both). Used in strawberry, chocolate, rose, grape, honey, spice, and ginger ale flavorings for beverages, ice cream, ices, candy, baked goods, gelatin desserts, chewing gum, and jelly. Used also in perfumes, especially those of the rose type. The FDA data bank, PAFA (see page 10), has fully up-to-date toxicology information available on this food additive.

RHODINYL ACETATE • Acetic Acid. An acidulant and synthetic flavoring, colorless to slightly yellow, with a light, fresh, roselike odor. Used in berry, coconut, apricot, floral, rose, and honey flavorings for beverages, ice cream, ices, candy, and baked goods. A skin irritant. The FDA data bank, PAFA, has fully up-to-date toxicology information available on this food additive.

RHODINYL BUTYRATE • Butyric Acid. A synthetic raspberry, strawberry, and fruit flavoring agent for beverages, ice cream, ices, candy, baked goods, and chewing gum. No known toxicity.

RHODINYL FORMATE • Formic Acid. A synthetic flavoring, colorless to slightly yellow, with a roselike odor. Used in raspberry, rose, apple, cherry, plum, pear, and pineapple flavorings for beverages, ice cream, ices, candy, baked goods, and gelatin desserts. The FDA data bank, PAFA, has fully up-to-date toxicology information available on this food additive. See Formic Acid for toxicity.

RHODINYL ISOBUTYRATE • Isobutyric Acid. A synthetic raspberry, floral, rose, apple, pear, pineapple, and honey flavoring agent for beverages, ice cream, ices, candy, baked goods, and gelatin desserts. The FDA data bank, PAFA (see page 10), has fully up-to-date toxicology information available on this food additive.

RHODINYL ISOVALERATE • Isovaleric Acid. A synthetic berry, floral, rose, and fruit flavoring agent for beverages, ice cream, ices, candy, and baked goods. The FDA data bank, PAFA, has fully up-to-date toxicology information available on this food additive.

RHODINYL PHENYLACETATE • Phenylacetic Acid. A synthetic flavoring used in beverages, ice cream, ices, candy, and baked goods. The FDA data bank, PAFA, has fully up-to-date toxicology information available on this food additive.

RHODINYL PROPIONATE • Propionic Acid. A synthetic berry, rose, plum, and honey flavoring agent for beverages, ice cream, ices, candy, and baked goods. The FDA data bank, PAFA, has fully up-to-date toxicology information available on this food additive.

RHODYMENIA PALMATA • *See* Dulse.

RHUBARB • The garden root of *Rheum rhaponticum,* used as a flavoring in alcoholic beverages only. Has been used as a laxative. The FDA data bank, PAFA (see page 10), has not yet done a toxicology literature search on this food additive.

RHYNCHOSIA PYRAMIDALIS • A genus of large, tropical twining plants with yellow flowers. Used as a flavoring. No known toxicity.

RIBOFLAVIN • Vitamin B_2. Lactoflavin. Formerly called vitamin G. Riboflavin is a factor in the vitamin B complex and is used in emollients. Every plant and animal cell contains a minute amount. Good sources are milk, eggs, and organ meats. It is necessary for healthy skin and respiration, protects the eyes from sensitivity to light, and is used for building and maintaining human body tissues. A deficiency leads to lesions at the corner of the mouth and to changes in the cornea. Recommended daily requirement for infants is 4,000 micrograms per day, and for adults, 1,300 micrograms. Its yellow to orange-yellow color is used to dye eggshells. It is permanently listed as a food color. Riboflavin and its more soluble form, riboflavin-5-phosphate, are added as enrichment to dry baby cereals, poultry stuffing, peanut butter, prepared breakfast cereals, enriched flour, enriched cornmeal, enriched corn grits, enriched macaroni, and enriched breads and rolls. GRAS. The FDA data bank, PAFA, has fully up-to-date toxicology information available on this food additive.

RIBOFLAVIN-5-PHOSPHATE • A more soluble form of riboflavin (*see*). The final report to the FDA of the Select Committee on GRAS Substances stated in 1980 that it should continue its GRAS status with no limitations other than good manufacturing practices. The FDA data bank, PAFA (see page 10), has not yet done a toxicology literature search on this food additive.

RIBONUCLEIC ACID (RNA) • Found in both the nucleus and cytoplasm of the cell, it is the material that contains directions for the genetic code of the cell, DNA.

D-RIBOSE • Prepared by the hydrolysis of yeast (*see*). The FDA data bank, PAFA, has not yet done a toxicology literature search on this food additive.

RICE BRAN OIL • Oil expressed from the broken coat of rice grain. Used as a coating for candy. Nontoxic.

RICE BRAN WAX • The wax obtained from the broken coat of rice grain. Used as a coating agent, as a chewing gum base, and a releasing agent (*see*). Although allowed as a food additive, there is no current reported use of the chemical, and therefore, although toxicology information may be available, the FDA is not updating it.

RICE STARCH • The finely pulverized grains of the rice plant used as an anticaking agent, thickener, and gelling agent. Also used in baby powders, face powders, and dusting powders. It is a demulcent and emollient and forms a soothing, protective film when applied. May cause mechanical irritation by blocking the pores and putrefying. May also cause an allergic reaction. The final report to the FDA of the Select Committee on GRAS Substances stated in 1980 that it should continue its GRAS status with no limitations other than good manufacturing practices.

RICINOLEATE • Salt of ricinoleic acid found in castor oil. Used in the manufacture of soaps. No known toxicity.

RICINOLEIC ACID • A mixture of fatty oils found in the seeds of castor beans. Castor oil contains 80 to 85 percent ricinoleic acid. The oily liquid is used in soaps, flavorings, antifungal agents, and contraceptive jellies. It is believed to be the active laxative in castor oil. Also used externally as an emollient. No known toxicity.

RIGHT-TO-KNOW • *See* Community Right-To-Know-List. Established by the Environmental Protection Agency and other government and civic organizations.

ROBENIDINE • Crystals from ethanol (*see*). Used to treat parasites in chickens. FDA residue limit of 0.2 ppm in skin and fat of chickens and 0.1 ppm in other chicken tissues. Moderately toxic by ingestion.

ROCHELLE SALT • Potassium Sodium Tartrate. Used in the manufacture of baking powder and in the silvering of mirrors. Translucent crystals or white crystalline powder with cooling saline taste. Slight efflorescence in warm air. Probably used in mouthwashes, but use not identified in cosmetics. No known toxicity.

RONNEL • Used in cattle feed. A systemic pesticide. *See* Organophosphates.

ROSA ALBA • *See* Rose, Absolute.

ROSA CANINA • *See* Rose Hips Extract.

ROSA CENTIFOLIA • *See* Rose, Absolute.

ROSE, ABSOLUTE • Same origin as for rose Bulgarian (*see*). Used as a berry, rose, fruit, and nut flavoring agent for beverages, ice cream, ices, candy, and baked goods. No known toxicity except for allergic reactions. GRAS. The FDA data bank, PAFA (see page 10), has not yet done a toxicology literature search on this food additive.

ROSE BENGAL • A bluish red, fragrant liquid taken from the rose of the Bengal region of the Asian subcontinent. Used to scent perfumes and as an edible color product to make lipstick dyes. Nontoxic.

ROSE BUDS, FLOWERS, FRUITS (HIPS), LEAVES • Flavoring. *See* Rose Extract. GRAS. There is no reported use of the chemical and no toxicology information is available, according to the FDA's data bank, PAFA.

ROSE BULGARIAN • True Otto Oil. Attar of Roses. Rose Otto Bulgaria. One of the most widely used perfume ingredients, it is the essential oil steam-distilled from the flowers of *Rosa damascena*. The rose flowers are picked early in the morning when they contain the maximum amount of perfume and are distilled quickly after harvesting. Bulgaria is the main source of supply, but Russia, Turkey, Syria, and Indochina also grow it. The liquid is pale yellow and has a warm, deep floral, slightly spicy, and extremely fragrant red-rose smell. It is used as a flavoring agent in loganberry, raspberry, strawberry, orange, rose, violet, cherry, grape, peach, honey, muscatel, maple, almond, pecan, and ginger ale flavorings for beverages, ice cream, ices, candy, baked goods, gelatin desserts, chewing gum, and jellies. Also used in mucilage, coloring matter, and as a flavoring in pills. May cause allergic reactions. GRAS. The FDA data bank, PAFA (see page 10), has not yet done a toxicology literature search on this food additive.

ROSE EXTRACT • An extract of the various species of rose, it is used in raspberry and cola beverages and in fragrances. No known toxicity except for allergic reactions. GRAS.

ROSE GERANIUM • Distilled from any of several South African herbs grown for their fragrant leaves. Used in perfumes and to scent toothpaste and dusting powders. May cause allergic reactions.

ROSE HIPS EXTRACT • Hipberries. Extract of the fruit of various species of wild roses, it is rich in vitamin C and is used as a natural flavoring. Widely used by organic food enthusiasts. The FDA data bank, PAFA, has not yet done a toxicology literature search on this food additive.

ROSE LEAVES EXTRACT • Derived from the leaves of the genus *Rosa*. Used in raspberry and cola beverages.

ROSE OIL • Attar of Roses. The fragrant, volatile essential oil distilled from fresh flowers. Colorless or yellow with a strong fragrant odor and taste of roses. Used in perfumes, toilet waters, and ointments. Nontoxic but may cause allergic reactions. *See* Rose Bulgarian.

ROSE OTTO BULGARIA • *See* Rose Bulgarian.

ROSELLE • *Hibiscus sabdariffa.* An herb cultivated in the East Indies, it is used for making tarts and jellies and gives a tart taste to acid drinks. It is also used as a natural red food coloring for soft drinks, tea-type products, punches, apple jelly, and pectin jelly, but it is not stable in carbonated beverages. No known toxicity. GRAS. There is no reported use of the chemical and no toxicology information is available, according to the FDA's data bank, PAFA (see page 10).

ROSEMARY EXTRACT • Garden Rosemary. A flavoring and perfume from the fresh, aromatic flowering tops of the evergreen shrub *Rosmarinus officinalis,* grown in the Mediterranean region. Light blue flowers and gray-green leaves. Used for beverages, condiments, and meat. It is also used in citrus, peach, and ginger flavorings for beverages, ice cream, ices, candy, baked goods, condiments, and meats. Also being studied as a natural antioxidant. A teaspoonful of the oil may cause illness in an adult, and an ounce may cause death. GRAS. The FDA data bank, PAFA, has not yet done a toxicology literature search on this food additive.

ROSIDINHA • Sideroxylon. A large genus of green tropical trees, family Sapotaceae, having hard wood and somewhat bell-shaped flowers with a few seeded berries. Used as a flavoring. The FDA data bank, PAFA (see page 10), has fully up-to-date toxicology information available on this food additive.

ROSIN • Colophony. Softener for chewing gum. It is a pale yellow residue left after distilling off the volatile oil from the oleoresin obtained from various species of pine trees chiefly produced in the U.S. Also used in the manufacture of varnishes and fireworks. It can cause contact dermatitis. The FDA data bank, PAFA, has fully up-to-date toxicology information available on this food additive.

ROSIN, METHYL ESTER, PARTIALLY HYDROGENATED • Used in the manufacture of food additives. The FDA data bank, PAFA, has fully up-to-date toxicology information available on this food additive.

ROSMARINUS OFFICINALIS • *See* Rosemary Extract.

ROXARSONE • An antibacterial for control of enteric infections and to improve growth and feed efficiency. Used in chicken and swine feeds. In drinking water of chickens, turkey, and swine.

RUBBER • Rubber as well as rubber-based adhesives are common causes of contact dermatitis. The natural gum obtained from the rubber tree is not allergenic; the offenders are the chemicals added to natural rubber gum to make it useful. Such chemicals are accelerators, antioxidants, stabilizers, and vulcanizers, many of which can cause allergies. Two are the most frequent but certainly not the only sensitizers. The FDA data bank, PAFA (see page 10), has fully up-to-date toxicology information available on this food additive.

RUBBER, BUTADIENE STYRENE • Latex. A chewing gum base. No known toxicity.

RUBBER, SMOKED SHEET • A chewing gum base. No known toxicity.

RUE OIL • A spice agent obtained from the fresh, aromatic blossoming plants grown in southern Europe and the Orient. It has a fatty odor and is used in baked goods. The oil is obtained by steam distillation and is used in fragrances and in blueberry, raspberry, coconut, grape, peach, rum, cheese, and spice flavorings for beverages, ice cream, ices, candy, baked goods, and condiments. Formerly used in medicine to treat certain disorders and hysteria. It is on the FDA list for study of mutagenic, teratogenic, subacute, and reproductive effects. It may cause photosensitivity. In 1976 the FDA confirmed rue as GRAS in all categories of food at a maximum of 2 ppm. The final report to the FDA of the Select Committee on GRAS Substances stated in 1980 that there is no available evidence that it is a hazard to the public when used as it is now and it should continue its GRAS status with limitations on amounts that can be added to food. The FDA data bank, PAFA, has not yet done a toxicology literature search on this food additive.

RUM ETHER • A synthetic flavoring consisting of water, ethanol, ethyl acetate, methanol, ethyl formate, acetone, acetaldehyde, and formaldehyde (*see all*). Used in butter, liquor, and rum flavorings for beverages, ice cream, ices, candy, baked goods, gelatin, chewing gum, and alcoholic beverages (1,600 ppm).

RUTIN • Pale yellow crystals found in many plants, particularly buckwheat. Used as a dietary supplement for capillary fragility. No known toxicity. The FDA data bank, PAFA (see page 10), has fully up-to-date toxicology information available on this food additive.

RYE FLOUR • Used in powders. Flour made from a hardy annual cereal grass. Seeds are used for feed and in the manufacture of whiskey and bread. May cause allergic reactions.

S

SACCHARIDE HYDROLYSATE • A mixture of sugars derived from using an alkali and water on a mixture of glucose and lactose (*see*).

SACCHARIDE ISOMERATE • *See* Saccharide Hydrolysate.

SACCHARIN • An artificial sweetener in use since 1879. It is three hundred times as sweet as natural sugar. Used as a sweetener for mouthwashes, dentifrices, and lipsticks. It sweetens dentifrices and mouthwashes in a 0.05 to 1 percent concentration. On the FDA's top-priority list to retest for mutagenic, subacute, and reproductive effects. White crystals or crystalline powder. Odorless or with a faint aromatic odor. It was used with cyclamates in the experiments that led to the ban on cyclamates. The FDA proposed restricting saccharin to fifteen milligrams per day for each kilogram of body weight or one gram a day for a 150-pound person. Then, on March 9, 1977, the FDA announced the use of saccharin in foods and beverages would be banned because the artificial sweetener had been found to cause malignant bladder tumors in laboratory animals. The ban was based on the findings of a study sponsored by the Canadian government that found that seven out of thirty-eight animals developed tumors, three of them malignant. In addition, one hundred offspring were fed saccharin, and fourteen of them developed bladder tumors. In contrast, one hundred control rats were not fed saccharin and only two developed tumors. At the time of the FDA's announcement, 5 million pounds of saccharin were being consumed per year, 74 percent of it in diet soda, 14 percent in dietetic food, and 12 percent as a tabletop replacement for sugar. There was an immediate outcry, led vociferously by the Calorie Control Council, an organization made up of commercial producers and users of saccharin. The FDA, urged by Congress, then delayed the ban. The moratorium on prohibiting the use of saccharin has been extended indefinitely. Since 1977, however, saccharin containers carry labels warning that saccharin may be hazardous to your health.

Saccharin has exhibited mutagenic activity (genetic changes) in the early-warning Ames Test (*see*) for carcinogens. When administered orally to mice, mutagenic activity was demonstrated in the urine of these animals as well as in tissue tests. Highly purified saccharin was not mutagenic in tissue tests, but the urine of mice fed saccharin was. Two other sweeteners, neohesperidin dihydrochalcone and xylitol, had no detectable mutagenic activity. Congress's Office of Technology Assessment, in view of the evidence to date, strongly endorsed the scientific basis of the FDA's proposed ban. "This review of animal studies leads to the conclusion that saccharin is a carcinogen for animals," the FDA panel said. Clouding the degree of risk, however, is that up to 20 ppm of unknown chemical impurities contaminated those doses fed the rats in the Canadian study that led to the FDA's original move. The impurities themselves proved mutagenic in the Ames Test.

On November 6, 1978, the Committee of the Institute of Medicine and National Research Council concluded that saccharin is a potential carcinogen in humans. The extremely low potency of saccharin as a carcinogen was emphasized by the committee. However, they expressed special concern that children under ten years of age were consuming diet sodas and other saccharin-containing products in increasing amounts. Exposure in children, the committee noted, may have special significance because of the long time required for some cancers to develop. There were some "worrisome data" regarding consumption by women of child-bearing age, children, and teenagers. The concern about fetal exposure grew out of earlier findings of increased bladder cancers in male rats fed high-saccharin diets or born to mothers that were on high-saccharin diets during pregnancy. The committee concluded that it is most likely that saccharin itself is the carcinogenic agent, rather than any impurities that may be associated with its manufacture. The fight to keep saccharin on the market spotlighted the Delaney Amendment, which prohibits known carcinogens from being added to food, and a move to weaken that amendment persists. In 1969, Britain banned saccharin except as an artificial sweetener. In 1950, France banned it except as a nonprescription drug. Germany restricts its use to certain foods and beverages, which must state on the label that it is in the product.

SAFFLOWER GLYCERIDE • *See* Safflower Oil.

SAFFLOWER OIL • The edible oil expressed from the seed of an Old World herb that resembles a thistle, with large bright red or orange flowers. Widely cultivated for its oil, which thickens and becomes rancid on exposure to air. It is used in salad oils and shortenings, and as a vehicle for medicines. As a dietary supplement it is alleged to be a preventative in the development of atherosclerosis—fat-clogged arteries. A drug consisting of the dried flowers of safflower is used in medicine in place of saffron (*see*). Used in creams and lotions to soften the skin. No known toxicity. American safflower (American saffron) is no longer authorized for use.

SAFFRON • Crocus. Vegetable Gold. Spanish or French Saffron. It is the dried stigma of the crocus, *Crocus sativus,* cultivated in Spain, Greece, France, and Iran. Orange-brown; strong, peculiar, aromatic odor; bitterish, aromatic taste. Almost entirely employed for coloring and flavoring. It has been permanently listed for use in foods since 1966. Used in bitters, liquors, and spice flavorings for beverages, baked goods, meats, and liquors. Cleared by the USDA Meat Inspection Department for coloring sausage casing, oleomargarine, shortening, and for marking ink. The *extract* is used in honey and rum flavorings for beverages, ice cream, ices, candy, baked goods, and condiments, and it goes into yellow coloring. The coloring is used in food and has been permanently listed since 1966. Formerly used to treat skin disease. GRAS. The FDA data bank, PAFA (see page 10), has fully up-to-date toxicology information available on this food additive.

SAFROLE • Found in certain natural oils such as star anise, nutmeg, ylang-ylang, it is a stable, colorless to brown liquid with an odor of sassafras and root beer. Used in the manufacture of heliotropin (*see*) and in expensive soaps and perfumes. Used as a beverage flavoring until it was banned in 1960. The toxicity of this fragrance ingredient is being questioned by the FDA. It is an animal-liver carcinogen.

SAGE • The flowering tops and leaves of the shrubby mints. Spices include Greek sage and Spanish sage. The genus is *Salvia,* so named for the plant's supposed healing powers. *Greek sage* is used in fruit and spice flavorings for beverages, baked goods, and meats (1,500 ppm). *Greek sage oil,* obtained by steam distillation, is used in berry, grape, liquor, meat, crème de menthe, nutmeg, and sage flavorings for beverages, ice cream, ices, candy, baked goods, chewing gum, condiments, meats, and pickles. *Greek sage oleoresin (see)* is used in sausage and spice flavorings for condiments and meats. *Spanish sage oil* is used in fruit and spice flavorings for beverages, ice cream, ices, candy, baked goods, condiments, and meats. It is also used as a meat preservative. Greek sage is used in medicine. Used by herbalists to treat sore gums, mouth ulcers, and to remove warts. The Arabs believed that it prevents dying. No known toxicity. GRAS. The FDA data bank, PAFA (see page 10), has not yet done a toxicology literature search on this food additive.

SAIGON CINNAMON • *See* Cinnamon.

SAIGON CINNAMON LEAF OIL • *See* Cinnamon.

SAINT JOHN'S BREAD • *See* Locust Bean Gum. GRAS.

SAINT-JOHN'S-WORT FLOWERS, LEAVES, AND CAULIS • *Hypericum perforatum.* Amber. Blessed. Devil's Scourge. God's Wonder Herb. Grace of God. Goatweed. Hypericum. Klamath Weed. A perennial native to Britain, Europe, and Asia, it is now found throughout North America. The plant contains volatile oil, tannin, resin, and pectin (*see all*) and glycosides. It was believed to have infinite healing powers derived from the saint, the red juice representing his blood. It was used as an antivenereal. It is used to treat pains and diseases of the nervous system, arthritic pains, and injuries. An infusion made from its leaves is used for stomach disorders, diarrhea, depression, and bladder problems and to remove threadworms in children. A salve made from the flowers is used by herbalists to treat scratches, swellings, and small wounds. The oil is used for burns. A spray has been used for colds. It reputedly also eases fibrositis, sciatica, and varicose veins. It is now being studied by researchers from the National Cancer Institute and universities as a potential treatment for cancer and AIDS. The FDA listed Saint-John's-wort as an "unsafe herb" in 1977. The FDA issued a notice in 1992 that Saint-John's-wort has not been shown to be safe and effective as claimed in OTC digestive-aid products. That does not mean, however, that it cannot be used for other purposes. There is no reported use of the chemical and no toxicology information is available, according to the FDA's data bank, PAFA.

SALAD OIL • Any edible vegetable oil. Dermatologists advise rubbing salad oils or fats on the skin, particularly on babies and older persons. Vegetable oils are used in commercial baby preparations, cleansers, emollient creams, face powders, hair-grooming preparations, hypoallergenic cosmetics, lipsticks, nail creams, shampoos, shaving creams, and wave sets. Nontoxic.

SALICARIA EXTRACT • Spiked Loose Strife. Extract of the flowering herb *Lythrum salicaria,* which has purple or pink flowers. Used since ancient Greek times as an herb that calms nerves and soothes skin.

SALICYLALDEHYDE • Salicylic Aldehyde. A synthetic flavoring made by heating phenol (very toxic) and chloroform. Occurs naturally in cassia bark.

Clear, bitter, almondlike odor, burning taste. White to slightly pink, crystalline, bitter powder. Gives a sensation of warmth on the tongue. Soluble in hot water. Used in butter flavorings for beverages, ice cream, ices, candy, baked goods, chewing gum, condiments, and liqueurs. Used chiefly in perfumery. Used as an analgesic, fungicide, and antiinflammatory agent to soothe the skin. Lethal dose in rats is one gram per kilogram of body weight. The FDA data bank, PAFA (see page 10), has fully up-to-date toxicology information available on this food additive.

SALICYLATES • Amyl. Phenyl. Benzyl. Menthyl. Glyceryl. Dipropylene Glycol Esters. Salts of Salicylic Acid. Those who are sensitive to aspirin may also be hypersensitive to FD and C Yellow No. 5, a salicylate, and to a number of foods that naturally contain salicylate, such as almonds, apples, apple cider, apricots, blackberries, boysenberries, cherries, cloves, cucumbers, currants, gooseberries, grapes, nectarines, oil of wintergreen, oranges, peaches, pickles, plums, prunes, raisins, raspberries, strawberries, and tomatoes. Foods with added salicylates for flavoring may be ice cream, bakery goods (except bread), candy, chewing gum, soft drinks, Jell-O, jams, cake mixes, and wintergreen flavors. The salts are used as sunburn preventatives and antiseptics.

SALICYLIC ACID • Occurs naturally in wintergreen leaves, sweet birch, and other plants and has a sweetish taste. Synthetically prepared by heating phenol with carbon dioxide, it is used as a preservative in food products. It is also used as a fungicide in the treatment of animals. Residues are prohibited in milk. EPA Genetic Toxicology Program (see). It is also used as a preservative and antimicrobial at 0.1 to 0.5 percent in skin softeners, face masks, hair tonics, deodorants, dandruff preparations, protective creams, hair dye removers, and suntan lotions and oils. It is antipuretic (antiitch) and antiseptic. In fact, in medicine, it is used as an antimicrobial at 2 to 20 percent concentration in lotions, ointments, powders, and plasters. It is also used in making aspirin. It can be absorbed through the skin. Absorption of large amounts may cause vomiting, abdominal pain, increased respiration, acidosis, mental disturbances, and skin rashes in sensitive individuals. It is poisonous by ingestion. Causes birth defects in experimental animals.

SALICYLIC ETHER • *See* Ethyl Salicylate.

SALICYLIDES • Any of several crystalline derivatives of salicylic acid (*see*) from which the water has been removed.

SALINOMYCIN • Coxistac. An antiparasite drug used in animal feed.

SALT • A compound formed by the interaction of an acid and a base. Sodium chloride, or common table salt, is an example. Sodium is the alkali or base and chloride provides the acidic factor.

SALTPETER • Potassium Nitrate. Niter. *See* Nitrate, Potassium. Acute intoxication is unlikely because a large dose causes vomiting and because it is rapidly excreted. Potassium poisoning disturbs the rhythm of the heart, and orally poisoned animals die from respiratory failure. Prolonged exposure to even small amounts may produce anemia, methemoglobinemia (lack of oxygen in the blood), and kidney damage.

SALTS OF FATTY ACIDS • Aluminum, calcium, magnesium, potassium, and sodium salts of capric, caprylic, myristic, oleic, palmitic, and stearic acids (*see all*) manufactured from fats and oils derived from edible sources. Used as anticaking agents, binders, and emulsifiers in various foods. The FDA data bank, PAFA (see page 10), has not yet done a toxicology literature search on this food additive.

SALVIA • *See* Sage.

SAMBUCUS **EXTRACT** • *See* Elder Flowers.

SANDALWOOD OIL, EAST INDIAN • It is the pale yellow, somewhat viscous volatile oil obtained by steam distillation from the dried ground roots and wood of the plant. A strong, warm, persistent odor; soluble in most fixed oils. Used in floral, fruit, honey, and ginger ale flavorings for beverages, ice cream, ices, candy, baked goods, and chewing gum. Used in perfume. Also used for incense and as a fumigant. May produce skin rash in the hypersensitive, especially if present in high concentrations in expensive perfumes. The FDA data bank, PAFA (see page 10), has not yet done a toxicology literature search on this food additive.

SANDALWOOD OIL, WEST INDIAN • Less soluble than the East Indian variety. *See* Amyris Oil.

SANDALWOOD OIL, YELLOW • Arheol. Same origin as East Indian sandalwood oil (*see*). A floral, fruit, honey, and ginger ale flavoring agent for beverages, ice cream, ices, candy, baked goods, and chewing gum. No known toxicity.

SANDARAC • Used in alcoholic beverages only. Resin from a plant grown in Morocco. Light yellow, brittle, insoluble in water. Used in tooth cements, varnishes, and for gloss and adhesion in nail lacquers. There is no reported use of the chemical and no toxicology information is available, according to the FDA's data bank, PAFA (see page 10).

SANTALOL • Alcohol from sandalwood used in fragrances. *See* Sandalwood Oil. The FDA data bank, PAFA, has not yet done a toxicology literature search on this food additive.

SANTALUM ALBUM • *See* Sandalwood Oil.

SANTALYL ACETATE • Acetic Acid. A synthetic flavoring agent obtained from sandalwood oils (*see*). Used in floral, pear, and pineapple flavorings for beverages, ice cream, ices, candy, baked goods, and chewing gum. The FDA data bank, PAFA, has fully up-to-date toxicology information available on this food additive.

SANTALYL PHENYLACETATE • Phenylacetic Acid. A synthetic flavoring obtained from sandalwood oils (*see*). Used in butter, caramel, fruit, and honey flavorings for beverages, ice cream, ices, candy, and baked goods. Although allowed as a food additive, there is no current reported use of the chemical, and therefore, although toxicology information may be available, the FDA is not updating it.

SANTOQUIN • Ethoxyquin. A yellow liquid antioxidant and herbicide. It has been found to cause liver tumors in newborn mice. *See* Sodium Acid Pyrophosphate (SAP).

SAPONIN • Any of numerous natural glycosides—natural or synthetic compounds derived from sugars—that occur in many plants such as soapbark, soapwort, or sarsaparilla. Characterized by their ability to foam in water. Yellowish to white, acrid, hygroscopic. In powder form they can cause sneezing. Extracted from soapbark or soapwort and used chiefly as foaming and emulsifying agents and detergents; also to reduce surface tensions, produce fine bubble lather in shaving creams, shampoos, bath oils, and dry shampoos. No known skin toxicity.

SARSAPARILLA EXTRACT • The dried root from tropical American plants, *Smilax* spp. Used in cola, mint, root beer, sarsaparilla, wintergreen, and birch beer flavorings for beverages, ice cream, ices, candy, and baked goods. Still used for psoriasis; formerly used for syphilis. The FDA data bank, PAFA (see page 10), has not yet done a toxicology literature search on this food additive.

SASSAFRAS BARK EXTRACT • Safrol. Safrol-free. It is the yellow to reddish yellow volatile oil obtained from the roots of the sassafras, *Sassafras albidum.* It is 80 percent safrole and has the characteristic odor and taste of sassafras. Used in rum and root beer flavorings for beverages, ice cream, ices, candy, and baked goods. Used in dentifrices, perfumes, soaps, and powders to correct disagreeable odors. Applied to insect bites and stings to relieve symptoms; also a topical antiseptic and used medicinally to break up intestinal gas. May produce dermatitis in hypersensitive individuals. The FDA data bank, PAFA, has not yet done a toxicology literature search on this food additive.

SASSAFRAS LEAVES • Safrol-free. Same origin as the bark extract. Used in soups (30,000 ppm). There is no reported use of the chemical and no toxicology information is available, according to the FDA's data bank, PAFA (see page 10). *See* Sassafras Bark Extract for toxicity.

SAUNDERS WHITE OIL • *See* Sandalwood Oil.

SAUSAGE CASINGS (HCL AND CELLUOSE FIBERS) • The FDA data bank, PAFA, is currently searching the toxicology literature concerning this additive.

SAVORY EXTRACT • An extract of *Satureia hortensis,* an aromatic mint known as summer or winter savory. The dried leaves of summer savory is a spice used in baked goods, condiments, and meats. *Summery savory oil* is obtained from the dried whole plant. It is used as a spice in condiments, candy, and baked goods. *Summer savory oil oleoresin (see)* is a spice used in candy, baked goods, and condiments. *Winter savory oil* and *oleoresin* spices are used in candy, baked goods, and condiments. Poisonous by skin contact. Moderately toxic by ingestion. A severe skin irritant. GRAS. The FDA data bank, PAFA, has not yet done a toxicology literature search on this food additive.

***SCHINUS MOLLE* OIL** • A natural flavoring extract from the tropical pepper tree, *Schinus molle.* Used in candy, baked goods, and condiments. The FDA data bank, PAFA (see page 10), has not yet done a toxicology literature search on this food additive. GRAS.

SCURVY GRASS EXTRACT • The extract of the leaves and flower stalks of *Cochlearia officinalis.* The bright green leaves of this northerly herb were collected and eaten in large quantities by European seamen to prevent scurvy. The plant has the strong odor of horseradish, to which it is related. No known toxicity.

SEBACIC ACID • Decanedioic acid. Colorless leaflets, sparingly soluble in water and soluble in alcohol. Manufactured by heating castor oil with alkalies or by distillation of oleic acid (*see*). The esters of sebacic acid are used as stabilizers. No known toxicity.

SELENIUM • Yellow solid or brownish powder, insoluble in water. Discovered in 1807 in the earth's crust. Used as a nutrient. Used in antidandruff shampoos. Can severely irritate the eyes if it gets into them while hair is being washed. Occupational exposure causes pallor, nervousness, depression, garlic odor of breath, gastrointestinal disturbances, and skin rash. Liver injury in experimental animals.

SENNA, ALEXANDRIA • Flavoring from the dried leaves of *Cassia senna* grown in India and Egypt. Has been used as a cathartic. The FDA data bank, PAFA, has not yet done a toxicology literature search on this food additive.

SENSITIVITY • Hypersensitivity. An increased reaction to substance that may be quite harmless to nonallergic persons.

SENSITIZE • To administer or expose to an antigen provoking an immune response so that, on later exposure to that antigen, a more vigorous secondary response will occur.

SEQUESTERING AGENT • A preservative that prevents physical or chemical changes affecting color, flavor, texture, or appearance of a product. Ethylenediamine tetraacetic acid (EDTA) is an example. It is used in carbonated beverages. It also prevents adverse effects of metals in shampoos.

SERINE • L and DL Forms. An amino acid (*see*), nonessential, taken as a dietary supplement. It is a constituent of many proteins (*see*). Since 1980, on the FDA list requiring further information. The FDA data bank, PAFA (see page 10), has fully up-to-date toxicology information available on this food additive.

SERPENTARIA EXTRACT • Snakeroot. Snakeweed. Extracted from the roots of *Rauwolfia serpentina,* its yellow rods turn red upon drying. Used in the manufacture of resins and as a bitter tonic. No known toxicity when applied to the skin but can affect heart and blood pressure when ingested. There is no reported use of the chemical and no toxicology information is available, according to the FDA's data bank, PAFA.

SERUM ALBUMIN • The major protein component of blood plasma derived from bovines. Used as a moisturizing ingredient.

SERUM PROTEINS • *See* Serum Albumin.

SESAME • Seeds and Oils. The edible seeds of an East Indian herb, *Sesamum indicum,* which has a rosy or white flower. The seeds, which flavor bread, crackers, cakes, confectionery, and other products, yield a pale yellow, bland-tasting, almost odorless oil used in the manufacture of margarine. The oil has been used as a laxative and skin softener and contains elements active against lice. May cause allergic reactions, primarily contact dermatitis. GRAS. The FDA data bank, PAFA (see page 10), has not yet done a toxicology literature search on this food additive.

SESQUITERPENE LACTONES • In recent years, more than six hundred plants have been identified as containing these substances, and more than fifty are known to cause allergic contact dermatitis. Among them are arnica, chamomile, and yarrow (*see all*).

354 • SHADDOCK EXTRACT

SHADDOCK EXTRACT • An extract of *Citrus grandis* and named for a seventeenth-century sea captain who brought the seeds back from the East Indies to Barbados. Shaddock is a large, thick-rinded, pear-shaped citrus fruit related to and largely replaced by the grapefruit. No known toxicity.

SHARK-LIVER OIL • A rich source of vitamin A, believed to be beneficial to the skin. A brown, fatty oil obtained from the livers of the large predatory fish. Used in lubricating creams and lotions. No known toxicity.

SHEA BUTTER • The natural fat obtained from the fruit of the karite tree, *Butyrosperum parkii.* Also called karite butter, it is chiefly used as a food but also in soap and candles. No known toxicity.

SHEA BUTTER UNSAPONIFIABLES • The fraction of shea butter that is not saponified during processing, that is, not turned into fatty alcohol.

SHELLAC • A resinous excretion of certain insects feeding on appropriate host trees, usually in India. As processed for marketing, the lacca, which is formed by the insects, may be mixed with small amounts of arsenic trisulfide for color and with rosin. White shellac is free of arsenic. Shellac is used as a candy glaze and polish up to 0.4 percent. Also used in hair lacquer and on jewelry and accessories. May cause allergic contact dermatitis. The FDA data bank, PAFA (see page 10), has not yet done a toxicology literature search on this food additive.

SHELLAC WAX • Bleached, refined shellac. *See* Shellac.

SHORTENINGS • A fat such as a butter, lard, or vegetable oil used to make cake, pastry, bread, etc., light and flaky. *See* Salad Oil.

SIBERIAN FIR OIL • *See* Pine Needle Oil.

SILICA • A white powder, slightly soluble in water, that occurs abundantly in nature and is 12 percent of all rocks. Sand is a silica. Upon drying and heating in a vacuum, hard transparent porous granules are formed that are used in absorbent and adsorbent material in toilet preparations, particularly skin protectant creams. Also used as a coloring agent.

SILICA AEROGEL • Silicon Dioxide. A fine, white powder, slightly soluble in water, that occurs abundantly in nature and is 12 percent of all rocks. Sand is a silica. Chemically and biologically inert, it is used as an antifoaming agent in beverages and as a surface-active agent. Used chiefly in the manufacture of glass. Upon drying and heating in a vacuum, hard, transparent, porous granules are formed that are used in absorbents and adsorbent material in toilet preparations, particularly skin-protectant creams. Also used as a coloring agent. The final report to the FDA of the Select Committee on GRAS Substances stated in 1980 that it should continue its GRAS status with no limitations other than good manufacturing practices. *See* Silicones.

SILICATES • Salts or esters derived from silicic acid (*see*). Any of numerous insoluble complex metal salts that contain silicon and oxygen that constitute the largest group of minerals and that with quartz make up the greater part of the earth's crust (as rocks, soils, and clays). Contained in building materials such as cement, concrete, bricks, and glass. No known toxicity. The simplest silicate is sand, a molecule formed by joining one silicon atom with two oxygen atoms.

SILICIC ACID • Silica Gel. White, gelatinous substance obtained by the action of acids on sodium silicate (*see*). Odorless, tasteless, inert, white, fluffy powder when dried. Insoluble in water and acids. Absorbs water readily. Used in face powders, dentifrices, creams, and talcum powders as an opacifier. Soothing to skin. No known toxicity.

SILICON DIOXIDE • Silica. Transparent, tasteless crystals or powder, practically insoluble in water. Occurs in nature as agate, amethyst, chalcedony, cristobalite, flint, quartz, sand, and tridymite. Used as a defoamer in beer production. Cleared for use as a food additive and as an anticaking agent at a level not to exceed 2 percent in salt and salt substitutes, in BHT (*see* Butylated Hydroxytoluene), in vitamins up to 3 percent, in urea up to 1 percent, and in sodium propionate up to 1 percent (*see all*). Also used in ceramics and in scouring and grinding compounds. Prolonged inhalation of the dust can injure lungs. The final report to the FDA of the Select Committee on GRAS Substances stated in 1980 that it should continue its GRAS status with no limitations other than good manufacturing practices. The FDA data bank, PAFA (see page 10), has fully up-to-date toxicology information available on this food additive.

SILICONES • Any of a large group of fluid oils, rubbers, resins, and compounds derived from silica (*see*) that are water repellent, skin adherent, and stable over a wide range of temperatures. Used as anticaking agents in foods and in waterproofing and lubrication. Used in aftershave preparations, hair-waving preparations, nail driers, hair straighteners, hand lotions, and protective creams. No known toxicity when used externally.

SIMPLESSE • A fat substitute developed by the same company that brought you NutraSweet. It is made from egg and milk protein. It can be used, according to the company, in margarine, ice cream, salad dressings, and yogurt. It cannot be used in baked food. Its introduction was delayed by the FDA, which said in 1988 that even though Simplesse was made from natural food, it should be pre-market-tested for safety.

SKATOLE • Used in perfumery as a fixative (*see*). A constituent of beetroot, feces, and coal tar. Gives a violet color when mixed with iron and sulfuric acid. The FDA data bank, PAFA (see page 10), has fully up-to-date toxicology information available on this food additive.

SLOE BERRIES • Blackthorn Berries. The fruit of the common juniper. The extract is a natural flavoring used in berry, plum, and liquor flavorings for beverages, ice cream, ices, candy, baked goods, and cordials (up to 43,000 ppm). Sloe gin is flavored with sloe berries. GRAS. The FDA data bank, PAFA, has not yet done a toxicology literature search on this food additive.

SMALLAGE • *See* Lovage.

SMELLAGE • *See* Lovage.

SMOKE FLAVORING SOLUTIONS • Condensates from burning hardwood in a limited amount of air. The solutions are used to flavor various foods, primarily meats, and as antioxidants to retard bacterial growth. Also permitted in cheese and smoke-flavored fish. The Select Committee of the Federation of American Societies for Experimental Biology (FASEB), under contract to the

FDA, concluded that smoke flavorings in general pose no hazard to the public when used at current levels and under present procedures, but uncertainties exist that require further study. The committee also said there are insufficient data upon which to base an evaluation of smoked-yeast flavoring, produced by exposing food-grade yeast to wood smoke. It is used to flavor soups, cheese, crackers, dip, pizza, and seasoning mixes.

SMOKED SHEET RUBBER • A chewing gum base. No known toxicity.

SNAKEROOT OIL • Canadian Oil. Derived from the roots of the plant *Asarum canadense,* which had a reputation for curing snakebites. Grown from Canada to North Carolina and Kansas. Used in ginger, ginger ale, wintergreen, and birch beer flavorings for beverages, ice cream, ices, candy, baked goods, and condiments. The FDA data bank, PAFA (see page 10), has fully up-to-date toxicology information available on this food additive.

SOAP • Sodium Oleate and Sodium Palmitate. Any salt of a fatty acid usually made by saponification of a vegetable oil with caustic soda. The oldest cleanser, usually a mixture of sodium salts of various fatty acids. In liquid soaps, potassium instead of sodium salts are used. Bar soaps vary in contents from brand to brand, depending on the fats or oils used. Sodium hydroxide makes a strong soap; fatty acids, a mild soap. So-called "neutral" soaps are actually alkaline, with pH around 10 (compared to skin, which is 5 to 6.5 pH) when dissolved in water. Soaps are usually in toothpastes, tooth powder, and shaving creams. Hard soap consists largely of sodium oleate or sodium palmitate and is used medicinally as an antiseptic, detergent, or suppository. Many people are allergic to soaps. They may also be drying to the skin, irritate the eyes, and cause rashes, depending upon ingredients. GRAS for food packaging.

SOAPBARK • *See* Quillaja Extract.

SODIUM • A metallic element that is soft, silvery, and oxidizes easily in air. It is waxlike at room temperature and brittle at low temperature. It has many uses in combination with other chemicals. Sodium chloride (*see*) is common table salt.

SODIUM ACETATE • Sodium Salt of Acetic Acid. Transparent crystals highly soluble in water. Used as a preservative, flavoring, and pH control agent in candy, cereals, fats, grain products, jams, jellies, meat products, oils, pasta, snack foods, soup mixes, soups, and sweet sauces. In industrial forms, it is used in photography, dyeing processes, and in foot warmers because it retains heat. Medicinally it is used as an alkalizer and as a diuretic. EPA Genetic Toxicology Program (*see*). Moderately toxic by ingestion. A skin and eye irritant. The final report to the FDA of the Select Committee on GRAS Substances stated in 1980 that it should continue its GRAS status with no limitations other than good manufacturing practices. The FDA data bank, PAFA (see page 10), has fully up-to-date toxicology information available on this food additive.

SODIUM ACID PHOSPHATE • A sequestrant in cheeses and frozen desserts. GRAS.

SODIUM ACID PYROPHOSPHATE (SAP) • A white mass or free-flowing powder used as a buffer. It is a slow-acting acid constituent of a leavening mixture for self-rising and prepared cakes, doughnuts, waffles, muffins, cupcakes, and other types of flours and mixes. Also used in canned tuna fish. The U.S.

Department of Agriculture has proposed that SAP be added to hot dogs and other sausages to accelerate the development of a rose-red color, thus cutting production time by some 25 to 40 percent. It is related to phosphoric acid, which is sometimes used as a gastric acidifier. No known toxicity. The final report to the FDA of the Select Committee on GRAS Substances stated in 1980 that it should continue its GRAS status with no limitations other than good manufacturing practices. The FDA data bank, PAFA (see page 10), is currently searching the toxicology literature concerning this additive.

SODIUM ACID SULFITE • *See* Sodium Bisulfite.

SODIUM ALGINATE • Dissolves in water to form a viscous, colloidal solution and is used in cosmetics as a stabilizer, thickener, and emulsifier. An emollient used in baby lotions, hair lacquers, wave sets, and shaving creams. It is the sodium salt of alginic acid extracted from brown seaweed. Occurs as a white to yellowish, fibrous or granular powder, nearly odorless and tasteless. No known toxicity. GRAS.

SODIUM ALUM • *See* Alum.

SODIUM ALUMINATE • A strong alkaline employed in the manufacture of lake colors used in foods (*see* FD and C Lakes). Also used in water-softening and printing. The final report to the FDA of the Select Committee on GRAS Substances stated in 1980 that it should continue its GRAS status with no limitations other than good manufacturing practices. There is no reported use of the chemical and no toxicology information is available, according to the FDA's data bank, PAFA.

SODIUM ALUMINUM PHOSPHATE • A white, odorless powder, insoluble in water, used as a buffer in self-rising flour. Used with sodium bicarbonate (*see*). Used also in various cheeses. No known toxicity. The final report to the FDA of the Select Committee on GRAS Substances stated in 1980 that it should continue its GRAS status with no limitations other than good manufacturing practices. The FDA data bank, PAFA (see page 10), has fully up-to-date toxicology information available on this food additive.

SODIUM ALUMINOSILICATE • A chemical substance used in dental compounds, colored lakes (*see* FD and C Lakes) for foods, and in washing compounds. The final report to the FDA of the Select Committee on GRAS Substances stated in 1980 that it should continue its GRAS status with no limitations other than good manufacturing practices. The FDA data bank, PAFA, has fully up-to-date toxicology information available on this food additive.

SODIUM ALUMINUM SULFATE • A flour-bleaching agent alone or in combination with potassium aluminum, calcium sulfate, and other compounds. No known toxicity. GRAS.

SODIUM ASCORBATE • Vitamin C. Sodium. Aside from its use in vitamin C preparations, it can serve as an antioxidant in chopped meat and other foods to retard spoiling; also used in curing meat. No known toxicity. The final report to the FDA of the Select Committee on GRAS Substances stated in 1980 that it should continue its GRAS status with no limitations other than good manufacturing practices. The FDA data bank, PAFA, has fully up-to-date toxicology information available on this food additive. *See* Ascorbic Acid.

SODIUM BENZOATE • White, odorless powder or crystals; sweet, antiseptic taste. Works best in slightly acid media. Used as a preservative in margarine, codfish, bottled soft drinks, maraschino cherries, mincemeat, fruit juices, pickles, confections, fruit jelly preserves, and jams. Also used in the ice for cooling fish. An antiseptic and preservative used in eye creams, vanishing creams, and toothpastes. Once used medicinally for rheumatism and tonsillitis. No known toxicity for external use. Moderately toxic by ingestion. Caused birth defects in experimental animals. Larger doses of eight to ten grams by mouth may cause nausea and vomiting. Small doses have little or no effect. The FDA data bank, PAFA, is currently searching the toxicology literature concerning this additive.

SODIUM BICARBONATE • Bicarbonate of Soda. Baking Soda. An alkali prepared by the reaction of soda ash with carbon dioxide and used in prepared pancake, biscuit, and muffin mixes; a leavening agent in baking powders; in various crackers and cookies; to adjust acidity in tomato soup, ices, and sherbets; in pastes and beverages; in syrups for frozen products; confections; and self-rising flours. Also used in cornmeals and canned peas. Also used in effervescent bath salts, mouthwashes, and skin-soothing powders. Its white crystals or powder are used as a gastric antacid, as an alkaline wash, and to treat burns. Used also as a neutralizer for butter, cream, milk, and ice cream. Essentially harmless to the skin, but when used on very dry skin in preparations that evaporate, it leaves an alkaline residue that may cause irritation. It may alter the urinary excretion of other drugs, thus making those drugs either more toxic or less effective. GRAS. The FDA data bank, PAFA (see page 10), has fully up-to-date toxicology information available on this food additive.

SODIUM BISULFATE • Sodium Acid Sulfite. Sodium Hydrogen Sulfite. Colorless or white crystals fused in water, with a disagreeable taste. It is used as a disinfectant in the manufacture of soaps, and in perfumes, foods, and pickling compounds. See Sodium Bisulfite.

SODIUM BISULFITE • Sodium Acid Sulfite. An inorganic salt. It is a white powder with a disagreeable taste, used as a bleaching agent in ale, wine, beer, and other food products. Commercial bisulfite consists chiefly of sodium metabisulfite (*see*). It is used as an antiseptic, as an antifermentative in cosmetic creams, mouthwashes, bleaches, perfumes, and hair dyes, to treat parasitic skin diseases, and to remove warts. In its aqueous solution, it is an acid. Concentrated solutions are highly irritating to the skin and mucous membranes. Sodium bisulfite can cause changes in the genetic material of bacteria and is a suspect mutagen. Not permitted in meats and other sources of vitamin B_1; strong irritant to the skin and tissue. The Select Committee on GRAS Substances found it did not present a hazard at present use levels but that additional data would be needed if higher use occurred. The committee said in 1980 that it should continue as GRAS with limitations on the amounts that can be added to food. The FDA data bank, PAFA, is currently searching the toxicology literature concerning this additive. See Sulfites.

SODIUM BORATE • Used as a preservative and emulsifier. Used in freckle lotions, nail whiteners, liquefying (cleansing) creams, and eye lotions. Hard, odorless powder insoluble in water, it is a weak antiseptic and astringent for mucous membranes. Used also in bath salts, foot preparations, scalp lotions, permanent-wave solutions, and hair-setting lotions. Has a drying effect on the skin and may cause irritation. Continued use of a shampoo containing it will cause the hair to become dry and brittle. There is no reported use of the chemical and no toxicology information is available, according to the FDA's data bank, PAFA (see page 10).

SODIUM BOROHYDRIDE • Prepared from methyl borate and sodium hydride, it is used as a reducing agent (*see*) for various food additive chemicals. It scavenges for traces of aldehyde, ketones, and peroxides in organic chemicals. The FDA data bank, PAFA, has not yet done a toxicology literature search on this food additive.

SODIUM BROMATE • Inorganic salt. Colorless, odorless crystals that liberate oxygen. Used as a solvent. *See* Potassium Bromate for toxicity.

SODIUM CALCIUM ALUMINOSILICATE • Used to prevent salt and dry mixes from caking. No known toxicity. The final report to the FDA of the Select Committee on GRAS Substances stated in 1980 that it should continue its GRAS status with no limitations other than good manufacturing practices. There is no reported use of the chemical and no toxicology information is available, according to the FDA's data bank, PAFA.

SODIUM CAPRYL LACTYLATE • *See* Palm Oil.

SODIUM CAPRYLATE • *See* Palm Oil.

SODIUM CARBONATE • Soda Ash. Small, odorless crystals or powder that occurs in nature in ores and is found in lake brines or seawater. Absorbs water from the air. Used as a neutralizer for butter, cream, fluid milk, and ice cream; in the processing of olives before canning; and in cocoa products. Has an alkaline taste and is used as an antacid and reagent in permanent-wave solutions, soaps, mouthwashes, shampoos, foot preparations, bath salts, and vaginal douches. A strong alkali used like lye. It is used to treat skin rashes and as a water softener. It caused scalp, forehead, and hand rashes when the hypersensitive used cosmetics containing it. Ingestion of large quantities may produce corrosion of the gastrointestinal tract, vomiting, diarrhea, circulatory collapse, and death. The final report to the FDA of the Select Committee on GRAS Substances stated in 1980 that it should continue its GRAS status with no limitations other than good manufacturing practices. The FDA data bank, PAFA (see page 10), has fully up-to-date toxicology information available on this food additive.

SODIUM CARBOXYMETHYLCELLULOSE • Made from a cotton byproduct, it occurs as a white powder or granules. Used as a stabilizer, thickener, gelling agent, and nonnutritive bulking aid. Used to prevent water loss, make food opaque, and to texturize food. Found in ice cream, beverages, confections, baked goods, icings, toppings, chocolate milk, chocolate-flavored beverages, gassed cream (pressure-dispensed whipped cream), syrup for frozen products, variegated mixtures, cheese spreads, and in certain cheeses. Also used in French dressing, artificially sweetened jellies, preserves, gelling ingredients, and mix-it-yourself and powdered drinks. Medicinally used as a laxative (1.5 grams orally), antacid (15–30 milligrams of 5 percent solution), and in pharmacies for preparing suspensions. Used in setting lotions, it is an artificial gum that dries and leaves a film on the hair. Prepared by treating alkali cellulose with sodium chloroacetate. Can cause digestive disturbances. *See* Cellulose Gums.

SODIUM CARRAGEENAN • Sodium salt of carrageenan (*see*).

SODIUM CASEINATE • Casein. The soluble form of milk protein in which casein is partially neutralized with sodium hydroxide and used as a texturizer in ice cream, frozen custard, ice milk, and sherbet. Cleared by the USDA Meat Inspection Department for use in imitation sausage, nonspecific loaves, soups, and stews. No known toxicity. GRAS. The final report to the FDA of the Select Committee on GRAS Substances stated in 1980 that it should continue its GRAS status with no limitations other than good manufacturing practices.

SODIUM CASTORATE • The sodium salt of the fatty acids derived from castor oil (*see*).

SODIUM CHLORIDE • Common table salt. In addition to seasoning it is used as a pickling agent, a preservative for meats, vegetables, and butter. Prevents browning in cut fruit. Used as an astringent and antiseptic in mouthwashes, dentifrices, bubble baths, soap, bath salts, and eye lotions. It consists of opaque white crystals. Odorless, with a characteristic salty taste, and absorbs water. Used topically to treat inflamed lesions. Diluted solutions are not considered irritating, but upon drying, water is drawn from the skin and may produce irritation. Salt workers have a great deal of skin rashes. Also reported to irritate the roots of the teeth when used for a long time in dentifrices. Not considered toxic but can adversely affect persons with high blood pressure and kidney disease. The final report to the FDA of the Select Committee on GRAS Substances stated in 1980 that it should continue its GRAS status with no limitations other than good manufacturing practices. The FDA data bank, PAFA (see page 10), is currently searching the toxicology literature concerning this additive.

SODIUM CHLORITE • A powerful oxidizer prepared commercially and used to modify food starch (*see* Modified Starch) up to 0.5 percent. Used as a bleaching agent for textiles and paper pulp and in water purification. Toxicity depends on concentration. The FDA data bank, PAFA, has not yet done a toxicology literature search on this food additive.

SODIUM CHOLATE • *See* Cholic Acid.

SODIUM CITRATE • White, odorless crystals, granules, or powder with a cool salty taste. Stable in air. Prevents "cream plug" in cream and "feathering" when cream is used in coffee; an emulsifier in ice cream, processed cheese, and evaporated milk; a buffer to control acidity and retain carbonation in beverages, in frozen fruit drinks, confections, fruit jellies, preserves, and jams. It attaches itself to trace metals present in water and inhibits their entering the living cell. Proposed as a replacement for phosphates in detergents, but also causes algae growth and removes the necessary trace metals from water as well as the toxic ones. Used as a sequestering agent (*see*) to remove trace metals in solutions and as an alkalizer in cosmetic products. Can alter urinary excretion of other drugs, thus making those drugs either less effective or more toxic. The final report to the FDA of the Select Committee on GRAS Substances stated in

1980 that it should continue its GRAS status with no limitations other than good manufacturing practices. The FDA data bank, PAFA (see page 10), has fully up-to-date toxicology information available on this food additive.

SODIUM COCO-HYDROLYZED ANIMAL PROTEIN • The sodium salt of the condensation product of coconut acid chloride and hydrolyzed animal protein. *See* Hydrolyzed Protein.

SODIUM COCOATE • *See* Coconut Oil.

SODIUM COCOYL GLUTAMATE • A softener. *See* Glutamate.

SODIUM DEHYDROACETATE • Dehydroacetic Acid. A preservative; white, odorless, powdered, with an acrid taste. Used in cut or peeled squash and as a plasticizer, fungicide, and bactericide in antienzyme toothpaste. Used as a plasticizer, fungicide, and bacteria killer in cosmetics; as an antienzyme ingredient in dentifrices, allegedly prevents decay; a kidney-tube blocking agent. Can cause impaired kidney function. Large doses can cause vomiting, ataxia, and convulsions. There are no apparent allergic skin reactions. The FDA data bank, PAFA (see page 10), has not yet done a toxicology literature search on this food additive.

SODIUM DIACETATE • A compound of sodium acetate and acetic acid (*see*); a white, crystalline solid. Smells like vinegar. Used as a preservative. Inhibits molds and rope-forming bacteria in baked goods. No known toxicity. The final report to the FDA of the Select Committee on GRAS Substances stated in 1980 that it should continue its GRAS status with no limitations other than good manufacturing practices. The FDA data bank, PAFA, has fully up-to-date toxicology information available on this food additive.

SODIUM DIALKYLPHENOXYBENZENEDISULFONATE • Used in lye mixtures for peeling fruits and vegetables.

SODIUM DIHYDROGEN PHOSPHATE • White, odorless powder or granules used as a buffer, dietary supplement, emulsifier, nutrient, and in poultry wash. Used in beverages, cheese, meat products, poultry, and soft drinks. In meat food products, where allowed, limited to 5 percent. Mildly toxic by ingestion. A human eye irritant.

SODIUM N, n-DIMETHYLDITHIOCARBAMATE • Vinstop. Sta-Fresh 615. An antimicrobial agent used on beets and sugarcane. FDA limits the additive to 3 ppm based on weight of raw product. Moderately toxic by ingestion. Has caused mutations in experimental animals.

SODIUM DODECYLBENZENESULFONATE • An anionic detergent, it is used to treat raw food products and in cosmetic bath products and creams. It may irritate the skin. Will cause vomiting if swallowed. Although allowed as a food additive, there is no current reported use of the chemical, and therefore, although toxicology information may be available, the FDA is not updating it.

SODIUM ERYTHORBATE • Sodium Isoascorbate. A white, odorless powder used as an antioxidant in pickling brine up to 7.5 ounces per 100 gallons and in meat products up to three-quarters of an ounce per 100 pounds. Also used in beverages and baked goods; in cured cuts and cured, pulverized products to accelerate color fixing in curing. No known toxicity. The final report to the FDA of the Select Committee on GRAS Substances stated in 1980 that it should continue its GRAS status with no limitations other than good manufacturing practices. The FDA data bank, PAFA (see page 10), has fully up-to-date toxicology information available on this food additive.

SODIUM 2-ETHYL 1-HEXYLSULFATE • A component of a commercial detergent for washing raw foods. The FDA data bank, PAFA, has fully up-to-date toxicology information available on this food additive.

SODIUM FERRIC EDTA • Prepared from disodium ethylenediaminetetraacetic acid and ferric nitrate. Used as an iron source. The final report to the FDA of the Select Committee on GRAS Substances stated in 1980 that there were insufficient biological and other studies upon which to base an evaluation of it when it is used as a food ingredient. Nothing new has been reported by the FDA since. *See* Iron Salts.

SODIUM FERRICITROPYROPHOSPHATE • A white powder used in food enrichment. It is less prone to induce rancidity than other orthophosphates. The final report to the FDA of the Select Committee on GRAS Substances stated in 1980 that there were insufficient biological and other studies upon which to base an evaluation of it when it is used as a food ingredient. There is no reported use of the chemical and no toxicology information is available, according to the FDA's data bank, PAFA (see page 10). *See* Iron Salts.

SODIUM FERROCYANIDE • Yellow crystals or crystalline powder used as an anticaking agent for table salt and as a processing aid in wine. FDA limits residue to 1 ppm in finished wine. GRAS.

SODIUM FORMATE • White, deliquescent crystals used in paper packaging. Moderately toxic by ingestion. There is no reported use of the chemical and no toxicology information is available, according to the FDA's data bank, PAFA.

SODIUM GLUCONATE • Gluconic Acid. Sodium Salt. A pleasant-smelling compound, it is used as a sequestering agent (*see*). The final report to the FDA of the Select Committee on GRAS Substances stated in 1980 that it should continue its GRAS status with no limitations other than good manufacturing practices. The FDA data bank, PAFA, has fully up-to-date toxicology information available on this food additive.

SODIUM GLUTAMATE • The monosodium salt of the L-form of glutamic acid (*see*).

SODIUM GLYCERYL OLEATE PHOSPHATE • *See* Glyceryl Monostearate.

SODIUM HEXAMETAPHOSPHATE • Sodium Polymetaphosphate. Graham's Salt. An emulsifier, sequestering agent (*see*), and texturizer. Used in breakfast cereals, angel food cake, flaked fish, ice cream, ice milk, beer, bottled beverages, reconstituted lemon juice, puddings, processed cheeses, and artificially sweetened jellies. Used in foods and potable water to prevent scale formation and corrosion. Because it keeps calcium, magnesium, and iron salts in solution, it is an excellent water softener and detergent. Used in bath salts, bubble baths, permanent-wave neutralizers, and shampoos. Phosphorus is an essential nutrient, but it has to be in balance with other minerals such as calcium in the diet. Too much phosphorus in foods could lead to an imbalance and adversely affect bones, kidney, and heart. Lethal dose in dogs is 140 milligrams per kilogram of body weight. Used in Calgon, Giltex, and other such products. The final report to the FDA of the Select Committee on GRAS Substances stated in 1980 that it should continue its GRAS status for packaging with no limitations other than good manufacturing practices.

SODIUM HYALURONATE • The sodium salt of hyaluronic acid. From the fluid in the eye; it is used as a gelling agent. No known toxicity.

SODIUM HYDROSULFATE • Sodium Dithionate. A bacterial inhibitor and antifermentative. Slight odor. White or grayish white, crystalline powder that oxidizes in air. No known toxicity to the skin.

SODIUM HYDROSULFITE • A bacterial inhibitor and antifermentative in the sugar and syrup industries. Slight odor. No known toxicity. The final report to the FDA of the Select Committee on GRAS Substances stated in 1980 that it should continue its GRAS status with no limitations other than good manufacturing practices. *See* Sulfites.

SODIUM HYDROXIDE • Caustic Soda. Soda Lye. An alkali and emulsifier. Readily absorbs water. Used as a modifier for food starch, a glazing agent for pretzels, and a peeling agent for tubers and fruits. An alkali and emulsifier in liquid face powders, soaps, shampoos, cuticle removers, hair straighteners, shaving soaps, and creams. The FDA banned use of more than 10 percent in household liquid drain cleaners. If too much alkali is used, dermatitis of the scalp may occur. Its ingestion causes vomiting, prostration, and collapse. Inhalation causes lung damage. The final report to the FDA of the Select Committee on GRAS Substances stated in 1980 that it should continue its GRAS status for packaging with no limitations other than good manufacturing practices. The FDA data bank, PAFA (see page 10), has fully up-to-date toxicology information available on this food additive.

SODIUM HYDROXIDE GELATINIZED STARCH • Starch (*see*) that has been gelatinized with sodium hydroxide. The final report to the FDA of the Select Committee on GRAS Substances stated in 1980 that there were insufficient biological and other studies upon which to base an evaluation of it when it is used as a food ingredient. Nothing new has been reported since.

SODIUM HYPOCHLORITE • A preservative used in the washing of cottage cheese curd. Also used medically as an antiseptic for wounds. Ingestion may cause corrosion of mucous membranes, esophageal or gastric perforation. The aqueous solutions are Eau de Javelle, Clorox, Dazzle. The FDA data bank, PAFA (see page 10), is currently searching the toxicology literature concerning this additive.

SODIUM HYPOPHOSPHATE • White crystals, soluble in water, used as a sequestering agent (*see*). The final report to the FDA of the Select Committee on GRAS Substances stated in 1980 that it should continue its GRAS status with no limitations other than good manufacturing practices.

SODIUM INOSINATE • *See* Inosinate.

SODIUM IRON PYROPHOSPHATE • *See* Sodium Pyrophosphate.

SODIUM ISOASCORBATE • *See* Erythrobic Acid.

SODIUM ISOSTEROYL LACTYLATE • The sodium salt of isostearic acid and lactyl lactate. *See* Stearic Acid and Lactic Acid.

SODIUM LACTATE • Plasticizer substitute for glycerin. Colorless, thick, odorless liquid miscible with water, alcohol, and glycerin. It is used as an antioxidant, bodying agent, and humectant. Solution is neutral. Used medicinally as a systemic and urinary alkalizer. The FDA data bank, PAFA (see page 10), has fully up-to-date toxicology information available on this food additive. GRAS.

SODIUM LAURATE • *See* Sodium Lauryl Sulfate.

SODIUM LAURETH SULFATE • The sodium salt of sulfated ethoxylated lauryl alcohol, widely used as a water softener, and in baby and other nonirritating shampoos as a wetting agent and cleansing agent. *See also* Surfactants.

SODIUM LAUROYL GLUTAMATE • A softener. *See* Glutamate.

SODIUM LAURYL SULFATE (SLS) • A detergent, wetting agent, and emulsifier. It is used to treat raw foods, followed by a water rinsing. It is employed as a whipping aid in cake mixes and dried-egg products. Also used in bubble baths, emollient creams, cream depilatories, hand lotions, cold permanent waves, soapless shampoos, and toothpastes. Prepared by sulfation of lauryl alcohol followed by neutralization with sodium carbonate. Faint fatty odor; also emulsifies fats. May cause drying of the skin because of its degreasing ability and is an irritant to the skin. On the FDA list for further studies on the safety of this widely used additive. The FDA data bank, PAFA, has fully up-to-date toxicology information available on this food additive.

SODIUM LIGNOSULFONATE • The sodium salt of polysulfonated lignin derived from wood. It is used as a dispersing agent. A tan, free-flowing powder, it is also used as an emulsifier, stabilizer, and cleaning agent. The FDA data bank, PAFA (see page 10), has fully up-to-date toxicology information available on this food additive.

SODIUM MAGNESIUM SILICATES • *See* Silicates.

SODIUM METABISULFITE • An inorganic salt. A bacterial inhibitor in wine, ale, and beer; an antifermentative in sugar and syrups; a preservative for fruit and vegetable juices; antibrowning agent in cut fruits, frozen apples, dried fruits, prepared fruit-pie mix, peeled potatoes, and maraschino cherries. The final report to the FDA of the Select Committee on GRAS Substances stated in 1980 that the additive did not present a hazard when used at present levels but that increased use would require additional safety data. The FDA data bank, PAFA, is currently searching the toxicology literature concerning this additive. *See* Sulfites.

SODIUM METAPHOSPHATE • Graham's Salts. A dough conditioner. Used in dental polishing agents, detergents, water softeners, sequestrants, emulsifiers, food additives, and textile laundering. The final report to the FDA of the Select Committee on GRAS Substances stated in 1980 that it should continue its GRAS status with no limitations other than good manufacturing practices. The FDA data bank, PAFA, is currently searching the toxicology literature concerning this additive. *See* Sodium Hexametaphosphate.

SODIUM METASILICATE • An alkali usually prepared from sand and soda ash. Used as a peeling solution for peaches and as a denuder for tripe "in amounts sufficient for the purpose." Used in detergents. Caustic substance, corrosive to the skin, harmful if swallowed, and cause of severe eye irritations. Preserves eggs in egg shampoos. There is no reported use of the chemical and no toxicology information is available, according to the FDA's data bank, PAFA (see page 10).

SODIUM METHYL COCOYL TAURATE • *See* Ox Bile.

SODIUM METHYL OLEYL TAURATE • *See* Ox Bile.

SODIUM n-METHYL-n-OLEYL TAURATE • *See* Ox Bile.

SODIUM METHYL SULFATE • Used in processing pectin (*see*). No known toxicity.

SODIUM MONO- AND DIMETHYL NAPHTHALENE SULFONATE • Anticaking agent and lye peeling agent used in cured fish and meats, and potable water. The FDA data bank, PAFA, has fully up-to-date toxicology information available on this food additive.

SODIUM MONOALKYLPHENOXYBENZENEDISULFONATE • Used in lye for peeling fruits and vegetables. No known toxicity.

SODIUM MONOHYDROGEN PHOSPHATE • Dibasic Sodium Phosphate. Used as a buffer, to retain juices, as a dietary supplement, emulsifier, hog wash, poultry wash, and in evaporated milk, poultry, instant pudding, and whipped products. Limited by FDA to 0.5 percent of total poultry product. Mildly toxic by ingestion. A skin and eye irritant.

SODIUM MYRISTATE • There is no reported use of the chemical and no toxicology information is available, according to the FDA's data bank, PAFA (see page 10). *See* Myristic Acid.

SODIUM MYRISTOYL ISETHIONATE • *See* Myristic Acid.

SODIUM NITRATE • The FDA data bank, PAFA, is currently searching the toxicology literature concerning this additive. *See* Nitrate, Sodium.

SODIUM NITRITE • The FDA data bank, PAFA, is currently searching the toxicology literature concerning this additive. *See* Nitrite, Sodium.

SODIUM OLEATE • Sodium Salt of Oleic Acid. White powder, fatty odor, alkaline. Used in soaps. The final report to the FDA of the Select Committee on GRAS Substances stated in 1980 that it should continue its GRAS status for packaging with no limitations other than good manufacturing practices. There is no reported use of the chemical and no toxicology information is available, according to the FDA's data bank, PAFA (see page 10).

SODIUM PALMITATE • There is no reported use of the chemical and no toxicology information is available, according to the FDA's data bank, PAFA. Sodium salt of palmitic acid (*see*).

SODIUM PANTOTHENATE • Vitamins D_1 and D_2. Used as a dietary supplement. The final report to the FDA of the Select Committee on GRAS Substances stated in 1980 that it should continue its GRAS status with no limitations other than good manufacturing practices. There is no reported use of the chemical and no toxicology information is available, according to the FDA's data bank, PAFA.

SODIUM PECTINATE • A stabilizer and thickener for syrups for frozen products, ice cream, ice milk, confections, fruit sherbets, French dressing and other salad dressings, fruit jelly, preserves, and jams. Used in quantities that reasonably compensate for the deficiency, if any, of natural pectin content of the fruit ingredients. There is no reported use of the chemical and no toxicology information is available, according to the FDA's data bank, PAFA. GRAS.

SODIUM PHOSPHATE • Buffer and effervescent used in the manufacture of nail enamels and detergents. White crystalline or granular powder, stable in air. Without water, it can be irritating to the skin but has no known skin toxicity. The final report to the FDA of the Select Committee on GRAS Substances stated in 1980 that it should continue its GRAS status with no limitations other than good manufacturing practices. The FDA data bank, PAFA, is currently searching the toxicology literature concerning this additive. *See* Phosphorous Sources.

SODIUM PHOSPHOALUMINATE • The acid salt of phosphoric acid. An ingredient of baking powders and other leavening mixtures. GRAS for packaging. *See* Phosphoric Acid for toxicity.

SODIUM POTASSIUM TARTRATE • Rochelle Salt. A buffer for confections, fruit jelly, preserves, and jams. For each hundred pounds of saccharin in the above products, three ounces of sodium potassium tartrate is used. Also used in cheese. Used medicinally as a cathartic. There is no reported use of the chemical and no toxicology information is available, according to the FDA's data bank, PAFA (see page 10). GRAS.

SODIUM PROPIONATE • Colorless or transparent, odorless crystals that gather water in moist air. Used as a preservative in cosmetics and foodstuffs to prevent mold and fungus. Used in baked goods, frostings, confections, and gelatin. It has been used to treat fungal infections of the skin, but can cause allergic reactions. There is no reported use of the chemical and no toxicology information is available, according to the FDA's data bank, PAFA. GRAS.

SODIUM PYROPHOSPHATE • Used to decrease the amount of cooked-out juices in canned hams, pork shoulders, and bacon at 5 percent phosphate in pickle; 0.5 percent phosphate in product (only clear solution may be injected into hams). It is also used in cold-water puddings and processed cheese. It is an emulsifier salt and a texturizer as well as a sequestrant. The FDA labeled it GRAS for use as a sequestrant. The FDA data bank, PAFA (see page 10), is currently searching the toxicology literature concerning this additive.

SODIUM RIBOFLAVIN PHOSPHATE • A B vitamin containing sodium phosphate (*see*).

SODIUM SACCHARIN • An artificial sweetener in dentifrices, mouthwashes, and lipsticks. In use since 1879. Pound for pound it is three hundred times as sweet as natural sugar but leaves a bitter aftertaste. It was used along with cyclamates in the experiments that led to their ban in 1969. The FDA has proposed restricting saccharin to fifteen milligrams per day for each kilogram of body weight or one gram a day for a 150-pound person. On the FDA's priority list for further safety testing.

SODIUM SALT • *See* Sodium Benzoate.

SODIUM SALTS OF FATTY ACIDS • The FDA data bank, PAFA, has not yet done a toxicology literature search on this food additive. *See* Sodium and Fatty Acids.

SODIUM SESQUICARBONATE • Lye. White crystals, flakes, or powder produced from sodium carbonate. Soluble in water. Used as a neutralizer for butter, cream, fluid milk, ice cream, in the processing of olives before canning, cacao products, and canned peas. Used as an alkalizer in bath salts, shampoos, tooth powders, and soaps. Irritating to the skin and mucous membranes. May cause an allergic reaction in the hypersensitive. The final report to the FDA of the Select Committee on GRAS Substances stated in 1980 that it should continue its GRAS status with no limitations other than good manufacturing practices. The FDA data bank, PAFA (see page 10), has not yet done a toxicology literature search on this food additive.

SODIUM SILICATE • Water Glass. Soluble Glass. An anticaking agent for preserving eggs, detergents in soaps, depilatories, and protective creams. Consists of colorless to white or grayish white, crystalline pieces or lumps. These silicates are almost insoluble in cold water. Strongly alkaline. As a topical antiseptic can be irritating and caustic to the skin and mucous membranes. If swallowed, it causes vomiting and diarrhea. The final report to the FDA of the Select Committee on GRAS Substances stated in 1980 that it should continue its GRAS status with no limitations other than good manufacturing practices. The FDA data bank, PAFA, has fully up-to-date toxicology information available on this food additive.

SODIUM SILICOALUMINATE • Anticaking agent used in table salt up to 2 percent; dried egg yolks up to 2 percent; in sugar up to 1 percent; and in baking powder up to 5 percent. Slightly alkaline. No known toxicity. *See* Silicates.

SODIUM SOAP • *See* Sodium Stearate.

SODIUM SORBATE • A food preservative. The final report to the FDA of the Select Committee on GRAS Substances stated in 1980 that it should continue its GRAS status with no limitations other than good manufacturing practices. There is no reported use of the chemical and no toxicology information is available, according to the FDA's data bank, PAFA (see page 10). *See* Calcium Sorbate.

SODIUM STEARATE • Alkaline; 92.82 percent stearic acid (*see*). Used as an emulsifier in foods. A fatty acid used in deodorant sticks, stick perfumes, toothpastes, soapless shampoos, and shaving lather. A white powder with a soapy feel and a slight tallowlike odor. Slowly soluble in cold water or cold alcohol. Also a waterproofing agent and has been used to treat skin diseases and in suppositories. One of the least allergy-causing of the sodium salts of fatty acids. Nonirritating to the skin. The FDA data bank, PAFA, has not yet done a toxicology literature search on this food additive.

SODIUM STEAROYL LACTYLATE • *See* Lactic Acid.

SODIUM STEAROYL-2-LACTYLATE • The sodium salt of a lactylic ester of fatty acid. Prepared from lactic acid and fatty acids. It is used as an emulsifier, plasticizer, or surface-active agent in an amount not greater than that required to produce the intended physical or technical effect, and where standards of identity (*see*) do not preclude use, in the following: bakery mixes, baked products, cake icings, fillings and toppings, dehydrated fruits and vegetables, dehydrated fruit and vegetable juices, frozen desserts, liquid shortenings for household use, pancake mixes, precooked instant rice, pudding mixes, solid-state edible vegetable fat–water emulsions used as substitutes for milk or cream in coffee, and with shortening and edible fats and oils when such are required in the foods listed above. The FDA data bank, PAFA (see page 10), has fully up-to-date toxicology information available on this food additive. *See* Lactic Acid for toxicity.

SODIUM STEARYL FUMARATE • Fine white powder used as a dough conditioner in bakery products, cereals processed for cooking, starch-thickened flour, and dehydrated potatoes. FDA limits are 0.5 percent of flour for yeast-leavened baked goods; 1 percent for non-yeast-leavened baked goods; 1 percent of dehydrated potatoes; 1 percent of dry processed cereals for cooking; and 0.2 percent for starch-thickened flour. The FDA data bank, PAFA, has fully up-to-date toxicology information available on this food additive.

SODIUM SULFACHLOROPYRIDAZINE MONOHYDRATE • An antibiotic used for chickens. FDA requires zero residue in uncooked edible tissues of chickens.

SODIUM SULFATE • Salt Cake. Occurs in nature as the minerals mirabilite and nardite. Used in chewing gum base and to preserve tuna fish and biscuits. Used medicinally to reduce body water. Used chiefly in the manufacture of dyes, soaps, and detergents. It is a reagent (*see*) and a precipitant; mildly saline in taste. Usually harmless when applied in toilet preparations. May prove irritating in concentrated solutions if applied to the skin and permitted to dry and then remain. May also enhance the irritant action of certain detergents. Taken by mouth, it stimulates gastric mucous production and sometimes inactivates a natural digestive juice—pepsin. Fatally poisoned animals show only diarrhea and intestinal bloating with no gross lesions outside the intestinal tract. The FDA data bank, PAFA (see page 10), has fully up-to-date toxicology information available on this food additive.

SODIUM SULFIDE • Composition in chewing gum base. Crystals or granules prepared from ammonia that easily absorb water. Also used in dehairing hides and wool pulling, engraving, and cotton printing.

SODIUM SULFITE • White to tan-pink, odorless or nearly odorless powder having a cooling, salty, sulfurlike taste. An antiseptic, preservative, and antioxidant used as a bacterial inhibitor in wine-brewing and distilled-beverage industries. Also an antifermentative in the sugar and syrup industries and a browning inhibitor in cut fruits, used in frozen apples, dried fruit, prepared fruit-pie mix, peeled potatoes, maraschino cherries, dried fruits, and glacéed fruits. Used to bleach straw, silk, and wool; a developer in photography; treats upset stomachs and combats fungus infections. Also used in hair dyes. Foods and drinks containing sulfites may release sulfur dioxide. If this is inhaled by people who suffer from asthma, it can trigger an asthmatic attack. Sulfites are known to cause stomach irritation, nausea, diarrhea, skin rash, or swelling in sulfite-sensitive people. People whose kidneys or livers are impaired may not be able to produce the enzymes that break down sulfites in the body. Sulfites may destroy thiamin and consequently are not added to foods that are sources of this B vitamin. The final report to the FDA of the Select Committee on GRAS Substances stated in 1980 that it did not present a hazard when used at present levels but that additional data would be necessary if a significant increase in consumption occurred. The FDA data bank, PAFA (see page 10), is currently searching the toxicology literature concerning this additive. *See* Sulfites.

SODIUM SULFO-ACETATE DERIVATIVES • Used as emulsifiers in margarine. *See* Sodium Sulfate.

SODIUM TARTRATE • A laxative, sequestrant, chemical reactant, and stabilizer in cheese and artificially sweetened jelly. There is no reported use of the chemical and no toxicology information is available, according to the FDA's data bank, PAFA. *See* Tartaric Acid. GRAS.

SODIUM TAUROCHOLATE • Taurocholic Acid. The chief ingredient of the bile of carnivorous animals. Used as an emulsifier in dried egg white up to 0.1 percent. It is a lipase accelerator. Lipase is a fat-splitting enzyme in the blood, pancreatic secretion, and tissues. There is no reported use of the chemical and no toxicology information is available, according to the FDA's data bank, PAFA.

SODIUM TETRAPHOSPHATE • Sodium Polyphosphate. Used as a sequestering agent. The final report to the FDA of the Select Committee on GRAS Substances stated in 1980 that it should continue its GRAS status with no limitations other than good manufacturing practices. *See* Phosphate.

SODIUM THIOSULFATE • An antioxidant used to protect sliced potatoes and uncooked french fries from browning and as a stabilizer for potassium iodide in iodized salt. Also used to neutralize chlorine and to bleach bone. It is an antidote for cyanide poisoning and has been used in the past to combat blood clots; used to treat ringworm and mange in animals. Poorly absorbed by the bowel. The final report to the FDA of the Select Committee on GRAS Substances stated in 1980 that it should continue its GRAS status with no limitations other than good manufacturing practices. The FDA data bank, PAFA (see page 10), has fully up-to-date toxicology information available on this food additive.

SODIUM *p*-TOLUENE-SULFOCHLORAMINE • Chloramine-T. Water-purifying agent and a deodorant used to remove weed odor in cheese. Suspected of causing rapid allergic reaction in the hypersensitive. Poisoning by chloramine-T is characterized by pain, vomiting, sudden loss of consciousness, circulatory and respiratory collapse, and death.

SODIUM TOLUENESULFONATE • Methylbenzenesulfonic Acid, Sodium Salt. An aromatic compound that is used as a solvent. *See* Benzene.

SODIUM TRIMETAPHOSPHATE • A starch modifier. *See* Sodium Metaphosphate.

SODIUM TRIPOLYPHOSPHATE (STPP) • A texturizer and sequestrant cleared for use in food-starch modifiers. A water softener. Also cleared by the USDA Meat Inspection Department to preserve meat by decreasing cooked-out juices in canned hams, pork shoulders, chopped ham, and bacon. Also used as a dilutant for Citrus Red No. 2 (*see*). It is used in angel food cake mix, beef, desserts, gelling juices, goat, canned ham, lamb, lima beans, meat loaf, meat toppings, meringues, mutton, canned peas, pork, poultry, sausage products, and veal. It may deplete the body of calcium if taken in sufficient amounts, and such a case of low calcium was reported in a patient poisoned with water softener. Used in bubble baths and as a texturizer in soaps. It is a crystalline salt, moderately irritating to the skin and mucous membranes. Ingestion can cause violent purging. The final report to the FDA of the Select Committee on GRAS Substances stated in 1980 that it should continue its GRAS status for packaging with no limitations other than good manufacturing practices. The FDA data bank, PAFA (see page 10), is currently searching the toxicology literature concerning this additive. *See* Sodium Phosphate.

SOLUBILIZATION • The process of dissolving in water such substances as fats and liquids that are not readily soluble under standard conditions by the action of a detergent or similar agent. Technically, a solubilized product is clear because the particle size in an emulsion is so small that light is not bounced off the particle. Solubilization is used in colognes and clear lotions. Sodium sulfonates (*see*) are common solubilizing agents.

SOLUBLE ANIMAL COLLAGEN • *See* Solubilization and Collagen.

SOLUBLE COLLAGEN • The protein derived from the connective tissue of young animals.

SOLVENT • A liquid capable of dissolving or dispersing one or more substances. Methyl ethyl ketone is an example of a solvent.

SORBATE, CALCIUM • *See* Calcium Sorbate.

SORBIC ACID • Acetic Acid. Hexadienic Acid. Hexadienoic Acid. Sorbistat. A white, free-flowing powder obtained from the berries of the mountain ash. It is also made from chemicals in the factory. It is used in cosmetics as a preservative and humectant. A mold and yeast inhibitor, it is used in foods, especially cheeses and beverages. It is also used in baked goods, chocolate syrup, fresh fruit cocktail, soda-fountain-type syrups, tangerine puree (sherbet base), salads (potato, macaroni, coleslaw, gelatin), cheesecake, pie fillings, cake, cheese in consumer-size packages, and artificially sweetened jellies and preserves. Percentages range from 0.003 in beverages to 0.2 percent in cheeses. Used as a replacement for glycerin in emulsions, ointments, embalming fluids, mouthwashes, dental creams, and various cosmetic creams. A binder for toilet preparations and plasticizers. Produces a velvetlike feel when rubbed on skin. In large amounts, sticky. Practically nontoxic but may cause skin irritation in susceptible people. When injected under the skin in 2,600-milligram doses per kilogram of body weight, it caused cancer in rodents. The final report to the FDA of the Select Committee on GRAS Substances stated in 1980 that it should continue its GRAS status with no limitations other than good manufacturing practices. The FDA data bank, PAFA (see page 10), is currently searching the toxicology literature concerning this additive.

SORBITAN • A compound from sorbitol that has the water removed.

SORBITAN DIISOSTEARATE • The diester of isostearic acid and hexitol (*see* Fatty Acids).

SORBITAN DIOLEATE • The diester of oleic acid and hexitol anhydrides derived from sorbitol. *See* Sorbitan Fatty Acid Esters.

SORBITAN FATTY ACID ESTERS • Mixture of fatty acids (*see*) and esters of sorbitol (*see*) and sorbitol with the water removed. Widely used in food and the cosmetics industry as an emulsifier and stabilizer. Also used to prevent irritation from other cosmetic ingredients.

SORBITAN ISOSTEARATE • *See* Sorbitan Fatty Acid Esters.

SORBITAN LAURATE • Span 20. Oily liquid, insoluble in water, soluble in alcohol and oils. An emulsifier in cosmetic creams and lotions; a stabilizer of essential oils in water. No known toxicity.

SORBITAN MONOOLEATE • Polysorbate 80. An emulsifying agent for special dietary products and pharmaceuticals, a defoamer in yeast production, and a chewing gum plasticizer. An unintentionally administered daily dose of 19.2 grams per kilogram of body weight for two days to a four-month-old baby caused no harm except loose stools. The FDA data bank, PAFA (see page 10), has fully up-to-date toxicology information available on this food additive.

SORBITAN MONOPALMITATE • An emulsifier and flavor-dispersing agent used as an alternate for sorbitan monostearate (*see*) in cake mixes. No known toxicity.

SORBITAN MONOSTEARATE • An emulsifier, defoamer, and flavor-dispersing agent. Used in cakes and cake mixes, whipped vegetable-oil toppings, cookie coatings, cake icings and fillings, solid-state edible vegetable fat–water emulsions used as substitutes for milk or cream in coffee, coconut spread, beverages, confectionery, baked goods. Percentages range from 1 to 0.0006 percent. No single dose is known to be lethal in animals, and man has been fed a daily single dose of twenty grams without harm. The FDA data bank, PAFA (see page 10), has fully up-to-date toxicology information available on this food additive.

SORBITAN OLEATE • Sorbitan Monooleate. An emulsifying agent, defoaming agent, and plasticizer. No known toxicity.

SORBITAN PALMITATE • Span 40. Derived from sorbitol (*see*). An emulsifier in cosmetic creams and lotions, a solubilizer of essential oils in water. Light yellow wax, insoluble in water, soluble in solvents. No known toxicity.

SORBITAN SESQUIOLEATE • An emulsifier. *See* Sorbitol and Oleic Acid.

SORBITAN SEQUISTEARATE • *See* Sorbitan Stearate.

SORBITAN STEARATE • Sorbitan Monostearate. An emulsifier in cosmetic creams and lotions, a solubilizer of essential oils in water. Used in antiperspirants, deodorants, cake makeup, hand creams, hair tonics, rouge, and suntan creams. Manufactured by reacting edible commercial stearic acid with sorbitol (*see both*). Light cream to tan-colored, hard, waxy solid, with a bland odor and taste. Soluble at temperatures above its melting point in toluene, ethanol, methanol, and other alcohols. No known toxicity.

SORBITAN TRIISOSTEARATE • *See* Stearic Acid.

SORBITAN TRIOLEATE • *See* Sorbitol.

SORBITAN TRISTEARATE • An emulsifier and alternate for sorbitan stearate (*see*). No known toxicity.

SORBITOL • An alcohol first found in the ripe berries of the mountain ash; it also occurs in other berries (except grapes), and in cherries, plums, pears, apples, seaweed, and algae. Consists of white, hygroscopic powder, flakes, or granules with a sweet taste. A sugar substitute for diabetics. Used as a thickener in candy, a sequestrant in vegetable oils, a stabilizer and sweetener in frozen desserts for special dietary purposes, and a humectant and texturizing agent in shredded coconut and dietetic fruits and soft drinks. Gives a velvety feel to skin. Used as a replacement for glycerin in emulsions, ointments, embalming fluid, mouthwashes, dental creams, and various cosmetic creams. A binder for toilet preparations and a plasticizer. Also used in hairsprays, beauty masks, cuticle removers, foundation cake makeup, hand lotions, liquid powders, dentifrices, aftershave lotions, deodorants, antiperspirants, shampoos, rouge, in writing inks to ensure a smooth flow from the point of the pen, and in pharmaceutical preparations to increase the absorption of vitamins. Medicinally used to reduce body water and for intravenous feedings. No known toxicity if it is applied to the skin. However, if ingested in excess, it can cause diarrhea and gastrointestinal disturbances. Eating as little as ten grams of sorbitol can cause diarrhea in some children, according to Dr. Laurel Prestridge, a gastroenterologist and assistant professor of pediatrics at the University of Texas Southwestern Medical Center at Dallas. One piece of hard, sugar-free candy contains about 2.6 grams of sorbitol, and one thin, sugar-free chocolate bar contains about ten grams. In adults and children, sorbitol may alter the absorption of other drugs, making them less effective or more toxic. The FDA data bank, PAFA (see page 10), has fully up-to-date toxicology information available on this food additive.

SORBOSE • Derived from sorbitol (*see*) by fermentation. Used in the manufacture of vitamin C (accounts for nearly a thousand tons of ascorbic acid [*see*] produced yearly). No known toxicity. The final report to the FDA of the Select Committee on GRAS Substances stated in 1980 that it should continue its GRAS status for packaging with no limitations other than good manufacturing practices. There is no reported use of the chemical and no toxicology information is available, according to the FDA's data bank, PAFA.

SORBUS EXTRACT • Service Tree Extract. The extract of *Sorbus domestica*. An extract was used by the Indians to make a wash for sore and blurred eyes from the sun as from climbing and hiking, and from dust.

SORGHUM • The second most widely grown feed grain in the U.S. Only 2 to 3 percent of the crop is used for human food in America, but it is the reverse in Africa and Asia. However, a new sorghum plant has been developed that is twice as nutritious in protein as the common variety and is 50 percent richer in lysine, an essential amino acid. The *syrup*, produced by evaporation from the stems and the juice, resembles cane sugar but contains a high proportion of invert sugars (*see*) as well as a starch and dextrin (*see both*). Very sweet, it is used as a texturizer and sweetener in foods. No known toxicity.

SORGHUM GRAIN SYRUP • Produced from dried sorghum juice. *See* Sorghum.

SORREL EXTRACT • Rumex Extract. An extract of the various species of *Rumex*. The Europeans imported this to America and the Indians adopted it. Originally the root was used as a laxative and as a mild astringent. It was also used for scabs on the skin and as a dentifrice. It was widely used by American medical circles in this century to treat skin diseases.

SOY EXTRACT • *See* Soybean Oil.

SOY FLOUR • *See* Soybean Oil.

SOY PROTEIN ISOLATES • The FDA data bank, PAFA, is currently searching the toxicology literature concerning this additive. *See* Soybean.
SOY SAUCE • Fermented or Hydrolyzed. A hydrolysis product of soybeans. A combination of mold fermentation and acid hydrolysis is used. The molds employed are *Aspergillus flavus, A. niger,* and *A. oryzae.* Soy sauce consists of a mixture of amino acids, peptides, polypeptides, peptones, simple proteins, purines, carbohydrates, and other organic compounds suspended in an 18 percent sodium chloride solution. In 1983, some manufacturers began producing soy sauce with a lower salt content. Used directly on food as a flavoring. The final report to the FDA of the Select Committee on GRAS Substances stated in 1980 that there is no available evidence that it is a hazard to the public when used as it is now and it should continue its GRAS status with limitations on the amounts that can be added to food.
SOY STEROL • *See* Soybean Oil.
SOY STEROL ACETATE • *See* Soybean Oil and Acetate.
SOYA FATTY ACIDS HYDROXYLATED • *See* Soybean and Hydroxylate. The FDA data bank, PAFA (see page 10), has fully up-to-date toxicology information available on this food additive.
SOYA HYDROXYETHYL IMIDAZOLINE • See Ethylenediamine and Urea.
SOYAMIDE DEA • *See* Soybean Oil.
SOYAMINE • *See* Soybean Oil.
SOYBEAN • An erect, bushy, hairy legume, *Glycine max,* native to Asia and extensively cultivated in China, Japan, and elsewhere, whose seeds yield valuable products. They contain glycerides of linoleic, oleic, linolenic, and palmitic acids. *See* Soybean Oil.
SOYBEAN OIL • Flour. Extracted from the seeds of plants grown in eastern Asia, especially Manchuria, and the midwestern U.S. The oil is made up of 40 percent protein, 17 percent carbohydrates, 18 percent oil, and 4.6 percent ash. It contains ascorbic acid, vitamin A, and thiamine. Pale yellow to brownish yellow. Also used in the manufacture of margarine. Debittered soybean flour contains practically no starch and is widely used in dietetic foods. Soybean oil is used in defoamers in the production of beet sugar and yeast, and in the manufacture of margarine, shortenings, candy, and soap. Soybean is used in many products including MSG, dough mixes, Lea and Perrins sauce, Heinz's Worcestershire sauce, soy sauce, salad dressings, pork link sausages, luncheon meats, hard candies, nut candies, and milk and coffee substitutes. It is made into soybean milk, soybean curd, and soybean cheese. Used in the manufacture of soaps, shampoos, and bath oils. About 300 million bushels of soybeans are grown yearly in the U.S., one-third more than in China. May cause allergic reactions, including hair damage and acnelike pimples. The final report to the FDA of the Select Committee on GRAS Substances stated in 1980 that it should continue its GRAS status with no limitations other than good manufacturing practices. The FDA data bank, PAFA (see page 10), has fully up-to-date toxicology information available on this food additive.
SOYBEAN OIL UNSAPONIFIABLES • The fraction of soybean oil that is not saponified (turned into fatty alcohol) in the refining of soybean oil fatty acids.

SPANISH HOPS • *See* Ditanny of Crete.

SPANISH ORIGANUM • *See* Origanum Oil.

SPEARMINT • Garden Mint. Green Mint. It is the essential volatile oil obtained by steam distillation from the fresh aboveground parts of the flowering plant *Mentha spicata,* grown in the United States, Europe, and Asia. It is colorless, yellow, or yellow-green with the characteristic taste and odor of spearmint. The principal active constituent of the oil contains at least 50 percent carvone (*see*). The fresh ground parts of the aromatic herb are used in spearmint flavoring for beverages, meats, and condiments (1,000 ppm). Widely cultivated in the U.S., it is used in butter, caramel, citrus, fruit, garlic, soy, and spice flavorings for beverages, ice cream, ices, candy, baked goods, condiments (100,000 ppm), fats, oils, and icings (50,000 ppm). Has been used to break up intestinal gas. Used in perfumes, perfumed cosmetics, and toothpaste. May cause allergic reactions such as skin rash. GRAS. The FDA data bank, PAFA (see page 10), has not yet done a toxicology literature search on this food additive.

SPERM OIL • Hydrogenated (*see*). Obtained from the sperm whale. Yellow, thin liquid; slightly fishy odor if not of good quality. Used as a releasing agent or lubricant in baking pans and as a coating on fresh citrus fruits. Also as an industrial lubricant. Although allowed as a food additive, there is no current reported use of the chemical, and therefore, although toxicology information may be available, the FDA is not updating it.

SPERMACETI • Cetyl Palmitate. Derived as a wax from the head of the sperm whale. Used to make creams glossy and increase their viscosity. Generally nontoxic but may become rancid and cause irritations.

SPIKE LAVENDER OIL • French Lavender. Used in perfumes. A pale yellow, stable oil obtained from a flower grown in the Mediterranean region. A lavenderlike odor. Used in fruit, floral, mint, and spice flavorings for beverages, ice cream, ices, candy, and baked goods. Used in cologne, toilet water, soaps, varnishes, and blended with lavender oil. Used also for fumigating to keep moths from clothes. Moderately toxic by ingestion. GRAS.

SPIKENARD EXTRACT • *Nardostachys jatamansi.* An East Indian aromatic plant. The dried roots and young stems are used for a soothing ointment and as an ingredient in flavorings and perfumes. The FDA data bank, PAFA (see page 10), has not yet done a toxicology literature search on this food additive.

SPINACH EXTRACT • An extract of the leaves of spinach, *Spinacea oleracea.*

SPIRAEA EXTRACT • Queen Meadow. An extract from the flowers of *Spiraea ulmaria.* Contains an oil similar to wintergreen oil (*see*). The roots are rich in tannic acid (*see*).

SPIRAL FLAG OIL • *See* Costus Root Oil.

SPIRIT OF NITROUS ETHER • *See* Ethyl Nitrite.

SPRUCE NEEDLES AND TWIGS • Extract of *Picea* spp. used in flavorings. There is no reported use of the chemical and no toxicology information is available, according to the FDA's data bank, PAFA (see page 10). *See* Spruce Oil.

SPRUCE OIL • Colorless to light yellow, pleasant-smelling oil obtained from the needles and twigs of various spruces and hemlocks. Used chiefly in scenting soaps and cosmetics but also used as a flavoring. The FDA data bank, PAFA, has not yet done a toxicology literature search on this food additive. *See* Hemlock Oil.

SQUALENE • Obtained by hydrogenation of shark-liver oil. Stable in air and oxygen. Occurs in smaller amounts in olive oil, wheat germ oil, and rice bran oil. A faint agreeable odor, tasteless, miscible with vegetable and mineral oils, organic solvents, and fatty substances. Insoluble in water. A lubricant and perfume fixative. A bactericide, an intermediate (*see*) in hair dyes, and used in surface-active agents. No known toxicity.

STABILIZER • A substance added to a product to give it body and to maintain a desired texture or consistency. Chocolate milk needs a stabilizer to keep the particles of chocolate from settling to the bottom of the container. Calcium (*see* Calcium Acetate) is used as a stabilizer in canned tomatoes to keep them from falling apart. Among the most widely used stabilizers are the gums, such as gum arabic and agar-agar (*see both*).

STANDARDS OF COMPOSITION • Regulate the amounts of cooked meat and poultry that processed products must contain. These standards dictate how much chicken goes into a chicken pot pie along with the peas and gravy. When shopping, you can compare foods for overall content. In "beef with noodles," beef is the main ingredient. In "noodles with beef," noodles are the main ingredient.

STANDARDS OF FILL • Guarantee that a minimum amount of food is placed in its container and prohibits excessive amounts of air or water.

STANDARDS OF IDENTITY • The FDA and USDA previously established a "recipe" for about three hundred foods such as peanut butter and mayonnaise, fixing the ingredients by law. Many of these foods were exempted from the need for ingredient listing. The new labeling law effective in 1994 requires manufacturers to give full ingredient listings for all foods.

STANDARDS OF QUALITY • Ensure that only those fruits and vegetables of high quality, free of defects, are used. Products of lesser quality might be so labeled (mandarin orange pieces instead of segments, for example).

STANILO • Spectinomycin. An antibiotic used on chickens. FDA limits residues to 0.1 ppm in chickens. Used to treat syphilis in humans. Potential adverse reactions in humans include hives, decreased urine output, fever, and chills.

STANNIC CHLORIDE • Tin Tetrachloride. A thin, colorless, fuming caustic liquid, soluble in water, used in cosmetics. May be highly irritating to the eyes and mucous membranes. There is no reported use of the chemical in foods and no toxicology information is available, according to the FDA's data bank, PAFA (see page 10).

STANNOUS CHLORIDE • Tin Dichloride. An antioxidant, soluble in water, and a powerful reducing agent, used in canned asparagus, canned soda (11 ppm), and other foods. Used to revive yeast. Low systemic toxicity but may be irritating to the skin and mucous membranes. On the FDA list for further study of mutagenic, teratogenic, subacute, and reproductive effects since 1980. GRAS. The FDA data bank, PAFA, has fully up-to-date toxicology information available on this food additive.

STAPHYBIOTIC • Bactopen. Cloxacillin. Tegopen. A penicillin antibiotic used on cattle. FDA permits residue of 0.01 ppm in uncooked edible tissues of cattle and in milk. Mildly toxic by ingestion but can cause allergic reactions.

STAR ANISE • Chinese Anis. Fruit of *Illicium verum* from China, called star because of the fruit's shape. The *extract* is used in fruit, licorice, anise, liquor, sausage, root beer, sarsaparilla, vanilla, wintergreen, and birch beer flavorings for beverages, ice cream, ices, candy, meats (1,000 ppm), and liqueurs. The *oil* is used in blackberry, peach, licorice, anise, liquor, meat, root beer, spice, wintergreen, and birch beer flavorings for beverages, ice cream, ices, candy, baked goods, meats, syrups, and liqueurs. The fruit is a source of anise oil (*see* Anise). Star anise has been used as an expectorant and carminative. Japanese star anise is *Illicium anisatum* and contains a toxic lactone called anisatin, unknown in the Chinese variety. No known toxicity. GRAS.

STARCH • Acid Modified. Pregelatinized and Unmodified. Starch is stored by plants and is taken from grains of wheat, potatoes, rice, corn, beans, and many other vegetable foods. Insoluble in cold water or alcohol but soluble in boiling water. Comparatively resistant to naturally occurring enzymes, and this is why processors "modify" starch to make it more digestible. Starch is modified with propylene oxide, succinic anhydride, 1-octenyl succinic anhydride, aluminum sulfate, or sodium hydroxide (*see all*). Starch is a major component of cereals and many vegetables. The average U.S. diet has about 180 grams per person daily. Modified starch contributes about a gram per person per day. The source of starch and the type of modification are not usually identified on the label, since the FDA does not require it. The modified starches used in foods are most often bleached starch, acetylated distarch adipate, distarch phosphate, acetylated distarch phosphate, and hydroxypropyl distarch phosphate. The later three are commonly used in baby foods. Starch is also used in dusting powders, dentifrices, hair colorings, rouge, dry shampoos, baby powders, emollients, and bath salts. Soothing to the skin and used to treat rashes. Used internally as a gruel for diarrhea. Allergic reaction to starch in toilet goods includes stuffy nose and other symptoms due to inhalation. Absorbs moisture and swells, causing blocking and distension of the pores leading to mechanical irritation. Particles remain in pores and putrefy, accelerated by sweat. The final report to the FDA of the Select Committee on GRAS Substances said there was no information that starch acetate was hazardous to the public when used as it is now and it should continue its GRAS status with limitations on amounts that can be added to food. On the other hand, starch sodium succinate, starch sodium octenyl succinate, and starch sodium hypochlorite oxidized were said not to demonstrate a hazard to the public at current use levels, but uncertainties do exist, requiring additional studies. However, GRAS status continues while tests are being completed and evaluated. Acid-modified and pregelatinized starches were said in the final report to be GRAS, requiring no limitations other than good manufacturing practices. The FDA data bank, PAFA (see page 10), has not yet done a toxicology literature search on this food additive.

STARCH DIETHYLAMINOETHYL ETHER • *See* Starch.

STARCH/ACRYLATES/ACRYLAMIDE COPOLYMER • *See* Starch and Acrylic Acid.

STARTER DISTILLATE • Butter Starter Distillate. Steam distillate of *Streptococcus lactis, S. cremoris, S. lactis* subsp. *diacetylactic, Leuconostoc citrovorum,* and *L. dextronicum.* Used as a flavoring agent in margarine.

STEARAMIDE • An emulsifier. Colorless leaflets, insoluble in water. No known toxicity. *See* Stearic Acid.

STEARAMINE • *See* Stearic Acid.

STEARAMINE OXIDE • *See* Stearyl Alcohol.

STEARATES • *See* Stearic Acid.

STEARETH-2 • A polyoxyethylene (*see*) ether of fatty alcohol. The oily liquid is used as a surfactant (*see*) and emulsifier (*see*). No known toxicity.

STEARETH-4 THROUGH -100 • The polyethylene glycol ethers of stearyl alcohol. The number indicates the degree of liquidity; the higher, the more solid. *See* Steareth-2.

STEARIC ACID • Octadecanoic Acid. Occurs naturally in some vegetable oils, cascarilla bark extract, and as a glyceride (*see*) in tallow and other animal fats and oils. A white, waxy, natural fatty acid, it is the major ingredient used in making bar soap and lubricants. Prepared synthetically by hydrogenation (*see*) of cottonseed and other vegetable oils. Slight tallowlike odor. Used in butter and vanilla flavorings for beverages, baked goods, and candy (4,000 ppm). Also a softener in chewing gum base. Also used in deodorants and antiperspirants, liquid powders, foundation creams, hand creams, hand lotions, liquefying creams, hair straighteners, protective creams, and shaving creams. A large percentage of all cosmetic creams on the market contain it. It gives pearliness to hand creams. It is also used for suppositories. It is a possible sensitizer for allergic people. Caused tumors in experimental animals. A human skin irritant. The final report to the FDA of the Select Committee on GRAS Substances stated in 1980 that it should continue its GRAS status with no limitations other than good manufacturing practices. In 1988, University of Texas researchers reported in the *New England Journal of Medicine* that it did not raise blood cholesterol levels as much as other saturated fats. The FDA data bank, PAFA (see page 10), has fully up-to-date toxicology information available on this food additive. *See* Fatty Acids.

STEARYL ACETATE • The ester of stearyl alcohol and acetic acid (*see both*).

STEARYL ALCOHOL • Stenol. A mixture of solid alcohols prepared from sperm whale oil. White flakes, insoluble in water, soluble in alcohol and ether. Used as a coating agent, emulsifier, lubricant, solvent, and texturizing agent in baked goods, cake, desserts, fruits, ice cream, nuts, peanut butter, puddings, shortening, and whipped topping. A substitute for cetyl alcohol (*see*) to obtain a firmer product at ordinary temperatures. Used in pharmaceuticals, cosmetic creams, for emulsions, as an antifoam agent, and lubricant; also in depilatories, hair rinses, and shampoos. Although allowed as a food additive, there is no current reported use of the chemical, and therefore, although toxicology information may be available, the FDA is not updating it.

STEARYL BETAINE • *See* Surfactants and Stearic Acid.

STEARYL CAPRYLATE • The ester of stearyl alcohol and citric acid (*see both*).
STEARYL CITRATE • The ester of stearyl alcohol and citric acid (*see both*). A metal scavenger to prevent adverse effects of trace metals in foods and an antioxidant to prevent rancidity in oleomargarine. The final report to the FDA of the Select Committee on GRAS Substances stated in 1980 that it should continue its GRAS status with no limitations other than good manufacturing practices. There is no reported use of the chemical and no toxicology information is available, according to the FDA's data bank, PAFA (see page 10).
STEARYL DIMETHYLAMINE • *See* Stearyl Alcohol.
STEARYL ERUCATE • *See* Stearyl Alcohol and Erucic Acid.
STEARYL GLYCYRRHETINATE • The ester of stearyl alcohol and glycyrrhetinic acid (*see both*).
STEARYL HEPTANOATE • The ester of stearyl alcohol and heptanoic acid (*see both*). Used as a wax.
STEARYL LACTATE • An emulsifier that occurs in tallow and other animal fats as well as vegetable oils. Used to emulsify shortening in non-yeast-leavened bakery products and pancake mixes. Also used to emulsify cakes, icing, and fillings. No known toxicity.
STEARYL MONOGLYCERIDYL CITRATE • The soft, practically tasteless, off-white, waxy solid used as an emulsion stabilizer in shortening with emulsifiers. Not over 0.15 percent in food. It is prepared by the chemical reaction of citric acid on monoglycerides of fatty acids (*see*). Although allowed as a food additive, there is no current reported use of the chemical, and therefore, although toxicology information may be available, the FDA is not updating it.
STEARYL OCTANOATE • The ester of stearyl alcohol and 2-ethylhexanoic acid. *See* Stearyl Alcohol.
STEARYL STEARATE • The ester of stearyl alcohol and stearic acid (*see both*).
STEARYL STEAROYL STEARATE • *See* Stearyl Alcohol.
STERCULEN • Sterculia. *See* Karaya Gum.
STERCULIA GUM • GRAS. *See* Karaya Gum.
STEROIDS • Class of compounds that includes certain drugs of hormonal origin, such as cortisone, and used to treat the inflammations caused by allergies. **STEROL** • Any class of solid complex alcohols from animals and plants. Cholesterol is a sterol and is used in hand creams. Sterols are lubricants in baby preparations, emollient creams and lotions, emulsified fragrances, hair conditioners, hand creams, and hand lotions. No known toxicity.
STONEROOT • Horse Balm. Used for its constituents of resin, saponin, and tannic acid (*see all*). An erect, smooth perennial; a strong-scented herb of eastern North America with pointed leaves. It produces a chocolate-colored powder with a peculiar odor and bitter, astringent taste. Soluble in alcohol. No known toxicity.
STORAX • Styrax. Sweet Oriental Gum from *Liquidambar* spp. Used in perfumes. It is the resin obtained from the bark of an Asiatic tree. Grayish brown, fragrant semiliquid, containing also styrene and cinnamic acid (*see both*). Once used in medicine as a weak antiseptic and as an expectorant. Used in strawberry, fruit, and spice flavorings for beverages, ice cream, ices, candy,

baked goods, chewing gum, and toppings. Moderately toxic when ingested. Can cause urinary problems when absorbed through the skin. Can cause skin irritation, welts, and discomfort when applied topically. A common allergen. The FDA data bank, PAFA (see page 10), has not yet done a toxicology literature search on this food additive.

STPP • *See* Sodium Tripolyphosphate.

STRAWBERRY ALDEHYDE • Synthetic flavoring. Little information available.

STRAWBERRY EXTRACT • *See* Strawberry Juice.

STRAWBERRY JUICE • Fresh ripe strawberries are reputed to contain ingredients that soften and nourish the skin. Widely used in natural cosmetics today. No scientific evidence of benefit or harm.

STRAWFLOWER EXTRACT • The extract of *Helichrysum italicum,* grown for its bright yellow strawlike flowers. Used in coloring.

STREPTOMYCIN • An aminoglycoside antibiotic, it is given by injection and is active against streptococcal endocarditis, an infection of the heart in humans. It is used as an animal antibiotic in chickens, swine, and turkeys. FDA limits residue to zero in these products, including eggs. EPA Genetic Toxicology Program (*see*). Potential adverse reactions in humans to streptomycin include ear problems, muscle problems, kidney dysfunction, local pain, irritation, and sterile abscesses at the site of injection and skin disorders. Has been implicated in aplastic anemia.

STRONTIUM HYDROXIDE • Used chiefly in making soaps and greases in cosmetics. Colorless, water-absorbing crystals or white powder. Absorbs carbon dioxide from the air. Very alkaline in solution. Also used in refining beet sugar and separating sugar from molasses. Irritating when applied to the skin.

STYRACIN • *See* Cinnamyl Cinnamate.

STYRAX • *See* Storax.

STYRENE • Obtained from ethylbenzene by taking out the hydrogen. Colorless to yellowish oil with a penetrating odor. Used in the manufacture of paper and paperboard and used as a chewing substance in chewing gum. May be irritating to the eyes and mucous membranes, and in high concentrations it is narcotic. The FDA data bank, PAFA (see page 10), has fully up-to-date toxicology information available on this food additive.

STYRYL CARBINOL • *See* Cinnamyl Alcohol.

STYRYLPYRIDINIUM CHLORIDE, DIETHYL CARBAMAZINE • Used in animal feed to combat worms.

SUBACUTE • A zone between acute and chronic or the process of a disease that is not overt. Subacute endocarditis, for example, is an infection of the heart. It is usually due to a "strep germ" and may follow temporary infection after a tooth extraction.

SUBSTITUTE • Means the product is equivalent to the food it resembles. *See* Imitation.

SUCCINIC ACID • Occurs in fossils, fungi, lichens, etc. Prepared from acetic acid (*see*). Odorless; acid taste. The acid is used as a plant-growth retardant. A buffer and neutralizing agent in food processing. A germicide and mouthwash and used in perfumes and lacquers; also a buffer and neutralizing agent. Has been employed medicinally as a laxative. No known toxicity in cosmetic use. Large amounts injected under the skin of frogs kills them. The final report to the FDA of the Select Committee on GRAS Substances stated in 1980 that it should continue its GRAS status with no limitations other than good manufacturing practices. The FDA data bank, PAFA (see page 10), has not yet done a toxicology literature search on this food additive.

SUCCINIC ANHYDRIDE • A starch modifier up to 4 percent. There is no reported use of the chemical and no toxicology information is available, according to the FDA's data bank, PAFA. *See* Succinic Acid.

SUCCINISTEARIN • Stearoyl Propylene Glycol Hydrogen Succinate. Emulsifier in or with shortenings and edible oils used in cakes, cake mixes, fillings, icings, pastries, and toppings. *See* Succinic Acid.

SUCCINYLATED MONOGLYCERIDES • Surfactants (*see*) used as dough conditioners to add loaf volume and firmness. The FDA data bank, PAFA (see page 10), has fully up-to-date toxicology information available on this food additive. *See* Glycerides and Succinic Acid.

SUCROSE • Sugar. Cane Sugar. Saccharose. A sweetening agent and food, a starting agent in fermentation production, a preservative and antioxidant in pharmacy, a demulcent, and a substitute for glycerin (*see*). Table sugar can stimulate the production of fat in the body, apart from its calorie content in the diet, and may be particularly fat-producing in women on the "pill." Workers who handle raw sugar often develop rashes and other skin problems. Sugar when it oxidizes with sweat draws water from the skin and causes chapping and cracking. Infections, erosions, and fissures around the nails can occur. No known toxicity in cosmetics. The final report to the FDA of the Select Committee on GRAS Substances stated in 1980 that it should continue its GRAS status with no limitations other than good manufacturing practices. The FDA data bank, PAFA (see page 10), has fully up-to-date toxicology information available on this food additive.

SUCROSE BENZOATE • *See* Benzoic Acid.

SUCROSE DISTEARATE • A mixture of sucrose and stearic acid (*see both*).

SUCROSE FATTY ACID ESTERS • Derived from sucrose (*see*) and edible tallow, the FDA gave permission in 1982 for their use as components of protective coatings for fruits. The FDA data bank, PAFA (see page 18), has fully up-to-date toxicology information available on this food additive.

SUCROSE LAURATE • A mixture of sucrose and lauric acid (*see both*).

SUCROSE OCTAACETATE • Prepared from sucrose (*see*). A synthetic flavoring used in bitters, spice, and ginger ale flavorings for beverages. Used in adhesives; a denaturant for alcohol. The FDA data bank, PAFA, has fully up-to-date toxicology information available on this food additive.

SUCROSE POLYESTER • *See* Olestra.

SUCROSE STEARATE • A mixture of sucrose and stearic acid (*see both*).

SUGAR BEET EXTRACT • A flavoring in foods. *See* Sucrose.

SUGAR SOLID EXTRACT • The FDA data bank, PAFA, has not yet done a toxicology literature search on this food additive. *See* Sucrose.

SULFABROMOMETHAZINE SODIUM • 5-Bromosulfamethazine. A widely used sulfa antibacterial to treat cattle. FDA limits residue to 0.1 ppm in uncooked edible tissues of cattle and 0.01 ppm in milk. Sulfa drugs can cause sensitivity to the sun. Mildly toxic by ingestion. Causes tumors and birth defects in experimental animals.

SULFAMIC ACID • A strong white crystalline acid used chiefly as a weed killer, in cleaning metals, and as a softening agent. Used as a plasticizer and fire retardant for paper and other cellulose products; as a stabilizing agent for chlorine and hypochlorite, bleaching paper pulp; and as a catalyst for urea-formaldehyde resin. A cleaning agent in cosmetics and used in the manufacture of hair dyes and lakes (*see* FD and C Lakes). Moderately irritating to the skin and mucous membranes. The final report to the FDA of the Select Committee on GRAS Substances stated in 1980 that it should continue its GRAS status with no limitations other than good manufacturing practices. The FDA data bank, PAFA (see page 10), has not yet done a toxicology literature search on this food additive.

6-SULFANILAMIDO-2,4-DIMETHOXYPYRIMIDINE • ABCID. Agribon. Albon. Bactrovet. A widely used sulfa antibacterial drug to treat cattle, poultry, and in animal feed. It is also used in catfish farming to prevent infections. FDA limits residues to 0.1 ppm in chickens, turkeys, cattle, ducks, salmon, and catfish. Caused birth defects in experimental animals. Sulfa drugs can cause sensitivity to sunlight and allergic reactions.

SULFANITRAN • A sulfa antibiotic used to treat chickens. FDA residue limit is zero in chickens. Sulfa drugs can cause sensitivity to light and allergic reactions in humans.

SULFAQUINOXALINE • A sulfa drug used in animal feed. Moderately toxic by ingestion. Sulfa drugs can cause sensitivity to light and allergic reactions in humans.

SULFATE • A salt or ester of sulfuric acid (*see*). A chemical is "sulfated" to help control the acid-alakali balance.

SULFATED GLYCERYL OLEATE • Produced by adding sulfuric acid to glyceryl oleate. *See* Sulfonated Oils.

SULFATED OIL • Sulphated Oil. A compound to which a salt of sulfuric acid has been added to help control the acid-alkali balance.

SULFATED TALLOW • Fat from fatty tissues of sheep and cattle that becomes solid at 40 to 46° F. It is a defoaming agent in yeast and beet sugar production in "amounts reasonably required to inhibit foaming." *See* Tallow Flakes for toxicity.

SULFIDES • Inorganic sulfur compounds that occur free or in combination with minerals. They are salts of weak acid and are used in dyes and hair dissolving agents in depilatories. They are skin irritants.

SULFITE DIOXIDE • *See* Sulfites.

SULFITES • Sodium, Potassium, and Ammonium. Preservatives, antioxidants, and antibrowning agents used in foods. Sulfites are also used for bleaching food starches and as a preventive against rust and scale in boiler water used in making steam that will come in contact with food. Some sulfites are used in the production of cellophane for food packaging. The FDA prohibits the use of sulfites in foods that are important sources of thiamine (vitamin B_1), such as enriched flour, because sulfites destroy the nutrient.

There are six sulfiting agents that are currently listed as GRAS chemical preservatives. They are sulfur dioxide, sodium sulfite, sodium and potassium bisulfite, and sodium and potassium metabisulfite (*see all*). Under the current listing, sulfiting agents may be used as preservatives in any food except recognized sources of vitamin B_1. These agents have been used in many processed foods and in cafeterias and restaurants to prevent fruits, green vegetables, potatoes, and salads from turning brown, as well as to enhance their crispness.

The FDA had sulfiting agents under review. As part of this review, a proposal to affirm the GRAS status of sulfur dioxide, sodium bisulfite, and sodium and potassium metabisulfite, with specific use limitations, was published in the *Federal Register* of July 9, 1982. The agency did not propose to affirm the GRAS status of sodium sulfite and potassium bisulfite because it had no evidence to indicate their current use in food.

Reactions to sulfites can include acute asthma attacks, loss of consciousness, anaphylactic shock, diarrhea, and nausea occurring soon after ingesting sulfiting agents. There have been seventeen deaths that the FDA has determined were "probably or possibly" associated with sulfites. The FDA banned the use of the preservative on fresh fruits and vegetables and at this writing is reviewing a proposal to prohibit it on fresh, precut potatoes. The FDA decided in 1988 against extending its ban on the use of sulfites to a variety of foods sold in supermarkets and served in restaurants, including wine, dried fruit, some seafood, and condiments. Sulfites must be declared on the labels of wine and packaged foods sold in supermarkets when they are added in excess of 10 ppm.

A citizens' petition was submitted by the Center for Science in the Public Interest, Washington, D.C., on October 28, 1982, that asked the agency to restrict the use of sulfiting agents to a safe residue level in food or require labels on those food products in which sulfiting agents must be used at higher levels to perform essential public health functions.

In the meantime, the California Grape and Tree Fruit League recommended that the Food and Drug Administration affirm as GRAS sulfiting agents used in sulfur dioxide fumigation within specific limitations and include its use as an ingredient to treat fresh grapes. Stating that the compound is essential to the marketing, transport, storage, and export of table grapes, the group claimed lack of any known substitute for the gaseous compound effective in preventing mold-rot and other storage fungi and in prolonging storage life. A spokesperson for the Wine Institute, which represents 460 domestic wine makers, said that many of the sulfur compounds in wine are natural parts of fermentation, but they are also added to many wines.

When dining in a restaurant, you have to have a lot of faith in your waiter if you are allergic to sulfites. Foods, especially potato products and some canned foods served in restaurants, could contain sulfites. You can ask, but you may not receive a proper answer.

You have to be cautious about "prepared" products in general if you are sulfite sensitive. For example, lemon juice from a lemon may be fine, but from a bottle it may contain sodium bisulfite.

The following are food categories with common levels of sulfur dioxide residues.[43]

baked goods	30 ppm
beer	25
canned vegetables	30
condiments & relishes	30
dairy products	200
dehydrated potatoes	500
dehydrated vegetables	200
dried fruit	2000
filled crackers	75
frozen potatoes	50
fruit juices (regular strength)	300
fruit juices (concentrates)	1000
gelatin	40
glacéed fruit	150
grain products	200
gravies & sauces	75
jams & jellies	30
lobster, frozen	100
maraschino cherries	150
molasses	300
nut products	25
plant protein isolates	110
processed seafood (other than dried or frozen)	25
shrimp, fresh or frozen	100
soup mixes (dry)	20
sugar	20
sweet sauces & syrups	60
tea	90
vegetable juice	100
vinegar	75
wine	275

The FDA data bank, PAFA (see page 18), has not yet done a toxicology literature search on this food additive.

SULFONATED OILS • Sulfated. Prepared by reacting oils with sulfuric acid. Used in soapless shampoos and hair sprays as an emulsifier and wetting agent.

SULFO-*p*-TOLUENE • Sodium Chloramine. A water-purifying agent and a deodorant used to remove onion and weed odors in cheese. Toluene may cause mild anemia and is narcotic in high concentrations.

43. Judith Foulke, "A Fresh Look at Food Preservatives," *FDA Consumer,* October 1993, p. 26.

SULFOACETATE DERIVATIVES OF MONOGLYCERIDES AND DIGLYCERIDES

• Used as emulsifiers. The final report to the FDA of the Select Committee on GRAS Substances stated in 1980 that there were insufficient biological and other studies upon which to base an evaluation of them when they are used as food ingredients.

SULFOMYXIN • A sulfa drug used to combat bacteria in chickens and turkeys. FDA limits residue to zero in uncooked edible tissues of chickens and turkeys. Sulfa drugs can cause sensitivity to light and allergic reactions in humans.

SULFUR DIOXIDE • A gas formed when sulfur burns. Used to bleach vegetable colors and to preserve fruits and vegetables; a disinfectant in breweries and food factories; a bleaching agent in gelatin, glue, and beet sugars; an antioxidant, preservative, and antibrowning agent in wine, corn syrup, table syrup, jelly, dried fruits, brined fruit, maraschino cherries, beverages, dehydrated potatoes, soups, and condiments. Should not be used on meats or on foods recognized as a source of vitamin A because it destroys the vitamin. Poisonous, highly irritating. Often cited as an air pollutant. EPA Extremely Hazardous Substances List and EPA Genetic Toxicology Program (*see both*). Inhalation produces respiratory irritation and death when sufficiently concentrated. The final report to the FDA of the Select Committee on GRAS Substances stated in 1980 that there is no available evidence that it is a hazard to the public when used as it is now and it should continue its GRAS status with limitations on amounts that can be added to food. The FDA data bank, PAFA (see page 10), has fully up-to-date toxicology information available on this food additive.

SULFURIC ACID • Oil of Vitriol. A clear, colorless, odorless, oily acid used to modify starch and to regulate acid-alkalinity balance in the brewing industry. It is corrosive and produces severe burns on contact with the skin and other body tissues. Inhalation of the vapors can cause serious lung damage. Dilute sulfuric acid has been used to stimulate appetite and to combat overalkaline stomach juices. It is used as a topical caustic in cosmetic products. If ingested undiluted, it can be fatal. The final report to the FDA of the Select Committee on GRAS Substances stated in 1980 that it should continue its GRAS status with no limitations other than good manufacturing practices. The FDA data bank, PAFA, has fully up-to-date toxicology information available on this food additive.

SUNFLOWER SEED OIL • Oil obtained by milling the seeds of the large flower produced in the USSR, India, Egypt, and Argentina. A bland, pale yellow oil, it contains vitamin E (*see* Tocopherols) and forms a "skin" after drying. Used in food, salad oils, and in resin and soap manufacturing. No known toxicity.

SUNFLOWER SEED OIL GLYCERIDE • *See* Sunflower Seed Oil and Glycerides.

SUPERGLYCERINATED FULLY HYDROGENATED RAPESEED OIL • Used in some margarines and emulsions. *See* Rapeseed Oil, Glycerin, and Hydrogenation.

SURFACE-ACTIVE AGENT • *See* Surfactants.

SURFACTANTS • These are wetting agents. They lower water's surface tension, permitting water to spread out and penetrate more easily. These surface-active agents are classified by whether or not they ionize in solution and by the nature of their electrical charges. There are four major categories—anionic, nonionic, cationic, and amphoteric. *Anionic surfactants,* which carry a negative charge, have excellent cleaning properties. They are stain and dirt removers in household detergents, powders, and liquids and in toilet soaps. *Nonionic surfactants* have no electrical charge. Since they are resistant to hard water and dissolve in oil and grease, they are especially effective in spray-on oven cleaners. *Cationic surfactants* have a positive charge. These are primarily ammonia derivatives and are antistatic and sanitizing agents used as friction reducers in hair rinses and fabric softeners. *Amphoteric surfactants* may be either negatively charged or positively charged depending on the acidity or alkalinity of the water. They are used for cosmetics where mildness is important, such as in shampoos and lotions. Surfactants may be classified as emulsifiers, dispersants, wetting and foaming agents, detergents, viscosity modifiers, or stabilizers. For example, in peanut butter, a surfactant keeps oil and water mixtures from separating; in cosmetics, it makes lotions more spreadable; salad dressings and cheeses are thickened by surfactants, which make them pour better.

SWEET BIRCH • *See* Methyl Salicylate.

SWEET CLOVER EXTRACT • The extract of various species of *Melilotus,* grown for hay and soil improvement. It contains coumarin (*see*) and is used as a scent to disguise bad odors.

SWEET FLAG • *See* Calamus.

SWEET MARJORAM OIL • Pot Marjoram. Used in perfumery and hair preparations. The natural extract of the flowers and leaves of two varieties of the fragrant marjoram. Also a food flavoring. No known toxicity.

SYLVIC ACID • *See* Abietic Acid.

SYNTHETIC • Made in the laboratory and not by nature. Vanillin, for example, made in the laboratory may be identical to vanilla extracted from the vanilla bean, but vanillin cannot be called "natural."

SYNTHETIC BEESWAX • A mixture of alcohol esters.

SYNTHETIC FATTY ALCOHOLS • Made from fatty alcohols (*see*) obtained by distillation. Used as substitutes for naturally derived fatty acids (*see*).

SYNTHETIC GLYCERIN • *See* Glycerin.

SYNTHETIC JOJOBA OIL • *See* Jojoba Oil.

SYNTHETIC PARAFFIN AND SUCCINIC DERIVATIVES • Used as a coating on fresh citrus, muskmelons, and sweet potatoes. *See* Paraffin Wax and Succinic Acid.

SYNTHETIC SPERMACETI • *See* Spermaceti.

SYNTHETIC WAX • A hydrocarbon wax derived from various oils.

T

TAGETES • Meal, Extract, and Oil. The *meal* is the dried, ground flower petals of the Aztec marigold, a strong-scented, tropical American herb, mixed with no more than 0.3 percent ethoxyquin, an herbicide and antioxidant. The *extract* is taken from tagetes peels. Both the meal and the extract are used to enhance the yellow color of chicken skin and eggs. They are incorporated in chicken feed, supplemented sufficiently with the yellow coloring xanthophyll. The coloring has been permanently listed since 1963 but is exempt from certification. The *oil* is extracted from the Aztec flower and used in fruit flavorings for beverages, ice cream, ices, candy, baked goods, gelatin, desserts, and condiments. The FDA data bank, PAFA (see page 18), has not yet done a toxicology literature search on this food additive.

TALC • French Chalk. The lumps are known as soapstone of steatite. An anticaking agent added to vitamin supplements to render a free flow; also to chewing gum base. Gives a slippery sensation to powders and creams. Talc is finely powdered native magnesium silicate, a mineral. The main ingredient of baby and bath powders, face powders, eye shadows, liquid powders, protective creams, dry rouges, face masks, foundation cake makeups, skin fresheners, foot powders, and face creams. It usually has small amounts of other powders such as boric acid or zinc oxide added as a coloring agent. Prolonged inhalation can cause lung problems because it is similar in chemical composition to asbestos, a known lung irritant and cancer-causing agent. There is no known acute toxicity, but there are suspicions about its being a cancer-causing agent upon ingestion. It is suspected that the high incidence of stomach cancer among the Japanese is due to the fact that they prefer that their rice be treated with talc. Talc is not considered food grade by the FDA as it contains asbestiform minerals. GRAS for packaging. The FDA data bank, PAFA, has fully up-to-date toxicology information available on this food additive.

TALL OIL • Liquid Rosin. A byproduct of the wood pulp industry. *Tall* is Swedish for "pine." Dark brown liquid. Acrid odor. A fungicide and cutting oil. It may be a mild irritant and sensitizer. The final report to the FDA of the Select Committee on GRAS Substances stated in 1980 that it should continue its GRAS status with no limitations other than good manufacturing practices. There is no reported use of the chemical and no toxicology information is available, according to the FDA's data bank, PAFA (see page 10).

TALL OIL BENZYL HYDROXYETHYL IMIDAZOLINIUM CHLORIDE • *See* Quaternary Ammonium Compounds and Tall Oil.

TALL OIL ROSIN AND GLYCEROL ESTER • Softener for chewing gum base. *See* Tall Oil.

TALLAMIDE DEA • *See* Tall Oil.

TALLAMPHOPROPIONATE • *See* Tall Oil.

TALLOW, HYDROGENATED • *See* Tallow Flakes and Hydrogenation. The FDA data bank, PAFA, has fully up-to-date toxicology information available on this food additive.

TALLOW ACID • *See* Tallow Flakes.

TALLOW AMIDE • *See* Tallow Flakes.

TALLOW AMIDOPROPYLAMINE OXIDE • *See* Tallow Flakes.

TALLOW AMINE • *See* Tallow Flakes.

TALLOW AMINE OXIDE • *See* Tallow Flakes.

TALLOW FLAKES • Suet. Dripping. The fat from the fatty tissue of bovine cattle and sheep in North America. White, almost tasteless when pure, and generally harder than grease. Used as a defoaming agent in yeast and beet sugar production. In miniature pigs in one year, feeding tallow caused moderate to severe atherosclerosis (clogging of the arteries) similar to that in humans. Used in shaving creams, lipsticks, shampoos, and soaps. May cause eczema and blackheads. The final report to the FDA of the Select Committee on GRAS Substances stated in 1980 that it should continue its GRAS status for packaging with no limitations other than good manufacturing practices. There is no reported use of the chemical and no toxicology information is available, according to the FDA's data bank, PAFA (see page 10).

TALLOW GLYCERIDES • A mixture of triglycerides (fats) derived from tallow.

TALLOW HYDROXYETHYL IMIDAZOLINE • *See* Tallow Flakes and Imidazole.

TALLOW IMIDAZOLINE • *See* Tallow Flakes.

TALLOWAMIDE DEA AND MEA • *See* Tallow Flakes.

TALLOWETH-6 • *See* Tallow Flakes.

TAMARIND EXTRACT • The extract of *Tamarindus indica,* a large tropical tree grown in the East Indies and Africa. Preserved in sugar or syrup, it is used as a natural fruit flavoring. The pulp contains about 10 percent tartaric acid (*see*). Has been used as a cooling laxative drink. The FDA data bank, PAFA (see page 10), has not yet done a toxicology literature search on this food additive. GRAS.

TANGERINE OIL • The oil obtained by expression from the peels of the ripe fruit from several related tangerine species. Reddish orange, with a pleasant orange aroma. Used in blueberry, mandarin, orange, tangerine, and other fruit flavorings for beverages, ice cream, ices, candy, baked goods, gelatin desserts, and chewing gum. A skin irritant. GRAS. The FDA data bank, PAFA, has not yet done a toxicology literature search on this food additive.

TANNIC ACID • It occurs in the bark and fruit of many plants, notably in the bark of the oak and sumac, and in cherries, coffee, and tea. It is used to clarify beer and wine, and as a refining agent for rendered fats. As a flavoring it is used in butter, caramel, fruit, brandy, maple, and nut flavorings for beverages, ice cream, ices, candy, baked goods, and liquor (1,000 ppm). Used medicinally as a mild astringent, and when applied, it may turn the skin brown. Used in sunscreen preparations, eye lotions, and antiperspirants. Tea contains tannic acid, and this explains its folk use as an eye lotion. Excessive use in creams or lotions in hypersensitive persons may lead to irritation, blistering, and increased pigmentation. Low toxicity orally, but large doses may cause gastric distress. Can cause tumors and death by injection, but not, evidently, by ingestion. International Agency for Research on Cancer (IARC) review and EPA Genetic Toxicology Program (*see both*). The final report to the FDA of the Select Committee on GRAS Substances stated in 1980 that there is no available evidence that it is a hazard to the public when used as it is now and it should continue its GRAS status with limitations on the amount that may be added to food. The FDA data bank, PAFA (see page 10), has fully up-to-date toxicology information available on this food additive.

TANNIN • Used in alcoholic beverages only. *See* Tannic Acid.

TANSY • A common herb, *Tanacetum vulgare,* which the Greeks believed prolonged life. Strong aromatic odor and bitter taste. Flavoring used in alcoholic beverages only. There is no reported use of the chemical and no toxicology information is available, according to the FDA's data bank, PAFA.

TAPIOCA STARCH • A preparation of cassava, the tapioca plant. Used for thickening liquid foods such as puddings, juicy pies, and soups. No known toxicity. The final report to the FDA of the Select Committee on GRAS Substances stated in 1980 that it should continue its GRAS status with no limitations other than good manufacturing practices.

TAR OIL • The volatile oil distilled from wood tar, generally from the family Pinaceae. Used externally to treat skin diseases. The principal toxic ingredients are phenols (very toxic) and other hydrocarbons such as the naphthalenes. Toxicity estimates are hard to make because even the U.S. Pharmacopoeia does not specify the phenol content of official preparations. However, if ingested, it is estimated that one ounce would kill. *See* Pine Tar Oil, which is a rectified tar oil used as a licorice flavoring.

TARA GUM • Peruvian Carob. Obtained by grinding the endosperms of the seeds of an evergreen tree common to Peru. The whitish yellow, nearly odorless powder that is produced is used as a thickening agent and stabilizer. No known toxicity. *See also* Locust Bean Gum.

TARAXACUM ERYTHROSPERUMUM • *See* Dandelion Leaf and Root.

TARDIVE DYSKINESIA • Abnormal grimacing about the mouth occurring as a side effect of some antipsychotic medications.

TARRAGON • Pale yellow oil derived from the dried leaves of a small European perennial wormwood herb. Grown for its aromatic, pungent foliage. Used in making pickles and vinegar. Also used in perfumery. GRAS. The FDA data bank, PAFA (see page 10), has not yet done a toxicology literature search on this food additive.

TARS • Any of the various dark brown or black, bituminous, usually odorous, viscous liquids or semiliquids obtained by the destructive distillation of wood, coal, peat, shale, and other organic materials. Used in hair tonics and shampoos and as a licorice food flavoring. Also used in antiseptics, deodorants, and insecticides. May cause allergic reactions.

TARTARIC ACID • Sodium Tartrate. Sodium Potassium Tartrate. Rochelle Salts. Described in ancient times as being a residual of grape fermentation. Widely distributed in nature in many fruits but usually obtained as a byproduct of wine making. Consists of colorless or translucent crystals or a white, fine-to-granular, crystalline powder, which is odorless and has an acid taste. It is the acidic constituent of some baking powders and is used to adjust acidity in frozen dairy products, jellies, bakery products, beverages, confections, dried egg whites, food colorings, candies, and artificially sweetened preserves up to 4 percent. Used as a sequestrant, especially in wines, as an emulsifier, and as a grape and sour flavoring for candies, canned sodas and colas, preserves, baked goods, dried egg white, lemon meringue pie mix, pasteurized processed cheese, cheese food and cheese spread, and some types of baking powder. Effervescent acid used in bath salts, denture powders, nail bleaches, hair-grooming aids, hair rinses, depilatories, and hair coloring. Large amounts may have a laxative effect. GRAS. The FDA data bank, PAFA (see page 10), has fully up-to-date toxicology information available on this food additive.

TARTRATE, SODIUM POTASSIUM • The final report to the FDA of the Select Committee on GRAS Substances stated in 1980 that it should continue its GRAS status with no limitations other than good manufacturing practices. *See* Sodium Potassium Tartrate.

TARTRAZINE • FD and C Yellow No. 5. Bright orange-yellow powder used in foods, drugs, and cosmetics and as a dye for wool and silk. Those allergic to aspirin are often allergic to tartrazine. Allergies have been reported in persons eating sweet corn, soft drinks, and cheese crackers—all colored with Yellow No. 5. It is derived from coal tar.

TAURINE • An amino acid found in almost every tissue of the body and high in human milk. Most infant soy-protein formulas are now supplemented with taurine. Taurine is almost absent from vegetarian diets. It is believed necessary for healthy eyes and it is an antioxidant. The FDA data bank, PAFA, has not yet done a toxicology literature search on this food additive.

TAUROCHOLIC ACID • Cholic Acid. Cholyltaurine. Occurs as a sodium salt in bile. It is formed by the combination of the sulfur-containing amino acid taurine and cholic acid. It aids digestion and absorption of fats. It is used as an emulsifying agent in foods. The final report to the FDA of the Select Committee on GRAS Substances stated in 1980 that it should continue its GRAS status with no limitations other than good manufacturing practices. There is no reported use of the chemical and no toxicology information is available, according to the FDA's data bank, PAFA.

TBHQ • *See* Tertiary Butylhydroquinone.

TCC • *See* Triclocarban.

TEA • The abbreviation for *triethanolamine* (*see*).

TEA • The leaves, leaf buds, and internodes of plant shaving leaves and fragrant white flowers, prepared and cured to make an aromatic beverage. Cultivated principally in China, Japan, Sri Lanka, and other Asian countries. Tea is a mild stimulant and its tonic properties are due to the alkaloid caffeine; tannic acid (*see*) makes it astringent. Used by natural cosmeticians to reduce the puffiness around the eyes. No known toxicity.

TEA-ABIETOYL HYDROLYZED ANIMAL PROTEIN • The salt of the condensation product of abietic acid and hydrolyzed protein (*see both*).

TEA-C12-15 ALCOHOLS SULFATE • *See* Triethanolamine, Alcohol, and Sulfate.

TEA-COCO-HYDROLYZED PROTEIN • *See* Hydrolyzed Protein and Surfactants, anionic.

TEA-COCO-HYDROLYZED PROTEIN • *See* Proteins.

TEA-COCYL GLUTAMATE • A softener. *See* Glutamate.

TEA-EDTA • *See* Ethylenediamine Tetraacetic Acid.

TEA EXTRACT • Essential oil. The FDA data bank, PAFA (see page 10), has not yet done a toxicology literature search on this food additive. *See* Tea. GRAS.

TEA-HYDROGENATED TALLOW GLUTAMATE • A softener. *See* Glutamate.

TEA-LAUROYL GLUTAMATE • A softener. *See* Glutamate.

TEA SORBATE • *See* Triethanolamine and Sorbic Acid.

TEA-STEARATE • *See* Triethanolamine and Stearic Acid.

TEA-SULFATE • *See* Triethanolamine and Sulfuric Acid.

TEA TREE OIL • *Melaleuca alternifolia.* Any of various shrubs or trees so named because their leaves are used as a substitute for tea leaves. The essential oil is obtained from the leaves and used as a germicide. The FDA data bank, PAFA (see page 10), has not yet done a toxicology literature search on this food additive.

TERA JAPONICA • *See* Catechu Extract.

TERATOGENIC • From the Greek *terat* (monster) and Latin *genesis* (origin): the origin or cause of a monster—or defective fetus.

TERGITOL • Tergemist. Sodium Etasulfate. Lye peeling agent, poultry scald agent, and washing-water agent used on fruits, poultry, and vegetables. FDA limits residue to 0.2 percent in wash water. Moderately toxic by ingestion and skin contact. A skin and eye irritant.

TERPENELESS OILS • Essential oils from which the terpene components have been removed by extraction and fractionation, either alone or in combination. The terpeneless grades are more highly concentrated than the original oil. Removal of the terpenes is necessary to inhibit spoilage, particularly of oils derived from citrus. It also makes the compound more soluble in alcohol. *See* Terpenes.

TERPENES • A class of unsaturated hydrocarbons (*see*). Its removal from products improves their flavor and gives them a more stable, stronger odor. However, some perfumers feel that the removal of terpenes destroys some of the original odor. Has been used as an antiseptic. The FDA data bank, PAFA, has fully up-to-date toxicology information available on these food additives.

TERPINEOL • A colorless, viscous liquid with a lilaclike odor, insoluble in mineral oil and slightly soluble in water. It is primarily used as a flavoring agent but is also employed as a denaturant to make alcohol undrinkable. It has been used as an antiseptic. It can be a sensitizer. The FDA data bank, PAFA (see page 10), has fully up-to-date toxicology information available on this food additive.

TERPINOLENE • A synthetic citrus and fruit flavoring agent for beverages, ice cream, ices, candy, and baked goods. The FDA data bank, PAFA, has fully up-to-date toxicology information available on this food additive. *See* Turpentine for toxicity.

TERPINYL ACETATE • Colorless liquid, odor suggestive of bergamot and lavender. Occurs naturally in cardamom. Slightly soluble in water and glycerol. Derived by heating terpineol with acetic acid (*see both*). Used in berry, lime, orange, cherry, peach, plum, and meat flavorings for beverages, ice cream, ices, candy, and baked goods. The FDA data bank, PAFA, has fully up-to-date toxicology information available on this food additive. *See* Turpentine for toxicity.

TERPINYL ANTHRANILATE • A synthetic fruit flavoring agent. Derived by heating terpineol with anthranilic acid (*see both*). Used as a synthetic fruit flavoring agent for beverages, ice cream, ices, candy, and baked goods. The FDA data bank, PAFA, has fully up-to-date toxicology information available on this food additive. *See* Turpentine for toxicity.

TERPINYL BUTYRATE • A synthetic fruit flavoring agent. Derived by heating terpineol with butyric acid (*see both*). Used as a synthetic fruit flavoring agent for beverages, ice cream, ices, candy, chewing gum, and baked goods. The FDA data bank, PAFA (see page 10), has fully up-to-date toxicology information available on this food additive. *See* Turpentine for toxicity.

TERPINYL CINNAMATE • A synthetic fruit flavoring agent. Derived by heating terpineol with cinnamic acid (*see both*). Used as a synthetic fruit flavoring agent for beverages, ice cream, ices, candy, and baked goods. The FDA data bank, PAFA, has fully up-to-date toxicology information available on this food additive. *See* Turpentine for toxicity.

TERPINYL FORMATE • Formic Acid. A synthetic fruit flavoring agent. Derived by heating terpineol with formic acid (*see both*). Used as a synthetic fruit flavoring agent for beverages, ice cream, ices, candy, liqueurs, and baked goods. The FDA data bank, PAFA, has fully up-to-date toxicology information available on this food additive. *See* Turpentine for toxicity.

TERPINYL ISOBUTYRATE • A synthetic fruit flavoring agent. Derived by heating terpineol with isobutyric acid (*see both*). Used as a synthetic fruit flavoring agent for beverages, ice cream, ices, candy, and baked goods. The FDA data bank, PAFA (see page 10), has fully up-to-date toxicology information available on this food additive. *See* Turpentine for toxicity.

TERPINYL ISOVALERATE • A synthetic fruit flavoring agent. Derived by heating terpineol with isovaleric acid (*see both*). Used as a synthetic fruit flavoring agent for beverages, ice cream, ices, candy, and baked goods. The FDA data bank, PAFA (see page 10), has fully up-to-date toxicology information available on this food additive. *See* Turpentine for toxicity.

TERPINYL PROPIONATE • A synthetic fruit flavoring agent, colorless with a lavender odor. Derived by heating terpineol with propionic acid (*see both*). Used as a synthetic fruit flavoring agent for beverages, ice cream, ices, candy, and baked goods. The FDA data bank, PAFA, has fully up-to-date toxicology information available on this food additive. *See* Turpentine for toxicity.

TERTIARY BUTYLHYDROQUINONE (TBHQ) • This antioxidant was put on the market after years of pushing by food manufacturers to get it approved. It contains petroleum-derived butane and is used either alone or in combination with the preservative-antioxidant butylated hydroxyanisole (BHA) and/or butylated hydroxytoluene (BHT) (*see both*). Hydroquinone combines with oxygen rapidly and becomes brown when exposed to air. The FDA said that TBHQ must not exceed 0.02 percent of the total oil and fat content in a food. Death has occurred from the ingestion of as little as five grams. Ingestion of a single gram (a thirtieth of an ounce) has caused nausea, vomiting, ringing in the ears, delirium, a sense of suffocation, and collapse. Industrial workers exposed to the vapors—without obvious systemic effects—suffered clouding of the eye lens. Application to the skin may cause allergic reactions.

TESTOSTERONE PROPIONATE • Agovirin. Androgen. Androsan. Testoviron. TP. Uniteston. Vulvan. The male hormone, a steroid (*see*) produced by cells of the testicles. It is used to increase growth in cattle. FDA limits residue to 0.60 ppb in muscle, 2.6 ppb in fat, 1.9 ppb in kidney, and 1.3 ppb in liver of heifers. International Agency for Research on Cancer (IARC) review (*see*). EPA Genetic Toxicology Program (*see*). Moderately toxic by ingestion. Given by injection or tablet, it stimulates target tissues to develop normally in androgen-deficient men. It is used to treat eunuchs and male hormonal-change symptoms. It is used for breast engorgement in nonnursing mothers and to treat breast cancer in women one to five years postmenopausal. Potential adverse reactions in women include acne, edema, oily skin, weight gain, hairiness, hoarseness, clitoral enlargement, changes in libido, flushing, sweating, and vaginitis with itching. In males prepuberty, premature epiphyseal closure, priapism, growth of body and facial hair, phallic enlargement; postpuberty, testicular atrophy, scanty sperm, decreased ejaculatory volume, impotence, enlargement of breast, and epididymitis. In both sexes, edema, gastroenteritis, nausea, vomiting, diarrhea, constipation, changes in appetite, bladder irritability, jaundice, liver toxicity, and high levels of calcium in the blood.

TETRACHLOROETHYLENE • Perchloroethylene. Tetrachloroethane. Ethylene Tetrachloride. 1,1,2,2-tetrachloroethylene. Perchlor. Carbon Dichloride. A clear, colorless, nonflammable liquid with an etherlike smell, it is the main solvent used in dry cleaning. It is also used in metal degreasing and during the production of fluorocarbons. It is used in some adhesives, aerosols, paints, and coatings. Used in food packaging. FDA limits residue to 0.3 percent in finished foamed polyethylene. International Agency for Research on Cancer (IARC) review (*see*). This chemical enters your body when you breathe its vapors in the air. Liquid perc can be absorbed through your skin, to a limited extent. The most common effects of overexposure are irritation of the eyes, nose, throat, or skin. Like most organic solvents, it affects the brain the same way as drinking alcohol does. The symptoms of short-term overexposure usually clear up within hours after exposure stops. The mildest effects may start occurring at exposure levels of about 1,090 ppm. Effects occur more quickly and become more noticeable and serious as the exposure level increases. Effects of this chemical on the nervous system include feeling "high," dizziness, headache, nausea, vomiting, fatigue, weakness, confusion, slurred speech, loss of balance, and poor coordination. At very high exposure (above 5,000 to 10,000 ppm) it can cause loss of consciousness and even death. Some studies, according to the California State Hazard Evaluation and Information System, show that overexposure to organic solvents over months or years may have long-lasting and possibly permanent effects on the nervous system. The symptoms of these long-term effects include fatigue, poor muscle coordination, difficulty in concentrating, loss of short-term memory, and personality changes such as increased anxiety, nervousness, and irritability. Tetrachloroethylene causes cancer in laboratory animals at exposure levels close to the level legally allowed in the workplace. Contamination of drinking water with this chemical in Massachusetts and New Jersey has been implicated in clusters of leukemia and birth defects among residents. In any case, do not use perc around an open flame or intense ultraviolet light. Like most solvents containing chlorine, perc can break down into hazardous compounds such as phosgene, hydrochloric acid, and chlorine.

TETRACHLOROISOPHTHALONITRILE • Bravo. Termil. TCPN. A fungicide and antiworm product used on broccoli, cabbage, cantaloupe, carrots, cauliflower, celery, citrus oil, cucumber, lettuce, onions, potatoes, tomatoes, and watermelon. Fungicide residue tolerance of 10 ppm in citrus oil. International Agency for Research on Cancer (*see*) review. Cyanide products are on the Community Right-To-Know List (*see*) and the EPA Genetic Toxicology Program (*see*). Causes cancer in experimental animals. Mildly toxic by ingestion.

TETRACHLORVINPHOS • A white powder that inhibits the transmission of nerve signals, it is used as an insecticide. Used as a feed additive for cattle and swine. FDA limits residue to 0.00015 pound per hundred pounds of body weight of cattle and horses when used in animal feed. Limitation of 0.00011 pound per hundred pounds of body weight of swine when used in animal feed. Found to be carcinogenic in feed by the National Cancer Institute. On the Community Right-To-Know List (*see*). Poisonous by ingestion. Also caused reproductive problems in experimental animals.

TETRACYCLINE • Achromycin. Introduced in 1953, tetracycline antibiotics are among the most widely prescribed. Used to treat cattle, chickens, lambs, swine and turkeys. FDA limits residues to 0.25 ppm in calves, swine, sheep, chickens, and turkeys. In humans, tetracyclines are used to treat acne, bronchitis, pneumonia, syphilis, gonorrhea, inflammation of the tube that carries urine, and chest infections. Also used to treat Rocky Mountain spotted fever, brucellosis, relapsing fever, cholera, trachoma, and arthritis due to infection, syphilis, gonorrhea, chlamydia, shigellosis, rickettsia, and *Mycoplasma*. Tetracyclines are also used to prevent and treat eye infections. Potential adverse effects of oral tetracyclines include nausea, vomiting, drop in white blood cells, dizziness, headache, pressure on the brain, sore throat, sore tongue, trouble swallowing, loss of appetite, colitis, inflammation around the anus, liver problems, kidney problems, and diarrhea. Tetracyclines may cause sensitivity to sunlight and result in a rash and discoloration of the skin. If tetracycline is taken during pregnancy, a child may have discolored teeth. Oral tetracyclines must be used with extreme caution if kidney or liver problems are present. The effects of antibiotics such as tetracycline in meat eaten by humans is a matter of controversy. It is believed by many scientists that it causes resistance to antibiotics used by humans and may cause allergic reactions in sensitive persons, even in minute amounts.

TETRADECANAL • *See* Myristaldehyde.

TETRADECANOIC ACID • *See* Ethyl Myristate.

TETRADECYL ALDEHYDE • *See* Myristaldehyde.

TETRAETHYLENE GLYCOL • Colorless or pale yellow liquid used as a finishing agent on twine used to tie meat. Mildly toxic by ingestion. *See* Glycols.

(E)-4,5,6-TETRAHYDRO-1-METHYL-2-(2-[2-THIENYL]ETHENYL)PYRIMIDINE • Banminth. Early Bird. Helmex. Pyrantel Tartrate. An animal drug used to treat worms in swine. FDA limits residue to 10 ppm in swine liver and kidney and 1 ppm in swine muscle. Poison by ingestion.

TETRAHYDROFURAN • Butylene Oxide. Oxolane. A colorless liquid with an etherlike odor, it is used as a solvent for packaging materials. FDA limits it to 1.5 percent of film. Moderately toxic by ingestion. Causes mutations in experimental animals. Human systemic effects by inhalation. Affects consciousness. Irritating to eyes and mucous membranes.

TETRAHYDROFURFURYL ACETATE • The FDA data bank, PAFA (see page 10), has fully up-to-date toxicology information available on this food additive. *See* Furfural.

TETRAHYDROFURFURYL ALCOHOL • A liquid that absorbs water and is flammable in air. A solvent for cosmetic fats, waxes, and resins. Mixes with water, ether, and acetone. Mildly irritating to the skin and mucous membranes. The FDA data bank, PAFA, has fully up-to-date toxicology information available on this food additive. *See* Furfural.

TETRAHYDROFURFURYL BUTYRATE • Butyric acid. A synthetic chocolate, honey, and maple flavoring agent for beverages, ice cream, ices, candy, and baked goods. May be irritating to the skin and mucous membranes. The FDA data bank, PAFA (see page 10), has fully up-to-date toxicology information available on this food additive.

TETRAHYDROFURFURYL PROPIONATE • Propionic Acid. A synthetic chocolate, honey, and maple flavoring agent for beverages, ice cream, ices, candy, and baked goods. Also used as a solvent for intravenous drugs. Moderately irritating to skin and mucous membranes. The FDA data bank, PAFA, has fully up-to-date toxicology information available on this food additive.

TETRAHYDROGERANYL HYDROXYL STEARATE • *See* Stearic Acid and Hydroxylation.

TETRAHYDROLINALOOL • Colorless liquid with a floral odor used as a flavoring agent in various foods. The FDA data bank, PAFA, has fully up-to-date toxicology information available on this food additive. *See* Linalool.

TETRAHYDROXYPROPYL ETHYLENEDIAMINE • Clear, colorless, thick liquid, a component of the bacteria-killing substance in sugarcane. It is strongly alkaline and is used as a solvent and preservative. It may be irritating to the skin and mucous membranes and may cause skin sensitization.

TETRAIODOFLUORESCEIN SODIUM • FD and C Red No. 3. Acid Red No. 3. Brown powder used as a color additive for candy, cherries, and confections. EPA Genetic Toxicology Program (*see*). Moderately toxic by ingestion. *See* FD and C Red No. 3.

TETRAKIS (HYDROXYMETHYL) PHOSPHONIUM CHLORIDE • Catalyst, humectant, emulsifier, and plasticizer. No known toxicity.

TETRAMETHYL DECYNEDIOL • *See* Fatty Alcohols.

TETRAMETHYL PYRAZINE • White crystals or powder with a fermented soybean odor. Used as a flavoring agent in various foods. Moderately toxic by ingestion. GRAS. The FDA data bank, PAFA (see page 10), has fully up-to-date toxicology information available on this food additive.

2,4,5,8-TETRAMETHYL-1,2,5,6-TETROXOCANE • Metason. Slug-Tox. A pesticide to kill slugs and other parasites on strawberries. Human poison by ingestion. Can cause convulsions. Causes mutations in experimental animals.

TETRAMETHYLTHIURAM • Sprayed on some bananas. Seed disinfectant; fungicide; bacteriostat in soap. Can cause contact dermatitis. Irritating to mucous membranes.

TETRAPOTASSIUM PHOSPHATE (TKPP) • An emulsifier. See Tetrasodium Pyrophosphate.

TETRAPOTASSIUM PYROPHOSPHATE • An emulsifier. See Tetrasodium Pyrophosphate.

TETRASODIUM EDTA • Sodium Edetate. Powdered sodium salt that reacts with metals. A sequestering agent and chelating agent (see both) used in cosmetic solutions. Can deplete the body of calcium if taken internally. See Ethylenediamine Tetraacetic Acid. No known toxicity on the skin.

TETRASODIUM PYROPHOSPHATE (TSPP) • Used in cheese emulsification, and as a sequestering agent in cheese and ice cream. Also used in cleansing compounds, oil-well drilling, water treatment, and as a general sequestering agent to remove rust stains. A sequestering agent, clarifying agent, and buffering agent for shampoos. Produced by molecular dehydration of dibasic sodium phosphate. Insoluble in alcohol. A water softener in bath preparations. It is alkaline and irritating and ingestion can cause nausea, diarrhea, and vomiting. GRAS for packaging.

TEXTURIZER • A chemical used to improve the texture of various foods. For instance, canned tomatoes, canned potatoes, and canned apple slices tend to become soft and fall apart, unless the texturizer calcium chloride (see), for example, or its salts are added, which keep the product firm.

TFC • Abbreviation for triclofurcarban, a disinfectant.

THALOSE • A blend of food-grade acidulants (see) that contains propylene glycol and citric, lactic, phosphoric, and tartaric acids (see all) and water and salt. Adding this compound to sugar permits a reduction in the amount of sugar required to achieve a desired sweetness (one ounce of liquid Thalose added to thirty-two pounds of sugar causes the perceived sweetness to be increased by 90 percent). One pint added to sugar will result in a saving of five hundred pounds of sugar without reducing sweetness. Thalose itself is not sweet and does not alter the flavor or aroma of the foods to which it is added. It does not contribute calories but will reduce the caloric level of the end product by lowering the amount of carbohydrates in the compound. Thalose can be used in beverages, bakery and confectionery products, and in ice cream, as long as the physical properties of the sugar are not needed (sugar is often used as a thickening agent and texturizer). All of the substances contained in this extender are GRAS and comply with the FDA provision for food-grade ingredients.

THAMNIDIUM ELEGANS • A grayish white mold used for aging meat. It is related to the tropical bread mold. No known toxicity.

THAUMATIN • A mixture of intensely sweet-tasting proteins extracted from the fruit of a West African plant, *Thaumatococcus daniellii*. The fruits of the plant have been used for centuries by the West Africans as a source of sweetness. It is also sold in Japan. Because of problems with stability, taste profile, and compatibility, thaumatin is used primarily as a flavor enhancer at levels below the sweet-taste threshold. There is no reported use of the chemical and no toxicology information is available, according to the FDA's data bank, PAFA (see page 10).

THBP • *See* 2,4,5-Trihydroxybutyrophenone. Antioxidant in fats and oils.

THEINE • *See* Caffeine.

THEOBROMA OIL • Cacao Butter. Cocoa Butter. Yellowish white solid with chocolatelike taste and odor. Derived from the cacao bean. Widely used in confections, suppositories, pharmaceuticals, soaps, and cosmetics. No known toxicity but may cause allergic reactions in the sensitive.

THEOBROMINE • The alkaloid found in cocoa, cola nuts, tea, and chocolate products, closely related to caffeine. It is used as a diuretic, smooth-muscle relaxant, heart stimulant, and blood-vessel dilator. In 1992, the FDA proposed a ban on theobromine sodium salicylate in oral menstrual-drug products because it has not been shown to be safe and effective for its stated claims. The FDA data bank, PAFA, has fully up-to-date toxicology information available on this food additive.

THIABENDAZOLE HYDROCHLORIDE • A mold retardant used on animal feed, apples, bananas, beef, citrus fruit, lamb, milk, pears, pheasant, pork, potato processing waste, and rice hulls. FDA limits are 0.1 ppm in cattle, goats, sheep, pheasant, and swine; 0.05 ppm in milk; 33 ppm in dried apple pomace; 150 ppm in dry or wet grape pomace; 30 ppm in potato processing waste; and 8 ppm in rice hulls when used for animal feed. Moderately toxic by ingestion.

THIAMINE HYDROCHLORIDE • Vitamin B_1. A white crystalline powder used as a dietary supplement in prepared breakfast cereals, peanut butter, poultry, stuffing, baby cereals, skimmed milk, bottled soft drinks, enriched flours, enriched farina, cornmeal, enriched macaroni and noodle products, and enriched bread and rolls. Acts as a helper in important energy-yielding reactions in the body. Practically all B_1 sold is synthetic. The vitamin is destroyed by alkalies and alkaline drugs such as phenobarbital. GRAS. The FDA data bank, PAFA (see page 10), has not yet done a toxicology literature search on this food additive.

THIAMINE MONONITRATE • A B vitamin. A white crystalline powder used as a diet supplement and to enrich flour. GRAS. The FDA data bank, PAFA, has not yet done a toxicology literature search on this food additive.

THIAMUTILIN • Tiamulin. Crystals from acetone (*see*) used in animal feed and as an animal drug to combat bacterial infections. Moderately toxic by ingestion and injection under the skin.

THIAZOLE • Colorless or pale yellow liquid. Used in organic synthesis of fungicides, dyes, and rubber accelerators. The FDA data bank, PAFA (see page 10), has fully up-to-date toxicology information available on this food additive.

2-(THIAZOLE-4-YL)BENZIMIDAZOLE • Thiabendazole. Arbotect. TBDZ. Mycozol. White to tan, odorless compound used as a fungicide in animal feed and for citrus fruit and to control fungal diseases in seed potatoes. Used therapeutically in animals to combat worms and fungus infections. EPA Genetic Toxicology Program. Poisonous by ingestion. Caused birth defects in experimental animals.

THIAZOLYLSULFANILAMIDE • Sulzol. Thiazamide. An antibiotic used to treat infections in swine. EPA Genetic Toxicology Program (*see*). Human poison.

THIBETOLIDE • *See* Pentadecalactone.

THICKENERS • Many natural gums and starches are used to add body to mixtures. Pectin (*see*), for instance, which is used in fruits naturally low in this gelling agent, enables manufacturers to produce jams and jellies of a marketable thickness. Algin (*see* Alginates) is used to make salad dressings that will not be runny. Also used to add body to lotions and creams. Those usually employed include such natural gums as sodium alginate and pectins.

2-THIENYL MERCAPTAN • A synthetic flavoring agent that occurs naturally in coffee. Used in coffee flavoring for candy and baked goods. No known toxicity. The FDA data bank, PAFA (see page 10), has fully up-to-date toxicology information available on this food additive.

THIETHYL CITRATE • An antioxidant used primarily in dried egg whites. *See* Citric Acid. GRAS.

THIOALLYL ETHER • *See* Allyl Sulfide.

THIOBIS(DODECYL PROPIONATE) • White crystalline flakes with a sweet odor used as an antioxidant in fats, oils, and packaging materials. FDA regulations limit it to 0.005 percent migrating from food package. An eye irritant.

THIOCYANATE • Colorless or white crystals derived from cyanide. Used in animal feeds as a growth stimulant.

THIODIPROPIONIC ACID • An acid freely soluble in hot water, alcohol, and acetone. Used as an antioxidant in general food use. Allowed up to 0.02 percent of fat or oil, including essential oil, content of food. Used also for soap products and polymers (*see*) of ethylene. The final report to the FDA of the Select Committee on GRAS Substances stated in 1980 that there is no available evidence that it is a hazard to the public when used as it is now and it should continue its GRAS status with limitations on the amounts that can be added to food. There is no reported use of the chemical and no toxicology information is available, according to the FDA's data bank, PAFA.

THISTLE, BLESSED • Holy Thistle. Extract of the prickly plant *Cnicus benedictus*. Cleared for use as a natural flavoring in alcoholic beverages. No known toxicity. The FDA data bank, PAFA (see page 10), has not yet done a toxicology literature search on this food additive.

THREONINE • L Form. An essential amino acid (*see*); the last to be discovered (1935). Prevents the buildup of fat on the liver. Occurs in whole eggs, skim milk, casein, and gelatin. On the FDA list for further study. GRAS. The FDA data bank, PAFA, has fully up-to-date toxicology information available on this food additive.

THUJA OIL • A constituent of many essential oils. Usually derived from the leaves of the white cedar. Colorless liquid, almost insoluble in water. Ingestion may cause convulsions. It is used in flavorings and perfumery.

4-THUJANOL • An alcohol from thuja oil (*see*). The FDA data bank, PAFA, has fully up-to-date toxicology information available on this food additive.

THYME, WHITE OIL • Obtained from the plant and used in fruit, liquor, and thyme. Used in fruit, peppermint, and spice flavorings for beverages, ice cream, ices, candy, baked goods, and chewing gum. Oral dose as medicine is 0.067 grams. It can cause vomiting, diarrhea, dizziness, and cardiac depression when taken in sufficient amounts. GRAS.

THYME OIL • It is a seasoning from the dried leaves and flowering tops of the wild creeping thyme grown in Eurasia and throughout the U.S., *Thymus vulgaris* and *Thymus zygis*. Colorless, yellow, or red, with a pleasant odor. Used in sausage, spice, and thyme flavorings for beverages, ice cream, ices, candy, baked goods, chewing gum, condiments, meats, and soups. Used to flavor toothpaste and mouthwashes and to scent perfumes, aftershave lotions, and soap. Used as a flavoring in cough medicines. May cause contact dermatitis and hay fever. GRAS. The FDA data bank, PAFA (see page 10), has not yet done a toxicology literature search on this food additive.

THYMOL • Obtained from the essential oil of lavender, origanum oil, and other volatile oils. It destroys mold, preserves anatomical specimens, and is a topical antifungal agent with a pleasant aromatic odor. Used in fruit, peppermint, and spice flavorings for beverages, ice cream, ices, candy, baked goods, and chewing gum. Used in mouthwashes and to scent perfumes, aftershave lotions, and soap. It is omitted from hypoallergenic cosmetics because it can cause allergic reactions. Oral dose as medicine is 0.067 grams. It can cause vomiting, diarrhea, dizziness, and cardiac depression when taken in sufficient amounts. The FDA data bank, PAFA (see page 10), has fully up-to-date toxicology information available on this food additive.

THYMUS CAPITATUS • Flavoring.

TIAMULIN • *See* Thiamutilin.

TIGLIC ACID • *See* Allyl Tiglate.

TIN CHLORIDE • Colorless crystals used as an antioxidant and reducing agent (*see*) in asparagus and carbonated beverages. FDA limits it to 20 ppm in asparagus packed in glass. EPA Genetic Toxicology Program (*see*). Poison by ingestion.

TINCTURE • A solution in alcohol of the flavors derived from plants, obtained by mashing or boiling.

TIPA • The abbreviation for *triisopropanolamine* (*see*).

TIPA-STEARATE • *See* Stearic Acid.

TITANIUM DIOXIDE • Occurs naturally in minerals. Used chiefly as a white pigment and as an opacifier; also a white pigment for candy, gum, and marking ink. The amount of dioxide may not exceed 1 percent by weight of food. A pound has been ingested without apparent ill effects. The greatest covering and tinting power of any white pigment used in bath powders, nail whites, depilatories, eyeliners, white eye shadows, antiperspirants, face powders, protective creams, liquid powders, lipsticks, hand lotions, and nail polish. In high concentrations the dust may cause lung damage. It has been permanently listed for use as a food color with a limit of 1 percent by weight of finished food since 1966. The FDA data bank, PAFA (see page 10), has fully up-to-date toxicology information available on this food additive.

TITANIUM HYDROXIDE • *See* Titanium Dioxide.

TITANIUM OXIDE • *See* Titanium Dioxide.

TOCOPHEROLS • Vitamin E. Obtained by the vacuum distillation of edible vegetable oils. Protects fat in the body's tissues from abnormal breakdown. Experimental evidence shows vitamin E may protect the heart and blood vessels and retard aging. Used as a dietary supplement and as an antioxidant for essential oils, rendered animal fats, or a combination of such fats with vegetable oils. Helps form normal red blood cells, muscle, and other tissues. The final report to the FDA of the Select Committee on GRAS Substances stated in 1980 that it should continue its GRAS status with no limitations other than good manufacturing practices. The FDA data bank, PAFA (see page 10), has fully up-to-date toxicology information available on this food additive.

TOCOPHERYL SUCCINATE • Vitamin E Succinate. Obtained by the distillation of edible vegetable oils and used as a dietary supplement and as an antioxidant for fats and oils. No known toxicity.

TOLERANCE • The ability to live with an allergen.

TOLU BALSAM • Extract and Gum. Extract from the Peruvian or Indian plant *Myroxylon* spp. Contains cinnamic acid and benzoic acid (*see both*). Used in butter, butterscotch, cherry, and spice flavorings for beverages, ice cream, ices, candy, baked goods, and chewing gum. The *gum* is used in fruit, maple, and vanilla flavorings for beverages, ice cream, ices, candy, baked goods, and syrups. Mildly antiseptic and may be mildly irritating to the skin. The FDA data bank, PAFA, has not yet done a toxicology literature search on this food additive.

a-TOLUALDEHYDE • *See* Phenylacetaldehyde.

TOLUALDEHYDE GLYCERYL ACETAL • A synthetic chocolate, fruit, cherry, coconut, and vanilla flavoring agent for beverages, ice cream, ices, candy, and baked goods. No known toxicity.

TOLUALDEHYDES (MIXED, *o, m, p*) • Synthetic berry, loganberry, fruit, cherry, muscatel, peach, apricot, nut, almond, and vanilla flavorings for beverages, ice cream, ices, candy, baked goods, chewing gum, gelatin desserts, and maraschino cherries. No known toxicity.

TOLUENE • Toluol. Methyl Benzene. Used in water purifying agents, to remove odors in cheese, and in a number of food processing compounds. Also used as a solvent for paints, nail polish, lacquers, thinners, coatings, shellacs, adhesives, metal cleaners, rust preservatives, fuel system antifreezes, asphalt removers, flame retardants, high-octane gasoline blends, rotogravure printing processes, and glue, and is being used to replace more toxic benzene solvents in many products. Obtained from petroleum or by distilling balsam of Tolu. Resembles benzene but is less volatile, flammable, or toxic. May cause mild anemia if ingested, and it is narcotic in high concentrations. Being tested at the U.S. Frederick Cancer Research Center for possible cancer-causing effects. It can cause liver damage and is irritating to the skin and respiratory tract. Halogenated hydrocarbons like toluene are assumed to be dangerous; illness may result from long-term, low-level exposure to such substances, which can be found in the drinking water of at least 20 U.S. cities. There is concern about the role of toluene on the brain and nervous system, because symptoms have been observed in workers chronically exposed in jobs such as spray painting. The chronic high-dose exposures seen in toluene abuse such as in glue sniffers have been associated epidemiologically with sudden death secondary to irregular heartbeat and liver and neurologic disorders. The current U.S. standard is 200 ppm in eight hours and maximum peaks up to 500 ppm for 10 minutes. NIOSH (*see*) currently recommends that toluene exposures be limited to 100 ppm. Brief exposure to 100 ppm causes statistical impairment of reflexes and thinking. Exposure to 800 ppm causes severe fatigue, confusion, and staggering that may persist for several days. Exposure to 10,000 ppm can cause loss of consciousness and death.

o-TOLUENETHIOL • Thiocresol. Cream to white, moist crystals with a musty odor. A skin irritant. Used as an intermediate (*see*) and as a germicide. The FDA data bank, PAFA (see page 10), has fully up-to-date toxicology information available on this food additive.

TOLYL ACETATE • Acetic Acid. A synthetic butter, caramel, fruit, honey, nut, and spice flavoring for beverages, ice cream, ices, candy, baked goods, chewing gum, and gelatin desserts. The FDA data bank, PAFA, has fully up-to-date toxicology information available on this food additive.

o-TOLYL ACETATE • Acetic Acid. A synthetic butter, caramel, fruit, honey, and cherry flavoring for beverages, ice cream, ices, candy, baked goods, chewing gum, and gelatin desserts. The FDA data bank, PAFA (see page 10), has fully up-to-date toxicology information available on this food additive.

p-TOLYL ACETATE • Acetic Acid. A synthetic butter, caramel, fruit, honey, nut, and spice flavoring for beverages, ice cream, ices, candy, baked goods, chewing gum, and condiments. The FDA data bank, PAFA, has fully up-to-date toxicology information available on this food additive.

4-(*p*-TOLYL)-2-BUTANONE • A synthetic fruit flavoring for beverages, ice cream, ices, candy, and baked goods. The FDA data bank, PAFA, has fully up-to-date toxicology information available on this food additive.

p-TOLYL ISOBUTYRATE • A synthetic fruit flavoring for beverages, ice cream, ices, candy, and baked goods. The FDA data bank, PAFA, has fully up-to-date toxicology information available on this food additive.

p-TOLYL LAURATE • Dodecanoic Acid. A synthetic butter, caramel, fruit, honey, and nut flavoring for beverages, ice cream, ices, candy, and baked goods. The FDA data bank, PAFA (see page 10), has fully up-to-date toxicology information available on this food additive.

p-TOLYL PHENYLACETATE • A synthetic butter, caramel, fruit, honey, and nut flavoring for beverages, ice cream, ices, candy, and baked goods. The FDA data bank, PAFA, has fully up-to-date toxicology information available on this food additive.

2-(*p*-TOLYL) PROPIONALDEHYDE • A synthetic caraway flavoring agent for beverages, ice cream, ices, candy, baked goods, and liqueurs. The FDA data bank, PAFA, has fully up-to-date toxicology information available on this food additive.

TOLYLACETALDEHYDE • A synthetic berry, loganberry, fruit, cherry, muscatel, peach, apricot, nut, almond, and vanilla flavoring agent for beverages, ice cream, ices, candy, baked goods, gelatin desserts, chewing gum, and maraschino cherries. The FDA data bank, PAFA, has fully up-to-date toxicology information available on this food additive.

p-**TOLYLALDEHYDE** • Colorless liquid derived from benzene. Used in perfumes and flavoring agents. The FDA data bank, PAFA, has fully up-to-date toxicology information available on this food additive.

TOMATO EXTRACT • Tomatine. Extract from the fruit of the tomato, *Solanum esculentum.* Used as a fungicide and as a precipitating agent. Nontoxic.

TONKA • Tonka Bean. Coumarouna Bean. Black-brownish seeds with a wrinkled surface and brittle, shining or fatty skins. A vanillalike odor and a bitter taste. Used in the production of natural coumarin (*see*), flavoring extracts, and toilet powders. Banned from food because of its coumarin content.

TORMENTIL EXTRACT • The extract of the roots of *Potentilla erecta.*

TORTUA YEAST • Dried *Candida utils.* Flavoring in food. *See* Yeast.

TOXAPHENE • Yellow, waxy solid with a pleasant pine odor, it is used as an insecticide in soybean oil. FDA regulations set a tolerance of 6 ppm in soybean oil. Human poison by ingestion. Can be absorbed through the skin. Causes cancer and birth defects in experimental animals. Lethal amounts of toxaphene can enter the body through the mouth, lungs, and skin.

TRAGACANTH • *See* Gum Tragacanth. GRAS.

TRALOMETHRIN • An insecticide. FDA residue tolerance in cottonseed oil is 0.02 ppm; on or in cottonseed, 0.02 ppm; on or in soybeans, 0.05 ppm.

TRENBOLONE • A synthetic anabolic steroid. A male sex hormone given to cattle to "build up," to stimulate growth, weight gain, strength, and appetite. Abuse of these drugs has caused problems, especially among young athletes who wish to build muscle and strength. Uncontrolled use can cause liver damage and cancer. On February 27, 1991, anabolic steroids became controlled drugs requiring security ordering and record keeping for humans. Increased tumors were evident in long-term studies of rats fed trenbolone. The FDA limits residues to 50 ppb in the muscle of beef, 100 ppb in liver, 300 ppb in kidney, and 400 ppb in fat in cattle. The FAO/WHO Expert Committee on Food Additives set a marginal no-effect level at 0.1 mg/kg diet equal to approximately 2 micrograms per kilogram of body weight. The committee set an ADI (*see*) of 0–0.02 micrograms per kilogram of body weight.

TRENBOLONE ACETATE AND ESTRADIOL • Hormones used as implants in feedlot cattle. For residues in cattle, *see* Trenbolone and Estradiol.

TRIACETIN • Glyceryl Triacetate. Primarily a solvent for hair dyes. Also a fixative in perfume and used in toothpaste. A colorless, somewhat oily liquid with a slight fatty odor and a bitter taste. Obtained from adding acetate to glycerin (*see both*). Soluble in water and miscible with alcohol. No known toxicity in above uses. Large subcutaneous injections are lethal to rats. GRAS.

TRIACETYL GLYCERIN • Colorless, oily liquid with a fatty odor and taste, it is used as a flavoring agent, a humectant (*see*), plasticizer, solvent, and carrier for food additives. Used in baked goods, baking mixes, beverages, candy, chewing gum, confections, fillings, frostings, frozen dairy desserts, dessert mixes, gelatins, and puddings. Poison by ingestion. An eye irritant.

TRIBASIC CALCIUM PHOSPHATE • Tricalcium Diorthophosphate. Tricalcium Phosphate. An anticaking agent and calcium supplement in grain products used in packaged cake mixes, candy, baked goods, gelatin desserts, powdered beverage mixes, seasoning mixes and powdered soups, and sugar. Too much phosphorus in the form of phosphates from processed foods could upset the body's mineral balance, particularly calcium, and could adversely affect teeth, bones, and kidneys.

TRIBUTYLACETYLCITRATE • A synthetic fruit flavoring agent for beverages. The FDA data bank, PAFA (see page 10), has fully up-to-date toxicology information available on this food additive.

TRIBUTYL CITRATE • The triester of butyl alcohol and citric acid (*see both*), it is a pale yellow, odorless liquid used as a plasticizer, antifoam agent, and solvent for nitrocellulose. Low toxicity.

TRIBUTYLCRESYLBUTANE • Used as a stabilizer. *See* Phenol.

TRIBUTYRIN • Glyceryl Tributyrate. A colorless, somewhat oily liquid that occurs naturally in butter. It has a characteristic odor and bitter taste. It is soluble in alcohol. Used as a flavoring agent in beverages, ice cream, candy, baked goods, margarine, and puddings. Moderately toxic by ingestion. *See* Glycerol and Butyric Acid.

TRICALCIUM PHOSPHATE • The calcium salt of phosphate (*see*). An anticaking agent in table salt and vanilla powder, and a dietary supplement. Used as a bleaching agent in flour at not more than 6 ppm by weight alone or in combination with potassium alum, calcium sulfate (*see*), and other compounds. Also used as a polishing agent in dentifrices. No known toxicity. *See* Calcium Phosphate. GRAS.

TRICALCIUM SILICATE • Used in table salt and baking powder as an anticaking agent up to 2 percent. On the FDA list to be studied for subacute, mutagenic, teratogenic, and reproductive effects. No known toxicity. GRAS.

(2,2,2-TRICHLORO-1-HYDROXYEXYETHYL)DIMETHYL PHOSPHONATE • Anthon. Chloroftalm. Chlorophos. Chlorofos. Dimetox. Dipterax. Dipterex. Trichlorfon. Widely used insecticide for the control of flies and roaches and also to fight worms in animals. Used in animal feed and on citrus pulp. FDA limits it to 2.5 ppm in dried citrus pulp when used for animal feed. Inhibits nerve signals. Poison by ingestion, inhalation, and other routes except skin. On skin, it is moderately toxic. Causes cancer and birth defects in experimental animals.

TRICHLOROETHYLENE (TCE) • Residue in decaffeinated coffee powder. Used in spice oleoresins as a solvent. Moderate exposure can cause symptoms similar to alcohol inebriation, and its analgesic and anesthetic properties make it useful for short operations. High concentrations have a narcotic effect. Deaths have been attributed to irregular heart rhythm. Tests conducted by the National Cancer Institute showed that this chlorinated hydrocarbon caused cancer of the liver in mice. Rats failed to show a significant response, a fact that may be attributed to the cancer resistance of the strain used. The findings serve as a warning of possible carcinogenicity in humans. International Agency for Research on Cancer (IARC) (*see*) review. However, the extent of the possible human risk cannot be reliably predicted on the basis of these studies alone. A related compound, vinyl chloride (*see*), does cause liver cancer in humans. FDA residue tolerance in decaffeinated ground coffee, 25 ppm (0.0025 percent); in decaffeinated soluble (instant) coffee extract, 10 ppm (0.001 percent); in spice oleoresins, 30 ppm. There is no reported use of the chemical and no toxicology information is available, according to the FDA's data bank, PAFA (see page 10).

TRICHLOROMETAFOS • Dermaphos. Ronnel. Fenchlorphos. White powder widely used as an insecticide in animal feed. Chlorophenol compounds are on the Community Right-To-Know List. Poisonous by ingestion. Causes birth defects in experimental animals. Inhibits nerve transmission.

n-TRICHLOROMETHYL MERCAPTO-4-CYCLOHEXENE-1,2-DICARBOXIMIDE • A fumigant. *See* Captan.

TRICLOCARBAN • Prepared from aniline and chlorophenyl isocyanate, it is used as an antiseptic in soaps and other cleaning products. *See* Aniline and Phenol.

TRICLOPYR • A preemergent herbicide. FDA residue tolerance, 0.01 in milk; 0.05 ppm in meat, fat, and meat byproducts of cattle, goats, hogs, and sheep; and 0.5 ppm in liver and kidneys of cattle, goats, hogs, and sheep.

TRICYCLAZOLE • A fungicide used on rice. The FDA tolerance for residues are 30 ppm in rice bran, rice hulls, and rice polishings.

TRICYCLOHEXYLTIN HYDROXIDE • Cyhexatin. TCTH. A pesticide used on animal feed. FDA residue tolerances are 8 ppm in dried apple pomace and dried citrus pulp resulting from application to growing crops; 90 ppm in dried hops; and 4 ppm in dried prunes. Irritating to the eyes.

2-TRIDECENAL • A synthetic citrus and flavoring for beverages, ice cream, ices, candy, baked goods, and chewing gum. The FDA data bank, PAFA (see page 10), has fully up-to-date toxicology information available on this food additive.

TRIDECYL ALCOHOL • Derived from tridecane, a paraffin hydrocarbon obtained from petroleum. Used as an emulsifier in cosmetic creams, lotions, and lipsticks. No known toxicity.

TRIETHANOLAMINE • A coating agent for fresh fruit and vegetables and widely used in surfactants (*see*) and as a dispersing agent and detergent in hand and body lotions, shaving creams, soaps, shampoo, and bath powders. Its principal toxic effect in animals has been attributed to overalkalinity. Gross pathology has been found in the gastrointestinal tract in fatally poisoned guinea pigs. It is an irritant. The FDA data bank, PAFA (see page 10), has fully up-to-date toxicology information available on this food additive.

TRIETHANOLAMINE STEARATE • Made from ethylene oxide. Used in brilliantines, cleansing creams, foundation creams, hair lacquers, liquid makeups, fragrances, liquid powders, mascara, protective creams, baby preparations, shaving creams and lathers, and preshave lotions. A moisture absorber, viscous, used in making emulsions. Cream colored, turns brown on exposure to air. May be irritating to the skin and mucous membranes, but less so than many other amine oxides (*see*). The FDA data bank, PAFA, has fully up-to-date toxicology information available on this food additive.

TRIETHYL CITRATE • Citric Acid. Ethyl Citrate. A plasticizer in nail polish. Odorless, practically colorless, bitter; also used in dried egg as a sequestering agent (*see*), and to prevent rancidity. Citrates may interfere with laboratory tests for blood, liver, and pancreatic function, but no known skin toxicity. The final report to the FDA of the Select Committee on GRAS Substances stated in 1980 that it should continue its GRAS status with no limitations other than good manufacturing practices. The FDA data bank, PAFA, is currently searching the toxicology literature concerning this additive.

TRIETHYLENE GLYCOL • Used in stick perfume. Prepared from ethylene oxide and ethylene glycol (*see both*). Used as a solvent.

TRIFLUMIZOLE • Fungicide used in animal feed. FDA residue tolerances are 2 ppm in apple pomace, 25 ppm in grape pomace, and 8 ppm in raisin waste.

TRIFORINE • White crystals used as a fungicide for animal feed and hops. FDA limits residue to 60 ppm in dried hops and in spent hops when used for animal feed.

TRIFURAN • A pesticide used in peppermint and spearmint oil. FDA residue tolerance is 2 ppm.

TRIHYDROXY STEARIN • Isolated from cork and used as a thickener. No known toxicity.

2-4-5-TRIHYDROXYBUTYROPHENONE (THBP) • An antioxidant used alone or in combination with other antioxidants. Total antioxidants not to exceed 0.02 percent of the oil or fat content of any product. Also used in the manufacture of food-packaging materials, with a limit of 0.005 percent in food. This widely used additive is on the FDA list for further study. May not be listed on labels. Although allowed as a food additive, there is no current reported use of the chemical, and therefore, although toxicology information may be available, the FDA is not updating it.

TRIISOPROPANOLAMINE (TIPA) • A crystalline, white solid. A mild base used as an emulsifying agent. A component of a coating used for fresh fruits and vegetables. No known toxicity.

TRIISOSTEARIN • *See* Glycerin and Isostearic Acid.

TRILAURIN • *See* Lauric Acid.

TRILAURYL CITRATE • *See* Lauryl Alcohol and Citric Acid.

2,6,6-TRIMETHYL-2-CYCLOHEXANE-1-ONE • Nicomol. Crystals from dilute acetic acid. Odorless and tasteless. Breaks down fats. The FDA data bank, PAFA (see page 10), has fully up-to-date toxicology information available on this food additive.

2,4,5-TRIMETHYL DELTA-3-OXAZOLINE • Yellow to orange liquid with a strong, nutlike odor. Used as a flavoring agent in various foods. GRAS. The FDA data bank, PAFA, has fully up-to-date toxicology information available on this food additive.

TRIPOLYPHOSPHATE • A phosphorus salt. A sequestering agent (*see*) in foods and a food additive. Used to soften water, as an emulsifier, and as a dispersing agent. A buffering agent in shampoos. Can be irritating because of its alkalinity. May cause esophageal stricture if swallowed. Moderately irritating to the skin and mucous membranes. Ingestion can cause violent vomiting.

TRISODIUM-3-CARBOXY-5-HYDROXY-1-*p*-SULFOPHENYL-4-*p*-SUFOPHENYL-AZOPYRAZOLE • *See* FD and C Yellow No. 5.

TRISODIUM EDTA • *See* Tetrasodium EDTA.

TRISODIUM HEDTA • Mineral suspending agents. *See* Sequestering Agent.

TRISODIUM HYDROXY EDTA • *See* Tetrasodium EDTA.

TRISODIUM HYDROXYETHYL ETHLENEDIAMINETRIACETATE • *See* Tetrasodium EDTA.

TRISODIUM NTA • *See* Sequestering Agent.

TRISODIUM PHOSPHATE • Obtained from phosphate rock. Highly alkaline. Used in shampoos, cuticle softeners, bubble baths, and bath salts for its water-softening and cleaning actions. Phosphorus was formerly used to treat rickets and degenerative disorders and is now used as a mineral supplement for foods; also in incendiary bombs and tracer bullets. Can cause skin irritation from alkalinity.

TRISTEARIN • Present in many animal and vegetable fats, especially hard ones such as tallow and cocoa butter, it is used in surfactants, quaternary ammonium compounds, and emollients. No known toxicity.

TRISTEARYL CITRATE • The triester of stearyl alcohol and citric acid (*see both*).

TRITHION • Acarithion. Akarithion. Endyl. Trithion Miticide. Insecticide and miticide used in animal feed, grapefruit, lemons, limes, oranges, tangelos, tangerines, and dried tea. FDA's insecticide residue tolerances are 20 ppm on dried tea and 10 ppm in dehydrated citrus pulp and citrus meal when used for cattle feed. EPA Extremely Hazardous Substances List. Poisonous by ingestion and skin contact. Inhibits nerve transmission.

TRITICALE • A man-made cross between wheat (*see* Dog Grass Extract) and rye (secale), but more nutritious than wheat. The protein content of bread made with it is 10 percent higher, and its essential amino acid, lysine (*see*), exceeds that in wheat bread by 50 percent. The crop is the result of seven years' development and is being offered both as an ingredient and as a basic food substance. A number of novel products are being made from it, including ethnic breads. Two slices of Tritibread (made with triticale) supply 12 percent of the U.S. recommended daily allowance for protein, 30 percent for thiamine, and 10 percent for riboflavin, niacin, and iron. Triticale is intended for baked goods, ready-to-eat cereals, and malt products; also as a thickener, emulsifier, fortifier, and supplement. Once accepted, triticale can be an important nutritious addition to the food supply.

TRITICUM • *See* Dog Grass Extract. GRAS.

TROMETHAMINE • Made by the reduction (*see*) of nitro compounds, it is a crystalline mass used in the manufacture of surfactants (*see*). Used as an emulsifying agent for cosmetic creams and lotions, mineral oil, and paraffin wax emulsions. Used medicinally to correct an overabundance of acid in the body. No known toxicity.

TRUE FIXATIVE • This holds back the evaporation of the other materials. Benzoin is an example. *See* Fixatives.

TRYPTOPHAN • (L form only.) A tremendous amount of research is now in progress with this amino acid (*see*). First isolated in milk in 1901, it is now being studied as a means to calm hyperactive children, induce sleep, and fight depression and pain. Although it is sold over the counter, it is not believed to be completely harmless and has been suspected of being a cocarcinogen and to affect the liver when taken in high doses. Like niacin, it is capable of preventing and curing pellagra. It is a partial precursor of the brain hormone serotonin and is indispensable for the manufacture of certain cell proteins. In cosmetics, it is used to increase the protein content of creams and lotions. Causes cancer in experimental animals. The FDA called for further study of this additive. GRAS. The FDA data bank, PAFA (see page 10), has fully up-to-date toxicology information available on this food additive.

TUBEROSE EXTRACT • Derived from a Mexican bulbous herb commonly cultivated for its spike of fragrant white single or double flowers that resemble small lilies. Used in peach flavorings for beverages, ice cream, ices, candy, and baked goods. Tuberose is used in perfumes. Can cause allergic reactions. GRAS.

TUMERIC • *See* Turmeric.

TUNG NUT OIL • China Wood Oil. Drying oil used to waterproof packaging materials. Toxic by ingestion. Causes contact dermatitis (skin rash). Ingestion causes nausea, vomiting, cramps, diarrhea, thirst, dizziness, lethargy, and disorientation. Large doses can cause fever, irregular heartbeat, and respiratory effects.

TUNU EXTRACT • Tuno. From a Central American tree, *Castilloa fallax cook,* closely related to the rubber tree. Cleared for use as a natural masticatory substance of vegetable origin in chewing gum base. The FDA data bank, PAFA (see page 10), has fully up-to-date toxicology information available on this food additive.

TURMERIC • Tumeric. Derived from an East Indian herb, *Curcuma longa.* An aromatic, pepperlike but somewhat bitter taste. The cleaned, boiled, sun-dried, pulverized root is used in coconut, ginger ale, and curry flavorings for puddings, condiments, meats, soups, and pickles; also for yellow coloring used to color sausage casings, oleomargarine, shortening, and marking ink. The *extract* is used in fruit, meat, and cheese flavorings for beverages, condiments, meats, soup bases, and pickles. The *oleoresin* (*see*) is obtained by extraction with one or more of the solvents acetone, ethyl alcohol, ethylene dichloride (*see all*), and others. It is used in spice flavorings for condiments, meats, pickles, and brine. Both turmeric and its oleoresin have been permanently listed for coloring food since 1966. GRAS. The FDA data bank, PAFA, has fully up-to-date toxicology information available on this food additive.

TURPENTINE • Gum and Steam Distilled. Any of the various resins obtained from coniferous trees. A yellowish, viscous exudate with a characteristic smell, both forms are used in spice flavorings for baked goods. Steam-distilled turpentine is used also in candy. Also used as a solvent in hair lotions, waxes, perfume soaps, and to soothe skin. It is the oleoresin from a species of pine. Readily absorbed through the skin. Irritating to the skin and mucous membranes. In addition to being a local skin irritant, it can cause allergic reactions. In addition, it is a central nervous system depressant. Death is usually due to respiratory failure. As little as fifteen milliliters has killed children. The FDA data bank, PAFA (see page 10), has not yet done a toxicology literature search on this food additive.

TYLOSIN • Tylon. Tylan. Antibiotic from *Streptomyces fradiae* used for beef, chicken, eggs, milk, pork, and turkey. FDA limitations are 0.2 ppm in chickens, turkeys, cattle, swine, and eggs; 0.05 ppm in milk. Moderately toxic by ingestion.

TYROSINE • L Form. Widely distributed amino acid (*see*), termed nonessential because it does not seem to be necessary for growth. It is used as a dietary supplement. It is a building block of protein and is used in cosmetics to help creams penetrate the skin. The FDA has asked for further study of this additive. GRAS. The FDA data bank, PAFA, has fully up-to-date toxicology information available on this food additive.

U

U • Symbol meaning "kosher" (*see*).

ULTRAMARINE BLUE • A color additive occurring naturally in the mineral lapis lazuli. Used for packaging material and a salt for animal feed. FDA limitation of 0.5 percent of salt. It is used for external use only. No longer permitted for use as a drug coloring. There is no reported use of the chemical and no toxicology information is available, according to the FDA's data bank, PAFA (see page 10).

2,3-UNDECADIONE • A synthetic butter flavoring agent for beverages, ice cream, ices, candy, and baked goods. The FDA data bank, PAFA, has fully up-to-date toxicology information available on this food additive.

γ-UNDECALACTONE • Peach Aldehyde. Colorless to light yellow liquid with a peachy odor. Derived from undecylenic acid with sulfuric acid. A synthetic fruit flavoring used for beverages, ice cream, ices, candy, baked goods, gelatin desserts, and chewing gum. Used also in perfumery. The FDA data bank, PAFA, has fully up-to-date toxicology information available on this food additive.

UNDECANAL • A synthetic flavoring agent. Colorless to slightly yellow, with a sweet, fatty odor. Used in lemon, orange, rose, fruit, and honey flavorings for beverages, ice cream, ices, candy, baked goods, and chewing gum. The FDA data bank, PAFA, has fully up-to-date toxicology information available on this food additive.

9-UNDECANAL • A synthetic citrus and fruit flavoring for beverages, ice cream, ices, candy, baked goods, and chewing gum. No known toxicity.

10-UNDECANAL • A synthetic citrus, floral, and fruit flavoring agent for beverages, ice cream, ices, and candy. No known toxicity.

1-UNDECANOL • Colorless liquid with a citrus odor used in perfumery and as a flavoring. *See* Undecylenic Acid.

2-UNDECANOL • Antifoaming agent, perfume fixative, and plasticizer. *See* Undecylenic Acid.

2-UNDECANONE • A synthetic flavoring agent that occurs naturally in rue and hops oil. Used in citrus, coconut, peach, and cheese flavorings for beverages, ice cream, ices, candy, baked goods, and puddings. The FDA data bank, PAFA (see page 10), has fully up-to-date toxicology information available on this food additive.

10-UNDECEN-1-YL ACETATE • A synthetic citrus and fruit flavoring agent for beverages, ice cream, ices, candy, and baked goods. The FDA data bank, PAFA, has fully up-to-date toxicology information available on this food additive.

10-UNDECENOIC ACID • Occurs in sweat. Obtained from ricinoleic acid (*see*). Used as an antifungal agent. The FDA data bank, PAFA, has fully up-to-date toxicology information available on this food additive.

2-UNDECENOL • White to slightly yellow liquid with a sweet floral odor used as a flavoring agent in various foods. Although allowed as a food additive, there is no current reported use of the chemical, and therefore, although toxicology information may be available, the FDA is not updating it.

UNDECYL ALCOHOL • A synthetic lemon, lime, orange, and rose flavoring agent for beverages, ice cream, ices, candy, and baked goods. The FDA data bank, PAFA (see page 10), has fully up-to-date toxicology information available on this food additive.

UNDECYLENIC ACID • 10-Undecenoic Acid. Occurs in sweat. Obtained from ricinoleic acid (*see*). A liquid or crystalline powder, with an odor suggestive of perspiration or citrus. Used as a fungicide, in perfumes, as a flavoring, and as a lubricant additive in cosmetics. Has been given orally, but it causes dizziness, headaches, and stomach upset. No known toxicity for the skin.

UNDECYLENYL ALCOHOL • Colorless liquid with a citrus odor. Used in perfumes. It is combustible but has a low toxicity.

UNDECYLIC ACID • *See* Undecylenic Acid.

UNDECYLPENTADECANOL • *See* Fatty Alcohols.

UNSAPONIFIABLE OLIVE OIL • The oil fraction that is not broken down in the refining of olive fatty acids.

UNSAPONIFIABLE RAPESEED OIL • The oil that is not broken down in the refining of rapeseed-oil fatty acids.

UNSAPONIFIABLE SHEA BUTTER • The fraction of shea butter that is not broken down during processing.

UNSAPONIFIABLE SOYBEAN OIL • The fraction of soybean oil that is not broken down in the refining recovery of soybean-oil fatty acids.

UPC • Abbreviation for Universal Product Code.

UREA • Carbamide. A product of protein metabolism and excreted in human urine. Used in yeast food and wine production up to two pounds per gallon. It is used to "brown" baked goods such as pretzels and consists of colorless or white, odorless crystals that have a cool, salty taste. An antiseptic and deodorizer used in liquid antiperspirants, ammoniated dentifrices, roll-on deodorants, mouthwashes, hair colorings, hand creams, lotions, and shampoos. Medicinally, urea is used as a topical antiseptic and as a diuretic. Its largest use, however, is a fertilizer, and only a small part of its production goes into the manufacture of other urea products. No known toxicity. The final report to the FDA of the Select Committee on

GRAS Substances stated in 1980 that it should continue its GRAS status with no limitations other than good manufacturing practices. The FDA data bank, PAFA (see page 10), has not yet done a toxicology literature search on this food additive.

UREASE • An enzyme that hydrolyzes urea (*see*) to ammonium carbonate (*see*). There is no reported use of the chemical and no toxicology information is available, according to the FDA's data bank, PAFA.

URIC ACID • Lithic Acid. White crystals contained in solution in the urine of mammals and in solid form in the urine of birds and reptiles.

UROCANIC ACID • Prepared from L-histidine (*see*).

USNIC ACID • Antibacterial compound found in lichens. Pale yellow, slightly soluble in water. No known toxicity.

V

VALBAZEN • Albendazole. Zental. A worm medicine for animals. Moderately toxic by ingestion. Causes birth defects in experimental animals.

VALERAL • *See* Valeraldehyde.

VALERALDEHYDE • Pentanal. A synthetic flavoring agent that occurs naturally in coffee extract. Used in fruit and nut flavorings for beverages, ice cream, ices, candy, and baked goods. Has narcotic properties and is a mild irritant. The FDA data bank, PAFA (see page 10), has fully up-to-date toxicology information available on this food additive.

VALERIAN • *Valeriana officinalis*. A perennial native to Europe and the U.S., it was reputed to be a love potion. Its vapor was found to kill the bacillus of typhoid fever after forty-five minutes. The herb has been widely studied in Europe and Russia, and the major constituents, the valepotriate, have been reported to have marked sedative, anticonvulsive, blood-pressure-lowering, and tranquilizing effects. It has been used for centuries to treat panic attacks. In Germany, valerian preparations have been used for more than a decade to treat childhood behavioral disorders, supposedly without the side effects experienced with pharmaceuticals for that purpose. It has been reported that it also helps concentration and energy. Prolonged use of valerian may result in side effects such as irregular heartbeat, headaches, uneasiness, nervousness, and insomnia. Very large doses may cause paralysis. The FDA data bank, PAFA, has not yet done a toxicology literature search on this food additive.

VALERIC ACID • Occurs naturally in apples, cocoa, coffee, oil of lavender, peaches, and strawberries. A synthetic flavoring agent used in butter, butterscotch, fruit, rum, and cheese flavorings for beverages, ice cream, ices, candy, and baked goods. Colorless, with an unpleasant odor. Usually distilled from valerian root. Used in the manufacture of perfumes. Some of its salts are used in medicine. Also used in peeling solutions for fruits and vegetables. Moderately toxic by ingestion. A corrosive irritant to skin, eyes, and mucous membranes. The FDA data bank, PAFA (see page 10), has fully up-to-date toxicology information available on this food additive.

VALERIC ALDEHYDE • *See* Valeraldehyde.

VALEROLACTONE • A synthetic vanilla flavoring agent for beverages, ice cream, ices, candy, and baked goods. Moderately toxic by ingestion. A skin irritant. The FDA data bank, PAFA, has fully up-to-date toxicology information available on this food additive.

VALINE • L Form. An essential amino acid (*see*). Occurs in the largest quantities in fibrous protein. It is indispensable for growth and nitrogen balance. Used in suntan lotions. No known toxicity in cosmetics, but the FDA asked for further study of this ingredient as a food additive in 1980. GRAS. The FDA data bank, PAFA, has fully up-to-date toxicology information available on this food additive.

VANADIUM TETRACHLORIDE • Derived from chlorination of ferrovanadium. Catalyst. Toxic by ingestion, inhalation, and skin absorption.

VANAY • *See* Triacetin.

VANILLA EXTRACT • Extracted from the full-grown unripe fruit of the vanilla plant of Mexico and the West Indies. Contains not less than 35 percent aqueous ethyl alcohol (*see*) and one or more of the following ingredients: glycerin, propylene glycol, sugar (including invert sugar), and corn syrup. Used in many foods and beverages as a flavoring. No known toxicity. GRAS. The FDA data bank, PAFA (see page 10), has not yet done a toxicology literature search on this food additive.

VANILLAL • *See* Ethyl Vanillin.

VANILLIN • Occurs naturally in vanilla extract (*see*) and potato parings but is an artificial flavoring. Odor and taste of vanilla. Made synthetically from eugenol (*see*); also from the waste of the wood pulp industry. One part vanillin equals four hundred parts vanilla pods. Used in butter, chocolate, fruit, root beer, and vanilla flavorings for beverages, ice cream, ices, candy, baked goods, gelatin desserts, puddings, syrups (30,000 ppm), toppings, margarine, chocolate products, and liqueurs. The lethal dose in mice is three grams (thirty grams to the ounce) per kilogram of body weight. A skin irritant that produces a burning sensation and eczema. May also cause pigmentation of the skin. GRAS. The FDA data bank, PAFA, has fully up-to-date toxicology information available on this food additive.

VANILLIN ACETATE • Vanillin. A synthetic spice and vanilla flavoring agent for beverages, ice cream, ices, candy, and baked goods. The FDA data bank, PAFA, has fully up-to-date toxicology information available on this food additive.

VEGETABLE GUMS • Includes derivatives from quince seed, karaya, acacia, tragacanth, Irish moss, guar, sodium alginate, potassium alginate, ammonium alginate, and propylene glycol alginate. All are subject to deterioration and always need a preservative. The gums function as liquid emulsions, that is, they thicken cosmetic products and make them cream. No known toxicity other than allergic reactions in hypersensitive persons. The FDA data bank, PAFA (see page 10), has not yet done a toxicology literature search on this food additive.

VEGETABLE JUICE • Used in food colorings consistent with good manufacturing practices. Permanently listed for coloring since 1966. The FDA data bank, PAFA, has fully up-to-date toxicology information available on this food additive.

VEGETABLE OILS • Peanut, sesame, olive, and cottonseed oil obtained from plants and used in many food additives and in baby preparations, cleansing creams, emollient creams, face powders, hair-grooming aids, hypoallergenic cosmetics, lipsticks, nail creams, shampoos, shaving creams, and wave sets. No known toxicity. *See* Vegetable Oils, Brominated.

VEGETABLE OILS, BROMINATED • Peanut, sesame, and cottonseed oil obtained from plants. Used in fruit-flavored beverages where not prohibited by standards. FDA tolerance, less than 15 ppm. Also used in baby preparations, cleansing creams, emollient creams, face powders, hair-grooming aids, hypoallergenic cosmetics, lipsticks, nail creams, shampoos, shaving creams, and wave sets. *See* Bromates.

VERATRALDEHYDE • A synthetic fruit, nut, and vanilla flavoring agent for beverages, ice cream, ices, candy, baked goods, and puddings. Derived from vanillin. May have narcotic and irritant effects, but no specific data. The FDA data bank, PAFA (see page 10), has fully up-to-date toxicology information available on this food additive.

VERATRIC ALDEHYDE • *See* Veratraldehye.

VERBENALOL • An alcohol made from *Verbena officinalis*. The FDA data bank, PAFA, has fully up-to-date toxicology information available on this food additive.

VERONICA • Extract of *Veronica officinalis*, a small herb of wide distribution that has pink or white flowers. Flavoring in alcoholic beverages only. The FDA data bank, PAFA, has not yet done a toxicology literature search on this food additive.

VERVAIN, EUROPEAN • *Verbena officinalis*. A class of medicinal plants used as a flavoring in alcoholic beverages only. There is no reported use of the chemical and no toxicology information is available, according to the FDA's data bank, PAFA.

VERXITE GRANULES • Hydrated magnesium-aluminum iron silicate. Soft and resilient. Used as an anticaking and blending agent in ruminant feeds.

VERXITE GRITS • Used as a roughage replacement in ruminant feeds.

VERY LOW SODIUM • Less than 35 mg per serving.

VETIVER OIL • Vetiverol. Khuskhus. Stable brown to reddish brown oil from the roots of a fragrant grass. It has an aromatic to harsh woodsy odor. Used as a flavoring in foods and as a scent in soaps and perfumes. The FDA data bank, PAFA (see page 10), has not yet done a toxicology literature search on this food additive.

VIBURNUM EXTRACT • Haw Bark. Black Extract. Extract of the fruit of a hawthorn shrub or tree. Used in fragrances and in butter, caramel, cola, maple, and walnut flavorings for beverages. Has been used as a uterine antispasmodic. No known toxicity.

VIBURNUM PRUNIFOLIUM • *See* Viburnum Extract.

VINEGAR • Used for hundreds of years to remove lime soap after shampooing. It is a solvent for cosmetic oils and resins. Vinegar is about 4 to 6 percent acetic acid. Acetic acid occurs naturally in apples, cheese, grapes, milk, and other foods. No known toxicity but may cause an allergic reaction in those allergic to corn.

VINEGAR NAPHTHA • *See* Ethyl Acetate.

VINYL • Made from acetylene with various other substances to form plastics.

VINYL ACETATE • A starch modifier not to exceed 2.5 percent in modified starch (*see*). Vapors in high concentration may be narcotic; animal experiments show low toxicity. There is no reported use of the chemical and no toxicology information is available, according to the FDA's data bank, PAFA (see page 10).

VINYL CHLORIDE • Chloroethylene. Prepared from ethylene dichloride and alcoholic potassium, it is a colorless gas that becomes liquid upon freezing. It is one of the most frequently used vinyl compounds and is a hazardous chemical by all avenues of exposure. It may be narcotic in high concentrations. If spilled on the skin, rapid evaporation causes local frostbite. It is a known cancer-causing agent, and because of that, it has been banned from aerosol sprays. It is used for many polyvinyl compounds in paper coating, adhesives, and refrigerants. It is permitted by the FDA for use in adhesives, and in food-contact coatings.

VINYL CHLORIDE-VINYLIDENE CHLORIDE COPOLYMER • Used as a coating on fresh citrus fruits. Vinyl chloride was banned in hairsprays because it is a cancer-causing agent. It is a proven liver-cancer-causing agent in people who work with the compound. Vinylidene chloride is an irritant to mucous membranes, narcotic in high concentrations, and has caused liver and kidney injury in experimental animals. There is no reported use of the chemical and no toxicology information is available, according to the FDA's data bank, PAFA.

VIOLA ODORATA • *See* Violet Extract.

VIOLAXANTHIN • Natural orange-red coloring isolated from yellow pansies and Valencia orange peel. Soluble in alcohol. *See* Xanthophyll. No known toxicity.

VIOLET EXTRACT • Flowers and Leaves. Green liquid with typical odor of violet. It is taken from the plant widely grown in the U.S. Used in berry, violet, and fruit flavorings for beverages, ice cream, ices, candy, and baked goods. Also in face powders and for coloring inorganic pigments. May produce skin rash in the allergic. No known toxicity. GRAS.

VIOLET LEAVES, ABSOLUTE • Essential oil of *Viola odorata*. *See* Violet Extract. GRAS. The FDA data bank, PAFA (see page 10), has not yet done a toxicology literature search on this food additive.

VIRGINIAMYCIN • Eskalin. Pristinamycin. Staphlyomycin. White powder from *Streptomyces* used as an antibiotic for chickens and swine. FDA limits residue in swine to 0.4 ppm in kidney, skin, and fat, 0.3 ppm in liver, and 0.1 ppm in muscle. In broiler chickens, the limit is 0.5 ppm in kidney, 0.3 ppm in liver, 0.2 ppm in skin and fat, and 0.1 ppm in muscle. Moderately toxic by ingestion.

VIRIDINE • *See* Phenylacetaldehyde Dimethyl Acetal.

VITAMIN A • Acetate and Palmitate. A yellow, viscous liquid insoluble in water. An anti-infective, antixerophthalmic vitamin, essential to growth and development. Deficiency leads to retarded growth in the young, diminished visual acuity, night blindness, and skin problems. Insoluble in water. Toxic when children or adults receive more than 100,000 units daily over several months.

Recommended daily dietary allowance is 1,500 units for infants and 4,500 units for adults and 2,000–3,500 units for children. It is used to fortify mellorine (vegetable-fat imitation ice cream), skim milk, dietary infant formula, blue cheese, Gorgonzola cheese, milk, and oleomargarine (one pound of margarine contains 15,000 units of vitamin A). Vitamin A is also used in lubricating creams and oils for its alleged skin-healing properties. Can be absorbed through the skin. The final report to the FDA of the Select Committee on GRAS Substances stated in 1980 that it should continue its GRAS status with no limitations other than good manufacturing practices. The FDA data bank, PAFA (see page 10), has not yet done a toxicology literature search on this food additive.

VITAMIN B$_1$ • *See* Thiamine Hydrochloride.

VITAMIN B$_2$ • Riboflavin. Lactoflavin. Formerly called vitamin G. Riboflavin is a factor in the vitamin B complex and is used in emollients. Every plant and animal cell contains a minute amount. Helps to metabolize protein, carbohydrate, and fat; maintains healthy skin, eyes; aids formation of red blood cells and antibodies. It is necessary for healthy respiration, protects the eyes from sensitivity to light, and is used for building and maintaining human body tissues. A deficiency leads to lesions at the corner of the mouth, to changes in the cornea, and to skin problems. Recommended daily allowances for infants to six months, 0.4 mg. Children one to three years, 0.8 mg. Children four to six years, 1.1 mg. Children seven to ten years, 1.2 mg. Males eleven to fourteen years, 1.5 mg. Males fifteen to eighteen years, 1.8 mg. Males nineteen to fifty years, 1.7 mg. Males fifty-one years and over, 1.4 mg. Females eleven to fifty years, 1.3 mg. Females fifty-one years and over, 1.4 mg. Pregnant women 1.6 mg. Lactating women, 1.7–1.8 mg. It is used to treat riboflavin deficiency or as an adjunct to thiamine treatment for nerve inflammation of lips secondary to pellagra. In 1992, the FDA proposed a ban on riboflavin in oral menstrual drug products because it has not been shown to be safe and effective for its stated claims.

VITAMIN B$_3$ • *See* Niacin.

VITAMIN B$_5$ • *See* Pantothenic Acid.

VITAMIN B$_6$ • Pyridoxine. Beesix. Hexa-Betalin. Hexacrest. Nestrex. Rodex. Vitabee 6. Metabolizes protein; helps produce red blood cells; maintains proper functioning of nervous system tissue. Vitamin B$_6$ is believed to act as a partner for more than one hundred different enzymes. A number of the brain chemicals that send messages back and forth between nerves depend upon it for formation. A deficiency in this vitamin is known to cause depression and mental confusion. The occurrence of seizures in experimental animals in response to vitamin B$_6$ antagonists has been observed by many. Similar seizures were observed in human infants inadvertently made vitamin B$_6$ deficient when they were fed a commercial infant formula in which the vitamin had not been properly preserved. Certain substances that deplete B$_6$ also produce deficiency seizures. Vitamin B$_6$ also reportedly helps rid the body tissues of excess fluid that causes some of the symptoms of premenstrual tension. Estrogen and cortisone deplete B$_6$. Storage over a long period of time diminishes the vitamin. Recommended daily allowance for newborns and infants to six months is 0.3 mg. Children four to six years, 1.1 mg. Children seven to ten years, 1.4 mg. Males eleven to fourteen years, 1.7 mg. Males fifteen years and over, 2 mg. Females eleven to fourteen years, 1.4 mg. Females fifteen to eighteen years, 1.5 mg. Females nineteen years and over, 1.6 mg. Pregnant women, 2.2 mg. Lactating women, 2.1 mg. Used to treat vitamin B$_6$ deficiency and responsive anemias. Also prevention of vitamin B$_6$ deficiency during isoniazid therapy to treat tuberculosis. Patients are likely to have a defiency of B$_6$ if they are alcoholics or have burns, diarrhea, heart disease, intestinal problems, liver disease, overactive thyroid, or are suffering the stress of long-term illness or serious injury. Patients on dialysis or who have their stomach removed are also probably deficient in the vitamin. Current research seems to indicate that B$_6$ enhances the immune response in the elderly and may alleviate some signs of carpal tunnel syndrome, a wrist problem. Overdosing on B$_6$ is unwise. A study reported in the *New England Journal of Medicine* in 1983 described the loss of balance and numbness suffered by seven young adults who took from two to six grams of pyridoxine daily for several months to a year. Other potential adverse reactions include drowsiness and a feeling of pins and needles in the limbs. In 1992, the FDA proposed a ban on pyridoxine in fever-blister and cold-sore treatment products because it has not been shown to be safe and effective for its stated claims.

VITAMIN B$_9$ • *See* Folic Acid.

VITAMIN B COMPLEX FACTOR • *See* Panthenol.

VITAMIN B$_{12}$ • Cyanocobalamin. Anacobin. Bedoce. Betalin 12. Bioglan B$_{12}$. Crystamine. Cyano-Gel. Dodex. Kaybovite. Poyamin. Redisol. Rubesol-1000. Rubramin. Sigamine. Alpha-Ruvite. Codroxomin. Droxomin. Helps form red blood cells; maintains healthy nervous system. Deficiency symptoms include anemia, brain damage, and nervousness. More than one in five Americans over the age of sixty may need to take vitamin B$_{12}$ by injection to prevent neurological disorders because their stomach acid does not enable them to absorb the vitamin from foods. The condition is known as atrophic gastritis. Recommended daily allowances: Neonates and infants to six months, 0.3 mcg. Infants six months to one year, 0.5 mcg. Children over one year to three years, 0.7 mcg. Children four to six years, 1 mcg. Adults and children eleven years and over, 2 mcg. Pregnant women, 2.2 mcg. Lactating women, 2.6 mcg. Some medicines cause malabsorption of vitamin B$_{12}$. Cobalt and its compounds are on the Community Right-To-Know List (*see*) and on EPA Genetic Toxicology Program (*see*). Causes adverse reproductive effects in experimental animals. The FDA data bank, PAFA (see page 10), has not yet done a toxicology literature search on this food additive.

VITAMIN C • *See* Ascorbic Acid.

VITAMIN D$_2$ • Calciferol. A pale yellow, oily liquid, odorless, tasteless, insoluble in water. Nutritional factor added to prepared breakfast cereals, mellorine (vegetable-fat imitation ice cream), vitamin D milk, evaporated and skim milks, margarine, infant dietary formulas, enriched flour, self-rising flour, enriched cornmeal and grits, enriched macaroni and noodle products (250–1,000 USP units), enriched farina and enriched bread, rolls, etc. Vitamin D speeds the body's production of calcium and has been found to cause calcium deposits and facial deformities and subnormal IQs in children of mothers given too much vitamin D. Nutritionists recommend four hundred units per day for pregnant women. Some women taking vitamin pills and vitamin enriched milk and foods consume as much as two thousand to three thousand units daily. Used for its alleged skin-healing properties in lubricating creams and lotions. The absence of vitamin D in the food of young animals can lead to rickets, a bone-affecting condition. It is soluble in fats and fat solvents and is present in animal fats. Absorbed through the skin. Its value in cosmetics has not been proven. No known toxicity to the skin. The final report to the FDA of the Select Committee on GRAS Substances stated in 1980 that there is no available evidence that it is a hazard to the public when used as it is now and it should continue its GRAS status with limitations on amounts that can be added to food. The FDA data bank, PAFA (see page 10), has not yet done a toxicology literature search on this food additive.

VITAMIN D$_3$ • Activated 7-Dehydrocholesterol. Approximately as effective as vitamin D$_2$ (*see*). The final report to the FDA of the Select Committee on GRAS Substances stated in 1980 that there is no available evidence that it is a hazard to the public when used as it is now and it should continue its GRAS status with limitations on the amounts that can be added to food. The FDA data bank, PAFA, has not yet done a toxicology literature search on this food additive.

VITAMIN E • *See* Tocopherols.

VITAMIN E ACETATE • *See* Tocopherols.

VITAMIN E SUCCINATE • *See* Tocopherols.

VITAMIN G • *See* Riboflavin.

VITAMIN H • *See* Biotin.

VITAMIN K • Recommended daily allowance for adults has not been established, but the safe and adequate daily dietary intake level is listed at 0.07 to 0.14 mg. It is necessary for blood clotting. Current research seems to indicate it helps maintain bone mass in the elderly and prevents osteoporosis, thinning of the bones. Vitamin K antagonizes the action of anticoagulants and has been used as an antidote in managing overdosages of or excessive responses to the latter. The excessive use of vitamin K–containing substances—drugs or dietary items such as green leafy vegetables—should be avoided in patients receiving anticoagulants. The FDA data bank, PAFA (see page 10), has not yet done a toxicology literature search on this food additive.

VIVERRA CIVETTA SCHREBER • *See* Civet, Absolute.

VIVERRA ZIBETHASCHREBER • *See* Civet, Absolute.

VOLATILE FATTY ACIDS • Including Isobutyric Acid, Isovaleric Acid, Methylbutyric Acid, and *m*-Valeric Acid (*see all*). Used in dairy-cattle feeds as a source of energy.

VOLATILE OILS • The volatility in oils is the tendency to give off vapors, usually at room temperature. The volatile oils in plants such as peppermint or rose produce the aroma. The volatile oils in plants stimulate the tissue with which they come in contact whether they are inhaled, ingested, or placed on the skin. They can relax or stimulate, irritate or soothe, depending upon their source and concentration.

W

WALNUT EXTRACT • An extract of the husk of the nut of *Juglans* spp., the English walnut tree. Used in walnut flavorings for beverages, ice cream, ices, candy, and baked goods. Also used for brown coloring. The FDA data bank, PAFA (see page 10), has not yet done a toxicology literature search on this food additive.

WALNUT OIL • *See* Walnut Extract.

WALNUT SHELL POWDER • The ground shell of English walnuts, *Juglans regia*. *See* Walnut Extract.

WATERCRESS EXTRACT • Extract obtained from *Nasturtium officinalis*.

WAX, PARAFFIN • Coating for certain cheeses. *See* Paraffin Wax.

WAXES • Obtained from insects, animals, petroleum, and plants. Waxes made in the U.S. are vegetable, petroleum, or bug based. One of the most common vegetable waxes, carnauba (*see*), is made from a palm leaf. Waxes from petroleum are the same as those used as chewing gum bases. The "shellac" used on some products is made from the secretion of the lac bug, native to Pakistan and India. More than twenty varieties of fruits and vegetables, including cantaloupes, eggplants, oranges, peaches, persimmons, squash, cucumbers, sweet potatoes, and tomatoes, are being waxed. Waxing reduces the loss of moisture and keeps produce from dehydrating. Some waxes are cosmetic. For example, oranges are waxed because consumers prefer a shiny surface rather than the natural dull matte of the rind. A wide application in the manufacture of cosmetics. Beeswax, for instance, is secreted by the bee's special glands on the underside of its abdomen. The wax is glossy and hard but plastic when warm. Insoluble in water but partially soluble in boiling alcohol. Used in candy and vegetable coatings as well as for packaging. Waxes are generally nontoxic but may cause allergic reactions in the hypersensitive depending upon the source of the wax. It is also difficult to know which items have been waxed. Some foreign imports may use beef tallow, for example, which is undesirable in vegetarian or kosher diets. In many cases, pesticides and fungicides are added to waxes to help prevent decay. The FDA does have regulations requiring all waxed products at the supermarket to be labeled as such, either with a card listing the specific ingredients in the wax above the bin or on the bin or container itself. Have you seen such a listing? Some companies, according to Cornell University professor of food science Joseph Regenstein, Ph.D., switch waxes three times a day depending on environmental conditions.

WAXY MAIZE • Cornstarch. The soft, sticky material from the inside of the corn kernel. The final report to the FDA of the Select Committee on GRAS Substances stated in 1980 that it should continue its GRAS status with no limitations other than good manufacturing practices.

WETTING AGENT • Any of numerous water-soluble agents that promote spreading of a liquid on a surface or penetration into a material such as skin. It lowers surface tension for better contact and absorption. *See* Surfactants.

WHEAT • A cereal grain that yields a fine white powder. Wheat is avoided by some allergic people. Bread, cakes, crackers, cookies, pretzels, pastries, and noodles are made of wheat; also, breakfast foods such as cream of wheat, pablum, Grape-Nuts, Wheaties, puffed wheat, shredded wheat, and bran; sauces, soups, gravies; Postum, Ovaltine, malted milk; sausages, hamburger, and meat loaf. Nontoxic.

WHEAT BRAN • The broken coat of *Triticum aestivum*. About 14.5 percent of the kernel. In addition to indigestible cellulose, it contains 86 percent of niacin, 73 percent of the pyridoxine, 50 percent of the pantothenic acid, 42 percent of the riboflavin, 33 percent of the thiamine, and 19 percent of the protein of the whole wheat kernel. *See* Wheat Germ.

WHEAT BRAN LIPIDS • An extract of the coat of wheat. *See* Wheat Germ.

WHEAT FLOUR • Milled from the kernels of wheat, *Triticum aestivum*. *See* Wheat Starch.

WHEAT GERM • The golden germ of the wheat is high in vitamin E. About 2.5 percent of the whole wheat kernel. The germ contains about 64 percent of the thiamine, 26 percent of the riboflavin, and 21 percent of the pyridoxine of the whole wheat kernel. *See* Tocopherols.

WHEAT GERM EXTRACT • *See* Tocopherols.

WHEAT GERM GLYCERIDES • *See* Tocopherols.

WHEAT GERM OIL • *See* Tocopherols.

WHEAT GERMAMIDOPROPYL BETAINE • *See* Surfactants.

WHEAT GERMAMIDOPROPYL DIMETHYLAMINE LACTATE • *See* Tocopherols.

WHEAT GERMAMIDOPROPYLAMINE • *See* Tocopherols.

WHEAT GLUTEN • A mixture of proteins present in wheat flour and obtained as an extremely sticky, yellowish gray mass by making a dough and then washing out the starch. It consists almost entirely of two proteins, gliadin and glutenin. It contributes to the porous and spongy structure of bread. Used in powders and creams as a base. The FDA data bank, PAFA (see page 10), has fully up-to-date toxicology information available on this food additive.

WHEAT STARCH • A product of cereal grain, it swells when water is added. A minor part of starch production in the U.S. Used as a demulcent, emollient, and in dusting and face powders. May cause allergic reactions such as red eyes and stuffy nose. The final report to the FDA of the Select Committee on GRAS Substances stated in 1980 that it should continue its GRAS status with no limitations other than good manufacturing practices.

WHEY • The serum that remains after removal of fat and casein (*see*) from milk. Used to make cheese. GRAS. The FDA data bank, PAFA (see page 10), has fully up-to-date toxicology information available on this food additive.

WHEY PROTEIN • Milk Serum. Serum Lactis. The water part of milk remaining after the separation of casein (*see*). Cleared by the U.S. Department of Agriculture's Meat Inspection Department to bind and extend imitation sausage, and for use in soups and stews. Also used as source of protein and non-protein nitrogen for cattle. It is used in emollients. The FDA data bank, PAFA, has not yet done a toxicology literature search on this food additive.

WHITE CEDAR LEAF OIL • Oil of Arborvitae. Stable, pale yellow volatile oil obtained by steam distillation from the fresh leaves and branch ends of the Eastern *Arborvitae*. Has a strong camphoraceous and sagelike scent. Used as a perfume and scent for soaps and room sprays. Also used as a flavoring agent. Soluble in most fixed oils. *See* Cedar for toxicity.

WHITE FLAG EXTRACT • *See* Orris.

WHITE LILY EXTRACT • Extract of the bulbs of *Lilium candidum*. Edible bulbs that were made into soup by the Indians. The lily is used in perfumery.

WHITE MINERAL OIL • Obtained from petroleum and used in baked goods. *See* Mineral Oil.

WHITE NETTLE EXTRACT • Obtained from the flowers of *Lamium album*. *See* Nettles.

WHOLE FISH PROTEIN CONCENTRATE • Dietary supplement for household use only. FDA tolerance is less than 20 mg per day when consumed regularly by children up to eight years of age. When used in manufactured food, less than 8 ppm.

WILD CHERRY • Wild Black Cherry Bark. The dried stem bark collected in autumn in North America. Used in cherry flavorings for food, lipsticks, and medicines. Also used medicinally as a sedative and expectorant. No known toxicity. GRAS.

WILD GINGER • Canadian Oil. *See* Snakeroot Oil.

WILD MARJORAM EXTRACT • Extract of the flowering ends of *Origanum vulgare*. Yellow or greenish yellow liquid containing about 40 percent terpenes (*see*). Used in flavoring and perfumery. *See* Marjoram, Pot.

WILD MINT EXTRACT • Extract of the leaves and tender twigs of *Mentha arvensis*. The Cheyenne Indians prepared a decoction of the ground leaves and stems of wild mint and drank the liquid to check nausea. Pulegone and thymol (*see*) are derived from an oil of wild mint. Its odor resembles peppermint. Used in flavoring. *See* Peppermint Oil.

WILD THYME EXTRACT • The flowering tops of a plant grown in Eurasia and throughout the U.S. The dried leaves are used as a seasoning in foods and in emollients and fragrances. Has also been used as a muscle relaxant. No known toxicity. GRAS.

WILLOW LEAF EXTRACT • The extract of the leaves of the willow tree, *Salix* spp. The willow has been used for pain-relieving and fever-lowering properties since ancient Greece. The American Indians used willow baths to cool fevers, and indeed, the extract of willows contains salicylic acid, a close cousin of aspirin.

WINTERGREEN OIL • Extract and Oil. Menthyl Salicylate. Checkerberry Extract. Obtained naturally from betula, sweet birch, or teaberry oil. Present in certain leaves and bark but usually prepared by treating salicylic acid with methanol (*see both*). Wintergreen *extract* is used in root beer and wintergreen flavorings for beverages and candy (5,000 ppm). The *oil* is used for checkerberry, raspberry, teaberry, fruit, nut, root beer, sassafras, spice, and wintergreen flavorings for beverages, ice cream, ices, candy, baked goods (1,500 ppm), and chewing gum (3,900 ppm). Used in toothpaste, tooth powder, and perfumes. Wintergreen is a strong irritant. Ingestion of relatively small amounts may cause severe poisoning and death. Average lethal dose in children is ten milliliters and in adults, thirty milliliters. It is irritating to the mucous membranes and skin and can be absorbed rapidly through the skin. Like other salicylates, it has a wide range of interaction with other drugs, including alcohol, antidiabetic medications, vitamin C, and tranquilizers. The FDA data bank, PAFA (see page 10), has not yet done a toxicology literature search on this food additive.

WOOD ROSIN • The exudate from a living Southern pine tree. Pale yellow to amber, slight turpentine odor. Used as a coating for fresh citrus fruits. No known toxicity.

WOODRUFF • Master of the Woods. Used as a flavoring in alcoholic beverages only. Made of the leaves of an herb grown in Europe, Siberia, North Africa, and Australia. It is a symbol of spring and has a clean, fresh smell. The FDA data bank, PAFA, has not yet done a toxicology literature search on this food additive.

WORMWOOD • Absinthium. A European woody herb with a bitter taste, used in bitters and liquor flavorings for beverages and liquors. The *extract* is used in bitters, liquor, and vermouth flavorings for beverages, ice cream, candy, and liquors, and in making absinthe. The *oil* is a dark green to brown and a narcotic substance. Used in bitters, apple, vermouth, and wine flavorings for beverages, ice cream, ices, candy, baked goods, and liquors. In large doses or frequently repeated doses, it is a narcotic poison, causing headache, trembling, and convulsions. Ingestion of the volatile oil or of the liquor, absinthe, may cause gastrointestinal symptoms, nervousness, stupor, coma, and death.

X

XANTHAN GUM • A gum produced by a pure culture fermentation of a carbohydrate with *Xanthomonas campestris.* Also called corn sugar gum. The U.S. Agriculture Department has asked for the use of xanthan gum as a necessary ingredient in packaging meat and poultry products. It is now used to thicken, suspend, emulsify, and stabilize water-based foods, such as dairy products and salad dressings. It is also used as a "pseudoplasticizer" in salad dressings to help them pour well. In animal feeds it is used as a stabilizer, thickener, and suspending agent. FDA tolerance is 0.25 percent in liquid feeds for ruminants and 0.1 percent in calf milk replacer. The FDA data bank, PAFA (see page 10), has fully up-to-date toxicology information available on this food additive.

XANTHENE • Colorants are divided into acid and basic groups. They are the second-largest category of certified colors. The acids are derived from fluorescein. The quinoid-acid type is represented by FD and C Red No. 3, erythrosine, used frequently in lipsticks. The phenolic formulations, often called bromo acids, are represented by D and C Red No. 2, used to "stain" lips. The only basic type certified is D and C Red No. 19, also called rhodamine B.

XANTHOPHYLL • Vegetable Lutein. A yellow coloring originally isolated from egg yolk, now isolated from petals of flowers. Occurs also in colored feathers of birds. One of the most widespread carotenoid alcohols (a group of red and yellow pigments) in nature. Provisionally listed for use in food. Although carotenoids can usually be turned into vitamin A, xanthophyll has no vitamin A activity.

XANTHOXYLUM AMERICANUM • *See* Zanthoxylum.

XYLENOL • 2-4-Dimethylphenol. A white crystalline solid that is derived from coal tar and is toxic by ingestion and skin absorption. It is used as a disinfectant and as a solvent in pharmaceuticals, as a solvent in insecticides and rubber manufacture, and as a wetting agent for dyestuffs. It caused cancer when painted on the skin of mice. The FDA data bank, PAFA (see page 10), has fully up-to-date toxicology information available on this food additive.

XYLITOL • Formerly made from birchwood, but now made from waste products from the pulp industry. Xylitol has been reported to have diuretic effect, but this has not been substantiated. It is used in chewing gum and as an artificial sweetener but costs more than sugar. It has been reported to sharply reduce cavities in teeth, because, unlike sugar, it doesn't ferment in the mouth. Therefore, it is sold for foods that stay in the mouth for some time, such as gum, toffee, and mints. FDA preliminary reports cited it as a possible cancer-causing agent. Xylitol is now used in eleven European countries and the United States and Canada. It is also used in large amounts in the former Soviet Union as a diabetic sweetener. Xylitol was evaluated by the joint FAO/WHO Expert Committee on Food Additives in Geneva, April 11–20, 1983. On the basis of submitted data, the committee accepted that the adverse effects observed in British studies, in which cancer-prone rats were fed large doses of xylitol, were species-specific and cannot be extrapolated to humans. Therefore, no limit on daily intake was set and no additional toxicological studies were recommended. It can cause stomach upsets when taken in large amounts. It may be of benefit to diabetics since xylitol metabolization does not involve insulin. There is no reported use of the chemical and no toxicology information is available, according to the FDA's data bank, PAFA.

D-XYLOSE • Xylo-Pfan. Wood Sugar. Used for evaluating intestinal absorption and diagnosing malabsorptive states. The FDA data bank, PAFA, has fully up-to-date toxicology information available on this food additive.

Y

YARA YARA • *See b*-Naphthyl Methyl Ether.

YARROW • Milfoil. A strong-scented, spicy, wild herb, *Achillea millefolium,* used in liquor, root beer, and spice flavorings for beverages and liquor. Also used in shampoos. Its astringent qualities have caused it to be recommended by herbalists for greasy skins. According to old herbal recipes, it prevents baldness when the hair is washed regularly with it. Used medicinally as an astringent, tonic, and stimulant. May cause a sensitivity to sunlight and artificial light, in which the skin breaks out and swells. The FDA data bank, PAFA (see page 10), has not yet done a toxicology literature search on this food additive.

YEAST • A fungus that is a dietary source of folic acid. It produces enzymes that will convert sugar to alcohol and carbon dioxide. It is used in enriched farina, enriched cornmeal and corn grits, and in bakery products. It is also used in hot dogs, hamburger and frankfurter buns and rolls, pretzels, milk fortified with vitamins, meat coated with cracker crumbs and fried, mushrooms, truffles, cheeses of all kinds, vinegars, catsup, barbecue sauce, fermented brews, and all dried fruits. Any yeast is a type of one-celled fungus. Ordinary yeast produces the enzymes invertase and zymase, which eventually convert cane sugar to alcohol and carbon dioxide in fermentation. Some of the living organisms pressed into starch, or other absorbent material give a product known as baker's yeast, which is not as potent as brewer's yeast. No known toxicity. GRAS. The FDA data bank, PAFA, has fully up-to-date toxicology information available on this food additive.

YEAST, MALT-SPROUT EXTRACT • Used as a flavor enhancer. The FDA data bank, PAFA, has fully up-to-date toxicology information available on this food additive. *See* Yeast.

YEAST AND TORTULA YEAST, DRIED • Dietary supplement used in food providing total folic acid content. The FDA data bank, PAFA, has fully up-to-date toxicology information available on this food additive. *See* Yeast.

YEAST AUTOLYZATES • Concentrated soluble components of hydrolyzed brewer's or baker's yeasts, a byproduct of brewing. They provide a good source of B vitamins. The final report to the FDA of the Select Committee on GRAS Substances stated in 1980 that while no available evidence on it demonstrates a hazard to the public at current use levels, uncertainties exist, requiring additional studies. The FDA said GRAS status should continue while tests were being completed and evaluated. There is no reported use of the chemical and no toxicology information is available, according to the FDA's data bank, PAFA (see page 10).

YEAST EXTRACT • *See* Yeast.

YELLOW BEESWAX • Obtained from bee honeycombs, it is brittle, with a honeylike odor and a balsamic taste. It is used in the manufacture of wax paper, candles, cosmetics, and shoe polish, and in pharmaceutical ointment and plasters. May cause allergic reactions.

YELLOW NO. 5 • All foods containing this coloring, which is the most widely used color additive in food, drugs, and cosmetics, are supposed to identify it on the label. The FDA ordered this so that those allergic to it could avoid it. *See also* Tartrazine and Salicylates.

YELLOW PRUSSIATE OF SODA • Sodium Ferrocyanide. An anticaking agent, it is used in table salt to prevent the formation of clumps and to keep it free-flowing. The additive is produced by heating sodium carbonate and iron with organic materials. The average daily diet in the U.S. contains 0.6 milligrams of sodium ferrocyanide per person. The UN Joint FAO/WHO Expert Committee on Food Additives considers 1.5 milligrams daily an acceptable and safe intake for a 132-pound human. The FDA data bank, PAFA (see page 10), has fully up-to-date toxicology information available on this food additive.

YELLOW WAX • *See* Yellow Beeswax.

YERBA SANTA FLUID EXTRACT • Holy Herb. Fruit flavoring derived from an evergreen shrub, *Eriodictyon californicum,* grown in California. Used in beverages, ice cream, ices, candy, and baked goods, and to mask the bitter taste of drugs. Also used as an expectorant. The FDA data bank, PAFA, has not yet done a toxicology literature search on this food additive.

YLANG-YLANG OIL • A light yellow, fragrant liquid obtained in the Philippines from flowers of *Canangium odoratum.* Used in raspberry, cola, violet, cherry, rum, and ginger ale flavorings for beverages, ice cream, ices, candy, baked goods, chewing gum, and icing. Used in perfumes, cosmetics, and soap. No known toxicity. GRAS. The FDA data bank, PAFA, has not yet done a toxicology literature search on this food additive.

YOGURT • A dairy product produced by the action of bacteria or yeast on milk. No known toxicity. Supposedly has emollient properties.

YUCCA EXTRACT • Mohave Extract. Joshua Tree. Adam's Needle. Derived from a southwestern U.S. plant, *Yucca* spp., and used as a base for organic cosmetics and as a root beer flavoring for beverages, ices, and ice cream. The FDA data bank, PAFA, has not yet done a toxicology literature search on this food additive.

Z

ZANTHOXYLUM • Xanthoxylum. Ash Bark. Toothache Tree. Angelica Tree. The dried bark or berries of this tree, which grows in Canada, south to Virginia and Missouri, is used to ease the pain of toothaches, to soothe stomachaches, and as an antidiarrheal medicine. No known toxicity. A member of the rue family.

ZEDOARY • A bark extract from the East Indies plant *Curcuma zeodaria*, used as a bitters and ginger ale flavoring for beverages. GRAS. The FDA data bank, PAFA (see page 10), has not yet done a toxicology literature search on this food additive.

ZEIN • It is the principal protein in corn. Obtained as a yellowish powder by extracting corn gluten with an alcohol. Used to make textile fibers, plastics, printing inks, varnishes, and other coatings and adhesives. The FDA data bank, PAFA, has not yet done a toxicology literature search on this food additive.

ZERANOL • Zearalanol. A hormone used to increase growth in animals. FDA residue limit is zero in uncooked edible tissue of cattle and sheep.

ZINC • A white, brittle metal insoluble in water and soluble in acids or hot solutions of alkalies. It is a mineral source and added as a nutrient to food. Widely used as an astringent for mouthwashes and as a reducing agent (*see*) and reagent (*see*). Ingestion of the salts can cause nausea and vomiting. It can cause contact dermatitis. *See* Zinc Chloride.

ZINC ACETATE • The zinc salt of acetic acid (*see*) used in medicine as a dietary supplement and as a cross-linking agent for polymers (*see*). For toxicity, *see* Zinc. GRAS. There is no reported use of the chemical and no toxicology information is available, according to the FDA's data bank, PAFA (see page 10).

ZINC BACITRACIN • Used in animal feed. *See* Bacitracin.

ZINC BORATE • The inorganic salt of zinc oxide and boric oxide, it is used as a fungistat and mildew inhibitor. *See* Zinc.

ZINC CARBONATE • A cosmetic coloring agent, it is a crystalline salt of zinc occurring in nature as smithsonite. *See* Zinc for toxicity. GRAS. There is no reported use of the chemical and no toxicology information is available, according to the FDA's data bank, PAFA.

ZINC CHLORIDE • Butter of Zinc. A zinc salt used as an antiseptic and astringent in shaving creams, dentifrices, and mouthwashes. Odorless and water absorbing; also a deodorant and disinfectant. Can cause contact dermatitis and is mildly irritating to the skin. Can be absorbed through the skin. GRAS. The FDA data bank, PAFA, is currently searching the toxicology literature concerning this additive.

ZINC GLUCONATE • The FDA data bank, PAFA (see page 10), has fully up-to-date toxicology information available on this food additive. *See* Zinc.

ZINC GLUTAMATE • The zinc salt of glutamic acid (*see*).

ZINC ION AND MANEB • A pesticide used on raisins, flours of barley, oats, rye, and wheat. Maneb is a fungicide. FDA residue tolerances: 28 ppm in raisins; 1 ppm in flours of barley, oats, rye, and wheat; 20 ppm in bran of barley, oats, rye, and wheat as well as milled feed fractions of those grains.

ZINC METHIONINE SULFATE • A nutrient. The FDA data bank, PAFA, has fully up-to-date toxicology information available on this food additive. *See* Zinc and Methionine.

ZINC OXIDE • GRAS. The FDA data bank, PAFA, is currently searching the toxicology literature concerning this additive. *See* Zinc.

ZINC RESINATE • The zinc salt of rosin (*see*).

ZINC RICINOLEATE • The zinc salt of ricinoleate (*see*). Used as a fungicide, emulsifier, and stabilizer.

ZINC ROSINATE • The zinc salt of rosin (*see*).

ZINC STEARATE • Nutrient. GRAS. The FDA data bank, PAFA (see page 10), is currently searching the toxicology literature concerning this additive. *See* Zinc.

ZINC SULFATE • White Vitriol. The result of the reaction of sulfuric acid with zinc. Mild crystalline zinc salt used in shaving cream, eye lotions, astringents, styptic, as a gargle spray, skin tonic, and aftershave lotion. Used medicinally as an emetic. Irritating to the skin and mucous membranes. May cause an allergic reaction. Injection under the skin of 2.5 milligrams per kilogram of body weight caused tumors in rabbits. *See* Zinc. GRAS. The FDA data bank, PAFA, is currently searching the toxicology literature concerning this additive.

ZINGERONE • A synthetic flavoring occurring naturally in ginger. Used in fruit, root beer, sarsaparilla, spice, ginger ale, wintergreen, and birch beer flavorings for beverages, ice cream, ices, candy, baked goods, and chewing gum. The FDA data bank, PAFA, has fully up-to-date toxicology information available on this food additive.

ZINGIBER OFFICINALE • *See* Ginger.

ZINGIBERONE • *See* Zingerone.

ZOALENE • Dinitolmide. Used in chicken and turkey feed to combat parasites. FDA tolerance residues are 2 ppm in uncooked fat of chickens; 3 ppm in uncooked muscle meat of chickens; 6 ppm in uncooked liver and kidneys of chickens; 3 ppm in uncooked muscle meat and liver of turkeys.

BIBLIOGRAPHY

Adams, Catherine F. *Nutritive Value of American Foods in Common Units.* Washington, D.C.: Agriculture Handbook No. 456, U.S. Department of Agriculture, 1975.

Bowes, Helen N., and Charles F. Church. *Food Values of Portions Commonly Used,* 11th ed., rev. Philadelphia: J.B. Lippincott Co., 1970.

Chemicals Used in Food Processing. Washington, D.C.: National Academy of Sciences, Publication 1274, 1965.

Code of Federal Regulations: Food and Drugs, Parts 100 to 169, revised April 1, 1993.

The Condensed Chemical Dictionary, 11th ed. Revised by N. Irving Sax and Richard J. Lewis, Sr. New York: Van Nostrand Reinhold, 1987.

Done, Alan. "Toxic Reactions to Common Household Products." Paper read at the Symposium on Adverse Reactions sponsored by the Drug Service Center for Disease Control, December 1976, San Francisco.

Evaluation of Certain Veterinary Drug Residues in Food. WHO Technical Report Series No. 800, thirty-fourth report of the Joint FAO/WHO Expert Committee on Food Additives, 1991.

Fisher, Alexander A. *Contact Dermatitis,* 3d. ed. Philadelphia: Lea & Febiger, 1986.

Food Additive Status List, Investigations Operations Manual, corrected to January 30, 1992. U.S. Food and Drug Administration.

Food Allergy: Adverse Reactions to Foods and Food Additives. Edited by Dean D. Metcalfe, M.D., Hugh Sampson, M.D., and Ronald A. Simon, M.D. Boston: Blackwell Scientific Publications, 1991.

Food Chemicals Codex, 1st ed. Washington, D.C.: National Academy of Sciences, Publication 1406, 1966.

Food Labeling: Questions and Answers for Guidance to Facilitate the Process of Developing or Revision of Labels for Foods Other Than Dietary Supplements. Office of Food Labeling, Center for Food Safety and Applied Nutrition, Food and Drug Administration, August 1993.

Gleason, Marion N., et al. *Clinical Toxicology of Commercial Products.* Baltimore: The Williams & Wilkins Co., 1969.

Gordon, Lesley. *A Country Herbal.* New York: Mayflower Books, 1980.

Handbook of Food Additives. Edited by Thomas E. Furia. Cleveland: The Chemical Rubber Co., 1971.

Hawley's Condensed Chemical Dictionary, 11th ed. Revised by N. Irving Sax and Richard J. Lewis, Sr. New York: Van Nostrand Reinhold, 1987.

Lewis, Richard, Sr. *Food Additives Handbook.* New York: Van Nostrand Reinhold, 1991.

Martin, Eric W., et al. *Hazards of Medications.* Philadelphia: J.B. Lippincott Co., 1971.

The Merck Index, 8th, 9th, 10th, and 15th editions. Rahway, N.J.: Merck, Sharp and Dohme Research Laboratories, 1989.

The Merck Manual, 15th ed. Edited by Robert Berkow, M.D. Rahway, N.J.: Merck, Sharp and Dohme Research Laboratories, 1987.

Miall, L. Mackenzie, and D. W. A. Sharp. *A New Dictionary of Chemistry,* 4th ed. New York: John Wiley & Sons, Inc., 1968.

Physicians' Desk Reference. Oradell, N.J.: Medical Economics, 1993.

Present Knowledge in Nutrition, 5th ed. Washington, D.C.: The Nutrition Foundation, Inc., 1984.

Recommended Dietary Allowances, rev. ed. Washington, D.C.: National Academy of Sciences, 1980.

Smith, Jim. *Food Additives User's Handbook.* New York: Blackie and Sons Ltd., Van Nostrand Reinhold, 1991.

Sourcebook on Food and Nutrition, 3d ed. Edited by Joannis Scarpa, Ph.D., Helen Kiefer, Ph.D., and Rita Tatum. Chicago: Marquis Academic Media, 1982.

Steadman's Medical Dictionary, 25th ed. Baltimore: The Williams & Wilkins Co., 1989.

Suspected Carcinogens: A Subfile of the NIOSH Toxic Substance List. Rockville, Md.: Tracor Jitco, Inc., U.S. Department of Health, Education and Welfare, 1975.

Suspected Carcinogens: A Subfile of the Registry of Toxic Effects of Chemical Substances. Cincinnati: U.S. Department of Health, Education and Welfare, Public Health Services, Center for Disease Control, 1976.

Toxicants Occurring Naturally in Foods, 2d ed. Washington, D.C.: National Academy of Sciences, 1973.

Toxicity Testing: Strategies to Determine Needs and Priorities. Washington, D.C.: National Research Council: National Academy Press, 1984.

Watt, Bernice, Annabel Merrill, et al. *Composition of Foods: Raw, Processed, Prepared.* Washington, D.C.: Agriculture Handbook No. 8, U.S. Department of Agriculture, 1963.

White, John Henry. *A Reference Book of Chemistry,* 3d ed. New York: Philosophical Library, 1965.

Winter, Ruth. *Cancer-Causing Agents: A Preventive Guide.* New York: Crown Publishers, Inc., 1979.

————. *A Consumer's Dictionary of Household, Yard and Office Chemicals.* New York: Crown Publishers, Inc., 1992.

————. *Poisons in Your Food,* rev. ed. New York: Crown Publishers, Inc. 1991.